Artificial Intelligence for Maximizing Content Based Image Retrieval

Zongmin Ma
Northeastern University, China

INFORMATION SCIENCE REFERENCE

Hershey · New York

Director of Editorial Content: Kristin Klinger
Director of Production: Jennifer Neidig
Managing Editor: Jamie Snavely
Assistant Managing Editor: Carole Coulson
Typesetter: Chris Hrobak
Cover Design: Lisa Tosheff
Printed at: Yurchak Printing Inc.

Published in the United States of America by
        Information Science Reference (an imprint of IGI Global)
        701 E. Chocolate Avenue, Suite 200
        Hershey PA 17033
        Tel: 717-533-8845
        Fax: 717-533-8661
        E-mail: cust@igi-global.com
        Web site: http://www.igi-global.com

and in the United Kingdom by
        Information Science Reference (an imprint of IGI Global)
        3 Henrietta Street
        Covent Garden
        London WC2E 8LU
        Tel: 44 20 7240 0856
        Fax: 44 20 7379 0609
        Web site: http://www.eurospanbookstore.com

Library of Congress Cataloging-in-Publication Data

Artificial intelligence for maximizing content based image retrieval / Zongmin Ma, editor.
      p. cm.
   Includes bibliographical references and index.
   Summary: "This book provide state of the art information to those involved in the study, use, design and development of advanced and emerging AI technologies"--Provided by publisher.
    ISBN 978-1-60566-174-2 (hardcover) -- ISBN 978-1-60566-175-9 (ebook)
   1. Artificial intelligence. 2. Image processing. I. Ma, Zongmin, 1965-
   Q335.A78736 2009
   006.4'2--dc22
                            2008022541

British Cataloguing in Publication Data
A Cataloguing in Publication record for this book is available from the British Library.

All work contributed to this book set is original material. The views expressed in this book are those of the authors, but not necessarily of the publisher.

Table of Contents

Section I

Danilo Avola, Institute of Research on Population and Social Policies - National Research Council, Italy
Fernando Ferri, Institute of Research on Population and Social Policies - National Research Council, Italy
Patrizia Grifoni, Institute of Research on Population and Social Policies - National Research Council, Italy

Dany Gebara, University of Calgary, Canada
Reda Alhajj, University of Calgary, Canada

Gang Zhang, College of Information Science and Engineering, Northeastern University, China
Z. M. Ma, College of Information Science and Engineering, Northeastern University, China
Li Yan, College of Information Science and Engineering, Northeastern University, China
Ji-feng Zhu, College of Information Science and Engineering, Northeastern University, China

Jafar M. Ali, Kuwait University, Kuwait

Section II

Section III

Detailed Table of Contents

Section I

Chapter I

Danilo Avola, Institute of Research on Population and Social Policies - National Research
Council, Italy
Fernando Ferri, Institute of Research on Population and Social Policies - National Research
Council, Italy
Patrizia Grifoni, Institute of Research on Population and Social Policies - National Research
Council, Italy

The novel technologies used in different application domains allow obtaining digital images with a high complex informative content, which can be exploited to interpret the semantic meaning of the images themselves. Furthermore, it has to be taken into account that the complex informative content extracted from the images, that is, the features, need of flexible, powerful, and suitable ways to be represented and managed. The metadata through which a set of images can be described are directly tied to the quality and quantity of the extracted features; besides the efficient management of the metadata depend on the practical and capable feature representation. The more used approaches to analyze the image content do not seem able to provide an effective support to obtain a whole image understanding and feature extraction process. For this reason, new classes of methodologies that involve computational intelligent approaches have been developed. In particular, genetic algorithms (GAs) and other artificial intelligent-(AI) based approaches seem to provide the best suitable solutions. The artificial intelligent technologies allow for the obtaining of a more semantically complex metadata image representation through which to develop advanced systems to retrieval and to handle the digital images. This new method to conceive a metadata description allows the user to make queries in a more natural, detailed, and semantically complete way. As a result it can overcome the always more sophisticated duties caused by the use of wide local and/or distributed databases with heterogeneous complex images.

    Dany Gebara, University of Calgary, Canada
    Reda Alhajj, University of Calgary, Canada

This chapter presents a novel approach for content-fbased image retrieval and demonstrates its applicability on non-texture images. The process starts by extracting a feature vector for each image; wavelets are employed in the process. Then the images (each represented by its feature vector) are classified into groups by employing a density-based clustering approach, namely OPTICS. This highly improves the querying facility by limiting the search space to a single cluster instead of the whole database. The cluster to be searched is determined by applying on the query image the same clustering process OPTICS. This leads to the closest cluster to the query image, and hence, limits the search to the latter cluster without adding the query image to the cluster, except if such request is explicitly specified. The power of this system is demonstrated on non-texture images from the Corel dataset. The achieved results demonstrate that the classification of images is extremely fast and accurate.

    Gang Zhang, College of Information Science and Engineering, Northeastern University,
       China
    Z. M. Ma, College of Information Science and Engineering, Northeastern University, China
    Li Yan, College of Information Science and Engineering, Northeastern University, China
    Ji-feng Zhu, College of Information Science and Engineering, Northeastern University, China

Texture feature extraction and description is one of the important research contents in content-based medical image retrieval. The chapter first proposes a framework of content-based medical image retrieval system. It then analyzes the important texture feature extraction and description methods further, such as the co-occurrence matrix, perceptual texture features, Gabor wavelet, and so forth. Moreover, the chapter analyzes the improved methods for these methods and demonstrates their application in content-based medical image retrieval.

    Jafar M. Ali, Kuwait University, Kuwait

Advances in data storage and image acquisition technologies have enabled the creation of large image datasets. Thus, it is necessary to develop appropriate information systems to efficiently manage these datasets. Image classification and retrieval is one of the most important services that must be supported by such systems. The most common approach used is content-based image retrieval (CBIR) systems. This paper presents a new application of rough sets to feature reduction, classification, and retrieval for image databases in the framework of content-based image retrieval systems. The suggested approach combines image texture features with color features to form a powerful discriminating feature vector for each image. Texture features are extracted, represented, and normalized in an attribute vector, followed by a generation of rough set dependency rules from the real value attribute vector. The rough set reduction technique is applied to find all reducts with the minimal subset of attributes associated with a class label for classification.

Section II

Chapter V

David García Pérez, University of Santiago de Compostela, Spain
Antonio Mosquera, University of Santiago de Compostela, Spain
Stefano Berretti, University of Firenze, Italy
Alberto Del Bimbo, University of Firenze, Italy

Content-based image retrieval has been an active research area in past years. Many different solutions have been proposed to improve performance of retrieval, but the large part of these works have focused on sub-parts of the retrieval problem, providing targeted solutions only for individual aspects (i.e., feature extraction, similarity measures, indexing, etc). In this chapter, we first shortly review some of the main practiced solutions for content-based image retrieval evidencing some of the main issues. Then, we propose an original approach for the extraction of relevant image objects and their matching for retrieval applications, and present a complete image retrieval system which uses this approach (including similarity measures and image indexing). In particular, image objects are represented by a two-dimensional deformable structure, referred to as "active net." Active net is capable of adapting to relevant image regions according to chromatic and edge information. Extension of the active nets has been defined, which permits the nets to break themselves, thus increasing their capability to adapt to objects with complex topological structure. The resulting representation allows a joint description of color, shape, and structural information of extracted objects. A similarity measure between active nets has also been defined and used to combine the retrieval with an efficient indexing structure. The proposed system has been experimented on two large and publicly available objects databases, namely, the ETH-80 and the ALOI.

Chapter VI

Ming Zhang, University of Calgary, Canada
Reda Alhajj, University of Calgary, Canada

Content-Based Image Retrieval (CBIR) aims to search images that are perceptually similar to the query-based on visual content of the images without the help of annotations. The current CBIR systems use global features (e.g., color, texture, and shape) as image descriptors, or usefeatures extracted from segmented regions (called region-based descriptors). In the former case, descriptors are not discriminative enough at the object level and are sensitive to object occlusion or background clutter, thus fail to give satisfactory result. In the latter case, the features are sensitive to the image segmentation, which is a difficult task in its own right. In addition, the region-based descriptors are still not invariant to varying imaging conditions. In this chapter, we look at the CBIR from the object detection/recognition point of view and introduce the local feature-based image representation methods recently developed in object detection/recognition area. These local descriptors are highly distinctive and robust to imaging condition change. In addition to image representation, we also introduce the other two key issues of CBIR: similarity measurement for image descriptor comparison and the index structure for similarity search.

Chapter VII

Chotirat "Ann" Ratanamahatana, Chulalongkorn University, Thailand
Eamonn Keogh, University of California, Riverside, USA
Vit Niennattrakul, Chulalongkorn University, Thailand

After the generation of multimedia data turning digital, an explosion of interest in their data storage, retrieval, and processing, has drastically increased in the database and data mining community. This includes videos, images, and handwriting, where we now have higher expectations in exploiting these data at hand. We argue however, that much of this work's narrow focus on efficiency and scalability has come at the cost of usability and effectiveness. Typical manipulations are in some forms of video/image processing, which require fairly large amounts for storage and are computationally intensive. In this work, we will demonstrate how these multimedia data can be reduced to a more compact form, that is, time series representation, while preserving the features of interest, and can then be efficiently exploited in Content-Based Image Retrieval. We also introduce a general framework that learns a distance measure with arbitrary constraints on the warping path of the Dynamic Time Warping calculation. We demonstrate utilities of our approach on both classification and query retrieval tasks for time series and other types of multimedia data including images, video frames, and handwriting archives. In addition, we show that incorporating this framework into the relevance feedback system, a query refinement can be used to further improve the precision/recall by a wide margin.

Chapter VIII

Hakim Hacid, University of Lyon 2, France
Abdelkader Djamel Zighed, University of Lyon 2, France

A multimedia index makes it possible to group data according to similarity criteria. Traditional index structures are based on trees and use the k-Nearest Neighbors (k-NN) approach to retrieve databases. Due to some disadvantages of such an approach, the use of neighborhood graphs was proposed. This approach is interesting, but it has some disadvantages, mainly in its complexity. This chapter presents a step in a long process of analyzing, structuring, and retrieving multimedia databases. Indeed, we propose an effective method for locally updating neighborhood graphs, which constitute our multimedia index. Then, we exploit this structure in order to make the retrieval process easy and effective, using queries in an image form in one hand. In another hand, we use the indexing structure to annotate images in order to describe their semantics. The proposed approach is based on an intelligent manner for locating points in a multidimensional space. Promising results are obtained after experimentations on various databases. Future issues of the proposed approach are very relevant in this domain.

Section III

Chapter IX

    Ruofei Zhang, Yahoo!, Inc., USA
    Zhongfei (Mark) Zhang, SUNY Binghamton, USA

This chapter studies the user relevance feedback in image retrieval. We take this problem as a standard two-class pattern classification problem aiming at refining the retrieval precision by learning through the user relevance feedback data. However, we have investigated the problem by noting two important unique characteristics of the problem: small sample collection and asymmetric sample distributions between positive and negative samples. We have developed a novel approach to empirical Bayesian learning to solve for this problem by explicitly exploiting the two unique characteristics, which is the methodology of **BA**yesian **L**earning in **AS**ymmetric and **S**mall sample collections, thus called **BALAS**. In **BALAS** different learning strategies are used for positive and negative sample collections, respectively, based on the two unique characteristics. By defining the relevancy confidence as the relevant posterior probability, we have developed an integrated ranking scheme in **BALAS** which complementarily combines the subjective relevancy confidence and the objective similarity measure to capture the overall retrieval semantics. The experimental evaluations have confirmed the rationale of the proposed ranking scheme, and have also demonstrated that **BALAS** is superior to an existing relevance feedback method in the current literature in capturing the overall retrieval semantics.

Chapter X

    Chia-Hung Wei, Ching Yun University, Taiwan
    Chang-Tsun Li, University of Warwick, UK

An image is a symbolic representation; people interpret an image and associate semantics with it based on their subjective perceptions, which involves the user's knowledge, cultural background, personal feelings and so on. Content-based image retrieval (CBIR) systems must be able to interact with users and discover the current user's information needs. An interactive search paradigm that has been developed for image retrieval is machine learning with a user-in-the-loop, guided by relevance feedback, which refers to the notion of relevance of the individual image based on the current user's subjective judgment. Relevance feedback serves as an information carrier to convey the user's information needs / preferences to the retrieval system. This chapter not only provides the fundamentals of CBIR systems and relevance feedback for understanding and incorporating relevance feedback into CBIR systems, but also discusses several approaches to analyzing and learning relevance feedback.

Chapter XI

    Paweł Rotter, European Commission, Joint Research Centre, Institute for Prospective
    Technological Studies, Spain & AGH-University of Science and Technology, Poland
    Andrzej M.J. Skulimowski, AGH-University of Science and Technology, Poland

In this chapter, we describe two new approaches to content-based image retrieval (CBIR) based on preference information provided by the user interacting with an image search system. First, we present the existing methods of image retrieval with relevance feedback, which serve then as a reference for the new approaches. The first extension of the distance function-based CBIR approach makes it possible to apply this approach to complex objects. The new algorithm is based on an approximation of user preferences by a neural network. Further, we propose another approach to image retrieval, which uses reference sets to facilitate image comparisons. The methods proposed have been implemented, and compared with each other, and with the earlier approaches. Computational experiments have proven that the new preference extraction and image retrieval procedures here proposed are numerically efficient. Finally, we provide a real-life illustration of the methods proposed: an image-based hotel selection procedure.

Chapter XII

Iker Gondra, St. Francis Xavier University, Canada

In content-based image retrieval (CBIR), a set of low-level features are extracted from an image to represent its visual content. Retrieval is performed by image example where a query image is given as input by the user and an appropriate similarity measure is used to find the best matches in the corresponding feature space. This approach suffers from the fact that there is a large discrepancy between the low-level visual features that one can extract from an image and the semantic interpretation of the image's content that a particular user may have in a given situation. That is, users seek semantic similarity, but we can only provide similarity based on low-level visual features extracted from the raw pixel data, a situation known as the semantic gap. The selection of an appropriate similarity measure is thus an important problem. Since visual content can be represented by different attributes, the combination and importance of each set of features varies according to the user's semantic intent. Thus, the retrieval strategy should be adaptive so that it can accommodate the preferences of different users. Relevance feedback (RF) learning has been proposed as a technique aimed at reducing the semantic gap. It works by gathering semantic information from user interaction. Based on the user's feedback on the retrieval results, the retrieval scheme is adjusted. By providing an image similarity measure under human perception, RF learning can be seen as a form of supervised learning that finds relations between high-level semantic interpretations and low-level visual properties. That is, the feedback obtained within a single query session is used to personalize the retrieval strategy and thus enhance retrieval performance. In this chapter we present an overview of CBIR and related work on RF learning. We also present our own previous work on a RF learning-based probabilistic region relevance learning algorithm for automatically estimating the importance of each region in an image based on the user's semantic intent.

Section IV

Chapter XIII

Zhiping Shi, Institute of Computing Technology, Chinese Academy of Sciences, China
Qingyong Li, Beijing Jiaotong University, China
Qing He, Institute of Computing Technology, Chinese Academy of Sciences, China
Zhongzhi Shi, Institute of Computing Technology, Chinese Academy of Sciences, China

Semantics-based retrieval is a trend of the Content-Based Multimedia Retrieval (CBMR). Typically, in multimedia databases, there exist two kinds of clues for query: perceptive features and semantic classes. In this chapter, we proposed a novel framework for multimedia database organization and retrieval, integrating the perceptive features and semantic classes. Thereunto, a semantics supervised cluster-based index organization approach (briefly as SSCI) was developed: the entire data set is divided hierarchically into many clusters until the objects within a cluster are not only close in the perceptive feature space, but also within the same semantic class; then an index entry is built for each cluster. Especially, the perceptive feature vectors in a cluster are organized adjacently in disk. Furthermore, the SSCI supports a relevance feedback approach: users sign the positive and negative examples regarded a cluster as unit rather than a single object. Our experiments show that the proposed framework can improve the retrieval speed and precision of the CBMR systems significantly.

Chapter XIV

Chia-Hung Wei, Ching Yun University, Taiwan
Chang-Tsun Li, University of Warwick, UK
Yue Li, University of Warwick, UK

As distributed mammogram databases at hospitals and breast screening centers are connected together through PACS, a mammogram retrieval system is needed to help medical professionals locate the mammograms they want to aid in medical diagnosis. This chapter presents a complete content-based mammogram retrieval system, seeking images that are pathologically similar to a given example. In the mammogram retrieval system, the pathological characteristics that have been defined in Breast Imaging Reporting and Data System (BI-RADS™) are used as criteria to measure the similarity of the mammograms. A detailed description of those mammographic features is provided in this chapter. Since the user's subjective perception should be taken into account in the image retrieval task, a relevance feedback function is also developed to learn individual users' knowledge to improve the system performance.

Chapter XV

Ying-li Tian, IBM T. J. Watson Research Center, USA
Arun Hampapur, IBM T. J. Watson Research Center, USA
Lisa Brown, IBM T. J. Watson Research Center, USA
Rogerio Feris, IBM T. J. Watson Research Center, USA
Max Lu, IBM T. J. Watson Research Center, USA
Andrew Senior, IBM T. J. Watson Research Center, USA
Chiao-fe Shu, IBM T. J. Watson Research Center, USA
Yun Zhai, IBM T. J. Watson Research Center, USA

Video surveillance automation is used in two key modes: watching for known threats in real-time and searching for events of interest after the fact. Typically, real-time alerting is a localized function, for example, an airport security center receives and reacts to a "perimeter breach alert," while investigations often tend to encompass a large number of geographically distributed cameras like the London bombing, or Washington sniper incidents. Enabling effective event detection, query and retrieval of surveillance video for preemption, and investigation, involves indexing the video along multiple dimensions. This chapter presents a framework for event detection and surveillance search that includes: video parsing, indexing, query and retrieval mechanisms. It explores video parsing techniques that automatically extract index data from video indexing, which stores data in relational tables; retrieval which uses SQL queries to retrieve events of interest and the software architecture that integrates these technologies.

This chapter introduces an advanced content-based image retrieval (CBIR) system, MMIR, where Markov model mediator (MMM) and multiple instance learning (MIL) techniques are integrated seamlessly and act coherently as a hierarchical learning engine to boost both the retrieval accuracy and efficiency. It is well-understood that the major bottleneck of CBIR systems is the large semantic gap between the low-level image features and the high-level semantic concepts. In addition, the perception subjectivity problem also challenges a CBIR system. To address these issues and challenges, the proposed MMIR system utilizes the MMM mechanism to direct the focus on the image level analysis together with the MIL technique (with the neural network technique as its core) to real-time capture and learn the object-level semantic concepts with some help of the user feedbacks. In addition, from a long-term learning perspective, the user feedback logs are explored by MMM to speed up the learning process and to increase the retrieval accuracy for a query. The comparative studies on a large set of real-world images demonstrate the promising performance of our proposed MMIR system.

Preface

Multimedia data comprising of images, audio, and video is becoming increasingly common. The decreasing costs of consumer electronic devices such as digital cameras and digital camcorders, along with the ease of transportation facilitated by the Internet, has lead to a phenomenal rise in the amount of multimedia data. Given that this trend of increased use of multimedia data is likely to accelerate, there is an urgent need for providing a clear means of capturing, storing, indexing, retrieving, analyzing, and summarizing such data. Image data is a very commonly used multimedia data type. The early image retrieval systems are based on manually annotated descriptions, called text-based image retrieval (TBIR). TBIR is a great leap forward, but has several inherent drawbacks. First, textual description is not capable of capturing the visual contents of an image accurately, and in many circumstances, the textual annotations are not available. Second, different people may describe the content of an image in different ways, which limits the recall performance of textual-based image retrieval systems. Third, for some images there is something that no words can convey. To resolve these problems, content-based image retrieval (CBIR) became an active and fast developing research area from the early 1990s, and has attracted significant research attention. CBIR aims to search images that are perceptually similar to the query based on visual content of the images without help of annotations.

CBIR systems are designed to support image retrieval as well as storage and processing activities related to image data management in multimedia information systems. So CBIR systems are the key to implementing image data management. Image data management requires CBIR system support. It should be noted, however, that not being the same as the traditional textual retrieval, a general CBIR framework contains several main components such as *feature extraction and representation, similarity measurement, databases of pre-analyzed image collections,* and *relevance feedback.* It has been shown that artificial intelligence (AI) plays an important role in the feature extraction, similarity measures, and relevance feedback of CBIR. CBIR using AI technology is emerging as a new discipline, which provides the mechanisms for retrieving image data efficiently and naturally by means of AI technology. Many researchers have been concentrating on CBIR using AI technology. The research and development of CBIR using AI technology are receiving increasing attention. By means of AI technology, large volumes of image data can be retrieved effectively and naturally from image databases. Intelligent CBIR systems are hereby built based on AI and databases to support various problem solving and decision making. Intelligent CBIR systems is a field that must be investigated by academic researchers and developers together, both from the CBIR and AI fields.

The book focuses on the following issues of AI for CBIR: AI for the feature extraction and representation; AI for the distance measurement and image indexing as well as query; AI for the relevance feedback, and the intelligent CBIR systems and applications; aiming at providing a single account of technologies and practices in AI for CBIR. The objective of the book is to provide the state-of-the-art information to academics, researchers, and industry practitioners who are involved or interested in the study, use, design, and development of advanced and emerging AI technologies for CBIR, with ultimate aim to empower individuals and organizations in building competencies for exploiting the opportunities of the knowledge society. This book presents the latest research and application results in AI for CBIR. The different chapters in the book have been contributed by different authors and provide possible solutions for the different types of technological problems concerning AI for CBIR.

INTRODUCTION

This book, which consists of 11 chapters, is organized into four major sections. The first section discusses the issues of AI for the feature extraction and representation in the first four chapters. The next four chapters, covering AI for the distance measurement and image indexing as well as query, comprise the second section. The third section includes four chapters about AI for the relevance feedback. The fourth section containing the final four chapters focuses on the intelligent CBIR systems and applications.

First of all, we take a look at the issues of AI for the feature extraction and representation.

Danilo Avola, Fernando Ferri, and Patrizia Grifoni introduce and discuss the different AI approaches used to extract and to represent the features of any image. In particular, the role of the Genetic Algorithms (GAs) has been highlighted. The authors start from a brief discussion about the feature extraction process, and then introduce a general description of some of the most interesting AI approaches along with their application in image feature extraction problems. They give a more complete and exhaustive description of the GAs. Finally the possibility of combined AI approaches (used in the hybrid systems) to solve more complex feature extraction problems is faced. Therefore, they present some of the most recent and powerful applications exploiting the AI image feature extraction.

Dany Gebara and Reda Alhajj present a novel approach for content-based image retrieval and demonstrate its applicability on non-texture images. The process starts by extracting a feature vector for each image; wavelets are employed in the process. Then the images (each represented by its feature vector) are classified into groups by employing a density-based clustering approach, namely OPTICS. This highly improves the querying facility by limiting the search space to a single cluster instead of the whole database. The cluster to be searched is determined by applying on the query image the same clustering process OPTICS; this leads to the closest cluster to the query image and hence limits the search to the latter cluster, without adding the query image to the cluster except if such a request is explicitly specified.

Texture feature extraction and description is one of the important research contents in content-based medical image retrieval. Gang Zhang *et al.* first propose a framework of content-based medical image retrieval system. Then they review the important texture feature extraction and description methods such as co-occurrence matrix, perceptual texture features, Gabor wavelet, and so forth. Moreover, they analyze each of the improved methods and demonstrate its application in content-based medical image retrieval.

Jafar M. Ali presents an application of rough sets to feature reduction, classification, and retrieval for image databases in the framework of content-based image retrieval systems. The suggested approach combines image texture features with color features to form a powerful discriminating feature vector for each image. Texture features are extracted, represented, and normalized in an attribute vector, followed by a generation of rough set dependency rules from the real value attribute vector. The rough set reduction technique is applied to find all reducts with the minimal subset of attributes associated with a class label for classification.

The next session takes a look at AI for the distance measurement and image indexing as well as query.

Many different solutions have been proposed to improve performance of content based image retrieval, but the large part of these works have focused on sub-parts of the retrieval problem, providing targeted solutions only for individual aspects (i.e., feature extraction, similarity measures, indexing, etc). David García Pérez *et al.* first shortly review some of the main practiced solutions for content-based image retrieval, evidencing some of the main issues. Then, they propose an original approach for the extraction of relevant image objects and their matching for retrieval applications, and present a complete image retrieval system which uses this approach (including similarity measures and image indexing). In particular, image objects are represented by a two-dimensional deformable structure, referred to as "active net," capable to adapt to relevant image regions according to chromatic and edge information. Extension of the active nets has been defined, which permits the nets to break themselves, thus increasing their capability to adapt to objects with complex topological structure. The resulting representation allows a joint description of color, shape, and structural information of extracted objects. A similarity measure between active nets has also been defined and used to combine the retrieval with an efficient indexing structure.

CBIR aims to search images that are perceptually similar to the query based on visual content of the images without help of annotations. The current CBIR systems use global features (e.g., color, texture, and shape) as image descriptors, or use features extracted from segmented regions (called region-based descriptors). In the former case, descriptors are not discriminative enough at the object level and are sensitive to object occlusion or background clutter, thus failing to give satisfactory results. In the latter case, the features are sensitive to the image segmentation, which is a difficult task in its own right. In addition, the region-based descriptors are still not invariant to varying imaging conditions. Ming Zhang and Reda Alhajj look at the CBIR from the object detection/recognition point of view and introduce the local feature-based image representation methods recently developed in object detection/recognition area. These local descriptors are highly distinctive and robust to imaging condition change. In addition to image representation, they also introduce the other two key issues of CBIR: similarity measurement for image descriptor comparison and the index structure for similarity search.

Chotirat "Ann" Ratanamahatana, Eamonn Keogh, and Vit Niennattrakul demonstrate how multimedia data can be reduced to a more compact form, that is, time series representation, while preserving the features of interest, and can then be efficiently exploited in Content-Based Image Retrieval. They introduce a general framework that learns a distance measure with arbitrary constraints on the warping path of the Dynamic Time Warping calculation. They demonstrate utilities of their approach on both classification and query retrieval tasks for time series and other types of multimedia data including images, video frames, and handwriting archives. In addition, they show that incorporating the framework into the relevance feedback system; a query refinement can be used to further improve the precision/recall by a wide margin.

Traditional index structures are based on trees and use the k-Nearest Neighbors (k-NN) approach to retrieve databases. Due to some disadvantages of such an approach, the use of neighborhood graphs has been proposed. While this approach is interesting, it suffers from some disadvantages, mainly in its complexity. Hakim Hacid and Abdelkader Djamel Zighed present a step in a long process of analyzing, structuring, and retrieving multimedia databases. They propose an effective method for locally updating neighborhood graphs, which constitute their multimedia index. Then, they exploit this structure in order to make the retrieval process easy and effective, using queries in an image form in one hand. In another hand, they use the indexing structure to annotate images in order to describe the semantics of images.

The third section deals with the issues of AI for the relevance feedback.

Ruofei Zhang and Zhongfei (Mark) Zhang take the user relevance feedback in image retrieval as a standard two-class pattern classification problem aiming at refining the retrieval precision by learning through the user relevance feedback data. They investigate this problem by noting two important unique characteristics of the problem: small sample collection and asymmetric sample distributions between positive and negative samples. They develop a novel approach to empirical Bayesian learning to solve this problem by explicitly exploiting the two unique characteristics, which is the methodology of Bayesian Learning in Asymmetric and Small (BALAS) sample collections. In BALAS, different learning strategies are used for positive and negative sample collections, respectively, based on the two unique characteristics. By defining the relevancy confidence as the relevant posterior probability, they develop an integrated ranking scheme in BALAS which complementarily combines the subjective relevancy confidence. The objective similarity measure to capture the overall retrieval semantics.

Chapter X

An image is a symbolic representation; people interpret an image and associate semantics with it based on their subjective perceptions, which involves the user's knowledge, cultural background, personal feelings, and so on. Content-based image retrieval (CBIR) systems must be able to interact with users and discover the current user's information needs. An interactive search paradigm that has been developed for image retrieval is machine learning with a user-in-the-loop, guided by relevance feedback, which refers to the notion of relevance of the individual image based on the current user's subjective judgment. Relevance feedback serves as an information carrier to convey the user's information needs/preferences to the retrieval system. Chia-Hung Wei and Chang-Tsun Li provide the fundamentals of CBIR systems and relevance feedback for understanding and incorporating relevance feedback into CBIR systems. Also they discuss several approaches to analyzing and learning relevance feedback.

Paweł Rotter and Andrzej M. J. Skulimowski describe two new approaches to content-based image retrieval (CBIR) based on preference information provided by the user interacting with an image search system. First, they present the existing methods of image retrieval with relevance feedback, which serve then as a reference for the new approaches. The first extension of the distance function-based CBIR approach makes it possible to apply this approach to complex objects. The new algorithm is based on an approximation of user preferences by a neural network. Further, they propose another approach to image retrieval, which uses reference sets to facilitate image comparisons. The methods proposed have been implemented, and compared with each other and the earlier approaches. Finally, they provide a real-life illustration of the methods proposed: an image-based hotel selection procedure.

Relevance feedback (RF) learning has been proposed as a technique aimed at reducing the semantic gap. By providing an image similarity measure under human perception, RF learning can be seen as a form of supervised learning that finds relations between high-level semantic interpretations and low-level visual properties. That is, the feedback obtained within a single query session is used to personalize the retrieval strategy and thus enhance retrieval performance. Iker Gondra presents an overview of CBIR and related work on RF learning. He also presents his own previous work on a RF learning-based probabilistic region relevance learning algorithm for automatically estimating the importance of each region in an image based on the user's semantic intent.

In the fourth section, we see the intelligent CBIR systems and applications.

Semantics-based retrieval is a trend of the Content-based Multimedia Retrieval. Typically, in multimedia databases, there exist two kinds of clues for query: perceptive features and semantic classes. Zhiping Shi *et al.* propose a framework for multimedia database organization and retrieval integrating the perceptive features and semantic classes. Thereunto, a semantics supervised cluster-based index organization approach (briefly as SSCI) is developed: the entire data set is divided hierarchically into many clusters until the objects within a cluster are not only close in the perceptive feature space, but also within the same semantic class; then an index entry is built for each cluster. Especially, the perceptive feature vectors in a cluster are organized adjacently in disk. Furthermore, the SSCI supports a relevance feedback approach: users sign the positive and negative examples regarded a cluster as unit rather than a single object.

As distributed mammogram databases at hospitals and breast screening centers are connected together through PACS, a mammogram retrieval system is needed to help medical professionals locate the mammograms they want to aid in medical diagnosis. Chia-Hung Wei, Chang-Tsun Li, and Yue Li present a complete content-based mammogram retrieval system, seeking images that are pathologically similar to a given example. In the mammogram retrieval system, the pathological characteristics that have been defined in Breast Imaging Reporting and Data System (BI-RADS™) are used as criteria to measure the similarity of the mammograms. A detailed description of those mammographic features is provided. Since the user's subjective perception should be taken into account in the image retrieval task, a relevance feedback function is also developed to learn individual users' knowledge to improve the system performance.

Video surveillance automation is used in two key modes: watching for known threats in real-time and searching for events of interest after the fact. Typically, real-time alerting is a localized function, for example,. an airport security center receives and reacts to a "perimeter breach alert;" while investigations often tend to encompass a large number of geographically distributed cameras like the London bombing, or Washington sniper incidents. Enabling effective event detection, query and retrieval of surveillance video for preemption and investigation, involves indexing the video along multiple dimensions. Ying-li Tian *et al.* present a framework for event detection and surveillance search that includes video parsing, indexing, and query and retrieval mechanisms. It explores video parsing techniques that automatically extract index data from video; indexing which stores data in relational tables; and retrieval which uses SQL queries to retrieve events of interest and the software architecture that integrates these technologies.

Min Chen and Shu-Ching Chen introduce an advanced content-based image retrieval (CBIR) system, MMIR, where Markov model mediator (MMM) and multiple instance learning (MIL) techniques are integrated seamlessly and act coherently as a hierarchical learning engine to boost both the retrieval accuracy and efficiency. The proposed MMIR system utilizes the MMM mechanism to direct the focus on the image level analysis together with the MIL technique (with the neural network technique as its core) to real-time capture and learn the object-level semantic concepts with some help of the user feedbacks. In addition, from a long-term learning perspective, the user feedback logs are explored by MMM to speed up the learning process and to increase the retrieval accuracy for a query.

Acknowledgment

The editor wishes to thank all of the authors for their insights and excellent contributions to this book and would like to acknowledge the help of all involved in the collation and review process of the book, without whose support the project could not have been satisfactorily completed. Most of the authors of chapters included in this book also served as referees for chapters written by other authors. Thanks go to all those who provided constructive and comprehensive reviews.

A further special note of thanks goes to all the staff at IGI Global, whose contributions throughout the whole process from inception of the initial idea to final publication have been invaluable. Special thanks also go to the publishing team at IGI Global. This book would not have been possible without the ongoing professional support from IGI Global.

The idea of editing this volume stems from the initial research work that the editor did in past several years. The assistances and facilities of Northeastern University, China, are deemed important, and are highly appreciated. The research work of the editor supported by the *Program for New Century Excellent Talents in University* (NCET-05-0288).

Zongmin Ma, PhD & Professor
April 2008

Section I

Chapter I
Genetic Algorithms and Other Approaches in Image Feature Extraction and Representation

Danilo Avola
Institute of Research on Population and Social Policies - National Research Council, Italy

Fernando Ferri
Institute of Research on Population and Social Policies - National Research Council, Italy

Patrizia Grifoni
Institute of Research on Population and Social Policies - National Research Council, Italy

ABSTRACT

The novel technologies used in different application domains allow obtaining digital images with a high complex informative content, which can be exploited to interpret the semantic meaning of the images themselves. Furthermore, it has to be taken into account that the complex informative content extracted from the images, that is, the features, need of flexible, powerful, and suitable ways to be represented and managed. The metadata through which a set of images can be described are directly tied to the quality and quantity of the extracted features; besides the efficient management of the metadata depend on the practical and capable feature representation. The more used approaches to analyze the image content do not seem able to provide an effective support to obtain a whole image understanding and feature extraction process. For this reason, new classes of methodologies that involve computational intelligent approaches have been developed. In particular, genetic algorithms (GAs) and other artificial intelligent-(AI) based approaches seem to provide the best suitable solutions. The artificial intelligent technologies allow for the obtaining of a more semantically complex metadata image representation through which to develop advanced systems to retrieval and to handle the digital images. This new method to conceive a metadata description allows the user to make queries in a more natural, detailed, and semantically complete way. As a result it can overcome the always more sophisticated duties caused by the use of wide local and/or distributed databases with heterogeneous complex images.

INTRODUCTION

Digital images, that describe objects and/or situations in the real world, are frequently used to support complex human being activities. Furthermore, the pervasive use of image capture devices, and the increasing relevance of the image analysis in specialized fields (such as: medical, military, satellite, engineering, and so on) have brought an exponential growth of the image data sets into the local and/or distributed image databases. This growth makes the database management, and in particular the image retrieval, a complex task. Moreover, the entropy level of the images contained in these databases makes the optimal exploitation of the images and the performance of several operations (such as: intelligent indexing, comparisons, inference, special query, analysis, processing, and so on) not easy. All these factors contribute to the data mining processes inefficiency. This kind of problems can be overcome exploiting the images themselves. In fact, the novel technologies used in the different application domains allow to obtain images with high level details. These images often possess an informative content that goes beyond the simple visual representation. That is, by observing the relationships among pixels (or clusters of pixels) meaningful features of what is represented in the image can be brought out. This information content is connected to features of an image (such as: textures, colours, patterns, local and global characteristics, and so on). For this reason, the feature extraction matter is one of the main issues in image processing, since the understanding of the meaningful image features implies understanding the image (and parts of it) with its own semantic content. These features can be exploited, by the image analysis processes, to evaluate deeply the semantic informative content of every image, that is, to understand the morphological structure of every object contained in the image and the whole image itself. By the semantic content, and the connected features, it is possible to obtain an exhaustive and great metadata image representation through which to accomplish more effectively the mentioned database operations. In particular, store and retrieval operations can be performed in powerful, efficient and effectiveness way.

It is important to observe that the complex features extracted from images with high level details need new approaches to be represented. In fact, as well known, high level semantic characteristics (such as: textures, objects, shapes, patterns, local and global characteristics, and so on) need of more complex logical structures than low level semantic characteristics (such as: colours, statistical content information, gradients, and so on) to be represented. Moreover, it has to be taken in account that a single high level semantic characteristic on an image (as the texture) can require several feature images (called feature space) to be expressed. The quality and the accuracy of the feature space allow to classify every image according to the connected semantic characteristic, while the capacity to manage of the feature space (that is, the related feature space representation) drive the effectiveness with which the developed systems can store and retrieve the images into the databases. This chapter introduces and discusses the different Artificial Intelligent (AI) approaches used to extract and to represent the features of any image. In particular, the role of the Genetic Algorithms (GAs) has been highlighted. The chapter starts from a brief discussion about the feature extraction process, then it introduces a general description of some of the most interesting AI approaches and their application in image feature extraction problems. A more complete and exhaustive description of the GAs is given. Finally the possibility of combined AI approaches (used in the hybrid systems) to solve more complex feature extraction problems is faced. Therefore, some of the most recent and powerful applications exploiting the AI image feature extraction are shown.

FEATURE EXTRACTION PROCESS

The image feature extraction process (Konstantinos et al., 2006; Woods, 2006) is the step through which it is possible to create the feature maps able to explain the semantic meaning of the image itself. These maps are represented by numerical, logical or symbolic elements. Every map identify a specific characteristic of the image (low level feature), several maps are needed to obtain a more complex features (high level feature). Images with high level of colours, objects and details (that is, with several complex features) need of several different set of maps to explain their own semantic content. Obviously, the complexity of the features extracted from the images depends on two main factors. The first one regards the intrinsic complexity of the image. In fact the content of an image can be more or less ambiguous and understandable. This depends on several factors that can influence the image layout, such as: the number and the complexity of the objects represented inside the image, the spatial relationships between these objects, the logical connections between these objects, the textures and the patterns through which these objects are expressed, the complex patterns, structures and shapes represented inside the image, and so on. Moreover, it has to be into account that there are graphical domains (such as: industrial, mechanical, and so on), which are less complex than others (such as: medical, biological, and so on), in fact, as well known (Zhang, 2006; Sarfraz, 2005), the image understanding in artificial domains have a low level of complexity than natural domains. The second factor related to the complexity of the features extracted from the images regards the kind of features that the user wants to obtain from the images. A digital image has a semantic information content distributed on several levels. In fact in an image it is possible to analyze simple features (as the colour scale) or complex features (as the morphological characteristics that make up the object inside the image). Likewise more deep analysis related the context of the image as well as conjectural analysis regarding the semantic meaning of the image can be performed. The quality, quantity and depth of the features extracted from the image depend on how the user intends to use the information. In particular, an image classification system based on simple colour variation (where a simple RGB query is used to identify images that have the specified amount of colours) is much less complex than one based on textural or semantic information (where a descriptive query is used to identify images that have, with a fixed degree of uncertainty, the required semantic features). Moreover, it is important to observer that the metadata description obtained by complex features allow to conceive store and retrieval image systems based on complex query. For example, a system based on texture analysis approach can adopt complex ways to formulate a query, such as: the natural language to describe a scene, the use of pattern template (query by example), the use of a mathematical description of a complex features, and so on. A further aspect that has to be taken into account regards the way through which the features are represented. This aspect is tightly tied to both the semantic meaning of each extracted feature and how this feature will be used by the user. In fact a same feature (for example, the corners measure of the objects in an image) can be represented in different ways (numerical representation, expressed by constraints between the strokes that make up the corner, vectorial representation, and so on). To explain the just mentioned concepts it is necessary to introduce the following example (see Figure 1).

In Figure 1 are represented twenty-one segments. A first set of simple extracted features may regard the identification of the segments and related spatial positions inside the graphical layout, moreover the texture of each element may be "easily" detected. Indeed, a more careful analysis can highlight more complex features. For example by a simple approach of pattern recognition two main patterns can be identified, as shown in Table 1.

Figure 1. An example of image understanding

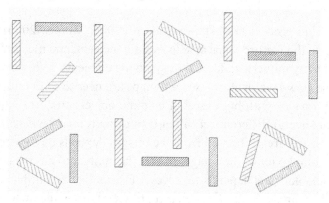

Table 1. Two different patterns

Brief Geometrical Description of the two Patterns	Representations of the two Patterns		
First Reference Pattern	Variation of the First Pattern		
△			
Second Reference Pattern	Variation of the Second Pattern		

Table 1 shows two different patterns, in particular the first pattern is made up by three segments in a triangular geometrical relationship, while the second pattern is made up by a more complex geometrical relationship. In fact, it is composed by four segments where: the two external verticals segments and one horizontal segment are equidistant in considering of a horizontal measure, besides the fourth segment is inner to the two external horizontal segments. Other geometrical consideration could be made for the elements involved in the second pattern. Indeed, the second pattern is an interpretation about some set of segments identified into the graphical layout, it is the more likely but not the only possible. These two patterns can be used to describe the semantic meaning of the image, other features, as shown in Figure 2, could be extracted to support the just extracted features.

In Figure 2 are shown two additional features that could be considered in the image understanding process. In particular, two different triangular relationships are identified for the three shapes belonging to the first and second pattern. Moreover, it can be observed that three segments (belonging to the shapes related to the first pattern) have the same texture. Obviously, other features (simple and/or complex) could be extracted. It depends from several factors, such as: application domain, type of image classification method, structure of the queries with which it is possible to interact with the store/retrieval system, and so on.

Figure 2. An example of further extracted features

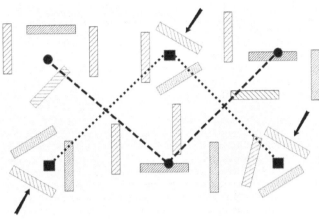

Also the representation of the extracted features covers a main role. In fact, every feature can be represented in several ways depending from how the user wants to apply the information. In this case, the bi-dimensional geometrical domain, the simple textures and the intuitive geometrical relationships between the elements suggest to use a simple numerical or vectorial representation. In Table 2 is shown a simple tree representation, expressed in XML like standard that can be used to describe every kind of 2D graphical shape (Quin, 1999), which resumes the main characteristics of the shape belonging to the first reference pattern.

The vectorial description provided in Table 2 highlights some main characteristics of the related shape. In particular, the spatial constraints (SpatialOnPrimitives) fix the spatial relationships between the three elements that make up the shape. The linkage constraints (LinkedTextures) identify specific textures associated (by a hash-table) to the elements. Furthermore, the approximate constraints (ApproximableSpatialOnPrimitives) identify the rotation degree of the elements respect the horizontal axis (x axis). Indeed, the constraints shown in Table 2 represent only a sub-set of the real complex constraints that need to describe the related shape in a vectorial way. Moreover, additional information regarding the relationships about all the shapes in the graphical layout can be needful to describe the whole shapes' situation.

All the described factors (that is, the features extracted from an image and the related representation) make up the theoretical basis through which to analyze and to create the store/retrieval systems. The different choices performed in these two main issues drive the capability, adaptability, reliability and goodness of the related implemented image store/retrieval systems.

The purpose of this kind approach is to provide a suitable and adaptable system for the definite application domain and to implement store and retrieve operations in effective and efficient way. All these kinds of reasoning can be applied on every type of image both in natural domain and artificial domain. The main goal of these efforts is to obtain a semantic description that goes beyond the simple explanation of the sum of the parts that make up the graphical layout of the image.

The last factor that has to be taken into account regards the "link" between the approach used to extract the image information and the way with which the images are stored and recovered in the system. In fact, these two aspects that compose the image retrieval framework are tightly connected. For example,

Table 2. XML-like shape representation

Shape	Vectorial XML like Representation
| | ```
<Description id="Shape 4">
    <GeneralizedPrimitives>
        <Segment id="Segment-1"/>
        <Segment id="Segment-2"/>
        <Segment id="Segment-3"/>
    </GeneralizedPrimitives>
    <Constraints>
        <SpatialOnPrimitives>
            <Coincident first="Segment-1" second="Segment-2"/>
            <AboutThirty first="Segment-1" second="Segment-2"/>
            <GreaterLength first="Segment-1" second="Segment-2"/>
            <Coincident first="Segment-2" second="Segment-3"/>
            <AboutThirty first="Segment-2" second="Segment-3"/>
            <GreaterLength first="Segment-2" second="Segment-3"/>
            <Coincident first="Segment-3" second="Segment-1"/>
            <AboutThirty first="Segment-3" second="Segment-1"/>
            <GreaterLength first="Segment-3" second="Segment-1"/>
            ..............................................................
        </SpatialOnPrimitives>
        <LinkedTextures>
            <TextureLink primitive="Segment-1" texture="type a"/>
            <TextureLink primitive="Segment-2" texture="type a"/>
            <TextureLink primitive="Segment-3" texture="type b"/>
        </LinkedTextures>
        <ApproximableSpatialOnPrimitives>
            <SegmentOrientation first="Segment-1" second="Segment-2"/>
            <SegmentOrientation first="Segment-2" second="Segment-3"/>
            <SegmentOrientation first="Segment-3" second="Segment-1"/>
            ..............................................................
        </ApproximableSpatialOnPrimitives>
        ..................................................................
    </Constraints>
</Description>
``` |

a query by example (Belkhatir, 2005; Vu et al., 2003) and a query by lexical description (Belkhatir et al., 2005; Dagli et al., 2004) systems require two completely different logical structures. Also the kind of information extracted from the images and the data structures in which the information are stored have to be conceived differently.

In the next two sections both a general description of some of the most interesting AI approaches applied in image feature extraction and a more exhaustive description of the GAs are introduced.

AI APPROACHES IN IMAGE FEATURE EXTRACTION

The current approaches to perform the feature extraction activity (from different images in different domains) can be aided by new technological software approaches (Saad et al., 2007). For this reason, in the early years, there has been much effort to adopt novel computer science approaches on feature extraction matter.

The Artificial Intelligence is a branch of Computer Science made up by several different complex areas. These areas have the common characteristic to exploit, from different points of view, the concepts that drive the capacities (and/or mechanisms) of the human intellect to solve different problems in different
```

application domains (*advanced human problem solving*). In this context, the AI allows a careful feature extraction activity from the image to obtain a higher (respect the conventional approaches) information content description. Indeed, the extracted features and their representations are usually distinguished concepts. In fact, the first one (extracted features) are tied up to both the image application domain (that determines complexity and quantity of the features that can be extracted from the given images) and the approach used to perform the feature extraction process. While the second one (related representations) are tied up according to the specific logical algorithms and logical data structure used to reach the prefixed aim. For example, it is possible to represent a particular image feature by several different logical data structure, such as: graphs, trees, set of mathematical constraints, statistical models, and so on. Therefore, the strategies and the algorithms used and/or created to manage the image representation are deeply tied up to the performed choice. This kind of choice is often driven by the way in which both the indexing of the images and the modality of the queries (such as: visual query, textual query, graphical query, and so on).

An interesting powerful approach used to extract meaningful features from an image belongs to the *Intelligent Agents* (IAs) area. Commonly, the IAs based approaches use an entity (the agent) which is aware of the assigned task, and this entity knows how to accomplish it (Jennings et al., 1998). This kind of algorithms is based on single elaboration entities, which work together on the same task and/or separately on different tasks (or parts of the same task). Each entity has to respect several characteristics such as (but not only): reactivity (the ability to interact timely with the environment and the events that occur in it), pro-activity (the ability to work in expected way, but if necessary it has to be also able to take initiatives), autonomy (the ability to work without external presence), social ability (the ability to interact with both other entities and humans). In particular, this last mentioned main property of the entities has a huge relevance in the image feature extraction. In fact, complex image domains require a large amount of feature maps to be described, therefore it is necessary to employ a large amount of agents able to understand the different peculiarity into the images. These agents have to interact each other to accomplish the relative assigned tasks. The complexity of the communication mechanism occurs according to the number and the complexity of the agents involved in the process. For this reason the features of whatever image are usually extracted by *Multi-Agent Systems* which work separately (but in

Figure 3. Simple image feature extraction conceptual scheme

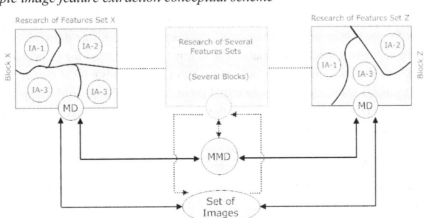

constant contact) on different aspects of the image (Liu et al., 2002). In Figure 3 a simple conceptual scheme of a common MAS architecture is given.

Figure 3 shows several blocks, each one made up by several IAs. Each block deals with a set of simple and/or complex features (or also a single feature), every agent inside a block can be considered an expert entity regarding a specific feature (such as: colours, corners, textures, and so on) or part of it. Every agent in a block can interact only with the agents of the same block. The coordination and interaction activities between blocks are performed by the mediator agents (MD) and a unique master mediator agent (MMD). The IA systems are particularly used in complex natural domain, such as: medical fields, biological fields, and so on. The reason is that these systems are particularly congenial to the statistical computation, that is, to identify: statistical patterns, stochastic situations, approximate models, and so on.

An interesting approach belonging to the IAs area, that follows the mentioned MAS architecture, is performed by *Pattern Recognition Agents* (PRA) (Konar, 2000; Liu et al., 2000). In this approach each agent is learned to recognize a particular feature (or parts of it) of the image (such as: set of primitive patterns, set of correlated colours, set or sub-set of textures, and so on). The agents can be grouped in teams, where every team deals with a specific feature (or set of features). The ability of interaction among PRAs drives the quality of extracted features. In fact a single pattern can be composed by several different aspects. Every agent belongs to a team has to interact with the other team agents to accomplish accuracy the connected feature extraction process. This reasoning can be used in a higher level to highlight the importance of interaction between teams.

The representation of the features extracted by agents depends on the kind of agents themselves. Several agents store the features to provide them to the other agents, in other cases the features have to be provided to the whole image retrieval system. Consequently, the data structures can have a wide range of representations, however the features exchange purely between agents have commonly a double-precision numerical representation.

Another considerable (and charming) application area regards the Neural Networks (NNs) also called Artificial Neural Networks (ANNs) (Hopgood, 2005). The applied paradigm, in this area, is connected to the cognitive information processing structure based on models of human brain function. The ANNs have been developed "to mimic" the elaboration way with which the central nervous system performs the information processing activity. ANNs (likewise to the hardware ANNs) can be considered like interconnected entities that work together to produce an output function. An ANN software architecture is composed by a number of interconnected units (called also neurons or nodes). Each unit can receive one (or more) input and can perform one output. Moreover the output performed by a unit can be used either as an input to other units or it can be part of the output of the whole network (I/O characteristics). Each unit implements a local mathematical or computational model for information processing. The output of any unit depends on several factors, such as (but not only): local model, interconnection (weighted) among units, I/O characteristics, external input, score feedback, and so on. The number and the kind of the factors (as well the complexity of the network topology) are related to the kind and the complexity of the specific application.

The topology of an ANN image feature extraction depends on both the application domain and the specified filters (that is, the algorithms) used to extract the features.

In general, there are several topologies of an ANN, both in learning and analysis phase, such as: State Space Neural Network (SSNN) (Zayan, 2006), Multi-Layer Perceptron Network (MLPN) (Eleuteri et al., 2005), Modular Feed-Forward Network (MFFN) (Boerrs et al., 1992), and so on. These topologies

Figure 4. Hierarchical ANN topology

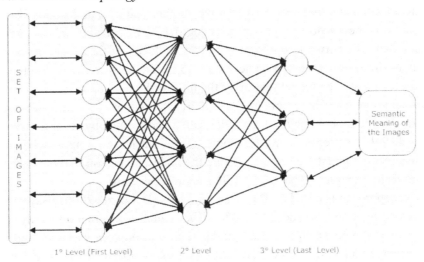

can be applied on one or more conceptual layers through which to implement the whole steps regarding the image retrieval system. Moreover there are several paradigms with which these topologies can be applied, such as: supervised, unsupervised and reinforcement. Indeed, as shown in Figure 4, in image feature extraction the hierarchical topology is widely used. Every image is firstly analyzed by several neurons (nodes belonging to the first level) that catch the lowest possible features, such as: colours, simple primitives, simple patterns, local characteristics, and so on. Afterwards, this set of simple features is analyzed by the neurons of the next level (in the example, second level) to make up a new set of more complex and semantically complete features. This activity is performed until the last ANN level (in the example, third level) to obtain a definitive complex version of the extracted features, such as: textures, complex patterns, objects relationships, and so on. This kind of step by step "refinement" can be performed using several different approaches. For example, a typical simple strategy can be performed catching simple statistical pattern about the image (as colour histograms about prefixed portion of the image) that, level by level, are correlated (by spatial information about cluster of pixels with the same histogram) to make up a more complex statistical scenario describing the object inside the images.

The final aim of the whole network is to provide a complete semantic description of the analyzed images. Indeed, the hierarchical network can have several variations to accomplish the requirements of a specific domain or a complex image retrieval system. The functionality of the algorithms inside each node is strongly subdivided according to the related level. In particular, while the algorithms belonging to the "low" levels work deeply on the image features, ones belonging to the "high" levels have to join and to interpret the information of the previous levels to provide, at the following level, high level descriptions.

A common algorithm based on ANN hierarchical topology is performed by *Complex Adaptive System* (CAS) (Arunkumar, 2004) paradigms. These systems can able to change their structure (topology, by adding nodes and functionalities) according to the external or internal information that flow through the network.

The employment of the ANNs in image feature extraction occurs usually after a hard phase of training process. In fact, these nets have to learn to recognize every single feature by a set of training data set. In particular, the net parameters are trained to recognize a first specific feature, afterwards the parameters are adjusted and managed to recognize another features, and so on. This phase can be very hard because every new feature that can be recognized can "invalidate" the previous choices. During this process both the network topology and the complexity of the model inside each net node can undergo changes. In particular, it can be necessary to introduce new nodes into the net otherwise to "complicate" (or to change) the model that drive the node task.

There are several approaches based on ANNs. The reason is that the same goal (for example the research of a particular roughness in a texture model) can be performed by several different nets. This involves possible different patterns of net topologies, different learning approaches (supervised or unsupervised), different computational models inside the nodes, and so on. All of this makes the classification of image feature extraction based on ANNs approaches hard.

A common ANN approach is based on Bayesian networks (Dol et al., 2006) (Bayesian Neural Network, BNN). This kind of networks is designed to learn very quickly and incrementally. They are based on probabilistic graphical models. In the graph nodes represent random variables and arcs represent dependencies between random variables with conditional probabilities at nodes. Frequently, BNNs are used to obtain many advantages over traditional methods of determining causal relationships (Limin, 2006). For example, the BNNs parameters of the models are expressed as a probability distribution rather than a single set of values. Other advantages regard the possibility (by the model) to support a powerful supervised ate learning phase and the opportunity to have a well knowledge feedback mechanisms to ensure an acceptable range of errors.

In image features extraction these causal relationships represent the desired image features. The BNNs (but also other ANNs) are made up by "reasoning layers" (that is, layers able to understand the effective structure of the image according to the layer knowledge) in which each layer attends to a specific feature level (for example a BNN with three levels can have: first level - global geometrical features, second level - stroke features, third level – shape/object features). Obviously, each layer is connected to each other, but the ability and the "knowledge" of nodes is tied up to the specific layer.

Differently from the previously introduced artificial intelligent areas, the input and output of the approaches belonging to the ANNs area are usually mathematical vectors.

An interesting AI area very frequently used for feature extraction is *Artificial Vision* (AV). The approaches belonging to this area aim to identify image features by "mimicking" human visual perception. The AV process tends to identify simple (such as: colours, simple shapes/patterns, and so on) and complex (such as: complex shapes/patterns, objects/models, relationship among objects/models, and so on) features exploiting the "mimicked" human ability to recognize them in the image.

Unlike the aforementioned thematic areas, the AV does not have specific common approaches. It includes a set of methods and techniques that are used in a lot of different ways in the image feature extraction matter. A common element of these approaches is the *Image Operator* (IO) concept (called also: image-filter, elaboration-mask, feature-extractor, etc., or simply feature). The IO is usually the computational unit that deals with a single feature (or part of it in complex features). The joined use of more IOs is performed to extract more complex feature and/or a set of simple/complex features. The *Spatial Gray Level Dependence Matrixes* (SGLDM) are commonly used to perform IOs able to recognize complex features (Haralick et al., 1973). These matrixes work on the spatial relationships that occur among pixels belonging to predefined portions of the image. There are several ways to effectively perform the matrixes, that is there are several ways to consider the distance between two pixels or cluster of pixels (such as: Euclidean, circular, eight neighbours, four neighbours, and so on). A common approach is to use the *Co-Occurrence Matrixes* (Vadivel, 2007). Through an opportune mathematical interpretation of these matrixes (that is, a mathematical norm that gives a single value from an entire matrix) the IOs can recognize complex textural visual features such as: regularity, roughness, coarseness, directionality, and so on.

Indeed, the image understanding/learning process by AV is also used to extract these features, which are visible only by an artificial sophisticated visual approach (advanced visual perception that goes beyond the common visual perception).

There are others AI areas that can be adopted in several ways to support the image feature extraction, such as: *Case-Base Reasoning* (CBR), *Knowledge-Based Systems* (KBSs), *Fuzzy Logic*, *Decision Trees*, and so on.

GENETIC ALGORITHMS IN IMAGE FEATURE EXTRACTION

One of the most recent interesting AI areas in the image feature extraction regards the *Evolutionary Algorithms* (EAs). Commonly, these kinds of algorithms use a heuristic approach to find approximate solutions to optimization and search problems.

The EAs are inspired by Darwin's theory about biological evolution. For this reason they use techniques driven by evolutionary biology (such as: reproduction, inheritance, mutation, selection, and crossover -also called recombination- survival of the fittest, and so on) to reach a solution. These algorithms start from a non-optimal solution and reach the optimal one toward their evolution. Indeed, there are several kinds of EAs (Freitas, 2002; Korolev, 2007; Zheng et al., 2007), such as: *Genetic Algorithms* (GAs), *Genetic Programming* (GP), *Evolutionary Programming* (EP), *Evolution Strategies* (ESs), and others. All these EAs follow the Darwin inspiration but, at the same time, they are distinguished by the different ways with which they have been applied, such as: different interpretation of evolution, different role of the solutions in evolutionary mechanism, different concept of mutation, and so on. The EAs adopt different *conceptual models* (paradigms) with which the Darwin evolution is performed.

Between the aforementioned algorithms the GAs use the paradigm that better than others adapts itself for the image feature extraction problems (Li et al., 2004; Brumby et al., 1999; Brumby et al., 2002) that is the "concept" behind the GA paradigm has a natural empathy with the image feature extraction problems. This paradigm can be expressed as follow: the GA is started with a set of abstract candidate solutions population. These solutions are represented by chromosomes (genotypes or genomes). The Solutions from one population are taken and used to form a new population. This last process is motivated by the hope that the new population will be better than the old one. In each generation, the fitness of each candidate solution is evaluated, multiple candidate solutions are stochastically selected from the current solutions (based on their fitness), and modified (recombined and/or mutated and/or others "genetic" operations) to form a new population of candidate solutions. The new population is then used in the next iteration of the algorithm.

The GAs, adopted with this paradigm, are generally used to perform optimization tasks in several different application domains. In image feature extraction this family of algorithms is used to increase both the quality and quantity of the features extracted from the image. They are used to catch particular kinds of features (such as: complex patterns or complex textures) that are hardly achievable with common approaches. All these factors play a relevant role in *graphical data mining* applications.

The GAs (and the EAs in general) applied to the image feature extraction allow to exploit and improve the just imposed conventional techniques based on statistical/synthetic pattern recognition, edge detection, shapes/objects analysis, model characterization/extraction, and so on. In fact, the GAs allow creating a framework through which the well known potentialities of the conventional techniques. Inside the GA framework, well known feature vectors otherwise specific mathematical image operators or even whole classical applications of image feature extraction are hosted. The framework allows improving the basic techniques through the GAs optimal research process. In Figure 5 a simple graphical explication about the GA paradigm applied to the image feature extraction is given.

As it is possible to observe by Figure 5, initial features are used to provide a start up to the retrieval system. These features can be randomly or empirically discovered in previous studies and/or analysis. The "temporary" solution is evaluated usually by a matching function on well-known pattern and/or configuration belonging to the images application domain. The best features are selected, modified, recombined and mutated to provide a new generation of features to restart the whole process. Usually, a rank on the matching function is used to decide the end of the process.

The candidate solutions of the GAs, differently from the case of their use for the image features extraction, are usually (but not only) represented by binary strings. The initial population may be created at random or some knowledge about previously known solutions may be used. In image feature extraction the candidate solutions tend to be considerably more complex. They are conveyed by several different heterogeneous ways such as: mathematical functions, formal descriptions, languages (such as the natural language), numerical feature vectors, and so on. For example, several GAs approaches use, as candidate solutions, selected (depending on a specific domain) image operators connected to the desired features. Other approaches to reach the same aim use well known experimental numerical feature vectors. In more complex approaches the candidate solutions can be also conveyed by high level description languages (such as: natural language, visual language, and so on), otherwise by autonomy algorithms (Cheng et al., 2005; Leveson et al., 2004) each one dedicated to catch a particular feature. An autonomy algorithm has the capability to improve the ability in problem solving activity, in particular it is able to face new situations and to integrate the developed behaviour as a new functionality.

Figure 5. General scheme of GA paradigm in image feature extraction

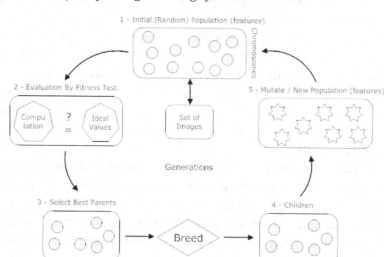

Seldom, the initial population in image feature extraction, is created in random way, because this could bring about problems in system's performance (more than in the common GAs application domains). In fact, a solution (such as a vector) for a single feature (such a kind of texture) can involve several vectors having high dimension.

These algorithms start from low level (or not sufficient) feature description and reach (by evolution) high level (or acceptable) feature description. The candidate solution is essentially driven by several factors: complexity of the image domain, methods through which to perform the evolutionary mechanism, quality and quantity of the desired features, and so on.

The evolution of solutions (included: the specific used "genetic" operators) and the fitness function can be performed in several different ways. They respectively depend on both: the solution's description and the way with which to measure the quality of the population (solutions). Some GAs set the evolution process based on objects/shapes identification by *edge detection* recognition (*segmentation* technique). The candidate solution, in this case, uses the first and second order derivatives to catch the edges in the images. Other kinds of GAs use a completely heuristic approach to find the best set of features able to describe the image. Usually they start from features expressed by numerical vectors, which should represent the meaningful features of the image application domain. Operators (usually: mutation and crossover) "change" the solutions with the aim to perform a more suitable segmentation on training image data set. Also in this case the fitness function works to guarantee a high level of the visual segmentation of the approach.

In general, the GAs will not necessarily achieve the optimal solution to the feature extraction problems, but they permit it by means of a careful manipulation of the solutions and they increase the chances of success choosing a suitable description to the image features.

There is an advanced way that tries to improve the GAs characteristics, the *Genetic Programming* (GP). In this technique not only the solution, but the whole GAs evolves. In this way the algorithm can adapt itself to different kinds of problems and give creative solutions for them. GP is often used to construct image-processing operators for specific tasks. The fitness of the parse tree is usually evaluated by comparison with training examples, where the task to be achieved has been performed manually.

There are several ways to perform the output of the AI image feature extraction approaches. Indeed, sometimes may be convenient to have a "standard" output structure contained the set point of interest about the features of an image, such as: graphs, trees, vectors, and so on. In other situations it could be convenient to have more complex "structures" that describe the extracted features, such as: raster images, diagrams, mathematical functions, and so on.

HYBRID SYSTEMS & RECENT APPLICATIONS

The collaborative use of more AI image feature extraction algorithms (*hybrid systems*) can be performed to extract features from complex domains otherwise to improve the performance of a specific AI algorithm. For example, GAs have been used to support the training process of the ANNs. The GAs can be also used to drive the whole structure of the net. Usually, the ANNs engage collaborative relationships with several kinds of EAs (not only GAs).

Several *hybrid systems* adopt at the same time more than one approach such as" *fuzzy logic* (a basic AI area) IAs, ANNs, EAs, and so on. A common strategy of *hybrid systems* is to use the different involved systems by a layer strategy. For example it is possible to use an ANN to recognize the main features of an image, and after, on the extracted features, it can be convenient to adopt a set of IAs to refine the aforementioned features.

Bellow are described some interesting feature extraction applications based on AI methods. For example GENIE (GENetic Imagery Exploration) (Perkins et al., 2000) uses a genetic programming approach to produce automatic feature extraction (AFE) tools for broad-area features in multispectral, hyperspectral, panchromatic, and multi-instrument imagery. Both spectral and spatial signatures of features are discovered and exploited.

Another interesting application, mentioned in (Del Buono, 2007) is Face Recognition ActiveX DLL. This application uses neural net back propagation algorithm with more artificial intelligence tools added for imaging optimization. Library works great even for a low resolution Web cam image and requires the user to align to a mirror frame on screen.

POOKA application (Porter et al., 2003) combines reconfigurable computing hardware with evolutionary algorithms to allow rapid prototyping of image and signal processing algorithms implemented at the chip level. This enables POOKA to rapidly produce customized automated feature extraction algorithms the run hundreds of times faster than equivalent algorithms implemented in software.

The efforts aimed to improve the actual systems in feature extraction field are in increasing growth.

CONCLUSION

The novel technologies, tied to the digital image environment, used to support the complex human being activities have brought an exponential growth of the image data sets into the local and/or distributed image databases.

The entropy of this kind of information makes the management of the images a hard task, moreover the high detail level of the actual images suggests that it is possible to explain the image content to develop innovative feature extraction mechanisms through which to perform store and retrieval activities in efficient and effective way. In particular, genetic algorithms (GAs) and other artificial intelligent (AIs) based approaches seem to provide the best suitable solutions in these feature extraction issues. In this way advanced systems both to retrieve and to handle the images in local and/or distributed databases can be developed.

FUTURE RESEARCH DIRECTIONS

Whole just described image feature extraction approaches have to use a training data set to learn particular patterns and/or specific features that have to be recognized by the related system. In the last years, the emerging trend is to use the training data set by Gaussian Pyramidal Approach (Heeger, 1995; Lowe, 2004). In this approach an image (source image) belonging to the training data set is analyzed to identify the desiderate patterns/features, moreover a new image (sub-sampled image) is generated. The sub-sampled image comes from the source image, the sub-sampling can depend on several factors, such as: lowering of resolution, replacing of pixel sets in the source image with pixel sets less dense (for example, due to an elaboration step), application of mathematical transformation, and so on. This process can be repetitively performed on the obtained image (sub-sampled image) to provide another sub-sampled image respect to the previous one. In this way from a single image, in training data set, it is possible to obtain several images, where every obtained image represents a level of the Gaussian Pyramid (source image is the pyramid base, and the other sub-sampled images represents respectively the first level, the second level, and so on).

All these images are used to understand the variation, quality and quantity of patterns/features into the image application domain. In fact in this way it is possible to obtain a more rich informative content about researched patterns/features. For example, by compared analysis of the different plans (obtained by a simple sub-sampled resolution) it is possible to observe information about the repetitions of specific patterns represented by different scale values.

An interesting opportunity that has to be taken into account in image feature extraction of complex and high resolution images is mathematical representation of the main patterns/features. That is, every pattern/feature (independently from the approach used to find it) can be expressed by a mathematical model, which can be exploited to perform provisional studies about the image application domain. For example, in medical image analysis mathematical models of different patterns representing the human tissues are used to estimate provisional models regarding: diagnosis, analysis, zones delineation, abnormal masses identification and irradiation, and so on.

REFERENCES

Arunkumar, S. (2004). *Neural network and its application in pattern recognition* (Dissemination Report). Department of Computer Science and Engineering, Indian Institute of Technology, Bombay.

Belkhatir, M. (2005). A symbolic query-by-example framework for the image retrieval signal/semantic integration. In *Proceedings of the 17th IEEE International Conference on Tools with Artificial Intelligence, ICTAI* (pp. 348-355). Washington, DC, IEEE Computer Society Press.

Belkhatir, M., Chiaramella, Y., & Mulhem, P. (2005). A signal/semantic framework for image retrieval. In *Proceedings of the 5th ACM/IEEE-CS Joint Conference on Digital Libraries, JCDL '05* (pp. 368-368). Denver, CO, USA, ACM Press.

Boerrs, E. J., & Kuiper, H., (1992). *Biological metaphors and the design of modular artificial neural networks*. Master's thesis, Department of Computer Science and Experimental Psychology, Leiden University.

Brumby, S. P., Theiler, J., Perkins, S., Harvey, N. R., & Szymanski, J. J. (2002). *Genetic programming approach to extracting features from remotely sensed imagery*. Paper presented at the internal meeting of Space and Remote Sensing Sciences, Los Alamos National Laboratory, Los Alamos, New Mexico.

Brumby, S. P., Theiler, J., Perkins, S. J., Harvey, N., Szymanskia, J. J., Bloch, J. J., & Mitchellb, M. (1999). *Investigation of image feature extraction by a genetic algorithm*. Paper presented at the internal meeting of the Los Alamos National Laboratory, Space and Remote Sensing Sciences, Santa Fe Institute.

Cheng, M. Y. K., Micacchil, C., & Cohen, R. (2005). Adjusting the autonomy of collections of agents in multiagent Ssystems. In *Advances in Artificial Intelligence, 3501, 2005* (pp. 33-37). Springer Berlin / Heidelberg Publisher.

Dagli, C., & Huang, T. S. (2004). A framework for grid-based image retrieval. *17th International Conference on Pattern Recognition, 2, ICPR'04* (pp. 1021-1024). IEEE Computer Society Press.

Del Buono, A. (2007). *An overview about sophisticatedfFace recognition systems.* (Tech. Rep No. 1). National Research Centre, Computer Science and Knowledge Laboratory (CSK Lab).

Dol, Z., Salam, R. A., & Zainol, Z. (2006). Face feature extraction using Bayesian network. *Proceedings of the 4th International Conference on Computer Graphics and Interactive Techniques* (pp. 261-264). ACM Press.

Eleuteri, A., Tagliaferri, R., & Milano, L. (2005). A novel information geometric approach to variable selection in MLP Networks. *International Journal on Neural Network, 18*(10), 1309-1318, Elsevier Science Publishing.

Freitas, A. A. (2002). A survey of evolutionary algorithms for data mining and knowledge discovery. *Advances in evolutionary computation: Theory and application, natural computing series* (pp. 819-845). Springer Publisher.

Haralick, R. M., & Shanmugam, K. (1973). Textural features for image classification. *IEEE Transaction on Systems Man Cysbern, 3*(6), 610-621. IEEE Press.

Heeger, D. J., & Bergen, J. R. (1995). Pyramid-based texture analysis/synthesis. *In Proceedings of the 22nd Annual Conference on Computer Graphics and Interactive Techniques* (pp. 229-238). ACM Press.

Hopgood, A. A. (2005). The state of artificial intelligence. In M. V.Zelkowitz (Ed.), *Advances in Computers* (pp. 1-75). Elsevier Publishing.

Jennings, N. R., Sycara, K., & Wooldridge M. (1998). A roadmap of agent research and development. *International Journal on Autonomous Agents and Multi-Agent Systems, 1*(1), 7-38. Boston, Kluwer Academic Publishers.

Konar, A. (Ed.). (2000). Artificial intelligence and soft computing - Behavioral and cognitive modeling of the human brain. CRC Press.

Konstantinos, N. P., & Rastislav, L. (Eds.). (2006). *Color image processing: Methods and applications.* CRC Press

Korolev, L. N. (2007). On evolutionary algorithms, neural-network computations, and genetic programming. Mathematical problems. *International Journal on Automation and Remote Control, 68*(5), 811-821. Plenum Press.

Li, Q., Hu, H., & Shi, Z. (2004). Semantic feature extraction using genetic programming in image retrieval. *Proceedings of the 17th International Conference on Pattern Recognition, ICPR 2004, 1(23-26),* pp. 648-651. IEEE Computer Society Press.

Leveson, N. G., & Weiss, K. A. (2004). Making embedded software reuse practical and safe. *Proceedings of the Twelfth International Symposium on ACM SIGSOFT* (pp. 171-178). ACM Press.

Limin, W. (2006). Learning Bayesian-neural network from mixed-mode data. In *Neural information processing* (pp. 680-687). Springer Publisher.

Liu, J., & Yin, J. (2000). Multi-agent integer programing. *Proceedings of the Second International Conference on Intelligent Data Engineering and Automated Learning* (pp. 301-307), Springer Press.

Liu, J., & Zhao, Y. (2002). On adaptive agentlets for distributed divide-and-conquer: A dynamical systems approach. *IEEE Transactions on Systems, Man and Cybernetics, 32(2)*, 214-227. IEEE Press.

Lowe, D. G. (2004). Distinctive image features from scale-invariant keypoints. *International Journal of Computer Vision, 60(2)*, 91-110.

Perkins, S., Theiler, J., Brumby, S. P., Harvey, N. R., Porter, R., Szymanski, J. J., & Bloch, J. J. (2000). *GENIE - A hybrid genetic algorithm for feature classification in multi-spectral images.* Los Alamos National Laboratory Internal Proceeding, SPIE 4120 (pp. 52-62).

Porter, R., Eads, D., Hush, D., & Theiler, J. (2003). Weighted order statistic classifiers with large rank-order margin. *Proceedings of the Twentieth International Conference on Machine Learning, ICML 20*, 600-607. Los Alamos National Laboratory, Washington DC.

Quin, L. (Ed.). (1999). *XML Specification Guide.* John Wiley Press.

Saad, A., Avineri, E., Dahal, K., Sarfraz, M., & Roy, R. (Eds.). (2007). *Soft computing in industrial applications: Recent and emerging methods and techniques.* Springer Verlag Press.

Sarfraz, M. (Ed.). (2005). *Computer-aided intelligent recognition techniques and applications.* John Wiley Press.

Vadivel, A., Sural, S., & Majumdar, A. K. (2007). An integrated color and intensity co-occurrence matrix. *Pattern Recognition Letter, 28*, 974-983. Elsevier Science Inc. Publisher.

Vu, K., Hua, K. A., & Jiang, N. (2003). Improving image retrieval effectiveness in query-by example environment. *Proceedings of the 2003 ACM Symposium on Applied Computing*, (pp. 774-781). Melbourne, Florida, USA, ACM Press.

Woods, J. W. (Ed.). (2006). *Multidimensional signal, image, and video processing and coding.* Elsevier Press.

Zayan, M. A. (2006). Satellite orbits guidance using state space neural network. *Aerospace Conference, 4, AERO 2006.* 16-22. IEEE Press.

Zhang, Y. J. (Ed.). (2006). *Advances in image and video segmentation.* Idea Group Inc (IGI) Press.

Zheng, B., & Li, Y. (2007). New model for multi-objective evolutionary algorithms. *Computational Science – ICCS 2007, 4490, 2007*, 037-1044. Springer Berlin/Heidelberg Publisher.

ADDITIONAL READING

Bazin, P. L., & Pham, D. L. (2007). Topology Correction of Segmented Medical Images Using a Algorithm. In *Computer Methods Prog. Biomed., Vol 88, Issue 2* (pp. 182-190). PubMed Press.

Campilho, A., & Kamel, M. (Eds.). (2006). *Image Analysis and Recognition.* Springer Press.

Cyganek, B. (2007). Road Signs Recognition by the Scale-Space Template Matching in the Log-Polar Domain. In *Pattern Recognition and Image Analysis, Vol. 4477/2007* (pp. 330-337). Springer Berlin / Heidelberg Publisher.

Guyon, I., Gunn, S., Nikravesh, M., & Zadeh, L. A. (Eds.). (2006). *Feature Extraction: Foundations and Applications (Studies in Fuzziness and Soft Computing).* Springer Press.

Haikonen, P. O. (Ed.). (2007). *Robot Brains: Circuits and Systems for Conscious Machines.* Wiley Press.

Julesz, B. (Ed.). (1995). *Dialogues on Perception.* Cambridge: Bradford/MIT Press.

Koskela, M., Sjöberg, M., Laaksonen, J., Viitaniemi, V., & Rushes, H. M. (2007). Summarization with Self-Organizing Maps. In *Proceedings of the TRECVID Workshop on Video Summarization, TVS'07* (pp. 45-49). Augsburg, Germany. ACM Press.

Koskela, M., & Smeaton., A. F. (2007). An Empirical Study of Inter-Concept Similarities in Multimedia Ontologies. In *Proceedings of the 6th ACM international conference on image and video retrieval, CIVR 2007* (pp 464-471). Amsterdam, The Netherlands, ACM Press.

Koskela, M., Smeaton, A. F, & Laaksonen J. (2007). Measuring Concept Similarities in Multimedia Ontologies: Analysis and Evaluations. In *IEEE Transactions on Multimedia, Vol. 9, Issue 5* (pp. 912-922). IEEE Computer Society Press.

McIntosh, C., & Hamarne, G. (2006). Genetic Algorithm Driver Statistically Deformed Models for Medical Image Segmentation. In *ACM Workshop on Medical Applications of Genetic and Evolutionary Computation Workshop* (pp. 1-8). ACM Press.

Pratt, W. K. (Ed.). (2007). *Digital Image Processing.* Wiley Press.

Roli, F., & Vitulano, S. (Eds.). (2005). *Image Analysis and Processing.* Springer-Verlag Publisher.

Yeung, D. Y., Kwok, J. T., Fred, A., Roli, F., & de Ridder, D. (Eds.). (2006). *Structural, Syntactic, and Statistical Pattern Recognition.* Springer Press.

Yixin, C., Jia, L., & James Z.W. (Eds.). (2004). *Machine Learning and Statistical Modeling Approaches to Image Retrieval.* Springer/Kluwer Press.

Zhirong, Y., & Laaksonen, J. (2006). A Fast Fixed-Point Algorithm for Two-Class Discriminative Feature Extraction. In *Proceedings of 16th International Conference on Artificial Neural Networks, ICANN 2006* (pp. 330-339). Athens, Greece, Springer Press.

Zhirong, Y., & Laaksonen, J. (2007). Face Recognition Using Parzenfaces. In *Proceedings of International Conference on Artificial Neural Networks, Vol. 4669, ICANN'07* (pp. 200-209). Porto, Portugal, Springer Verlag Publisher.

Zhirong, Y., Zhijian, Y., & Laaksonen, J. (2007). Projective Non-Negative Matrix Factorization with Applications to Facial Image Processing. *International Journal of Pattern Recognition and Artificial Intelligence*, *21*(8), 1353-1362.

Zwiggelaar, R., Blot, L., Raba, D., & Denton., E. R. E. (2003). Set-Permutation-Occurrence Matrix Based Texture Segmentation. In *Pattern Recognition and Image Analysis*, IbPRIA, *Vol. 2652* (pp. 1099-1107). Springer Berlin / Heidelberg Publisher.

Chapter II
Improving Image Retrieval by Clustering

Dany Gebara
University of Calgary, Canada

Reda Alhajj
University of Calgary, Canada

ABSTRACT

This chapter presents a novel approach for content-fbased image retrieval and demonstrates its applicability on non-texture images. The process starts by extracting a feature vector for each image; wavelets are employed in the process. Then the images (each represented by its feature vector) are classified into groups by employing a density-based clustering approach, namely OPTICS. This highly improves the querying facility by limiting the search space to a single cluster instead of the whole database. The cluster to be searched is determined by applying on the query image the same clustering process OPTICS. This leads to the closest cluster to the query image, and hence, limits the search to the latter cluster without adding the query image to the cluster, except if such request is explicitly specified. The power of this system is demonstrated on non-texture images from the Corel dataset. The achieved results demonstrate that the classification of images is extremely fast and accurate.

INTRODUCTION

Since the early 1990's, there has been considerable research carried out into **content-based image retrieval (CBIR)** systems. A few systems have been installed commercially, including Query-By-Image-Content (QBIC) (Niblack, Barber, Equitz, Flickner, Glasman, Petkovic, Yanker, Faloutsos, and Taubin, 1993), the VIR Image Engine (Bach, Fuller, Gupta, Hampapur, Gorowitz, Humphrey, Jain, and Shu, 1996), the AltaVista Photofinder, Multimedia Analysis and Retrieval System (MARS) (Huang,

Mehrotra, and Ramchandran, 1996), Photobook (Pentland, Picard, and Sclaroff, 1994), Netra (Ma and Manjunath, 1999), RetrievalWare (Dowe, 1993), etc. Actually, the problem of sorting through images to find a particular object of interest is not new. Whether it is paintings in old museum archives, or browsing through the family albums looking for a particular photograph, extracting information from graphic objects has presented many challenges. With the recent advent and growth of the internet, this problem has been taken to a whole new level. Further, as the hardware needed to capture and store images in digital format has become cheaper and more accessible, the number of people and businesses that have started collecting large numbers of images has grown. The first strategy for dealing with such large collections of images was to tag each image with one or more keywords, allowing existing text-based search systems to work with images. This was a great leap forward, but still had limitations; the biggest of which is that someone had to choose and enter keywords for every image. In addition to being a very tedious task, selection of keywords is a very subjective function. Another method was to sort images by type and place them in file folders much like photographs would be placed in albums. This also suffers from similar drawbacks.

In general, images could be classified into two classes, texture and non-texture. **Texture images** form an important class, where an object within the image is repeated periodically throughout the image. x Some medical images such as X-rays and some topographic images fall under this category. **Non-texture images** tend to have objects of interest clustered in one or more regions of an image. Figure 1 shows one image from each class.

In order to be able to compare images by content, a feature vector (or representative signature) needs to be calculated for each image. This feature vector is the description of the image to the **content-based image retrieval** (CBIR) system, which will then conduct its search based on these calculated vectors. Generally, the algorithms used to calculate these feature vectors perform well on some class of images and poorly on others. It therefore follows that a **CBIR** system should classify an image first, and then use an appropriate algorithm based on the classification.

In terms of querying speed, a faster system is naturally preferred. Hence, if there is a way to avoid scanning the entire database every time a query is submitted, this should result in faster responses to the user. **Clustering** can be applied to the calculated feature vectors, where the signatures for similar images are grouped as one cluster. When querying, a **CBIR** system need only to look at a representative for each cluster to narrow the search.

To handle the classification and querying of images better in a more concise and effective way, this chapter proposes a system that combines both wavelet analysis and clustering into the image retrieval

Figure 1. Example of Texture and Non-Texture

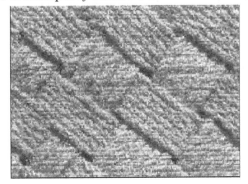

process. The proposed system has a learning phase to understand the images in the database. The learning phase is comprised of different parts. First, a feature vector is calculated for each image. These vectors are then clustered so that similar images are grouped together; we use **OPTICS** clustering approach which does not require the number of clusters be specified in advance. In the querying phase, the query image is first classified, and a feature vector is calculated for the image. The vector is compared to representatives of the clusters only, instead of every stored image in the database. After locating the cluster representing the closest match, the query image is compared to the images within that cluster and the best matches are returned to the user. Finally, the main contributions of this chapter may be enumerated as follows. A simple and efficient classification algorithm has been adapted, developed and tested with excellent results. The developed system can scale well for large databases. **Clustering** has been adapted to reduce the search space, and thus the querying times. It is worth noting that there is no significant deterioration of matching rates as a result of introducing clustering. The **Daubechies wavelet transform** is used to extract feature vectors. It has been demonstrated to be very effective when dealing with general-purpose images (Wang, Wiederhold, Firschein, and Wei, 1997). The proposed approach has been tested using both texture and non-texture images. The results on texture images are reported in (Gebara and Alhajj, 2007). The successful results on texture images motivated extending the approach to work for non-texture images. We describe in this chapter the results on non-texture images from the Corel dataset. Although the results reported on the non-texture images are good compared to those described in the literature, we feel that still we have room for improvement; this is one of the aspects we are currently concentrating on.

The balance of this chapter is organized as follows. Section 2 is a brief overview of the background. The proposed system is presented in Section 3. Section 4 is conclusion. Section 5 is future research directions.

BACKGROUND

In this section, we first present an overview of wavelets as required for understanding how images are analyzed to extract their feature vectors; then we briefly cover the basic CBIR systems described in the literature and/or available online.

Wavelets

Wavelets are basis functions defined over a finite interval. Like any basis function, a set of linear combinations of wavelets (or basis functions) can be used to represent any function $f(x)$. These functions are derived from one wavelet function called the mother wavelet, ψ, by dilations (scaling) and translations:

$$\psi_{a,b}(x) = \frac{1}{\sqrt{|a|}} \psi \left(\frac{x - b}{a} \right) \tag{2.1}$$

where a is the scaling factor and b is the translation (Hong, Wang, and Gardner, 2004; Hubbard, 1998; Unser and Blu, 2000).

The basic idea behind wavelets is to examine a signal, in this case an image, at different resolutions. This is called multi-resolution analysis. The big wavelets correspond to an approximation of the original signal and the small wavelets correspond to the signal details. According to Hubbard as stated in "The World According to Wavelets" (Hubbard, 1998), wavelet transforms are useful to analyze signals with "interesting components at different scales."

There are two functions that play a fundamental role in wavelet analysis. The wavelet (also called mother) function, ψ, defined previously and a scaling function φ. They produce a set of functions that can be used to decompose or reconstruct a signal or an image (Boggess and Narcowich. 2001). Their aim is to transform signal information into coefficients that can be used later on to compress or reconstruct the original image.

Since images contain distinct coefficients corresponding to image pixels, the discrete wavelet transform is obtained by applying discrete filters to the image. The two filters used are one high pass and one low pass filter, defined based on the wavelet used. The simplest wavelet transform is the Haar wavelet and its corresponding high (h_H) and low (l_H) pass filters are given in Equation 2.2:

$$\left. \begin{array}{ll} l_H = & (\frac{1}{2}, \frac{1}{2}), \\ h_H = & (-\frac{1}{2}, \frac{1}{2}) \end{array} \right\} \quad \text{Haar Filters} \qquad (2.2)$$

To see how the Haar wavelet decomposition works, consider the following 1-dimensional image with pixel values: $I = [7\ 5\ 1\ 3]$.

To decompose this image using the **Haar wavelet transform**, it is first passed through the low pass filter l_H to calculate its approximation at a lower resolution. Then, it is passed through the high pass filter h_H to calculate the coefficients that will help in reconstructing the original image later on. The basic premise when decomposing an image is to reduce its size. To accomplish this, one starts by taking every other coefficient. This is called down-sampling. Therefore, the image I is first passed through the low pass filter as shown next:

$$\begin{bmatrix} \frac{1}{2} & \frac{1}{2} & 0 & 0 \\ 0 & 0 & \frac{1}{2} & \frac{1}{2} \end{bmatrix} \bullet \begin{bmatrix} 7 \\ 5 \\ 1 \\ 3 \end{bmatrix} = \begin{bmatrix} \frac{7}{2} + \frac{5}{2} \\ \frac{1}{2} + \frac{3}{2} \end{bmatrix} = \begin{bmatrix} 6 \\ 2 \end{bmatrix}$$

It is then passed through the high pass filter as follows:

$$
\begin{bmatrix} -\frac{1}{2} & \frac{1}{2} & 0 & 0 \\ 0 & 0 & -\frac{1}{2} & \frac{1}{2} \end{bmatrix} \bullet \begin{bmatrix} 7 \\ 5 \\ 1 \\ 3 \end{bmatrix} = \begin{bmatrix} -\frac{7}{2} + \frac{5}{2} \\ -\frac{1}{2} + \frac{3}{2} \end{bmatrix} = \begin{bmatrix} -1 \\ 1 \end{bmatrix}
$$

Therefore, the Haar wavelet decomposition of I=[7 5 1 3] yields an approximation of I at a lower resolution [6 2] and some coefficients [-1 1] to be able to reconstruct the original image from its approximation.

The **Haar wavelet transform** can also be applied to a 2-dimensional image. In this case, first each row of pixel values in the image passes through Haar's low pass filter (l_H), then through the high pass filter (h_H). Later on, each column of pixel values in the newly generated image also passes through Haar's low and high pass filters. This will generate an approximation of the original image at a lower resolution, corresponding to the horizontal and vertical low pass filters (LL). Three more sub-bands with dimensions equal half of the original image will be generated, each corresponding to some detail coefficients in the original image. The sub-band HL, which corresponds to the horizontal high and vertical low filters, contains the vertical coefficients of the original image. The LH sub-band, corresponding to the horizontal low and vertical high filters, contains the horizontal coefficients. Finally, the HH sub-band, which corresponds to the horizontal and vertical high filters, contains the diagonal coefficients.

Another wavelet transform is the **Daubechies wavelet transform**. The mother wavelet is continuous, and in the case of general-purpose images, performs better than the Haar wavelet (Wang, Wiederhold, Firschein, and Wei, 1997). The low (l_D) and high (h_D) **Daubechies filters** are given in Equation 2.3

$$
\left.
\begin{aligned}
l = (l_0, l_1, l_2, l_3) &= (\frac{1+\sqrt{3}}{4\sqrt{2}}, \frac{3+\sqrt{3}}{4\sqrt{2}}, \frac{3-\sqrt{3}}{4\sqrt{2}}, \frac{1-\sqrt{3}}{4\sqrt{2}}), \\
h = (h_0, h_1, h_2, h_3) &= (\frac{1-\sqrt{3}}{4\sqrt{2}}, -\frac{3-\sqrt{3}}{4\sqrt{2}}, \frac{3+\sqrt{3}}{4\sqrt{2}}, -\frac{1+\sqrt{3}}{4\sqrt{2}})
\end{aligned}
\right\} \quad \text{Daubechies Filters} \quad (2.3)
$$

The same principles described earlier for the Haar wavelet apply to the Daubechies wavelet with the difference that there are now four filter coefficients instead of two. This may be a problem when the boundaries of the image are reached.

To apply the **Daubechies wavelet transform** to a 2-dimensional image, the same steps shown earlier for the Haar wavelet are taken, except that the **Daubechies filters** are used. The sequence starts by applying the Daubechies low (l_D in Equation 2.3) and high (h_D in Equation 2.3) pass filters to each row in the image. Then, the **Daubechies filters** are applied to each column of the resulting image, to get four sub-bands: LL, HL, LH and HL.

CBIR Systems

Since the early 1990's, there has been considerable research carried out into **CBIR** systems. Below is a list of the most popular systems, with a brief description of what makes each one unique. For an exhaustive survey and listing of **CBIR** systems, readers are directed towards several papers, e.g., (Zachary and Iyengar, 1999).

Query By Image Content (QBIC) (Niblack, Barber, Equitz, Flickner, Glasman, Petkovic, Yanker, Faloutsos, and Taubin, 1993), developed at IBM, is perhaps the best known example of a CBIR system, and represents the first instance of a commercially installed system. The QBIC system can be experienced on the world wide web. Querying in QBIC can be by color, shape or texture patterns, user-specified sketches, and example image. QBIC is a very important project which helped influence the shape of many CBIR systems that followed it.

The VIR Image Engine (Bach, Fuller, Gupta, Hampapur, Gorowitz, Humphrey, Jain, and Shu, 1996) was developed by Virage Inc.; it is similar to QBIC in that it supports querying by color, layout, texture and shape. It also supports querying by any combination of the aforementioned criteria, where users can adjust the weighting of each criterion to suit their own requirements. The VIR Image Engine is essentially a software development kit where developers are provided with the tools to develop their own graphical user interfaces, support is provided for keyword-based searches, and several image file formats are supported. The AltaVista Photofinder is an example of a system based on VIR technology.

Initially developed at the University of Illinois at Urbana- Champaign, Multimedia Analysis and Retrieval System (MARS) (Hubbard, 1998) supports queries based on color, shape, texture and keywords. It incorporates elements of computer vision, database management and image retrieval. **Texture feature vectors** are extracted using wavelets. MARS attempts to dynamically adapt to different users and environments. There is a feedback architecture built in to help the system learn and adapt.

Photobook (Pentland, Picard, and Sclaroff, 1994) was developed at MIT and works by comparing the features associated with the images rather than the images themselves. The features are typically based on color, shape, and texture. Photobook uses one of a number of algorithms, some based on wavelets, to compare features. More recent versions allow any linear combination of algorithms to be used. An interactive learning agent has been developed to work within Photobook which combines texture, color and shape based on user examples, helping users make their intentions clear to the system.

Netra (Ma and Manjunath, 1999) was developed at the University of California at Santa Barbara, for the Alexandria Digital Library (ADL) project. Netra uses segmentation, followed by extraction of color, spatial location, shape and texture information. Gabor wavelets are used to extract texture feature vectors, and Fast Fourier transforms (FFT) are used to calculate shape feature vectors. Querying can be done by image example or by entering color and spatial location information directly.

RetrievalWare (Dowe, 1993) was developed by Excalibur Technologies Corp. It is another software development kit for building image manipulation applications. Tools for image processing, feature extraction and content-based retrieval are included. Queries may be run, for example, on a combination of color, shape and texture. To run a query, a user specifies the relative importance of the aforementioned three attributes, then selects one of the images that the system returns as the query image. RetrievalWare has been used by both Yahoo! and InfoSeek search engines, and is available for sale.

WebSEEK (Smith and Chang, 1997) was developed at Columbia University and is a web-based search engine. WebSEEK supports queries based on text and or visual content. It is made up of three main modules; one to collect images and video from the internet, another module to classify and index the collected content, and a third to allow users to search or browse. A working demo can be accessed on the world wide web.

WBIIS (Wang, Wiederhold, Firschein, and Wei, 1997) is a CBIR system using **Daubechies wavelets**. In WBIIS, Wang *et al.* propose an image indexing and retrieval system that uses the **Daubechies wavelet transform** of the three color components, Red, Green, and Blue (RGB) to extract features. Indexing of the images is performed by storing the standard deviations and the wavelet coefficients of the fourth and fifth level Daubechies wavelet transform.

The retrieval phase is divided into two parts. First, a coarse selection is done based on the standard deviation; then a finer selection criteria are performed that is based on feature vector matching. The advantage of WBIIS is that it is invariant to size since all images are first normalized to the same size before extracting the feature vectors.

In Simplicity, Wang *et al.* (2001) developed a pre-processing phase, in which an image is first classified as texture vs. non-texture, or graph vs. photograph, before extracting its feature vector. They also segment the image into regions. They use the LUV color component to extract texture features. Some of these features are extracted directly from the color components and some from the wavelet transform of the L component, whereas, the shape/non-texture feature is derived from the normalized inertia. The advantage of Simplicity is its ability to limit the search space by grouping images that belong to the same category together. However, the disadvantage is the time needed to perform the classification. This is done by calculating a feature vector for every 4×4 pixel block and then clustering them to find out which category the image belongs to.

Natsev *et al.* in WALRUS (Natsev, Rastogi, and Shim, 2004) tackle the problem of finding objects of different sizes and locations within an image. They do that by calculating the wavelet transform of sliding windows or variable sizes in an image. A feature vector consisting of the sum wavelet coefficients is calculated for each sliding window. Then, the feature vectors are clustered to determine the regions in an image belonging to the same object. In the image matching phase, the regions of the im-

Figure 2. Information flow within phases of the proposed approach

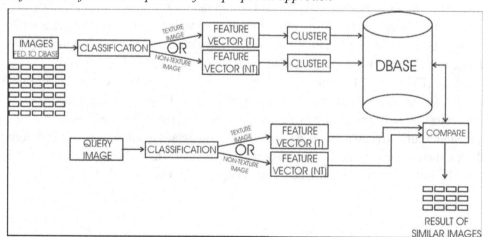

ages are compared and the one with the highest percentage of matching regions with the query image is returned as a query match. The advantage of WALRUS is its ability to retrieve matching images of different object size and location within images. The disadvantage of WALRUS is the high computational complexity due to wavelet transforms of the sliding windows and the large search space from all the sub-images generated.

THE PROPOSED SYSTEM

Figure 2 depicts the information flow within the learning and querying phases of the proposed system. Like most **content-based image retrieval (CBIR)** systems, the proposed system consists of two major phases: the learning phase and the querying phase. In the learning phase, all the images in the database go through an indexing stage, where each image is classified as either **texture** or **non-texture**. Then, based on the image type, a signature, also referred to as a feature vector, is extracted from the image. Each image is represented in the database by a feature vector. After deriving feature vectors for all images in the database, clustering is applied to **texture** and **non-texture** images separately. Each cluster contains a set of images that are most similar to each other. Then for each cluster a representative feature vector is calculated. This representative vector is then used in the querying phase.

The querying phase undergoes the same process of extracting a feature vector for the query image as the learning phase. A distance function is then calculated between the query image feature vector and the representative feature vectors of all clusters having the same class of images (texture/non-texture) as the query image. The cluster with the minimum distance from the query image is then searched for matches.

Feature Extraction

The proposed system classifies images by using the LUV color space, which is device-independent and has "good perception correlation properties" (Li, Wang, and Wiederhold, 2000; Wang, Li, and Wiederhold, 2001), i.e., the Euclidean distance between two colors approximately equals to the perceived color difference (Healey and Enns, 1999). While L encodes luminance, which corresponds to the perceived brightness (or gray scale level) of a color, U and V encode the color information of a pixel. U corresponds approximately to the red-green color from the RGB spectrum, and V to the blue-yellow color (Healey and Enns, 1999). The values of L, U and V for each pixel can be calculated from the RGB pixel components as shown in Equation 3.1.

$$\begin{bmatrix} X \\ Y \\ Z \end{bmatrix} = \begin{bmatrix} 0.431 & 0.342 & 0.178 \\ 0.222 & 0.707 & 0.071 \\ 0.020 & 0.130 & 0.939 \end{bmatrix} \begin{bmatrix} R \\ G \\ B \end{bmatrix}$$

$$L = \begin{cases} 116 \times \left(\sqrt[3]{\frac{Y}{Y_n}} \right) & if \frac{Y}{Y_n} > 0.008856 \\ 903.3 \times \frac{Y}{Y_n} & if \frac{Y}{Y_n} \le 0.008856 \end{cases}$$

$$u = 13L \times \left(\frac{4X}{X + 15Y + 3Z} - U_n \right)$$

$$v = 13L \times \left(\frac{9Y}{X + 15Y + 3Z} - V_n \right)$$

(3.1)

where $(Y_n, U_n, V_n) = (1.0, 0.2009, 0.4610)$ for white point reference.

The next step is to calculate the energy of one of the color components. Experiments conducted on both U and V components showed that the U component is better suited for the application under consideration. The energy formula is given in Equation 3.2.

$$e = \frac{1}{MN} \sum_{i=1}^{M} \sum_{j=1}^{N} pixel(m,n)$$

(3.2)

where M and N are the width and height of the image, respectively, and pixel(m,n) is the value of the pixel located at index (m,n).

The standard deviation is a statistic from which one can tell how tightly objects are packed about a mean in a set of data objects. If the objects are closely packed, then the standard deviation is small. If they are scattered, the standard deviation is relatively large. Based on the definition of texture, the standard deviation of the U component is calculated for every pixel. In textured images the energy of the image will be close in value to a larger number of pixels. This leads to a smaller value for the standard deviation.

For feature extraction, **Daubechies wavelet** decomposition is applied to the L component of the image. The L component is used because it corresponds to the gray scale of the image without considering the color information. The proposed system can read colored images, but it converts them to gray scale, and uses the L component to classify and extract features. The feature vectors calculated for all the images are stored and used in the clustering step.

Apply the Daubechies low and high pass filters to all the columns in the image yields a Daubechies wavelet decomposed image with four sub-bands: LL, HL, LH, and HH. While LL is an approximation of the original image at a lower resolution, HL and LH correspond to the vertical and horizontal wavelet coefficients, respectively. The fourth sub-band HH corresponds to the diagonal coefficients.

After completing the Daubechies decomposition, the next step is to calculate the feature vectors. The texture feature vector is made up of several components. There are some statistical features including energy (Equation 3.2) and standard deviation. There are also some wavelet co-occurrence features, such as contrast, energy, entropy and local homogeneity. Wavelet decomposition is carried out to the third level, and statistical and wavelet co-occurrence features are recorded from these sub-bands. The level 1 low frequency sub-band LL1 is further decomposed by **Daubechies wavelet** and the energy and standard deviation are calculated for the level 2 high frequency sub-bands. This process is repeated for a third level decomposition, where LL2 is decomposed and the wavelet statistical features are calculated for LH3, HL3 and HH3.

Texture features can be extracted in several ways. One of the earliest methods developed uses statistical features of a pixel's grey level (L component) (Howarth and Rüger, 2004). Haralick proposed the use of grey level co-occurrence matrices to extract second order statistics from an image (Haralick, 1979). Instead of using the co-occurrence matrix on the original image, it is calculated for the level 1 Daubechies decomposed sub-bands. The size of the co-occurrence matrix is determined by the highest grey level in the sub-band. Finally, the texture feature vector also contains the average of contrast, energy, entropy and local homogeneity over all four orientations: horizontal, vertical and the two diagonals.

For calculating the non-texture feature vector, we adapted the method of Kubo *et al* (2003), with the only difference of using the **Daubechies wavelet transform** instead of the **Haar wavelet**. **Daubechies wavelets** are used because they are better than **Haar wavelets** when working with general purpose images (Wang, Wiederhold, Firschein, and Wei, 1997).

The non-texture feature vector method takes a level 1 Daubechies decomposed image as input and uses the LH and HL sub-bands to construct an edge image. The HL sub-band embodies the vertical edges and the LH sub-bands contains the coefficients of the horizontal edges. The edge image is built by combining the elements of the LH and HL sub-bands together using the following equation:

$$e_{m,n} = \sqrt{v_{m,n}^2 + h_{m,n}^2} \qquad (3.3)$$

where $1 < m <$ height of LH & HL sub-bands, $1 < n <$ width of LH & HL sub-bands, $v_{m,n}$, $h_{m,n}$, and $e_{m,n}$ are elements of the HL sub-band, LH sub-band and the edge image, respectively.

The edge image constructed is used to calculate the higher order autocorrelation features, which are the primitive edge features (Kubo, Aghbari, and Makinouchi. 2003). Due to the large number of autocorrelation functions, Kubo *et al* limited them by limiting the autocorrelation functions to the second order and the range of displacement to a 3×3 window. By doing these limitations, 25 features are extracted.

$$R^N(a_1, a_2, ..., a_N) = \sum I(r)I(r + a_1)I(r + a_2)...I(r + a_N) \qquad (3.4)$$

Equation 3.4 is used to calculate the order autocorrelation features. $I(r)$ represents the image and i is the translation of $I(r)$ by a displacement vector i.

Higher order autocorrelation features are shift-invariant, i.e., the features are not dependant on the positions of objects within an image. However, these features are not invariant to scale and grey levels. That is, if two images were presented to a content-based image retrieval system, with the only difference being scaling or brightness, the system would not return a match. A remedy for this could be by normalization using the following process:

$$\frac{1}{wh} \sum N\sqrt{I(r)I(r + a_1)I(r + a_2)...I(r + a_N)} \qquad (3.5)$$

Figure 3. Example of □-neighborhood

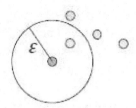

Figure 4. Clusters with Different Densities (Ankerst, Breunig, Kriegel, and Sander, 1999)

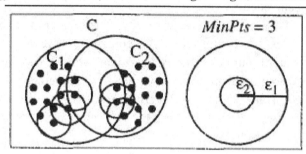

To make the features scale-invariant, Equation 3.4 is divided by the size of the original image, *wh*; and to make them grey-level invariant, Equation 3.4 is raised to the power $1/N$, where N is the order of autocorrelation. Thus, two similar images of different size or brightness should match during a query.

Clustering

To cluster the images, the proposed system employs the **OPTICS** clustering algorithm (Ankerst, Breunig, Kriegel, and Sander, 1999), which was developed by M. Ankerst *et al.*. **OPTICS** orders the points in the database following the concept of density-based clustering algorithms. This results in a set of ordered points that are useful to determine clusters at different densities. In a density-based clustering algorithm, each point in a cluster should have a minimum number of points that are within a specified distance ε from it; this can be seen in Figure 3. Clusters that have a higher density, i.e., a smaller ε value, can be totally included (or nested) in clusters of lower density, i.e., larger ε value; this can be seen in Figure 4. Taking this into consideration, **OPTICS** orders the points in the database so that clusters of different densities can be derived concurrently. Finally, some basic concepts to be used in the sequel are introduced next.

Given two objects *p* and *q*, object *p* is in the ε-neighborhood of *q* if the distance from *p* to *q* is less than ε. An object is said to be core if and only if it has a minimum number of points (MinPts) in its ε-neighborhood. Object *p* is directly density-reachable from *q* if *q* is a core object and *p* is in the ε-neighborhood of *q*. Object *p* is density-reachable from object *q* if there is a chain of objects 1*n*, where 1 = *q* and *n* = *p* such that *j*+1 is directly density-reachable from *j*. The core-distance is the smallest distance between a given object *p* and an object in its ε-neighborhood such that *p* would be a core object with respect to . The reachability-distance of a given object *p* is the smallest distance such that *p* is density-reachable from a core object *o*.

The only parameter needed by **OPTICS** is MinPts, the minimum number of points that should be in the ε-neighborhood of a point *p* in order for it to be considered a core object. Previous research (Ankerst,

Breunig, Kriegel, and Sander, 1999) has shown that good results can be obtained by using any value for MinPts between 10 and 20. We decided to set MinPts to 15. The higher the value of MinPts, the more continuous and even the reachability curve is; and the lower the value, the more rough the curve is.

The value of ε is an important consideration in this clustering system. There are many ways to calculate ε. It is important to use a sensible value because if ε is too small, many potential clusters may be lost. Therefore, it is desired to obtain the smallest value for ε that would result in one large cluster containing almost all points in the database. Then, all the smaller clusters can be assumed to be contained within this large cluster.

Using simple heuristics, and assuming random distribution of points within the database (i.e no clusters), the k-nearest-neighbor distance is calculated, i.e., the distance ε for a point to have k-objects within its neighborhood, where k=MinPts. This value is computed for a data space DS containing N points. ε is equal to the radius of a d-dimensional hypersphere S within DS, where S contains k points (Ankerst, Breunig, Kriegel, and Sander, 1999).

To calculate ε consider the following equations for the volume of a hypersphere S.

$$Volume_S = \frac{Volume_{DS}}{N} \times k \tag{3.6}$$

$$Volume_S(r) = \frac{\sqrt{\pi}^d}{\Gamma(\frac{d}{2}+1)} \times r^d$$

S in Equation 3.6 holds because we assume that the points are randomly distributed. Note that N and k are the total number of points in DS and S, respectively. Whereas, $Volume_S(r)$ in Equation 3.6 also, is the volume of a hypersphere S with radius r and dimension d. And ε is the Gamma function defined in Equation 3.8. Now, if we equate these two equations (since they both represent the volume of a hypersphere), we can calculate the value of r (ε):

$$\frac{Volume_{DS}}{N} \times k = \frac{\sqrt{\pi}^d}{\Gamma(\frac{d}{2}+1)} \times r^d$$

$$r^d = \frac{Volume_{DS} \times k \times \Gamma(\frac{d}{2}+1)}{N \times \sqrt{\pi}^d} \tag{3.7}$$

$$r = \sqrt[d]{\frac{Volume_{DS} \times k \times \Gamma(\frac{d}{2}+1)}{N \times \sqrt{\pi}^d}}$$

Thus, ε is calculated by setting its value to r in Equation 3.7.

$$\Gamma(n) = \begin{cases} \frac{\sqrt{\pi^n}}{(\frac{n}{2})!} \times r^n & \text{if n is even} \\ 2^n \times \pi^{\frac{n-1}{2}} \times \frac{(\frac{n-1}{2})!}{n!} \times r^n & \text{if n is odd} \end{cases} \tag{3.8}$$

The value for ε is calculated as described previously. After calculating ε, OPTICS sorts the set of d-dimensional points being clustered. It takes a d-dimensional Origin point (0,...,0), and calculates the Euclidean distance, given in Equation 3.9 between all points and the Origin. The list is sorted in ascending order based on the Euclidean distance. This is done to facilitate the extraction of points later in the algorithm. The Euclidean distance is given by:

$$D(p,q) = \sqrt{\sum_{i=1}^{N} (p_i - q_i)^2} \tag{3.9}$$

where p and q are points of dimension N and i and i are their respective coordinates in dimension i.

It is required to determine whether p is a core object or not, and to calculate its core and reachability distances. This is achieved by considering points that are in the ε-neighborhood of p. If there are more than *MinPts* in p's ε-neighborhood, then p is a core object with a core distance equal to the distance of its neighbor, where $n=MinPts$. Second, the reachability-distance for each point q in p's ε-neighborhood is updated. This is done by first checking whether q is processed or not. If not, then q is added to *NeighborList*, which is arranged to preserve the heap properties based on q's reachability-distance. However, if q is processed, this means that it is already *NeighborList*, because it is in another point's ε-neighborhood. So, q's reachability has to be modified *NeighborList* to correspond to the smallest reachability of q. This is the only way to ensure that clusters with higher densities, i.e., smaller ε values are completed first. Finally, the point currently being processed is written with its core and reachability distances recorded in a file called *OutputFile*.

Looking at the reachability distances should be sufficient to determine which points belong to a cluster. To extract the clusters from the ordered list of reachabilities, every object o in the list is checked, and the clusters are created or updated based on the reachability and core distance values. If the reachability of o is greater than , this means that o is not reachable from any object before it in the *OrderedFile*. If it were reachable then it would have been assigned a reachability-distance that is less than or equal to . So, the core distance of o is checked. If o is a core object with respect to and *MinPts*, then a new cluster is created and o is added to it. Otherwise, o belongs to the *NOISE* cluster. If the reachability of o is at most , then o is reachable from the points that precede it *OrderedFile*; and thus, o is added to the current cluster. After performing some experiments, was taken to be the average of all non-infinity reachabilities times 0.7.

While adding objects to clusters, a feature vector, for each cluster except *NOISE*, is calculated to represent this cluster. The representative feature vector is the mean of all feature vectors belonging to the same cluster. This representative feature vector is used later on in the querying phase to speed up the process.

Experimental Analysis

This section focuses on testing the proposed system to highlight its strength, applicability and effectiveness as compared to similar approaches described in the literature. So, it is desired to test on databases of images that have been previously used to test other image retrieval systems.

The proposed system was developed in Java-based software development environment. The testing has been carried out on a desktop PC equipped with an Intel Pentium CPU clocked at 3.0 GHz, and has 1.00GB of RAM. The operating system installed is Microsoft Windows XP Professional Edition SP2.

Table 1. Corel images

Categories				
Africa people & villages	Beach	Buildings	Buses	Dinosaurs
Mountains & glaciers	Elephants	Flowers	Horses	Food

We tested the power of the proposed system in classifying and querying non-texture images. We also compared the performance of proposed system to other **CBIR** systems already described in the literature.

The images used in the experiments were taken from the Corel database, which is a set of non-texture images. A subset of this database, available online, is used in the conducted experiments. 1000 images, of size 256×384 and jpeg format, containing ten different categories listed in Table 1, were used, where each category contains 100 images. With the images belonging to known categories, this made it easier to track the results and gauge system performance.

We demonstrate the power of the proposed system by primarily comparing the achieved results with those reported by two already developed systems (Chang and Kuo, 1993; Wang, Li, and Wiederhold, 2001), which were tested on the same set of images.

The first criteria analyzed is the effectiveness and speed of classification as compared to the one used by Wang *et al* (Li, Wang, and Wiederhold, 2000; Wang, Li, and Wiederhold, 2001), along with the time needed to classify an image. It was easy to analyze the effectiveness of the proposed system because it was known in advance what the total number of correct non-texture images would be.

The effectiveness of the classification process is important. As the first step in both the learning and the querying phases, correct classification is vital in order to extract feature vectors correctly and cluster them effectively. If the classification rate is low, then less matching images would be returned as a result of a query because either the query image was classified incorrectly, or in the learning phase the images that were grouped together did not belong to the same image type. The time taken to classify is also important because as the database size is increased, the run time would also increase significantly within the learning phase.

The second parameter being considered is the precision of querying based on the feature vectors extracted; the higher the system's precision, the higher the percentage of matching images returned to a query. The most favorable condition would be for 100% matching of images, since the idea behind a **CBIR** system is to retrieve from the database the maximum number of images that match a query image. For the evaluation, the definition given in Equation 3.10 is used for precision.

$$\mathrm{Precision} = \frac{Number\ of\ correct\ images\ returned}{Number\ of\ images\ returned} \qquad (3.10)$$

The third factor under consideration is determining the effectiveness of incorporating clustering on the performance. This was tested by comparing the querying results obtained by applying clustering with those obtained by using the feature vectors of all the images in the database. The hypothesis being tested is that clustering would be useful due to the fact that it reduces the search space without significantly affecting the accuracy of the query results. This is demonstrated in Equation 3.11.0

$$\text{Clustering Precision} = \frac{\textit{Number of correct images returned from Clusters}}{\textit{Number of correct images returned from entire database}} \qquad (3.11)$$

To test the benefits of the classification method, the Corel image sets were first processed according to the algorithm used by Wang *et al* (Li, Wang, and Wiederhold, 2000; Wang, Li, and Wiederhold, 2001). They were then processed again by the proposed system. It was known that the 1000 Corel images are non-texture. Executing both algorithms on the 1000 images from the Corel database also showed that the proposed system performed a little better; 4 out of the 1000 Corel images were classified as texture, that is wrong, and 996 were classified as true-positives, which is correct because they are not texture images. For the algorithm of Wang *et al* (Li, Wang, and Wiederhold, 2000; Wang, Li, and Wiederhold, 2001), 30 of the original 1000 images were classified wrongly as textures and 970 were classified as non-textures. Therefore, the percentage of true-positives is 99.6% for the proposed system and 97% for Wang *et al*'s algorithm.

Another experiment was conducted to test the matching performance of the proposed system on non-texture images. The images used are the 1000 images from the Corel database, with ten categories of 100 images each. Each image in the collection was presented as a query image and the output from the proposed system was recorded. Generally, it is more difficult to extract features from non-texture images, since there is likely to be more than one object within the image. Another significant factor in classification is the time required to perform the task. The size of image databases is usually large and a fast learning phase is naturally preferred. **Classification** is part of the learning phase, and the faster the classification can be done the better. Overall, it takes almost 10 hours to classify 1000 Corel images using Wang et al's approach, while our approach needs only 53 minutes to complete the classification, with a better rate of true-positives.

The clustering efficacy is tested by calculating the number of images returned by using clusters with respect to the number of images returned when no clusters are used.

For each image submitted as a query, the number of correct images returned when clusters were considered is divided by the number of correct images returned when all images in the database were checked. The results for all images belonging to one category are averaged and recorded in Table 2.

Table 2. Corel clustering precision

Category	No. sampled images	Precision
African people	100	72.55%
Buildings	100	75.88%
Dinosaurs	100	91.62%
Flowers	100	51.82%
Mountains	100	62.91%
Beach	100	76.27%
Buses	100	75.03%
Elephants	100	66.31%
Horses	100	58.25%
Food	100	60.23%
Total & Average	1000	69.09%

Figure 5. Sample query 1

Figure 6. Sample query 2

Figure 7. Sample query 3

Figure 8. Sample query 4

Figure 9. Sample query 5

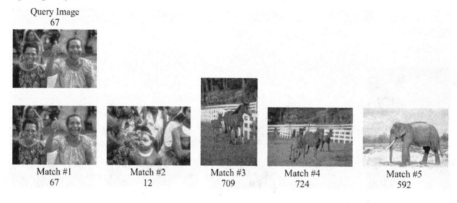

Figure 10. Sample query 6

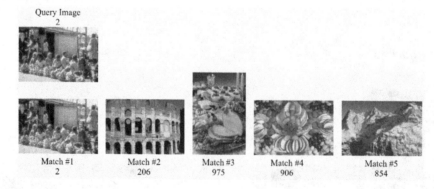

Figure 11. Segmentation

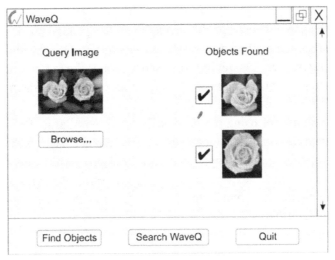

The relatively low precision and clustering precision values for the tested images merited a closer look. Several queries were run with selected images. The aim of the extra experiments is to try and pinpoint the reasons for the reported precision values.

The first two queries run are shown in Figures 5 and 6. The query image is shown first (on the left) followed by the top five matches returned by the proposed system. From Figures 5 and 6, it can be concluded that the feature vector calculated by the proposed system is accurate for images containing only a single object.

The next two queries run are shown in Figures 7 and 8. These two queries demonstrate that the proposed algorithm is able to extract the feature vectors when the image contains only one object of interest, but there is a prominent background.

The final two queries run are shown in Figures 9 and 10. The query images contain multiple objects. As seen from these images, the performance of the proposed system deteriorate when the query image contain multiple objects. One way to overcome this limitation would be to introduce segmentation into the proposed algorithm. This would improve the rate of matches when multiple objects are concerned.

During the learning phase, several distinct samples would be taken from each image, where each sample would correspond to an object in the image. Feature vectors would then be calculated and stored for objects within each image instead of one feature vector for the whole image.

When a query image is then presented to the proposed system, it would also be segmented as previously, and multiple objects could be identified. The user interface could also then be designed to allow matching on any of the objects or on multiple objects. This idea is presented in Figure 11. Both the learning and querying phases would be expected to take more time to complete, where multiple objects are found within an image. However, it is expected that matching precision would be improved.

CONCLUSION

The research scope for this paper focused on the development of a general purpose content-based image retrieval system. A classification method was adapted from an existing algorithm and this proved to be very efficient at classifying images. **Clustering** was used to reduce the search space by grouping similar images together in order to make querying faster. Some of the conclusions drawn from the experimentation are presented here. The classification algorithm is very fast and accurate in classifying images. This is very encouraging, especially for using the proposed system with large databases of images. Many of the queries that were run returned 100% matches, i.e., no wrong images were returned. The feature vectors generated lower matching rates. There are several reasons for this, the first of which is that in non-texture images, there tended to be more than one object, even if the extra objects were just part of the background. Another factor that contributed to the lower matching rate on non-texture images is the categorizing of the images themselves.

FUTURE RESEARCH DIRECTIONS

As was noted, there were images in some categories that did not really fit in with the rest of the images in their category. Hence, they would not be expected to return as matches from the same category. The clustering that was implemented yielded query results that were very close to the results generated when clustering was disabled. This led to the conclusion that the clustering does not result in significant deterioration in performance. Despite all that has been accomplished, both in this paper and in all the research done to date in the area, there is still much to do in the field of CBIR systems. There is also lot to be done to improve the performance of the proposed system. The concept of segmentation is important and should improve system performance where multiple objects are found in an image. This improvement in extracting non-texture feature vectors should also improve the matching rate when clustering is turned on.

REFERENCES

Ankerst, M., Breunig, M.M., Kriegel, H.-P., & Sander, J. (1999). Optics: Ordering points to identify the clustering structure. In Proceedings ACM SIGMOD International Conference on Management of Data, pp. 49–60.

Bach, J., Fuller, C., Gupta, A., Hampapur, A., Gorowitz, B, Humphrey, R., Jain, R., & Shu, C. (1996). Virage image search engine: An open framework for image management. In Poceedings of the SPIE Conference on Storage and Retrieval for Image and Video Databases IV, pp. 76–87.

Boggess, A., & Narcowich, F.J. (2001). A first course in wavelets with Fourier analysis, chapter Haar wavelet analysis, pp. 155-178. Prentice Hall.

Chang, T., & Jay, C.C., & Kuo. (1993). Texture analysis and classification with tree-structured wavelet transform. *IEEE Transactions on Image Processing, 2*(3), 429–441.

Columbia University. WebSeek. Available at http://persia.ee.columbia.edu:8008/

Convera. Purchasing RetrievalWare. Available at http://www.convera.com/.

COREL. Corel images. Accessed on 12/3/2005. Available at http://wang.ist.psu.edu/docs/related.

Dowe, J. (1993). Content-based retrieval in multimedia imaging. In Poceedings of the SPIE Conference on Storage and Retrieval for Image and Video Databases.

Duce, D. (Ed.). W3C Portable Network Graphics Specification Version 2.0. Available at http://www.w3.org/TR/PNG-Glossary.html.

Gebara, D., & Alhajj, R. (2007). WaveQ: Combining wavelet analysis and clustering for effective image retrieval. Proceedings of IEEE International Symposium on Data Mining and Information Retrieval.

Haralick, R. (1979). Statistical and structural approaches to texture. *Proc. IEEE*, 67, 786–804.

Healey, C.G., & Enns, J.T. (1999). Large datasets at a glance: Combining textures and colors in scientific visualization. *IEEE Transactions on Visualization and Computer Graphics*, 5(2), 145–167.

Hong, D., Wang, J., & Gardner, R. (2004). Real analysis with an introduction to wavelets and applications, chapter Orthonormal wavelet basis, pp. 209-270. Academic Press.

Howarth, P., & Rüger, S. (2004). Evaluation of texture features for content-based image retrieval. In International Conference on Image and Video Retrieval, pp. 326–334.

Huang, T.S., Mehrotra, S., & Ramchandran, K. (1996). Multimedia analysis and retrieval system (MARS) project. In Proceedings of 33rd Annual clinic on Library Application of Data Processing - Digital Image Access and Retrieval.

Hubbard, B. (1998). The World According to Wavelets. A K Peters, Ltd Natick.

IBM. QBIC IBM's Query by Image Content. Available at http://wwwqbic.almaden.ibm.com.

Kubo, M., Aghbari, Z., & Makinouchi, A. (2003). Content-based image retrieval technique using wavelet-based shift and brightness invariant edge feature. *International Journal of Wavelets, Multiresolution and Information Processing*, 1(2) 163–178.

Li, J., Wang, J., & Wiederhold, G. (2000). Classification of textured and non-textured images using region segmentation. In Proc. of the 7th International Conference on Image Processing, pp. 754–757.

Ma, W.Y., & Manjunath, B.S. (1999). Netra: A toolbox for navigating large image databases. *Multimedia Systems*, 7(3), 184–198.

Natsev, A., Rastogi, R., & Shim, K. (2004). WALRUS: A similarity retrieval algorithm for image databases. *IEEE Transactions on Knowledge and Data Engineering, 16*(3), 301-316.

Niblack, W., Barber, R., Equitz, W., Flickner, M., Glasman, E., Petkovic, D., Yanker, P.,Faloutsos, C., & Taubin, G. (1993). The QBIC project: Quering images by content using color, texture, and shape. In Poceedings of the SPIE Conference on Storage and Retrieval for Image and Video Databases, pp. 173–187.

Pentland, A., Picard, R., & Sclaroff, S. (1994). Photobook: Tools for content-based manipulation of image databases. In Proceedings of the SPIE Conference on Storage and Retrieval for Image and Video Databases II.

Smith, J.R., & Chang, S.F. (1997). Visually searching the Web for content. *IEEE Multimedia Magazine, 4*(3), 12-20.

Unser, M., & Blu, T. (2000). Wavelets and radial basis functions: A unifying perspective. In Proceedings of the SPIE Conference on Mathematical Imaging: Wavelet Applications in Signal and Image Processing VIII, pp. 487-493.

Veltkamp, R.C., & Tanase, M. Content-based image retrieval systems: Available at http://give-lab.cs.uu.nl/cbirsurvey/.

Wang, J., Li, J., & Wiederhold, G. (2001). Simplicity: Semantics-sensitive integrated matching for picture libraries. *IEEE Transactions On Pattern Analysis And Machine Intelligence, 23*(9), 947–963.

Wang, J.Z., Wiederhold, G., Firschein, O., & Wei, S.X. (1997). Content-based image indexing and searching using Daubechies' wavelets. *International Journal on Digital Libraries, 1*, 311–328.

Zachary, J.M., & Iyengar, S.S. (1999). Content-based image retrieval systems. In Proceedings of the IEEE Symposium on Application-Specific Systems and Software Engineering and Technology, pp. 136–143.

ADDITIONAL READING

Agrawal, R., Gehrke, J., Gunopulos, D., & Raghavan, P. (1998). Automatic subspace clustering of high dimensional data for data mining applications. In Proceedings of ACM SIGMOD International Conference on Management of Data, (pp. 94-105).

Arivazhagan, S., & Ganesan, L.. (2003). Texture classification using wavelet transform. *Pattern Recognition Letters, 24*(9-10), 1513-1521.

Berkhin, P. (2002). Survey of clustering data mining techniques. Technical report, Accrue Software, San Jose, CA.

Bovik, A.C. (1991). Analysis of multichannel narrow-band filters for image texture segmentation. *IEEE Transactions on Signal Processing, 39*, 2025-2043.

Chellappa, R. (1985). Two-dimensional discrete Gaussian Markov random field models for image processing. *Pattern Recognition, 2*, 79-112.

Chuang, G.C., & Kuo, C.J. (1996). Wavelet descriptor of planar curves: Theory and applications. *IEEE Transactions on Image Processing, 5*(1), 56-70.

Cohen, F.S., & Cooper, D.B. (1987). Simple parallel hierarchical and relaxation algorithms for segmenting noncausal Markovian random fields. *IEEE Transactions on Pattern Analysis and Machine Intelligence, 9*, 195-219.

Cross, G.R., & Jain, A.K. (1983). Markov random field texture models. *IEEE Transactions on Pattern Analysis And Machine Intelligence, 5,* 25-39.

Davis, L.S., & Johns, S.A., & Aggarwal, J.K. (1979). Texture analysis using generalized co-occurrence matrices. *IEEE Transactions on Pattern Analysis And Machine Intelligence, 1*(3), 251-259.

Dempster, A.P., Laird, N.M., & Rubin, D.B. (1977). Maximum likelihood from incomplete data via the em algorithm. *Journal of the Royal Statistical Society, Series B, 39*(1), 1-38.

Derin, H. (1986). Segmentation of textured images using Gibbs random fields. Computer Vision, *Graphics and Image Processing, 35,* 72-98.

Derin, H., & Elliott, H. (1987). Modeling and segmentation of noisy and textured images using Gibbs random fields. *IEEE Transactions on Pattern Analysis And Machine Intelligence, 9,* 39-55.

Derin, H., Elliott, H., Cristi, R., & Geman, D. (1984). Bayes smoothing algorithms for segmentation of binary images modeled by Markov random fields. *IEEE Transactions on Pattern Analysis and Machine Intelligence, 6,* 707-720.

Elder, J.H., & Zucker, S.W. (1998). Local scale control for edge detection and blur estimation. *IEEE Transactions on Pattern Analysis And Machine Intelligence, 20*(7), 699-716.

Ester, M., Kriegel, H.P., Sander, J., & Xu, X. (1996). A density-based algorithm for discovering clusters in large spatial databases with noise. In Proceedings of the 2nd International Conference on Knowledge Discovery and Data Mining, pages 226-231.

Geman, S., & Geman D. (1984). Stochastic relaxation, Gibbs distributions, and the Bayesian restoration of images. *IEEE Transactions On Pattern Analysis And Machine Intelligence, 6,* 721-741.

Gross, M.H., Koch, R., Lippert, L., & Dreger, A. (1994). Multiscale image texture analysis in wavelet spaces. In Proceedings of IEEE International Conference on Image Processing.

Gupta, A., Santini, S., & Jain, R. (1997). In search of information in visual media. *Communication ACM, 40*(12), 34-42.

Han, J., & Kamber, M. (2001). Data mining: concepts and techniques, chapter cluster analysis, pp. 335-388. Morgan Kaufmann.

Haralick, R.M., Shanmugam, K., & Dinstein, I. (1973). Texture features for image classification. *IEEE Transactions Systems, Man, and Cybernetics, 8*(6), 610-621.

Jain, A.K., Murty, M.N., & Flynn, P.J. (1999). Data clustering: A review. *ACM Computing Surveys, 31*(3), 264-323.

Kapur, D., Lakshman, Y.N., and Saxena, T. (1995). Computing invariants using elimination methods. In Proceedings of IEEE International Conference on Image Processing.

Kashyap, R.L., & Chellappa, R. (1983). Estimation and choice of neighbors in spatial interaction models of images. *IEEE Transactions on Information Theory, 29,* 60-72.

Kashyap, R.L., & Chellappa, R. (1985). Texture synthesis using 2-D non-causal autoregressive models. *IEEE Transactions on Acoustics, Speech and Signal Processing, 33,* 194 -203.

Kundu, A., & Chen, J.L. (1992). Texture classification using qmf bank-based subband decomposition. *Computer Vision, Graphics and Image Processing, 54,* 369-384.

Kurani, A., Xu, D., Furst, J., & Raicu, D. (2004). Co-occurrence matrices for volumetric data. In Computer graphics and imaging, pp. 85 -91.

Laine, A., & Fan, J. (1993). Texture classification by wavelet packet signatures. *IEEE Transactions on Pattern Analysis and Machine Intelligence, 15*(11), 1186 -1191.

Laws, K.I. (1980). Texture image segmentation. Ph.D. Dissertation, University of Southern California.

Li., J. (2003). A wavelet approach to edge detection. Master of Science, Sam Houston State University.

Ma, W.Y. and Manjunath, B.S. (2000) EdgeFlow: A technique for boundary detection and image segmentation. *IEEE Transactions on Image Processing, 9*(8), 1375-1388.

Mallat, S., & Hwang, W.L. (1992). Singularity detection and processing with wavelets. *IEEE Transactions On Information Theory, 38*(2), 617-643.

Mallat, S., & Zhong, S. (1992). Characterization of signals from multiscale edges. *IEEE Transactions On Pattern Analysis And Machine Intelligence, 14*(7), 710-732.

Manjunath, B.S., Shekhar, C., & Chellappa, R. (1996). A new approach to image feature detection with applications. *Pattern Recognition, 31,* 627-640.

Marimont, D.H., Rubner, Y. (1998). A probabilistic framework for edge detection and scale selection. In International Conference on Computer Vision, pp. 207-214.

Rui, Y. (1999). Efficient indexing, browsing and retrieval of image/video content. Ph.D. Dissertation, University of Illinois at Urbana-Champaign.

Rui, Y., She, A., & Huang, T.S. (1996). Modified Fourier descriptors for shape representation - A practical approach. In Proceedings of First International Workshop on Image Databases and Multi Media Search.

Sheikholeslami, G., Chatterjee, S., & Zhang, A. (1998). WaveCluster: A multiresolution clustering approach for very large spatial databases. In Proceedings of the 24th International Conference on Very Large Databases, pp. 428-439.

Sklansky, J. (1978). Image segmentation and feature extraction. *IEEE Transactions on Systems, Man, Cybernetics, 8,* 237-247.

Tabb, M., & Ahuja, N. (1997). Multiscale image segmentation by integrated edge and region detection. *IEEE Transactions on Image Processing, 6*(5) 642 -655.

Tamura, H., Mori, S., & Yamawaki, T. (1978). Texture features corresponding to visual perception. *IEEE Transactions Systems, Man, and Cybernetics, 8*(6) 460-473.

Thyagarajan, K.S., Nguyen, T., & Persons, C. (1994). A maximum likelihood approach to texture classification using wavelet transform. In Proceedings of IEEE International Conference on Image Processing.

Woods, J.W., Dravida, S., & Mediavilla, R. (1987). Image estimation using doubly stochastic Gaussian random field models. *IEEE Transactions On Pattern Analysis And Machine Intelligence, 9*, 245 -253.

Yang, L., & Albregtsen, F. (1994). Fast computation of invariant geometric moments: A new method giving correct results. In Proceedings of the 12th IAPR International Conference on Computer Vision & Image Processing, pp. 201-204.

Chapter III
Review on Texture Feature Extraction and Description Methods in Content–Based Medical Image Retrieval

Gang Zhang

College of Information Science and Engineering, Northeastern University, China

Z. M. Ma

College of Information Science and Engineering, Northeastern University, China

Li Yan

College of Information Science and Engineering, Northeastern University, China

Ji-feng Zhu

College of Information Science and Engineering, Northeastern University, China

ABSTRACT

Texture feature extraction and description is one of the important research contents in content-based medical image retrieval. The chapter first proposes a framework of content-based medical image retrieval system. It then analyzes the important texture feature extraction and description methods further, such as the co-occurrence matrix, perceptual texture features, Gabor wavelet, and so forth. Moreover, the chapter analyzes the improved methods for these methods and demonstrates their application in content-based medical image retrieval.

1. INTRODUCTION

Content-based medical image retrieval has been one of the most vivid research areas in the medical field over the last 10 years. With the development of computer technology and medical imaging technology, amount of medical images increase exponentially. Text-based medical image retrieval hasn't met the needs of medical image retrieval, management, and maintenance. So it is urgent to develop an efficient technology for medical image retrieval (Liu *et al*, 2007). Under the circumstance, content-based medical image retrieval has received a wide concern. Now it isn't only used for medical image retrieval, management and maintenance, but also used to assist physicians in diagnosis and treatment of diseases (Müller *et al*, 2004; Lau and Ozawa, 2004; Tourassi and Floyd, 2004; Ogawa *et al*, 1998).

Now there are many conceptual frameworks of content-based medical image retrieval system (Smeulders *et al*, 2000; Wei *et al*, 2005; Zhang *et al*, 2007). A simple framework (See Figure 1) is used to demonstrate the problems which are studied in the chapter. The framework consists of feature extraction, feature selection, feature description, dimension reduction, indexing, relevance feedback, and similarity measure. Feature extraction is usually thought to be a transformation for a medical image from high dimension feature space description to low dimension feature space description. Feature selection is used to select some of most discriminative features from a group of features to reduce feature space dimension. A group of representative features from a medical image are used to describe the content of the medical image in feature description. Feature description emphasizes how to organize the features effectively to describe the content in the medical image. In dimension reduction, transformations are used to reduce feature space, which decreases computation complexity in medical image retrieval. Indexing is used to speed up retrieval process. Relevance feedback is introduced into medical image retrieval by the participation of users in which retrieval patterns are submitted many times with interactivity to improve precision of retrieval system. Similarity measure is used to measure similarity between medical images. To improve both efficiency and effectiveness of a retrieval system, a typical content-based medical image retrieval system is divided into offline processing and online retrieval. Feature extraction, feature selection, feature description, dimension reduction and indexing for each image in a medical image database are performed by offline (See dashed frame in Figure 1). But feature extraction, feature selection, feature description, dimension reduction and indexing for a query image are performed by online. In addition, relevance feedback, similarity measure and result

Figure 1. Conceptual framework of content-based medical image retrieval

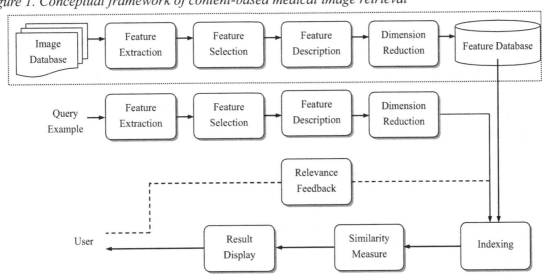

display are performed by online. The chapter will analyze some of the important methods for texture feature extraction and description of medical images.

Although there is no strict definition of image texture, it is easily perceived by humans and is believed to be a rich source of visual information – about the nature and three-dimensional shape of physical objects. Generally speaking, textures are complex visual patterns composed of entities, or subpatterns, that have characteristic brightness, colour, slope, size, etc. Thus texture can be regarded as a similarity grouping in an image (Rosenfeld and Kak, 1982). The local subpattern properties give rise to the perceived lightness, uniformity, density, roughness, regularity, linearity, frequency, phase, directionality, coarseness, randomness, fineness, smoothness, granulation, etc., of the texture as a whole (Levine, 1985). For medical image databases, it is clear that the texture structures of different organ tissues of human are quite different. Also the difference between the texture structures of the same organ tissue is obvious. Therefore, texture for medical images, being important low level visual feature, is receiving a wide attention. And texture feature extraction and description for medical images have been one of important research areas in content-based medical image retrieval (Ma and Manjunath, 1996; Glatard *et al*, 2004).

The methods for texture feature extraction and description can usually be categorized into structural, statistical, spectral and transform methods. Relatively comprehensive overview for these methods is given in Materka and Strzelecki (1998). Structural methods, such as mathematical morphology, represent texture by well-defined primitives (microtexture) and a hierarchy of spatial arrangements (macrotexture) of those primitives. Mathematical morphology is used for texture feature extraction and description of bone image to detect changes in bone microstructure (Chen and Dougherty, 1994). Statistical methods, such as gray co-occurrence matrix, represent the texture indirectly by the non-deterministic properties that govern the distributions and relationships between the grey levels of an image. Gray co-occurrence matrix is used for mammogram images to extract and describe texture features in Wei *et al* (2005). Model-based methods, such as computational model of grating cells, attempt to interpret the texture of an image by use of generative image model (fractal model, etc.) and stochastic model respectively. Modified computational model of grating cells is used for texture feature extraction and description of chest CT images in Zhang *et al* (2007). Transform-based methods, such as wavelet transform and Gabor wavelet, use mappings to transform feature space. Then they extract and describe texture features in the transformed feature space. Gabor wavelet is used for texture feature extraction and description of chest CT images in Zhang *et al* (2007). The chapter still uses the aforementioned classification method. Furthermore, it analyzes some representative methods in structural methods, statistical methods, spectral methods, and transform methods further.

2. TEXTURE FEATURE EXTRACTION AND DESCRIPTION USING GRAY CO-OCCURRENCE MATRIX

Gray co-occurrence matrix is one of most elementary and important methods for texture feature extraction and description. Its original idea is first proposed in Julesz (1975). Julesz found through his famous experiments on human visual perception of texture, that for a large class of textures no texture pair can be discriminated if they agree in their second-order statistics. Then Julesz used the definition of the joint probability distributions of pairs of pixels for texture feature extraction and description, and first used gray level spatial dependence co-occurrence statistics in texture discrimination experiments. Weid *et al.* (1970) used one-dimensional co-occurrence for a medical application. Haralick *et al* (1973) suggested two-dimensional spatial dependence of the gray levels in a co-occurrence matrix for each fixed distance and/or angular spatial relationship, and used statistics of this matrix as measures of texture in an image. In recent years, the gray co-occurrence matrix has been widely used for content-based medical image retrieval. For example, it is used for automated chest X-ray analysis in Chien and Fu (1974). And it used for cervical cell image discrimination in Pressman (1976).

Given a medical image $f(x, y)$ of size $L_r \times L_c$ with a set of N_g gray levels, if $P(k, j, d, \theta)$ denotes the estimate of the joint probability of two pixels with a distance d apart along a given direction θ having particular values k and j, it is called gray co-occurrence matrix of the image with a distance d apart along a given direction θ having particular values k and j and denoted as follows.

$$P(k,j,d,\theta) = N\{((x_1, y_1),(x_2, y_2)) \in (L_r \times L_c)(L_r \times L_c)|$$
$$(x_2, y_2) = (x_1, y_1) + (d\cos\theta, d\sin\theta), f(x_1, y_1)=k, f(x_2, y_2)=j, 0<k, j<N_g\} \quad (1)$$

where the parameter d denotes the distance between pixels (x_1, y_1) and (x_2, y_2) in the medical image, the parameter θ denotes the direction aligning (x_1, y_1) and (x_2, y_2) (See Figure 2). If the conditional co-occurrence probabilities are based on the undirected distances typically used in the symmetric co-occurrence probabilities, $\theta \in [0°, 180°)$. And $N\{\}$ denotes the amount of elements in the set.

Haralick *et al* (1973) extracted the fourteen statistical features from the co-occurrence matrix P(k, j, d, θ), and used them to describe various texture properties in the image. The fourteen statistical features are angular second moment, contrast, correlation, variance, inverse difference moment, sum average, sum variance, sum entropy, entropy, different variance, different entropy, measure of correlation-1, measure of correlation-2, and max correlation coefficient respectively. The parameter d is usually selected based on texture granularity, and parameter θ is selected as 0°, 45°, 90° and 135° (Andrysiak and Chora, 2005; Moyo *et al*, 2006) in P(k, j, d, θ). It is found in Conners and Harlow (1980) that only five among fourteen features, *i.e.* energy, entropy, correlation, local homogeneity (or inverse different moment) and inertia, were truly useful in real applications.

When the gray co-occurrence matrix is used for texture feature extraction and description, it is susceptible to noise and entity rotation in an image. Furthermore, it is proposed in Zhang *et al* (2007) that directions 0°, 45°, 90° and 135° aren't usually dominant directions for images of specific parts in a medical image database, and dominant directions of images of different parts are usually different. So directed filter for dominant directions is proposed in Zhang *et al* (2007).

Figure 2. Gray co-occurrence of direction θ and distance d

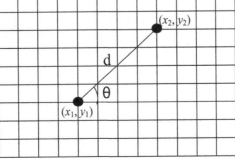

Suppose $(\ldots)^\theta$ denotes the rotary operator, G denotes the filter, and G^θ denotes that G rotate angle θ from the original point. If there is a set $A = \{G^{\theta(i)} \mid 1 \leq i \leq M\}$, and the arbitrary direction filter can be computed by the linear combination of the elements from set A, the element in A is called basic direction filter, denoted by $G^{\theta(i)}$.

Suppose interpolation function set $K = \{k_i(\theta) \mid 1 \leq i \leq M\}$. If an arbitrary direction filter G^θ can be computed using set A and K, filter G is called directed filter, denoted by G^θ.

$$G^\theta = \sum_{i=1}^{M} k_i(\theta) G^{\theta(i)} \tag{2}$$

The G^θ is computed for each element in the direction set $\theta = \{\theta \mid \theta \in [0, 360°) \wedge \theta \% 5 = 0\}$. And then the filtered results of G^θ in direction θ of each image in a medical image database are computed. The gray co-occurrence matrix of direction θ is computed for every medical image. And the texture features, *i.e.* energy, entropy, correlation, local homogeneity and inertia, are extracted from each co-occurrence matrix to form a texture feature vector. Statistical method is used for these texture feature vectors to make clustering analysis, and fuzzy theory is used to compute the membership of dominance of direction θ.

The process is repeated for each direction in the direction set θ to compute dominance of each direction. Dominant direction set is determined using dominance of each direction in the direction set θ. When entity in a medical image has small rotation angle, performance of content-based medical image retrieval system in which the gray co-occurrence matrix is used for the dominant direction set to extract and describe texture features can be strengthened further.

The gray co-occurrence matrix encodes the intensity relationship between pixels in different position. The texture feature extraction and description method is susceptible to noise and change in illumination. A texture feature extraction and description method using motif co-occurrence matrix is proposed in Jhanwar *et al* (2004). The method doesn't encode the intensity relationship between pixels in different positions, but encode the relationship between texture primitives in different positions. The method can reduce the effect of noise and change in illumination effectively. Moreover, the actual gray levels in the image are irrelevant.

The method first defined the six texture primitives over a 2×2 grid (See Figure 3). Each texture primitive, *i.e.* a motif, depicts a distinct sequence of pixels starting from the top left corner (See Figure 4). If texture primitives are rotated 90°, 180° and 270° respectively, and a sequence of pixels are started from the top right corner, the bottom right corner and the bottom left corner respectively, twenty-four texture primitives are computed including the original texture primitives. All the texture primitives form a texture primitive set.

Then each image in the medical image database can be divided into a group of 2×2 grid of pixels. And the texture primitive that each 2×2 grid of pixels corresponds to is detected. When all 2×2 grids

Figure 3. Texture primitives

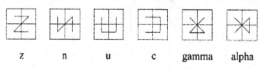

Figure 4. Construction of a motif

Figure 5. 8 × 8 image and motif transformed image

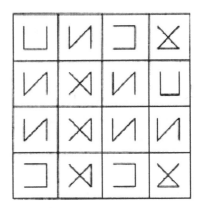

Table 1. Comparison of co-occurrence matrix methods

	Functionary unit	Functionary direction	Illumination effect	Effect of noise
Method in Andrysiak and Choras	pixel	0°, 45°, 90°, 135°	Yes	Yes
Method in Zhang *et al*	pixel	dominant directions	Yes	Yes
Method in Jhanwar *et al*	motif	0°, 45°, 90°, 135°	No	No

of pixels are detected in the image, the motif transformed image of the image are formed. Figure 5 shows an image of size 8 × 8 and its motif transformed image.

Co-occurrence matrix is used for the motif transformed image to extract and describe the texture features. The parameters k and j of $P(k, j, d, \theta)$ in formula (1) denote two motif. The parameter d denotes the distance from the motif k to the motif j. And the parameter θ is used to constrain the angle from the motif k to the motif j. The $P(k, j, d, \theta)$ denotes the estimate of the joint probability of two motifs with a distance d along a given direction θ having particular values k and j. When the motif co-occurrence matrix is computed, the method in Haralick *et al* (1973) is used to extract and describe the texture features. The similar method was used to discard gray level information to achieve illumination invariance and robustly handle large amount of noise in Ojala *et al* (2002).

Table 1 shows the comparison of methods for texture feature extraction and description using the co-occurrence matrix in Andrysiak and Choras (2005), Zhang *et al* (2007) and Jhanwar *et al* (2004).

3. EXTRACTION AND DESCRIPTION OF PERCEPTUAL TEXTURE FEATURES

Tamura *et al* (1978) proposed a texture feature extraction and description method based on psychological studies of human perceptions. The method consists of six statistical features, including coarseness, contrast, directionality, line-likeness, regularity and roughness, to describe various texture properties (Lin *et al*, 2003). And what is more, Tamura features are visually meaningful. This advantage makes Tamura features very attractive in content-based medical image retrieval.

Coarseness is the most fundamental feature in texture analysis. It refers to texture granularity, that is, the size and number of texture primitives. A coarse texture contains a small number of large primitives, whereas a fine texture contains a large number of small primitives. Suppose $f(x, y)$ denotes an image of size $n \times n$, coarseness (f_{crs}) can be computed as follows.

$$f_{crs} = \frac{2^k}{n^2} \sum_i^n \sum_j^n f(i, j) \tag{3}$$

where k is obtained as the value which maximizes the differences of the moving averages $(1/2^{2k}) \Sigma\Sigma p$ (i, j), taken over a $2^k \times 2^k$ neighborhood, along the horizontal and vertical directions. The k is selected as 1, 2, 3, 4 and 5 in Lin *et al* (2003).

Contrast refers the difference in intensity among neighboring pixels. A texture on high contrast has large difference in intensity among neighboring pixels, whereas a texture on low contrast has small difference. Contrast (f_{con}) can be computed as follows.

$$f_{con} = \frac{\delta}{(\mu_4 / \delta^4)^{1/4}} \tag{4}$$

where δ is standard deviation of the image and μ_4 is fourth moment of the image.

Directionality refers the shape of texture primitives and their placement rule. A directional texture has one or more recognizable direction of primitives, whereas an isotropic texture has no recognizable direction of primitives. Directionality (f_{dir}) can be computed as follows.

$$f_{dir} = 1 - r \cdot n_p \cdot \sum_p^{n_p} \sum_{\varphi \in wp} (\varphi - \phi_p)^2 \cdot H_D(\varphi) \tag{5}$$

where H_D is the local direction histogram, n_p is the number of peaks of H_D, ϕ_p is the pth peak position of H_D, w_p is the range of pth peak between valleys, r is a normalizing factor, and ϕ is the quantized direction code. H_D is selected as 16, $\phi \in [0, 15]$ and r as 0.025 in Lin *et al* (2003).

Line-likeness refers only the shape of texture primitives. A line-like texture has straight or wave-like primitives whose direction may not be fixed. Often the line-like texture is simultaneously directional. Line-likeness (f_{lin}) can be computed as follows.

$$f_{lin} = \sum_i^n \sum_j^n P_{Dd}(i, j) \cos[(i - j)\frac{2\pi}{n}] / \sum_i^n \sum_j^n P_{Dd}(i, j) \tag{6}$$

where $P_{Dd}(i, j)$ denotes the $n \times n$ local direction co-occurrence matrix of distance d in the image.

Regularity refers to variations of the texture-primitive placement. A regular texture is composed of identical or similar primitives, which are regularly or almost regularly arranged. An irregular texture is composed of various primitives, which are irregularly or randomly arranged. Regularity (f_{reg}) can be computed as follows.

$$f_{\text{reg}} = 1 - r \left(\delta_{\text{crs}} + \delta_{\text{con}} + \delta_{\text{dir}} + \delta_{\text{lin}} \right) \tag{7}$$

where r is a normalizing factor and δ_{xxx} means the standard deviation of f_{xxx}. The normalizing factor is selected as 0.25 in Lin *et al* (2003).

Roughness refers tactile variations of physical surface. A rough texture contains angular primitives, whereas a smooth texture contains rounded blurred primitives. Roughness (f_{rgh}) can be computed as follows.

$$f_{\text{rgh}} = f_{\text{crs}} + f_{\text{con}} \tag{8}$$

It is found in Tamura *et al* (1978) that coarseness, contrast, and directionality achieve successful correspondences with psychological measurements. But line-likeness, regularity, and roughness require further improvement due to their discrepancies with psychological measurements. Based on the research results of Tamura, Flickner *et al.* used three of Tamura features, including coarseness, contrast, and directionality, to design the QBIC system, in which a texture image is described by the three features. And the image comparison is achieved by evaluating the weighted Euclidean distance in the 3D feature space, and each weight is the inverse variance on the feature (Flickner *et al*, 1995). Rui *et al* (1999) also used the three features in the MARS system. Liu and Picard (1996) presented a Wold representation for textures in the Photobook system, in which a texture image is regarded as a homogeneous 2D discrete random field, which can be decomposed into three features, including periodicity, directionality, and randomness. The Wold representation can effectively model the human perception subjectivity for finding similar textures. And it produces compact texture descriptions but preserves perceptual attributes of textures. Furthermore, MPEG proposed a texture feature extraction and representation method, which consists of a perceptual browsing component (PBC) and a similarity retrieval component (SRC) in the MPEG-7 standard (Wu *et al*, 1999). The method is a perceptual texture feature extraction and description method, which use regularity, directionality and coarseness to describe various texture information.

After Gabor wavelet is used for an image, the image is decomposed into a set of filtered images. Each image represents the image information at a certain scale and at a certain direction. After observing these images, researchers found that structured textures usually consist of dominant periodic patterns; that a periodic or repetitive pattern, if it exists, could be captured by the filtered images. This behavior is usually captured in more than one filtered output; that the dominant scale and direction information can also be captured by analyzing projections of the filtered images. Based on these observations, Texture browsing component was denoted as follows.

$$\text{PBC} = [v_1, v_2, v_3, v_4, v_5] \tag{9}$$

The computation of the browsing descriptor is described in detail, and the descriptor was used for image classification in Wu *et al* (2000). The descriptor is a compact descriptor that requires only 12 bits to characterize the texture features of an image. Here regularity, directionality, and coarseness are described by 2 bits, 4 bits and 6 bits respectively. Moreover, a texture may have more than one dominant directions and associated scales. So MPEG-7 specification allows a maximum of two different directions and coarseness values.

The regularity of a texture is graded on a scale of 0 to 3, with 0 indicating an irregular or random texture. A value of 3 indicates a periodic pattern with well-defined directionality and coarseness values.

There is some flexibility (or implied ambiguity) in the two values in between. The regularity of a texture has close relation to the direction of the texture. The regularity of a texture having a well-defined directionality in the absence of a perceivable micro-pattern texture (texture primitives) is compared with that of a texture that lacks directionality and periodicity and where the individual micro-patterns are clearly identified in Manjunath *et al* (2001). And it is found in Manjunath *et al* (2001) that the former is more regular that the latter.

The directionality of a texture is quantized to six values, ranging from 0° to 150° in steps of 30°. Three bits are used to represent the different directions. The value 0 is used to signal textures that do not have any dominant directionality, and the remaining directions are represented by values from 1 to 6. Associated with each dominant direction is a coarseness component. Coarseness is related to image scale or resolution. It is quantized to four levels, with 0 indicating a fine grain texture and 3 indicating a coarse texture.

Table 2 shows the comparison of texture feature extraction and description methods using the perceptual texture features in Lin *et al* (2003) and Wu *et al* (2000).

4. TEXTURE FEATURE EXTRACTION AND DESCRIPTION USING GABOR WAVELET TRANSFORM AND POST-GABOR

4.1 Texture Feature Extraction and Description Using Gabor Wavelet Transform

The discovery of direction-selective cells in the primary visual cortex of monkeys almost 40 years ago and the fact that most of the neurons in this part of the brain are of this type triggered a wave of research activity aimed at a more precise, quantitative description of the functional behavior of such cells in Hubel and Wiesel (1974). So far, some computational models of direction-selective visual neurons such as simple cells, complex cells, grating cells, etc., have been proposed (Petkov and Kruizinga, 1997). Moreover, some computational models that simulate the principle of operation of these cells (e.g., Gabor filters) have been proposed (Arivazhagan *et al*, 2006). Gabor wavelet transform is a wavelet transform whose mother wavelet is Gabor function. The wavelet transform with rotation-invariance of Gabor function and scale-invariance of wavelet transform is used for direction-invariant and scale-invariant texture feature extraction and description. Gabor wavelet is usually thought be a complex planar wave restricted by 2-D Gaussian envelope. Aside from scale and direction, the only thing that can make two Gabor wavelets differ is the ratio between wavelength and width of the Gaussian envelope. Every Gabor wavelet has a certain wavelength and direction, and is then convolved with an image to estimate the magnitude of local frequencies of that approximate wavelength and direction in the image. The Gabor wavelets can be considered as a class of self-similar functions. If Gabor function is mother wavelet, other wavelets can be obtained by appropriate dilations and rotations of the mother wavelet.

Table 2. Comparison of methods using perceptual texture features

	Functionary unit	Feature description	Compact descriptor
Method in Lin *et al*	texture primitive	magnitude	No
Method in Wu *et al*	texture primitive	bit	Yes

For a given image $f(x, y)$ of size $m \times n$, its 2-D discrete Gabor wavelet transform is denoted as follows.

$$G_{pq}(x,y) = \sum_s \sum_t f(x-s, y-t) \psi_{pq}^*(s,t)$$

(10)

Here s, t are the filter mask size variables, and p, q are the scale and direction values respectively. Also ψ_{pq}^* is the complex conjugate of ψ_{pq}, which is a self-similar function generated from the dilation and rotation of the mother wavelet ψ.

$$\Psi_{pq}(x, y) = a^p \Psi(x', y')$$

(11)

where a is the factor of scale and greater than 1. Also $p = 0$, 1...P-1 and $q = 0$, 1...Q-1 respectively. P and Q are the total number of scales and directions respectively. And $x' = a^p (x \cos \theta + y \sin \theta)$ and $y' = a^p (-x \sin \theta + y \cos \theta)$ where $\theta = q \pi / Q$.

$$\Psi(x, y) = (\frac{1}{2\pi\sigma_x\sigma_y}) \exp(-\frac{1}{2}(\frac{x^2}{\sigma_x^2} + \frac{y^2}{\sigma_y^2})) \exp(2\pi j W x)$$

(12)

where W defines the frequency bandwidth of Gabor filter. It has been found in neurophysiology that $W = 0.5$ is completely consistent with visual system of human (Ro *et al*, 2001). The parameters σ_x and σ_y are constants of Gaussian envelope along x and y axles in time domain respectively.

The self-similar functions from rotation and change of scale of the mother wavelet form a non-orthogonal basis of functions for the multi-resolution decomposition (Manjunath and Ma, 1996). When using the basis of functions for an image, there is redundant information in the filtered images. So the strategy in Manjunath *et al* (2000) can be used to reduce this redundancy. Let U_l and U_h denote the lower and upper center frequencies of interest. Let Q be the total number of directions and P be the total number of scales in the multi-resolution decomposition. The design strategy is to ensure that the half-peak magnitude supports of the filter responses in the frequency spectrum touch each other as shown in Figure 6. The parameters σ_x and σ_y can be computed based on the strategy. The Fourier transform of the formula (12) can first be denoted as follows.

$$G(u,v) = \exp(-\frac{1}{2}(\frac{(u-W)^2}{\sigma_u^2} + \frac{v^2}{\sigma_v^2}))$$

(13)

Here $\sigma_u = 1/2\pi\sigma_x$ and $\sigma_v = 1/2\pi\sigma_y$. Then the parameters σ_u and σ_v can be computed as follows. The parameters σ_x and σ_y can be computed using the parameters σ_u and σ_v.

$$a = (U_h - U_l)^{1/(P-1)}$$

(14)

$$\delta_u = \frac{(a-1)U_h}{(a+1)\sqrt{2\ln 2}}$$

(15)

$$\delta_v = \tan(\frac{\pi}{2k})[U_h - 2\ln 2(\frac{\sigma_u^2}{U_h})] \times [2\ln 2 - \frac{(2\ln 2)^2 \sigma_u^2}{U_h^2}]^{-1/2} \tag{16}$$

Furthermore, to eliminate sensitivity of the filter response to absolute intensity values, the real (even) components of the 2-D Gabor filters are biased by adding a constant to make them zero mean (This can also be done by setting G(0, 0) in the equation (13) to zero.)

After formula (10) is used for the image, energy can be computed and denoted as follows.

$$E_{pq} = \sum_x \sum_y |G_{pq}(x, y)| \tag{17}$$

The method in Arivazhagan (2006) and Manjunath (2000) can be used to compute the mean μ_{pq} and standard deviation δ_{pq} as texture features using E_{pq} computed. Suppose μ_{pq} and δ_{pq} denote the mean and standard deviation computed from scale p and direction q respectively, the μ_{pq} and δ_{pq} can be denoted as follows respectively.

$$\mu_{pq}(x) = \frac{E_{pq}(x)}{MN} \tag{18}$$

$$\sigma_{pq}(x) = \sqrt{\frac{\sum_x \sum_y (|G_{pq}(x, y)| - \mu_{pq})^2}{MN}} \tag{19}$$

The aforementioned method extracts and describes the texture features in spatial domain, and uses the information from frequency domain to compute the transform parameters. Previous extensive works on the feature descriptor have shown that this descriptor is robust, effective, and easy to compute (Manjunath and Ma, 1996; Haley and Manjunath, 1999; Li *et al*, 1999; Ro, 1998). During the MPEG-7 Core Experiments, it was realized that the computational complexity of this descriptor can be reduced significantly by computing the values in the frequency domain rather than in the spatial domain.

Figure 6. half-peak magnitude of the filter responses in the Gabor filter bank

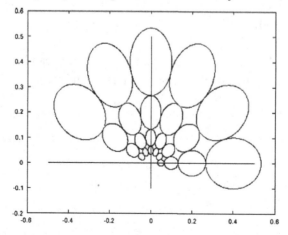

A texture feature extraction and description of polar frequency domain is proposed in Ro *et al* (2001). The method is based on the principle of operation of human visual system and corresponds well to some results from psychophysical experiments. In these experiments, the response of the visual cortex is turned to a band-limited portion of the frequency domain. And the human brain decomposes the spectra into perceptual channels that are bands in spatial frequency (Manjunath and Ma, 1996). For texture featuring, the best sub-band representation of HVS is a division of the spatial frequency domain in octave-bands (4~5 divisions) along the radial direction and in equal-width angles along the angular direction. These sub-bands are symmetrical with respect to the origin of the polar coordinate. Based on these research results, homogeneous texture descriptor is proposed in Ro *et al* (2001).

In the method, the frequency space is partitioned into 30 channels with equal divisions in the angular direction (at 30° intervals) and octave division in the radial direction (five octaves), as shown in Figure 7. In a normalized frequency space ($0 \leq w \leq 1$), the normalized frequency w is given by $w = \Omega / \Omega_{max}$ where Ω_{max} is the maximum frequency value of the image. The center frequencies of the feature channels are spaced equally in 30 degrees along the angular direction such as $\theta_r = 30° \times r$. Here r is an angular index with $r \in \{0, 1, 2, 3, 4, 5\}$. The angular width of all feature channels is 30 degree. In the radial direction, the center frequencies of the feature channels are spaced with octave scale such as $w_s = w_0 \times 2^{-s}$, $s \in \{0,1,2,3,4\}$ where s is a radial index and w_0 is the highest center frequency specified by 3/4. The octave bandwidth of the feature channels in the radial direction is written as $B_s = B_0 \times 2^{-s}$, $s \in \{0,1,2,3,4\}$ where B_0 is the largest bandwidth specified by 1/2.

The frequency layout in Figure 7 is actually realized with a set of ideal filter banks that have abrupt channel boundaries. Suppose $G_{s,r}(w, \theta)$ denotes the Fourier-transformed Gabor function at s-th radial index and r-th angular index in polar coordinate, then $G_{s,r}(w, \theta)$ is denoted as follows.

$$G_{s,r}(w,\theta) = \exp(\frac{-(w - w_s)^2}{2\sigma_{w_s}^2}) \exp(\frac{-(\theta - \theta_r)^2}{2\sigma_{\theta_r}^2}) \qquad (20)$$

where the parameters σ_{ws} and $\sigma_{\theta r}$ are the standard deviations of the Gabor function in the radial direction and the angular direction respectively. And the parameter σ_{ws} is dependent on the octave bandwidth.

When using Gabor filter bank, channels overlap over boundary regions. So the neighboring channels affect each other. To reduce the redundant information, the method in Manjunath (2000) is used. The method makes Gabor function touch other Gabor function in half peak of the radial direction and the angular direction. And then it computes the standard deviation of Gabor function. When the frequency

Figure 7. Frequency layout for texture feature extraction

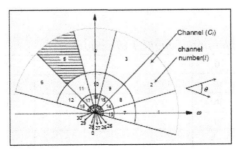

Figure 8. 5 × 6 Gabor filer in polar coordinate

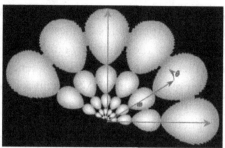

space is divided into six in the angular direction and five in the radial direction, the 5 × 6 Gabor filter where redundant information has been reduced is shown in Figure 8.

For the frequency layout in Figure 7, the parameters σ_{ws} 和 $\sigma_{\theta r}$ can be computed as follows.

$$\sigma_{\theta_r} = 15° / \sqrt{2\ln 2} \text{ and } \sigma_{w_s} = \frac{B_S}{2\sqrt{2\ln 2}} \tag{21}$$

Table 3 and table 4 show the parameters of channels and Gabor function respectively.

After the $G_{s,r}(w, \theta)$ has been computed, the method in Ro *et al* (2001) can be used for every channel in Figure 7 to compute the energy and energy deviation. Suppose the energies and energy deviations of 30 channels are denoted as $e_1, e_2, e_3, \cdots, e_{30}$ and $d_1, d_2, d_3, \cdots, d_{30}$ respectively, then homogeneous texture descriptor of the image can be denoted as follows.

$$TD = [f_{DC}, f_{SD}, e_1, e_2, e_3, \cdots, e_{30}, d_1, d_2, d_3, \cdots, d_{30}] \tag{22}$$

where f_{DC} and f_{SD} denote the brightness mean and standard deviation of the image respectively.

In recent years, the texture feature extraction and description methods using Gabor wavelet has received a wide concern in content-based medical image retrieval. The imaginary part of Gabor filter is used for the edge information extraction of CT cerebrovascular medical image in Lei *et al* (2007).

Table 3. Parameters of octave band in the radial direction

Radial index(s)	0	1	2	3	4
Centre frequency(w_s)	3 / 4	3 / 8	3 / 16	3 / 32	3 / 64
Octave bandwidth(B_s)	1 / 2	1 / 4	1 / 8	1 / 16	1 / 32
σ_{ws}	$\dfrac{1}{4\sqrt{2\ln 2}}$	$\dfrac{1}{8\sqrt{2\ln 2}}$	$\dfrac{1}{16\sqrt{2\ln 2}}$	$\dfrac{1}{32\sqrt{2\ln 2}}$	$\dfrac{1}{64\sqrt{2\ln 2}}$

Table 4. Parameters of angular band in the angular direction

Angular index(r)	0	1	2	3	4	5
Centre frequency(θ_r)	0°	30°	60°	90°	120°	150°
Angular bandwidth	30°	30°	30°	30°	30°	30°
$\sigma_{\theta r}$	$\dfrac{30°}{2\sqrt{2\ln 2}}$	$\dfrac{30°}{2\sqrt{2\ln 2}}$	$\dfrac{30°}{2\sqrt{2\ln 2}}$	$\dfrac{30°}{2\sqrt{2\ln 2}}$	$\dfrac{30°}{2\sqrt{2\ln 2}}$	$\dfrac{30°}{2\sqrt{2\ln 2}}$

Gabor filter bank is used for blood image segmentation in Safabakhsh and Zamani (2006). In Zhao *et al* (2004), Gabor filters are used for the texture feature extraction of liver CT image.

After the texture features from Gabor filters are used for content-based medical image retrieval, it is found for the different kinds of medical images that the texture information only from part of 30 channels has main effect on the performance of retrieval system. Moreover, the channels in which the texture information which has main effect on the retrieval system, is computed, can be different.

A texture feature extraction and description of medical images using multi-scale and multi-direction Gabor wavelet is proposed in Clark *et al* (1987). The method extracts energy information for each image in a medical image database from each of 30 channels respectively. Then the energy mean of each channel is computed for each kind of medial images in the medical image database. And the *k* scales and directions with the maximum energy means are selected to form a dominant multi-scale and multi-direction fuzzy set. The standardized energy means are used for the measure of dominance of each element in the fuzzy set. Then Gabor wavelet is used for each element in the multi-scale and multi-direction fuzzy set to compute the texture information which forms a texture feature vector.

4.2 TEXTURE FEATURE EXTRACTION AND DESCRIPTION USING POST-GABOR WAVELET

The texture features from Gabor filters can be used directly for medical image retrieval, medical image segment, medical image classification, etc. Or they can be transformed into new features which are used for the aforementioned application. In Clark (1987), Bovik (1992), Fogel and Sagi (1989), Tan (1995), Turner (1986), Manjunath and Chellappa (1993), the pairs of Gabor features that correspond to the same preferred direction and spatial frequency but differ in the value of a phase parameter are combined in a quantity to form new texture features. The method is called the Gabor energy. In Bigün and du Buf (1994) and Schroeter and Bigün (1995), complex moments are derived from Gabor features. In Petkov and Kruizinga (1997), Kruizinga and Petkov (1995), Kruizinga and Petkov (1998) and Kruizinga and Petkov (1999), grating cell operator features, inspired by the function of a special type of visual neuron, are computed using Gabor features.

Grating cells are found in the same cortical area (V1) as simple and complex cells and similarly to simple and complex cells show direction selectivity. In contrast to other direction-selective cells, grating cells respond very weakly or not at all to single bars, i.e., the bars which are isolated and do not form the parts of a grating. However, Grating cells respond vigorously to a grating of bars of appropriate direction, position and periodicity. And what's more, grating cell operator can react only to texture patterns, not to other patterns such as shape patterns. In Petkov and Kruizinga (1997), grating cells were modeled by two stages. In the first stage, the responses of so-called grating subunits were computed by using as input the responses of centre-on and centre-off simple cells with symmetric receptive fields. In the second stage, the responses of grating subunits of a given preferred direction and periodicity were summed together within a certain area in order to compute the response of a grating cell. The computational model of grating cells uses as input the responses of simple cells. And the simple cells are modeled by a family of two-dimensional Gabor functions as follows in Petkov and Kruizinga (1997).

$$G(x,y) = \frac{1}{2\pi\delta_x\delta_y}\exp(-\frac{1}{2}(\frac{x^2}{\delta_x^2} + \frac{\gamma^2 y^2}{\delta_y^2}))\exp(-2\pi i \frac{x}{\lambda} + \varphi) \qquad (23)$$

To strengthen the information in the position (x, y) of a light impulse in the visual field when the Gabor function is acted on the (x, y) central symmetry area, the real part of the Gabor function can be used and denoted as follows.

$$G(x,y) = \frac{1}{2\pi\delta_x\delta_y}\exp(-\frac{1}{2}(\frac{x^2}{\delta_x^2}+\frac{\gamma^2 y^2}{\delta_y^2}))\cos(2\pi\frac{x}{\lambda}+\varphi) \qquad (24)$$

Here the parameters δ_x and δ_y denote the standard deviation of the Gaussian factor, which are used to determine the size of the receptive field. The parameter λ denotes the wavelength and $1/\lambda$ denotes the spatial frequency of the harmonic factor $\cos(2\pi x/\lambda+\varphi)$. Here δ_x/λ and δ_y/λ are used to determine the spatial frequency bandwidth of the simple cells along x and y direction. Usually, $\delta_x/\lambda = 0.56$ and $\delta_y/\lambda = 0.56$. The parameter γ denotes the spatial aspect ratio and is used to determine the eccentricity of the receptive field ellipse. Generally the parameter γ has a range from 0.23 to 0.92. The parameter φ denotes the phase offset in the argument of the harmonic factor $\cos(2\pi x/\lambda+\varphi)$ and is used to determine the symmetry of the function $G(x, y)$. In Burr *et al* (1989), $G(x, y)$ is symmetric for $\varphi = 0$ and $\varphi = \pi$ with respect to the center of the receptive field. It is shown in Petkov and Kruizinga (1997) that a cell with a symmetric receptive field reacts strongly (but not exclusively) to a bar which coincides in direction, width and polarity with the central lobe of the receptive field.

$$x = (x' - \xi')\cos\theta - (y' - \eta')\sin\theta \text{ and } y = (x' - \xi')\sin\theta + (y' - \eta')\cos\theta \qquad (25)$$

Here the arguments x' and y' specify the position of a light impulse in the visual field, and ξ' and η' specify the centre of a receptive field within the visual field. The argument θ is the direction, in which Gabor filters perform and specifies the direction of the normal to the parallel excitatory and inhibitory stripe zones.

4.2.1 Response of a Simple Cell

If a luminance distribution image is $f(x, y)$ of size m×n, the response R of a simple cell in the visual field Ω is denoted as follows.

$$R = \begin{cases} X(\dfrac{R_1/R_2 * C_1}{R_1/R_2+C_2}) = \begin{cases} 0 & G'(x,y)=0 \\[2mm] \begin{cases} 0 & \dfrac{R_1/R_2 * C_1}{R_1/R_2+C_2} < 0 \\[2mm] \dfrac{R_1/R_2 * C_1}{R_1/R_2+C_2} & \dfrac{R_1/R_2 * C_1}{R_1/R_2+C_2} \geq 0 \end{cases} & G'(x,y) <> 0 \end{cases} \end{cases} \qquad (26)$$

Here the parameters C1 and C2 are the maximum response level and the semi-saturation constant, respectively. The parameters R1 and R2 are denoted as follows.

$$R_1 = \sum_x\sum_y(\sum_s\sum_t f(x-s, y-t)G(s,t)) \qquad (27)$$

$$R_2 = \sum_x \sum_y (\sum_s \sum_t f(x-s, y-t) G'(s,t)) \qquad (28)$$

Here the parameters s and t are the Gabor filter mask size variables. The function G'(x, y) can be denoted as follows.

$$G'(x,y) = \frac{1}{2\pi\delta_x\delta_y} \exp(-\frac{1}{2}(\frac{x^2}{\delta_x^2} + \frac{\gamma^2 y^2}{\delta_y^2})) \qquad (29)$$

4.2.2 Computational Model of Grating Cells

Suppose that a grating subunit of three bars is a segment of length 3λ passing through point (ξ,η) in direction θ. The segment is divided in the intervals of length $\lambda/2$ and the maximum activity of one sort of simple cell, centre-on or centre-off, is determined in each interval. The point (ξ,η) is selected as the center and each interval is marked with a value in $\{-3, -2, -1, 0, 1, 2\}$. The results are shown in Figure 9.

It can be found from Figure 9 that the subunit of a grating cell is activated if centre-on and centre-off cells of the same preferred direction θ and spatial frequency $1/\lambda$ are alternately activated in the intervals of length $\lambda/2$ along a line segment of length 3λ centered on point (ξ,η) and passing in direction θ.

Suppose that the center of visual field is (ξ',η') and the position of grating subunit is (ξ,η). If $n = \{-3, -1, 1\}$, the parameter φ in formula (24) is 0. If $n = \{-2, 0, 2\}$, the parameter φ in formula (23) is π. The centre-on and centre-off can be computed with the formula as follows.

$$M(n) = \max\{R \,|\, \xi',\eta' : n\frac{\lambda}{2}\cos\theta \leq (\xi'-\xi) < (n+1)\frac{\lambda}{2}\cos\theta, n\frac{\lambda}{2}\sin\theta \leq (\eta'-\eta) < (n+1)\frac{\lambda}{2}\sin\theta\} \qquad (30)$$

Based on the responses of grating subunit, the method in Petkov and Kruizinga (1997) can be used for texture feature extraction and description. The method simulates the function of direction selectivity cells in visual cortex and show good performance in texture feature extraction and description. However, current computational models of grating cells use two-valued logic, which limits its expression on uncertain information during feature description. A modified computational model of grating cell is proposed in Zhang *et al* (2007) and used for the texture feature extraction and description of chest CT images. Multi-valued logic is introduced into the computational model of grating cells to improve performance of the method in Petkov and Kruizinga (1997) further.

Zhang *et al* (2007) proposed that it cannot be determined by the method in Petkov and Kruizinga (1997) that whether or not a grating cell can be activated if adjacent centre-on and centre-off have adjacent responses. In Zhang *et al* (2007), multi-valued logic is introduced into the computational model of grating cell for this problem. Having been normalized, $M(n)$ in formula (30) can be denoted as follows.

Figure 9. Grating subunit of three bars

$$M'(n) = \frac{M(n)}{\max\{M(n) \mid n = -3 \cdots 2\}} \qquad (31)$$

The response of a grating subunit can be computed as follows.

$$Q = \begin{cases} 1 & \forall n, n \in [-3,1], |M'(n) - M'(n+1)| < L_1 \\ 1 - \min\{|M'(n) - M'(n+1)|\} & \forall n, n \in [-3,1], L_1 < |M'(n) - M'(n+1)| < L_2 \end{cases} \qquad (32)$$

Here the parameter L_1 denotes the maximum threshold with that human can distinguish the difference between $M'(n)$ and $M'(n+1)$, and L_2 denotes the minimum threshold with that human can distinguish the similarity between $M'(n)$ and $M'(n+1)$. If $|M'(n)-M'(n+1)|$ is between L_1 and L_2, fuzzy values that are $1-\min\{|M'(n)-M'(n+1)|\}$ are used to describe the response of grating subunit.

In the second stage of the model, the response of a grating cell is computed by the weighted summation of the responses of the grating subunits. Furthermore, the sum of grating subunits with direction θ and $\theta+\pi$ is used so that the model is made symmetric for opposite directions. The response of grating cell can be denoted as follows.

$$G(\theta) = \sum_{\xi'}\sum_{\eta'} \exp\left(-\frac{(\xi - \xi')^2 + (\eta - \eta')^2}{2(\beta\delta^2)}\right)(Q(\theta) + Q(\theta + \pi)) \qquad (33)$$

Here the parameter β determines the size of the area over which the effective summation takes place. A value of $\beta = 5$ results in a good approximation of the spatial summation properties of grating cells and $\theta \in [0,\pi)$ (Petkov and Kruizinga, 1997). The method in Petkov and Kruizinga (1997) can be used to compute a texture feature vector.

Table 5 shows the comparison of texture feature extraction and description methods using Gabor filters and post-Gabor filters in Zhang *et al* (2007), Petkov and Kruizinga (1997), Ro *et al* (2001), Manjunath *et al* (2000) and Clark *et al* (1987).

Table 5. Comparison of methodes using Gabor filters and post-Gabor filters

	Using dominant directions	Extracting texture features only
Method in Ro *et al*	No	No
Method in Manjunath *et al*	No	No
Method in Clark *et al*	Yes	No
Method in Petkov and Kruizinga	Yes	Yes
Method in Zhang *et al*	Yes	Yes

5. CONCLUSION

Texture feature extraction and description is one of important research areas in content-based medical image retrieval. The chapter first presents a theory framework of content-based medical image retrieval. Then it makes classification for current texture feature extraction and description methods. Moreover, it analyzes co-occurrence matrix, perceptual texture features, Gabor filter, post-Gabor filter, and the modified methods of these methods further. In addition, the chapter makes comparison for different methods in each kind.

6. FUTURE RESEARCH DIRECTIONS

In recent years, texture feature extraction and description methods have been developed. The development doesn't only contain that of low level texture feature extraction and description methods, but also that of texture semantic feature extraction and description methods. However, the following issues are open.

1. **Thorough researches on low level texture feature extraction and description methods:** Many low level texture feature extraction and description methods are demonstrated in the chapter, such as gray co-occurrence matrix, perceptual texture feature, Gabor filter, etc. But the following issues are open. The first is selection of the texture features with dominant discrimination. The second is how low level texture feature extraction and description methods are combined to improve the efficiency and effectiveness of a retrieval system further.

2. **Researches on texture semantic feature extraction and description methods:** Texture semantic feature extraction and description makes term-based retrieval possible. But the following issues need be researched further. The first is creation of terms. The second is the description of uncertain information in a term. The third is the combination of terms. The fourth is the optimization of terms using relevance feedback.

3. **Mapping from low level texture feature to texture semantic feature:** Low level texture feature extraction and description can extract and describe the texture information of an image. But what users make use of are texture semantic features. So the issue of the mapping from low level texture feature to texture semantic feature is open. Though fuzzy clustering, neural network, and so on are proposed, the mappings need be searched further.

4. **Comparison of texture feature extraction and description methods:** In recent years, many texture feature extraction and description methods are proposed, low level texture feature extraction and description methods or texture semantic feature extraction and description methods. The performance of some texture feature extraction and description methods are compared using the user-defined image set and different test methods, but some issues such as standardization of image test sets and selection of test methods are open.

5. **Texture feature extraction and description of special part medical images:** The texture information of different parts in body can be different for medical images. The performance of the systems in which the same texture feature extraction and description method is used for the medical images of the different part can be different. And the performance of the systems in which the different texture feature extraction and description methods are used for the medical images of

the same part can also be different. So the issues about the selection of texture feature extraction and description methods for the special parts in body are open.

REFERENCES

Andrysiak T., & Choras M. (2005). Image retrieval based on hierarchical Gabor filters. *International Journal of Applied Mathematics and Computer Science. 15*(4), 471-480.

Arivazhagan S., Ganesan L., & Priyal S. P. (2006). Texture classification using Gabor wavelets-based rotation invariant features. *Pattern Recognition Letters, 27*(16), 1976-1982.

Bigün, J., & du Buf, J. M. H. (1994). N-folded symmetries by complex moments in Gabor space and their application to unsupervised texture segmentation. *IEEE Transactions on Pattern Analysis and Machine Intelligence, 16*(1), 80-87.

Bovik, A. C., Gopal, N., Emmoth, T., & Restrepo, A. (1992). Localized measurement of emergent image frequencies by Gabor wavelets. *IEEE Transactions on Information Theory, 38*(2), 691-712.

Chen, Y. D., & Dougherty, E. R. (1994). Gray-scale morphological granulometric texture classification. *Optical Engineering, 33*(8), 2713-2722.

Burr, D. C., Morrone, M. C., & Spinelli, D. (1989). Evidence for edge and bar detectors in human vision. Vision Research, *29*(4), 419-431.

Chien, Y. P., & Fu, K. S. (1974). Recognition of X-ray picture patterns. *IEEE Transactions on Systems Man and Cybernetics. 4*(2), 145-156.

Clark, M., Bovik, A. C., & Geisler, W. S. (1987). Texture segmentation using Gabor modulation/demodulation. *Pattern Recognition Letters, 6*(4), 261-267.

Conners R. W., & Harlow C. A. (1980). Towards a structural textural analyzer based on statistical methods. *Computer Graphics and Image Processing, 12*(3), 224-256.

Flickner, M., Sawhney, H., Niblack, W., Ashley, J., Huang, Q., Dom, B., Gorkani, M., Hafner, J., Lee, D., Petkovic, D., Steele, D., & Yanker, P. (1995). Query by image and video content: The QBIC system. *IEEE Computer Magazine, 28*(9), 23-32.

Fogel, I., & Sagi, D. (1989). Gabor filters as texture discriminator. *Biological Cybernetics, 61*(2), 103-113.

Glatard, T., Montagnat, J., & Magnin, I.E. (2004). Texture-based medical image indexing and retrieval: application to cardiac imaging. In *Proceedings of ACM SIGMM international workshop on Multimedia information retrieval* (pp. 135-142). New York, NY: Association for Computing Machinery.

Haley, G. M., & Manjunath, B. S. (1999). Rotation invariant texture classification using a complete space-frequency model. *IEEE Transactions on Image Processing, 8*(2), 255-269.

Haralick, R. M., Shanmugam, K., & Dinstein, I. (1973). Texture features for image classification. *IEEE Transactions on Systems Man and Cybernetics. 3*(6), 610-621.

Hubel, D. H., & Wiesel, T.N. (1974). Sequence Regularity and Geometry of Direction Columns in the Monkey Striate Cortex. *Journal of Comparative Neurology, 158*(3), 267-293.

Julesz, B. (1975). Experiments in the Visual Perception of Texture. *Scientific American, 232*(4): 34-43.

Jhanwar, N., Chaudhuri, S., Seetharaman, G., & Zavidovique, B. (2004). Content based image retrieval using motif cooccurrence matrix. *Image and Vision Computing, 22*(14), 1211-1220.

Kruizinga, P., & Petkov, N. (1995). A computational model of periodic-pattern-selective cells. In: J. Mira & F. Sandoval, (Eds.), *International Workshop on Artificial Neural Networks* (pp. 90-99). Berlin: Springer-Verlag.

Kruizinga, P., & Petkov, N. (1998). Grating cell operator features for oriented texture segmentation. In A. Jain, S. Venkatesh, & B. Lovell, (Eds.), *International Conference on Pattern Recognition* (pp. 1010-1014). Brisbane: IEEE Press.

Kruizinga, P., & Petkov, N. (1999). Non-linear operator for oriented texture. *IEEE Transactions on Image Processing, 8*(10), 1395-1407.

Lei, Y. S., Wang, M. S., & Qin R. (2007). Edge information extraction algorithm of CT cerebrovascular medical image based on imaginary part of gabor filter. *Journal of Tianjin University Science and Technology, 40*(7), 833-838.

Levine, M. (Ed.). (1985). Vision in Man and Machine. New, York: McGraw-Hill.

Lau, P.Y., & Ozawa, S. (2004). An image-based analysis for classifying multimodal brain images in the image-guided medical diagnosis model. In: D. Hudson (Ed.), *Annual International Conference of the IEEE Engineering in Medicine and Biology Society: Vol. 26.* (pp. 3400-3403). New, Jersey: Institute of Electrical and Electronics Engineers Inc.

Li, C.S., Smith, J.R., Castelli, V., & Bergman, L. (1999). Comparing texture feature sets for retrieving core images in petroleum applications. In *Proceedings of Storage and Retrieval for Image and Video Databases VII: Vol. 3656. The International Society for Optical Engineering* (pp. 2-10). Bellingham, WA: Society of Photo-Optical Instrumentation Engineers.

Lin H. C., Chiu C. Y., & Yang S. N. (2003). Finding textures by textual descriptions, visual examples, and relevance feedbacks. *Pattern Recognition Letters, 24*(14), 2255-2267.

Liu, F., & Picard, R. (1996). Periodicity, directionality, and randomness: World features for image modeling and retrieval. *IEEE Transactions on Pattern Analysis and Machine Intelligence, 18*(7), 722-733.

Liu, Y., Zhang, D. S., Lu, G. J., & Ma, W. Y. (2007). A survey of content-based image retrieval with high-level semantics. *Pattern Recognition, 40*(1), 262-282.

Ma, W. Y., & Manjunath, B. S. (1996). Texture-based pattern retrieval from image databases. *Journal Multimedia Tools and Applications, 2*(1), 35-51.

Manjunath, B. S., & Chellappa, R. (1993). A unified method to boundary perception: Edges, textures and illusory contours. *IEEE Transactions on Neural Networks, 4*(1), 96-108.

Manjunath, B. S., & Ma, W. Y. (1996). Texture features for browsing and retrieval of image data. *IEEE Transactions on Pattern Analysis and Machine Intelligence, 18*(8), 837-842.

Manjunath, B. S., Ohm, J. R., vasudevan, V. V., & Yamada, A. (2001). Color and texture descriptors. *IEEE Transactions on Circuits and Systems for Video Technology, 11*(6), 703-715.

Manjunath B.S., Wu P., Newsam S., and Shin H.D. (2000). A texture descriptor for browsing and similarity retrieval. *Signal Processing: Image Communication, 16*(1-2), 33-43.

Materka, A., & Strzelecki, M. (1998). *Texture Analysis Methods-A Review* (Tech. Rep. No. COST B 11). Brussels: Technical University of Lodz, Institute of Electronics.

Moyo T., Bangay S., & Foster G. (2006). The identification of mammalian species through the classification of hair patterns using image pattern recognition. In *Proceedings of the 4th international conference on Computer graphics, virtual reality, visualisation and interaction in Africa.* (pp. 177-181). Cape Town: ACM Press.

Müller, H., Michoux, N., Bandon, D., & Geissbuhler A. (2004). A review of content-based image retrieval systems in medical applications-clinical benefits and future directions. *International Journal of Medical Informatics, 73*(1), 1-23.

Ogawa, K., Fukushima, M., Kubota, K., & Hisa, N. (1998). Computer-aided diagnostic system for diffused liver diseases with ultrasonography by neural networks. *IEEE Transactions on Nuclear Science, 45*(6), 3069-3074.

Ojala, T., Pietikainen, M., & Maenpaa, T. (2002). Multiresolution gray-scale and rotation invariant texture classification with local binary patterns. *IEEE Transactions on Pattern Analysis and Machine Intelligence, 24*(7), 971–987.

Petkov, N., & Kruizinga, P. (1997). Computational Models of Visual Neurons Specialized in the Detection of Periodic and Aperiodic Oriented Visual Stimuli: Bar and Grating Cells. *Biological Cybernetics, 76*(2), 83-96.

Pressman, N. J. (1976). Markovian analysis of cervical cell images. *Journal of Histochemistry and Cytochemistry. 24*(1), 138-144.

Ro, Y. M. Matching pursuit: Contents featuring for image indexing. (1998). In *Proceedings of Multimedia Storage and Archiving Systems III: Vol. 3527. The International Society for Optical Engineering* (pp. 89–100). Boston, MA: The International Society for Optical Engineering.

Ro, Y. M., Kim M., Kang H. K., Manjunath B. S., & Kim J. (2001). MPEG-7 Homogeneous Texture Descriptor. *ETRI Journal, 23*(2), 41-51.

Rosenfeld, A., and Kak, A. (Ed.). (1982). *Digital Picture Processing*. New, York: Academic Press.

Rui, Y., Huang, T. S., & Chang, S. F. (1999). Image retrieval: Current techniques, promising directions, and open issues. *Journal of Visual Communication and Image Representation, 10*(1), 39-62.

Safabakhsh, R., & Zamani, F. (2006). A robust multi-direction Gabor based system for discriminating touching white and red cells in microscopic blood image. In *Proceedings of the International Confer-*

ence on Information & Communication Technologies: Vol. 1. from Theory to Applications (1135- 1139). Damascus: IEEE Press.

Schroeter, P., & Bigün, J. (1995). Hierarchical image segmentation by multidimensional clustering and direction adaptive boundary refinement. *Pattern Recognition, 28*(5), 695-709.

Smeulders, A. W. M., Worring, M., Santini, S., Gupta, A., & Jain, R. (2000). Content-based image retrieval at the end of the early years. *IEEE Transactions on Pattern Analysis and Machine Intelligence, 22*(12), 1349-1380.

Tamura, H., Mori, S., & Yamawaki, T. (1978). Texture features corresponding to visual perception. *IEEE Transactions on Systems Man and Cybernetics, 8*(6), 460-473.

Tan, T. N. (1995). Texture edge detection by modeling visual cortical channels. *Pattern Recognition, 28*(9), 1283-1298.

Tourassi, G. D., & Floyd, C. E. (2004). Computer-assisted diagnosis of mammographic masses using an information-theoretic image retrieval scheme with BIRADs-based relevance feedback. In *Proceedings of Progress in Biomedical Optics and Imaging - Medical Imaging 2004: Vol. 5370(2). Imaging Processing* (pp. 810-817). Bellingham, WA: International Society for Optical Engineering.

Turner, M. R. (1986). Texture discrimination by Gabor functions. *Biological Cybernetics, 55*(2-3), 71-82.

Wei, C. H., Li, C. T., & Wilson, R. (2005). A content-based method to medical image database retrieval. In Z. M. Ma (Ed.), *Database Modeling for Industrial Data Management* (pp. 258-292). Hershey, PA: Idea Group publishing.

Wied, G., Bahr, G., & Bartels, P. (1970). Automatic analysis of cell images. In G. Wied, & G. Bahr (Ed.), Automated Cell Identification and Cell Sorting (pp. 195-360). New, York: Academic Press.

Wu, P., Manjunath, B. S., Newsam, S., & Shin, H. D. (2000). A texture descriptor for browsing and image retrieval. *Signal Processing: Image Communication, 16*(1-2), 33-43.

Wu, P., Ma, W., Manjunath, B.S., Shin, H., & Choi, Y. (1999). MPEG-7 Document, ISO/IEC JTC1/SC29/WG11/P77.

Zhang, G., Ma, Z. M., Deng, L. G., & Cai, Z. P. (2007). Oriented Filter Based on Dominant Directions in Content-based Image Retrieval. *Journal of Northeastern University, 28*(7), 978-981.

Zhang, G. Ma, Z.M., Cai, Z. P., & Wang, H. L. (2007). Texture analysis using modified computational model of grating cells in content-based medical image retrieval. In *Proceedings of International Conference on Medical Imaging and Informatics* (pp. 184-191). Beijing: Middlesex University Press.

Zhang, G., & Ma, Z.M. (2007). Texture feature extraction and description using Gabor wavelet in content-based medical image retrieval. In *Proceedings of International conference on wavelet analysis and pattern recognition* (pp. 169-173). Beijing: IEEE Press.

Zhang G., Ma Z.M., & Cai Z.P. (2007). Directed filter for dominant direction fuzzy set in content-based image retrieval. In *Proceedings of the 22th ACM Symposium on Applied Computing.* (pp. 76–77). Seoul: ACM Press.

Zhao, C.G., Cheng, H.Y., Huo, Y.L., & Zhuang, T.G. (2004). Liver CT-image retrieval based on Gabor texture. In *Proceedings of the 26th Annual International Conference of the IEEE Engineering in Medicine and Biology Society: Vol. 26 II.* (pp. 1491-1494). San Francisco, CA: Institute of Electrical and Electronics Engineers Inc.

ADDITIONAL READING

Duan, L. J., Gao, W, Zeng, W., & Zhao, D. B. (2005). Adaptive relevance feedback based on Bayesian inference for image retrieval. *Signal Processing, 85*(2), 395-399.

Dubois, S. R., & Glanz, F. H. (1986). An autoregressive model method to two-dimensional shape classification. *IEEE Transactions on Pattern Analysis and Machine intelligence. 8*(1), 55–66.

Dy, J. G., Brodley, C. E., Kak, A., Broderick L. S., & Aisen, A. M. (2003). Unsupervised feature selection applied to content-based retrieval of lung images. *IEEE Transactions on Pattern Analysis and Machine intelligence, 25*(3), 373-378.

Greenspan, H. & Pinhas, A. T. (2005). Medical image categorization and retrieval for PACS using the GMM-KL framework. *IEEE Transactions on Information Technology in BioMedicine, 11*(2), 190-202.

Hung, M. H., Hsieh, C. H., & Kuo, C. M. (2006). Similarity retrieval of shape images based on database classification. *Journal of Visual Communication & Image Representation, 17*(5), 970-985.

Kim, D. H., Chung, C. W., & Barnard, K. Relevance feedback using adaptive clustering for image similarity retrieval. *The Journal of Systems and Software, 78*(1), 9-23.

Kunttu, I., Lepistö, L., Rauhamaa, J., & Visa, A. (2006). Multiscale Fourier descriptors for defect image retrieval. *Pattern Recognition Letters, 27*(2), 123-132.

Saha, S. K., Das, A. K., & Chanda B. (2007). Image retrieval based on indexing and relevance feedback. *Pattern Recognition Letters, 28*(3), 357-366.

Cross, G., & Jain, A. (1983). Markov random field texture models. *IEEE Transactions on Pattern Analysis and Machine Intelligence, 5*(1), 25–40.

Amari, S., & Cardoso, J. (1997). Blind source separation — semiparametric statistical approach. *IEEE Transactions on Signal Processing, 45*(11), 692–700.

Bar-Joseph, Z., El-Yaniv, R., Lischinski, D., & Werman, M. (2001). Texture mixing and texture movie synthesis using statistical learning. *IEEE Transactions on Visualization and Computer Graphics, 7*(2), 120–135.

Bauer, D., Deistler, M., & Scherrer, W. (1999). Consistency and asymptotic normality of some subspace algorithms for systems without observed inputs. *Automatica, 35*(7), 1243–1254.

Bigun, J., & du Buf, J. M. (1994). N-folded symmetries by complex moments in gabor space and their application to unsupervised texture segmentation. *IEEE Transactions on Pattern Analysis and Machine Intelligence, 16*(1), 80–87.

Hassner, M., & Sklansky, J. (Eds.). (1981). *The use of markov random fields as models of texture in image modeling*. San Diego, CA: Academic Press.

Kailath, T. (Ed.). (1980). *Linear Systems*. Englewood Cliffs, NJ: Prentice Hall.

Mallat, S. (1989). A theory of multiresolution signal decomposition: The wavelet representation. *IEEE Transactions on Pattern Analysis and Machine Intelligence, 11*(7), 674–693.

Nelson, R.C., & Polana, R. (1992). Qualitative recognition of motion using temporal texture. *Computer Vision, Graphics, and Image Processing. Image Understanding, 56*(1), 78–89.

Simoncelli, E., Freeman, W., Adelson, E., & Heeger, D. (1992). Shiftable multi-scale transforms. *IEEE Transactions on Information Theory, 38*(2), 587–607.

Sims, K. (1990). Particle animation and rendering using data parallel computation. *Computer Graphics, 24*(4), 405–413.

Van Overschee, P., & De Moor, B. (1993). Subspace algorithms for the stochastic identification problem. *Automatica, 29*(3), 649–660.

Van Overschee, P., & De Moor, B. (1994). N4sid: Subspace algorithms for the identification of combined deterministic-stochastic systems. *Automatica, 30*(1), 75–93.

Zhu, S., Wu, Y., & Mumford, D. (1997). Minimax entropy principle and its application to texture modeling. *Neural Computation, 9*(9), 1627–1660.

Carmona, R. A., & Zhong, S. F. (1998). Adaptive smoothing respecting feature directions. *IEEE Transactions on Image Process. 7*(3), 353–358.

Derin, H., & Cole, W. S. (1986). Segmentation of textured images using Gibbs random fields. *Comput. Vision, Graphics Image Process. 35*(1), 72–98.

Dunn, D., & Higgins, W. E. (1995). Optimal gabor filters for texture segmentation. *IEEE Transactions on Image Process. 4*(7), 947–964.

Geman, S., & Geman, D. (1984). Stochastic relaxation, Gibbs distributions, and the Bayesian restoration of images. *IEEE Transactions on Pattern Analysis and Machine Intelligence, 6*(6), 721–741.

Li, X.P., & Chen, T.W. (1994). Nonlinear diffusion with multiple edginess thresholds. *Pattern Recognition, 27*(8), 1029–1037.

Pichler, O., Teuner, A., & Hosticka, B. J. (1998). Optimal Gabor filters for texture segmentation. *IEEE Transactions on Image Process, 7*(1), 53–61.

Chapter IV
Content–Based Image Classification and Retrieval:
A Rule–Based System Using Rough Sets Framework

Jafar M. Ali
Kuwait University, Kuwait

ABSTRACT

Advances in data storage and image acquisition technologies have enabled the creation of large image datasets. Thus, it is necessary to develop appropriate information systems to efficiently manage these datasets. Image classification and retrieval is one of the most important services that must be supported by such systems. The most common approach used is content-based image retrieval (CBIR) systems. This paper presents a new application of rough sets to feature reduction, classification, and retrieval for image databases in the framework of content-based image retrieval systems. The suggested approach combines image texture features with color features to form a powerful discriminating feature vector for each image. Texture features are extracted, represented, and normalized in an attribute vector, followed by a generation of rough set dependency rules from the real value attribute vector. The rough set reduction technique is applied to find all reducts with the minimal subset of attributes associated with a class label for classification.

INTRODUCTION

There is a pressing need for efficient information management and mining of the huge quantities of image data that are routinely being used in databases (Cios, Pedrycz, & Swiniarski, 1998; Laudon, & Laudon, 2006; Starzyk, Dale, & Sturtz, 2000). These data are potentially an extremely valuable source of information, but their value is limited unless they can be effectively explored and retrieved, and it is becoming increasingly clear that in order to be efficient, data mining must be based on semantics. However, the extraction of semantically rich metadata from computationally accessible low-level features poses tremendous scientific challenges (Laudon & Laudon; Mehta, Agrawal, & Rissanen, 1996; Mitra, Pal, & Mitra, 2002). Content-based image retrieval (CBIR) systems are needed to effectively and efficiently use the information that is intrinsically stored in these image databases. The image retrieval system has gained considerable attention, especially during the last decade. Image retrieval based on content is extremely useful in many applications (Carson, Thomas, Belongie, Hellerstein, & Malik, 1999; Huang, Tan, & Loew, 2003; Koskela, Laaksonen, & Oja, 2004; Ma & Manjunath, 1999; Molinier, Laaksonen, Ahola, & Häme, 2005; Smeulders, Worring, Santini, Gupta, & Jain, 2000; Smith, 1998; Viitaniemi & Laaksonen, 2006; Yang & Laaksonen, 2005) such as crime prevention, the military, intellectual property, architectural and engineering design, fashion and interior design, journalism and advertising, medical diagnosis, geographic information and remote sensing systems, cultural heritage, education and training, home entertainment, and Web searching. In a typical CBIR system, queries are normally formulated either by example or similarity retrieval, selecting from color, shape, skeleton, and texture features or a combination of two or more features. The system then compares the query with a database representing the stored images. The output from a CBIR system is usually a ranked list of images in order of their similarity to the query.

Image searching (Graham, 2004) is one of the most important services that need to be supported by such systems. In general, two different approaches have been applied to allow searching on image collections: one based on image textual metadata and another based on image content information. The first retrieval approach is based on attaching textual metadata to each image and uses traditional database query techniques to retrieve them by keyword. However, these systems require a previous annotation of the database images, which is a very laborious and time-consuming task. Furthermore, the annotation process is usually inefficient because users, generally, do not make the annotation in a systematic way. In fact, different users tend to use different words to describe the same image characteristic. The lack of systematization in the annotation process decreases the performance of the keyword-based image search. These shortcomings have been addressed by so-called content-based image retrieval. In CBIR systems, image processing algorithms are used to extract feature vectors that represent image properties such as color, texture, and shape (Hassanien & Ali, 2004; Ma & Manjunath, 1999; Viitaniemi & Laaksonen, 2006). In this approach, it is possible to retrieve images similar to one chosen by the user (i.e., query by example). One of the main advantages of this approach is the possibility of an automatic retrieval process, contrasting with the effort needed to annotate images.

The work introduced in this article is based on the second retrieval approach. Image similarity is typically defined using a metric on a feature space. Numerous similarity metrics have been proposed so far. The search results are combined with existing textual information and collections of other features via intelligent decision-support systems. In this article, we use a new similarity function based on the rough set theory (Grzymala-Busse, Pawlak, Slowinski, & Ziarko, 1999; Kent, 1994; Pawlak, 1982, 1991; Pawlak, Grzymala-Busse, Slowinski, & Ziarko, 1995). This theory has become very popular among scientists around the world. Rough sets data analysis was used for the discovery of data dependencies, data reduction, approximate set classification, and rule induction from databases. The generated rules represent the underlying semantic content of the images in the database. A classification mechanism is developed by which the images are classified according to the generated rules.

RELATED WORK AND PROBLEM DEFINITION

Image classification and retrieval methods aim to classify and retrieve relevant images from an image database that are similar to the query image. The ability to effectively retrieve nonalphanumeric data is a complex issue. The problem becomes even more difficult due to the high dimension of the variable space associated with the images. Image classification is a very active and promising research domain in the area of image management and retrieval. A representative example is presented by Lienhart and Hartmann (2002) who implemented and evaluated a system that performs a two-stage classification of images: First, photo-like images are distinguished from nonphotographic ones, and second, actual photos are separated from artificial, photo-like images, and nonphotographic images are differentiated into presentation slides, scientific posters, and comics. This scheme is neither exclusive nor exhaustive; many images fall into multiple categories. Some systems have used edge and shape information that is either supplied by the user or extracted from training samples (Saber & Tekalp, 1998). However, such systems require detailed region segmentation. Segmentation has been used to extract region-based descriptions of an image by NeTra, Blobworld, and SIMPLIcity (Carson et al., 1999; Ma & Manjunath, 1999; Wang, Li, & Wiederhold, 2001). NeTra and Blobworld present a user with the segmented regions of an image. The user selects regions to be matched, together with attributes such as color and texture. SIMPLIcity is able to match all segmented regions automatically. However, a user's semantic understanding of an image is at a higher level than the region representation. Often it is difficult for a user to select a representative region for the entire image; coupled with the inaccuracy of automatic segmentation, the retrieved results do not match the user's intuition or understanding of the images. An object is typically composed of multiple segments with varying color and texture patterns. One or more segmented regions are usually not sufficient to address semantic object representation.

A key feature of our approach is that segmentation and detailed object representation are not required. Our approach is a texture color-based image retrieval system using a similarity approach on the basis of the matching of selected texture color features. Image texture features are generated via a gray-level co-occurrence matrix, and color features are generated via an image histogram. Since they are computed over gray levels, color images of the database are first converted to 256 gray levels. For each image of the database, a set of texture color features is extracted. They are derived from a modified form of the gray-level co-occurrence matrix over several angles and distances from the image histogram. Five texture features and one color feature are extracted from the co-occurrence matrix and image histogram. These features are represented and normalized in an attribute vector, then the rough set dependency rules are generated directly from the real-value attribute vector. The rough set reduction technique is applied to find all reducts of the data that contain the minimal subset of attributes associated with a class label for classification. To measure the similarity between two images, a new distance measure between two feature vectors based on rough sets is calculated and evaluated.

- **Problem definition:** Assume that we have an image database that contains a collection of images $IDB=\{I_1, I_2, \ldots I_n\}$. Let Q be a query image and y be a real inter-image distance between two images I_i and I_j. The user can specify a query to retrieve a number of relevant images. Let m be the number of images that are close to the query Q that the user wants to retrieve such that $m < n$. This image retrieval problem can be defined as the efficient retrieval of the best of m images based on IDB from a database on n images.

ROUGH SET THEORY: THEORETICAL BACKGROUND

Basically, the rough set theory (Hassanien & Ali, 2004; Pawlak, 1982, 1991; Pawlak et al., 1995; Slowinski, 1995) deals with the approximation of sets that are difficult to describe with the available information. In a medical application, a set of interest could be the set of patients with a certain disease or outcome. In rough set theory, the data are collected in a table, called a decision table. Rows of the decision table correspond to objects, and columns correspond to attributes. In the data set, we assume we are given a set of examples with a class label to indicate the class to which each example belongs. We call the class label the decision attributes, and the rest of the attributes the condition attributes. Rough set theory defines three regions based on the equivalent classes induced by the attribute values: lower approximation, upper approximation, and boundary. Lower approximation contains all the objects that are definitely classified based on the data collected, and upper approximation contains all the objects that can probably be classified. The boundary is the difference between the upper approximation and the lower approximation. So, we can define a rough set as any set defined through its lower and upper approximations.

On the other hand, the notion of indiscernibility is fundamental to rough set theory. Informally, two objects in a decision table are indiscernible if one cannot distinguish between them on the basis of a given set of attributes. Hence, indiscernibility is a function of the set of attributes under consideration. For each set of attributes, we can thus define a binary indiscernibility relation, which is a collection of pairs of objects that are indiscernible to each other. An indiscernibility relation partitions the set of cases or objects into a number of equivalence classes. An equivalence class of a particular object is simply the collection of objects that are indiscernible to the object in question. Some formal definitions of the rough sets are given as follows.

Information Systems

Knowledge representation in rough sets is done via information systems, which are a tabular form of an OBJECT→ATTRIBUTE VALUE relationship, more precisely, an information system, $\Gamma = <U, \Omega, V_q, f_q>_{q \in \Omega}$, where U is a finite set of objects, $U = \{x_1, x_2, x_3, ..., x_n\}$, and Ω is a finite set of attributes (features). The attributes in Ω are further classified into disjoint condition attributes A and decision attributes D, $\Omega = A \cup D$. For each $q \in \Omega$, V_q is a set of attribute values for q. Each $f_q: U \to V_q$ is an information function that assigns particular values from domains of attributes to objects such that $f_q(x_i) \in V_q$ for all $x_i \in U$ and $q \in \Omega$. With respect to a given q, the function partitions the universe into a set of pairwise disjoint subsets of U:

$$R_q = \{x : x \in U \wedge f(x, q) = f(x_0, q) \forall x_0 \in U. \tag{1}$$

Assume a subset of the set of attributes, $P \subseteq A$. Two samples, x and y in U, are indiscernible with respect to P if and only if $f(x, q) = f(y, q) \forall q \in P$. The indiscernibility relation for all $P \subseteq A$ is written as $IND(P)$. $U / IND(P)$ is used to denote the partition of U given $IND(P)$ and is calculated as follows:

$$U / IND(P) = \otimes \{q \in P : U / IND(P)(\{q\})\}, \tag{2}$$

$$A \otimes B = \{X \cap Y : \forall q \in A, \forall Y \in B, X \cap Y \neq \{\}\}. \tag{3}$$

Approximation Spaces

A rough set approximates traditional sets using a pair of sets named the lower and upper approximations of the set. The lower and upper approximations of a set $P \subseteq A$, are defined by Equations 4 and 5, respectively.

$$PY = \bigcup \{X : X \in U / IND(P), X \subseteq Y\} \tag{4}$$

$$\overline{P}Y = \bigcup \{X : X \in U / IND(P), X \cup Y \neq \{\}\} \tag{5}$$

Assuming P and Q are equivalence relationships in U, the important concept of the positive region $POS_p(Q)$ is defined as:

$$POS_p(Q) = \bigcup_{X \in Q} PX. \tag{6}$$

A positive region contains all patterns in U that can be classified in attribute set Q using the information in attribute set P.

Degree of Dependency

The degree of dependency $\gamma(P, Q)$ of a set P of attributes with respect to a set Q of class labeling is defined as:

$$\gamma(P, Q) = \frac{|POS_P(Q)|}{|U|}, \tag{7}$$

where $|S|$ denotes the cardinality of set S.

The degree of dependency provides a measure of how important P is in mapping the data set examples into Q. If $\gamma(P, Q) = 0$ then classification Q is independent of the attributes in P, hence the decision attributes are of no use to this classification. If $\gamma(P, Q) = 1$ then Q is completely dependent on P, hence the attributes are indispensable. Values $0 < \gamma(P, Q) < 1$ denote partial dependency, which shows that only some of the attributes in P may be useful, or that the data set was flawed to begin with. In addition, the complement of $\gamma(P, Q)$ gives a measure of the contradictions in the selected subset of the data set.

A RULE-BASED SYSTEM FOR IMAGE CLASSIFICATION

Figure 1 shows the typical architecture of a content-based image retrieval system. It contains two main subsystems. The first one is concerned with the data insertion that is responsible for extracting appropriate features from images and storing them in the image database. This process is usually performed off line. The second subsystem is concerned with the query processing, which is organized as follows. The interface allows a user to specify a query by means of a query pattern and to visualize the retrieved similar images. The query processing module extracts a feature and rule vector from a query pattern and applies a metric distance function to evaluate the similarity between the query image and the database images. Next, the module ranks the database images in decreasing order of similarity to the query image and forwards the most similar images to the interface module.

Texture and Color Feature Extraction

Texture is one of the most important defining characteristics of an image. Texture is characterized by the spatial distribution of gray levels in a neighborhood (Kundu & Chen, 1992; Mari, Bogdan, Moncef, & Ari, 2002). In order to capture the spatial dependence of gray-level values that contribute to the perception of texture, a two-dimensional dependence texture analysis matrix is discussed for texture consideration. In the literature, different kinds of textural features have been proposed, such as multichannel filtering features, fractal-based features, and co-occurrence features (Haralick, 1979; Li, Gray, & Olshen, 2000; Zhang, Gong, Low, & Smoliar, 1995). For our classification purposes, the co-occurrence features are selected as the basic texture feature detectors due to their good performance in many pattern recognition applications, including medical image processing, remote sensing, and content-based retrieval. In the following paragraph, we describe the co-occurrence matrices and the features we computed from them.

A co-occurrence matrix is the two-dimensional matrix of joint probabilities $P_{d,r}(i,j)$ between pairs of pixels, separated by a distance d in a given direction r.

Figure 1. Content-based image classification and retrieval architecture

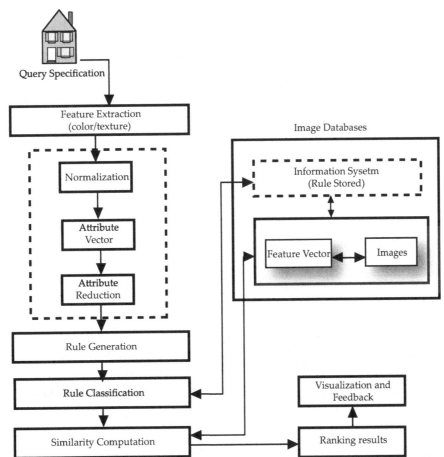

Definition 1 (Descriptor). Using a co-occurrence matrix, different properties of the pixel distribution can be obtained by applying mathematical operations to the matrix values. These operations are called descriptors. Each descriptor is related to a particular visual feature about the texture.

Haralick (1979) proposed a set of 14 descriptors derived from the co-occurrence matrix. In this article, five features (descriptors) were selected for further study: maximum probability (MP), contrast (Cont), inverse different moment (IM), angular second moment (AM), and entropy (Entro).

- Maximum probability is defined as follows:

$$MP = \max \sum_{i,j} P(i, j). \tag{8}$$

- The contrast feature is a measure of the image contrast or the number of local variations present in an image. It takes the following form:

$$Cont = \sum_{i,j} (i - j)^2 P(i, j). \tag{9}$$

- Inverse different moment is a measure of the image contrast or the amount of local variations present in an image. It takes the following form:

$$IM = \sum_{i,j} \frac{1}{1 + (i - j)^2} P(i, j). \tag{10}$$

This descriptor has large values in cases in which the largest elements in P are along the principal diagonal.

- Angular second moment takes the form

$$AM = \sum_{i,j} P(i, j)^2. \tag{11}$$

For homogeneous textures, the value of angular second moment turns out to be small compared to nonhomogeneous ones.

- Entropy is a measure of information content. It measures the randomness of intensity distribution.

$$Entro = \sum_{i,j} P(i, j) \log(P(i, j), \tag{12}$$

where $P(i, j)$ refers to the normalized entry of the co-occurrence matrices. That is, $P(i, j) = P_d(i, j)/R$, where R is the total number of pixel pairs (i, j) for a displacement vector $d=(dx,dy)$ and image of size NxM; R is given by $(N - dx)(M - dy)$.

In order to obtain better retrieval results, the image texture features can be combined with the color features to form a powerful discriminating feature vector for each image. Various color identification schemes have been proposed and used. The RGB (red, green, blue) model has been widely adopted because of its implementation simplicity (Ahuja & Rosefeld, 1978; Yining & Manjuncth, 1999; Zhang et al., 1995). Despite this, the RGB model has proved unable to separate the luminance and chromatic components; furthermore, it results in perceptual nonuniformity, that is, perceptual changes in color that are not linear with numerical changes. The HVC (hue, value, chroma) color model completely separates the luminance and chromatic components, with hue representing the color type, value representing the luminance, and chroma representing the color purity. The transformation from the RGB model to the HVC model can be performed in several ways; in this work, the transformation is obtained through the CIE L*a*b* model. Assuming a 24-bit-per-pixel context, the RGB components are transformed into the CIE XYZ components using the following equations:

$$\begin{cases} X = 0.607*R + 0.17*G + 0.210*B \\ Y = 0.299*R + 0.587*G + 0.114*B \\ Z = 0.066*G + 1.117*B \end{cases}.$$

Then, the HVC values are finally obtained as follows:

$$H = \arctan\left[\frac{200*\left[\left(\frac{Y}{Y_0}\right)^{\frac{1}{3}} - \left(\frac{Z}{Z_0}\right)^{\frac{1}{3}}\right]}{500*\left[\left(\frac{X}{X_0}\right)^{\frac{1}{3}} - \left(\frac{Y}{Y_0}\right)^{\frac{1}{3}}\right]}\right]$$

$$V = 116*\left(\frac{Y}{Y_0}\right)^{\frac{1}{3}} - 16$$

$$C = \sqrt{500x\left[\left(\frac{X}{X_0}\right)^{\frac{1}{3}} - \left(\frac{Y}{Y_0}\right)^{\frac{1}{3}}\right]^2 + 200x\left[\left(\frac{Y}{Y_0}\right)^{\frac{1}{3}} - \left(\frac{Z}{Z_0}\right)^{\frac{1}{3}}\right]^2},$$

where X_0, Y_0, Z_0 are the values for pure white.

Rough Set Attribute Reduction

In an information system, there often exist some condition attributes that do not provide any additional information about the objects in U. So, we should remove those attributes since the complexity and cost of the decision process can be reduced if those condition attributes are eliminated (Bazan, Skowron, & Synak, 1994; Kryszkiewicz & Rybinski, 1994; Stefanowski, 1993; Zhong & Skowron, 2000).

Definition 2 (Reduct). Given a classification task mapping a set of variables C to a set of labeling D, a reduct is defined as any $R \subseteq C$, such that $\gamma(C, D) = \gamma(R, D)$.

Definition 3 (Reduct Set). Given a classification task mapping a set of variables C to a set of labeling D, a reduct set is defined with respect to the power set $\mathbf{P}(C)$ as the set $R \subseteq \mathbf{P}(C)$ such that $R = \{A \in \mathbf{P}(C): \gamma(A, D) = \gamma(C, D)\}$. That is, the reduct set is the set of all possible reducts of the equivalence relationship denoted by C and D.

Definition 4 (Significance). Given P, Q, and the object $x \in P$, the significant $\sigma_x(P, Q)$ of x in the equivalence relation denoted by P and Q is $\sigma_x(P, Q) = \gamma(P, Q) - \gamma(P - \{x\}, Q)$.

Definition 5 (Minimal Reduct). Given a classification task mapping a set of variables C to a set of labeling D, and R, the reduct set for this problem space, a minimal reduct is defined as any reduct R such that $|R| \leq |A|$, $\forall A \in R$. That is, the minimal reduct is the reduct of least cardinality for the equivalence relationship denoted by C and D.

Algorithm 1: Reduct (Minimal number of attributes)

Input: A decision table DT(C, D), where C is the set of all conditional attributes and D is the set of decisional attributes

Processing:

```
  Red ← {}
     Do
DT ← Red
Loop x ∈ (C – Red)
      if γ_{R∪{x}}(D) > γ_T(D)
      DT = Red ∪ {x}
     Red ← DT
  Until (γ_T (D) = γ_C (D)
  Return Red
Output: Red, a set of minimum attribute subsets Red ⊆ C
```

A data set has at least one reduct in its reduct set: the trivial reduct (i.e., the data set itself). It also has one or more minimal reducts.

Rule Generation and Classifier Building

The main task of the rule generation method is to compute reducts relative to a particular kind of information system. The process by which the maximum number of condition attribute values is removed without losing essential information is called value reduction, and the resulting rule is called maximally general or minimal length. Computing maximally general rules is of particular importance in knowledge discovery since they represent general patterns existing in the data. In this subsection, we discuss a method to simplify the generated decision rules by dropping some condition attributes. The rule generation algorithm is described as follows (Algorithm 2).

Algorithm 2: Rule generation algorithm

Input: A set of specific decision rules RULE

Processing:
```
GRULE ← Φ
N←|RULE|
For i=0 to N-1 do
       r ← r_i
       M ← |r|
     For j = 0 to M-1 do
     Remove the j^th condition attribute a_j in rule r
```

> If *r* inconsistent with any rule $r_n \in$ RULE then restore the dropped condition a_j
>
> End if
>
> End for
>
> Remove any rule $r^i \in$ GRULE that is logically included in rule *r*
>
> If rule *r* is not logically included in a rule $r^i \in$ GRULE then
>
> GRULE $\leftarrow r \cup$ GRULE
>
> End if

End for

Output: A set of general rules GRULE

The rule generation algorithm initializes general rules GRULE to an empty set and copies one rule $r_i \in$ RULE to rule *r*. A condition is dropped from rule *r*, and then rule *r* is checked for decision consistency with every rule $r_j \in$ RULE. If rule *r* is inconsistent, then the dropped condition is restored. This step is repeated until every condition of the rule has been dropped once. The resulting rule is the generalized rule. Before rule *r* is added to GRULE, the rule is checked for rule redundancy. If rule *r* is logically included in any rule $r_a \in$ GRULE, rule *r* is discarded. If any rules in GRULE are logically included in rule *r*, these rules are removed from GRULE. After all rules in RULE have been processed, GRULE contains a set of general rules.

The goal of classification is to assign a new object to a class from a given set of classes based on the attribute values of this object. To classify objects, which has never been seen before, rules generated from a training set will be used (Algorithm 3). The classification algorithm is based on the method for decision rule generation from decision tables. The nearest matching rule is determined as the one whose condition part differs from the attribute vector of the reimage by the minimum number of attributes.

Algorithm 3: Classification of a new object

Input: A new image to be classified, the attribute vector of the new image, and the set of rules

Processing:

Begin

    For each rule in Rule set Do

        If match (rule, new object) Then

        Measure = |Objects|, K $\longrightarrow$ |Classes|;

    For i=1 to K Do

          Collect the set of objects defining the

          concept X^i

          Extract Mrule(X^i, u^t) = {r $\in$ Rule}

    For any rule r $\in$ Mrule(X^i, u^t) Do

          T=Match^A(r) $\cap X^i$ and LL=LL $\cup$ T ;

          Strength=Card(LL)/Card(X^i)

          Vote=Measure * Strength

          Give Vote(Class(Rule),Vote)

          Return Class with highest Vote

End

Output: The final classification

A similarity measure is required to calculate the distance between a new object and each object in the reduced decision table, and classify the object to the corresponding decision class. In this section, we adopt a new similarity measure in rough sets. Let $U=\{x_1, x_2, ... x_n\}$ be the features sets; then the similarity between two values is defined as follows:

$$SM(x_i, x_j)=\sum_{}^{n}Similar(x_i, x_j)=$$
$$\begin{cases} 1, & \text{if } ([x]_R) \text{ contains } x_i \text{ and } x_j, \\ 0, & \text{otherwise} \end{cases}$$

a category in equivalence relationship R containing an object $x \in U$.

EXPERIMENTAL RESULTS AND DISCUSSION

In our experiment, we used two image databases. The first one consisted of 521 images, whose sizes were adjusted to 512x512, acquired from ground level using the Sony Digital Mavica camera. The second one consisted of 630 24-bit color images, whose sizes were adjusted to 1024x1024 (http://www.visualdelights.net). We converted the images from RGB to HVC space. The transformation from RGB to HVC was obtained through the CIE L*a*b* model. The weight vector was set to be 1/3.

Once the feature values associated with the images were computed and stored, queries were done. Various models have been proposed for similarity analysis in image retrieval systems (Swets & Weng, 1999; Wu & Huang, 2000). In this work, we used the vector space model, which is widely used in textual

Figure 2. Images retrieved

Table 1. Retrieval by image classification, where T, R, and C are the total, retrieved, and correct number of images in structure class

Distance measure	T,R,C	Re=C/T%	Pr=C/R%	Fm=(2*Pr*Re)/(Re+Pr)
Rough distance	305,262,235	77.00%	89.697%	82.86%
Histogram inter-section	305,189,152	49.83%	80.42%	61.73%
Euclidean distance	305,155,96	31.47%	42.58%	36.19%

Figure 3. A comparative between similarities measures

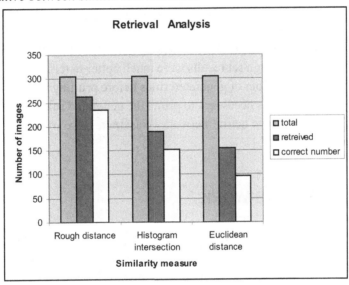

document retrieval systems. A new similarity distance function was adopted to measure the similarity in the classification results. The query was performed by providing a query image from a data set that contained visual features (i.e., color) and five texture features (maximum probability, contrast, inverse difference moment, angular second moment, and entropy) calculated from each occurrence matrix. Their values were saved in the feature vector of the corresponding image. Then the rules were generated and ordered. The similarity between the images was estimated by summing up the distance between the corresponding features in their feature vectors. Images having feature vectors closest to the feature vector of the query image were returned as best matches. The results were then numerically sorted, and the best images were displayed along with the query image.

All inputs to the rough set classifier (the image's mixed textual and color vectors) were normalized, and a set containing a minimal number of features (attributes) was contracted based on the rough set criteria. Then we trained the model to have a mean of 0 and variance of 1.

Our visual system then analyzed the sample images associated with each subtask. If the query image was deemed to be a color image by the system, the set of the top 50 textual images was processed; those images deemed to be in color were moved to the top of the list. Within that list, the ranking was based on the ranking of the textual results. The introduced image classification system was created using the MATLAB and ROSETTA[1] software. Figure 2 shows an example of the retrieved results.

The precision-recall measure is the conventional information retrieval performance measure. Precision is defined as the number of relevant images retrieved relative to the total number of retrieved images, while recall measures the number of relevant images retrieved relative to the total number of relevant images in the database. Table 1 displays the results for retrieval rates measured in terms of recall (Re), precision (Pr), and F-measure (Fm) for the above-mentioned distance measures. We have partitioned the databases into two classes: structure and nonstructure. These two partitioned classes are based upon the measure of structure present in an image.

Figure 3 shows the comparative analysis between the three different similarity measures used in this article. We observe that the rough-based similarity measure is better in terms of the number of retrieved and correct images in a class.

It has been shown that a rough distance measure can lead to perceptually more desirable results than Euclidean distance and histogram intersection methods as a rough distance measure considers the cross-similarity between features.

Table 2 compares the results of rough sets and neural networks (Parekh, Yang, & Honavar, 2000; Zhou, Jiang, & Chen, 2000). The rough set results were much better in terms of the number of rules and the classification accuracy. The number of generated rules before pruning was very large, which makes the classification slow. Therefore, it is necessary to prune the generated rules as we have done, reducing the number of rules. Moreover, in the neural networks classifier, more robust features are required to improve the performance.

CONCLUSION AND FUTURE WORK

The ability to classify images from databases is of great importance for a wide range of applications. This article presents an efficient algorithm for image classifying and retrieval based on a set of generated rules from large databases in the context of the rough set theory. We show that a feature is extracted and represented in the attribute vector, and then the decision rules within the data are extracted. The current system is a small prototype demonstrating the basic capabilities of a database system for retrieval and classification based on the rough set theory as a new intelligent system. The rough sets similarity measure has not yet been proven, but this article, to a certain extent, is able to identify common features that are probably derived from actual structures present in each location and therefore present in the images. The computational requirements for the similarity matrix increase as the square of the number of images. It is envisaged that larger classes of data would be divided up into parts before analysis, and a hierarchy of exemplars would be generated. Retrieval tasks would make use of such a hierarchy to identify clusters likely to contain target images rather than attempt to carry out an exhaustive search. It is expected that as an image collection expands, new classes would be introduced and new clusters would emerge based on entirely different sets of features in common. Future work will investigate the effectiveness of unsupervised clustering with application to much larger bodies of data where the number of clusters is unknown and the data are not labeled.

REFERENCES

Ahuja, N., & Rosefeld, A. (1978). A note on the use of second-order gray-level statistics for threshold selection. *IEEE Transactions on Systems, Man, and Cybernetics, 8,* 895-898.

Bazan, J., Skowron, A., & Synak, P. (1994). Dynamic reducts as a tool for extracting laws from decision tables. In *Proceedings of the Symposium on Methodologies for Intelligent Systems*, 346-355.

Carson, C., Thomas, M., Belongie, S., Hellerstein, J. M., & Malik, J. (1999). Blobworld: *A system for region-based image indexing and retrieval*. Third International Conference on Visual Information Systems, 509-516.

Cios, K., Pedrycz, W., & Swiniarski, R. (1998). *Data mining methods for knowledge discovery*. Norwell, MA: Kluwer Academic Publishers.

Graham, M. E. (2004). Enhancing visual resources for searching and retrieval: Is content based image retrieval solution? *Literary and Linguistic Computing, 19*(3), 321-333.

Grzymala-Busse, J., Pawlak, Z., Slowinski, R., & Ziarko, W. (1999). Rough sets. Communications of the ACM, 38(11), 88-95.

Haralick, R. M. (1979). Statistical and structural approaches to texture. In *Proceedings of the IEEE, 67*(5), 786-804.

Hassanien, A., & Ali, J. (2004). Enhanced rough sets rule reduction algorithm for classification digital mammography. *Intelligent System Journal, 13*(2), 117-151.

Huang, W., Tan, C. L., & Loew, W. K. (2003). Model-based chart image recognition. In *Proceedings of the International Workshop on Graphics Recognition (GREC)*, 87-99.

Kent, R. E. (1994). Rough concept analysis, rough sets, fuzzy sets knowledge discovery. In *Proceedings of the International Workshop on Rough Sets, Knowledge, Discovery*, 248-255.

Koskela, M., Laaksonen, J., & Oja, E. (2004). Entropy-based measures for clustering and SOM topology preservation applied to content-based image indexing and retrieval. In *Proceedings of 17th International Conference on Pattern Recognition* (ICPR 2004), 1005-1009.

Kryszkiewicz, M., & Rybinski, H. (1994). Finding reducts in composed information systems, rough sets, fuzzy sets knowledge discovery. In *Proceedings of the International Workshop on Rough Sets, Knowledge, Discovery*, 261-273.

Kundu, A., & Chen, J. L. (1992). Texture classification using QMF Bank-based subband decomposition. *CVGIP: Graphical Models and Image Processing*, 54, 369-384.

Laudon, K. C., & Laudon, J. P. (2006). *Management information systems: Managing the digital FIRM* (9th ed.). NJ: Prentice Hall.

Li, J., Gray, R. M., & Olshen R. A. (2000). Multiresolution image classification by hierarchical modeling with two-dimensional hidden Markov models. *IEEE Transactions on Information Theory, 46*(5), 1826-1841.

Lienhart, R., & Hartmann, A. (2002). Classifying images on the Web automatically. *Journal of Electronic Imaging, 11*, 31-40.

Ma, W. Y., & Manjunath, B. S. (1999). NeTra: A toolbox for navigating large image databases. *Multimedia Systems, 7*(3), 184-198.

Mari, P., Bogdan, C., Moncef, G., & Ari, V. (2002, October). *Rock texture retrieval using gray level co-occurrence matrix.* Paper presented at the NORSIG-2002, Fifth NORDIC Signal Processing Symposium, Hurtigruten from Tromsø to Trondheim, Norway.

Mehta, M., Agrawal, R., & Rissanen, J. (1996). SLIQ: A fast scalable classifier for data mining. In *Proceedings of the Fifth International Conference on Extending Database Technology*, Avignon, France.

Mitra, S., Pal, S. K., & Mitra, P. (2002). Data mining in soft computing framework: A survey. *IEEE Transactions on Neural Networks, 13*(1), 3-14.

Molinier, M., Laaksonen, J., Ahola, J., & Häme, T. (2005, October). Self-organizing map application for retrieval of man-made structures in remote sensing data. In *Proceedings of ESA-EUSC 2005, Image Information Mining: Theory and Application to Earth Observation*, Frascati, Italy.

Parekh, R., Yang, J., & Honavar, V. (2000). Constructive neural network learning algorithms for pattern classification. *IEEE Transactions on Neural Networks, 11*(2), 436-451.

Pawlak, Z. (1982). Rough sets. *International Journal of Computer and Information Science, 11*, 341-356.

Pawlak, Z. (1991). *Rough sets: Theoretical aspect of reasoning about data.* Norwell, MA: Kluwer Academic Publishers.

Pawlak, Z., Grzymala-Busse, J., Slowinski, R., & Ziarko, W. (1995). Rough sets. *Communications of the ACM, 38*(11), 89-95.

Saber, E., & Tekalp, A. M. (1998). Integration of color, edge, shape and texture features for automatic region-based image annotation and retrieval. *Electronic Imaging, 7*, 684-700.

Slowinski, R. (1995). Rough set approach to decision analysis. *AI Expert Magazine, 10*(3), 18-25.

Smeulders, A., Worring, M., Santini, S., Gupta, A., & Jain, R. (2000). Content-based image retrieval at the end of the early years. *IEEE Transactions on Pattern Analysis and Machine Intelligence, 22*, 1349-1380.

Smith, J. R. (1998). Image retrieval evaluation. In *Proceedings of IEEE Workshop on Content-based Access of Images and Video Libraries*, 112-113.

Starzyk, J. A., Dale, N., & Sturtz, K. (2000). A mathematical foundation for improved reduct generation in information systems. *Knowledge and Information Systems Journal, 2*, 131-147.

Stefanowski, J. (1993). Classification support based on the rough sets. Foundations of Computing and Decision Sciences, 18, 371-380.

Swets, D., & Weng, J. (1999). Hierarchical discriminant analysis for image retrieval. *IEEE Transactions on Pattern Analysis and Machine Intelligence, 21*(5), 386-401.

Viitaniemi, V., & Laaksonen, J. (2006). Techniques for still image scene classification and object detection. In *Proceedings of 16th International Conference on Artificial Neural Networks* (ICANN 2006).

Wang, J. Z. , Li, J., & Wiederhold, G. (2001). SIMPLIcity: Semantics-sensitive integrated matching for picture libraries. *IEEE Transactions on Pattern Analysis and Machine Intelligence*, 23, 947–963.

Wu, Q. T., & Huang, T. (2000). Discriminant algorithm with application to image retrieval. In *Proceedings to the IEEE Conference on Computer Vision and Pattern Recognition, 1*, 222-227.

Yang, Z., & Laaksonen, J. (2005). Partial relevance in interactive facial image retrieval. In *Proceedings of 3rd International Conference on Advances in Pattern Recognition* (ICAPR 2005), 216-225.

Yining, D., & Manjuncth, B. S. (1999). An efficient low-dimensional color indexing scheme for region-based image retrieval. In *Proceedings of the IEEE International Conference on Acoustics, Speech, and Signal Processing* (ICASSP), 3017-3020.

Zhang, H., Gong, Y., Low, C. Y., & Smoliar, S. W. (1995). Image retrieval based on color feature: An evaluation study. In *Proceedings of SPIE, 2606*, 212-220.

Zhong, N., & Skowron, A. (2000). Rough sets in KDD: Tutorial notes. *Bulletin of International Rough Set Society, 4*(1/2), 9-30.

Zhou, Z. H., Jiang, Y., & Chen, S. F. (2000). A general neural framework for classification rule mining. *International Journal of Computers, Systems, and Signals, 1*(2), 154-168.

ENDNOTE

[1]   ROSETTA is a general C++ rough sets toolkit offering the most common rough sets structure and operations

This work was previously published in International Journal of Intelligent Information Technologies, Vol. 3, Issue 3, edited by V. Sugumaran, pp. 41-58, copyright 2007 by IGI Publishing, formerly known as Idea Group Publishing (an imprint of IGI Global).

Section II

Chapter V
Content Based Image Retrieval Using Active–Nets

David García Pérez
University of Santiago de Compostela, Spain

Antonio Mosquera
University of Santiago de Compostela, Spain

Stefano Berretti
University of Firenze, Italy

Alberto Del Bimbo
University of Firenze, Italy

ABSTRACT

Content-based image retrieval has been an active research area in past years. Many different solutions have been proposed to improve performance of retrieval, but the large part of these works have focused on sub-parts of the retrieval problem, providing targeted solutions only for individual aspects (i.e., feature extraction, similarity measures, indexing, etc). In this chapter, we first shortly review some of the main practiced solutions for content-based image retrieval evidencing some of the main issues. Then, we propose an original approach for the extraction of relevant image objects and their matching for retrieval applications, and present a complete image retrieval system which uses this approach (including similarity measures and image indexing). In particular, image objects are represented by a two-dimensional deformable structure, referred to as "active net." Active net is capable of adapting to relevant image regions according to chromatic and edge information. Extension of the active nets has been defined, which permits the nets to break themselves, thus increasing their capability to adapt to objects with complex topological structure. The resulting representation allows a joint description of color, shape, and structural information of extracted objects. A similarity measure between active nets has also been defined and used to combine the retrieval with an efficient indexing structure. The proposed system has been experimented on two large and publicly available objects databases, namely, the ETH-80 and the ALOI.

INTRODUCTION

Effective access to modern archives of digital images requires that conventional searching techniques based on textual keywords are extended by content-based queries addressing visual features of searched data. To this end, many solutions have been experimented which permit to represent and compare images in terms of quantitative indexes of visual features. In particular, different techniques have been identified and experimented to represent content of single images according to low-level features, such as color, texture, shape and structure, intermediate-level features of saliency and spatial relationships, or high-level traits modeling the semantics of image content (Del Bimbo, 1999; Gupta & Jain, 1997; Lew et al., 2006; Smeulders et al., 2000). In so doing, extracted features may either refer to the overall image (e.g., a color histogram), or to any subset of pixels constituting a spatial entity with some visual cohesion in the user perception (e.g., an object).

Among these approaches, image representations based on chromatic indexes have been largely used for general purpose image retrieval systems, as well as for object based search partially robust to changes in objects shape and pose. Several low level features have been considered. In particular, representations based on chromatic indexes have been widely experimented and comprise the basic backbone of most commercial and research retrieval engines such as QBIC (Flickner et al., 1995), Virage (Swain et al., 1991), Visual Seek (Smith & Chang, 1996) or Simplicity (Wang et al., 2001). This mainly depends on the capability of color-based models in combining robustness of automatic construction with a relative perceptual significance of the models.

However, approaches based on global image features are not appropriate for precise retrieval, accounting for perceptual details in the image. More suited to this end are region based solutions. In fact, much research has recently focused on region based techniques that allow the user to specify a particular region of an image and search for images containing similar regions. However, most existing region or object-based systems rely on color segmentation only.

Together with color, texture is a powerful discriminating feature, present almost everywhere in nature. Textures may be described according to their spatial, frequency or perceptual properties. Features of the appearing shape of imaged objects have also been used to represent image content through a variety of approaches. For the purpose of retrieval by shape similarity, representations are preferred such that the salient perceptual aspects of a shape are captured, and the human notion of closeness between shapes corresponds to the topological closeness in the representation space. As a consequence, as opposed to color information, other retrieval schemes are entirely based on shape content. Most of the work on region-shape recognition relies on matching sets of local image features (e.g., edges, lines and corners), usually through statistical analysis which disregard relational information among extracted features. Most of these methods have been proved to be adequate only for simple, flat, and man-made objects, but shape features alone are rarely adequate to discriminate objects for the purpose of object based retrieval. Only few approaches have tried to conjugate color and shape information to improve the significance of object representations.

Objective of this chapter is to present a complete content based image retrieval system, which is mainly targeted to provide effective and efficient object-based retrieval using chromatic as well as shape information of image objects. To this end, solutions are proposed for each of the components constituting a modern image retrieval system, namely, *feature extraction*, *similarity matching* and *image indexing*.

In particular, we propose a descriptor modeled through a graph which accounts for structural elements and color of regions (objects) of interest in an image. The graph directly corresponds to an elastic structure (*active net*) that, through a deformation process, is used to separate regions from the background. In particular, due to their deformable structure, active nets can adapt to the borders and internal part of a region encoding, at the same time, information of color, shape and spatial structure of the region. The use of illumination invariant color space for the detection of region borders, makes the model partially robust also to changes in illumination conditions. The basic structure and the deformation process of active nets have been extended to make a net capable to break the edges connecting its nodes. This permits the net to better adapt to regions of complex shape or regions with complex topology (e.g., regions with holes). Once the net is adapted to a region, it is transformed to a graph accounting for the region chromatic content of the nodes, and for their relative distance and spatial position. Then, based on a similarity measure defined between graph representations, graph models are compared to support region-based retrieval. Finally, graph representations are stored into an efficient secondary memory access structure using M-Tree indexing. Separate evaluations are carried out in order to demonstrate the effectiveness of active-nets for the purpose of image objects representation, and to show the efficiency of image indexing. The performances of the overall retrieval system are evaluated based on two large and publicly available image object databases, by using the commonly used indicators of precision and recall.

The chapter is organized in the following sections: In Sect.2, active nets are defined and feature extraction based on active nets is discussed; In Sect.3, a graph based modeling of the active nets is proposed, and a similarity measure between active nets is defined; Efficient image indexing of active nets is proposed in Sect.4; An experimental evaluation of the efficiency and effectiveness of the retrieval system and of its components is reported in Sect.5, using the ETH-80 and the ALOI objects databases; Discussion and summary of the chapter are given in Sect.6; Finally, in Sect.7 future research directions are delineated.

Related Work

The literature on content based image retrieval is extremely large, and comprehensive surveys on the state of the art in this field can be found in (Datta et al., 2008; Liua et al., 2007; Lew et al., 2006; Smeulders et al., 2000; Rui et al., 1999). In the following, we shortly review some recent and relevant works that address image retrieval based on the chromatic content of salient image regions or objects in the image.

Many of the first works on content based image retrieval focused on global image descriptors, like color histograms (Swain & Ballard, 1991), mainly for the simplicity in extracting and comparing them. However, since these initial approches, it has been clear that more powerful descriptors, based on local properties of the images, are necessary to permit effective retrieval. Region based descriptors have been investigated to this end.

A scheme that implements a recursive *HSV*-space segmentation technique to identify perceptually prominent color areas is presented in (Androutsos et al., 1999). Authors motivate their proposal with the lack of good perceptual histogram similarity measures, the global color content of histograms, and the erroneous retrieval results due to gamma non-linearity. The average color vectors of these extracted areas are then used to build the image indices, requiring very little storage. Retrieval is performed by implementing a *combination* distance measure, based on the vector angle between two vectors. The system provides accurate retrieval results and high retrieval rate. It allows for queries based on single or multiple colors and, in addition, it allows for certain colors to be excluded in the query. This flexibility is due to the distance measure and the *multidimensional query space* in which the retrieval ranking of the database images is determined. Furthermore, the scheme proves to be very resistant to gamma non-linearity providing robust retrieval results for a wide range of gamma non-linearity values, which proves to be of great importance since, in general, the image acquisition source is unknown.

In (Gevers & Smeulders, 2000), the *PicToSeek* image retrieval system is described and it is demonstrated the power of color when invariants are used for finding back a specific object. The system exploits geometric and color invariant indexes to allow retrieval that is robust against scene-incidental imaging conditions. Through analysis of the dichromatic reflection model, a class of color ratios is derived that is invariant to major viewpoint distortions. After automatically collecting and cataloging images from the Web by means of an autonomous Web crawler, invariant representations are derived and combined to form a high-dimensional index that is independent of the disturbing influences of: an arbitrary viewpoint from which the shape of the physical object will appear differently for each view; photometric variations in the recordings due to changes in shadowing, shading, highlights and illumination; object fragmentation, occlusion and clutter by the presence of other objects in the scene.

In the SIMPLIcity system (*Semantics Sensitive Integrated Matching for Picture LIbraries*) (Wang et al., 2001), an integrated region matching approach based upon image segmentation is proposed, which uses semantics classification methods and a wavelet-based solution for feature extraction. As in other region based retrieval systems, an image is represented by a set of regions, roughly corresponding to objects, which are characterized by color, texture, shape, and location. The system classifies images into semantic categories, such as textured\nontextured, graph\photograph. Potentially, the categorization enhances retrieval by permitting semantically-adaptive searching methods and narrowing down the searching range in a database. A measure for the overall similarity between images is also developed using a region-matching scheme that integrates properties of all the regions in the images. Compared with retrieval based on individual regions, the overall similarity approach proposed in this work has some advantages: reduces the adverse effect of inaccurate segmentation; helps to clarify the semantics of a particular region; and enables a simple querying interface for region-based image retrieval systems. The SIMPLIcity system has been applied to several databases, including a database of about 200,000 general-purpose images, demonstrating that the system performs significantly better and faster than other existing ones. In addition, the system is fairly robust to image alterations.

In (Carson et al., 2002), authors presented a new image representation that provides a transformation from the raw pixel data to a small set of image regions that are coherent in color and texture. This so called *Blobworld* representation is created by clustering pixels in a joint color-texture-position feature space. The segmentation algorithm is fully automatic and has been run on a collection of 10,000 natural images. A system is described that uses the Blobworld representation to retrieve images from this collection. An important aspect of the system is that the user is allowed to view the internal representation of the submitted image and the query results. Similar systems do not offer the user this view into the workings of the system; consequently, query results from these systems can be inexplicable, despite the availability of knobs for adjusting the similarity metrics. By finding image regions that roughly correspond to objects, querying is allowed at the level of objects rather than global image properties. Results indicate that querying for images using Blobworld produces higher precision than does querying using color and texture histograms of the entire image in cases where the image contains distinctive objects.

In (Hoiem et al., 2003), a Bayesian approach to object-based image retrieval with relevance feedback is proposed. Although estimating the object posterior probability density from few examples seems infeasible, authors show that they are able to approximate this density by exploiting statistics of the image database domain. Unlike previous approaches that assume an arbitrary distribution for the unconditional density of the feature vector, in this work both the structure and the parameters of this density are learnt. These density estimates enable to construct a Bayesian classifier. Traditional region-based image retrieval systems require segmentation of the image; instead, using this Bayesian classifier, a windowed scan over images for objects of interest is performed. The user's feedback on the search results is used to train a second classifier that focuses on eliminating difficult false positives. This algorithm is incorporated into an object-based image retrieval system. Authors also demonstrated the effectiveness of the approach with experiments using a set of categories from the Corel database.

An approach to represent spatial color distributions using local Principal Component Analysis (PCA) is presented in (Heidemann, 2004). The representation is based on image windows which are selected by two complementary data driven attentive mechanisms: a symmetry based saliency map and an edge and corner detector. The eigenvectors obtained from local PCA of the selected windows form color patterns that capture both low and high spatial frequencies, so they are well suited for shape as well as texture representation. Projections of the windows selected from the image database to the local PCs serve as a compact representation for the search database. Queries are formulated by specifying windows within query images. System feedback makes both the search process and the results comprehensible for the user.

ACTIVE NETS

One-dimensional (1D) deformable models were first introduced by Kass et al. (Kass et al., 1988) using *snakes*. Deformable contours–*snakes*–have been defined as elastic curves that act over an image, and have been used as an extraction method for ill-defined contours in 2D images. The curve of the snake changes its shape and position with the objective to adjust to some particular characteristic of an image. In particular, deformations of the snake are the result of the action of external energies that push the contour to some characteristics of the image, and the action of internal energies that make the deformations of the net to be smooth. The final objective is to minimize the total amount of energies that act over the active model. The initial 1D deformable structures proposed by Kass et al., has been extended to 2D structures, the *active nets* (Tsumiyama et al., 1989), and to 3D structures (Bro-Nielsen, 1994; Takanashi et al., 1998; Doi et al., 2002).

In their original formulation, active nets were theoretically introduced as a variation of the classical deformable models (Tsumiyama et al., 1989). Later, Bro-Nielsen provided the first implementation of an active net, but in this first formulation the active net model had a lot of restrictions about the kind of objects it could detect (Bro-Nielsen, 1994). In (Ansia et al., 1999; Ansia et al., 2000), the implementation of Bro-Nielsen was extended making the model more capable to extract information from generic images without any particular restriction. More recently, the active net model has been applied to medical images and modified to get a better fit to different objects in the image (Barreira & Penedo, 2004; Ibáñez et al., 2006; Barreira et al., 2007). Applications of active nets to content based image retrieval, was first addressed in (García-Perez et al., 2006a; García-Perez et al., 2006b).

Finally, it is relevant to note that the active nets approach is somewhat related to *deformable grids* or *deformable graphs*. In particular, some authors use the term *deformable grids* as synonimous of active nets (Moreau et al., 2002). However, at the best of our knowledge, deformable grids and deformable graphs have been mainly used in contexts different from image retrieval, like face recognition (Duc et al., 1999), or the analysis of medical images (Moreau et al., 2002).

Feature Extraction using Active Nets

An *active net* is a discrete implementation of a two-dimensional elastic sheet (Ansia et al., 2000). It can be defined using the value $u(.,.)$, that the active net assumes in the planar domain defined by the horizontal (x) and vertical (y) coordinates of the plane. In parametric form, this can be expressed as: $u(r,s)$ = $(x(r,s), y(r,s))$, where $(r,s) \in ([0,1] \times [0,1])$. The domain of parameters (r, s) is discretized to a regular grid of *nodes* defined by the internode spacing (k, l) (see Figure 1). This parameterization defines a two-dimensional net in the two-dimensional space of an image. The net can deform under the control of the following energy function:

$$E(u) = \sum_{(r,s)} \left(E_{\text{int}}\left(u\left(r,s\right)\right) + E_{\text{ext}}\left(u\left(r,s\right)\right) \right) \tag{1}$$

The internal energy of the net E_{int}, controls the shape and structure of the net and is defined as:

$$E_{\text{int}}\left(u\left(r,s\right)\right) = \alpha\left(\left|u_r\left(r,s\right)\right|^2 + \left|u_s\left(r,s\right)\right|^2\right) + \beta\left(\left|u_{rr}\left(r,s\right)\right|^2 + 2\left|u_{rs}\left(r,s\right)\right|^2 + \left|u_{ss}\left(r,s\right)\right|^2\right) \tag{2}$$

where the subscripts indicate the orthogonal partial derivatives, and α and β are coefficients controlling the first and second order smoothness of the net. In particular, the first derivatives make the net contract and the second derivatives enforce smoothness and rigidity of the net.

The external energy of the net E_{ext}, accounts for external forces acting on the net, and is defined as:

$$E_{ext}(u(r,s)) = f[i(u(r,s))] \tag{3}$$

where f is a function of the properties of the image $I(u(r,s))$. The objective is to find a function f that makes the nodes of the net to be attracted to significant zones of an image according to an energy minimization process (*fitting*).

The energy minimization technique used in this work for the active nets fitting was originally proposed by Bro-Nielsen (Bro-Nielsen, 1994). In his work, the energy was minimized independently for each node with respect to every other node of the active net using an improved version of the *Greedy algorithm* proposed in (Williams & Shah, 1992). In order to avoid local minima, the Greedy algorithm is combined with ideas derived from *Simulated Annealing* (Geman & Geman, 1984). Moreover, the Greedy algorithm is further improved using the *Iterated Conditional Modes* algorithm (ICM) (Besag, 1986).

Image Attractors for an Active Net

Active nets are used to represent relevant zones of an image due to their capability to adapt to contours of image regions and capture their internal information. However, this requires that relevant image features are extracted and used as attractors for the nodes of the net. To this end, nodes are divided into *border* nodes (i.e., nodes belonging to the border of the net $\{u(r,s):r,s = 0, 1 \}$), and *internal* nodes (i.e., nodes that do not belong to the border of the net $\{u(r,s):r,s \neq 0, 1 \}$) as shown in Figure 1.

Figure 1. Basic structure of an active net. The grey area is the influence zone of an internal node (the Voronoi region of its second level neighbor nodes).

In our approach, color information is used to drive the fitting process which controls the deformation of a net. This is obtained by creating two external energy images, one locating the borders of a relevant region, and the other describing its internal area. During the fitting process of the active net, the border nodes are guided to the border of a region by the internal nodes, while the internal nodes are attracted to the internal zones of a region.

The energy images attracting the internal nodes, are created by clustering the image color content using a modified version of the clustering algorithm proposed by Uchiyama and Arbib (Uchiyama & Arbib, 1994). This algorithm iteratively selects a pixel randomly from the image and assigns it to a winner cluster by calculating the Euclidean distance between the color of the pixel and the centroid of the cluster (both expressed in the $L^*a^*b^*$ color space). While in the original formulation the maximum number of clusters is fixed a priori, and the creation of new clusters depends on the number of elements in the existing clusters, here this number can adaptively change on the basis of the cluster color variance and the median color of the image. Figure 2(b) shows the two energy images identified for the image in Figure 2(a).

Positioning of border nodes is guided by energy images associated to the border of an object. These energy images are based on the color edge detector proposed by Gevers and Smeulders (Gevers & Smeulders, 1999). It uses a color space defined by the relation of the *R, G, B* color components existing

Figure 2. Active net attractors for the image in (a). The clustering algorithm finds two color clusters, one for the background (white areas, upper image in (b)), and one for the apple (white areas, lower image in (b)). White pixels are associated with the lowest energy, thus resulting the best attractors for the internal nodes of the net. In (c), the color edges of the white regions are detected. The black pixels of the edges indicate energy barriers that the border nodes of an active net should not cross. In (d), an active net is fitted to each cluster. As final result, the image is represented by two nets modeling the background and the apple, respectively

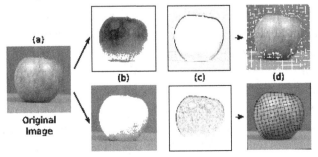

between two neighbor pixels of an image. This results in a high robustness to illumination changes of image objects (Figure 2(c)). Unlike internal nodes, border nodes have a low external energy where there is no border, and a high energy value near to or in the border of an object. In this way, border nodes can move in zones of low energy, but cannot cross the border of a region in that this would increase their energy. The result is that border nodes act as anchor around the edges of the region, while internal nodes are positioned inside the region, In doing so, the border of an object acts like a barrier for the border nodes and anchor their position.

According to this modeling approach, the equation for the external energy is given by:

$$E_{ext}\left(v(r,s)\right) = \begin{cases} \gamma f\left(I_{cluster}(r,s)\right) & \text{Internal nodes} \\ \delta f\left(I_{border}(r,s)\right) & \text{Border nodes} \end{cases} \qquad (4)$$

where γ and δ are constants that ponderate the effect of each external energy component. $f(I_{cluster}(r, s))$ depends on the intensity of color cluster image, while $f(I_{border}(r, s))$ depends on the intensity of the color border image.

Changes of the Topology of Active Nets

According to the active deformation process, a net can adaptively reshape itself to a region of interest. However, due to the physical properties of a net, the precision of the fitting process can be hampered by two main problems.

First, if an object has a complex shape (i.e., like the horse in Figure 3), the net can adapt to the shape of the object with some difficulties. To have a perfect fit, the net needs to increase the distance between its nodes, but this increases its internal energy value (in that the internal energy makes the net contract over itself). To solve this problem, a rupture algorithm, that breaks links (*edges*) between border nodes, has been developed.

The rupture algorithm only acts over the border nodes and is activated once the net has finished its fitting process. At this point, the algorithm looks for *candidate* border nodes for which an edge can be broken. When an edge is broken, two internal nodes are converted to border ones (see Figure 3(a)) and they start to be under the influence of $\delta f(I_{border}(r, s))$ instead of $\gamma f(I_{cluster}(r, s))$. After an edge is broken, the net tries to reach a new stable position and the cycle restarts until no more edges are broken. A particular case occurs for the border nodes located at the corners of the net. In fact, a corner node is not allowed to break one of its edges thus avoiding the creation of a threat in the net structure.

The distance of a border node to the borders of a region of interest is considered to identify *candidate* border nodes. In particular, only border nodes that are far from the borders of the object are taken into consideration. The border node with the greatest distance from the object boundary is selected. If its neighbors nodes are also candidates to rupture, the two neighbors with the highest distance are selected and the edge between them is removed.

A second difficulty, can occur when an active net is filled to an object with holes inside it (see Figure 3(d)). In order to manage such objects, the fitting process is modified by searching for holes inside of objects. In particular, this is obtained by considering the external energy of the internal nodes ($\gamma f(I_{cluster}(r, s))$). In fact, internal nodes in the hole areas of a region, have a high energy value compared with the energy of well positioned nodes (energy value near or equal to 0). This selection is automatically done

Figure 3. Typical problems in the adjusting process of an active net. The leftmost image in (b) shows the problem of adapting a net around the legs of a horse. If the rupture of the net is allowed (rightmost image), the net can adapt itself to the contour of the legs and obtain a better fitting. The problem of creating a hole inside of a net is shown in figure (d). In this case, the active net is attracted to the blue background of the image and, in the image on the left, several nodes cannot move outside the apple because an equilibrium between its internal and border nodes is reached. If a hole is created, as shown in the rightmost image in (d), the net gets a better fit to the image background

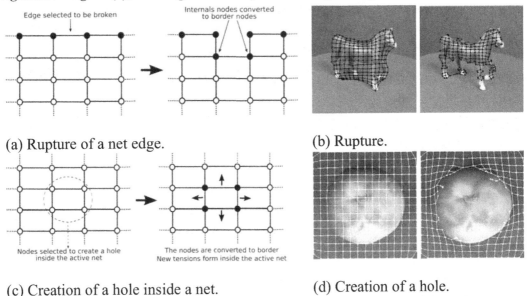

(a) Rupture of a net edge.

(b) Rupture.

(c) Creation of a hole inside a net.

(d) Creation of a hole.

by constructing an external energy histogram for the internal nodes. A histogram thresholding is used to select a value T, that distinguishes between nodes which are in a bad or in a good position (Figure 3(c)). If all the nodes have a similar energy, they are all considered in good position. Otherwise, the algorithm searches for the node with the highest energy value and checks if this node has four neighbors inside the hole with the highest external energy value. Once four candidates internal nodes are found, these are converted to border nodes. In this way, combining the internal energy, which makes the active net to contract, and the rupture algorithm all the nodes can move from the hole area to the internal or border part of the object (Figure 3(d)).

Fitting Process of an Active Net

The fitting process of an active net is performed according to the following steps. First, the energy images of a given picture are computed, and an active net is created for each color selected by the clustering algorithm (Figure 4(a)). Then, each net is adapted to the relevant regions of an image (Figure 4(b)). The main orientation of each zone is evaluated by computing its main geometric moment. In a second step, the region is rotated according to the orientation angle, and a second net is created and initialized on the minimum embedding rectangle of the region (Figure 4(c)). This new net is adapted over the particular region of the image identified during the first step (Figure 4(d)). In this way, the final configuration of the net is independent from the initial position and orientation of the object in the image. At the end of

Figure 4. The fitting process of an active net. (a) In the first step, the active net starts with its nodes equally distributed over all the image. (b) Since the region of interest is in a corner of the image, some nodes reach the region before other nodes of the net. As a consequence, some nodes take a good position over the object, while other nodes remain out of it. (c) To solve the previous problem, a second net is initialized on the minimum embedding rectangle of the region selected by the previous net. At the same time, the image is rotated according to the principal moments of the object. In this way, the net is more robust to rotations of the object. (d) In the second fitting process, all the nodes reach the object at the same time, allowing a better distribution of the nodes according to the external energies

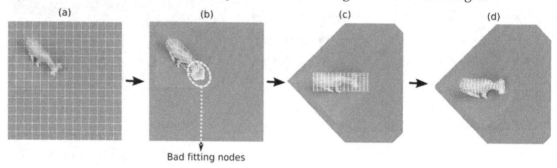

the second fitting process, the algorithm that allows the net to break is run, thus permitting the net to modify its topology (Figure 4(d)).

SIMILARITY MATCHING

In the proposed approach, an image is represented by a set of active nets capturing the relevant objects in the image. In the perspective to compare objects for retrieval purposes, a distance measure between two active nets has been defined. To this end, an active net is regarded as an attributed relational graph so that graph properties can be usefully exploited to enhance the net representation. In this way, the comparison between two nets is reduced to the problem of matching their corresponding graphs.

Given an active net $u(r, s)$, it is cast to a graph G by mapping nodes of the net to vertices of the graph, and links between nodes of the net to edges of the graph:

$$G \stackrel{def}{=} \langle V, E, \Phi, \Psi \rangle$$

$V =$ set of vertices

$E \subseteq V \times V =$ set of edges $\qquad\qquad (5)$

$\Phi : V \mapsto L_V$, vertices labeling function

$\Psi : E \mapsto L_E$, edge labeling function

where L_V and L_E are the sets of vertices and edge labels, respectively.

In our framework, active nets adapt to image regions according to the overall energy function of Eq.(1) so that nodes are constrained to some relevant points of the image (those providing the stable minimal configuration for the energy of the net). In so doing, the average color (in the $L^*a^*b^*$ color space) of the

Voronoi regions surrounding the nodes in the image is used as the vertices labeling function Φ of the graph (an example is the grey region shown in Figure 1). Vertex attributes are compared by exploiting the metric properties of the $L^*a^*b^*$ color space. In particular, given two vertices v_1 and v_2, their distance is evaluated as:

$$D_v(v_1,v_2)=\sqrt{\left(L^*_{v_1}-L^*_{v_2}\right)^2+\left(a^*_{v_1}-a^*_{v_2}\right)^2+\left(b^*_{v_1}-b^*_{v_2}\right)^2} \qquad (6)$$

In order to account for the deformation of the net with respect to its initial configuration, the normalized distance existing between two nodes n_1 and n_2 is used as edge labeling function Ψ of the edge e_{v_1,v_2} connecting the graph vertices v_1 and v_2 to which n_1 and n_2 are mapped, respectively, in the graph representation. The distance between edges e_j and e_k is defined as:

$$D_e\left(e_j,e_k\right)=\left|l_{e_j}-l_{e_k}\right| \qquad (7)$$

being l_{e_j} and l_{e_k} the labels associated to e_j and e_k, and measuring their length.

Before to convert an active net to a graph, all the edges broken during the fitting process are reconstructed to recover the original net topology (Figure 5). In this way, edges of the net are removed during the net adaptation process to increase its capability to deform according to the shape of complex objects; then, the complete topological structure of the net is recovered by inserting the missing edges so as to include this information in the graph representation.

The comparison of the graph models of a *query net* Q and an archive *description net* D involves the association of the vertices in the query with a subset of the vertices in the description. Using an additive composition, and indicating with Γ an injective function which associates vertices v_k in the query graph with a subset of the vertices in the description graph, this is expressed as follows (Berretti et al., 2001):

$$\mu^\Gamma(Q,D)\overset{def}{=}\lambda\sum_{k=1}^{N_q}D_v\left(v_k,\Gamma(v_k)\right)+(1-\lambda)\sum_{k=1}^{N_q}\sum_{h\in C(k)}D_e\left(\left|v_k,v_h\right|,\left|\Gamma(v_k),\Gamma(v_h)\right|\right) \qquad (8)$$

where N_q is the number of vertices in the query graph Q, $C(k)$ is the set of graph vertices directly connected to the vertex k (i.e., $v_h \in C(k)$ if an edge $e_{h,k}=e_{k,h}$ connecting the vertices v_h and v_k exists in the

Figure 5. After an active net is stable, the rupture and hole detection algorithm is executed. This can delete edges, allowing a better fit of the active net to regions of complex shape. When this process is completed, the edges are re-inserted into the net so as to fully account for the deformation of the active net

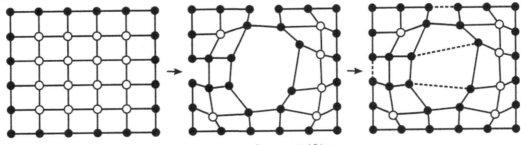

- - - - - - Reconstructed Edge

set of graph edges E), and $\lambda \in [0, 1]$ balances the mutual relevance of edge and vertex distance (e.g., for $\lambda = 1$, the distance only accounts for the chromatic distance).

In general, given Q and D, a combinatorial number of different interpretations Γ are possible each scoring a different value of distance. The distance is thus defined as the minimum under any possible interpretation: $\mu(Q, D) = \min_\Gamma \mu^\Gamma(Q, D)$. In so doing, computation of the distance between two nets becomes an *optimal error-correcting (sub)graph isomorphism problem,* which is a NP-Complete problem with exponential time solution algorithm (Berretti et al., 2001).

However, due to the particular structure of active nets, it is possible to find the optimal match between their graph representations in polynomial time. In fact, we assume that nets with the same number of nodes are used to describe every object in the image database (i.e., $N_q = N_d = n \times m$, being n and m the number of nodes in the rows and columns of a net, respectively). This is motivated by the fact that nets with the same number of nodes represent image objects at the same spatial resolution. A second basic assumption is that, during comparison, only homologous graph vertices can match (i.e., vertices having the same position in the grid $u(r, s)$). This corresponds to assume that the injective function Γ of Eq.(5) maps any vertex v_k in the graph Q to the homologous vertex d_k in D (i.e., $\Gamma(v_k) = d_k$).

INDEXING OF ACTIVE NETS

In order to make efficient the retrieval process in large databases, M-Tree indexing (Ciaccia et al., 1997) is used. This is motivated by the fact that the graph model proposed in this work is not a feature vector space, so it is not possible to use the traditional tree structures for its indexing. The M-Tree is a paged metric tree. It is a balanced tree, able to deal with dynamic data fill, and it does not require periodical reorganizations. M-Tree can index objects using features compared by distances functions which either do not fit into a vector space or do not use a L_p metric. Using a specific distance function d, the M-Tree can partition objects, and store these objects into fixed nodes, which correspond to constrained regions in the metric space. The only requirement is that the distance follows the metric axioms. If the metric assumption is true, the M-Tree can index any kind of data without knowing their structure. It can be easily proved that the distance between active nets (defined in the previous Section) is a metric, thus fitting the M-tree requirements.

Organization and Access

A M-Tree of graphs is a tree of *nodes*, each containing a fixed maximum number m of *entries*. In turn, each entry is constituted by a routing graph D; a reference to the root sub^D of a (sub)index containing the graphs in the so-called *covering region* of D; and a *radius* μ^D providing an upper bound for the distance between D and any graph in its covering region (Figure 6):

$$
\begin{aligned}
&<\text{node}> \quad ::= \quad \{<\text{entry}>\}^m \\
&<\text{entry}> \quad ::= \quad D, sub^D, \mu^D
\end{aligned}
\tag{9}
$$

The index tree can be constructed using different schemes for the insertion of new graphs and the selection of routing graphs (Ciaccia et al., 1997). In our particular case, the index is constructed dynami-

Figure 6. M-tree structure

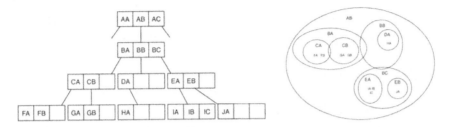

(a) A M-Tree with a maximum of 3 objects per node.

(b) Covering regions for the routing objects in (a).

cally by inserting graphs from the bottom layer and by splitting nodes and promoting routing graphs when insertion overflows occur (see Figure 7). In so doing, the tree is kept balanced while its depth grows through splits of the root node. Different policies can be implemented to select the most suitable leaf node for the insertion, the entries moved in the split of a node, and the graphs which is promoted in the split. Most common policies include "Minimum of Maximum of Radii" (which reduces the size of regions) and "Maximum Lower Bound on Distance" (which reduces the overlap between different regions) (Ciaccia et al., 1997).

In our case, we used the *Minimum Sum of Radii* policy. This algorithm considers all the possible pairs of objects, partitions the set of entries to each one of those combinations and promotes the pair of objects for which the sum of covering radius, $\mu^{D_1} + \mu^{D_2}$ is minimum. This algorithm is the most complex in terms of distance computations.

During retrieval, triangular inequality can be used to support efficient processing of range queries, i.e., queries seeking for all the graphs in the archive which are within a given range of distance from a query graph Q. To this end, the distance between Q and any graph in the covering region of a routing graph D can be lower-bounded using the radius μ^D and the distance between D and Q. Specifically, if μ_{max} is the range of the query, the following condition can be employed to check whether all the graphs in the covering region of D can be discarded, based on the sole evaluation of the distance $\mu(Q,D)$:

Figure 7. Split process of the M-tree. The new object XX needs to be inserted into a full leaf node: this induces a split of the node. Two new routing objects are selected, and the leaf node splits into two different leaf nodes. The new routing objects create a new split into a routing node. The split process propagates towards the root of the tree and ends up when no more splits are needed.

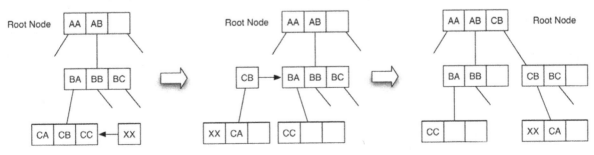

$\mu(Q,D) \geq \mu max + \mu^D \rightarrow$ no graph in sub^D is acceptable $\hspace{2cm}$ (10)

In a similar manner, the following condition checks whether all the graphs in the covering region of D fall within the range of the query (in this case, all the graphs in the region can be accepted):

$\mu(Q,D) \leq \mu max - \mu^D \rightarrow$ every graph in sub^D is acceptable $\hspace{2cm}$ (11)

In the critical case that neither one of the previous two inequalities holds, the covering region of D may contain both acceptable and non acceptable graphs, and the search must be repeated on the sub-index sub^D.

K-Nearest Neighbor (KNN) queries seeking for the K graphs that are most similar to the query in the archive can be also managed in a similar manner, but with lower efficiency. This is obtained by regarding the query as a particular case in which the range μ_{max} is determined during the search. This is the solution implemented in this work.

To manage KNN queries, Ciaccia et al. (Ciaccia et al., 1997) proposed the use of a branch-and-bound technique similar to that designed for the R-Trees (Roussopoulos et al., 1995). This technique uses two global structures, a priority queue PR, and a result array NN.

PR is a structure that contains pointers to every subtree that may contain valid objects for a given query Q. For every pointer, a lower bound in the distance of any graph in sub^{D_r} is kept:

$$d_{min}\left(sub^{D_r}\right) = \max\left\{d\left(D_r,Q\right) - \mu^{D_r}, 0\right\} \hspace{2cm} (12)$$

At each step of the algorithm, the entry in PR with the lower d_{min} is considered in order to find objects relevant to the given query.

NN is the sorted array that at the end of the execution contains the final results of the search. Each element of the array stores a graph D_j and its distance to the query, $d(D_j, Q)$. We denote the distance d_k as the distance of the last element in the array. As a consequence, any subtree so that $d_{min}\left(sub^{D_r}\right) > d_k$ can be safely pruned from the search. In so doing, d_k plays the role of a dynamic search radius.

Apart from the lower bound, an upper bound is also considered:

$$d_{max}\left(sub^{D_r}\right) = d\left(D_r,Q\right) + \mu^{D_r} \hspace{2cm} (13)$$

After analyzing the root graph of a branch, if $d_{max} < d_k$, this root graph is added to NN with d_{max} as distance value, and d_k is updated. This may cause a pruning in PR, thus reducing the number of necessary computations.

RESULTS

The proposed approach for objects representation and retrieval has been experimented on the *ETH-80* (Leibe & Schiele, 2003) and *ALOI* (Geusebroek et al., 2006) objects databases.

The *ETH-80* database includes natural and artificial objects organized in eight basic categories: *apples, tomatoes, pears, dogs, cows, horses, cups* and *cars*. For each category, 10 different objects are provided, being each object represented by 41 images taken from different viewpoints. This results in a total of 3280 images. For each object, a reference segmentation mask is also provided in the *ETH-80* database, for comparison and evaluation purposes.

The *ALOI* database, (*Amsterdam Library of Object Images)*, is an object image database composed of 1000 objects recorded under various imaging circumstances (Geusebroek et al., 2006). In order to capture the sensory variation in object recordings, the viewing angle, illumination angle, and illumination color of each object are systematically varied. Additionally, wide-baseline stereo images are captured. They recorded over a hundred images for each object, yielding a total of 110250 images for the entire collection.

One of the key factors in the fitting process of an active net is the creation of the energy images. One of the energies selected for this work depends on the efficiency of the color clustering algorithm shown in Section 2. Since the ETH-80 image database includes a perfect mask for every image, we tested the efficiency of our algorithm against these masks (Figure 8 shows some clustering examples). The color clustering algorithm shows the following efficiency in correctly segmenting image objects: 89.27% for apple images; 79.02% for cow images; 90.98% for cup images; 77.80% for dog images; 77.56% for horse images; 86.10% for pear images, and 93.66% for tomato images. In particular, this percentual values indicate the relative number of images that are correctly segmented with respect to the ideal segmentation mask and to the requirements of the active-nets.

The adjustment of the parameters of equations (3) and (4) has been done by visual inspection of the active net fitting process of the images of the ETH-80 database. We found out that the best results were achieved for $\alpha = 3$, $\beta = 0.01$, $\gamma = 1$ and $\delta = 9$ (with these parameters, good results have been obtained for the active nets of different size used in this work).

In Figures 9 to 11 *precision-recall* (P-R) curves are reported for active nets of different size (i.e., n × m nodes) using different images of the ETH-80 database. *Precision* is defined for each query as the number of correctly retrieved images relative to the number of images retrieved from the database. *Recall* is the number of correctly retrieved images relative to the overall number of relevant images in the database to a given query. The ideal result is to get precision equal to one for every value of recall.

Results show that nets of size 5 × 5 or 10 × 10 are not able to capture enough details of the objects in comparison with net of size 15 × 15 (an exception is that reported in Figure 11c: the cups object have a very simple structure, and adding more nodes to the active net does not give better results. In fact, the additional nodes make the active nets more sensible to small changes in the images). In our experiments, this size resulted as a reasonable tradeoff between the effectiveness of retrieval and the efficiency of the match, in that further increasing the size of the nets has not provided significant improvements in the P-R curves.

P-R graphs have been computed also for the ALOI database. Figures 12, 13 and, 14 show the P-R graphs using different query images of the ALOI database. In this case, a net of size 15 × 15 is used.

Figure 8. Some results of the color clustering algorithm. These are compared against the ideal segmentation masks provided in the ETH-80 object database

Original   Ideal   Result   Original   Ideal   Result

Figure 9. ETH-80 images: (a) cup8-090-248; (b) cup9-090-248. (c) P-R results for images (a) and (b) using active nets of size 5x5. (d) P-R results for images (a) and (b) using active nets of size 10x10. (e) P-R results for images (a) and (b) using active nets of size 15x15

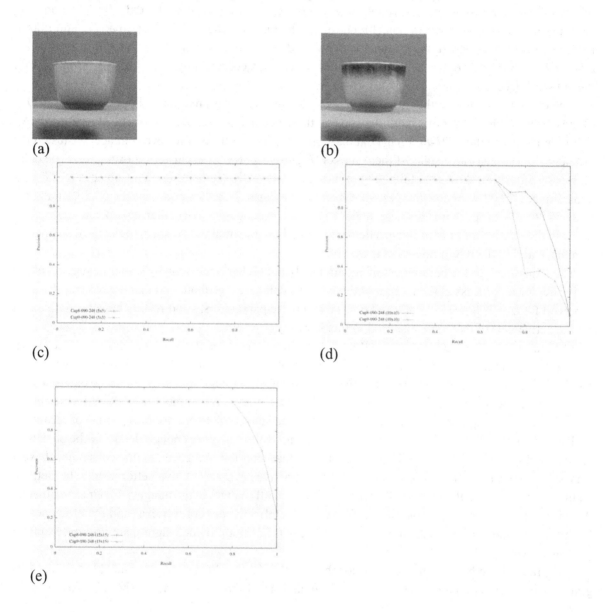

Leibe and Schiele (Leibe & Schiele, 2003) performed a series of tests using state of the art image classification algorithms to check how they perform on this database. The tests consisted in selecting an image of one category and checking if the algorithm could provide the correct category for the image (i.e., if we introduce a tomato as query, the system will produce tomato as result). It is simple to modify the system proposed here as an image classifier. To this end, we assumed that the query image is from the same category to which the first 10 replies belongs to (if we have images from different categories,

Figure 10. ETH-80 images: (a) tomato1-000-000; (b) tomato2-000-000; (c) tomato3-000-000; (d) tomato4-000-000; (e) tomato5-000-000; (f) tomato8-000-000; (g) the tomato9-000-000. (h) P-R results for images (a)-(g) using active nets of size 5x5. (i) P-R results for images (a)-(g) using active nets of size 10x10. (j) P-R results for images (a)-(g) using active nets of size 15x15.

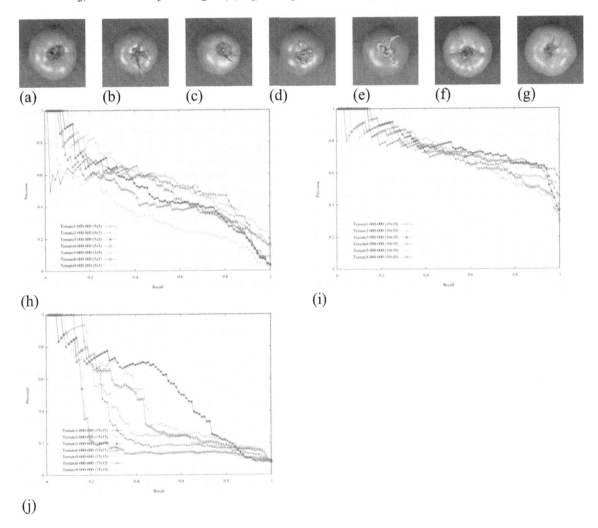

we assign the category which has the larger number of replies). Using this simple technique we have compared our method with those considered by Leibe and Schiele (Leibe & Schiele, 2003). For the sake of the comparison, the algorithms used by Leibe and Schiele (and reported in the comparison of Table 1) are shortly summarized in the following.

The Color approach, uses a global RGB histogram of all the pixels of the image belonging to the object and compares object histograms using a divergence measure (Swain & Ballard, 1991). $D_x D_y$ and Mag-Lap use texture information: $D_x D_y$ is a rotation variant descriptor and uses only the first deriva-

Figure 11. ETH-80 images: (a) horse3-033-270; (b) horse4-022-270; (c) horse6-022-270; (d) horse7-022-270; (e) horse10-022-270. (f) P-R curves for images (a)-(e) using active nets of size 5x5. (g) P-R curves for images (a)-(e) using active nets of size 10x10. (h) P-R curves for images (a)-(e) using active nets of size 15x15

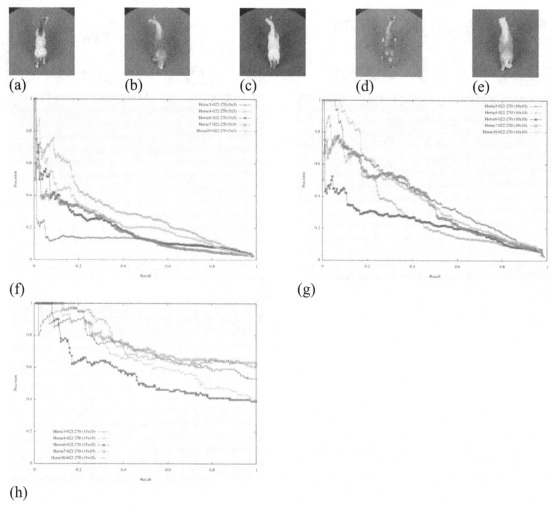

tives in x and y directions over 3 scales; Mag-Lap uses rotation invariant features, namely the gradient magnitude and the Laplacian, over 3 scales (Schiele & Crowley, 2000). PCA Masks and PCA Grey use shape cues for image categorization. In PCA masks, one single global eigenspace for all categories is built. Recognition becomes a nearest-neighbor search in the eigenspace (Murase & Naya, 1995). The PCA Grey approach, builds separate eigenspaces for each category and measures the reconstruction error, which is defined as the quality by which class-specific eigenspace can represent the test image (Turk & Pentland, 1991). In the two last methods, Cont. Greedy and Cont. DnyProg, the shape of the object is represented by a discrete set of points sampled regularly along the internal or external contours. For every point, a log-polar histogram, the Shape Context, is computed that approximates the distribution of adjacent point locations relative to the reference point. Correspondence between different shapes can be found by matching the log-polar histograms. In their original method, Belongie et al. (Belongie et al., 2001) matched shapes by iteratively deforming one contour using thin plate splines. Leibe and Schiele used two simpler approaches. In the Cont. DnyProg method, they searched a continuous path around the main object contour using a dynamic programming approach. In the Cont. Greedy approach, a one-to-one matching between contour points using a greedy strategy is used.

Results obtained by comparing the approach proposed in this work against the methods addressed are summarized in Table 1.

From Table 1, it can be observed the proposed approach attains the best performance for five of the seven classes (namely, *apple, cow, dog, horse, tomato*). In the two cases in which the proposed approach does not score the best result (*cup* and *pear*), it is very close to the best with a difference of about 1%. For the classes *apple* and *dog,* the proposed approach shows a significant increment in the classification rate with respect to the second best approach (about 10%). Moreover, the classification rate of the proposed approach is more than 91% for all the classes, clearly showing an average performance that outperforms the other solutions.

Indexing Efficiency

To evaluate the M-Tree indexing algorithm, we used the ETH-80 image database. This database includes 3280 images. After the database images have been processed by our algorithm, the database comprised 7016 objects. This approximately corresponds to represent each image with two active nets, one active net for the object in the image and one for the background. A linear scan of this database, comparing one query object against all the objects in the database, requires 7016 comparisons and about 347646 mil-

Figure 12. ALOI images: (a) 4-r0; (b) 82-r0; (c) 164-r0; (d) 444-r0. (e) P-R results for images (a)-(d) using active nets of size 15x15

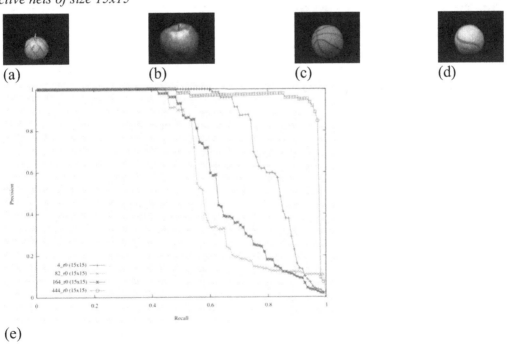

(a)   (b)   (c)   (d)

(e)

Figure 13. ALOI images: (a) 707-r0; (b) 713-r0; (c) 82-r0; (d) 257-r0. (e) P-R for images in (a)-(d) using active nets of size 15x15

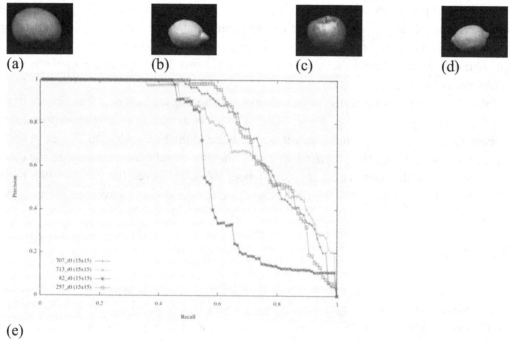

(a)   (b)   (c)   (d)

(e)

Figure 14. ALOI images: (a) 24-r0; (b) 235-r0; (c) 236-r0; (d) 249-r0. (e) P-R results for images in (a)-(d) using active nets of size 15x15

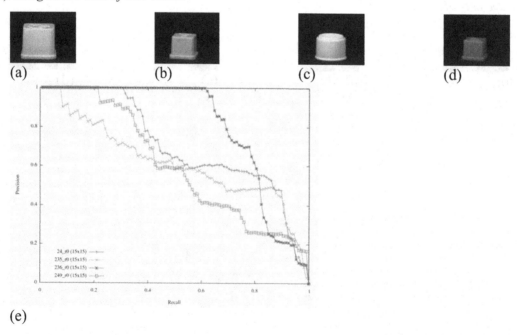

(a)   (b)   (c)   (d)

(e)

Table 1. Classification rates for different classes of objects and different approaches.

	Apple	Cow	Cup	Dog	Horse	Pear	Tomato
Color	57.56%	86.59%	79.76%	34.63%	32.68%	66.10%	98.54%
$D_x D_y$	85.37%	82.68%	66.10%	62.44%	58.78%	90.00%	94.64%
Mag-Lap	80.24%	94.39%	77.80%	74.39%	70.98%	85.37%	97.07%
PCA Masks	78.78%	75.12%	96.10%	72.20%	77.80%	99.51%	67.80%
PCA Grey	88.29%	62.44%	96.10%	66.34%	77.32%	99.76%	76.59%
Cont. Greedy	77.07%	86.83%	99.76%	81.95%	84.63%	90.73%	70.73%
Cont. DnyProg	76.34%	86.34%	99.02%	82.93%	84.63%	91.71%	70.24%
Proposal	**98.05%**	**96.01%**	**99.27%**	**94.39%**	**91.22%**	**98.54%**	**99.51%**

Table 2. Search efficiency comparison. Time and number of comparisons are reported for M-tree search. Gain with respect to a linear scan of the database is also reported. In the worst cases, it can be observed that the indexing algorithm performs as a linear scan of the database. In general, the M-Tree reduces considerably the number of necessary computations and the time users wait for a query

Leafs per Branch 10	Time (millisecond)	Comparisons (Number of)	Performance Gain vs Linear Scan (Time)	Performance Gain vs Linear Scan (Comparisons)
Query 1	206264	2337	1.68	3.00
Query 2	119894	1279	2.89	5.48
Query 3	259289	3058	1.34	2.29
Query 4	81569	903	4,26	7.77
Leafs per Branch 15	Time (millisecond)	Comparisons (Number of)	Performance Gain vs Linear Scan (Time)	Performance Gain vs Linear Scan (Comparisons)
Query 1	198023	2266	1.75	3.10
Query 2	136621	1336	2.54	5.25
Query 3	261834	3124	1.32	2.24
Query 4	84047	899	4.13	7.80
Leafs per Branch 20	Time (millisecond)	Comparisons (Number of)	Performance Gain vs Linear Scan (Time)	Performance Gain vs Linear Scan (Comparisons)
Query 1	182913	2156	1.90	3.25
Query 2	126806	1355	2.74	4.21
Query 3	256015	3042	1.35	2.31
Query 4	85438	951	4.06	7.37
Leafs per Branch 30	Time (millisecond)	Comparisons (Number of)	Performance Gain vs Linear Scan (Time)	Performance Gain vs Linear Scan (Comparisons)
Query 1	211128	2274	1.64	3.08
Query 2	154981	1666	2.24	4.21
Query 3	280959	2314	1.23	3.03
Query 4	104521	1197	3.32	5.86

liseconds using an active net of size 15x15. This time also includes I/0 access to the disk (the tests have been run on an Intel Core Duo machine at 2.4GHz, 2 GB of RAM and a Java 6.0 Virtual Machine).

To check the influence of the size of the nodes (i.e., the number of objects per node), trees with different node size have been constructed, namely: 10, 15, 20 and 30.

Every tree was tested with the same query images, and results obtained for different node size have been compared each other and against a linear scan. The results are resumed in Table 2.

CONCLUSION

In this work, we have proposed a content based image retrieval system which relies on an original approach for the extraction and representation of significant perceptual regions (objects) of an image. This is obtained by first extracting relevant regions and their borders on the basis of image chromatic content, then by using active nets to identify and represent image regions. In particular, we extended the basic structure and adaptation process of active nets in order to allow the rupture of edges of the net and the creation of holes inside the net. In this way, we found that a better fit of the active net to objects of complex shape can be attained. Casting an active net to a graph representation allows for the embedding of additional information in the model and for an efficient matching algorithm. At the same time, the metric similarity measure used to compare two graphs allows to index all the objects in the database into a M-Tree indexing structure. This speeds up the retrieval process making necessary less computations with respect to a linear scan. Experimental results validated the proposed approach on two different databases of object images.

FUTURE RESEARCH DIRECTIONS

Future work will mainly address the inclusion of texture information in the active nets model. Currently, the system uses chromatic and spatial information in the form of energy images to guide the fitting process of an active net to relevant regions of an image. The combination of these two features with texture information should result in the creation of better energy images for the fitting of active nets. In particular, the inclusion of texture information is expected to improve the identification of image attractors, making them more close to the actual contours of image objects.

An interesting area of current and future research in the field of image retrieval by content is the investigation of techniques capable to reduce the *semantic gap* between the user's needs and the system. To this end, the proposed approach will be investigated in order to be used as the starting point to learn mappings between low level image features and intermediate or high level semantic concepts.

REFERENCES

Androutsos, D., Plataniotis, K. N., & Venetsanopoulos, A. N. (1999). A novel vector-based approach to color image retrieval using vector angular-based distance measure. *Computer Vision and Image Understanding, 1/2*, 46-58.

Ansia, F., Penedo, M., Mariño, C., López, J., & Mosquera, A. (1999). Morphological analysis with active nets. In *4th International Conference on Advances in Pattern Recognition and Digital Techniques*.

Ansia, F., Penedo, M. Mariño, C., López, J., & Mosquera, A. (2000). Automatic 3D shape reconstruction of bones using active net-based segmentation. In *15th International Conference on Pattern Recognition, Barcelona, Spain*.

Barreira, N., & Penedo, M. G. (2004). Topological active volumes for segmentation and shape reconstruction of medical images. In *Lecture Notes in Computer Science: Image Analysis and Recognition* (pp. 132-140).

Barreira, N., Penedo, M. G., Ibázes, O., & Santos, J. (2007). Automatic topological active net division in genetic-greedy hybrid approach. In *Lecture Notes in Computer Science: Pattern Recognition and Image Analysis* (pp. 226-233).

Belongie, S., Malik, J., & Puchiza, J. (2001). Matching Shapes. In *Proceeeding International Conference on Computer Vision*.

Berretti, S., Del Bimbo, A., & Vicario, E. (2001). Efficient matching and indexing of graph models in content-based retrieval. *IEEE Transactions on Pattern Analysis and Machine Intelligence, 23*(10), 1089-1105.

Besag, J. (1986). On the statistical analysis of dirty pictures. *Journal Royal Statistical Society, Series B, 33*(3), 259-302.

Bro-Nielsen, M. (1994). *Active nets and active cubes.* (Tech. Rep. No. 94-13). IMM.

Carson, C., Belongie, S., Greenspan, H., & Malik, J. (2002). Blobworld: Image segmentation using expectation-maximization and its application to image querying. *IEEE Transactions on Pattern Analysis and Machine Intelligence, 24*(8), 1026-1038.

Ciaccia, P., Patella, M., & Zezula, P. (1997). M-tree: An efficient access method for similarity search in metric spaces. In *23rd VLDB Conference*.

Datta, R., Joshi, D., Li, J., & Wang, J.Z. (in press). Image retrieval: Ideas, influences, and trends of the new age. *ACM Computing Surveys*.

Del Bimbo, A. (1999). *Visual information Rretrieval.* Morgan Kaufmann Plublisers, Inc.

Duc, B., Fischer, S., & Bigun, J. (1999). Face authentication with Gabor information on deformable graphs. *IEEE Transactions on Image Processing, 8*(4), 504-516.

Doi, A., Fujiware, S., Matsuda, K., & Kameda, M. (2002). 3D Volume extraction and mesh generation using energy minimization techniques. In *Proceedings of the first International on 3D Data Processing Visualization and Transmission* (pp. 83-86).

Finlayson, G. D., Hordley, S. D., & Hubel, P. M. (2001). Color by correlation: A simple, unifying framework for color constancy. *IEEE Transactions on Pattern Analysis and Machine Intelligence, 23*(11), 1209-1221.

Flickner, M., Niblack, W., Sawhney, H., Ashley, J., Huang, Q., Dom, B., Gorkani, M., Hafner, J., Lee, D., Petkovic, D., Steele, D., & Yanker, P. (1995). Query by image and video content: The QBIC system. *IEEE Computer, 28*(9), 23-32.

García-Pérez, D., Mosquera, A., Berretti, S., & Del Bimbo, A. (2006a). Object-based image retrieval using active nets. In *Proceedings International Conference on Pattern Recognition* (ICPR'06), (pp. 750-753). Honk-Kong, China.

García-Pérez, D. Mosquera, A., Berretti, S., & Del Bimbo, A. (2006b). Topological active-nets for object-based image retrieval. In *International Conference on Image Analysis and Recognition* (pp. 636-647). Pòvoa de Varzim, Portugal.

Geusebrock, J., Burghouts, G., & Smeulders, A. (2006). The Amsterdam library of object images. *International Journal of Computer Vision, 66*(1), 103-112.

Geman, S., & Geman, D. (1984). Stochastic relaxation, Gibbs distributions, and the Bayesian restoration of images. *IEEE Transactions on Pattern Analysis and Machine Intelligence, 6*(6).

Gevers, T., & Smeulders, A. W. M. (1999). Color-based object recognition. *Pattern Recognition, 32*, 453-464.

Gevers, T., & Smeulders, A. W. M. (2000). Pictoseek: Combining color and shape invariant features for image retrieval. *IEEE Transactions on Image Processing, 9*(1), 102-110.

Gupta, A., & Jain, R. (1997). Visual information retrieval. *Communications of the ACM, 40*(5), 70-79.

Heidemann, G. (2004). Combining spatial and colour information for content-based image retrieval. *Computer Vision and Image Understanding, 94*(1-3) 234-270.

Hoiem, D., Sukthankar, R., Schneiderman, H., & Huston, L. (2004). Object-based image retrieval Using the statistical structure of images. In *IEEE Conference on Computer Vision and Pattern Recognition*.

Ibáñez, O., Barreira, N., Santos, J., & Penedo, M. G. (2006). Topological active nets optimization using genetic algorithms. In *Lecture Notes in Computer Science: Image Analysis and Recognition* (pp. 272-282).

Kass, M., Witkin, A., & Terzopoulos, D. (1988). Snakes: Active contour models. *International Journal of Computer Vision, 1*, 312-331.

Leibe, B., & Schiele, B. (2003). Analyzing appearance and contour-based methods of object categorization. In *Proceedings of the IEEE Computer Society Conference on Computer Vision and Pattern Recognition (CVPR'03)*.

Lew, M. S., Sebe, N., Djeraba, C., & Jain, R. (2006). Content-based multimedia information Retrieval: State-of-the-art and Challenges. *ACM Transactions on Multimedia Computing, Communications and Applications, 2*(1), 1-19.

Liua, Y., Zhanga, D., Lua, G., & Mab, W.-Y. (2007). A survey of content-based image retrieval with high-level semantics. *Pattern Recognition, 40*(1), 262-282.

Moreau, V., Cohen, L. D., & Pellerin, D. (2002). Estimation and analysis of the deformation of the cardiac wall using Doppler tissue imaging. In *Proceedings International Conference on Pattern Recognition.*

Murase, H., & Naya, S. K. (1995). Visual learning and recognition of 3D objects for appearance. *International Journal of Computer Vision, 14,* 5-14.

Nayar, S. K., & Bolle, R. M. (1996). Reflectance-based object recognition. *International Journal of Computer Vision, 17*(3), 219-240.

Roussopoulos, N., Kelly, S., & Vincent, F. (1995). Nearest neighbor queries. In *ACM SIGMOD*, (pp. 71–79).

Rui, Y., Huang, T. S., & Chang, S.-F. (1999). Image retrieval: Current techniques, promising directions, and open issues. *Journal of Visual Communications and Visual Representations*, 10, 39-62.

Schiele, B., & Crowley, J. L. (2000). Recognition without correspondence using multidimensional receptive field histograms. *International Journal of Computer Vision, 36*(1), 31-52.

Smeulders, A., Worring, M., Santini, S., Gupta, A., & Jain, R. (2000). Content-based image retrieval at the end of the early years. *IEEE Transactions on Pattern Analysis and Machine Intelligence, 22*(12), 1349-1380.

Smith, J. R., & Chang, S. F. (1996). VisualSEEk: a Fully Automated content-based image query system. In *ACM Multimedia '96*. Boston, MA.

Swain, M. J., & Ballard, D. H. (1991). Color indexing. *International Journal of Computer Vision, 7*(1), 11-32.

Takanashi, T., Muraki, S., & Kaufman, A. (1998). Three-dimensional active Net for volume extraction. In *Proceedings of SPIE 3289* (pp. 184-193).

Tsumiyama, Y., Sakane, K., & Yamamoto, K. (1989). Active net: Active Net model for region extraction. *IPSJ SIG Notes, 89*(96), 1-8.

Turk, M., & Pentland, A. (1991). Eigenfaces for recognition. *Journal of Cognitive Neuroscience, 3,* 71-86.

Uchiyama, T., & Arbib, M. (1994). Color image segmentation using competitive learning. *IEEE Transactions on Pattern Analysis and Machine Intelligence, 10*(12), 1197-1206.

Wang, J. Z., Li, J., & Wiederhold, G. (2001). Simplicity: Semantics-sensitive integrated matching for picture libraries. *IEEE Transactions on Pattern Analysis and Machine Intelligence, 23*(9), 947-963.

Williams, D., & Shah, M. (1992). A fast algorithm for active contours and curvature estimation. *CVIGP: Image Understanding, 55*(1), 1-26.

ADDITIONAL READING

Low Level Features: COLOR

Berretti, S., Del Bimbo, A., & Vicario, E. (2002). Spatial arrangement of color in retrieval by visual similarity. *Pattern Recognition,* 35(8), 1661-1674.

Eakins, J. P., Boardman, J. M., & Graham, M. E. (1998). Similarity retrieval of trademark images. *IEEE Multimedia*, 5(2), 53-63.

Funt, B. V., & Finlayson, G. D. (1995). Color constant color indexing. *IEEE Transactions on Pattern Analysis and Machine Intelligence*, 17(5), 522-529.

Gevers, T., & Stokman, H. M. G. (2003). Robust histogram construction from color invariants for object recognition. *IEEE Transactions on Pattern Analysis and Machine Intelligence*, 25(10).

Gevers, T. (2000). Color based image retrieval. *Multimedia Search. Springer Verlag.*

Hafner, J., Sawhney, H. S., Equitz, W., Flickner, M., & Niblack, W. (1995). Efficient Color Histogram Indexing for Quadratic Form Distance Functions. *IEEE Transactions on Pattern Analysis and Machine Intelligence,* 17(7), 729-736.

Low Level Features: TEXTURE

Belongie, S., Carson, C., Greenspan, H., & Malik, J. (1998). Color- and texture-based image segmentation using em and its application to content-based image retrieval. In *Sixth International Conference on Computer Vision.*

Chui, C. K., Montefusco, L., & Puccio, L. (1994). Wavelets: theory, algorithms, and applications. *Academic Press*, San Diego.

Daubechies, I. (1992). Ten lectures on wavelets. *Society for Industrial and Applied Mathematics*, Philadelphia.

Gevers, T. (2002). Image segmentation and matching of color-texture objects. *IEEE Transactions on Multimedia*, 4(4).

Hoang, M. A., Geusebroek, J. M., & Smeulders, A. W. M. (2005). Color texture measurement and segmentation. *Signal Processing.*

Laine, A., & Fan, J. (1993). Texture classification by wavelet packet signature, *IEEE Transactions on Pattern Analysis and Machine Intelligence*, 15(11), 1186-1191.

Li, J., & Wang, J. Z. (2003). Automatic linguistic indexing of pictures by a statistical modeling approach. *IEEE Transactions on Pattern Analysis and Machine Intelligence,* 25(9), 1075-1088.

Liu, F., & Picard, R. (1996). Periodicity, directionality, and randomness: Wold features for image modelling and retrieval. *IEEE Transactions on Pattern Analysis and Machine Intelligence*, 18 (7), 517-549.

Ma, W. Y., & Manjunath, B. S. (1997). Edge flow: a framework of boundary detection and image segmentation. In *Proc. IEEE International Conference on Computer Vision and Pattern Recognition* (CVPR'97) (pp. 744-749). San Juan, Puerto Rico.

Mao, J., & Jain, A. K. (1992). Texture classification and segmentation using multiresolution simultaneous autoregressive models. *Pattern Recognition*, 25(2).

Ojala, T., Pietikainen, M., & Harwood, D. (1996). A comparison study of texture measures with classification based on feature distributions. *Pattern Recognition*, 29, 51-59.

Panjwani, D. K., & Healey, G. (1995). Markov random field models for unsupervised segmentation of textured color images. *IEEE Transactions on Pattern Analysis and Machine Intelligence*, 17(10), 939-954.

Pentland, A., Picard, R. W., & Sclaroff, S. (1996). Photobook: Content-based manipulation of image databases. *International Journal of Computer Vision*, 18(3), 233-254.

Randen, T., & Hakon Husoy, J. (1999). Filtering for texture classification: a comparative study, *IEEE Transactions on Pattern Analysis and Machine Intelligence*, 21(4), 291-310.

Low Level Features: SHAPE

Belongie, S., Malik, J., & Puzicha, J. (2002). Shape Matching and Object Recognition Using Shape Contexts. *IEEE Transactions on Pattern Analysis and Machine Intelligence*, 24(4), 509-522.

Berretti, S., Del Bimbo, A., & Pala, P. (2000). Retrieval by Shape Similarity with Perceptual Distance and Effective Indexing. *IEEE Transactions on Multimedia*, 2(4), 225-239.

Berretti, S., & Del Bimbo, A. (2004). Multiresolution Spatial Partitioning for Shape Representation. In *Proc. IEEE International Conference on Pattern Recognition* (ICPR'04) (pp. 775-778). Cambridge, United Kingdom.

Bober, M. (2001). MPEG-7 Visual Shape Descriptors. *IEEE Transactions on Circuits and Systems for Video Technology*, 11(6), 716-719.

Del Bimbo, A., & Pala, P. (1997). Visual image retrieval by elasting matching of user sketches. *IEEE Transactions on Pattern Analysis and Machine Intelligence*, 19(2), 121-132.

Geiger, D., Liu, T.-L., & Kohn, R. (2003). Representation and Self-Similarity of Shapes. *IEEE Transactions on Pattern Analysis and Machine Intelligence*, 25(1), 86-99.

Grosky, W. I., & Mehrotra, R. (1990). Index-Based Object Recognition in Pictorial Data Management. *Computer Vision, Graphics and Image Processing*, 52, 416-436.

Jain, A. K., & Vailaya, A. (1998). Shape-based retrieval: a case study with trademark image database. *Pattern Recognition*, 31(9), 1369-1390.

Latecki, L. J., & Lakamper, R. (2000). Shape Descriptors for Nonrigid Shapes with a Single Closed Contour. In *Proc. IEEE Conference on Computer Vision and Pattern Recognition*.

Latecki, L. J., & Lakamper, R. (2000). Shape Similarity Measure Based on Correspondence of Visual Parts. *IEEE Transactions on Pattern Analysis and Machine Intelligence*, 22(10), 1-6.

Liao, S. X., & Pawlak, M. (1996). On Image Analysis by Moments. *IEEE Transactions on Pattern Analysis and Machine Intelligence*, 18(3), 254-266.

Loncaric, S. (1998). A Survey of Shape Analysis Techniques. *Pattern Recognition*, 34(8), 983-1001.

Mehrotra, R., & Gary, J. E. (1995). Similar-shape retrieval in shape data management. *IEEE Computer*, 28(9), 57-62.

Mokhtarian, F., & Mackworth, A. K. (1992). A Theory of Multiscale, Curvature-Based Shape Representation for planar curves. *IEEE Transactions on Pattern Analysis and Machine Intelligence*, 24(4), 789-805.

Mokhtarian, F. (1995). Silhouette-based isolated object recognition through curvature scale space. *IEEE Transactions on Pattern Analysis and Machine Intelligence*, 17(5), 539-544.

MPEG-7 Visual Part of Experimentation Model Version 8.0, A.Yamada, M.Pickering, S.Jeannin, L.Cieplinski, J.-R.Ohm and M.Editors, Eds, October 2000, ISO/IEC JTC1/SC29/WG11/N3673.

Petrakis, E., Diplaros A., & Milios, E. (2002). Matching and Retrieval of Distorted and Occluded Shapes Using Dynamic Programming. *IEEE Transactions on Pattern Analysis and Machine Intelligence*, 24(11), 1501-1516.

Sclaroff, S., & Pentland, A. (1995). Modal Matching for Correspondence and Recognition. *IEEE Transactions on Pattern Analysis and Machine Intelligence*, 17(6), 545-561.

Sikora, T. (2001). The MPEG-7 Visual Standard for Content Description - An Overview. *IEEE Transactions on Circuits and Systems for Video Technology*, 11(6), 696-702.

Tieng, Q. M., & Boles, W. W. (1997). Recognition of 2D object contours using the wavelet transform zero-crossing representation. *IEEE Transactions on Pattern Analysis and Machine Intelligence*, 19(8), 910-916.

Low Level Features: STRUCTURE

Iqbal, Q., & Aggarwal, J. K. (1999). Using Strcture in Content-based Image Retrieval. In *Proceedings of the IASTED International Conference Signal and Image Processing* (SIP) (pp. 129-133). Nassau, Bahamas.

Iqbal, Q., & Aggarwal, J. K. (1999). Applying perceptual grouping to content-based image retrieval: Building images. In *IEEE Int. Conference on Computer Vision and Pattern Recognition*, 1, 42-48.

Maybank, S. J. (2004). Detection of Image Structures Using the Fisher Information and the Rao Metric. *IEEE Transactions on Pattern Analysis and Machine Intelligence*, 26(12), 1579-1589.

Kar-Han, T., & Ahuja, N. (2001). A representation of image structure and its application to object selection using freehand sketches. In *IEEE International Conference on Computer Vision and Pattern Recognition*, CVPR 2001 (pp. 677-683).

Wardhani, A. W., & Gonzalez, R. (1998). Automatic image structure analysis. In *IEEE International Conference on Multimedia Computing and Systems* (pp. 180-188).

Zhou, X. S., & Huang, T. S. (2001). Edge Based Structural Features for Content-based Image Retrieval. *Pattern Recognition Letters,* 22(5), 457-468.

Intermediate Level Features: SALIENCY

Lowe, D. G. (2004). Distinctive image features from scale-invariant keypoints. *International Journal of Computer Vision*, 60(2), 91-110.

Lowe, D. G. (1999). Object recognition from local scale-invariant features. In *Proc. IEEE Conf. on Computer Vision*, 1150-1157.

Mindru, F., Tuytelaars, T., Van Gool, L., & Moons, T. (2004). Moment invariants for recognition under changing viewpoint and illumination. *Computer Vision and Image Understanding*, 94(1-3), 3-27.

Schmid, C., Mohr, R., & Bauckhage, C. (2000). Evaluation of interest point detectors. *International Journal on Computer Vision*, 37(2):151-172.

Tuytelaars, T., & Van Gool, L. (2004). Matching widely separated views based on affine invariant regions. *International Journal on Computer Vision*, 59(1), 61-85.

Intermediate Level Features: SPATIAL RELATIONSHIPS

Berretti, S., Del Bimbo, A., & Vicario, E. (2003). Weighted Walkthroughs between Extended Entities for Retrieval by Spatial Arrangement. *IEEE Transactions on Multimedia*, 5(1), 52-70.

Chang, S. K. Shi, Q. Y., & Yan, C. W. (1987). Iconic Indexing by 2-D Strings. *IEEE Transactions on Pattern Analysis and Machine Intelligence*, 9(3), 413-427.

Chang, S. K., & Jungert, E. (1991). Pictorial Data Management Based upon the Theory of Symbolic Projections. *Journal of Visual Languages and Computing*, 2(2), 195-215.

Egenhofer, M. J., & Franzosa, R. (1991). Point-Set Topological Spatial Relations. *International Journal of Geographical Information Systems*, 5(2), 161-174.

Frank, A. U. (1992). Qualitative spatial reasoning about Distances and Directions in Geographic Space. *Journal of Visual Languages and Computing*, 3(3), 343-371.

Tao, Y., & Grosky, W. I. (1999). Spatial Color Indexing: A Novel Approach for Content-Based Image Retrieval. In *Proceedings of the IEEE Int. Conf .on Multimedia Computing and Systems*, (ICMCS`99). Firenze: Italy

Gudivada, V. N., & Raghavan, V. V. (1995). Design and Evaluation of Algorithms for Image Retrieval by Spatial Similarity. *ACM Transactions On Information Systems*, 13(2).

Gupta, A., & Jain, R. (1997). Visual Information Retrieval. *Communications of the ACM*, 40(5), 70-79.

Huang, J., Kumar, S. R., Mitra, M., Zhu, W.-J., & Zabih, R. (1997). Image Indexing Using Color Correlograms. In *Proceedings of the IEEE Conference on Computer Vision and Pattern Recognition*, San Juan, Puerto Rico, 762-768.

Lee, S. Y., & Hsu, F. (1992). Spatial Reasoning and Similarity Retrieval of Images using 2D C-strings Knowledge Representation. *Pattern Recognition*, 25(3), 305-318.

Matsakis, P., & Wendling, L. (1999). A new way to represent the relative Position between Areal Objects. *IEEE Transaction on Pattern Analysis and Machine Intelligence*, 21(7), 634-643.

Miyajima, K., & Ralescu, A. (1994). Spatial Organization in 2D Segmented Images: Representation and Recognition of Primitive Spatial Relations. *International Journal of Fuzzy Sets and Systems*, 65, 225-236.

Pass, G., Zabih, R., & Miller, J. (1996). Comparing images using color coherence. *ACM International Multimedia Conference* (pp. 65-73).

Smith, J. R., & Li, C.-S. (1999). Image Classification and Querying Using Composite Region Templates. *Computer Vision and Image Understanding*, 75(1/2), 165-174.

Wang, Y., & Makedon, F. (2003). R-Histogram: Qualitative Representation of Spatial Relations for Similarity-Based Image Retrieval. *ACM Multimedia*, MM'03. Berkeley: CA.

Chapter VI
Content–Based Image Retrieval:
From the Object Detection/Recognition Point of View

Ming Zhang
University of Calgary, Canada

Reda Alhajj
University of Calgary, Canada

ABSTRACT

Content-Based Image Retrieval (CBIR) aims to search images that are perceptually similar to the query-based on visual content of the images without the help of annotations. The current CBIR systems use global features (e.g., color, texture, and shape) as image descriptors, or use features extracted from segmented regions (called region-based descriptors). In the former case, descriptors are not discriminative enough at the object level and are sensitive to object occlusion or background clutter, thus fail to give satisfactory result. In the latter case, the features are sensitive to the image segmentation, which is a difficult task in its own right. In addition, the region-based descriptors are still not invariant to varying imaging conditions. In this chapter, we look at the CBIR from the object detection/recognition point of view and introduce the local feature-based image representation methods recently developed in object detection/recognition area. These local descriptors are highly distinctive and robust to imaging condition change. In addition to image representation, we also introduce the other two key issues of CBIR: similarity measurement for image descriptor comparison and the index structure for similarity search.

1. INTRODUCTION

The explosive growth of digital images in our lives requires efficient image data management systems for image storage and retrieval. The early image retrieval systems are based on manually annotated descriptions and have the following drawbacks (Chang and Hsu, 1992): 1. manually annotating is too expensive for large database; 2. the annotation is subjective and context-dependent. From the early 1990s, **content-based image retrieval (CBIR)** became an active and fast developing research area. Simply speaking, **CBIR** is a method of image retrieval that searches images (from the database) that are similar to the query image based on visual content (by "appearance" according to human perception). More formally, we may define the CBIR as follows:

Definition of content-based image retrieval: Given a large image database U, an image representation method based on image primitives (e.g., pixel intensities) and a dissimilarity measure D(p,q) defined on the image representation, find (using certain index) the M images $p \in U$ with the lowest dissimilarity to the query image q, the resulting M images are ranked by ascending dissimilarity.

According to the above definition, the **CBIR** is query by example. Our definition is narrower than the general case **CBIR** as query by example is the most common form of **CBIR**. Our chapter is based on this definition.

As the ultimate goal of image retrieval system is to find images that the users are interested in and the result images are determined by the content of the query image, the first problem we have to deal with is: Can the query image always express clearly what the users are interested in?

In a traditional database, a query is a formally phrased information request that clearly expresses the user's information needs. Put it in the context of CBIR, the user's information request should be unambiguously determined by the visual content of the query image. If a user is looking for a specific object or the objects that are very similar to a specific object by appearance, for example, his lost dog or the dogs that look very much like his dog, he may use a photo of his dog as the query image. In this case, the photo is better than any words to express clearly the user's interest. However, users who are only interested in a generic category of objects, for instance, "animal", can never be able to express this information need by submitting an image of a specific dog. They will not get satisfactory result by doing so. Some researchers refer to this as the semantic gap problem. To bridge the semantic gap is to make the system generalize semantic concept from a single specific image, which is, in our opinion, impossible, because a high level concept can only be generalized from a large number of instances using machine learning techniques.

In this chapter, we will not consider the semantic gap problem. We assume that the CBIR is used when the users' information need is better expressed by image than by words. Specifically, query by example is preferred when the user is looking for a specific object/scene or a narrow category of objects/scenes that the instances belonging to this category are similar by appearance, in both cases the user's information need cannot be expressed unambiguously by simple words. From this perspective, the content-based image retrieval can be roughly regarded as an object detection/recognition problem. Therefore, we may use some techniques originally developed for object detection/recognition in CBIR system.

In this chapter, we discuss three key issues of the CBIR:

1. Image representation methods;
2. Dissimilarity measurements;
3. Index methods to facilitate the search;

Section 2 mainly introduces the local feature-based image representation originally developed for object detection/recognition, but we believe can be applied to content-based image retrieval. Section 3 gives a brief introduction of the dissimilarity measurements to compare the image descriptors. Section 4 is devoted to the index approaches for similarity search, especially in metric space. Section 5 is the conclusion and possible research directions.

2. IMAGE REPRESENTATION

The early CBIR systems, such as QBIC (Flickner, et al., 1995), Virage, Photobook (Pentland, Picard and Sclaroff, 1994), use global features to represent images. These global features includes: color, texture and shape. Color histogram (Swain and Ballard, 1991) is the standard color representation, which characterizes the color distributions of the pixels. Color coherence vector and color correlogram (Huang, et al., 1997) incorporate spatial information to the histogram. "Color moments" is a compact histogram of the first three color moments (mean, variance and skewness). Texture is the presence of approximately periodically repeated primitive patterns.

Early work in texture feature extraction proposed to use co-occurrence matrices at different distances and orientations. Tamura *et al* (1978) designed, based on the studies of human perception of texture, a set of features, include: *coarseness, contrast, directionality, linelikeness* and *regularity*. Later, the Markov Random Field models were introduced for texture analysis, e.g. the *multi-resolution simultaneous auto-regressive model* (Mao and Jain, 1992). Wavelet transforms (Laine and Fan, 1993) and Gabor filters were applied to generate texture features and achieve good performance for texture images. Shape features are important for non-texture images, early work include the boundary-based Fourier descriptor (Arbter, et al., 1990), finite element models (Sclaroff and Pentland, 1995) and region-based moment invariants (Yang and Algregtsen, 1994). Recently, S. Belongie *et al* (2002) proposed shape context. Shape features can be extracted after the image has been segmented or object contours have been obtained by edge detection.

Researchers realized that global features lose the spatial information and fail to capture the similarity on object-level. The recent CBIR systems use region-based features, which are extracted from segmented image regions. For example, the SIMPLIcity (Wang, et al., 2001) system first segments the image using k-means clustering and then extracts color, texture and shape features from each region. An image is represented by a set of region descriptors. Blobworld (Carson, et al., 1999) system segments the image using the Expectation-Maximization algorithm and the segmented regions (called blobs) are described by color distributions and mean texture descriptors. The system described in (Jing, et al., 2004) segments the images using the JSEG algorithm (Deng and Manjunathl 2001) and uses color moments to describe each region.

The **global features** can not be used in situations of occlusion or background clutter. For example, we can not compute the contour of a partially occluded object. Interest object in different background produces different color histograms. Therefore, these global features can only be used for 2D texture images and fail to get good performance in real-world object-based images. The region-based feature extraction is sensitive to the image segmentation, which is a very difficult task in its own. No ideal image segmentation method exists that can perfectly segment the image into interested objects and background. In addition, the region-based features are still "global" in each region and not invariant to varying imaging conditions.

The recent development in object detection/recognition from the computer vision community sheds light on the image representation methods. Recall that in CBIR, users are interested in the images that are perceptually similar to the query image. The result images are ranked by the similarity. The highest ranked images should be the images of the same object as in the query image (if exist in the database). From this point of view, finding the most desirable image can be regarded as the object detection problem, that is, to decide if the given object (in the database) is the query object. The candidate images may be taken under different imaging conditions: 1. from different viewpoints and at different distance; 2. under different illumination condition; 3. in different background and objects are partially occluded. The only constraint is that the viewpoint difference is not too big to lose all the overlapped part. The global features do not satisfy these requirements. Instead, the state-of-the-art techniques employ local features computed from a small region of the image and describe the property of the supporting region. Each image is represented by a set of sparsely distributed local features (called descriptors). These image descriptors are expected to have the following properties:

1.   Robust: invariant to scale, rotation, view point change and illumination change;
2.   Discriminative: highly informative to distinguish the image;
3.   Efficient: with reasonable computation complexity.

Before deciding what the descriptors are, the locations (called interest points) and support regions of descriptors should be determined. Support region refers to the area on which the descriptor is computed. Section 2.1 introduces the interest point and support region detection. Section 2.2 describes the descriptors.

2.1 Interest Point Detection

Interest points or regions are locations at which the **image descriptors** are to be extracted. There are many interest point detectors proposed in the literature, Schmid *et al* (1998) compared these detectors by proposing a quantitative evaluation measurement: *repeatability*. A good detector has high repeatability. Schmid also indicated that a good interest point should have high information content, which is measured by entropy.

Before introducing the formal definition of *repeatability*, let us look at the basic requirement of a good interest point detector. As we mentioned before, the interest point detector determines the locations of image descriptors. When applied independently to two images of the same object (under different imaging condition), an ideal detector should detect the same set of interest points, i.e., the same set of locations at which image descriptors are to be extracted. Formally, given a 3-D object A, M_1 and M_2 are two images of A from different imaging conditions. When we apply an ideal interest point detector to M_1 and M_2 independently, the interest points detected from M_1 and M_2 should correspond to the same set of physical points on object A. In practice, we can not expect to find an ideal detector. The percentage of overlapped interest points, called *repeatability*, is a good quality indicator of the detectors. The formal definition of **repeatability**, denoted by R, is:

$R_{1,2}=C(M_1,M_2)/\min(n_1,n_2)$

where $C(M_1,M_2)$ is the number of one-to-one correspondence of interest points from M_1 and M_2, n_1 and n_2 are the number of interest points detected in M_1 and M_2, respectively. In practice, an interest point p_1 from M_1 and an interest point p_2 from M_2 have correspondence if they can be back-projected to the same physical point or two physical points with distance below a very small threshold. Obviously, $0\le R_{1,2}\le 1$ and $R_{1,2}=1$ for ideal detector.

Schmid compared the following detectors: Harris (1988), Heitger, Forstner (1994) , Horaud (1990) and Cottier. They were compared under varying imaging conditions: rotation, scale change, viewpoint change and illumination change. It was shown that, under all these conditions, the Harris detector gave the best performance. That is, it has the highest repeatability.

Harris detector finds the corner points--points with large intensity change in all directions. Formally, corner points are the points with local maximal corner strength which is defined based on the *windowed second moment matrix*. Let $I(x,y):R^2\to R$ be an image, the *windowed second moment matrix* of pixel $q(x,y)$ is defined as:

$$\mu_L(q) = E_q \begin{pmatrix} I_x^2 & I_xI_y \\ I_xI_y & I_y^2 \end{pmatrix}$$

where L_x and L_y are, respectively, gradients at q in x and y direction, E_q is an averaging operator to compute the local weighted mean using a symmetric window function (e.g., convolve with a Gaussian function W centered at q).

The corner strength at $q(x,y)$ is defined as:

strength $(q)=\det(\mu_L(q))-k(\text{trace}(\mu_L(q)))^2=\lambda_1\lambda_2-k(\lambda_1+\lambda_2)^2$,

where λ_1, λ_2 are the eigenvalues of the second moment matrix $\mu_L(q)$, and k is a empirically determined constant in the range of 0.04~0.06.

Given an image, we compute Harris corner strength for every pixel. Interest points are the pixels whose strength attain local maximal and above a predefined threshold. Theoretically, Harris detector is invariant to rotation and linear intensity change. However, it is not scale invariant.

The other interest point (region) detectors involve scale space selection;, they will be discussed after the introduction of scale space representation.

2.1.1 Scale Space Representation

Consider the images of the same object or scene taken by different image devices (e.g., cameras) and at different distances (the other conditions remain the same: the same viewpoint and illumination), the way the object/scene appears in the images depends on the resolution of the image devices and the distance at which each image is taken. In short, these images are in different scales. Lindeberg (1994) indicates:

Any real-world image has a limited extent determined by two scales, the outer scale corresponding to the finite size of the image and inner scale given by the resolution; ....The outer scale of an object or a feature may be said to correspond to the (minimum) size of a window that completely contains the object or the feature, while the inner scale may be loosely said to correspond the scale at which substructures of the object or the feature begin to appear."

The image in coarse scale is a blurred (smoothed) copy of the image in fine scale. The blurring suppresses the details, and thus loses the fine structure (feature) in the image. In other words, the features of images only exist over a restricted range of scales (Koenderink, 1984).

As we make no assumption on the imaging conditions in the object detection problem, i.e., we do not have a priori information on what particular features we are looking for, we cannot decide on the right scales (that the desired features exist). Image descriptors computed at inappropriately chosen scales would be highly unstable (Lindeberg, 1998). Therefore, the only solution is to provide a multi-scale representation, treating the image at all resolutions (inner scale) simultaneously. Koenderink (1984) put forward the concept of **scale-space representation**, which is the representation of an image at various resolutions (inner scales). The scale-space representation is created by embedding the original image into a one-parameter family of derived images, with the resolution (inner scale) being the parameter. Let $I(x,y)$ be a 2-D image, the scale-space representation is a 3-D image $L(x,y,\sigma)$ with initial condition $L(x,y,0)=I(x,y)$, where σ is the scale. $L(x,y,\sigma)$ is constructed by convolution of $I(x,y)$ with a smoothing kernel with increasing width σ. Koenderink (Koenderink. 1984) proved that, under a few general constraints, Guassian kernel is the unique choice to generate the scale space. Formally, the scale space of an image $I(x,y)$, denoted by $L(x,y,\sigma)$, is defined by

$$L(x,y,\sigma)=I(x,y)*G(\sigma)$$

where * denotes convolution and $G(\sigma)$ is the two dimensional Guassian kernel with width σ in both dimensions, defined by

$$G(\sigma)= (1/2\pi\sigma)\exp(-(x^2+y^2)/2\sigma)$$

2.1.2 Automatic Scale Selection

Given the scale space representation of an image, we need to determine the location of interest point/region not only spatially, but also in the scale axis. The interest point detectors introduced in section 2.1 only give the spatial location; we still require a mechanism to select the appropriate scale. The basic idea of scale selection is to study the over scale evolution properties of a function and determine the **characteristic scale** at which the function attains local extrema (Lindeberg, 1998). Lindeberg (1998) proposed to use the class of normalized derivatives as the scale selection function. As stated by Lindeberg, the **principle for scale selection** is:

In the absence of other evidence, assume that a scale level, at which some (possibly non-linear) combination of normalized derivatives assumes a local maximum over scales, can be treated as reflecting a characteristic length of a corresponding structure in the data.

The justification for using the normalized derivatives is that they have the scale invariant property:

If the input image is rescaled by a constant scaling factor s, then the scale at which the maximum is assumed will be multiplied by the same factor.

Formally, consider two images $I(x,y)$ and $I'(x', y')$, related by $I(x,y)=I'(sx, sy)$, then the scale space representation of I and I' are:

$$L(x,y,\sigma)=G(\sigma)*I(x,y)$$
$$L'(x',y',\sigma')=G(\sigma')*I(x',y')$$

If we let $\sigma'=s^2\sigma$, we have $L=L'$ and the mth order spatial derivatives of L and L' is related by

$$\partial x^p y^q L(x,y,\sigma)=s^m \partial x'^p y'^q L'(x',y',\sigma')$$

where $m=p+q$. Obviously, when $s>1$, $\partial x^p y^q L(x,y,\sigma)>\partial x'^p y'^q L'(x',y',\sigma')$. That means the amplitude of derivatives decrease with the scale increase (smoothing). In order to compensate for such decrease and make the derivative operators scale invariant, scale normalization is needed.

In particular, the class of derivatives under consideration is the homogeneous polynomial differentials (the sum of orders of differentiation is the same for each term in the polynomial, e.g., $aL_{xx}+bL_{xy}+cL_{yy}$). Let DL and DL' be the homogeneous polynomial differentials of order m at scale σ and σ', respectively, by scale normalization, we have

$$\sigma^{m/2} DL = \sigma'^{m/2} DL'$$

That is, the normalized homogeneous polynomial differentials are scale invariant.

Lindeberg proposed to use the normalized homogeneous polynomial differentials to simultaneously detect the spatial and scale location. That is, to find a location at the scale-space representation that the normalized differential expression simultaneously attains local extremum with respect to both spatial and scale parameters. The exact type of differential expression to be used depends on the type of expected features. Lindeberg described the differential expressions for blob detection, junction detection, edge detection and ridge detection. For example, he proposed to use the *trace* and *determinant* of the normalized Hessian matrix to detect blob like feature.

$$Trace(H_{norm}(L))= \sigma (L_{xx}+L_{yy})$$
$$Det((H_{norm}(L))= \sigma^2(L_{xx}L_{yy}-L_{xy}^2)$$

where

$$H_{norm}(L) = \sigma \begin{pmatrix} L_{xx} & L_{xy} \\ L_{xy} & L_{yy} \end{pmatrix}$$

2.1.3 Scale Invariant Interest Point (Region) Detection

Based on Lindeberg's scale selection principle, Baumberg (2000) introduced **Multi-Scale Harris Detector**, which computes Harris strength (see section 2.1) at all scales and the *n* points with highest strength response over all scales are selected as interest points.

Brown *et al* (2005) used a slightly **modified Multi-Scale Harris Detector**. The basic idea is similar to Baumberg's, the difference lies in the selection process of interest points. Instead of directly selecting the top *n* largest strength, it employed an adaptive non-maximal suppression (ANMS) strategy in the interest point selection process. As we know, the Harris interest points are those whose strength is local maxima in a neighborhood of radius *r* pixels, where *r* is a parameter. The basic idea of ANMS is to adjust the *r* value such that only a fixed number of interest points are retained (e.g., by increasing *r* from 0 monotonically until *n* interest points are obtained).

Mikolajczyk and Schmid (2001) proposed a detector, referred to it as **Harris-Laplace detector**, which is a combination of Harris detector and Laplacian. It first detects candidate points using Harris detector in the scale-space representation of the image. From the candidate points, use the normalized Laplacian-of-Gaussian (the trace of normalized Hessian matrix) to select interest points at characteristic scale. Normalized Laplacian is defined as:

$$Lap(x,y,\sigma) = |\sigma^2(L_{xx}(x,y,\sigma)+L_{yy}(x,y,\sigma))|$$
$$= |\sigma^2(G_{xx}(\sigma)+G_{yy}(\sigma))*I(x,y)|$$

where σ is the scale, L_{xx} and L_{yy} are second order derivatives of scale space image at x and y directions. Formally, the characteristic scale is the scale σ_n at which $Lap(x,y,\sigma_n)>Lap(x,y,\sigma_{n-1})$ and $Lap(x,y,\sigma_n)>Lap(x,y,\sigma_{n+1})$.

They also compared Laplacian with several other functions for scale selection:

1. Square gradient : $\sigma^2(L_x^2(x,y,\sigma)+L_y^2(x,y,\sigma))$
2. Difference-of-Gaussian: $|I(x,y)*G(\sigma_{n-1})- I(x,y)*G(\sigma_n)|$
3. Harris function: $\det(H)- \alpha \, trace^2(H)$ where H is normalized second moment matrix.

It shows that Laplacian produces highest percentage of correct characteristic scale detection. "The selected scale for a point is correct if the ratio between characteristic scales in corresponding points is equal to the scale factor between the images." Formally, suppose A is an image and B is the scaled copy of A with scale factor k, for a given point *a* in A and its corresponding point *b* in B, let S_a be the characteristic scale of *a* in A and S_b be the characteristic scale of *b* in B, the scale selection is correct if $S_b/S_a=k$.

In summary, from the 3-D scale space representation $L(x,y,\sigma)$, the Harris-Laplace detector uses the Harris function to determine the spatial location (x-y coordinates) and the normalized Laplacian function to determine the scale location (the σ coordinate).

Lowe (2004) used **Difference-of-Gaussian (DoG)** to detect interest points (called Key Point in Lowe's SIFT framework, SIFT will be introduced in the image descriptor section) in the scale space. DoG is an approximation to Laplacian-of-Gaussian, but with faster computation. From section 2.2, we know that the scale space representation is a set of increasingly blurred images. Difference-of-Gaussian images are generated from the difference of adjacent blurred images. Interest points (key points) are the local extrema (maxima or minima) of DoG images across scales. A point is a local maximum if it is larger than its 8 neighbors at the same scale and the 9 corresponding neighbors at neighboring scales. Formally, DoG images are defined by:

$$D(x,y,\sigma_n)=G(x,y,\sigma_{n+1})*I(x,y)- G(x,y,\sigma_n)*I(x,y)$$

A point $p(x,y,\sigma_n)$ in the DoG images is a local maximum if for all $i, j, k \in \{-1,0,1\}$

$$p(x,y,\sigma_n)>p(x+i, y+j, \sigma_{n+k})$$

where i, j, and k do not all take 0.

Kadir and Brady (2001) proposed a method to detect interest regions, called **Scale Salient Regions**. The scale salient region detector is invariant to rotation, scaling and intensity shift. Generally speaking, a salient region is a highly informative region that exists in a narrow range of scales.

Recall that a good location for image descriptor should have high information content. From information theory, we know that entropy measures information content. In an image, the amount of information is not determined by the magnitude of intensity value, but by the variation of intensities. A region with constant intensity has little information.

The saliency of a region is defined as a product of two factors: 1. maximal entropy of the intensity histogram of the region over scales; 2. self-dissimilarity of the region at the scale that the entropy is maximized;

Formally, the saliency of the region around a pixel X, denoted by $Y(S_p, X)$, is defined as:

$$Y(S_p, X)=H(S_p,X) \times W(S_p,X)$$

where $H(S_p,X)$ is the entropy of the intensity histogram of the region at scale S_p, and $W(S_p,X)$ is the self-dissimilarity measure of the region at scale S_p.

Here, entropy is defined as:

$$H(S,X)=-\sum P_{d,S} \log_2(P_{d,S})$$

where $P_{d,S}$ is the probability of pixels with intensity d (within the region around X and at scale S). By varying scale S, a set of entropies are obtained. We select the scale that maximizes the entropy, and use that entropy to compute the saliency.

A constant region has peaked intensity histogram (peaked PDF of intensity) and produces low entropy, while a region with high intensity variations has flat histogram and produces high entropy. The entropy is a good indicator of the information contained in the region. The higher the entropy, the more information is in the region. In addition, entropy is invariant to rotation as it is based on the statistical measure only. However, entropy loses all the spatial information and an arbitrary permutation of the pixels produces the same entropy. In other words, entropy is not a discriminative descriptor. The self-dissimilarity measure is used to solve this problem.

The self-dissimilarity measure is defined as:

$$W(S,X)=(S^2/2S-1)\sum |P_{d,S} - P_{d,S-1}|$$

Where $P_{d,S}$ and $P_{d,S-1}$ are the probabilities of pixels with intensity d (within the region around X) at scales S and S-1, respectively. Here, S is the scale that maximizes the entropy. It is shown that small value of W(S,X) indicates stable region over scales (feature that exist over a large range of scales) and large value of W(S,X) suggests the feature that only exists over narrow range of scales, or self-dissimilar over scales.

In summary, a salient region is an over-scale self-dissimilar and highly informative region.

2.1.4 Affine Invariant Region Detection

The image descriptors are extracted from neighborhoods of the interest points, the neighborhood is called support region of the descriptor. Recall that robust image descriptors are expected to be invariant to viewpoint change; therefore, the support region of the potential descriptors should be invariant to viewpoint change. That is, the support regions independently extracted from two images (taken from different viewpoint) of the same object should correspond to the same physical region on the object. In other words, the support region should be adaptive to certain geometric transformation.

The images of the same object from different viewpoints are related by a perspective transformation. Mikolajczyk and Schmid (2004) indicated "a perspective transformation of a smooth surface can be locally approximated by an affine transformation." Since the descriptors are extracted on very small regions (around the interest point), the existing methods described in the literature only deal with the affine transformation (Mikolajczyk, et al., 2006), which is simpler than the general perspective transformation.

Affine transformations preserve parallel lines, but do not preserve angles and length ratios. A general affine transformation is a combination of three types of operations (Baumberg, 2000) : 1. rotation; 2. scale; 3. skew.

Baumberg (2000) introduced an affine-invariant region detector. Mikolajczyk and Schmid (2004) extended their Harris-Laplace detector to an affine invariant **Harris-Affine detector**. A region is affine invariant if it is adaptive to the affine transformation in the sense that the regions independently detected on the two affine-related images (of the same object) correspond to the same physical region on the object. The affine adaptation strategies of the **Harris-Affine detector** and Baumberg's detector are similar. The basic idea comes from Lindeberg and Garding's method (1997). Before describing the affine adaptation, we need to introduce the concept of **affine Gaussian scale space** (Lindeberg and Garding, 1997).

Figure 1.

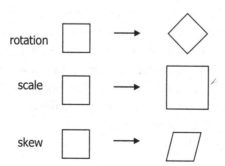

An affine transformation can be represented by a 2×2 invertible matrix.

Recall that the conventional scale space representation introduced in Section 2.2 is generated by convolution with 2-D rotationally symmetric (isotropic) Gaussian kernel. That is, the smooth wide σ is same for all directions. In other words, the degree of smoothing is the same for all directions. However, in affine transformation, shapes are not preserved; for example, a circle region is transformed to an ellipse. The degree of smoothing is not same for all directions. **Affine Gaussian scale space** is the natural generalization of the isotropic scale space. The affine Gaussian scale space of an image I is the convolution of I with a 2-D non-uniform Gaussian kernel, i.e., with different smoothing wide (scale) for the x and y axes. Formally, the non-uniform Gaussian is

$$G(\Sigma_\sigma) = (1/2\pi|\Sigma_\sigma|^{1/2})\exp(-(x, y)^T \Sigma_\sigma^{-1}(x, y)/2)$$

where Σ_σ is the covariance matrix and $|\Sigma_\sigma|$ denotes the determinant of Σ_σ.

The affine scale space of image I(x,y) is defined by

$$L(x,y,\Sigma_\sigma) = I(x,y) * G(\Sigma_\sigma).$$

As we know, Σ_σ is 2×2 matrix with 3 degrees of freedom. The affine scale space representation is a 3-parameter family of derived images.

The affine adaptation is based on the 2×2 windowed second moment matrix (introduced in Section 2.1). For easy understanding, we rewrite it by

$$\mu_L(q) = G(\sigma_t) * \begin{pmatrix} I_x^2(x,y,\sigma_s) & I_x(x,y,\sigma_s)I_y(x,y,\sigma_s) \\ I_x(x,y,\sigma_s)I_y(x,y,\sigma_s) & I_y^2(x,y,\sigma_s) \end{pmatrix}$$

where $I_x(x,y,\sigma_s) = I(x,y) * G_x(\sigma_s)$ and $I_y(x,y,\sigma_s) = I(x,y) * G_y(\sigma_s)$.

The computation of $\mu_L(q)$ involves two scales: σ_t and σ_s. σ_t is the integration scale used to compute the Gaussian weighted mean within a neighborhood of wide σ_t, and σ_s is the local scale used to compute the partial derivatives. When we compute $\mu_L(q)$ in the affine scale space, it becomes

$$\mu_L(q) = G(\Sigma_t) * \begin{pmatrix} I_x^2(x,y,\Sigma_s) & I_x(x,y,\Sigma_s)I_y(x,y,\Sigma_s) \\ I_x(x,y,\Sigma_s)I_y(x,y,\Sigma_s) & I_y^2(x,y,\Sigma_s) \end{pmatrix}$$

The second moment matrix of pixel q(x,y) computed at integration scale Σ_t and local scale Σ_s is denoted by $\mu_L(q, \Sigma_t, \Sigma_s)$.

For an arbitrary affine transformation A, which is a 2×2 invertible matrix, we have the following relationship between the second moment matrix of the pixel q from the original image and the pixel Aq from the A transformed image.

$$\mu_L(q, \Sigma_t, \Sigma_s) = A^T\mu_R(Aq, A\Sigma_t A^T, A\Sigma_s A^T)A$$

where A^T denotes the transpose of A and μ_R is the second moment matrix of pixel Aq computed on the A transformed image.

If we compute the second moment matrix under certain Σ_t, Σ_s such that,

$$\Sigma_t = t \, (\mu_L(q, \Sigma_t, \Sigma_s))^{-1}$$

$$\Sigma_s = s \, (\mu_L(q, \Sigma_t, \Sigma_s))^{-1}$$

then, on the A transformed image we still have these relationship

$$A\Sigma_t A^T = t \, (\mu_R(Aq, A\Sigma_t A^T, A\Sigma_s A^T))^{-1}$$

$$A\Sigma_s A^T = s \, (\mu_R(Aq, A\Sigma_t A^T, A\Sigma_s A^T))^{-1}$$

For simplicity, we use M_L to denote $\mu_L(q, \Sigma_t, \Sigma_s)$ and M_R to denote:

$$\mu_R(Aq, A\Sigma_t A^T, A\Sigma_s A^T).$$

The most important property is as follows: If we transform the original image by $M_L^{-1/2}$ and the A-transformed copy by $M_R^{-1/2}$, then the two resulting images are related by a rotation. This property enables using the components of second moment matrix to express the affine transform A. As the second moment matrix has only 3 degrees of freedom, but the affine transform A has 4 degrees of freedom, we can not uniquely determine affine transform A. A is determined up to a rotation. Formally,

$$A = M_R^{-1/2} R \, M_L^{1/2}$$

where R is an arbitrary rotation. That is, we can determine the affine transform A up to a rotation only from the second moment matrix computed independently on the two images without any a priori knowledge of the affine transform. Thus, the affine adaptation problem reduces to the problem of finding the appropriate scale matrix Σ_t, Σ_s such that

$$\Sigma_t = t \, M_L^{-1}$$

$$\Sigma_s = s \, M_L^{-1}$$

An iterative algorithm is used to find such scale matrix and the second moment matrix.

J. Matas (2004) proposed the concept of affine invariant **Maximally Stable Extremal Region (MSER)**. The definition of MSER is as follows: Given an image, the extremal regions are the connected regions (under 4-neighborhoods) of a thresholded image, which is a binary image with pixels whose intensity above the threshold being white and pixels whose intensity below the threshold being black. The computation process of extremal regions is the same as *watershed algorithm* (Vincent, Soille, 1991). By monotonically increasing thresholds (start from 0 to the highest possible intensity), we obtain a set of nested extremal regions. The black regions are the minimum intensity extremal regions and the white regions the maximum intensity extremal regions. The Maximal Stable Extremal Regions are the extremal regions whose size change rate attains local minimum over varying thresholds.

Kadir *et al* (2004) extended the entropy-based Salient Region detector to an affine invariant detector, called **Affine Salient Region detector**. Other affine-invariant region detector include Tuytelaars's **Edge-based Region Detector** and **Intensity Extrema-based Region Detector** (Tuytelaars and van Gool, 2004); refer to (Mikolajczyk, et al., 2006) for comparison of these affine invariant region detectors.

2.2 Image Descriptors

Image descriptors (or called feature descriptors) are extracted from the interest points or neighborhoods of the interest points. These image descriptors are used to represent the image. The object detection is to establish correspondence between the descriptors from the two images. In ideal scenario (ideal interest point detector and ideal feature descriptors), we can establish one-to-one correspondence between the descriptors from two images of the same object or scene. In other words, if a complete one-to-one correspondence exists between the two set of descriptors, we say an object or scene is detected. The first thing is to define the descriptor according to the basic requirements.

As we make no assumptions on the imaging condition, the descriptors must be invariant to two types of transformation:

1.   Geometric transformation (affine transformation);
2.   Photometric transformation (illumination change).

In the recent comparative study of local descriptors, Mikolajczyk and Schmid (2005) classified the descriptors into three categories:

1.   Distribution-based descriptors;
2.   Spatial-frequency based descriptors;
3.   Differential descriptors.

We can also classify the descriptors into the following three types:

1.   Local geometric descriptor;
2.   Local statistical descriptor;
3.   Local statistical-geometric descriptor;

Generally speaking, the geometric descriptor is more discriminative and the statistical descriptor is more stable (insensitive to noises/outlier pixels). The statistical-geometric descriptor is a combination of the first two and performs best.

Among the requirements of invariance (rotation, scale, skew, illumination), scale invariance is achieved by the scale selection process discussed before, so in the following discussions we'll not talk about the descriptor's scale invariance. Local statistical descriptor is usually rotation invariant if the support region of the descriptor is chosen appropriately. Illumination invariance (we only consider linear illumination change) can be obtained by intensity normalization. Skew invariance is mainly determined by the support region selection method.

2.2.1 Local Geometric Descriptor

Koenderink (1987) proposed to use **Local Jet**, a set of derivatives up to a certain order, to characterize the local geometric structure in the small neighborhood of a point. The Local Jet of order N at a scale space pixel (x,y,σ), denoted by $J^N(x,y,\sigma)$, is defined by

$$J^N(x,y,\sigma)=\{\ L_{i_1...i_n}(x,y,\sigma) \mid n=0,...,N\ ;\ i_k \in \{x,y\}\ \}.$$

As indicated by Koenderink, "the order of the jet determines the amount of geometry represented." For example, the second order local jet detects "line orientation". The third order jet can capture, in addition to "line orientation", the "line curvature". Romeny *et al* (1992)(1993)(1994) studied the differential invariants from the combinations of the local jet components. Schmid and Mohr (1997) used a vector of invariant derivatives from the third order local jet as the descriptor. This descriptor is rotation invariant and highly discriminative.

2.2.2 Local Statistical Descriptor

Geodesic-Intensity-Histogram (Ling and Jacobs. 2005) is the intensity histogram of the pixels on the geodesic level curves around the interest point.

In an image, the intensity value of pixels is regarded as height of the pixels. That is, the image is treated as a surface in 3-D space. The geodesic distance between two pixels p and q is the length of the shortest path from p to q. For a given interest point X in the image, a geodesic level curve of X consists of a set of pixels that have same geodesic distance to X. By varying the geodesic distance, we obtain a set of geodesic level curves. For a given image $I(x,y,z)$, where z is the pixel intensity, weight the third coordinate z with aspect weight α, and weight the first two coordinates x-y with 1-α. When the aspect weight $\alpha \to 1$, the geodesic distance is deformation invariant. The Geodesic-Intensity-Histogram is computed on the weighted image.

The Geodesic-Intensity-Histogram of a given interest point X is generated as follows:

1. Extract geodesic level curves of X at interval δ;
2. Sample points from each level curve at interval δ;
3. Divide the obtained points into K×M bins, where K is the intensity interval and M is the geodesic distance interval. Bin (k,m) contains the number of points falling into the kth intensity interval and m[th] geodesic distance interval;
4. Normalize each set of bins representing the same geodesic distance;
5. Normalize all the bins.

Because of its deformation invariance, the geodesic-intensity-histogram is especially useful to represent non-rigid objects.

Multi-Scale Oriented Patches (Brown, Szeliski and Winder, 2005) is the wavelet coefficients of the intensities of 8×8 sampled points around the interest point. Low frequency sampling is employed to make the descriptor robust to interest point location error.

Intensity-domain spin image (Lazebnik, Schmid and Ponce, 2005) is a 2-dimensional histogram of pixel intensities in the circular neighborhood (the normalized circular region) of the reference point. A bin at (d,i) can be regarded as the number of pixels who are at distance d from the center point and has intensity i. However, the value of each bin is not the exact number of pixels meeting the above condition. The 2-dimensional histogram is a "soft histogram", where each pixel contributes to multiple bins. That is, a pixel with intensity i and at distance d from the center contributes not only to the bin (d,i), but also to the other bins. From the bin's point of view, bin (d,i) receives contributions not only from pixels who are at distance d from the center point and has intensity i, it also receives contributions (with less amount) from other pixels. Suppose a pixel is at location x, its contribution to bin (d,i) is defined by

$$\exp(-(|x-x_0|-d)^2/2\alpha^2-|I(x)-i|^2/2\beta^2)$$

where x_0 is the location of the center point, $I(x)$ is the intensity of x, α and β are two parameters defining the "soft width" of the bins. Obviously, the contribution ranges from 0 to 1.

2.2.3 Statistical-Geometric Descriptor

SIFT (Lowe, 2004) is orientation histograms (each with 8-bin corresponding to 8 directions) in 4×4 sub-regions around the interest point. Therefore, it is a 128 dimensional descriptor. SIFT is computed as follows: First assign a consistent orientation to each interest point based on the dominant orientation of local gradients around the interest point. Compute the gradient magnitude and orientations of 16×16 samples around the interest point. The orientations are rotated relative to the interest point orientation so that they are rotation invariant. The magnitudes are weighted by a Gaussian window such that the samples far away from the interest point are given less weight. Divide the 16×16 samples into 4×4 sub-regions and form one orientation histogram for each sub-region. Each histogram has 8 bins covering 8 directions. The value of each bin is the sum of magnitude of the gradient near the corresponding direction. Finally, the descriptor is normalized to length one to become invariant to linear illumination change. Theoretically, SIFT is not affine invariant. But, it gives very good performance under view point change, possibly due to its high distinctiveness.

Rotation-Invariant Feature Transform (RIFT) (Lazebnik, Schmid and Ponce, 2005) is a 2-dimensional histogram of gradient orientation over a set of equally spaced concentric rings. At each pixel on the rings, orientation is measured relative to the direction pointing outward from the center. Histogram bin (d, θ) is the number of pixels who are on the ring at distance d from the center and with orientation θ. RIFT uses 4 rings and 8 orientations, thus a histogram with 32 bins.

2.3 Image Ranking Based on Local Descriptors

For each image in the database, a collection of local descriptors are extracted at interest points of the characteristic scales. There are two ways to represent the image:

1. Regard the descriptors as the building blocks of the image and each image is represented by a variable-sized set of descriptors (Lowe, 2004);
2. Cluster the descriptors and form an image signature for each image (Rubner, Tomasi and Guibas, 2000). An image signature S is a set of cluster centers associated with corresponding normalized cluster size: $S=\{(m_1,u_1), (m_2, u_2), ..., (m_k,u_k)\}$, where k is the number of clusters, m_i is the center of the cluster i and u_i is the relative weight of the cluster (Lazebnik, Schmid and Ponce, 2005).

For the first type of representation, we find the nearest neighbor for each descriptor of the query image and employ a "voting" strategy by giving a vote to the owner of the nearest descriptor (Lowe, 2004). In the object detection task, this strategy works as the system only needs to check the votes and accepts the images with the votes above a threshold. However, it is more complicated in image retrieval as the system needs to rank the result images instead of answering simple "yes/no" questions. Rank by votes might be an option, but may not reflect the perceptual similarity because the descriptors have different distinctiveness.

For the second type of representation, the image signatures are compared and ranked by Earth Mover's Distance (Rubner, Tomasi and Guibas, 2000). This method was used in (Lazebnik, Schmid and Ponce, 2005) for texture image recognition. Note that recognition is a supervised learning problem which requires a large number of training instances. In image retrieval, the user only provides one or at most a small number of query images. In addition, the image signature is less distinctive than the original descriptors. This method might miss the most similar image.

3. DISSIMILARITY MEASURES

As the aim of CBIR is to find perceptually similar images, the dissimilarity function used to give quantitative measure of difference between two descriptors should be able to match the perceptual difference. For simple color descriptors, we may choose the LUV color space, in which the Euclidean distance between two colors approximately equals the perceived color difference. However, it is no longer a simple case when more complicated descriptors are compared. From section 2, we know that most up-to-date descriptors are histograms of image primitives (instead of image primitives themselves in order to increase robustness). The dissimilarity measure for histogram comparison can be classified into two categories (Rubner, Tomasi and Guibas, 2000):

1. Bin-by-bin measures that only compare the corresponding pair of bins;
2. Cross-bin measures that also compare non-corresponding bins.

Here we will not enumerate all the measures, but mention some representatives. The most commonly used Minkowski-form distance (also called L_p norm) is a bin-by-bin measure: $L_p(X,Y)=(\sum(x_i-y_i)^p)^{1/p}$. When p=2, it is the Euclidean distance. Another bin-by-bin measure is the χ^2 distance defined as
$\chi^2(X,Y)= 1/2\sum(x_i-y_i)^2/(x_i+y_i)$, which is recently used to compare the Geodesic-Intensity-Histogram discussed in the previous section. The main drawback of bin-by-bin measure is their sensitivity to bin size because all features fall into the same bin are consider to be same although they are not so close in case of big bin size, but very close features may fall into two bins (on two side of the bin boundary) and are considered to be different; therefore, slight shift of the bin size would make abrupt change of the descriptor. One solution is to use soft histogram (Lazebnik, Schmid and Ponce, 2005; Lowe, 2004), in which each feature contributes to multiple bins weighted based on its distance to central value of each bin. On the other hand, the cross-bin measures, although do not have the boundary problem, have their own demerits. For example, the quadratic-form distance (Niblack, et al., 1993) may overestimate the mutual similarity and produce false positives in retrieval results.

The above mentioned dissimilarity measures are applicable in comparing single feature vectors. As we mentioned in the pervious section, an image could be represented by an image signature, which is a set of weighted feature vectors, the following dissimilarity measures are used to compare image signatures.

Rubner *et al* (2000) proposed the Earth Mover's Distance (EMD), which can compare image signatures of different sizes and is claimed to better match the perceptual similarity. Simply speaking, the EMD between two signatures is the minimal cost to transform one into another. Mathematically, computing EMD is a linear programming problem. It is based on the solution of the transportation problem (Hitchcock, 1941), and needs to resort to the simplex method (Hillier and Liberman. 1990). IRM (Integrated Region Matching) (Li, Wang and Wiederhold, 2000) is another dissimilarity measure to compare image signatures. The IRM distance between two images is the weighted sum of individual region distances. A "soft matching" scheme is employed for individual region matching, i.e., a region feature in one image can match multiple region features in another image. The weight (called significance credit) to calculate the IRM distance is determined following the "most similar highest priority" principle: most similar regions are given highest weight. IRM is claimed to have similar performance as EMD in reflecting the perceptual similarity of images and is faster to compute. The Hausdorff distance (from image A to image B) is defined to be the maximum of the matching distances of the region feature vectors in image A to the region feature vectors in image B, where, for a feature vector x in image A, the matching distance of x is the distance from x to the closest feature vector in image B. The symmetrized Hausdorff distance is used to compare image signatures in (Ko and Byun, 2002).

4. INDEX FOR SIMILARITY SEARCH

From Section 2, we know that each local descriptor is a high dimensional vector. The search process can be regarded as similarity search (in particular, the k-nearest neighbor search) of the query image descriptor under certain dissimilarity (distance) measure as discussed in Section 3. Similarity search includes two types of queries:

1. Range query: Given a query point q and range r, find all the data points $p \in S$ (S is the data set) that satisfy D(p,q)<r, where D(p, q) gives the distance between p and q;
2. K-nearest neighbor query: given a query point q, find the k nearest points to q;

Although in CBIR systems, usually we are interested in nearest neighbor search only, we will discuss these two types of queries because in some indexes, the nearest neighbor query is transformed to range query in the query processing. **K-nearest neighbor search** can be regarded as a dynamic range query with r being constantly updated by the distance to the current k^{th} nearest neighbor.

The distance measurements can be classified into two categories: metric and non-metric. If a metric measurement is employed, we called the search space a metric space. A metric space is a pair (S, D), where S is a data space, D is a distance metric defined on S. D has the following properties:

1. $\forall x \in S, \ D(x,x) = 0$;
2. $\forall x, y \in S, \ D(x,y) = D(y,x) \geq 0$;
3. $\forall x, y, z \in S, \ D(x,y) + D(y,z) \geq D(x,z)$;

The third property is called the metric triangle inequality.

In real applications, the image database is large with huge amount of data residing on the disks. In addition, as the local image descriptors are high dimensional (tens to hundreds dimensions), sometimes the computation of similarity measure is expensive, (e.g., computation of EMD). Therefore, linear search is not acceptable and an index is needed to facilitate the search. In this section, we will introduce the index structures or other related techniques for the following two objectives in similarity search:

1. Reduce the number of disk accesses;
2. Reduce the number of expensive distance computations.

Indexing high-dimensional space for similarity search has been an active area for long time. In Section 4.1 and Section 4.2, we will give an overview of the two types of index structures: tree index and hash index, respectively, for similarity search. The tree indexes can give exact k-nearest neighbors; hash indexes only produce approximate result but more efficiently in high-dimensional space. In Section 4.3, we will describe the techniques for saving distance computations.

4.1 Tree Index for Similarity Search

The tree indexes for similarity search aim at partitioning the data set/space into many parts with each part being contained in one node, such that, for any given query, the query result can be produced by searching a small number of nodes. Specifically, the tree indexes are constructed (when use full data set/space) as follows: recursively partition the data set/space into many parts based on certain criteria, each node corresponds to one part and is associated with a concise data summary of the data points in this part. Given a query point, the search starts from the root and the concise data summary is used to decide whether a path needs to be followed for further search. In other words, the data summary is used to prune the search space. If the tree is dynamic with data points being inserted gradually, the data point is inserted to the appropriate node such that the good property of data summary is maintained.

The **tree indexes** can be classified into two types based on the partitioning objective:

1. **Space-based partitioning:** Partition the data space using coordinate planes. Thus, each partition is a hyper-rectangle. Some early work such as K-D tree (Bentley, 1975), K-D-B-tree (Robinson, 1981), grid-file (Nievergelt, Hinterberger and Sevcik, 1984) are space partitioning methods. The obtained partitions are disjoint. The main disadvantages of the space partitioning methods are: (1) The total number of partitions is exponential in the number of dimensions, so the query hyper-sphere may intersect a huge number of partitions; (2) Some of the partitions may contain very few points or even empty; for disk-based index, one partition is stored in one disk page, the page storage utilization is very low.
2. **Data-based partitioning:** Partition the data set based on the distribution of the data points. Data-based partitioning methods overcome the above demerits. Many data-based partitioning methods can be found in the literature. We can classify them into two categories:
    a. Convex Description Index (Shaft and Ramakrishnan, 2005);
    b. Distance-based Index.

The difference between them lies on the data summary associated with each node. In Convex Description Index, the data summary is a convex bounding region covering all the data points in this partition.

In Distance-based Index, the data is evenly partitioned based on the distance to a reference point; the data summary of each partition is the cutting values on both sides. The data summary is the key element as we will show that it determines the way of data set partitioning and the query search process.

4.1.1 Convex Description Index

A convex description index structure has the following properties (Shaft and Ramakrishnan. 2005):

a.   Data points are divided into partitions (redundancy is permitted);
b.   Each partition is associated with a convex bounding region covering all the data points in this partition.
c.   The parameters of the convex bounding region are used to decide whether the partition is fetched for further search.
d.   If a partition is fetched, all the data points in the partition are searched.

In the search process, only the partitions whose convex bounding regions are intersecting the query hyper-sphere need to be fetched for further search. Therefore, a tree index with compact bounding regions that have small overlapping (or ideally, disjoint) will give better performance because small disjoint bounding regions have less chances to intersect the query sphere. The index tree designers always try to reduce size of the bounding regions and the overlaps between them so as to improve the search efficiency.

Most existing tree indexes for similarity search belong to this category; they differ in the partitioning strategy and the definition of the bounding region (e.g., shape and size of the region).

R-tree (Guttman, 1984) and its variants (R*-tree (Beckmann, et al., 1990), X-tree (Berchtold, Keim and Kriegel, 1996), SS-tree (White and Jain, 1996), SR-tree (Katamaya and Satoh, 1997)) were initially designed for searching spatial objects (i.e., objects of non-zero size). They can be used to index high-dimensional point data. However, they only perform well in low dimensional space. For example, R-tree is found to degenerate for dimensions higher than 7, and the performance of X-tree degenerates to sequential scan for dimensions higher than 20 (Berchtold, Keim and Kriegel, 1996).

To the best of our knowledge, M-tree (Ciaccia, Patella, and Zezula, 1997) is the first dynamic index tree for similarity search in high-dimensional metric space. M-tree uses hyper-sphere as minimum bounding region in each node. For similarity query, search starts from the root and along all the paths that intersect the query hyper-sphere. M-tree uses the triangle inequality to prune the search space and save distance computations. It uses a priority queue to keep all the active sub-trees (i.e., the sub-trees that are not pruned by the triangle inequality). The search order of these active sub-trees is based on the distance from the query point to the possible closest point in the sub-tree. Earlier work like Gh-tree (Uhlmann, 1991) and GNAT (Geometric Near-Neighbor Access Tree) (Brin, 1995) can be regarded as the static version of M-tree.

Slim-tree (Traina, et al., 2000) is an improved version of M-tree with reduced overlapping of MBRs (Minimum Bounding Regions) by (1) using minimal spanning tree in node splitting; (2) using a slim-down post-processing to diminish the number of data points in the overlapped regions. DBM-tree (Vieira, et al., 2004) further reduces the overlapping by relaxing the height-balancing property. It does not partition the data set into same-sized parts. The denser region has larger number of data points. Therefore, the tree height is larger in denser regions.

The Telescopic-Vector Tree (TV-tree) (Lin, Jagadish and Faloutsos, 1994) is a Convex Description Index with dynamic-dimensional Minimum Bounding Region: dimension of the MBR is determined by the data points it encloses. For example, in n dimensional space, for a MBR A, if all the data points in A agree on k (k≤n) dimensions, these k dimensions are called inactive and the rest n-k dimension are active, and A can be specified as a n-k dimension MBR. Obviously, lower dimensional MBR causes less chances of overlap between the MBRs. However, the downside is that it is not straightforward to determine if two MBRs with different dimensions intersect. Unfortunately, this is the frequent operation in the searching process.

Δ+-tree (Cui, Ooi, Su and Tan, 2005) first transform the data points into PCA-space and partitions the data set by clustering. At each level, only a subset of the dimensions (the principal components) is used in data clustering. However, using less number of dimensions for partitioning sacrifices the pruning rate because the distance shrinks in lower dimensional space.

4.1.2 Distance Based Index

The Distance Based Indexes have the following property: they partition the data set based on distances to selected reference points. Data points with similar distances are grouped together in the same node and the lower&upper bounds of the distances work as the data summary (for the node), which is used, in the query processing, to determine whether the node is fetched for further search.

The early work on distance based index includes VP-tree (Vantage-point tree)(Uhlmann, 1991) and its variants MVP-tree (Bozkaya and Ozsoyoglu, 1997). VP-tree is a height-balanced tree. The tree construction is top-down using the full data set. It selects one data point as reference point and computes its distances to the other data points. Based on the distances, the data set is divided into equal-sized partitions. The partitioning strategy is applied recursively and finally a hierarchical disjoint partition is obtained. In the query searching process, a depth-first search is performed and the triangle inequality (of metric space) is used to prune the search space—specifically, at each level, the search space is confined to a subset of consecutive nodes. The original VP-tree (Uhlmann, 1991) selects the reference points randomly. P. Yianilos (1993) proposed to use sampling techniques to select reference point. MVP-tree (Bozkaya and Ozsoyoglu, 1997) uses multiple reference points in each node and stores the distances from each data point to the reference points along the path from root to the leaf node that contains it. These pre-computed distances are used to avoid unnecessary distance computation. Therefore, in the leaf node, it does not need to compute the distance from every data points to query point. The original VP-tree and MVP-tree are both static, no insert operations were introduced. A.W.-C. Fu, *et al* (2000) proposed the insert and delete operations for the VP-tree, turning it into a dynamic structure.

Recently, two distance based indexes, called Omni-family (Filho, Traina, Traina, and Faloutsos, 2001) and iDistance (Jagadish, el al., 2005), were proposed for similarity search in high dimensional space. Both of them are based on the well know B$^+$-tree. Omni-family (Filho, Traina, Traina, and Faloutsos, 2001) selects k reference points, where k is determined by the intrinsic dimension (the fractal dimension (Pagel, korn and Faloutsos, 2000) of the data set. For each data point, it computes its distances to all the references points and use these distances (called omni-coordinates) to represent the data point. For each reference point, it builds a B$^+$-tree with the key being the distances from the data points to this reference. So there are k B$^+$-trees for k reference points. Given a range query (q, r), for each reference point f_i, the candidate points fall into a range [dist(f_i, q)-r, dist(f_i,q)+r]. It computes the intersection M of the candidate points with respect to all the reference points. Finally, it searches M to get the result. For nearest neighbor query, it uses an estimated initial search range r, and successively corrects it until the desired nearest neighbors are obtained. The iDistance method (Jagadish, el al., 2005) first partitions the data set by k-means clustering and then computes the distance from each data point to their respective reference point (the cluster centroid). It maps all the data points into a real line based on their cluster number and distance to the reference point. Since all the data points are on one-dimensional line, B⁺-tree is employed to index the data. For a nearest neighbor query, the search starts with an estimated initial search range and gradually increases the search range until obtaining desired number of nearest neighbors. For nearest neighbor search in both of Omni-family and iDistance, it is not easy to decide on the initial search range and the following adjustment value. For different query points, the distances to their nearest neighbors vary significantly, it is very hard (if not impossible) to determine an initial range and adjustment value that work efficiently for all the queries.

4.2 Hash Index: Locality Sensitive Hashing for ε-Approximate Nearest Neighbor Search

When searching one dimensional space, hash index performs better than tree index as the former needs O(1) steps and the latter needs O(log N) steps by binary search. The Locality Sensitive Hash (LSH) (Indyk and Motwani, 1998) (Gionis, Indyk, and Motwani, 1999) (Datar, et al., 2004) is a hash index scheme for nearest neighbor search in high-dimensional space.

LSH does not guarantee to find exact nearest neighbor, instead it aims to find ε-approximate nearest neighbor with high probability. Given a query point q, an ε-approximate nearest neighbor of q is a data point within distance (1+ε)r from q, where r is the distance from q to its exact nearest neighbor. In CBIR systems, usually the database is huge and system response time is a crucial factor. In some cases, quick response is more important than accuracy and it is worth sacrificing certain accuracy in exchange for efficiency. LSH is claimed to be much faster than the tree indexes that aims at finding exact nearest neighbors.

Generally speaking, LSH is to hash the data points by several hash functions such that for each function, the probability of collision of close points is much high than the probability of collision of far apart points. Thus, closer points are more likely to be in the same bucket.

Definition of Locality Sensitive Hashing in a domain S with distance measure D:

A hash function family $H=\{h: S \rightarrow U\}$ is called (r_1, r_2, p_1, p_2) sensitive for D if for any $v, q \in S$
If $D(q,v) \leq r_1$ then $Pr(h(q) = h(v)) \geq p_1$;
If $D(q,v) > r_2$ then $Pr(h(p) = h(v)) \leq p_2$,
where $p_1 > p_2, r_1 < r_2$.

The earlier work on LSH (Indyk and Motwani, 1998) (Gionis, Indyk and Motwani, 1999) only work in Hamming space with distance defined by l_1 norm. The recent work (Datar, et al., 2004) extends LSH to work in l_p space, where p≤2, by using p-stable distributions to construct the hash functions.

Definition of p-Stable distribution:

A distribution D over R is called p-stable if there exists $p \geq 0$ such that for any n real numbers $v_1 \ldots v_n$ and i.i.d. variables $X_1 \ldots X_n$ with distribution D, the random variable $\sum v_i X_i$ has the same distribution as the variable $(\sum |v_i|^p)^{1/p} X$, where X is a random variable with distribution D.

A Gaussian (normal) distribution is 2-stable.

Given a d-dimensional data space, generate a random d-dimensional vector $\alpha = (\alpha_1, \ldots, \alpha_d)$, where each dimension α_i is chosen independently from a p-stable distribution. Let v be a d-dimensional vector, the inner product $\alpha \cdot v = \sum \alpha_i v_i$ is a random variable with distribution as $\|v\|_p X = (\sum |v_i|^p)^{1/p} X$, where X is random variable with p-stable distribution.

Each hash function in the family H is defined as:

$$h(v) = \lfloor (\alpha \cdot v + b)/w \rfloor$$

where w is a constant, α is chosen as above and b is a real number chosen uniformly from [0, w]. It is equivalent to map the multi-dimensional data points to a line and divide the line into slots of equal length w. The slots are numbered from left to right and h(v) gives the number of slot that v falls in.

Given two data points v_1 and v_2, the distance $\alpha \cdot v_1 - \alpha \cdot v_2$ is distributed as $\|v_1 - v_2\|_p X$. Thus, if the hash function is drawn uniformly at random from the hash family, the probability of collision $\Pr(h(v_1) = h(v_2))$ decreases monotonically with $\|v_1 - v_2\|_p$.

The LSH index is constructed as follows:

1. Define a function family $G = \{g: S \rightarrow U^M\}$, for $v \in S$, $g(v) = (h_1(v), h_2(v), \ldots h_M(v))$ where $h_i \in H$.
2. Choose L functions $g_1, \ldots, g_L$ independently and uniformly at random from G to construct L hash tables (i.e., each function for one hash table)
3. For each data point v, put v into the bucket pointed to by $g_i(v)$ in the ith hash table, for $1 \leq i \leq L$. That is, each data point is in L hash tables.

M and L are two parameters closely related to the performance.

Given a query point q, fetch the buckets pointed by $g_i(q)$, for $1 \leq i \leq L$. Search all the points in these L buckets to find the nearest neighbor. Note that, in one hash table, for two far apart points v_1 and v_2, $\Pr(h_i(v_1) = h_i(v_2)) \leq p_2$, thus $\Pr(g(v_1) = g(v_2)) \leq p_2^M$. That is, the collision probability decreases greatly for far apart points. However, the collision probability of close points is also reduced. That is the reason to use multiple hash tables.

The Locality Sensitive Hashing scheme introduced above (referred to as basic LSH in the following description) only searches one bucket in each hash table, thus needs a large number of hash tables to obtain good result. Q. Lv, *et al* (2007) proposed to probe multiple buckets (i.e. the bucket pointed by the hash value and its nearby buckets) in each hash table, these buckets are visited in the order of descending probability of containing query result. This method can reduce the number of hash tables by an order of magnitude and maintains same search quality.

Given a query point q, the basic LSH only visits bucket $g(q) = (h_1(q), h_2(q), \ldots h_M(q))$. The proposed method also visits buckets $g(q) + \delta$, where $\delta = (\delta_1, \delta_2, \ldots \delta_M)$, $\delta_i \in \{-1, 0, 1\}$. Two probing orders are proposed:

1. **Step-wise probing:** A bucket g(q)+δ is a called a n-step bucket of g(p) if n coordinates of δ are non-zero. The step-wise probing method visits all n-step buckets before the (n+1)-step buckets.

2. **Query-directed probing:** The buckets g(q)+δ are sorted based on descending probability that it contains the nearest neighbor. Search is started from the bucket with highest probability until a pre-defined number of points are fetched.

4.3 Techniques for Saving Distance Computations

As we indicated earlier, the number of disk accesses and distance computations determine the performance of similarity search. In some cases, the distance computation is very expensive (e.g. the Earth Mover's Distance (Rubner, Tomasi and Guibas, 2000)) and dominates the cost of search. The index schemes discussed in the previous sections mainly deal with the issue of disk access. In this section, we introduce some techniques for saving distance computations. They can be used alone or combined with the tree indexes.

4.3.1 Saving Distance Computations for Range Query

J. Venkateswaran, et al (2006) proposed a method for range query (q,r) in metric space, where q is the query point and r is the range.

1. Select a number of reference points, denoted by v_i;
2. For each data point, compute its distance to all the reference points;
3. Given a query point q, compute its distance to all the reference points and divide the data points s into three categories (w.r.t this q) based on lower bound and upper bound defined as follows:
   a. Lower bound: $\max(D(q, v_i) - D(s, v_i))$
   b. Upper bound: $\min(D(q, v_i) + D(s, v_i))$
   If r < lower bound, s can be pruned because (by triangular inequality of metric)
   $$r < \max(D(q,v_i) - D(s,v_i)) \leq D(q,s).$$
   If r > upper bound, s must be in the result because
   $$r > \min(D(q,v_i) + D(s,v_i)) \geq D(q,s).$$
   If lower bound < r < upper bound, add s to the candidate set.
4. Search the candidate set to filter out the false positives.

Note that in this method, the distances between data points to the reference points are computed off-line, when q is coming, we only compute the distance between q and the points in the candidate set plus the distance between q and the reference points.

Earlier than (Venkateswaran, et al., 2006), similar technique was used in the MVP-tree (Bozkaya and Ozsoyoglu, 1997). The difference is that MVP-tree only tests the lower bound to prune data points without identifying (by testing upper bound) the data points that are guaranteed to be in the result.

4.3.2 Multi-Step Algorithm to Save Distance Computation for k-Nearest Neighbor Search

In the case that, for the given expensive distance measure D, if an easily-computable lower-bound distance measure D_L is available, we can use multi-step method for **k-nearest neighbor** search (Korn, et al., 1996). A lower-bound distance measure D_L of D has the following property: for any data points x,y, $D_L(x,y) \leq D(x,y)$.

The multi-step algorithm consists of two stages:

1. A filtering stage that produces a candidate set using D_L;
2. A refinement stage that refines the candidate set using D to give the final result.

All the data points that can not be in the answer set are dropped in the filtering stage. Therefore, the computation of the expensive D is only performed for the candidate set.

The algorithm proposed in (Korn, et al., 1996) is as follows:

Given query q and the number k
1. Find the k-nearest neighbor under D_L, denote the result set by R_L; For all the points $p \in R_L$, determine $d_{max} = max\{D(p,q)\}$.
2. Perform a range query (q, d_{max}) under D_L, the result is the candidate set; Sort the points in the candidate set under D and report the top k points;

The k-nearest neighbor and range query under D_L can be performed using any desirable index defined for D_L, the expensive distance measure D is confined to the candidate set.

(Korn, et al. 1996) only proved that there are no false drops in the filtering stage. In other words, it only guarantees that the filtered points do not belong to the k-nearest neighbor set. However, this algorithm does not guarantee the optimality of the candidate set. That is, some points in the candidate set are unnecessary in the sense that they can be removed based on the information under D_L.

T. Seidl and H.P. Kriegel (1998) proposed an optimal algorithm that prevent unnecessary point from entering the candidate set. Specifically, the algorithm is optimal in the sense that only the data points whose distance under D_L not larger than the distance (under D) of the exact k^{th} nearest neighbor will be added into the candidate set in the filtering stage. In other words, all the points in the candidate set are necessary based on the information under D_L.

The optimal algorithm is as follows:

Given a query q and the number k
1. Assume there is an *index* that can incrementally gives nearest neighbor under D_L; Let S be a sorted list *<point, distance>* to contain candidate points and their distance to q, where *distance* is the sort key; initially S is empty, and $d_{max} = \infty$.
2. **while** p=*index*.getnext and $D_L(p, q) \leq d_{max}$ **do**
3.   **if** $D(p,q) \leq d_{max}$ **then** S.insert(p, D(p,q))
4.   **if** S.length$\geq$k **then** $d_{max} = S[k].distance$
5.   remove all entries from S whose *distance*$>d_{max}$
6. **endwhile**
7. report all entries from S where *distance*$\leq d_{max}$

The performance of this algorithm depends on the availability of a lower bound distance measure that can closely approximate the real distance measure. Recently, Assent, *et al* (2006) proposed some lower bounding distance measures for the Earth Mover's distance.

Seidl's algorithm outputs the answer (at line 7) after all the search stops, Kriegel *et al* (2007) proposed to deliver the result to the user earlier by using an additional upper bound distance measure. However, to find an easily computable close upper bound measure is a difficult task in its own.

5. CONCLUSION

In this chapter, we discussed **CBIR** from the object detection/recognition point of view. The most common form of CBIR, "query by example", can be roughly regarded as an object detection/recognition problem. Therefore, the local feature based image representation methods developed for object detection/recognition are applicable in CBIR. However, not all of them can be used directly without any modification.

6. FUTURE RESEARCH DIRECTIONS

There are differences between CBIR and object detection/recognition. Strictly speaking, object detection and object recognition are two different problems. The former aims to detect a specific object and require highly distinctive descriptors, whereas the latter tries to recognize a category of objects, thus uses less distinctive descriptors (to accommodate intra-class variations) and requires a large number of training instances for learning. On the contrary, the objective of CBIR (query by example) is to return ranked images perceptually similar to the query image. In other words, it tries to find a category of images using one or very few query images, and requires exact match be given highest rank. It can be regarded as a combination of object detection and recognition but without a learning process. Therefore, we need to design or modify the local descriptors to keep an adequate balance between distinctiveness and flexibility (to deal with intra-class variation). Or we may use less distinctive descriptors, which are usually easy to compute, and devise a "clever" ranking method. As the existing tree index structures do not give satisfactory performance in very high dimensional space (e.g., over 100 dimensions) and the faster LSH index only work under certain distance measures, developing efficient index for similarity search in high dimensional space is also promising research direction, especially for non-metric space.

REFERENCE

Assent, I., Wenning, A., and Seidl, T., (2006). Approximation techniques for indexing the earth mover's distance in multimedia databases. In Proc. of IEEE ICDE.

Arbter, K., et al. (1990). Application of affine-invariant Fourier descriptors to recognition of 3D objects. IEEE PAMI, 12, 640-647.

Baumberg, A. (2000). Reliable feature matching across widely separated views. CVPR, pp.774-781.

Beckmann, N., et al. (1990). The R*-tree : An efficient and robust access method for points and rectangles. Proc. of ACM SIGMOD.

Belongie, S., Malik, J., & Puzicha, J. (2002). Shape matching and object recognition using shape contexts. *IEEE PAMI 24*(24), 509-522.

Bentley, J.L. (1975). Multi-dimensional binary search tree used for associative searching. *Communications of ACM, 18*(9), 509-517.

Berchtold, S., Keim, D., & Kriegel, H.P. (1996). The X-tree: An index structure for high-dimensional data. Proc. of VLDB.

Bozkaya, T., & Ozsoyoglu, M. (1997). Distance-based indexing for high-dimensional metric spaces. *ACM SIGMOD*, 357-368.

Brin, S. (1995). Near neighbor search in large metric spaces. *VLDB*, 574-584.

Brown, M., Szeliski, R., & Winder, S. (2005). Multi-image matching using multi-scale oriented patches. *CVPR*, 510-517.

Carson, C., et al. (1999). Blobworld : A system for region-based image indexing and retrieval. Proc. of International Conference on Visual Information Systems.

Chang, S.K., & Hsu, A. (1992). Image information systems: Where do we go from here? *IEEE Trans. on Knowledge and Data Engineering, 5*(5), 431-442.

Ciaccia, P., Patella, M. & Zezula, P. (1997). M-Tree: An efficient access method for similarity search in metric spaces. *VLDB Journal*, 426-435.

Cui, B., Ooi, B.C., Su, J., & Tan, T. (2005). Indexing high-dimensional data for efficient in-memory similarity search. *IEEE Trans. on Knowledge and Data Engineering, 17*(3), 339-353.

Datar, M., et al. (2004). Locality-sensitive hashing scheme-based on P-Stable distributions. *ACM SoCG.*

Deng, Y., Manjunath, B.S. (2001). Unsupervised segmentation of color-texture regions in images and video. *IEEE Trans. PAMI, 23*(8), 800-810.

Filho, R.F.S., Traina, A.J.M., Traina, C., & Faloutsos, C. (2001). Similarity search without tears: The OMNI family of all-purpose access ,ethods. *ICDE*, 623-630, 2001.

Flickner, M., et al. (1995). Query by image and video content : The QBIC system. *IEEE Computer, 28*(9), 23-32.

Florack, L.M.J., et al. (1993). Cartesian differential invariants in scale-space. J. mathematical imaging and vision, 3, 327-348.

Florack, L.M.J., et al. (1994). General intensity transformation and differential invariants. *J. Mathematical Imaging and Vision, 4*(2), 171-187.

Forstner, W. (1994). A framework for low level feature extraction. *ECCV*, 383-394.

Fu, A.W.-C., et al. (2000). Dynamic VP-tree indexing for N-Nearest search given pair-wise distances. *VLDB Journal.*

Gionis, A., Indyk, P.,Motwani, R. (1999). Similarity search in high dimensions via hashing. Proc. of VLDB.

Guttman, A. (1984). R-Trees: A dynamic index structure for spatial searching. Proc. of ACM SIG-MOD.

Harris, C., & Stephens, M. (1988) A combined corner and edge detector. In Alvey Vision Conference.

Hitchcock, F.L. (1941). The distribution of a product from several sources to numerous locations. *J. Math. Phys.,* 20, 224-230.

Hillier, F.S., & Liberman, G.J. (1990). Introduction to mathematical programming. McGraw-Hill.

Horaud, R., Skordas, T., & Veillon, F.. (1990). Finding geometric and relational structures in an image. *ECCV,* 374-384.

Huang, J., et al. (1997). Image indexing using color correlogram. *CVPR,* 762-768.

Indyk, P., & Motwani, R. (1998). Approximate nearest neighbors: Towards removing the curse of dimensionality. *Proc. of ACM STOC.*

Jagadish, H.V., el al. (2005). iDistance: An adaptive B+-tree based indexing method for nearest neighbor search. *ACM Trans. Database Syst., 30*(2), 364-397.

Jing, F., *et al.* (2004). An efficient and effective region-based image retrieval framework. *IEEE Transactions on Image Processing, 13*(5), 699-709.

Kadir, T., & Brady, M. (2001), Saliency, scale, and image description. *IJCV 45*(2), 83-105.

Kadir, T., Zisserman, A., & Brady, M. (2004). An affine invariant salient region detector. *ECCV,* 1, 228-241.

Katamaya, N., & Satoh, S. (1997). The SR-tree: An index structure for high-dimensional nearest neighbor queries. *Proc. of ACM SIGMOD.*

Ko, B., & Byun, H. (2002). Integrated region-based image retrieval using region's spatial relationships. *EEE ICPR.*

Koenderink, J.J. (1984). The Structure of images. *Biological Cybernetics*, 50, 363-370.

Koenderink, J.J., & van Doorn, A.J. (1987) Representation of local geometry in the visual system. *Biological Cybernetics, 55*, 367-375.

Korn, F. *et al.* (1996). Fast nearest neighbor search in medical image databases. *VLDB,* 215-226.

Kriegel, H.P., *et al.* (2007). Optimal multi-step K-Nearest neighbor search. In Proc. of the International Symposium on Spatial and Temporal Databases.

Laine, A., & Fan, J. (1993). Texture classification by wavelet packet signatures. *IEEE Trans. PAMI, 15*(11), 1186-1191.

Lazebnik, S., Schmid, C., & Ponce, Jean. (2005). A sparse texture representation using local affine regions. *IEEE PAMI, 27*(8).

Li, J., Wang, J.Z., & Wiederhold, G. (2000). Irm: Integrated region matching for image retrieval. *ACM Multimedia.*

Lin, K., Jagadish, H.V., & Faloutsos, C. (1994). The TV-tree: An idex structure for high-dimensional data. *VLDV Journal, 3*, 517-542.

Ling, H., & Jacobs, D.W. (2005). Deformation invariant image matching. *ICCV.*

Lindeberg, T. (1994). Scale-space theory: A basis tool for analyzing structures at different scales. *Journal of Applied Statistics, 21*(2), 225-270.

Lindeberg, T., & Garding, J. (1997). Shape-adapted smoothing in estimation of 3-d shape cues from affine distortions of local 2-D brightness structure. *Image and Vision Computing, 15*(6), 415-434.

Lindeberg, T. (1998). Feature detection with automatic scale selection. *IJCV, 26*(3), 79-116.

Lowe, D.G. (2004). Distinctive image features from scale invariant features. *IJCV, 60*(2), 91-110.

Lv, Q., et al. (2007). Multi-probe LSH: Efficient indexing for high-dimensional similarity Search. *Proc. of VLDB.*

Mao, J., & Jain, A.K. (1992). Texture classification and segmentation using multiresolution simultaneous autoregression models. *Pattern Recognition, 25*(2), 173-188.

Matas, J., Chum, O., Urban, M., & Pajdla, T. (2004). Robust wide-baseline stereo from maximally stable external regions. *Image and Vision Computing, 22*, 761-767.

Mikolajczyk, K., & Schmid, C. (2001). Indexing based on scale invariant interest points. *ICCV.*

Mikolajczyk, K., & Schmid, C. (2004). Scale & affine invariant point detectors. *IJCV 60*(1), 63-86.

Mikolajczyk, K., & Schmid, C. (2005). A performance evaluation of local descriptors. *IEEE PAMI, 27*(10), 1615-1630.

Mikolajczyk, K., et al. (2006). A comparison of affine region detectors. *IJCV.*

Niblack, W., *et al.* (1993). Querying images by content, using color, texture, and shape. SPIE Conference on Storage and Retrieval for Image and Video Databases.

Nievergelt, J., Hinterberger, H., Sevcik, K.C.. (1984). The grid file: An adaptable, symmetric multikey file structure. ACM Trans. *Database Syst. 9*(1).

Pagel, B.-U., Korn, F., & Faloutsos, C. (2000). Deflating the dimensionality curse using multiple fractal dimensions. *Proc. of IEEE ICDE*, 589-598.

Pentland, A., Picard, A., & Sclaroff, S. (1994). Photobook: Tools for content-based manipulation of image databases. In *Proc. of SPIE.*

Robinson, J.T. (1981). The K-D-B tree: A search structure for large multi-dimensional dynamic indexes. *Proc. of ACM SIGMOD*, 10-18.

Rubner, Y., Tomasi, C. & Guibas, L. (2000). The earth mover's distance as a metric for image retrieval. *IJCV, 40*(2), 99-121.

Salden, A.H., et al. (1992). A complete and irreducible set of local orthogonally invariant features of 2-dimensional images. *ICPR*, 180-184.

Schmid, C., & Mohr, R. (1997) Local grayvalue invariants for image retrieval. *IEEE PAMI, 19*(5), 530-535.

Schmid, C., Mohr, R., & Bauskhage, C. (1998). Comparing and evaluating interest points. *ICCV*, 230-235.

Sclaroff, S., & Pentland, A. (1995). Modal matching for correspondence and recognition. *IEEE PAMI, 17*(6), 545-561.

Seidl, T., & Kriegel, H.P. (1998). Optimal multistep K-Nearest neighbor search. *SIGMOD*.

Shaft, U., & Ramakrishnan, R. (2005). When is nearest neighbors indexable? *ICDT*, 158-172.

Swain, M., & Ballard, D. (1991). Color indexing. *IJCV, 7*(1), 11-32.

Tamura, H., et al. (1978). Texture features corresponding to visual perception. IEEE Trans. on Systems, Man, and Cybernetics.

Traina, C., et al. (2000). Slim-Trees: High performance metric trees minimizing overlap between nodes. *EDBT*, 51-65.

Tuytelaars, T., & van Gool, L. (2004). Matching widely separated views based on affine invariant regions. *IJCV, 59*(1), 61-85.

Uhlmann, J.K. (1991). Satisfying general proximity/similarity queries with metric trees. *Information Processing Letters, 40,* 175-179.

Venkateswaran, J. et al. (2006). Reference-based indexing of sequences databases. *VLDB*.

Vieira, M.R., et al. (2004). DBM-Tree : A dynamic metric access method sensitive to local density data. In *SBBD*, 163-177.

Vincent, L., & Soille, P. (1991). Watershed in digital spaces : an efficient algorithm based on immersion simulations. *IEEE PAMI, 13*(6), 583-598.

Wang, J., et al. (2001). Simplicity: Semantics-sensitive integrated matching for picture libraries. IEEE Trans. *PAMI, 23*(9), 947-963.

White, D.A., & Jain, R. (1996). Similarity indexing with the ss-tree. Proc. of IEEE ICDE.

Yang, L., & Algregtsen, F. (1994). Fast computation of invariant geometric moments: A new method giving correct results. Proc. IEEE Int. Conf. on Image Processing.

Yianilos, P. (1993) Data structures and algorithms for nearest neighbor search in general metric spaces. Proceedings of the third annual ACM-SIAM symposium on Discrete Algorithms, 311-321.

ADDITIONAL READING

Bach, J., *et al.* (1996). Virage image search engine: an open framework for image management. In Proc. of SPIE.

Pass, G., & Zabith, R. (1996). Histogram refinement for content-based image retrieval. IEEE workshop on application of computer vision, 96-102.

Chen, C.C., & Chen, C.C. (1999). Filtering methods for texture discrimination. *Pattern Recognition Letters, 20*(8).

Natsev, A., Rastogi, R., & Shim, K. (2004). WALUS: A similarity retrieval algorithm for image databases. *IEEE Transactions on Knowledge and Data Engineering, 16*(3), 301-316.

Witkin, A.P. (1983). Scale-space filtering. Int. Joint Conf. of AI, 1019-1022.

Chapter VII
Making Image Retrieval and Classification More Accurate Using Time Series and Learned Constraints

Chotirat "Ann" Ratanamahatana
Chulalongkorn University, Thailand

Eamonn Keogh
University of California, Riverside, USA

Vit Niennattrakul
Chulalongkorn University, Thailand

ABSTRACT

After the generation of multimedia data turning digital, an explosion of interest in their data storage, retrieval, and processing, has drastically increased in the database and data mining community. This includes videos, images, and handwriting, where we now have higher expectations in exploiting these data at hand. We argue however, that much of this work's narrow focus on efficiency and scalability has come at the cost of usability and effectiveness. Typical manipulations are in some forms of video/image processing, which require fairly large amounts for storage and are computationally intensive. In this work, we will demonstrate how these multimedia data can be reduced to a more compact form, that is, time series representation, while preserving the features of interest, and can then be efficiently exploited in Content-Based Image Retrieval. We also introduce a general framework that learns a distance measure with arbitrary constraints on the warping path of the Dynamic Time Warping calculation. We demonstrate utilities of our approach on both classification and query retrieval tasks for time series and other types of multimedia data including images, video frames, and handwriting archives. In addition, we show that incorporating this framework into the relevance feedback system, a query refinement can be used to further improve the precision/recall by a wide margin.

1 INTRODUCTION

Much of the world's data is in the form of time series, and many other types of data, such as video, image, and handwriting, can also be trivially transformed into time series. Generally, we can use various image processing techniques (Deselaers, Keysers, & Ney, 2003; Käster, Wendt, & Sagerer, 2003; Krishnamachari & Abdel-Mottaleb, 1999; Wang, Yang, & Acharya, 1997; Yeung & Liu, 1995) to complete multimedia data mining tasks, by measuring similarities among the raw images, using certain features such as color, texture, or shape. However, time series representation of these data can significantly help speed up the process since they can be compared much easier and faster using distance measurements. This fact has fueled enormous interest in time series retrieval in the database and data mining community. We argue, however, that much of this work's narrow focus on efficiency and scalability has come at the cost of usability and effectiveness. For example, the lion's share of previous work has utilized the Euclidean distance metric, presumably because it is very amenable to indexing (Agrawal, Lin, Sawhney, & Shim, 1995; Chan, Fu, & Yu, 2003; Faloutsos, Ranganathan, & Manolopoulos, 1994). However, there is increasing evidence that the Euclidean metric's sensitivity to small differences in the time axis makes it unsuitable for most real world problems (Aach & Church, 2001; Bar-Joseph, Gerber, Gifford, Jaakkola, & Simon, 2002; Diez & González, 2000; Kadous, 1999; Schmill, Oates, & Cohen, 1999).

It has long been known that Dynamic Time Warping (DTW) is superior to Euclidean distance for classification and clustering of time series. However, until lately, most research has utilized Euclidean distance because it is more efficiently calculated. A recently introduced technique that greatly mitigates DTW demanding CPU time has sparked a flurry of research activities. However, the technique and its many extensions still only allow DTW to be applied to moderately large datasets. In addition, almost all of the research on DTW has focused exclusively on speeding up its calculation; there has been relatively little work done on approving its accuracy.

In this work, we target the accuracy aspect of correct classification and introduce a new framework that learns arbitrary constraints on the warping path of the DTW calculation. Apart from improving the accuracy of content-based image retrieval, our technique as a side effect speeds up DTW by many orders of magnitude as well. We show the utility of our approach on datasets from diverse domains and demonstrate significant gains in accuracy and efficiency. Moreover, some additional training or human intervention can also be further incorporated into the classic information retrieval technique of relevance feedback to achieve even much superior results.

1.1 The Ubiquity of Time Series Data

In this section, we wish to expand the readers' appreciation for the ubiquity of time series data. Rather than simply list the traditional application domains, i.e., stock market, weather data, electrocardiograms, etc., we will consider some less obvious applications of multimedia/image data that can benefit from efficient and effective retrieval.

Video retrieval: Video retrieval is one of the most important issues in multimedia database management systems. Generally, research on content-based video retrieval represents the content of the video as a set of image frames, leaving out the temporal features of frames in the shot. However, for some domains, including motion capture editing, gait analysis, and video surveillance, it may be fruitful to extract time series from the video, and index *just* the time series (with pointers back to the original video). Figure 1 shows an example of a video sequence that is transformed into a time series. There are

Figure 1. Stills from a video sequence; the right hand from each image frame is tracked, and converted into a time series

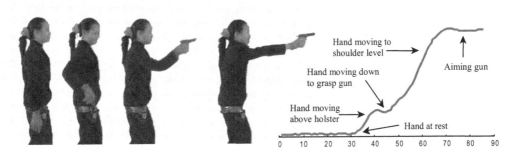

several reasons why using the time series representation may be better than working with the original data. One obvious point is the massive reduction in dimensionality, enhancing the ease of storage, transmission, analysis, and indexing; it is also much easier to make the time series representation invariant to distortions in the data, e.g., time scaling and time warping.

Image retrieval: Image Retrieval has become increasingly crucial in our information-based community. Large and distributed collections of scientific, artistic, technical, and commercial images have become more prevalent, thus requiring more sophisticated and precise methods for users to perform similarity- or semantic-based queries. For some specialized domains, it can be useful to convert the images into "pseudo time series". For example, consider Figure 2, where an image of a leaf is converted into a time series by observing the local angle measurement of its perimeter's trace.

Note that there are many other ways to convert shapes to time series. For example, Figure 3 shows a 'centroid' method (Keogh, Wei, Xi, Lee, & Vlachos, 2006) where a distance from every point on the shape profile to the center is measured and recorded as a time series.

The utility of such a transform is similar to that for video retrieval. In particular, for indexing of natural images, such as leaves, human faces, or insect wings, we can more easily handle the natural variability of living creatures in the time domain with dynamic time warping (Gandi, 2002) (which is

Figure 2. Many image indexing/classification/clustering problems can be solved more effectively and efficiently after converting the image into a "pseudo time series"

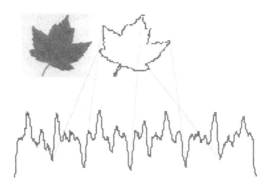

Figure 3. An image can be transformed into time series by recording the distance from every point on the shape profile to the image's center.

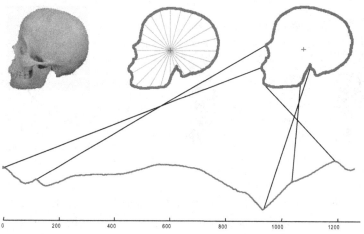

discussed in detail in upcoming sections). Working in the time domain also makes scale, offset, and rotation invariance trivial to handle.

Handwriting retrieval: While the recognition of *online* handwriting (Jain & Namboodiri, 2003) may be largely regarded as a solved problem, the problem of transcribing and indexing existing historical archives remains a challenge. The usefulness of such ability is obvious. For even such a major historical figure as Isaac Newton, there exists a body of unpublished, handwritten work exceeding one million words. For other historical figures, there are even larger collections of handwritten text. Such collections are potential goldmines for researchers/biographers.

The problem of indexing historical archives is difficult, because unlike the online handwriting problem, there is no pen-acceleration information. In addition, the archives may be degraded and stained. Finally, while humans learn to adapt their handwriting to make online handwriting recognition easier (i.e., "Graffiti" for Palm Pilots), archival handwriting is often highly stylized and written only with the intent of being legible to the writer. For example, Figure 4 A) shows an example of text written by George Washington, which is all but illegible to modern readers with little experience with cursive writing. Many off-line handwritten document image-processing algorithms have recently been proposed in the

Figure 4. A) An example of handwritten text by George Washington. B) A zoom-in on the word "Alexandria," which has been processed to remove slant. Many techniques exist to convert 2-D handwriting into a time series, e.g., the projection profile shown in C) and the upper and lower word profiles shown in D) (figure created by R. Manmatha)

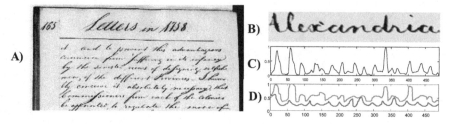

interest of word recognition and indexing (Kavallieratou, Dromazou, Fakotakis, & Kokkinakis, 2003; Tomai, Zhang, & Govindaraju, 2002; Weliwitage, Harvey, & Jennings, 2003), mostly without associating with problem with time series. While handwriting is not a time series, there exist several techniques to convert handwriting to (one or more) time series; many of these transformations were pioneered by Manmatha and students (Rath & Manmatha, 2003). Recent work suggests that this representation may still allow the high precision in indexing historical archives while simplifying the problem from 2-dimentional to 1-dimentional domain (Rath & Manmatha, 2003).

1.2 Existing Work on Time Series Retrieval

The explosion of interest in time series indexing in the last decade has been extraordinary, with well over a thousand papers devoted to the subject (Keogh & Kasetty, 2003). However, the vast majority of the work has focused on the Euclidean distance, which assumes that the ith point on the query time series maps onto the ith point in the candidate match. However, recent work has demonstrated that this similarity model generally does not work well for many real-world problems. The problem is that even very similar time series often demonstrate some variability in the time axis. As a concrete example, the actor shown in Figure 1 might attempt to repeat the action, but fumble slightly when retrieving the gun from the holster. These would lead to two time series having the same overall patterns, in which the local patterns may not align perfectly. The problem of distortion in the time axis can be addressed by Dynamic Time Warping (DTW), a distance measure that has long been known to the speech processing community (Kruskall & Liberman, 1983; Myers, Rabiner, & Rosenberg, 1980; Sakoe & Chiba, 1978). This method allows for non-linear alignments between the two time series to accommodate sequences that are similar but out of phase. The superiority of DTW over Euclidean distance for classification/ clustering and indexing has been demonstrated by several authors on a diverse set of domains, including bioinformatics, music retrieval, handwritten document archives, biometrics, chemical engineering, industry, and robotics (Aach & Church, 2001; Bar-Joseph et al., 2002; Caiani et al., 1998). Our approach takes this recent work on DTW as its starting point. In particular, DTW is currently viewed as a "one-size-fits-all" algorithm, which is applied to diverse domains in a black box fashion. We note, however, that we may be able to fine-tune the algorithm, for a particular domain, and even a particular query, by selectively limiting the amount of warping we allow along various parts of the query. As we will demonstrate, by selectively limiting the amount of warping allowed (learning from training data), we can actually improve the accuracy of DTW, and as an important side effect, we can drastically improve the indexing performance. Before formally introducing our technique, we must review the basic DTW algorithm in some detail.

2 BACKGROUND

The measurement of similarity between two time series is an important subroutine in many data mining applications, including rule discovery (Das, Lin, Mannila, Renganathan, & Smyth, 1998), clustering (Aach & Church, 2001; Deselaers et al., 2003), anomaly detection (Dasgupta & Forrest, 1996), motif discovery (Dasgupta & Forrest, 1996), and classification (Diez & González, 2000; Kadous, 1999). The superiority of DTW over Euclidean distance for these tasks has been demonstrated by many authors (Aach & Church, 2001; Bar-Joseph et al., 2002; Caiani et al., 1998; Keogh & Pazzani, 2000; Yi, Jagadish,

& Faloutsos, 1998); nevertheless, DTW is less familiar to the data mining community. We will therefore begin with overview of DTW and its recent extensions.

2.1 Review of DTW

Suppose we have two time series, a sequence Q of length n, and a sequence C of length m, where:

$$Q = q_1, q_2, \ldots, q_i, \ldots, q_n \tag{1}$$

$$C = c_1, c_2, \ldots, c_j, \ldots, c_m \tag{2}$$

To align these two sequences using DTW, we construct an n-by-m matrix where the (i^{th}, j^{th}) element of the matrix corresponds to the squared distance, $d(q_i, c_j) = (q_i - c_j)^2$, which is the alignment between points q_i and c_j. To find the best match between these two sequences, we can find a path through the matrix that minimizes the total cumulative distance between them, as illustrated in Figure 5. A warping path, W, is a contiguous set of matrix elements that characterizes a mapping between Q and C. The kth element of W is defined as $w_k = (i,j)_k$. So, we have:

$$W = w_1, w_2, \ldots, w_k, \ldots, w_K \; ; \; \max(m,n) \leq K < m + n - 1 \tag{3}$$

By definition, the optimal path W_o is the path that minimizes the warping cost:

$$DTW(Q,C) = \min_{\forall w \in P} \left\{ \sqrt{\sum_{k=1}^{K} d_{w_k}} \right\} \tag{4}$$

where P is a set of all possible warping paths, and K is the length of the warping path. This path can be found using dynamic programming to evaluate the following recurrence which defines the cumulative distance $\gamma(i,j)$ as the distance $d(i,j)$ found in the current cell and the minimum of the cumulative distances of the adjacent elements:

$$\gamma(i,j) = d(q_i, c_j) + \min\{ \gamma(i-1, j-1), \gamma(i-1, j), \gamma(i, j-1) \} \tag{5}$$

In practice, we do not evaluate all possible warping paths, since many of them correspond to pathological warpings (for example, a single point on one ECG mapping to an entire heartbeat in another ECG). Instead, we consider the following constraints that decrease the number of paths considered during the matching process. This reduction in the number of paths considered also has the desirable side effect of speeding up the calculations, although only by a (small) constant factor.

Boundary conditions: The path must start in $w_1 = (1,1)$ and end in $w_K = (m,n)$, that is, the warping path has to start at the bottom left and end at the top right of the matrix.

Continuity condition: Every point in the query and candidate sequences must be used in the warping path, and both i and j indexes can only increase by 0 or 1 on each step along the path. In other words, if we take a point (i, j) from the matrix, the previous point must have been $(i-1, j-1)$, $(i-1, j)$, or $(i, j-1)$.

*Figure 5. A) Two sequences **Q** and **C** which are similar, but out of phase. B) To align the sequences, we construct a warping matrix, and search for the optimal warping path, shown with solid squares. Note that the "corners" of the matrix (shown in dark gray) are excluded from the search path as part of an adjustment window condition. C) The resulting alignment*

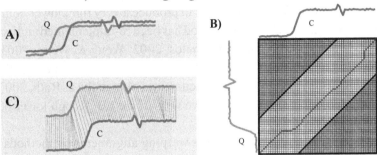

Monotonic condition: Given $w_k = (a,b)$ then $w_k-1 = (a',b')$ where $a-a' \geq 0$ and $b-b' \geq 0$. The warping path cannot go backward in time; both i and j indices either stay the same or increase. They can never decrease.

Slope constraint condition: The path should not be too steep or too shallow. This prevents very short subsequences to match very long ones. The condition is expressed as a ratio a/b, where b is the number of steps in the x direction and a is the number in the y direction. After b steps in x, it must make a step in y, and vice versa.

Adjustment window condition: An intuitive alignment path is unlikely to drift very far from the diagonal. The distance that the path is allowed to wander is limited to a window (or "band") of size r, directly above and to the right of the diagonal.

By applying these conditions, we can restrict the moves that can be made from any point in the path and therefore reduce the number of paths that need to be considered. Figure 5 B) illustrates a particular example of the last condition with the Sakoe-Chiba Band (Sakoe & Chiba, 1978). Since a good path is unlikely to wander very far from the diagonal, the distance that the path is allowed to wander is within the window of size r, above and to the right of the diagonal. As we will see in Section 4, it is this type of constraint that we will exploit to improve DTW.

The Euclidean distance between two sequences can be seen as a special case of DTW where k^{th} element of W is constrained such that $w_k = (i,j)_k$, $i = j = k$. Note that it is only defined in the special case where the two sequences have the same length. The time and space complexity of DTW is $O(nm)$. However, the constraints above mitigate this only by a constant factor.

This review of DTW is necessarily brief; we refer the interested reader to (Kruskall & Liberman, 1983; Rabiner & Juang, 1993; Ratanamahatana & Keogh, 2005) for more details.

2.2 Related Work

While there has been much work on indexing time series under the Euclidean metric over the past decade (Chan et al., 2003; Faloutsos et al., 1994; Keogh, Chakrabarti, Pazzani, & Mehrotra, 2001a, 2001b; Yi & Faloutsos, 2000), there has been much less progress on indexing under DTW. Additionally, all of the work on DTW has focused exclusively on speeding up DTW; it does not appear that researchers have considered the possibility of making DTW more accurate.

Keogh (Keogh, 2002) introduced a novel technique for exact indexing of DTW using global constraints and Piecewise Constant Approximation (Keogh et al., 2001a). The proposed lower bounding measure, *LB_Keogh*, exploits the global constraints to produce a very tight lower bound that prunes off numerous expensive DTW computations. The method has been re-implemented and extended by several other research groups (Vlachos, Kollios, & Gunopulos, 2002; Wong & Wong, 2003; Zhu & Shasha, 2003), and is now the basis of a successful "query-by-humming" system (Zhu, Shasha, & Zhao, 2003) and a system for indexing historical handwriting documents (Manmatha & Rath, 2003). Because of the power and widespread adoption of this approach, we will utilize LB_Keogh lower bounding function as a starting point for this work.

We note there has been some work on obtaining warping alignments by methods other than DTW (Bar-Joseph et al., 2002; Kwong, He, & Man, 1996). For example, Kwong et al. consider a genetic algorithm based approach (Kwong et al., 1996), and recent work by Bar-Joseph et al. considers a technique based on linear transformations of spline-based approximations (Bar-Joseph et al., 2002). However, both methods are stochastic and require multiple runs (possibly with parameter changes) to achieve an acceptable alignment. In addition, both methods are clearly non-indexable. Nevertheless, both works do reiterate the superiority of warping over non-warping for pattern matching.

Moreover, there has been relatively little work on relevance feedback for both time series and multimedia retrieval. However, relevance feedback in text-mining community has been the subject of much research since the 1970's (Attar & Fraenkel, 1977; Rickman, 1972; Rocchio, 1971) and still is an active area of research. It is only in recent years that the researchers started to expand relevance feedback into time series (Keogh & Pazzani, 1999), image (Wu & Manjunath, 2001), and multimedia (Yang & Kuo, 2000) retrieval domains. Before addressing the relevance feedback system with DTW, we first review the lower bounding measures and introduce our representation, the *R-K Band*, which will be used for the DTW distance measure in the classification task and relevance feedback.

3 LOWER BOUNDING THE DTW DISTANCE

In this section, we explain the importance of lower bounding and briefly review the LB_Keogh lower bounding distance measure (Keogh, 2002).

3.1 The Utility of Lower Bounding Measures

Time series similarity search under the Euclidean metric is heavily I/O bound; however, similarity search under DTW is also very demanding in terms of CPU time. One way to address this problem is to use a fast lower bounding function to help prune sequences that could not possibly be the best match (see (Keogh, 2002) for full algorithm detail).

There are only two desirable properties of a lower bounding measure:

- It must be fast to compute. Clearly, a measure that takes as long to compute as the original measure is of little use. In our case, we would like the time complexity to be at most linear in the length of the sequences.

- It must be a relatively tight lower bound. A function can achieve a trivial lower bound by always returning zero as the lower bound estimate. However, in order for the algorithm to be effective, we require a method that more tightly approximates the true DTW distance.

While lower bounding functions for string edit, graph edit, and tree edit distance have been studied extensively (Kruskall & Liberman, 1983), there has been far less work on DTW, which is very similar in spirit to its discrete cousins. We will review global constraints, which can be exploited to produce tight lower bounds.

3.2 Existing Lower Bounding Measures

As previously noted, virtually all practitioners using DTW constrain the warping path in a global sense by limiting how far it may stray from the diagonal (Berndt & Clifford, 1994; Chu, Keogh, Hart, & Pazzani, 2002; Gollmer & Posten, 1996; Itakura, 1975; Keogh & Pazzani, 2000; Myers et al., 1980; Sakoe & Chiba, 1978; Tappert & Das, 1978). The subset of matrix that the warping path is allowed to visit is called a warping window or a band. Figure 6 illustrates two of the most frequently used global constraints in the literature, the Sakoe-Chiba Band (Sakoe & Chiba, 1978) and the Itakura Parallelogram (Itakura, 1975).

In addition to helping to speed up the DTW distance calculation, the warping window prevents a pathological warping, where a relatively small section of one sequence maps onto a relatively large section of another. The importance of global constraints was documented by the originators of the DTW algorithm, Sakoe and Chiba, who were exclusively interested in aligning speech patterns (Sakoe & Chiba, 1978). However, it has been empirically confirmed in many other settings, including music (Hu, Dannenberg, & Tzanetakis, 2003; Zhu et al., 2003), finance (Berndt & Clifford, 1994), medicine (Gollmer & Posten, 1996), biometrics (Gavrila & Davis, 1995; Munich & Perona, 1999), chemistry (Gollmer & Posten, 1996), and robotics (Schmill et al., 1999).

As mentioned earlier, a lower bounding distance measure, LB_Keogh, has been introduced for the task of indexing DTW. This lower bounding technique uses the warping window, e.g., Sakoe-Chiba Band or Itakura Parallelogram, to create a bounding envelope above and below the query sequence. Then the squared sum of the distances from every part of the candidate sequence not falling within the bounding envelope, to the nearest orthogonal edge of the bounding envelope, is returned as its lower

Figure 6. Global constraints limit the scope of the warping path, restricting them to the gray areas. The two most common constraints in the literature are the Sakoe-Chiba Band and the Itakura Parallelogram

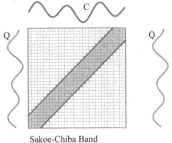
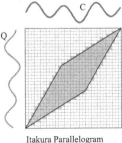

Sakoe-Chiba Band   Itakura Parallelogram

*Figure 7: The Sakoe-Chiba Band A) can be used to create an envelope B) around a query sequence **Q**. The Euclidean distance between any candidate sequence C and the closest external part of the envelope C) is a lower bound for the DTW distance.*

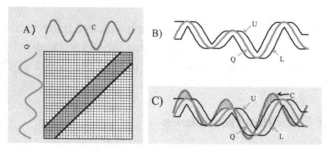

bound. The technique is illustrated in Figure 7. This lower bound can prune off numerous number of expensive DTW computations, using the simple algorithm described in (Keogh, 2002).

4 THE R-K BAND

The 'Adjustment Window Condition' of DTW has been almost universally applied to DTW, primarily to prevent unreasonable warping and to speed up its computation. However, surprisingly little research has looked at discovering the best shape and size of the window. Most practitioners simply use one of the well-known bands, e.g. Sakoe-Chiba Band (Sakoe & Chiba, 1978) or Itakura Parallelogram (Itakura, 1975), proposed in the context of speech recognition several decades ago. In addition, there is a widespread (and as we shall see, unwarranted) belief that having wider bands improves accuracy, and having narrower bands decreases accuracy. The use of smaller-size band is seen as a compromise made to make the algorithm tractable. This belief has been proved to be false by our extensive experiments on wide variety of datasets; surprisingly, the accuracies often peak at smaller-size window, and degrade or become stable for wider window sizes (Keogh & Ratanamahatana, 2005). In any case, the optimal size is typically smaller than 10%, the classic number most researchers normally have been using in DTW researches (Sakoe & Chiba, 1978). The motivation for our work has sparked from this discovery; we find that in general, the effect of the window size on accuracy is very substantial, and is strongly domain dependent. If the width of the band can greatly affect accuracy, then the *shape* of the band could also have similarly large effects. Our ideal solution would be to find an optimal band (both shape and size) for a given problem that will potentially increase the accuracy. We will first introduce the representation, the *Ratanamahatana-Keogh Band* (*R-K Band*) (Ratanamahatana & Keogh, 2004), which allows arbitrary shaped constraints.

4.1 A General Model of Global Constraints

We can represent any warping window as a vector R:

$$R_i = d; 0 \leq d \leq m, 1 \leq i \leq m \tag{6}$$

where R_i is the height above the diagonal in the y direction, as well as the width to the right of the diagonal in the x direction. Note that $|R| = m$, and the above definition forces R to be symmetric, i.e., the constraint above the diagonal is the mirror image of the one below the diagonal.

To represent a Sakoe-Chiba Band of overall width of 11 (width 5 strictly above and to the right of the diagonal) with the definition:

$$R_i = \begin{cases} 5 & ;1 \leq i \leq m-5 \\ m-i & ;m-5 < i \leq m \end{cases} \tag{7}$$

or an Itakura Parallelogram with the definition:

$$R_i = \begin{cases} \left\lfloor \frac{2}{3}i \right\rfloor & ;1 \leq i \leq \left\lfloor \frac{3}{8}m \right\rfloor \\ \left\lfloor \frac{3}{8}m \right\rfloor - \left\lfloor \frac{2}{5}i \right\rfloor & ;\left\lfloor \frac{3}{8}m \right\rfloor < i \leq m \end{cases} \tag{8}$$

The classic Euclidean distance can also be defined in terms of $R_i = 0$; $1 \leq i \leq m$; only the diagonal path is allowed. More generally, we can define any arbitrary constraint with a suitable vector R. Figure 8 illustrates some examples of *R-K Bands*.

An interesting and useful property of our representation is that it also includes the ubiquitous Euclidean distance and classic DTW as special cases. We also can exploit the *R-K Bands* for both classification and indexing (query retrieval) problems, depending on the task at hand. In particular,

- For classification, we can use a different *R-K Band* for each class; we denote the band learned for the cth class, as the *R-K$_c$ Band*.
- For indexing (query by content), we can use *one R-K Band* that maximizes the tradeoff between efficiency and precision/recall.

With *R-K Band*, we can easily represent any arbitrary warping windows. However, we are left with the question of how to *discover* the optimal *R-K Band* for the task at hand. In some cases, it maybe is possible to manually construct the bands, based on domain knowledge. For example, a cardiologist may

Figure 8. We can use R to create arbitrary global constraints. A) Note that the width of the band may increase or decrease. We can also use R to specify all existing global constraints, e.g., B) Sakoe-Chiba Band and C) Itakura Parallelogram

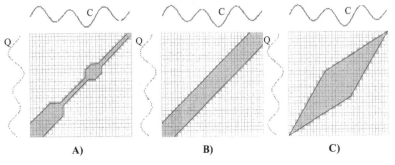

know from experience that the Romano-Ward syndrome may manifest itself with high variability in the length of one part of the heartbeat (the QT-wave), but little variability in the other section of a heartbeat (the UP-wave) (Viskin, 2000). We could explicitly attempt to encode this insight into an *R-K Band* for retrieving instances of the disease, by allowing R_i to be large where variability is expected. Unfortunately, our preliminary attempts to manually construct *R-K Bands* met with limited success, even for simple toy problems. Furthermore, since the number of possible *R-K Bands* is exponential, exhaustive search over all possibilities is clearly not an option. In the following sections, however, we will show how we can *learn* the high-quality bands automatically from data with the help of AI techniques.

4.2 Learning Multiple R-K$_c$ Bands for Classification

While it is generally not possible to handcraft accurate *R-K Bands*, it *is* possible to pose the problem as a search problem, and utilize classic search techniques from the artificial intelligence community. However, the higher the number of classes, the more the time complexity, we have to search through such a large space.

Since determining the optimal *R-K Bands* for each training set is highly computationally intensive, a hill climbing and heuristic functions have been introduced to guide which part of space should be evaluated. A space is defined as a segment of a band to be increased or decreased. In the original work, two heuristic functions, accuracy metric and distance metric, are used to evaluate a state. The accuracy metric is evaluated from the training accuracy using leave-one-out 1-NN, and the distance metric is a ratio of the mean DTW distances of correctly classified and incorrectly classified objects. However, these heuristic functions do not reflect the true quality of a band because empirically, we have found that the resulting bands tend to 'overfit' the training data.

Two searching directions are considered, i.e., forward searching, and backward searching. In forward search, we start from the Euclidean distance (all R_i equal to 0), and parts of the band are gradually

*Figure 9. An illustration of the concept in **R-K Band** forward searching algorithm. (Ratanamahatana & Keogh, 2004)*

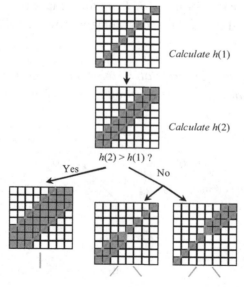

Table 1. The pseudo code for multiple R-K Bands learning

Function [*band*] = learning(*T*, *threshold*)	
1	N = size of T;
2	L = length of data in T;
3	initialize *band*$_i$ for $i = 1$ to c;
4	**foreachclass** $i = 1$ to c
5	enqueue(1, L, *Queue*$_i$);
6	**endfor**
7	*best_evaluate* = evaluate(*T*, *band*);
8	**while** !empty(*Queue*)
9	**foreachclass** $i = 1$ to c
10	**if** !empty(*Queue*$_i$)
11	[*start*, *end*] = dequeue(*Queue*$_i$)
12	*adjustable* = adjust(*band*$_i$, *start*, *end*);
13	**if** *adjustable*
14	*evaluate* = evaluate(*T*, *band*);
15	**if** *evaluate* > *best_evaluate*
16	*best_evaluate* = *evaluate*;
17	enqueue(*start*, *end*, *Queue*$_i$);
18	**else**
19	undo_adjustment(*band*$_i$, *start*, *end*);
20	**if** (*start* − *end*) / 2 ≥ *threshold*
21	enqueue(*start*, *mid*-1, *Queue*$_i$);
22	enqueue(*mid*, *end*, *Queue*$_i$);
23	**endif**
24	**endif**
25	**endif**
26	**endif**
27	**endfor**
28	**endwhile**

increased in each searching step. In the case where two bands have the same heuristic value, the wider band is selected. On the other hand, in backward search, we start from a very large band (all R_i equal to n, where n is the length of time series), and parts of the band are gradually decreased in each searching step. If two bands have the same heuristic value, the tighter band is chosen.

Our learning algorithm starts from first enqueuing the starting- and ending-parts of the *R-K Band*. In each iteration, these values are dequeued, and used as a boundary for a band increase/decrease. And then the adjusted band is evaluated. If the heuristic value is higher than the current best heuristic value, the same start and end values are enqueued. If not, this part is further divided into two equal subparts before being enqueued, as shown in Figure 9. The iterations are continued until a termination condition is met. Table 1 shows the pseudo code for this multiple *R-K Bands* learning.

We can illustrate the utility of our *R-K$_c$ Bands* for classification by the following simple experiment. We tested various similarity measures (Euclidean, DTW with 10% warping, DTW with best uniform warping, and DTW with *R-K$_c$ Bands*) on the Leaf dataset (dataset details in Section 5.3.2) and measure their classification error rates. Euclidean is very fast but inaccurate, giving 32.13% error rate. DTW with

Figure 10. The R-K Bands learned from the 6 different leaf species after transformation to pseudo time series

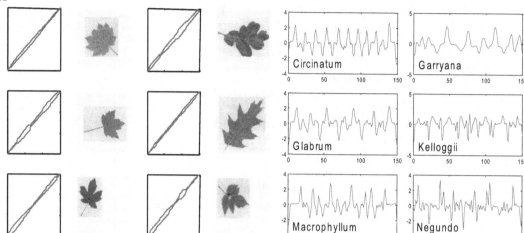

10% uniform warping gives a big improvement with 4.52%. However, the best uniform warping size for this dataset is at 13% window size, giving 4.3%. With *R-K Bands*, we produce 6 different bands, one for each class shown in Figure 10. Classification using these bands gives us almost a perfect result, a mere 0.9% error rate. These promising results suggest that *R-K Bands* are very effective in improving accuracy in classification.

To test the proposed *R-K Band*, we perform the following set of experiment. We use three classification datasets -- Gun, Trace, and Word Spotting from the UCR time series data mining archive [http://www.cs.ucr.edu/~eamonn/time_series_data/]. Trace dataset is a subset of the Transient Classification Benchmark (trace project), a synthetic dataset designed to simulate instrumentation failures in a nuclear power plant, created by Davide Roverso. The full dataset consists of 16 classes, 50 instances in each class. Details on Gun and Word Spotting data are available in section 5.3. We perform classification using the following approaches:

- Euclidean Distance,
- Dynamic Time Warping with Sakoe-Chiba Band (uniform warping window) of size 1% up to 100%. The best accuracy with smallest-size band is to be reported, and
- Dynamic Time Warping with *R-K Bands* that we learn from the input data.

Note that we only compare Dynamic Time Warping with Euclidean Distance metric in this work. It has been forcefully shown in (Keogh & Kasetty, 2003) that many of the more complex similarity measures proposed in other work have higher error rates than a simple Euclidean Distance metric, and therefore by transitivity have higher error rates than DTW itself. We therefore exclude those techniques from our consideration in this experiment.

We measure the accuracy and CPU time on each dataset, using the 1-nearest-neighbor with "train-test" classification method. The lower bounding technique introduced in (Keogh, 2002) is also integrated in all the DTW calculations to help achieve some speedup. All codes are written in C++ language, and

Table 2. Classification Error Rates (%) for all three datasets, using Euclidean distance, DTW with the best uniform band reported, DTW with 10% uniform band, and DTW with our framework, R-K$_c$ Bands

	Euclidean	Best Uniform	10% Uniform	R-K Bands
Gun	5.50%	1.00% at $R_i = 4$	4.50% at $R_i = 15$	0.50% with max(R_j) = 4
Trace	11.00%	0.00% at $R_i = 8$	0.00% at $R_i = 27$	0.00% with max(R_j) = 7
Word Spotting	4.78%	1.10% at $R_i = 3$	2.21% at $R_i = 10$	0.37% with max(R_j) = 4

Table 3. CPU time (msec) for all three datasets, both with and without the use of lower bounding measure

	Euclidean	Best Uniform	10% Uniform	R-K Bands
Gun (LB)	N/A	2,440	5,430	1,440
No LB	60	11,820	17,290	9,440
Trace (LB)	N/A	16,020	34,980	7,420
No LB	210	144,470	185,460	88,630
Word Spotting (LB)	N/A	6,100	14,770	1,940
No LB	40	8,600	12,440	7,480

all experiments are performed on an IBM R40 Intel ® Pentium 4 notebook with 960 MB of DDR RAM with Microsoft Windows ® XP as an operating system. Table 2 compares the classification accuracies in terms of error rates (percentage of misclassified images) for all approaches, and Table 3 compares the CPU time for each method to achieve these accuracies, both with using lower bounding measure and without. Note that the CPU time is timed only in the testing phase because in training (learning) phase, offline searching of a *R-K Band* for each class can be computed. Euclidean distance metric is essentially a DTW with uniform band of width 0% (no warping allowed). For the uniform (Sakoe-Chiba) band, we report the best accuracy within the window width between 1% and 100%. We also report the accuracy at 10% warping window size since it is the number most researchers typically have been using in DTW researches (Keogh, 2002; Sakoe & Chiba, 1978).

We can readily see from the figures and tables that the learned *R-K Bands* usually are of smaller sizes than the uniform case; some portions of the band even have zero width. This speeds up the time needed for classification. We can improve the DTW calculation from running several hundred times slower than Euclidean to running about only 30 times or so slower (or even less than 5 times slower in some other datasets). In addition, classification with *R-K Bands* always achieves higher accuracies than Euclidean or any-size uniform bands (or at least as accurate as the better of the two methods).

In the three datasets discussed previously, it is known that there is some distortion in the time axis. Where no distortion exists (and assuming Gaussian noise), Euclidean distance is known to be the optimal metric (Faloutsos et al., 1994). If we were to apply DTW in these cases, we may get lower accuracy, and we will certainly waste a lot of extra time. For real-world problems, we usually never know if Euclidean distance is the best approach. So, it would be very desirable if our approach could discover this automatically.

To see if this is the case, we performed an additional classification experiment on the well-known Cylinder-Bell-Funnel datasets (Diez & González, 2000; Kadous, 1999), on which Euclidean distance is known to perform extremely well, with sufficient number of instances. With 100 instances in each of the three classes, the Euclidean distance metric achieves 100% accuracy in 0.16 seconds. DTW also achieves perfect accuracy, but wastes a large amount of classification time without realizing the trivial solution.

The DTW algorithm with 10% warping window size requires 27.63 seconds. Our approach, learning $R\text{-}K_c$ *Bands*, quickly discovers that perfect accuracy can be achieved with three bands of size zero. In other words, our approach is capable of learning the optimal-size bands for this problem. With the resultant $R\text{-}K_c$ *Bands* of size 0, we also get the perfect accuracy using only 0.89 seconds. This is slightly slower than the Euclidean distance since the $R\text{-}K_c$ *Bands* are the special case of DTW thus a distance matrix has to be created during the computation. However, it is still much faster than the classic 10%-uniform DTW. It is also trivial to force the algorithm to perform the original Euclidean metric calculation instead of the DTW calculation of the zero band size.

4.3 Learning One R-K Band for Indexing

In addition to creating $R\text{-}K_c$ *Bands* for classification, we can learn one single *R-K Band* for indexing or query retrieval. The one-band learning algorithm is very similar to the multiple-band learning in the previous section, except that we only maintain one single band that represents the whole problem and that we measure the precision/recall instead of the accuracy.

We re-illustrate this approach by another simple experiment, measuring precision and recall for indexing. We take 10 examples of *Cylinders* from the Cylinder-Bell-Funnel dataset (Diez & González, 2000; Kadous, 1999) and place them in a database containing another 10,000 *random-walk* sequences that are similar in shape but do not belong in the class. Another 30 examples of *Cylinders* with 470 *random-walk* sequences are used in the *R-K Band* training process. To evaluate our method, another 10 different *Cylinder* examples are used to make 10 iterations of *k*-nearest neighbor queries to the dataset, using various distance measures (Euclidean, DTW with 10% warping, and DTW with *R-K Band*).

We measure the precision from 1-object (10%) to 10-object (100%) recall levels. The results are shown in Figure 11. It is apparent that utilizing an *R-K Band* in this problem improves both precision and recall

*Figure 11. The Precision/Recall curves from 10% to 100% recall for various distance measures: Euclidean, DTW with 10% window size, and our proposed method – **R-K Band** that gives **perfect** precision for all recall levels*

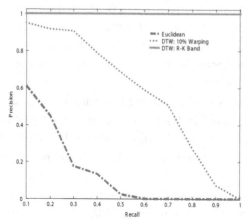

Figure 12. Starting from the neck area, the head profile is converted into a "pseudo time series"

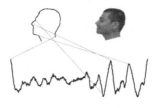

by a wide margin, compared to Euclidean and DTW with 10% warping. However, an *R-K Band* needs to be learned from a training data, which may not be practical or available in many circumstances. To resolve this problem, we can build a training data through relevance feedback system, with a little help from the user in identifying the positive and negative examples to the system. We will explain how this works in Section 5, but first we will attempt to develop the readers' intuition as to *why* the *R-K Bands* can produce superior performance

4.4 Intuition Behind *R-K Bands* Learning

After seeing some examples of our *R-K Band*'s utility, we would like to further convince readers by giving an intuition why *R-K Band* improve accuracy. Consider the following problem of face classification based on the head profile. We took a number of photos (20-35) of each individual with different expressions on the face, e.g., talking, smiling, frowning, etc. We then use the similar method (see section 1.1) to extract each of the head profile into a time series as shown in Figure 12.

We will show by experiment how *R-K Bands* may play an important role in this problem. First, we consider a 2-class problem: a dataset that contains only the collection of profiles from 2 different individuals that look rather different (1 male, 1 female). The $R-K_c$ *Bands* learned from our framework discover the bands both of size zero, the Euclidean distance measure, with 2% error rate. The result suggests that these two individuals are very distinguishable, i.e., the set of time series within each class is much different from another, just by looking at their Euclidean distances. Hence, no warping is necessary; in fact, too much warping could potentially hurt the accuracy because one person could be forced to match with another.

We then extend our experiment by adding 2 more male individuals into our problem (112 instances total). The corresponding *R-K Bands* are learned which give very low error rate of 1.8% (vs. 6.25% for Euclidean).

5 RELEVANCE FEEDBACK

In text-mining community, relevance feedback is well known to be an effective method to improve the query performance (Attar & Fraenkel, 1977; Rickman, 1972; Rocchio, 1971; Salton & Buckley, 1997). However, there has been relatively little research in non-text domains, such as images or multimedia data. In section 1, we have introduced time series as an alternative in representing certain types of multimedia data, including special cases of images and video. We will explain in this section how we utilize and incorporate the technique into the relevance feedback system using our proposed framework, *R-K Band.*

5.1 Query Refinement

Relevance feedback methods attempt to improve performance for a particular informational need by refining the query, based on the user's reaction to the initial retrieved documents or objects. In text retrieval in particular, the user's ranking of the document allows reweighing the query terms.

Working with time series retrieval is rather similar to the text retrieval; a user can draw or provide an example of a query and retrieve the set of best matches' retrieval of images/videos/time series. Once the user ranks each of the results, a query refinement is performed such that a better-quality query is produced for the next retrieval round. For real time series retrieval (i.e., electrocardiograms or stock market data), the querying interface can show the time series directly. For transformed data of images or video, the underlying time series representation is hidden from the user, and the user sees only thumbnails of the actual images or video snippets. In our system, the user is asked to rank each result in a 4-point scale as shown based on relevance to their informational needs. These rankings are converted into appropriate weights which are used in the query refinement process (averaging the weighted positive results with the current query).

However, averaging a collection of time series that are not perfectly time-aligned is non-trivial and DTW is needed (Gupta, Molfese, Tammana, & Simos, 1996). Each pair of time series are averaged according to their weights and warping alignment. The results from each pairs are hierarchically combined. Figure 13 illustrates this averaging process using equal weights for all sequences; in practice, the weights may all be different. In the next section, we will show how the relevance feedback system can benefit from our proposed *R-K Band* framework.

5.2 R-K Band in Relevance Feedback

We will empirically demonstrate that our proposed *R-K Band* combined with the query refinement can improve precision and recall of retrieval. Table 4 shows our relevance feedback algorithm.

In the first iteration, given a query, the system uses the initial *R-K Band* (the special case of Euclidean distance) to retrieve the 10 nearest neighbors, and then shows them to the user (line 1). When the user finishes their ranking, the positive and negative responses are noted and collected as a training data (lines 3-4). The algorithm uses this training data to learn an *R-K Band* that best represents the positive objects in the training set while being able to correctly differentiate the positive from the negative in-

Figure 13. An example of averaging 4 sequences with DTW. Pairs of sequences are hierarchically combined by DTW with their weights until the final averaged sequence is obtained

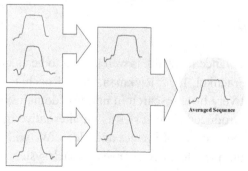

Table 4. R-K Band learning with Relevance Feedback

	Algorithm RelFeedback (*initial_query*)
1	**repeat** until all rankings are positive.
2	Show the 10 best matches to the current query to the user.
3	Let the user rank how relevant each result is.
4	According to the ranking, accumulatively build the training set; positive result → class 1, negative result → class 2.
5	Learn a single envelope (*R-K Band*) that represents the given training data.
6	Generate a new query, by averaging (with DTW) the positive results with the current query according to their weights (rankings).
7	**end**

stances (line 5). The training data will be accumulated during each round, developing a larger training set, thus producing progressively finer results. The process is complete when only positive feedbacks are given to the system or the user abandons the task. A simple screenshot of the image retrieval with relevance feedback system is shown in Figure 14.

Figure 14. A screenshot of the relevance feedback system that allows users to rank the retrieved content.

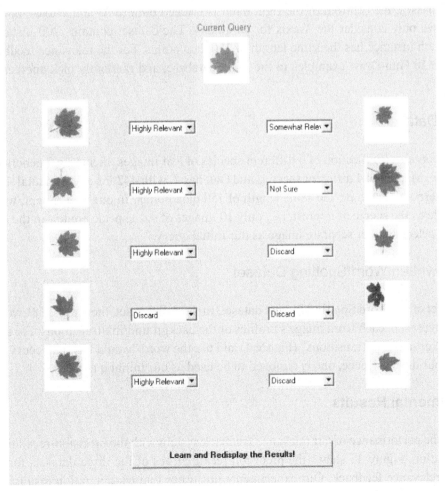

In our experiments, we consider 3 multimedia datasets to be tested using the relevance feedback technique.

5.3 Datasets

To evaluate our framework, we measure the precision and recall for each round of the relevance feedback retrieval. Since we only return the 10 best matches to the user and we would like to measure the precision at all recall levels, we purposely leave only 10 relevant objects of interest in all the databases.

5.3.1 Gun Problem

This dataset comes from the video surveillance domain (see Figure 1). The dataset has two classes, each containing 100 examples:

Gun-Draw: The actors have their hands by their sides. They draw a replicate gun from a hip-mounted holster, point it at a target for approximately one second, and then return the gun to the holster, and their hands to their sides.

Point: The actors have their hands by their sides. They point with their index fingers to a target for approximately one second, and then return their hands to their sides.

For both classes, the centroid of the right hand is tracked both in X- and Y-axes; however, in this experiment, we only consider the X-axis for simplicity. The dataset contains 200 instances, 100 for each class. Each instance has the same length of 150 data points. For the relevance feedback purpose, we only leave 10 Gun-Draw examples in the Point database, and randomly pick another example for an initial query.

5.3.2 Leaf Dataset

This dataset contains a collection of 6 different species of leaf images, including 2 genera of plant, i.e., oak and maple. Maple has 4 different species, and Oak has 2, with 442 instances in total. Each instance is linearly interpolated to have the same length of 150 data points. In our experiment, we choose Circinatum maple as the specie of interest, i.e., only 10 images of such specie are left in the database, and we randomly select another separate image as our initial query.

5.3.3 Handwritten Word Spotting Dataset

This is a subset of the Word Spotting Project dataset. In the full dataset, there are 2,381 words with four features that represent each word image's profiles or the background/ink transitions. For simplicity, we pick the "background/ink transitions" (Figure 4) and use the word "would" which occurs in the dataset 11 times for our query. Hence, one is removed to be used as our initial query.

5.4 Experimental Results

We measure the performance of our relevance feedback system with the precision-recall plot from each round of iteration. Figure 15 shows the precision-recall curves of the three datasets for the first five iterations of relevance feedback. Our experiments illustrates that each iteration results in significant improvement in both precision and recall.

Figure 15. The precision-recall plots for the Gun, Leaf, and Word Spotting datasets with 5 iterations of relevance feedback

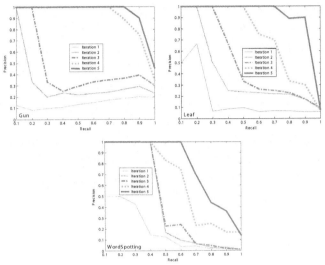

6 DISCUSSION AND CONCLUSIONS

In this work, we have introduced a framework for both classification and time series retrieval. The *R-K Band* allows for any arbitrary shape and size of the warping band. We have also introduced a heuristic search algorithm that automatically learns the *R-K Bands* from the data. With an extensive empirical evaluation, we have shown that our approach can reduce the error rate and the CPU time of DTW by an order of magnitude. An attractive property of our approach is that it includes the two most used distance measures, Euclidean distance and DTW as special cases. One advantage of this fact is that it enables us to simply "slot-in" our representation to the sophisticated techniques available for indexing time series envelopes (Hu et al., 2003; Manmatha & Rath, 2003; Wong & Wong, 2003; Zhu et al., 2003), thus achieving even greater speedup than shown here. With our extensive evaluation, we then have shown that our framework incorporated into relevance feedback can reduce the error rate in classification, and improve the precision at all recall levels in video and image retrieval.

7 FUTURE RESEARCH DIRECTIONS

We plan to extend this work in several directions. First we intend to investigate the theoretical properties of *R-K Bands*, and the search algorithms defined on them. We also plan to consider a more generalized form of our framework, in which a single *R-K Band* is learned for an application domain. For example, what is the best *single* band for indexing George Washington's handwriting (Manmatha & Rath, 2003), does it differ from the best band for, say Isaac Newton's handwriting? Finally, for some applications, it may be possible to examine the *R-K Bands* to glean knowledge about the domain. For example, if we learn to classify normal heartbeats versus supraventricular arrhythmias, and discover that *R-K Bands* are narrow at both ends, but wide in the center, this would suggest that the discriminating difference is contained within the T-U wave of the ECG (Caiani et al., 1998).

8 ADDITIONAL READING

Time series classification and retrieval was first discussed in data mining community to find patterns in time series by Berndt and Clifford (Berndt & Clifford, 1994). Since the DTW is high in computational cost, a lower bounding function is needed. Many lower bounding functions has been proposed to prune off numerous data in the database, i.e., LB_Yi (proposed in 1998 by Yi et al. (Yi et al., 1998)) , LB_Kim (proposed in 2001 by Kim et al. (Kim, Park, & Chu, 2001)), and LB_Keogh (proposed in 2002 by Keogh (Keogh, 2002)). Keogh specifically proposed a time series indexing algorithm using a general multi-dimensional indexing algorithm (GEMINI framework (Faloutsos et al., 1994)) proposed by Faloutsos. Later, Zhu and Shasha (Zhu & Shasha, 2003) have proposed yet a tighter lower bounding function for indexing, followed by a new algorithm, fast similarity search under the time warping distance (Sakurai, Yoshikawa, & Faloutsos, 2005) by Sakurai et al., that can drastically reduce computational cost.

9 REFERENCES

Aach, J., & Church, G. M. (2001). Aligning gene expression time series with time warping aalgorithms. *Bioinformatics, 17*(6), 495-508.

Agrawal, R., Lin, K.-I., Sawhney, H. S., & Shim, K. (1995). Fast similarity search in the presence of noise, scaling, and translation in time-series databases. *Proceedings of 21th International Conference on Very Large Data Bases* (pp. 490-501). San Francisco, CA, USA: Morgan Kaufmann Publishers Inc.

Attar, R., & Fraenkel, A. S. (1977). Local feedback in full-text retrieval systems. *Journal of the ACM, 24*(3), 397-417.

Bar-Joseph, Z., Gerber, G., Gifford, D. K., Jaakkola, T. S., & Simon, I. (2002). A new approach to Aanalyzing gene expression time series data. *Proceedings of 6th Annual International Conference on Computational Biology* (pp. 39 - 48). Washington, DC, USA: ACM.

Berndt, D. J., & Clifford, J. (1994). Using dynamic time warping to find patterns in time series. *AAAI Workshop on Knowledge Discovery in Databases* (pp. 229-248).

Caiani, E. G., Porta, A., Baselli, G., Turiel, M., Muzzupappa, S., Pieruzzi, F., et al. (1998). *Warped-average template technique to track on a cycle-by-cycle basis the cardiac filling phases on left ventricular volume, computers in cardiology* (pp. 73-76). Cleveland, OH, USA.

Chan, F. K.-P., Fu, A. W.-C., & Yu, C. (2003). Haar wavelets for efficient similarity search of time-series: With and without time warping. *IEEE Transactions on Knowledge and Data Engineering, 15*(3), 686-705.

Chu, S., Keogh, E., Hart, D., & Pazzani, M. (2002). Iterative deepening dynamic time warping. *Proceedings of 2nd SIAM International Conference on Data Mining.* Maebashi City, Japan.

Das, G., Lin, K.-I., Mannila, H., Renganathan, G., & Smyth, P. (1998). Rule discovery from time series. *Proceedings of 4th International Conference on Knowledge Discovery and Data Mining* (pp. 16-22). New York, NY, USA: AAAI Press.

Dasgupta, D., & Forrest, S. (1996). Novelty detection in time series data using ideas from immunology. *Proceedings of 5th International Conference on Intelligent Systems* (pp. 82-87). Reno, Nevada, USA.

Deselaers, T., Keysers, D., & Ney, H. (2003). Clustering visually similar images to improve image search engines. *Proceedings of Informatiktage 2003 der Gesellschaft für Informatik.* Bad Schussenried, Germany.

Diez, J. J. R., & González, C. A. (2000). Applying boosting to similarity literals for time series classification. *Proceedings of 1st International Workshop on Multiple Classifier Systems* (pp. 210-219). Cagliari, Italy.

Faloutsos, C., Ranganathan, M., & Manolopoulos, Y. (1994). Fast subsequence matching in time-series databases. *Proceedings of the 1994 ACM SIGMOD International Conference on Management of Data* (pp. 419-429). Minneapolis, Minnesota, United States: ACM.

Gandi, A. (2002). *Content-based image retrieval: Plant species identification.* Oregon State University.

Gavrila, D. M., & Davis, L. S. (1995). Towards 3-D model-based tracking and recognition of human movement: A multi-view approach. *Proceeding of International Workshop on Face and Gesture Recognition* (pp. 272-277).

Gollmer, K., & Posten, C. (1996). Supervision of bioprocesses using a dynamic time warping algorithm. *Control Engineering Practice, 4*(9), 1287-1295.

Gupta, L., Molfese, D. L., Tammana, R., & Simos, P. G. (1996). Nonlinear alignment and averaging for estimating the evoked potential. *IEEE Transactions on Biomedical Engineering, 43*(4), 348-356.

Hu, N., Dannenberg, R. B., & Tzanetakis, G. (2003). Polyphonic audio matching and alignment for music retrieval *Proceedings of the 2003 IEEE Workshop on Applications of Signal Processing to Audio and Acoustics* (pp. 185-188).

Itakura, F. (1975). Minimum prediction residual principle applied to speech recognition. *IEEE Transactions on Acoustics, Speech, and Signal Processing, 23*(1), 67-72.

Jain, A. K., & Namboodiri, A. M. (2003). Indexing and retrieval of on-line handwritten documents. *Proceedings 7th International Conference on Document Analysis and Recognition* (pp. 655-659).

Kadous, M. W. (1999). Learning Comprehensible Descriptions of Multivariate Time Series. *Proceedings of 16th International Conference on Machine Learning* (pp. 454-463). Bled, Slovenia: Morgan Kaufmann Publishers Inc.

Käster, T., Wendt, V., & Sagerer, G. (2003). Comparing Clustering Methods for Database Categorization in Image Retrieval. *Proceedings of 25th Deutsche Arbeitsgemeinschaft für Mustererkennung Symposium* (pp. 228-235). Magdeburg, Germany.

Kavallieratou, E., Dromazou, N., Fakotakis, N., & Kokkinakis, G. (2003). An Integrated System for Handwritten Document Image Processing. *International Journal of Pattern Recognition and Artificial Intelligence, 17*(4), 617 - 636

Keogh, E. (2002). Exact indexing of dynamic time warping. *Proceedings of 28th International Conference on Very Large Data Bases* (pp. 406 - 417). Hong Kong, China.

Keogh, E., Chakrabarti, K., Pazzani, M., & Mehrotra, S. (2001a). Dimensionality reduction for fast similarity search in large time series databases. *Knowledge and Information Systems, 3*(3), 263-286.

Keogh, E., Chakrabarti, K., Pazzani, M., & Mehrotra, S. (2001b). Locally adaptive dimensionality reduction for indexing large time series databases. *Proceedings of the 2001 ACM SIGMOD International Conference on Management of Data* (pp. 151-162). Santa Barbara, California, United States: ACM Press.

Keogh, E., & Kasetty, S. (2003). On the need for time series data mining benchmarks: A survey and empirical demonstration. *Data Mining and Knowledge Discovery, 7*(4), 349-371.

Keogh, E., & Pazzani, M. (1999). Relevance feedback retrieval of time series data. *Proceedings of 22nd Annual International ACM SIGIR Conference on Research and Development in Information Retrieval* (pp. 183-190). Berkeley, CA, USA: ACM.

Keogh, E., & Pazzani, M. (2000). Scaling up dynamic time warping for data mining applications. *Proceedings of 6th ACM SIGKDD International Conference on Knowledge Discovery and Data Mining* (pp. 285-289). Boston, MA, USA: ACM.

Keogh, E., & Ratanamahatana, C. A. (2005). *Exact Indexing of Dynamic Time Warping. Knowledge and Information Systems, 7*(3), 358-386.

Keogh, E., Wei, L., Xi, X., Lee, S.-H., & Vlachos, M. (2006). LB_Keogh Supports Exact Indexing of shapes under rotation invariance with arbitrary representations and distance measures. *Proceedings of 32nd International Conference on Very Large Data Bases* (pp. 882-893). Seoul, Korea.

Kim, S.-W., Park, S., & Chu, W. W. (2001). An index-based approach for similarity search supporting time warping in large sequence databases. *Proceedings 17th International Conference on Data Engineering* (pp. 607-614). Heidelberg, Germany.

Krishnamachari, S., & Abdel-Mottaleb, M. (1999). Image Browsing Using Hierarchical Clustering. *Proceedings of the 1999 IEEE International Symposium on Computers and Communications* (pp. 301-307).

Kruskall, J. B., & Liberman, M. (1983). The Symmetric Time Warping Algorithm: From Continuous to Discrete. Time Warps, String Edits, and Macromolecules.

Kwong, S., He, Q. H., & Man, K. F. (1996). Genetic Time warping for isolated word recognition. *International Journal of Pattern Recognition and Artificial Intelligence, 10*(7), 849-865.

Manmatha, R., & Rath, T. M. (2003). *Indexing handwritten historical documents - recent progress, the 2003 symposium on document image understanding* (pp. 77-86).

Munich, M. E., & Perona, P. (1999). Continuous dynamic time warping for translation-invariant curve alignment with applications to signature verification. *Proceedings of 7th IEEE International Conference on Computer Vision* (Vol. 1, pp. 108-115). Kerkyra, Greece.

Myers, C., Rabiner, L., & Rosenberg, A. (1980). Performance tradeoffs in dynamic time warping algorithms for isolated word recognition. *IEEE Transactions on Acoustics, Speech, and Signal Processing, 28*(6), 623-635.

Rabiner, L., & Juang, B.-H. (1993). *Fundamentals of speech recognition.* Prentice-Hall, Inc.

Ratanamahatana, C. A., & Keogh, E. (2004). Making Time-Series Classification More Accurate Using Learned Constraints. *Proceedings of 4th SIAM International Conference on Data Mining* (pp. 11-22). Lake Buena Vista, FL, USA.

Ratanamahatana, C. A., & Keogh, E. (2005). Three Myths about Dynamic Time Warping. *Proceedings of 5th SIAM International Conference on Data Mining* (pp. 506-510). Newport Beach, CA, USA.

Rath, T. M., & Manmatha, R. (2003). Word image matching using dynamic time warping. *Proceedings of the 2003 IEEE Computer Society Conference on Computer Vision and Pattern Recognition* (Vol. 2, pp. 512-527). Madison, WI, USA.

Rickman, J. T. (1972). Design considerations for a boolean search system with automatic relevance feedback processing. *Proceedings of the ACM Annual Conference* (pp. 478 - 481). Boston, MA, USA: ACM.

Rocchio, J. (1971). Relevance feedback in information retrieval. In G. Salton (Ed.), *The SMART Retrieval System - Experiments in Automatic Document Processing* (pp. 313-323): Prentice-Hall, Inc.

Sakoe, H., & Chiba, S. (1978). Dynamic programming algorithm optimization for spoken word recognition. *IEEE Transactions on Acoustics, Speech, and Signal Processing, 26*(1), 43-49.

Sakurai, Y., Yoshikawa, M., & Faloutsos, C. (2005). FTW: Fast Similarity Search under the Time Warping Distance. *Proceedings of 24th ACM SIGMOD-SIGACT-SIGART Symposium on Principles of Database Systems* (pp. 326 - 337). Baltimore, MD, USA: ACM.

Salton, G., & Buckley, C. (1997). Improving Retrieval Performance by Relevance Feedback. *Journal of the American Society for Information Science, 41*(4), 288-297.

Schmill, M., Oates, T., & Cohen, P. (1999). Learned Models for Continuous Planning. *Proceedings of 7th International Workshop on Artificial Intelligence and Statistics* (pp. 278-282).

Tappert, C., & Das, S. (1978). Memory and Time Improvements in a Dynamic Programming Algorithm for Matching Speech Patterns. *IEEE Transactions on Acoustics, Speech, and Signal Processing, 26*(6), 583-586.

Tomai, C. I., Zhang, B., & Govindaraju, V. (2002). Transcript Mapping for Historic Handwritten Document Images. *Proceedings of 8th International Workshop on Frontiers in Handwriting Recognition* (pp. 413-418).

Viskin, S. (2000). Cardiac pacing in the long QT syndrome: Review of available data and practical recommendations. *Journal of Cardiovascular Electrophysiology, 11*(5), 593-600.

Vlachos, M., Kollios, G., & Gunopulos, D. (2002). Discovering similar multidimensional trajectories. *Proceedings of 18th International Conference on Data Engineering* (pp. 673-684). San Jose, CA, USA.

Wang, J., Yang, W.-J., & Acharya, R. (1997). Color Clustering Techniques for Color-Content-Based Image Retrieval from Image Databases. *Proceedings of the 1997 IEEE International Conference on Multimedia Computing and Systems* (pp. 442-449). Ottawa, Canada.

Weliwitage, C., Harvey, A., & Jennings, A. (2003). Whole of Word Recognition Methods for Cursive Script. *Proceedings of the 2003 APRS Workshop on Digital Image Computing* (pp. 111-116). Brisbane, Australia.

Wong, T. S. F., & Wong, M. H. (2003). Efficient subsequence matching for sequences databases under time warping. *Proceedings of 7th International Database Engineering and Applications Symposium* (pp. 139-148).

Wu, P., & Manjunath, B. S. (2001). Adaptive nearest neighbor search for relevance feedback in large image databases. *Proceedings of 9th ACM International Conference on Multimedia* (pp. 89-97). Ottawa, Canada: ACM.

Yang, Z., & Kuo, C.-C. J. (2000). Learning image similarities and categories from content analysis and relevance feedback. *Proceedings the 2000 ACM Workshops on Multimedia* (pp. 175-178). Los Angeles, CA, USA: ACM.

Yeung, M. M., & Liu, B. (1995). Efficient Matching and Clustering of Video Shots. *Proceedings of the 1995 International Conference on Image Processing* (Vol. 1, pp. 338-341). Washington D.C., WA, USA.

Yi, B.-K., & Faloutsos, C. (2000). Fast time sequence indexing for arbitrary Lp norms. *Proceedings of 26th International Conference on Very Large Data Bases* (pp. 385-394). San Francisco, CA, USA: Morgan Kaufmann Publishers Inc.

Yi, B.-K., Jagadish, H. V., & Faloutsos, C. (1998). Efficient Retrieval of Similar Time Sequences under Time Warping. *Proceedings of 14th International Conference on Data Engineering* (pp. 201-208). Washington D.C., WA, USA.

Zhu, Y., & Shasha, D. (2003). Warping Indexes with Envelope Transforms for Query by Humming. *Proceedings of the 2003 ACM SIGMOD International Conference on Management of Data* (pp. 181-192). San Diego, CA, USA: ACM.

Zhu, Y., Shasha, D., & Zhao, X. (2003). Query by humming: In action with its technology revealed. *Proceedings of the 2003 ACM SIGMOD International Conference on Management of Data* (pp. 675-675). San Diego, CA, USA: ACM.

Chapter VIII
A Machine Learning–Based Model for Content–Based Image Retrieval

Hakim Hacid
University of Lyon 2, France

Abdelkader Djamel Zighed
University of Lyon 2, France

ABSTRACT

A multimedia index makes it possible to group data according to similarity criteria. Traditional index structures are based on trees and use the k-Nearest Neighbors (k-NN) approach to retrieve databases. Due to some disadvantages of such an approach, the use of neighborhood graphs was proposed. This approach is interesting, but it has some disadvantages, mainly in its complexity. This chapter presents a step in a long process of analyzing, structuring, and retrieving multimedia databases. Indeed, we propose an effective method for locally updating neighborhood graphs, which constitute our multimedia index. Then, we exploit this structure in order to make the retrieval process easy and effective, using queries in an image form in one hand. In another hand, we use the indexing structure to annotate images in order to describe their semantics. The proposed approach is based on an intelligent manner for locating points in a multidimensional space. Promising results are obtained after experimentations on various databases. Future issues of the proposed approach are very relevant in this domain.

INTRODUCTION

Data interrogation is a fundamental problem in various scientific communities. The database and statistics communities (with their various fields such as data mining) are certainly the most implied. Each community considers the interrogation from a different point of view. The database community, for example, deals with great volumes of data by organizing them in an adequate structure in order to be able to answer queries in the most effective way. This is done by using index structures. The statistics community deals only with data samples in order to produce predictive models that are able to draw conclusions on phenomena; these conclusions then are generalized to the whole items. This is achieved using various structures such as decision trees (Mitchell, 2003), Kohonen maps (Kohonen, 2001), neighborhood graphs (Toussaint, 1991), and so forth.

Dealing with multimedia databases means dealing with content-based retrieval. There are two fundamental problems associated with content-based retrieval systems: (a) how to specify a query and (b) how to access the intended data efficiently for a given query. The main objective is to capture the semantics of the considered data. For traditional database systems, the semantics of content-based access are finding data items that are match exactly the specified keywords in queries. For multimedia database systems, both query specification and data access become much harder (Chiueh, 1994).

To give the computer the ability to mimic the human being in scene analysis needs to explicit the process by which it moves up from the low level to the highest one. Multimedia processing tools give many ways to transform an image/video into a vector. For instance, MPEG-7 protocol associates a set of quantitative attributes to each image/video. The computation of these features is integrated and automated fully in many software platforms. In return, the labels basically are given by the user, because they are issued from the human language. The relevance of the image/video retrieval process depends on the vector of characteristics. Nevertheless, if we assume that the characteristics are relevant in the representation space, that it is supposed to be R^p, the images that are neighbors should have very similar meanings.

In order to perform an interrogation in a multimedia database, it must be structured in an adequate way. For that, an index is used. Indexing a multimedia database consists of finding a way to structure the data so that the neighbors of each multimedia document can be located easily according to one or more similarity criteria. The index structures used in databases are generally in a tree form and aim to create clusters, which are represented by the sheets of the tree and contain rather similar documents. However, in addition to the fact that a traditional index cannot support data with dimensions higher than 16, dealing with multimedia databases needs more operations such as classification and annotation. This is why the use of models issued from the automatic learning community can be very helpful.

The rest of this chapter is organized as follows. The next section introduces the point location and the database indexing problems. Section 3 presents the motivation and the contributions of our work. Section 4 describes the neighborhood graphs that are the foundation of this contribution. Our contributions are addressed in Section 5. The indexing method and the optimization of the neighborhood graphs are discussed in Section 5.1. Semi-automatic annotation is discussed in Section 5.2. Section 6 gives some experiments that were performed in order to evaluate and validate our approach. We conclude and give some future issues in Section 7.

POINT LOCATION AND DATABASES INDEXING PROBLEMS

Point Location Problem

Neighborhood search is a significant problem in several fields. It is handled in data mining (Fayyad, Piatetsky-Shapiro, & Smith, 1996), classification (Cover, & Hart, 1967), machine learning (Cost, &

Salzberg, 1993), data compression (Gersho, & Gray, 1991), multimedia databases (Flickner et al., 1995), information retrieval (Deerwester, Dumais, Landauer, Furnas, & Harshman, 1990), and so forth. Several works in connection with the neighborhood search in databases exist, such as Berchtold, Böhm, Keim, and Kriegel (1997), Lin, Jagadish, and Faloutsos (1994), and White and Jain (1996). The point location problem is a key question in automatic multidimensional data processing. This problem can be defined as follows: Having a data set Ω of n items in a multidimensional space R^p, the problem is to find a way to preprocess the data so that if we have a new query item α, we will be able to find its neighbors n as little time as possible.

The point location problem in one-dimensional space can be solved by sorting the data and by applying a binary search that is rather fast and inexpensive in term of resources with a complexity of $O(n \log n)$. In a two-dimensional space, this problem can be solved by using a voronoi diagram (Preparata & Shamos, 1985), as illustrated in Figure 1.

Unfortunately, when the dimension increases, the problem becomes more complex and more difficult to manage. Several methods for point location in a multidimensional space were proposed. For example, we can quote the ones based on points projection on only one axis (Friedman, Baskett, & Shustek, 1975; Guan & Kamel, 1992; Lee & Chen, 1994) or the work based on partial distances calculation between items (Bei & Gray, 1985). In the database community, the point location problem is known as the indexing problem.

Database Indexing Problem

There are two main classes of databases indexing methods:

- **Point access methods (PAM):** In this class of methods, data are considered as points in a multidimensional space. The indexing structures generally are based on the *kd-Tree* principle (Bentley, 1975).
- **Space access methods (SAM):** In this class of methods, the data are in various geometrical forms (e.g., lines, rectangles, etc.). The structures used are alternatives of *R*-Tree (Guttman, 1984).

Several content-based information retrieval systems are based on these structures (trees) and use the *k*-nearest neighbors principle (Fix & Hudges, 1951; Velkamp & Tanase, 2000). This principle is based on

Figure 1. A Voronoi diagram in a bi-dimensional space

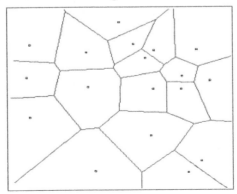

sorting items by taking into account their distances to the query item; fixed k nearest items are turned over by the system as an answer to the query. For example, the QBIC system in its implementation for the Hermitage museum (Faloutsos et al., 1994) returns the 12 nearest images to a query submitted by a user.

Disadvantages of the k-NN Approach

There are two main disadvantages related to the use of the *k-NN* approach: (i) the symmetry (the most important one) and (ii) the subjectivity problems. The first one is due to the fact that the principle of the *k-NN* is based only on data sorting according to their distances to the query point.

Figure 2 illustrates the symmetry problem of the *k-NN* on one axis using five points (*a, b, c, d, e*).

Let us consider a *k-NN* with *k*=3. So, if we take point *a* in the first case as a query point, its three neighbors are {*b, c, d*}. In the other case, if we consider point *d* as a query point, then its three nearest neighbors are {*b, c, e*}. So, we can see clearly that the neighborhood is not coherent, because in the neighborhood of point *a*, we find point *d*, but in the neighborhood of point *d*, we do not find point *a*. The symmetry problem raises other problems in the decision-making process related to other important functions in image databases, such as images classification and their automatic annotation. The navigation process also is affected by this problem.

The second problem, which is relatively a subjective one, concerns the manner of the determination of *k*. Indeed, some questions rise from that: Is the use of only a distance measure sufficient for the interrogation of an image database (neighborhood determination)? If this is the case, what is the maximum distance an item must respect to be a neighbor of a query item? What is the optimal number of neighbors of a query item? Dealing with image databases needs more operations (image classification, for example), so are the used techniques (trees and *k-NN*) sufficient and effective for that?

MOTIVATION AND CONTRIBUTION

The structuration model of image databases is (or can be seen) as a graph that is based on similarity relations among items (e.g., *k-NN* [Mitchell, 2003] or a relative neighborhood graph [Scuturici, Clech, Scuturici, & Zighed, 2005]). The goal is to explore an image database through the similarity among images. Exploring the similarity can result in the search of the images' neighbors. The structuration model is very important, because the performances of a content-based information retrieval system depend strongly on the representation structure (i.e., index structure), which manages the data.

The main motivation of this work is the following: We believe that the problem of image database retrieval, navigation, automatic annotation, and other tasks in this field cannot be solved by using tradi-

Figure 2. Illustration of the symmetry problem in the k-NN approach

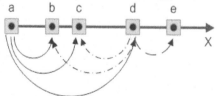

tional approaches such as *k-NN* and trees. We believe that the problems related to the use of traditional approaches can be solved by using only more adequate structures. In addition, the combination among various methods seems important for us, which is why, in our case, we introduce neighborhood graphs (issued from the automatic learning community) for indexing, retrieving, and semi-automatically annotating image databases.

There are two main contributions in this chapter. The first one concerns the accommodation of neighborhood graphs for indexing image databases using low-level features. The second is the exploitation of the proposed structure in order to annotate an image database. So, the proposed approach presents multiple advantages. Indeed, we take into account the two possible retrieval functions; namely, retrieval by visual contents and retrieval by keywords. Hence, a user can submit his or her query using either an image or textual description in order to recover the images that relate to a same concept.

- **Retrieval by visual content:** In this case, the query is expressed in an image form and analyzed to extract its low-level characteristics. After that, it is inserted in the neighborhood graph, and its neighbors are turned over as an answer. In addition, with the graph representation of the database, the navigation becomes more interesting and more coherent for the user.
- **Retrieval by keywords:** In this case, the interrogation is ensured by the use of keywords that are expressed in a natural language and describing the wished semantics of the expected images.

Moreover, we show how we exploit the proposed approach for annotating image databases. The next section introduces the neighborhood graphs. These structures can help us to bring some answers to the previous questions and can serve as a solution for the disadvantages of the *k-NN* approach.

Neighborhood Graphs

Neighborhood graphs are used in various systems. Their popularity is due to the fact that the neighborhood is recovered by coherent functions that reflect, in some points of view, the human intuition mechanism. Their use is varied from information retrieval systems to geographical information systems.

Neighborhood graphs are geometrical structures that use the neighborhood concept in order to find the closest points to a given one in a multidimensional space R^p. For that, they are based on proximity measures (Toussaint, 1991). We will use the following notations throughout this chapter:

Let Ω be a set of points in a multidimensional space R^p. A graph $G(\Omega, \rho)$ is composed by a set of points Ω and a set of edges ρ. Then, for any graph we can associate a binary relation $\Re$ upon Ω in which two points $(\alpha, \beta) \in \Omega^2$ are in binary relation if and only if the pair $(\alpha, \beta) \in \rho$. In other words, (α, β) are in binary relation if and only if they are connected directly in graph G. From that, the neighborhood $N(\alpha)$ of a point α in the graph G can be considered as a subgraph that contains point α and all the points that are connected directly to it.

Several possibilities were proposed for building neighborhood graphs. Among them, we can quote the Delaunay triangulation (Preparata & Shamos, 1985), the relative neighborhood graph (Toussaint, 1980), the Gabriel graph (Gabriel & Sokal, 1969), and the minimum spanning tree (Preparata & Shamos, 1985). In this chapter, we consider only one of them: the relative neighborhood graph.

Figure 3. Relative neighborhood graph in a bi-dimensional space

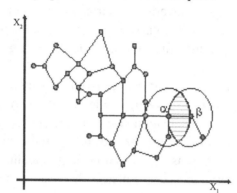

Relative Neighborhood Graph

In the relative neighborhood graph, $G_{rng}(\Omega, \rho)$, two points $(\alpha, \beta) \in \Omega^2$ are neighbors if they check the relative neighborhood property defined as follows: Let $H(\alpha, \beta)$ be the hypersphere of radius $\delta(\alpha, \beta)$ and centered on α, and let $H(\beta, \alpha)$ be the hypersphere of radius $\delta(\beta, \alpha)$ and centered on β ($\delta(\alpha, \beta)$, and $\delta(\beta, \alpha)$ are the distance measures between two points α and β. ($\delta(\alpha, \beta) = \delta(\beta, \alpha)$). So, α and β are neighbors if and only if the intersection of the two hyperspheres $H(\alpha, \beta)$ and $H(\beta, \alpha)$ is empty (Toussaint, 1980). Formally:

Consider $A(\alpha, \beta) = H(\alpha, \beta) \cap H(\beta, \alpha)$ So $(\alpha, \beta) \in \rho$ iff $A(\alpha, \beta) \cap \Omega = \phi$

Figure 3 illustrates the relative neighborhood graph.

Advantages and Disadvantages

The advantages of the use of a model issued from the automatic learning community are primarily the possibility for a user to exploit the powerful decision-making functions of these structures. Also, their construction respects some geometrical properties that result from the use of both a similarity measure and the topology of the items in the multidimensional space for the neighborhood determination. The direct consequence is the number of neighbors associated with each item. Indeed, because of the geometry properties, the number of neighbors is not fixed by a user and is variable from one item to another. This avoids the repetitious calculation of the neighbors at each interrogation of the index structure. Another advantage of these structures is the neighborhood symmetry. This offers the effectiveness of the decision-making process related to different operations such as automatic annotation of images.

However, several problems concerning neighborhood graphs are under research and require more investigation to solve them. These problems primarily are related to their high construction cost and to their updating difficulties. For these reasons, optimizations are necessary for their construction and updating in order to make their application possible on image databases. In the following, we give a description of some neighborhood graph construction algorithms.

Neighborhood Graph Construction Algorithms

One of the common approaches to the various neighborhood graph construction algorithms is the use of a refinement technique. In this approach, the graph is built by steps. Each graph is built starting from the previous graph, containing all connections, by eliminating some edges that do not check the considered neighborhood property. Pruning (edge elimination) generally is done by taking into account the construction function of the graph or through geometrical properties.

The construction principle of neighborhood graphs consists of seeking for each point if the other points in the space are in its proximity. The cost of this operation has a complexity of $O(n^3)$ (n is the number of points in the space). Toussaint (1991) proposed an algorithm with a complexity of $O(n^2)$. He deduced the *RNG* starting from a Delaunay triangulation (Preparata & Shamos, 1985). Using the Octant neighbors, Katajainen (1988) also proposed an algorithm with the same complexity. Smith (1989) proposed an algorithm of complexity $O(n^{23/12})$ that is less significant than $O(n^3)$.

The major problem of these algorithms is the fact that they are not able to update the initial structure without rebuilding it. Indexing image databases using these structures needs to adapt them in order to support rapid interrogation and updating operations. The next section presents the optimization of these structures for indexing and annotating image databases.

NEIGHBORHOOD GRAPHS FOR IMAGE INDEXING AND SEMI-AUTOMATIC ANNOTATION

Neighborhood Graphs Indexing-Based Approach

Neighborhood graphs for navigation in image databases were used in Scuturici et al. (2005). The proposed approach focuses mainly on neighborhood graphs locally updating technique. This method really does not offer the anticipated results. Indeed, the graph actually is not updated, but the neighbors of each query point are considered those of the nearest neighbor. This approach is not effective, because actually, the neighbors of a point are not only/always those of its nearest neighbor. So, the use of this method deteriorates the graph.

We can consider two situations when dealing with the neighborhood graphs optimization problem. The first situation is when we have an existing graph. In this situation, if one uses an approximation method, he or she risks having another graph with other properties; we can obtain, for example, more or less neighbors for some items. In this case, we have to find a solution for effectively updating the graph when inserting or deleting a point without rebuilding it. The second situation is when the graph is not built yet. In this situation, we can apply an approximation method in order to obtain a graph that is as close as possible to the one that we can obtain using a standard algorithm. In this chapter, we are interested in the first case. We propose an effective method with a low complexity for locally updating neighborhood graphs. This algorithm can be extended for incrementally building neighborhood graphs.

A neighborhood graph locally updates task passes by the location of the inserted (or removed) point in the multidimensional space as well as the points that can be affected by the modifications. To achieve this, we proceed into two main stages: initially, we look for an optimal space area that can contain a maximum number of potentially close points to the query point. The second stage is done in the aim of filtering the items found beforehand in order to recover the real closest points to the query point, and this by applying an adequate neighborhood property. This last stage causes the effective updating of the neighborhood relations among the concerned points.

The main stage of this method is the *space area* determination. This can be considered a problem of determining a hypersphere of center a (the query point), maximizing the chance of containing the neighbors of a while minimizing the number of items that it contains.

We take advantage of the general neighborhood graph structure in order to establish the radius of the hypersphere. We focus especially on the nearest neighbor and the farthest neighbor concepts. So, two observations in connection with these two concepts seem to be interesting:

The neighbors of the nearest neighbor of a are potential candidates to the neighborhood of the query point a.

From that, by generalization, we can deduce that:

All the neighbors of a point are also candidates to the neighborhood of a query point for which it is a neighbor.

With regard to the first step, the radius of the hypersphere, which respects the above properties, is the one that includes all the neighbors of the nearest neighbor of the query point. So, considering that the hypersphere is centered at α, its radius will be the sum of the distances between α and its nearest neighbor and the one between this nearest neighbor and its furthest neighbor.

That is, let us consider α the query point and β its nearest neighbor with a distance δ_1; and let us consider λ the furthest neighbor of β with a distance δ_2. The radius *SR* of the hypersphere can be expressed as:

$$SR = \delta_1 + \delta_2 + \varepsilon$$

ε is a relaxation parameter that can be set according to the state of the data (e.g., their dispersion) or by a domain knowledge. We set experimentally this parameter to 1.

The content of the hypersphere is processed in order to check whether there are some neighbors (or all the neighbors). The second step constitutes a reinforcement step and aims to eliminate the risk of losing neighbors or including bad ones. So, we take all the neighbors of the query point, recovered beforehand (those returned in the first step), as well as their neighbors, and update the neighborhood relations among these points.

The computation complexity of this method is very low and meets perfectly our starting aims (i.e., locating the neighborhood of points in as short a time as possible). It is expressed by:

$$O(2n + n'^3)$$

in which n is the number of items in the database, and n' is the number of items in the hypersphere ($\ll n$).

This complexity includes the two previously described stages; namely, the determination of the radius of the hypersphere and the determination of the points that are in it, corresponding to the term $O(2n)$. The second term corresponds to the necessary time for effectively updating the neighborhood relations.

Figure 4. Illustration of the principle of the proposed method

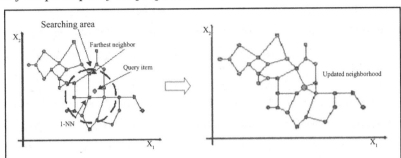

This complexity constitutes the worst case complexity and can be optimized in several ways. The most obvious way is to use a fast nearest neighbor search algorithm. The example hereafter (Figure 4) illustrates graphically and summarizes the principle of the method.

With this method, neighborhood graphs are adequate to be used for indexing image databases. More details about this method are described in Hacid and Zighed (2005).

In the next section, we present the exploitation of this indexing structure for semi-automatic image annotation.

From Indexing to Semi-Automatic Annotating

Another important function when we deal with image database is the semantic association to its visual contents. This function is known as the annotation process. Image annotation is the process that consists of assigning for each image a keyword or a list of keywords that makes it possible to describe its semantic content. This function can be considered a function that allows a mapping between the visual aspects of the image and its low-level characteristics.

Image annotation is not an easy task. There are three types of image annotation: manual, semi-automatic, and automatic. The first one is carried out manually by a human who is charged with alloting a set of keywords for each image. The automatic annotation is carried out by a machine and aims to reduce the user's charge. The first annotation type increases precision and decreases productivity. The second type decreases precision and increases productivity. In order to make a compromise between these two tasks, their combination became necessary. This combination is named semi-automatic annotation.

Moreover, image annotation can be performed on two levels: the local level and the global level. In the local level, the image is regarded as a set of objects. The annotation aims to affect for each object a keyword or a list of keywords in order to describe it. The global level concerns the whole image and assigns a list of keywords to describe its general aspect. The two approaches, the first one more than the second one, depend considerably on the quality of the image segmentation. Unfortunately, the segmentation remains a challenge, and a lot of works concentrate on this topic (Shi & Malik, 2000). In this section, we are interested in the semi-automatic annotation of images at the global level. We consider the semi-automatic annotation because it requires user intervention in order to validate the system's decisions.

There is not a lot of work on image annotation. There are methods that apply a clustering of images and their associated keywords in order to make it possible to attach a text to images (Barnard, Duygulu,

& Forsyth, 2001; Barnard & Forsyth, 2001). With these methods, it is possible to predict the label of a new image by calculating some probabilities. Picard and Minka (1995) proposed a semi-automatic image annotation system in which the user chooses the area to be annotated in the image. A propagation of the annotations is carried out by considering textures. Maron and Ratan (1998) studied the automatic annotation using only one keyword at a same time. Mori Takahashi, and Oka (1999) proposed a model based on co-occurrences between the image and keywords in order to find the most relevant keywords for an image. The disadvantage of this model is that it requires a large training sample in order for it to be effective. Duygulu, Barnard, De Freitas, and Forsyh (2002) proposed another model, the *translation model*, which is an improvement of the co-occurrence model suggested by Mori et al. (1999) and this by integrating a training algorithm. Probabilistic models such as the Cross Media Relevance Model (Jeon, Lavrenko & Manmatha, 2003) and the Latent Semantic Analysis (Monay & Gatica-Perez, 2003) also were proposed. Li and Wang (2003) use the two-dimensional hidden Markov chains to annotate images.

Our work as well as the work of Barnard et al. (2001) concerns the global level. We use a prediction model (neighborhood graphs) to annotate an image collection. The method that we propose can be adapted easily for a local level annotation. So, we will try to answer the following question: Having a set of annotated images, how can we proceed in order to annotate a new image introduced without annotations? For that, we exploit the indexing structure proposed beforehand in the previous section of this chapter.

Formally, let Ω be a set of n images $\Omega = \{I_1, I_2, ... I_n\}$. Each image is described by a set of features $<f_1, f_2, ..., f_m>$ that represents the low-level characteristics (color, texture, etc.) and a list of keywords $W = w_1, w_2, ..., w_k$ $(m \neq k)$. So, an image I_i can be described by a vector $I_i = <f_1, f_2, ..., f_m, W_i>$ in which each image can have a different number of keywords. From that, having a new unlabeled image $I_x = <f_1, f_2, ..., f_m>$, it is then a problem of finding a model that can assign to the image I_x the labels that can describe its semantics. In other words, the goal is to pass from a representation in the form of $I_x = <f_1, f_2, ..., f_m>$ to a representation in the form of $I_x = <f_1, f_2, ..., f_m, W_x>$.

In our approach, image annotation problem passes by two levels: data modeling (indexing) and decision making (effective annotation). The first level is described in detail in the previous sections. The result of this step is a graph representation of the image database based only on the low-level characteristics. This representation aims to keep the neighborhood relations among items.

After the data modeling process, the annotation phase can start. The main principle is the following: each point in the graph is considered a *judge*. The unlabeled image is then situated in the multidimensional space (using only its low-level features), and its neighbors are located. From there, the potential annotations of the image are deduced from the annotations of its neighbors. This is done by using vote techniques. So, we can decide, according to the decision of the judges (neighbors), which are the most suitable annotations to assign to an unlabeled image.

The effective annotation requires user intervention on two levels: setting up the decision parameters (decision threshold) and the validation of the machine's decisions. In the following, we detail the decision-making process.

Decision Making

At this stage, we consider that the database is indexed by using a neighborhood graph. The goal here is the effective association of annotations to a new unlabeled image. The main idea is the *heritage.*

Indeed, we may inherit an image after its insertion in the neighborhood graph from the annotations of its neighbors by calculating scores for each potential annotation.

We can consider two simple ways to calculate the scores for the inherited annotations (the two scoring methods are given for illustration; other more sophisticated functions can be used for this purpose):

- **Naive method:** In this case, a score is calculated for each annotation by considering only the neighbors count of the unlabeled image. In other words, we give the same decision power for each judge. One then can see the following formula:

$$S_t = \frac{\sum_{j=1}^{l} [t \in A(\beta_j) \ and \ \beta_j \in V(\alpha)]^1}{|V(\alpha)|}$$

in which $V(\alpha)$ is the set of the neighbors of the query image α; t is a specific annotation in the neighborhood; l is the number of neighbors of the query image α; and B_j is the neighbor j of the query image α.

The calculated score represents the number of close images that contain the annotation t compared to the total number of neighbors. The scores are calculated for each annotation that belongs to the neighborhood of the unlabeled image.

This approach is rather simple. However, it presents the disadvantage of allotting the same decision power for each judge that takes part in the decision-making process.

- **Weighting method:** The second possibility consists of considering the distances between the query point and its neighbors. In this case, we introduce a weighting function and give a more important decision power to the nearest neighbors. So, the more an image is near, the more its decision power is important. The weights affectation can be performed using the following formula:

$$W_i = 1 - \frac{\delta(\beta_i, \alpha)}{\sum_{j=1}^{l} \delta(\beta_j, \alpha)}$$

With W_i, the affected weight to the ith neighbor, $\delta(\beta_i, \alpha)$: the distance between the neighbor β_i and the query image α.

The scores assignation is performed in the same way as the previous one. However, in this case, we consider the weights instead of the items. The formula of the score calculation becomes:

$$S_t = \frac{\sum_{j=1}^{l} [t \in A(\beta_j) \ and \ \beta_j \in V(\alpha)] W_j}{\sum_{j=1}^{l} W_j}$$

At the end of the score calculation process, an annotation is assigned to an image if its score is equal to or higher than a threshold fixed by the user.

Table 1. A set of image neighbors and their associated labels

Items	Concepts	Weights
$I1$	$c1, c2, c3, c4$	0.4
$I2$	$c1, c3$	0.3
$I3$	$c1, c2$	0.2
$I4$	$c1, c2, c3$	0.1

Table 2. Scores calculated using the naïve decision-making method

Concepts	Scores
$c1$	*100%*
$c2$	*75%*
$c3$	*75%*
$c4$	*25%*

Table 3. Scores calculated using the weighting decision-making method

Concepts	Scores
$c1$	100%
$c2$	70%
$c3$	80%
$c4$	10%

Example 2. In order to illustrate the different functions, let us consider the following example: consider a query image having four neighbors, I_1, I_2, I_3, I_4 (recovered using only the low-level characteristics from the graph). These images contain four concepts, c_1, c_2, c_3, c_4, as shown in Table 1.

The last column in Table 1 represents the weight of each neighbor according to its distance to the query point (needed in the second function). Using the naïve decision-making method, the scores one can obtain are illustrated in Table 2, which obtains the scores of Table 3 by using the second decision-making method.

If we consider a threshold of 75%, then the annotations of the query image using the first method will be c_1, c_2, and c_3 but will be only c_1 and c_3 using the weighting method.

Propagation of the Annotations

The annotation of a new image depends on its neighborhood. This means that the annotation of a new image and its insertion in the graph can generate possible modifications in the labels of its neighbors (because a user can add new annotations to a query image). This is what we call the *annotations propagation*. In our case, we consider only the new inserted annotations.

We consider that the propagation scope follows the same schema as the neighborhood updating one (Hacid & Zighed, 2005). So, we use a hypersphere of ray $SR = \delta_1 + \delta_2 + \varepsilon$ to propagate the annotations and to recalculate the score for each new annotation.

That is, to update the annotations of the neighborhood, we calculate initially the ray of the hypersphere and recover the images in it. The next stage is the calculation of the scores for each image by considering each one as a query item. Annotation assignment follows the same principle of the previous one (i.e., the score must be equal to or higher than a given threshold). The new annotation, of course, is assigned to the inserted item without any calculation.

From that, we can notice that the annotation process that we propose is an incremental process. Indeed, the annotations of the images are updated incrementally as other images are inserted into the database. This enables us to have rather complete semantics at a given moment.

Experiments and Results

The interest of neighborhood graphs for content-based image retrieval is shown and discussed in Scuturici et al. (2005). The comparison tests done with several configurations of *k-NN* were conclusive and showed the utility of these structures in this field.

In what concern us, we are interested in this section in three different tests:

- Testing the validity of the obtained results using the suggested method.
- Testing the execution times of the proposed method.
- Testing the annotation performances.

Evaluation of the Validity of the Proposed Method

By the validity of the obtained results, we mean the ability of our method to find for each new inserted item in the graph the same neighbors as the ones we can find using the standard algorithm. For that, we carried out several tests on various data sets.

The principle of these experiments is as follows: We take m data sets S_1, S_2, ..., S_m with different items count n_1, n_2, ..., n_m, we build a relative neighborhood graph on each dataset, and we save the corresponding graph structure, which will serve as a reference graph. Once the reference graphs are built, we take each dataset and build new graphs using $n-1$ items. We then use our method in order to insert

Figure 5. Recall variations on one dataset using different items

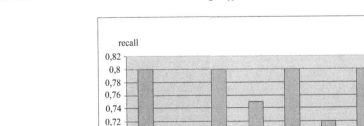

the remaining item, and we calculate the recall on the variously built graphs. This operation is repeated using several items on the *m* data sets.

We used various supervised datasets for these experiments; for example, Iris (Anderson, 1935; Fisher, 1936), UCI Irvine (Hettich, Blake, & Merz, 1998), and Breiman's waves (Breiman, Friedman, Olshen, & Stone, 1984). The graphic of Figure 5 illustrates the recall variation on one dataset with various insertions by considering three situations: the recall is calculated on the reference graph, then on a graph with *n−1* items, and finally after the insertion of the remaining item.

The first experiment constitutes our reference. The experiments carrying numbers 2, 4, and 6 are carried out with an item in less (*n−1* items) and experiments 3, 5, and 7 after the insertion of the remaining item in the corresponding previous experiment. That is, after the insertion of the remaining item, we always find the recall of the reference graph, which means that the method finds the good neighbors (i.e., exactly the same neighborhood as the reference graph) of the inserted item in each experiment, and the whole graph structure is well-updated.

EVALUATION OF THE EXECUTION TIME

In this section, we are interested in the response times of the suggested method (i.e., the time that the method takes to insert a query item in an existing structure). The evaluation protocol is rather similar to the previous one, but instead of recovering the recall, we recover the execution time. One of the used datasets in these experiments is an artificial dataset containing 30,000 items represented in 24 dimensions. We also used a machine with an INTEL Pentium 4 processor (2.80 GHz) and 512 Mo of memory. The response times for 20 items, always arbitrarily taken from the same dataset, are shown in the graphic of Figure 6. Note that we do not give a comparison with the execution time using the standard algorithm for legibility facilities.

The response times (expressed in milliseconds) are interesting according to the volume of the used data set. They vary between 20 and 60 milliseconds per item (average of the execution time). This is very interesting, considering that by using a standard method, the same neighborhood can be obtained

Figure 6. Illustration of the execution time variations using a sample of 20 local insertions into a dataset containing 30,000 items

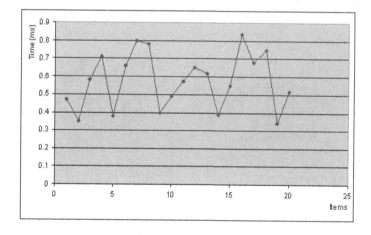

in four hours approximately in the same conditions. The variation of the execution times from one item to another is due especially to the fact that various amounts of candidate items for the neighborhood determination are used at each iteration.

Semi-Automatic Annotation Performances

In order to show the interest and performances of the proposed method for images annotation, we use an image database (Nene, Nayar, & Murase, 1996). This image database contains 7,200 images that represent 100 objects taken from various views. After the transformation of the image database into a vector representation using some image analysis techniques and the low-level features extracted, we have annotated the entire image database with a list of keywords that describe the semantic content of each image. So, each image is represented by a vector containing a set of descriptive features (24 low-level features) and from two to six keywords (we used a simple image database because the inter-

Figure 7. Retrieving a database using only the low-level characteristics indexed with a neighborhood graph

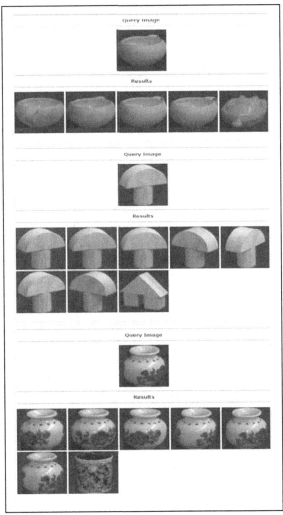

Table 4. The initial configuration of the neighborhood of the first query image

Images	Weights	Existing Annotations
1	0.35	Cup, Brown, Pottery, Bowl
2	0.25	Cup, Brown, Pottery, Bowl
3	0.15	Cup, Brown, Pottery, Bowl
4	0.1	Cup, Brown, Pottery, Bowl
5	0.15	Boat, Red

Table 5. Calculated scores for the candidate annotations

Annotations	Scores
Cup	85%
Brown	85%
Pottery	85%
Bowl	85%
Boat	15%
Red	15%

est here is not to show the performances of segmentation methods but only the utility of the proposed approach for annotating images).

We use approximately the same evaluation protocol as the previous tests. We first build a neighborhood graph using $n-1$ images considering only the low-level features (Figure 7 illustrates three retrieval examples using low-level characteristics). The second step consists of the insertion of the remaining item (the query images in Figure 7) in the graph previously built using the low-level characteristics. By applying the weighting annotation technique, we can predict the most suitable annotation that can be associated with the query image.

In order to illustrate the principle, let us consider the case of the first image of Figure 7. The associated weights and annotations for all images are summarized in Table 4.

According to this configuration, we calculate scores for each annotation. We obtain the scores illustrated in Table 5. Considering that the threshold is fixed to 75%, the image will be annotated as follows: Cup, Brown, Pottery, and Bowl with a score of 85%. These annotations are exactly the affected annotations to the query image. At the end, the user intervenes in order to accept the predicted annotations, discarding them or adding new free annotations. These last ones will be propagated in order to find out if other images can be annotated using them.

Generally speaking, the system has about 90% correct annotations of the images in the database. Of course, the images of the used database are rather simple; using a more complex image databases can affect the performances of the annotation approach but not considerably.

CONCLUSION

Content-based image retrieval is a complex task, primarily because of the nature of the images and the attached subjectivity to their interpretation. The use of an adequate index structure is primordial. In order to fix some problems related to the traditional indexing and retrieval approaches, we introduced neighborhood graphs as a substitution of the traditional tree structures and the *k-NN* approach. The introduction of neighborhood graphs in image databases indexing and retrieval is motivated by (a) the need for improving the neighborhood quality and (b) the necessity for automatic learning methods integration into the indexing process, which seems to us extremely important for mining image databases and for being able to discover possible hidden information in this type of data.

We also proposed a method for locally updating neighborhood graphs. Our method is based on the location of the potential items, which can be affected by the updating task, allowing an effective interaction with the index by supporting the most frequently applied operations on an index (insertion and deletion of an item). We also exploited the proposed indexing structure to help the user in the annotation of an image collection. The experiments performed on various datasets show the effectiveness and the utility of the proposed approach.

As future work, we plan to fix the problem of the relaxation parameter determination by setting up an automatic determination function. This can be achieved by taking into account some statistical parameters on the data, such as dispersion. On another side, we plan to use the proposed approach to annotate a more complex image collection. Finally, we plan to find a way to integrate user feedback in the system in order to make automatic the annotation process.

REFERENCES

Anderson, E. (1935). The irises of the Gaspé Peninsula. *Bulletin of the American Iris Society, 59*, 2–5.

Barnard, K., Duygulu, P., & Forsyth, D. A. (2001). Clustering art. *Computer Vision and Pattern Recognition (CVPR), 2*, 434–441.

Barnard, K., & Forsyth, D. A. (2001). Learning the semantics of words and pictures. In *Proceedings of the International Conference on Computer Vision (ICCV)* (pp. 408–415).

Bei, C.-D., & Gray, R. M. (1985). An improvement of the minimum distortion encoding algorithm for vector quantization. *IEEE Transactions on Communications, 33*, 1132–1133.

Bentley, J. L. (1975). Multidimensional binary search trees used for associative searching. *Communication of the ACM, 18*(9), 509–517.

Berchtold, S., Böhm, C., Keim, D.A., & Kriegel, H.-P. (1997). A cost model for nearest neighbor search in high-dimensional data space. In *Proceedings of the 16th ACM SIGACT-SIGMOD-SIGART Symposium on Principles of Database Systems* (pp. 78–86).

Breiman, L., Friedman, J. H., Olshen, R. A., & Stone, C. J. (1984). *Classification and regression trees.* Belmont, CA: Wadsworth International Group.

Chiueh, T.-C. (1994). Content-based image indexing. In *Very large databases* (pp. 582–593).

Cost, R. S., & Salzberg, S. (1993). A weighted nearest neighbor algorithm for learning with symbolic features. *Machine Learning, 10,* 57–78.

Cover, T. M., & Hart, P. E. (1967). Nearest neighbor pattern classification. *IEEE Transaction in Information Theory, 13,* 57–67.

Deerwester, S. C., Dumais, S. T., Landauer, T. K., Furnas, G. W., & Harshman, R. A. (1990). Indexing by latent semantic analysis. *Journal of the American Society for Information Science (JASIS), 41*(6), 391–407.

Duygulu, P., Barnard, K., De Freitas, J. F. G., & Forsyth, D. A. (2002). Object recognition as machine translation: Learning a lexicon for a fixed image vocabulary. In *Proceedings of the European Conference on Computer Vision, (ECCV)* (pp. 97–112).

Faloutsos, C., et al. (1994). Efficient and effective querying by image content. *Journal of Intelligent Information Systems, 3*(3/4), 231–262.

Fayyad, U. M., Piatetsky-Shapiro, G., & Smyth, P. (1996). From data mining to knowledge discovery: An overview. In *Advances in Knowledge Discovery and Data Mining* (pp. 1–34). Menlo Park: AAAI Press.

Fisher, R. (1936). The use of multiple measurements in taxonomic problems. *Annals of Eugenics, 7,* 179–188.

Fix, E., & Hudges, J. L. (1951). *Discriminatory analysis: Non parametric discrimination: Consistency properties* (Tech. Rep. No. 21-49-004). Randolph Field, TX: USAF School of Aviation Medicine.

Flickner, M., et al. (1995). Query by image and video content: The QBIC system. *IEEE Computer, 28*(9), 23–32.

Friedman, J. H., Baskett, F., & Shustek, L. J. (1975). An algorithm for finding nearest neighbors. *IEEE Transactions on Computers, 24*(10), 1000–1006.

Gabriel, K. R., & Sokal, R. R. (1969). A new statistical approach to geographic variation analysis. *Systematic Zoology, 18,* 259–278.

Gersho, A., & Gray, R. M. (1991). *Vector quantization and signal compression.* Boston: Kluwer Academic.

Guan, L., & Kamel, M. (1992). Equal-average hyperplane partitioning method for vector quantization of image data. *Pattern Recognition Letters, 13*(10), 693–699.

Guttman, A. (1984). R-trees: A dynamic index structure for spatial searching. In *Proceedings of the SIGMOD Conference* (pp. 47–57).

Hacid, H., & Zighed, A.D. (2005). An effective method for locally neighborhood graphs updating. *Database and Expert Systems Applications* (LNCS 3588, 930-939).

Hettich, S., Blake, C., & Merz, C. (1998). UCI repository of machine learning databases.

Jeon, J., Lavrenko, V., & Manmatha, R. (2003). Automatic image annotation and retrieval using cross-media relevance models. In *Proceedings of the SIGIR* (pp. 119–126).

Katajainen, J. (1988). The region approach for computing relative neighborhood graphs in the LP metric. *Computing, 40*, 147–161.

Kohonen, T. (2001). *Self-organizing maps* (Vol. 30). New York: Springer.

Lee, C.-H., & Chen, L.H. (1994). Fast closest codeword search algorithm for vector quantisation. In *IEEE Proceedings: Vision, Image, and Signal Processing* (Vol. 141, pp. 143–148).

Li, J., & Wang, J. Z. (2003). Automatic linguistic indexing of pictures by a statistical modeling approach. *IEEE Transactions on Pattern Analysis and Machine Intelligence, 25*(9), 1075–1088.

Lin, K.-I., Jagadish, H. V., & Faloutsos, C. (1994). The TV-tree: An index structure for high-dimensional data. *Very Large Databases Journal, 3*(4), 517–542.

Maron, O., & Ratan, A. L. (1998). Multiple-instance learning for natural scene classification. In *Proceedings of the International Conference on Machine Learning* (pp. 341–349).

Mitchell, T. M. (2003). Machine learning meets natural language. In *Proceedings of the Progress in Artificial Intelligence 8th Portuguese Conference on Artificial Intelligence, EPIA '97* (p. 391).

Monay, F., & Gatica-Perez, D. (2003). On image auto-annotation with latent space models. In *Proceedings of the ACM International Conference on Multimedia (ACM MM)*, Berkeley, CA (pp. 275–278).

Mori, Y., Takahashi, H., & Oka, R. (1999). Image-to-word transformation based on dividing and vector quantizing images with words. *Proceedings of the International Workshop on Multimedia Intelligent Storage and Retrieval Management* (pp. 341–349).

Nene, S. A., Nayar, S. K., & Murase, H. (1996). (Tech. Rep. No. CUCS-006-96). Columbia Object Image Library (coil-100).

Picard, R. W., & Minka, T. P. (1995). Vision texture for annotation. *Multimedia Systems, 3*(1), 3–14.

Preparata, F., & Shamos, M. I. (1985). *Computational Geometry: Introduction*. New York: Springer-Verlag.

Scuturici, M., Clech, J., Scuturici, V. M., & Zighed, A. D. (2005, January-June). Topological representation model for image databases query. *Journal of Experimental and Theoretical Artificial Intelligence (JETAI), 17*(1-2), 145–160.

Shi, J., & Malik, J. (2000). Normalized cuts and image segmentation. *IEEE Transactions on Pattern Analysis and Machine Intelligence, 22*(8), 888–905.

Smith, W. D. (1989). *Studies in computational geometry motivated by mesh generation* [doctoral thesis]. Princeton University.

Toussaint, G. T. (1980). The relative neighborhood graphs in a finite planar set. *Pattern Recognition, 12*, 261–268.

Toussaint, G. T. (1991). Some unsolved problems on proximity graphs. In *Proceedings of the First Workshop on Proximity Graphs*, Las Cruces, NM.

Veltkamp, R. C., & Tanase, M. (2000). *Content-based image retrieval systems: A survey* (Tech. Rep. No. UU-CS-2000-34). Utrecht University.

White, D. A., & Jain, R. (1996). Similarity indexing: Algorithms and performance. *Storage and Retrieval for Image and Video Databases (SPIE)*, 62–73.

This work was previously published in Semantic-Based Visual Information Retrieval, edited by Y. Zhang, pp. 230-251, copyright 2006 by IRM Press (an imprint of IGI Global).

Section III

Chapter IX
Solving the Small and Asymmetric Sampling Problem in the Context of Image Retrieval

Ruofei Zhang
Yahoo!, Inc., USA

Zhongfei (Mark) Zhang
SUNY Binghamton, USA

ABSTRACT

*This chapter studies the user relevance feedback in image retrieval. We take this problem as a standard two-class pattern classification problem aiming at refining the retrieval precision by learning through the user relevance feedback data. However, we have investigated the problem by noting two important unique characteristics of the problem: small sample collection and asymmetric sample distributions between positive and negative samples. We have developed a novel approach to empirical Bayesian learning to solve for this problem by explicitly exploiting the two unique characteristics, which is the methodology of **BA**yesian **L**earning in **AS**ymmetric and **S**mall sample collections, thus called **BALAS**. In **BALAS** different learning strategies are used for positive and negative sample collections, respectively, based on the two unique characteristics. By defining the relevancy confidence as the relevant posterior probability, we have developed an integrated ranking scheme in **BALAS** which complementarily combines the subjective relevancy confidence and the objective similarity measure to capture the overall retrieval semantics. The experimental evaluations have confirmed the rationale of the proposed ranking scheme, and have also demonstrated that **BALAS** is superior to an existing relevance feedback method in the current literature in capturing the overall retrieval semantics.*

INTRODUCTION

Very large collections of images have become ever more common than before. From stock photo collections and proprietary databases to the World Wide Web, these collections are diverse and often poorly indexed; unfortunately, image retrieval systems have not kept pace with the collections they are searching. How to effectively index and retrieve semantically relevant images according to users' queries is a challenging task. Most existing image retrieval systems, such as image search engines in Yahoo! (Yahoo! Search website) and Google (Google search website), are textual based. The images are searched by using the surrounding text, captions, keywords, etc. Although the search and retrieval techniques based on textual features can be easily automated, they have several inherent drawbacks. First, textual description is not capable of capturing the visual contents of an image accurately and in many circumstances the textual annotations are not available. Second, different people may describe the content of an image in different ways, which limits the recall performance of textual-based image retrieval systems. Third, for some images there is something that no words can convey. Try to imagine an editor taking in pictures without seeing them or a radiologist deciding on a verbal description. The content of images is beyond words. They have to be seen and searched as pictures: by objects, by style, by purpose.

To resolve these problems, Content-Based Image Retrieval (CBIR) has attracted significant research attention (Marsicoi et al., 1997; Ratan & Grimson, 1997; Sivic & Zisserman, 2003; Liu et al., 1998). In CBIR, a query image (an image to which a user tries to find similar ones) is imposed to the image retrieval system to obtain the semantically relevant images. The similarity between the query image and the indexed images in the image database is determined by their visual contents, instead of the textual information. Early research of CBIR focused on finding the "best" representation for image features, e. g., color, texture, shape, and spatial relationships. The similarity between two images is typically determined by the distances of individual low-level features and the retrieval process is performed by a *k-nn* search in the feature space (Del Bimbo, 1999). In this context, high level concepts and user's perception subjectivity cannot be well modeled. Recent approaches introduce more advanced human-computer interaction (HCI) into CBIR. The retrieval procedure incorporates user's interaction into the loop, which consists of several iterations. In each iteration, the user cast *positive samples* (relevant images) as well as *negative samples* (irrelevant images) for the returned results from the previous iteration. Based on user's feedback, the retrieval system is able to adaptively customize the search results to the user's query preference. This interaction mechanism is called relevance feedback, which allows a user to continuously refine his/her querying information after submitting a coarse initial query to the image retrieval system. This approach greatly reduces the labor required to precisely compose a query and easily captures the user's subjective retrieval preference.

However, most approaches to relevance feedback, e. g., (Rui et al., 1998; Picard et al., 1996; Porkaew et al., 1999; Zhang & Zhang, 2004), are based on heuristic formulation of empirical parameter adjustment, which is typically ad hoc and not systematic, and thus cannot be substantiated well. Some of the recent work (Wu et al., 2000; MacArthur et al., 2000; Tieu & Viola, 2000; Tong & Chan, 2001; Tao & Tang, 2004) formulates the relevance feedback problem as a classification or learning problem. Without further exploiting the unique characteristics of the training samples in the relevance feedback for image retrieval, it is difficult to map the image retrieval problem to a general two-class (i.e., relevance vs. irrelevance) classification problem in realistic applications.

Before we design a specific relevance feedback methodology, two unique characteristics of the relevance feedback problem in image retrieval must be observed and addressed when compared with the general pattern classification problems. The first is the small sample collection issue. In relevance feedback for image retrieval, the number of the training samples is usually small (typically < 20 in each iteration of interaction) relative to the dimensionality of the feature space (from dozens to hundreds, or even more), whereas the number of image classes or categories is usually large for typical image databases. The second characteristic is the asymmetric training sample issue. Most classification or learning techniques proposed in the literature of pattern recognition and machine learning, such as discriminant analysis (Duda & Hart, 1973) and Support Vector Machine (SVM) (Vapnik, 1995) consider the positive and negative examples interchangeably, and assume that both sets are distributed approximately equally. However, in relevance feedback for image retrieval, while it is reasonable to assume that all the positive samples conform to a single class distribution, it is typically not valid to make the same assumption for the negative samples, as there may be an arbitrary number of semantic classes for the negative samples to a given query; thus, the small, limited number of negative examples is unlikely to be representative for all the irrelevant classes, and this asymmetry characteristic must be taken into account in the relevance feedback learning.

In this chapter, we investigate the relevance feedback problem in image retrieval using empirical Bayesian learning. Specifically, we apply Bayesian learning by explicitly exploiting the two unique characteristics through developing a novel user relevance feedback methodology in image retrieval — **BA**yesian **L**earning in **A**symmetric and **S**mall sample collections, called **BALAS**. In **BALAS**, we introduce specific strategies to estimate the probability density functions for the positive and negative sample collections, respectively. It is shown that an optimal classification can be achieved when a scheme for measuring the relevancy confidence is developed to reflect the *subjective* relevancy degree of an image w.r.t. a query image. The relevancy confidence is integrated with the measure of feature-based distance, which reflects the *objective* proximity degree between image feature vectors, to order the ranking of the retrieved images from an image database.

The rest of the chapter is organized as follows. Beginning with the discussion of the related work in Section 2, we describe **BALAS** methodology in Section 3, in which the probability density estimations for the positive and negative sample distributions are introduced, and the measurement of the relevancy confidence is presented. In Section 4 the ranking scheme of **BALAS**, *session semantic distance*, is defined and developed. **BALAS** is evaluated as a prototype system, and the evaluations are reported in Section 5. Finally, this chapter is concluded in Section 6.

RELATED WORK

The problem of relevance feedback for image retrieval was identified and then received focused attention even in the early days of the CBIR research. Some of the early efforts attempted to learn a new query and the relative importance of different features or feature components (Rui et al., 1998; Nastar et al., 1998; Peng et al., 1999), while others attempted to learn a linear transformation in the feature space taking into account correlations among feature components (Ishikawa et al., 1998; Rui & Huang, 2000), or to map the learning problem to a two-class discriminant classification problem (Vasconcelos & Lippman, 2000). In particular, inspired by term weighting and relevance feedback techniques in textual document retrieval, some of those efforts focused on heuristics-based techniques to adjust parameters empirically, such as (Rui et al, 1998; Picard et al, 1996). The intuition was to emphasize more on the features that best cluster the positive samples and maximize the separation between the positive and negative samples. To achieve this goal, Kohonen's Learning Vector Quantization (LVQ) algorithm (Wood et al, 1998) and the tree-structured self-organizingmap (TS-SOM) (Laakdonen et al, 1999) were used for dynamic data clustering during the relevance feedback. For example, Laaksonen et al. (Laakdonen et al, 1999) applied TS-SOMs to index images along different feature dimensions such as color and texture. Positive and negative examples were mapped to positive and negative impulses and a low-pass filtering was applied to generate a map to implicitly reveal relative importance of different features, as a "good" map always keeps positive examples well clustered while negative examples are scattered away. Similarly, Peng et al. (Peng et al, 1999) used the same intuition to capture the feature relevance but took the probabilistic approach instead. Santini and Jain (Santini & Jain, 2000) proposed a method to optimize a parametric similarity metric according to the feedback from users.

Recently, the problem of the relevance feedback for image retrieval was investigated in the literature from a more systematic point of view by formulating it into an optimization problem. In the work of Ishikawa et al. (Ishikawa et al, 1998) and Rui and Huang (Rui & Huang, 2000), based on the minimization of the total distance of positive examples from the new query, an optimal solution was shown to be the weighted average as the new query and a whitening transform in the feature space. Moreover, Rui and Huang (Rui & Huang, 2000) adopted a two-level weighting scheme to cope with the singularity issue due to the small number of training samples. MacArthur et al. (MacAuthur et al., 2000) cast the relevance feedback problem into a two class learning problem, and used a decision tree algorithm to sequentially "cut" the feature space until all the points in the feature space within a partition are of the same class. The image data set was classified by the resulting decision tree: images that fell into a relevant leaf were collected and the nearest neighbors of the query were returned.

Classification techniques fromMachine Learning community were extensively used in the recent literature to solve for the relevance feedback problem of image retrieval, such as the BiasMap (Zhou & Huang, 2001) and the SVM active learning method (Tong & Chan, 2001), both using a kernel form to deal with the nonlinear classification boundaries, with the former emphasizing the small sample collection issue while the latter exploring the active learning issue. Active learning in image retrieval has been attracting attentions recently and several methods have been proposed (Geman & Moquet, 2000; Wang et al., 2003). Different metrics were proposed to select the most informative images for the user's labeling and the objective is to minimize the feedback rounds for the expected retrieval results by quickly learning a boundary that separates the images that satisfy the user's query concept from the rest of the database. Although interesting and promising, the evaluation and performance comparison between the active leaning methods and the traditional learning methods need more investigation. For more related work in the two-class classification problem with a small number of samples, see Zhou and Huang (Zhou & Huang, 2001); for related work in the two-class classification problem with asymmetric samples, see Lindgren and Spangeus (Lindgren & Spangeus, 2004).

Alternatively one-class classifiers were proposed, which formalized the relevance feedback in image retrieval as a one class (relevant images) classification problem (Tax & Duin, 2001; Chen et al., 2001). In this formalization, only positive examples are used while the presentation of users' query interests in terms of irrelevancy is not exploited. Compared to the methodologies using both positive and negative examples, the performance of one-class classifiers in the context of image retrieval is limited (Jing et al., 2003; Yan et al., 2003). In two-class classification category, Wu et al. (Wu et al., 2000) developed the D-EM algorithm within the transductive learning framework based on the examples both from the user feedback data (called labeled data) and from other data points (called unlabeled data); the method performs discriminant analysis through the EM (i.e., expectation and maximization) iterations to select a subspace of features, such that the two-class (i.e., the positive and negative sample classes) assumption on the data distribution has a better support. One notable work employing Bayesian relevance feedback is PicHunter (Cox et al., 2000). Also using Bayesian reasoning, there are three major differences between PicHunter and **BALAS**. First, the motivation is different. PicHunter addresses the "target search" problem, in which users seek to find a specific target image, i. e., exactly the same image as the query image, while **BALAS** attempts to find more semantically relevant images for a query image, which is harder compared with "target search". Second, PicHunter assumes that the probability of any given image being the target is independent of who the user is; in other words, all users are identical. This assumption does not hold true in the semantically relevant image retrieval. Third, the **BALAS** methodology is different from PicHunter's methodology. In PicHunter, a user model is derived from the offline learning and tuning to obtain the correlation between users' action and the displayed image set, whereas in **BALAS** we determine the relevancy/irrelevancy degree of each image by the online density estimation.

All these learning methods in relevance feedback for image retrieval are based on the assumption that both positive and negative samples conform either implicitly or explicitly to a well formed distribution. Considering the two unique characteristics of the relevance feedback problem of image retrieval, this assumption is often hardly valid, especially for negative samples, consequently limiting the performance of these methods. In this chapter, we propose **BALAS** methodology that not only generates an optimal classifier but also exploits the two unique characteristics of the problem to arrive at a novel *relevancy confidence* measure solving for the relevance feedback problem in image retrieval. In addition, **BALAS** offers an effective ranking scheme to integrate the *relevancy confidence* measure with a conventional feature-based distance to model the semantic similarity more precisely than the existing methods.

BALAS METHODOLOGY

Given a query image, it is natural that an indexed image data set can be classified into two classes of images, one is relevant in semantic content to the query and the other is irrelevant. A "good" relevance feedback method would, after learning, allow as many as relevant images to be retrieved and reject as many as irrelevant images from being retrieved. Consequently, this learning problem is reduced to a two-class classification problem in essence.

Given a feature space in which each image is represented as a feature vector, we apply Bayesian theory to determine the degree in which an image in the image data set is classified as a relevant or an irrelevant one to the query image. It is proven that the Bayesian rule is optimal in terms of the expected misclassification rate (Duda & Hart, 1973). In other words, no other rule has a lower expected error rate.

We define the notations as follows. We always use boldface symbols to represent vectors or matrices, and non-boldface symbols to represent scalar variables. Given a query image, Let R and I be the events of the relevancy and irrelevancy for all the images in the image data set to a query image, respectively, and let Img_i be the ith image in the image data set. We use $P()$ to denote a probability, and use $p()$ to denote a probability density function (pdf). Thus, $P(R)$ and $P(I)$ are the prior probabilities of relevancy and irrelevancy for all the images in the indexed data set to the query image, respectively; $p(Img_i)$ is the pdf of the ith image in the image data set; $P(R|Img_i)$ and $P(I|Img_i)$ are the conditional probabilities of the ith image's relevancy and irrelevancy to the query image, respectively; and $p(Img_i|R)$ and $p(Img_i|I)$ are the pdfs of the ith image given the relevant and irrelevant classes, respectively, in the image data set to the query image. Based on the Bayes's rule the following equations hold:

$$P(R|\mathrm{Img}_i) = \frac{p(\mathrm{Img}_i|R)P(R)}{p(\mathrm{Img}_i)} \tag{1}$$

$$P(I|\mathrm{Img}_i) = \frac{p(\mathrm{Img}_i|I)P(I)}{p(\mathrm{Img}_i)} \tag{2}$$

where $i = 1, \ldots, M$ and M is the number of images in the indexed data set.

Definition 1 *Given a specific image Img_i in an image data set, for any query image, the relevancy confidence of this image to the query image is defined as the posterior probability $P(R|Img_i)$. Similarly, the irrelevancy confidence of this image to the query image is defined as the posterior probability $P(I|Img_i)$. Obviously, the two confidences are related as $P(R|Img_i) + P(I|Img_i) = 1$.*

The relevancy confidence and irrelevancy confidence of an image are used to quantitatively describe the *subjective* relevance and irrelevance degrees to the query image, respectively.

From equations 1 and 2, the problem of determining whether an image Img_i is (ir)relevant to the query image and the corresponding (ir)relevancy confidence is reduced to estimating the conditional pdfs $p(Img_i|R)$ and $p(Img_i|I)$, respectively, the prior probabilities $P(R)$ and $P(I)$, respectively, and the pdf $p(Img_i)$ in the continuous feature space. These probabilities and pdfs may be estimated from the positive and negative samples provided by the user relevance feedback, as we shall show.

Since in CBIR, each image is always represented as a feature vector or a group of feature vectors (e.g., when each feature vector is used to represent a region or an object in the image (Carson et al., 2002)) in a feature space, to facilitate the discussion we use a feature vector to represent an image in this chapter. Consequently, in the rest of this chapter, we use the terminologies vector and image interchangeably. Due to the typical high dimensionality of feature vectors, we perform vector quantization before the pdf estimations to ease the computation intensity. Typically, as a preprocessing, uniform quantization is applied to every dimension of feature vectors and each interval is represented by its corresponding representative value. In the rest of this chapter, all the feature vectors in the image data set are meant to be the quantized feature vectors.

It is straightforward to estimate the pdf $p(Img_i)$ by statistically counting the percentage of the quantized feature vectors in the feature space of the whole image data set. Note that this estimation is performed offline and for each image it is only required to be computed once, resulting in no complexity for online retrieval. For image databases updated with batch manner (most practical databases are updated in this way), the content of databases does not change during the working periods and periodically updating $p(Img_i)$ with data set updating is feasible.

While the relevance feedback problem in image retrieval is a typical two class classification problem, due to the asymmetry nature between the positive and negative samples collected in the relevance feedback, the often-used assumption in the literature that the positive and the negative samples both conform to their corresponding well-formed distribution functions is not typically valid. In fact, posi-

Figure 1. Quantile-quantile test of a standardized feature dimension for images in one semantic category

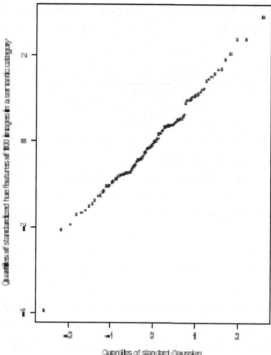

tive samples typically have a compact, low-dimensional support while negative samples can have arbitrary configurations (Zhou & Huang, 2001). Moreover, in relevance feedback, the sample collection, either positive or negative, is typically small. To address these characteristics explicitly and precisely, the **BALAS** methodology employs different strategies to estimate the conditional pdfs $p(Img_i|R)$ and $p(Img_i|I)$, respectively.

Estimating the Conditional PDF of the Positive Samples

It is well observed that all the positive (i.e., the relevant) samples "are alike in a way" (Zhou & Huang, 2001). In other words, some features of the class-of-interest usually have compact support in reality. We assume that the pdf of each feature dimension of all the relevant images to a given query image satisfies the Gaussian distribution.

$$p(x_k|R) = \frac{1}{\sqrt{2\pi}\sigma_k} \exp[-\frac{(x_k - m_k)^2}{2\sigma_k^2}] \tag{3}$$

where x_k is the kth dimension of the feature vector of an image, m_k is the mean value of the x_k of all relevant images to the query image, and σ_k is the standard deviation of the kth dimension of the relevant images.

To verify this model for positive samples, we have tested it on images of several predefined semantic categories. The experiment confirms that the model is practically acceptable. Figure 1 shows a quantile-quantile test (Ripley & Venables, 2002) of the standardized *hue* feature of 100 images in one predefined semantic category. It is shown that the quantile of the standardized feature dimension and the quantile of the standard Gaussian distribution are similar, which means that the feature dimension of the 100 images in this semantic category can be approximated as a Gaussian.

Assume that $L = \{l_1, l_2, \ldots, l_N\}$ is the relevant sample set provided by a user. Applying the maximum-likelihood method (Blom, 1989), we obtain the following unbiased estimations of the mean m_k and the standard deviation σ_k for the kth dimension of the features.

$$\widehat{m_k} = \frac{1}{N} \sum_{i=1}^{N} l_{ki} \tag{4}$$

and

$$\widehat{\sigma_k} = \frac{1}{N-1} \sum_{i=1}^{N} (l_{ki} - \widehat{m_k})^2 \tag{5}$$

where l_{ki} denotes the kth dimension of the feature vector l_i.

In order to ensure that these estimates are close to the true values of the parameters, we must have sufficient relevant samples. However, the number of relevant samples in each relevance feedback iteration is typically limited. Hence, we develop a cumulative strategy to increase the number of available relevant samples. Specifically, the relevant samples in each iteration in a query session are recorded over the iterations; when we estimate the parameters using equations 4 and 5, we not only use the relevant samples labeled by the user in the current iteration, but also include all the relevant samples recorded in the previous iterations to improve the estimation accuracy.

It is notable that not every feature dimension of the relevant images conforms to a Gaussian distribution equally well. It is possible that, for one semantic category, some feature dimensions are more semantically related than other dimensions such that these dimensions appear to conform to a Gaussian model better, while other dimensions' distributions in the feature space are jumbled, and thus do not conform to a Gaussian model well. To describe the different conformity degrees to Gaussian distributions among different dimensions in the feature space we introduce a measure, called *trustworthy degree*, to each feature dimension. The trustworthy degree depicts the goodness of model fitting on each feature dimension. It is defined as follows:

$$w_k = \frac{\sigma_k^{-1}}{\max_{j=1}^{T} \sigma_j^{-1}} \tag{6}$$

for each dimension k, $k = 1, \ldots, T$, where T is the number of dimensions of the feature space. This is a heuristic measure. The justification follows. If the standard deviation of the relevant samples is large along the dimension k, then we can deduce that the values on this dimension are not very relevant to the query image and thus the Gaussian distribution might not be a good model for this dimension because the features are not centered well around a prominent mean. Consequently, a low trustworthy degree w_k is assigned. Otherwise, a high trustworthy degree w_k is assigned. Note that the concept of the trustworthy degree is always relative to different image databases with different feature distributions. That is why we use the max function in the denominator, which maps $w_k \in [0, 1]$ for $k = 1, \ldots, T$.

To simplify the estimation of the class probability, we assume that all dimensions of one feature are independent (the raw features *per se* are independent, e. g., color and texture features, or we can always apply K-L transform (Dillon & Goldstein, 1984) to generate uncorrelated features from the raw features, resulting in the strengthened support to the assumption); this is just a justifiable design decision. Thus, the pdf of positive samples is determined as a trustworthy degree pruned joint pdf:

$$p(x|R) = \prod_{\substack{k=1 \\ w_k \geq \delta}}^{T} p(x_k|R) \tag{7}$$

where δ is a threshold for incorporating only high trustworthy dimensions (conforming to the Gaussian model well) to determine $p(x_k|R)$; it is determined empirically as 0.70 in the experiment by using cross-validation. Those dimensions that do not conform to the Gaussian distribution well would result in inaccurate pdf estimations, and consequently are filtered out.

Estimating the Conditional pdf of the Negative Samples

Unlike the positive samples which may be assumed to conform to a single, well-formed distribution function, negative (i.e., the irrelevant) samples may not be assumed to follow a single distribution function, as there may be many different irrelevant semantics to a query image. While the relevance feedback problem may be tackled as a general two-class classification problem (the relevance class and the irrelevance class), due to the fact that each negative sample is "negative in its own way" (Zhou & Huang, 2001), samples from the irrelevance class may come from different semantic classes. Consequently, it is neither reasonable nor practical to assume that all negative samples conform to one single distribution function as is assumed for the positive samples.

In order to correctly and accurately estimate the conditional pdf distribution for the negative samples, we assume that each negative sample represents a unique potential semantic class, and we apply the kernel density estimator (Silverman, 1986) to determine the statistical distribution function of all negative samples. In case two negative samples happen to come from the same semantic class, it is supposed that they would exhibit the same distribution function, and thus this assumption is still valid. Consequently, the overall pdf for the negative samples is the agglomeration of all the kernel functions.

We choose the kernel function in the estimator as an isotropic Gaussian function (assuming all the feature vectors have been normalized). The window of the estimation is a hyper-sphere centered at each negative sample x_j, $j = 1, 2, \ldots, N$, assuming that there are N negative samples in total. Let the radius of the jth hyper-sphere be r_j, which is called the *bandwidth* of the kernel density estimation in the literature (Chiu, 1996). Typically it is practical to assume that $r_j = r$ for all the different j, where r is a constant bandwidth. Hence, the conditional pdf to be estimated for the sample x_i in the feature space is given by

$$p(x_i|I) = \sum_{j=1}^{N} kernel(x_i, x_j) = \sum_{j=1}^{N} \exp\left\{-\frac{\|x_i - x_j\|_2^2}{2r_j^2}\right\} \tag{8}$$

where $\|x_i - x_j\|_2$ is the Euclidian distance between the neighboring sample x_j and the center feature vector x_i.

The choice of the bandwidth r has an important effect in the estimated pdfs. If the bandwidth is too large, the estimation would suffer from low resolution. On the other hand, if the bandwidth is too small, the estimation might be locally overfitted, hurting the generalization of the estimation. In this consideration, the optimal Parzen window size has been studied extensively in the literature (Chiu, 1996; Terrell & Scott, 1992). In practice, the optimal bandwidth may be determined by minimizing the *integrated squared error* (ISE), or the *mean integrated squared error* (MISE) (Chiu, 1996). The adaptive bandwidth is also proposed in the literature (Terrell & Scott, 1992). For simplicity, we choose a constant bandwidth r based on the maximum distance from all the negative samples to their closest neighbor D defined as follows:

$$r = \lambda D = \lambda \max_{x_k}[\min_{x_l}(\|x_k - x_l\|_2)] \tag{9}$$

where λ is a scalar. We find in our experiments that with well-normalized feature vectors, a λ between 1 and 10 often gives good results.

The computational overhead in estimating conditional pdf with Eq. 8 is tractable due to the limited number of negative samples and the use of dimensionality reduction techniques, while the estimation accuracy is satisfactory.

Since negative samples may potentially belong to different semantic class, and since each such semantic class only has a very limited number of samples thus far in one typical relevance feedback iteration, we must "generate" a sufficient number of samples to ensure that the estimated pdf for the negative samples is accurate. This problem has been studied in a semi-supervised learning framework in the community, e.g., Szummer and Jaakkola formulated a regularization approach (Szummer & Jaakkola, 2002) to linking the marginal and the conditional in a general way to handle the partially labeled Data. Although reported effective, the approach is very computation-intensive for a large scale database. Similarly performed in the semi-supervised learning framework, we address this "scarce sample collection" problem from another perspective. We actually generate additional negative samples based on the kernel distributions for each semantic classes defined in Eq. 8. These generated additional samples are the hypothetical images. For the sake of discussion, we call the original negative samples provided by the user in the relevance feedback iterations as the *labeled* samples, and the generated samples as the *unlabeled* samples. To ensure that the number of the generated samples is sufficiently large, for each labeled negative sample in one relevance feedback iteration, we generate q additional unlabeled negative samples, where q is a parameter. To ensure a "fair sampling" to the kernel function in Eq. 8, the generation of the unlabeled samples follows a probability function defined by the following Gaussian pdf function:

$$p(y) = \frac{1}{\sqrt{2\pi}\sigma} \exp\left\{-\frac{\|y - x_i\|_2^2}{2\sigma^2}\right\} \tag{10}$$

where $\|y - x_i\|_2$ is the Euclidian distance between the unlabeled sample y and the corresponding labeled sample x_i and σ is the standard deviation, which is set to be the average distance between two feature vectors in the labeled negative feature space defined as follows:

$$\sigma = \frac{1}{N(N-1)} \sum_{i=1}^{N} \sum_{\substack{j=1 \\ j \neq i}}^{N} \|x_i - x_j\|_2 \tag{11}$$

Equation 10 may be represented in another form as a function of the Euclidian distance, z, between the unlabeled sample y and the labeled sample x_i:

$$p(z) = \frac{1}{\sqrt{2\pi}\sigma} \exp(-\frac{z^2}{2\sigma^2}) \tag{12}$$

Based on Eq. 12, a vector is more likely to be selected as unlabeled negative sample if it is closer to a labeled negative sample than if it is farther away from a labeled negative sample. The probability density defined in Eq. 12 decays when the Euclidian distance to the labeled sample increases.

The following algorithm, called SAMPLING, is designed to perform the unlabeled sample selection based on Eq. 12. In the algorithm, *NUM* is the number of the unlabeled negative samples we intend to generate for each labeled sample. τ is a parameter to adjust the range centered at the positions with a distance d to the labeled sample, in which we select the unlabeled samples. In our experiments, τ is set to d/NUM.

In essence, SAMPLING implements a roulette wheel sampling strategy (Blom, 1989) to select unlabeled samples. The vectors with smaller distances to a labeled sample have larger probabilities to be selected as unlabeled samples. However, those potential unlabeled samples farther away from a labeled sample are not completely eliminated from being selected, though their chances of being selected are small. This random selection principle is reasonable. After generating unlabeled samples, Eq. 8 is ap-

Box 1. Algorithm SAMPLING

```
input   : S, Labeled negative example set
output  : R, Extended negative sample set
begin

    R = {};

    for each labeled negative example s ∈ S do

        i = 0;

        Create an array A with NUM + 1 elements, each element v_k = (k/NUM) * (1/√2πσ), where k ∈ [0, NUM];

        while i < NUM do

            d = 0;

            Generate a random number t = rand() in [0, 1/√2πσ];

            Search array A to find the k with v_{k-1} < t ≤ v_k;

            Determine the distance d based on the function v_k = p(d) defined in Eq. 12;

            Randomly sample the feature space until a feature V is found with a distance s in [d − τ, d + τ];

            R = R ∪ {V};

            i = i + 1;

        end

    end

    return R;

end
```

plied to both labeled and unlabeled samples. Since in general the feature space is huge and has loose cluster presentation for the distribution of features, the feature vectors selected in this algorithm are statistically possible to be the true negative samples. With the extended number of the negative samples, the accuracy of the pdf estimation defined in Eq. 8 is significantly improved as shown in the experiments. In addition, the cumulative learning principle adopted in the estimation of the conditional pdf for the positive samples is also applied in the estimation of the conditional pdf for the negative samples to further improve the estimation accuracy. While the estimation obtained from this method is still biased towards the given negative samples, it is noticeable that under the circumstances where there is no other information given, this is the best we can do. Compared to the existing approaches to handling unlabeled examples (Szummer & Jaakkola, 2000), SAMPLING algorithm is simple and does not use the unlabeled examples explicitly, yet more efficient and scalable.

Determining the Prior Probabilities

In order to determine the relevancy and irrelevancy confidences defined as the posterior probabilities in equations 1 and 2, we must solve for the prior probabilities *P(R)* and *P(I)* first. Unlike the typical approach in the classical pattern classification problems in which a prior probability is usually estimated from the supervised training samples, in the problem of the relevance feedback in image retrieval the relevancy or irrelevancy of an image is subject to different query images and different user subjective preferences. Thus, the relevancy and irrelevancy of an image vary to different queries and in different query sessions. Consequently, it is impossible to estimate the prior probabilities in advance. In other words, these prior probabilities must also be estimated online in solving for the relevance feedback problem. In **BALAS**, we propose the following method to solve for the prior probabilities. Given a query image, for each image Img_i in the image data set, we have:

$$p(\text{Img}_i) = p(\text{Img}_i|R) \, P(R) + p(\text{Img}_i|I) \, P(I) \tag{13}$$

and for the query image we also have

$$P(R) + P(I) = 1 \tag{14}$$

Combining equations 13 and 14, we immediately have:

$$P(R) = \frac{p(\text{Img}_i) - p(\text{Img}_i|I)}{p(\text{Img}_i|R) - p(\text{Img}_i|I)} \tag{15}$$

From equation 15, it is clear that since we have already developed methods to determine *p(Img_i|R)*, *p(Img_i|I)*, and *p(Img_i)*, the prior probability *P(R)* can be uniquely determined immediately. Thus, *P(I)* can also be immediately determined from equation 14. This reveals that for each given query image, the *overall* relevancy and irrelevancy of *all* the images in the image data set may be uniquely determined by *any individual* image Img_i in the image data set. In other words, any individual image Img_i in the image data set may be used to determine the prior probabilities, and given a query image, the prior probabilities are independent of the selection of any of the images in the data set. The experimental results have verified this conclusion. Nevertheless, due to the noise in the data, in practice, the estimated prior probabilities based on different individual images in the data set may exhibit slight variations. In order to give an accurate estimation of the prior probabilities that are not subject to the bias towards a specific image in the data set, we denote $P_i(R)$ as the prior probability determined in equation 15 using the individual image Img_i, i.e.,

$$P_i(R) = \frac{p(\text{Img}_i) - p(\text{Img}_i|I)}{p(\text{Img}_i|R) - p(\text{Img}_i|I)} \tag{16}$$

Thus, the final prior probability P(R) is determined by an average of all the images in the data set, i.e.,

$$P(R) = \frac{1}{M} \sum_{i=1}^{M} P_i(R) \tag{17}$$

where M is the number of images in the database, as defined in equations 1 and 2.

The prior probability $P(I)$ is determined accordingly from equation 14. It is noted that although this estimation of $P(R)$ is not really legitimate from the perspective of strict statistics, it is effective in empirical Bayes approaches.

RANKING SCHEME

Given a query image, for each image Img_i in the data set, there is a corresponding relevancy confidence $P(R|Img_i)$, which represents the relevancy degree of this image to the query image learned from the user's subjective preference through the relevance feedback. Hence, this relevancy confidence captures the *subjective* relevancy degree of each image in the data set to a query. On the other hand, for any CBIR system, there is always a feature-based distance measure used for similarity comparisons. The feature-based distance measure typically does not incorporate the user relevance preferences, and thus, only captures the *objective* proximity degree in the feature space of each image in the data set to a query. Consequently, in order to design a ranking scheme in image retrieval that "makes the best sense", it is ideal to consider to integrate the subjective relevancy confidence and the objective distance measure together through taking advantage of the labeled sample image set to define an comprehensive ranking scheme.

Noting that the relevancy confidence and the feature-based distance measure are complementary to each other, we define a unified ranking scheme, called *Session Semantic Distance* (SD), to measure the relevance of any image Img_i within the image data set in terms of both the relevancy confidence $P(R|Img_i)$, the irrelevancy confidence $P(I|Img_i)$, and the feature based distance measure $FD(Img_i)$ (e.g., for the Euclidean distance in the feature space between the query image and Img_i, $FD(\text{Im } g_i) = \|Q_u - \text{Im } g_i\|_2$, where Qu is the query image).

The SD for any image SD(Img_i) is defined using a modified form of the Rocchio's formula (Rocchio, 1971). The Rocchio's formula for relevance feedback and feature expansion has proven to be one of the best iterative optimization techniques in the field of information retrieval. It is frequently used to estimate "optimal query" Q' with an initial query Q in the relevance feedback for sets of relevant documents D_R and irrelevant documents D_I given by the user. The Rocchio's formula is:

$$Q' = \alpha Q + \beta(\frac{1}{N_R} \sum_{d_j \in D_R} d_j) - \gamma(\frac{1}{N_I} \sum_{d_j \in D_I} d_j) \tag{18}$$

where α, β, and γ are suitable constants; N_R and N_I are the numbers of documents in D_R and D_I, respectively. Based on the Rocchio's formula, $SD(Img_i)$ is defined as follows:

$$
\begin{aligned}
SD(\mathrm{Img}_i) \;=\; & \log(1 + P(R|\mathrm{Img}_i))FD(\mathrm{Img}_i) \\
& + \; \beta\{\frac{1}{N_R} \sum_{k \in D_R} [(1 + P(R|\mathrm{Img}_k))U_{ik}]\} \\
& - \; \gamma\{\frac{1}{N_I} \sum_{k \in D_I} [(1 + P(I|\mathrm{Img}_k))U_{ik}]\}
\end{aligned}
\tag{19}
$$

where N_R and N_I are the sizes of the positive and negative labeled sample sets D_R and D_I, respectively, in the relevance feedback, and U_{ik} is the feature-based distance between the images Img_i and Img_k (e.g., $U_{ik} = \|\mathrm{Im}\,g_i - \mathrm{Im}\,g_k\|_2$). We have replaced the first parameter α in the original Rocchio's formula with the logarithm of the relevancy confidence of the image Img_i. The other two parameters β and γ are assigned a value of 1.0 in our current implementation of the system for the sake of simplicity. However, other values may be given to emphasize the different weights between the last two terms.

With this definition of the $SD(Img_i)$, the relevancy confidence of Img_i, the relevancy confidence of images in the labeled relevant set, the irrelevancy confidence of images in the labeled irrelevant set, and the objective feature distance measure are integrated in a unified approach. The (ir)relevancy confidences of images in the labeled sample set act adaptively as weights to correct the feature-based distance measure. In the ranking scheme, an image is ranked high in the returned list if it is similar, in relevancy confidence measure and/or feature-based distance measure, to the query image and images in the labeled relevant image set, and it is dissimilar to images in the labeled irrelevant image set in both relevancy confidence and feature-based distance measure; otherwise, its rank is low. Thus, the robustness and precision of the semantic distance measure is improved, resulting in lower false-positives, by using both subjective and objective similarity measures to form a more accurate and unified measure for semantic similarity.

EXPERIMENTS AND DISCUSSIONS

The focus of this chapter is on user relevance feedback in image retrieval rather than on a specific image indexing and retrieval method. The relevance feedback methodology we have developed in this chapter, **BALAS**, is independent of any specific image indexing and retrieval methods, and in principle, may be applied to any such image indexing and retrieval methods. The objective of this section is to demonstrate that **BALAS** can effectively improve the image retrieval relevancy through the user relevance feedback using a prototype CBIR system.

For the evaluation purpose, we have implemented an image indexing and retrieval prototype system. In such a prototype system, many kinds of low-level features may be used to describe the content of images. In the current implementation, we use color moment, which is shown to be robust and effective (Stricker & Oregno, 1996). We extract the first two moments from each channel of CIE-LUV color space, and the simple yet effective L2 distance is used to be the ranking metric. Since the objective is to test the relevance feedback learning method rather than to evaluate the effectiveness of the features, the features we used are not as sophisticated as those used in some existing CBIR systems (Zhang & Zhang, 2003; Cox et al., 2000).

The following evaluations are performed on a general-purpose color image database containing 10,000 images from the COREL collection with 96 categories. All images are indexed as described previously, and 1,500 images are randomly selected from all categories to be the query set. A retrieved image is considered semantically relevant if it is in the same category of the query image. We note that the category information is only used to ground-truth the evaluation, and we do not make use of this information in the indexing and retrieval procedures. Figure 2 shows a few samples of the indexed images.

We have implemented the **BALAS** methodology on a prototype CBIR system, which we also call **BALAS** for the purpose of the discussion in this chapter. For a more general discussion on the implementation methods, see (Zhang, 2005). Since user relevance feedback requires subjective feedback, we have invited a group of 5 users to participate the evaluations. The participants consist of CS graduate students as well as lay-people outside the CS Department. We asked different users to run **BALAS** initially without the relevance feedback interaction, and then to place their relevance feedbacks after the initial retrievals. Figure 3 is a screen shot of the **BALAS** system. Users check (+) or (-) radio buttons in the interface to place their relevance/irrelevance votes for each returned image. All the reported results are the averages of the whole group of users. The average time for each round of retrieval after the relevance input is about 2 seconds on a Pentium IV 2GHz computer with 512MB memory.

The feature-based distance FD describes the difference between image content details while the relevancy confidence depicts the perceptual aspects, i. e., semantic concepts, of images to users. To compare the capabilities of the two similarity measures as well as the session semantic distance (SD) we have defined to deliver an effective image retrieval, we test the three similarity metrics on images of 10 different semantic categories (each category has 100 images). These 10 categories are selected

Figure 2. Sample images in the testing image database. The images in each column are assigned to one category. From left to right, the categories are "Africa rural area," "historical building," "waterfalls," and "British royal event," respectively

Figure 3. A screen shot of the BALAS system. The query image is "city skyline" and the first page of the retrieved images is shown. In this example, 12 of the top 16 returned images are relevant

such that no semantic overlap existing among them. The categories are {Africa, beach, buildings, buses, dinosaurs, elephants, flowers, horses, mountains, food}. In the comparison, FD is defined as Euclidean distance metric due to its effectiveness and simplicity. The average precisions of top 20(30, 50) returned images based on FD, the relevancy confidence $P(R|Img)$, and the SD for each category are recorded in Table 1. In the experiment, the number of the positive and negative samples are both 30 for the learning relevancy confidence. It shows that for the categories which have clear foreground/background and/or prominent objects, such as "dinosaur", "flowers", "horses", the feature-based distance performs well while the relevancy confidence is comparable. For the categories which do not have clear definitions of the objects in the images, such as "Africa", "beach", "food", the relevancy confidence is noticeably better for capturing the semantics. The integrated distance metric, SD, performs the best or is comparable to the better one of FD and $P(R|Img)$ in all the 10 categories.

To evaluate the systematic performance on the 10,000 image database, we have run the implemented CBIR system with **BALAS** for the 1,500 query image set with varying number of truncated top retrieved images and have plotted the curves of the average retrieval precision vs. the number of truncated top retrieved images (called scope). Figure 4 shows the average precision-scope plot for the system with and without **BALAS** enabled. In other words, one test is based solely on the feature distance FD and the other test is based on the session semantic distance SD with different numbers of provided sample images. The notation (m/n) in the figure denotes the number of positive sample images vs. the number of negative sample images for the learning. In the evaluations, the sampling multiplier for the negative samples (*NUM* in the algorithm SAMPLING) is set to 5. From this figure, it is clear that the **BALAS**

Table 1. The precision in top N returned images based on FD, P(R|Img), and SD metrics for the 10 categories. The "Average" column for each distance metric is the average of the corresponding three left columns (Top 20, Top 30, and Top 50, respectively)

Category	FD				P(R|Img)				SD			
	Top 20	Top 30	Top 50	Average	Top 20	Top 30	Top 50	Average	Top 20	Top 30	Top 50	Average
Africa	0.23	0.20	0.12	0.18	0.41	0.26	0.22	0.30	0.59	0.31	0.25	0.38
beach	0.32	0.25	0.20	0.26	0.62	0.55	0.48	0.55	0.60	0.58	0.50	0.56
buildings	0.38	0.30	0.24	0.31	0.51	0.31	0.29	0.37	0.49	0.38	0.30	0.39
buses	0.62	0.58	0.52	0.57	0.51	0.49	0.50	0.50	0.62	0.60	0.55	0.59
dinosaurs	0.80	0.72	0.69	0.74	0.73	0.65	0.58	0.65	0.81	0.75	0.70	0.75
elephants	0.58	0.50	0.43	0.50	0.61	0.59	0.50	0.57	0.60	0.55	0.51	0.55
flowers	0.81	0.72	0.70	0.74	0.90	0.81	0.82	0.65	0.91	0.86	0.80	0.83
horses	0.91	0.85	0.60	0.79	0.69	0.65	0.61	0.65	0.91	0.86	0.80	0.86
mountains	0.52	0.46	0.30	0.43	0.76	0.69	0.60	0.68	0.80	0.73	0.65	0.73
food	0.41	0.32	0.20	0.31	0.81	0.73	0.69	0.74	0.79	0.75	0.68	0.74

relevance feedback learning capability enhances the retrieval effectiveness substantially. In addition, we also calculate average precision-recall with the same configuration for 10 randomly picked queries on a 60 image data set, shown in Figure 5. Again, **BALAS** demonstrates a better performance.

In order to compare the performance of **BALAS** with those of the state-of-the-art user relevance feedback methods in the literature, we have used the same image data set and the query set to compare **BALAS** with the relevance feedback method developed by Yong and Huang (Rui & Huang, 2000), which is a combination and improvement of its early version and MindReader (Ishikawa et al., 1998) and represents the state-of-the-art relevance feedback research in the literature. Two versions of (Rui & Huang, 2000) are implemented. The first uses the color moments (called CM here) computed in the same way as described previously and the other uses the correlogram (called CG here) (Huang et al., 1997). For the latter, we consider RGB color space with a quantization of 64 total buckets. The distance set D = {1, 3, 5, 7} is used for computing the autocorrelograms, which results in a feature vector of 256 dimensions. The overall comparison evaluations are documented in Figure 6. The average precision in this evaluation is determined based on the top 100 returned images for each query out of the 1,500 query image set. From the figure, it appears that during the first two iterations, CG performs noticeably better than **BALAS** while CM performs comparably with **BALAS**. After the second iteration, **BALAS** exhibits a significant improvement in performance over that of (Rui & Huang, 2000) in either of the two versions, and as the number of iterations increases, the improvement of the performance of **BALAS** over (Rui & Huang, 2000) appears to increase also. For example, after five iterations of the feedback, **BALAS** boosts its retrieval precision (i.e., the precision is 14%) more than those of (Rui & Huang, 2000) using both CG (the precision is 10.5%) and CM (the precision is 9.5%), which means that **BALAS** has more potential. This also confirms with the cumulative learning strategy employed in **BALAS** and the fact that when more iterations of relevance feedback are conducted, more learning samples are given, and thus better performance is expected from **BALAS**.

To evaluate the effectiveness of explicitly addressing the asymmetry issue of relevance feedback in CBIR, we compare **BALAS** with the SVM (Vapnik, 1995) classification method. SVM classifier adopts the two-class assumption and treats positive and negative samples equally, which is not valid in CBIR as we have discussed. In addition, for SVM there is no satisfied method to optimally select

Figure 4. Average precisions vs. the numbers of the returned images with and without BALAS enabled.

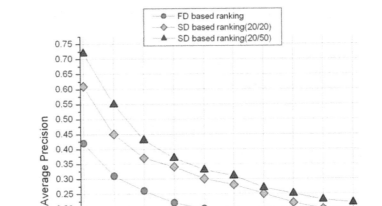

kernel function and its parameters yet except for empirically testing. In the comparison experiment, the RBF kernel $K(x, y) = e^{-\|x-y\|^2/2\sigma^2}$ is used in the SVM classifier and the best σ is determined by using offline cross-validation (Chang & Lin, 2001)[1]. The original SVM classifier only gives a decision boundary without providing confidence of each object belonging to each class. To utilize SVM classifiers in image retrieval, a ranking scheme is needed. In the comparison, *Larger margin first* retrieval scheme (Vapnik, 1995) is adopted for SVM to determine the rank of retrieved images. A smaller query set composed of randomly selected 100 images from the 1,500 image query set is applied to **BALAS** and SVM, respectively; the average precision in the top 100 images are recorded for different numbers of negative sample images with the number of positive sample images fixed. Figure 7 shows the comparison. It indicates that **BALAS** outperforms SVM consistently. The unsatisfactory performance of SVM is due to the false assumption that the two classes are equivalent and the negative samples are representative of the true distributions. With this invalid assumption in the SVM learning, we have found that the positive part "spills over" freely into the part of the unlabeled areas in the feature space in the SVM classification. The result of this "spill-over" effect is that after the user's feedback, the machine returns a totally different set of images, with most of them likely to be negative. In **BALAS**, this phenomenon did not occur due to the asymmetric density estimations.

CONCLUSION

This chapter is about the work on user relevance feedback in image retrieval. We take this problem as a standard two-class pattern classification problem with investigating two important unique characteristics of the problem: small sample collection and asymmetric sample distributions between positive and

Figure 5. Average precisions-recall with and without BALAS enabled

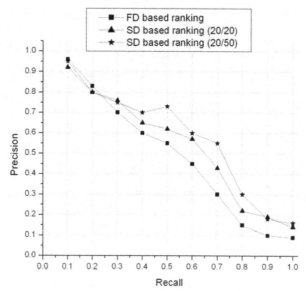

Figure 6: Retrieval precision comparison using relevance feedback between BALAS, CM, and CG

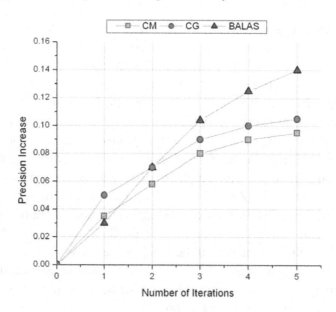

negative samples. We have developed a novel approach, called **BALAS,** to empirical Bayesian learning to solve for this problem by explicitly exploiting the two unique characteristics. Different learning strategies are used for positive and negative sample collections, respectively. By defining the relevancy confidence as the relevant posterior probability, we have developed an integrated and unified ranking scheme in **BALAS** which complementarily combines the subjective relevancy confidence and the

Figure 7. Comparison between BALAS and SVM on the average precision in the top 100 images returned. The number of positive sample images is set as 20

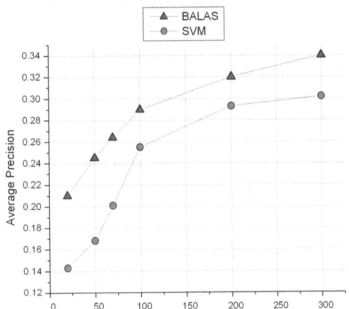

objective feature-based distance measure to capture the overall retrieval semantics. The experimental evaluations have confirmed the rationale of the proposed ranking scheme, and have also demonstrated that **BALAS** is superior to an existing relevance feedback method in the literature in capturing the overall retrieval semantics. We also show that the standard SVM classifier does not perform well in the relevance feedback of CBIR and that **BALAS** outperforms SVM in this problem.

FUTURE RESEARCH DIRECTIONS

BALAS has laid down a nice foundation on solving the small and asymmetric sampling problem in the context of image retrieval. Future research may focus on the following two directions. Methodologically, instead of using the Naïve Bayesian classification method, we may use more sophisticated Bayesian models such as Bayesian Networks. Experimentally, more extensive, larger scale experimental evaluations may be conducted to further validate the **BALAS** model as well as the related algorithm. In particular, the problem of small and/or asymmetric sampling in two-class classification has received special attention in the recent literature, and experimental performance comparison with the recently proposed models from the literature on this classification problem may be studied.

REFERENCES

Blom, G. (1989). *Probability and Statistics: Theory and Applications*. London, U. K.: Springer Verlag.

Carson, C., Belongie, S, Greenspan, H., & Malik, J. (2002). Blobworld: Image segmentation using expectation-maximization and its application to image querying. *IEEE Trans. on PAMI*, 24(8):1026–1038.

Chang, C.C., & Lin, C.J. (2001). Libsvm: a library for support vector machines. Software available at http://www.csie.ntu.edu.tw/~cjlin/libsvm.

Chen, Y., and Zhou, X., & Huang, T. (2001). One-class SVM for learning in image retrieval. In *Proceedings of the IEEE International Conference on Image Processing*.

Chiu., S.-T. (1996). A comparative review of bandwidth selection for kernel density estimation. *Statistica Sinica*, 16:129–145.

Cox, I.J., Miller, M.L., Minka, T.P., Papathomas, T.V., & Yianilos, P.N. (2000). The Bayesian image retrieval system, PicHunter: Theory, implementation and psychophysical experiments. *IEEE Trans. on Image Processing*, 9(1):20–37.

Del Bimbo, A. (1999). *Visual Information Retrieval*. San Francisco, CA: Morgan kaufmann Pub.

Dillon, W.R., & Goldstein, M. (1984). *Multivariate Analysis, Mehtods and Applications*. New York: John Wiley and Sons.

Duda, R.O., & Hart, P.E. (1973). *Pattern Classification and Scene Analysis*. New York: John Wiley and Sons.

Geman, D., & Moquet, R. (2000). A stochastic model for image retrieval. In *Proceedings of RFIA 2000*, Paris, France.

Google Image Search.http://www.google.com/imghp.

Huang, J., Kumar, S.R., Mitra, M., Zhu, W.-J., & Zabih, R. (1997). Image indexing using color correlograms. In *IEEE Int'l Conf. Computer Vision and Pattern Recognition Proceedings*, Puerto Rico.

Ishikawa, Y., Subramanya, R., & Faloutsos, C. (1998). Mindreader: Query databases through multiple examples. In *the 24th VLDB Conference Proceedings*, New York.

Jing, F., Li, M., Zhang, H.-J., & Zhang, B. (2003). Support vector machines for region-based image retrieval. In *Proceedings of the IEEE International Conference on Multimedia & Expo*, Baltimore, MD.

Laakdonen, J., Koskela, M., & Oja, E. (1999). Picsom: Self-organizing maps for content-based image retrieval. In *IJCNN'99 Proceedings*,Washington DC.

Lindgren, D., & Spangeus, P. (2004). A novel feature extraction algorithm for asymmetric classification. *IEEE Sensors Journal*, 4(5):643–650.

Liu, Y., Rothfus, W., & Kanade, T. (1998). Content-based 3D neuroradiologic image retrieval: Preliminary results. In *IEEE International Workshop on Content-based Access of Image and Video Databases*, pages 91 – 100, January 1998. in conjunction with International Conference on Computer Vision (ICCV98).

MacArthur, S.D., Brodley, C.E., & Shyu, C. (2000). Relevance feedback decision trees in content-based image retrieval. In *IEEE Workshop CBAIVL Proceedings*, South Carolina.

Marsicoi, M.D., Cinque, L., & Levialdi, S. (1997). Indexing pictorial documents by their content: a survey of current techniques. *Imagee and Vision Computing*, 15:119–141.

Nastar, C., Mitschke, M., & Meilhac, C. (1998). Efficient query refinement for image retrieval. In *IEEE Conf. Computer Vision and Pattern Recognition Proceedings*, CA.

Peng, J., Bhanu, B., & Qing, S. (1999). Probabilistic feature relevance learning for content based image retrieval. *Computer Vision and Pattern Recognition*, 75:150–164.

Picard, R.W., Minka, T.P., & Szummer, M. (1996). Modeling user subjectivity in image libraries. In *IEEE International Conference on Image Processing Proceedigns*, Lausanne, Switzerland.

Porkaew, K., Mehrotra, S., & Ortega, M. (1999). Query reformulation for content based multimedia retrieval in MARS. In *IEEE Int'l Conf. Multimedia Computing and Systems*.

Ratan, A.L., & Grimson, W.E.L. (1997). Training templates for scene classification using a few examples. In *IEEE Workshop on Content-Based Access of Image and Video Libraries Proceedings*, pages 90–97.

Ripley, B.D., & Venables, W.N. (2002). *Modern Applied Statistics with S*. New York: Springer Verlag.

Rocchio, J.J.J. (1971). Relevance feedback in information retrieval. In *The SMART Retrieval System — Experiments in Automatic Document Processing*, pages 313–323. Englewood Cliffs, NJ: Prentice Hall, Inc.

Rui, Y., & Huang, T.S. (2000). Optimizing learning in image retrieval. In *IEEE Conf. Computer Vision and Pattern Recognition*, South Carolina.

Rui, Y., Huang, T.S., Ortega, M., & Mehrotra, S. (1998). Relevance feedback: A power tool in interactive content-based image retrieval. *IEEE Trans. on Circuits and Systems for Video Tech*, 8(5):644–655.

Santini, S., & Jain, R. (2000). Integrated browsing and querying for image databases. *IEEE Multimedia*, 7:26–39.

Silverman, B.W. (1986). *Density Estimation for Statistics and Data Analysis*. New York: Chapman and Hall.

Sivic, J., & Zisserman, A. (2003). Video google: A text retrieval approach to object matching in videos. In *Proceedings of the International Conference on Computer Vision*.

Stricker, M.A., & Oregno, M. (1996). Similarity of color images. In *SPIE Storage and Retrieval of Still Image Video Databases IV*, volume 2420, pages 381–392.

Szummer, M., & Jaakkola, T. (2000). Kernel expansions with unlabeled examples. In *Proceedings of the Neural Information Processing Systems (NIPS)*.

Szummer, M. & Jaakkola, T. (2002). Information regularization with partially labeled data. In *Proceedings of the Neural Information Processing Systems (NIPS)*.

Tao, D., & Tang, X. (2004). Random sampling based SVM for relevance feedback image retrieval. In *Proceedings of the IEEE Conf. Computer Vision and Pattern Recognition*.

Tax, D.M.J., & Duin, R.P.W. (2001). Combining one-class classifiers. In *Proceedings of the Second International Workshop on Multiple Classifiers systems*, pages 299–308.

Terrell, G.R., & Scott, D.W. (1992). Variable kernel density estimation. *The Annals of Statistics*, 20:1236–1265.

Tieu, K., & Viola, P. (2000). Boosting image retrieval. In *IEEE Conf. Computer Vision and Pattern Recognitin Proceedings*, South Carolina.

Tong, S., & Chan, E. (2001). Support vector machine active learning for image retrieval. In *ACM Multimedia 2001 Proceedings*, Ottawa, Canada.

Vapnik, V. (1995). *The Nature of Statistical Learning Theory*. New York: Springer.

Vasconcelos, N., & Lippman, A. (2000). Learning from user feedback in image retrieval. In S. A. Solla, T. K. Leen, and K. R. Muller, editors, *Adv. in Neural Information Processing Systems 12*. MIT Press.

Wang, L., Chan, K.L., & Zhang, Z. (2003). Bootstrapping SVM active learning by incorporating unlabelled images for image retrieval. In *Proceedings of IEEE International Conference on Computer Vision and Pattern Recognition (CVPR)*, Madison, WI.

Wood, M.E.J., Campbell, N.W., & Thomas, B.T. (1998). Iterative refinement by relevance feedback in content-based digital image retrieval. In *ACM Multimedia 98 Proceedings*, Bristol, UK.

Wu, Y., Tian, Q., & Huang, T.S. (2000). Discriminant EM algorithm with application to image retrieval. In *IEEE Conf. Computer Vision and Pattern Recognition Proceedings*, South Carolina.

Yan, R., Hauptmann, A., & Jin, R. (2003). Negative pseudo-relevance feedback in content based video retrieval. In *Proceedings of the ACM Multimedia 2003*, Berkeley, CA.

Yahoo! Search. http://images.search.yahoo.com/.

Zhang, R. (2005). *Semantics-Oriented Modeling and Retrieval in Image Databases*, SUNY Binghamton PhD Dissertation.

Zhang, R., & Zhang, Z. (2003). Addressing CBIR efficiency, effectiveness, and retrieval subjectivity simultaneously. In *the 5th ACM Int'l Workshop on Multimedia Information Retrieval*, Berkeley, CA, November 2003. in conjunction with ACM Multimedia (ACM MM).

Zhang, R., & Zhang, Z. (2004). Hidden semantic concept discovery in region based image retrieval. In *IEEE International Conference on Computer Vision and Pattern Recognition (CVPR)*.

Zhou, X.S., & Huang, T.S. (2001). Small sample learning during and multimedia retrieval using biasmap. In *IEEE Conf. Computer Vision and Pattern Recognition Proceedings*, Hawaii.

ADDITIONAL READINGS

Guo, Z., Zhang, Z., Xing, E.P., & Faloutsos, C. (2007). A max margin framework on image annotation and multimodal image retrieval. In *Proceedings of the IEEE Annual International Conference on Multimedia and Expo*, Beijing, China.

Guo, Z., Zhang, Z., Xing, E.P., & Faloutsos, C. (2007). Enhanced max margin learning on multimodal data mining in a multimedia database. In *Proceedings of the 13th ACM International Conference on Knowledge Discovery and Data Mining*, San Jose, CA, USA.

Viola, P., & Jones, M. (2002). Fast and robust classification using asymmetric AdaBoost and a detector cascade, *NIPS*.

Zhang, R., Sarukkai, R., Chow, J.-H., Dai, W., Zhang, Z (2006). Joint categorization of queries and clips for Web-based video search. In *Proceedings of International Workshop on Multimedia Information Retrieval*, Santa Barbara, CA, USA.

Zhang, R., & Zhang, Z. (2004). A robust color object analysis approach to efficient image retrieval, *EURASIP Journal on Applied Signal Processing* (6), 871-885.

Zhang, R. & Zhang, Z. (2005). Image database classification based on concept vector model. In *Proceedings of the 2005 IEEE International Conference on Multimedia and Expo,* Amsterdam, The Netherlands.

Zhang, R. & Zhang, Z. (2005). FAST: Towards more effective and efficient image retrieval. *ACM Multimedia Systems Journal, the special issue on Multimedia Information Retrieval*, 10(6):529-543. Springer.

Zhang, R., & Zhang, Z. (2007). Effective image retrieval based on hidden concept discovery in image database. *IEEE Transaction on Image Processing*, 16(2):562-572.

Zhang, R., Zhang, Z., & Khanzode, S. (2004). A data mining approach to modeling relationships among categories in image collection. In *Proceedings of the 10th ACM International Conference on Knowledge Discovery and Data Mining*, Seattle, WA, USA.

Zhang, R., Zhang, Z., Li, M., Ma, W.-Y., & Zhang, H.-J. (2006). A probabilistic semantic model for image annotation and multi-modal image retrieval. *ACM Multimedia Systems Journal*, the special issue on Using Machine Learning Approaches to Multimedia Information Retrieval, 12(1):27-33. Springer.

Zhang, Z., Guo, Z., Faloutsos, C., Xing, E.P., & Pan, J.-Y. (2007). On the scalability and adaptability for multimodal image retrieval and image annotation. In *Proceedings International Workshop on Visual and Multimedia Digital Libraries*, Modena, Palazzo Ducale, Italy.

Zhou, X.S., & Huang, T.S. (2001). Relevance feedback in image retrieval: A comprehensive review. *Proceedings of Workshop on Content-based Access of Image and Video Libraries*. IEEE Computer Society Press.

ENDNOTE

[1]   Because the trained SVM classifiers are dynamic (i.e., for each query image, a different SVM classifier is trained), no validation data are available for online cross-validation. We used offline validation data for the emulation purpose, hopefully to obtain a good σ for the online SVM classifiers.

Chapter X
Content Analysis from User's Relevance Feedback for Content–Based Image Retrieval

Chia-Hung Wei
Ching Yun University, Taiwan

Chang-Tsun Li
University of Warwick, UK

ABSTRACT

An image is a symbolic representation; people interpret an image and associate semantics with it based on their subjective perceptions, which involves the user's knowledge, cultural background, personal feelings and so on. Content-based image retrieval (CBIR) systems must be able to interact with users and discover the current user's information needs. An interactive search paradigm that has been developed for image retrieval is machine learning with a user-in-the-loop, guided by relevance feedback, which refers to the notion of relevance of the individual image based on the current user's subjective judgment. Relevance feedback serves as an information carrier to convey the user's information needs / preferences to the retrieval system. This chapter not only provides the fundamentals of CBIR systems and relevance feedback for understanding and incorporating relevance feedback into CBIR systems, but also discusses several approaches to analyzing and learning relevance feedback.

1. INTRODUCTION

The rapid growth in the amount of digital images has highlighted the importance of effective retrieval approaches in order to facilitate the searching and browsing of large image databases. Although the design of content-based image retrieval (CBIR) systems is based on the nature of the underlying images and the system's purposes, one of the common purposes of all image retrieval systems is to satisfy human information needs and support human activities in an efficient and effective way. The development of an image retrieval system has to take human factors into account. Among human factors, subjective perception is one of the most challenging issues. An image is a symbolic representation; people interpret an image and associate semantics with it based on their subjective perceptions, which involves the user's knowledge, cultural background, personal feelings and so on (Jaimes, 2006b).

An important assumption in image retrieval is that each user's information need is different and time varying (Zhou & Huang, 2003). This assumption indicates that humans exhibiting subjective perceptions when interpreting images can be classified as *different information seekers* or *same information seekers* (Jaimes, 2006a). Different information seekers normally have different interpretations for the same image based on their individual perceptions. As a result, when different information seekers provide the same query example, they will have different satisfactory degrees for the same search results; even the same information seekers have different subjective perceptions as time evolves.

Another challenging issue arises from the difference between two descriptions of an object by high-level semantics and representations of low-level pixel data (Liu, Zhang, Lu, & Ma, 2007; Vasconcelos, 2007). The difference, known as the semantic gap, exists because low-level features are more easily computed in the system design process, but high-level queries are used as the starting point of the retrieval process. The semantic gap involves not only the conversion between low-level features and high-level semantics, but also the understanding of contextual meaning of the query involving human knowledge and emotion. Figure 1 shows that visual similarity mismatches human similarity judgments, resulting in a semantic gap between the user and the CBIR system. The "riding bicycle" query contains color gradients and two circular shapes that might guide a CBIR system, which utilizes shape and color as features for discriminating images, to associate it with objects, such as earphones, glasses, binoculars and two coins, with similar low-level features. However, the user actually looks for "riding bicycle" images, correlating the query example with high-level semantic context.

To compensate for the vagueness of subjective human perceptions, image retrieval systems must be able to interact with users and discover the current user's information needs. Due to the vagueness of subjective human perceptions, a retrieval system cannot adopt a fixed clustering structure to deal with the problem. An interactive search paradigm that has been developed for image retrieval is machine learning with a user-in-the-loop, i.e. in the search process users will be required to interact with the

Figure 1. Visual similarity does not match with human similarity judgments, resulting in a semantic gap. (a) A query example. (b) Visual feature matches. (c) Semantic matches.

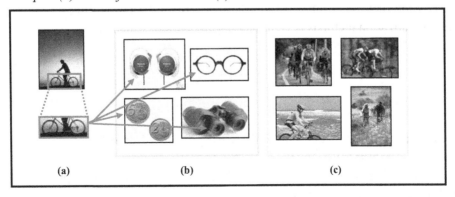

system in an iterative loop. The interactive search process is guided by relevance feedback, which refers to the notion of the relevance of the individual images based on the current user's subjective judgment. Relevance feedback serves as an information carrier to convey the user's information needs to the retrieval system. For a given query, the retrieval system returns initial results based on predefined criteria. Then, the user is required to identify the positive and/or negative examples by labeling those which are relevant and/or irrelevant to the query. A retrieval system can employ this relevance information to construct a better sketch and use it to provide better results to this user (Ortega-Binderberger & Mehrotra, 2003). Relevance feedback plays a more vital role in image-based search than in text-based search. This is because the features derived from images are more complex than the keywords used for text-based searches. As a result, in image-based search users cannot easily modify the features of the query example whereas in text-based search users can directly modify their query formulation, thereby making relevance feedback an indispensable function in image retrieval.

The main purpose of this chapter is to disseminate the knowledge of relevance feedback in content-based image retrieval and to attract greater interest from various research communities to rapidly advance research in this field. The rest of the chapter is organized as follows: section 2 introduces the background information on image representation, content-based image retrieval and relevance feedback. section 3 describes current challenges. section 4 indicates fundamental requirements for implementing a relevance feedback function in image retrieval systems. A content-based mammogram retrieval system is taken as an example to illustrate the approach to learning relevance feedback in section 5. section 6 discusses the major approaches to analyzing and learning relevance feedback in image retrieval. Section 7 discusses some future research issues. The last section concludes this chapter.

2. BACKGROUND

To enable content-based image retrieval, images are described by a set of proper features, which may be general features or specific features. General features refer to common properties most images possess, such as color, shape, and texture, while specific features refer to those features definded for describing specific properties in certain images. Let a set of features $\mathbf{f}^i = (f_1^i, f_2^i, ..., f_n^i)$ denote a feature vector representing image i, where n is the number of features. For example, $\mathbf{f}^i$ might represent a color histogram with n being the number of histogram bins.

In addition to extracting a set of features describing the contents of the images, a feature normalization process and a feasible distance metrics are required to measure similarity between images in the database. The purpose of normalization is to make all features possess an equal emphasis so that no single feature can dominate the results of similarity measure unless a weighting scheme is applied. One of the feature normalization methods is Gaussian normalization, which is expressed as

$$f_j^i = \frac{f_j^i - \mu_j}{\sigma_j} \tag{1}$$

where f_j^i is the jth feature of the ith image, μ_j and σ_j are the mean and standard deviation of the jth feature of the images in the database, respectively.

To measure image similarity, a general method is to represent each feature set as a point in a multi-dimensional feature space and then to calculate the distances between the multi-dimensional points.

Although Euclidean metrics is the most common metrics used to measure the distance between two points in multi-dimensional feature space, it does not always reflect human perceived similarity for some applications. Thus, a number of metrics (Feng, Siu, & Zhang, 2003), such as Mahalanobis distance, cosine distance, and proportional transportation distance, have been proposed for various applications. In image retrieval, distance is usually defined in the range [0, 1] with 0 denoting perfect similarity and 1 complete dissimilarity.

A typical content-based image retrieval system consists of an offline database construction and an online image retrieval parts as shown in Figure 2. The offline database construction part is intended to ensure high efficiency by extracting a feature set for each of the images in the database in an offline manner and storing the feature set along with its corresponding image in the database so that when a query image is presented to the system, the system does not have to perform online feature extraction on each database image.

To access the database, the user initiates the online image retrieval process by providing a query image as input, and then the system starts with extracting the features from the query image. Afterwards, the system measures the similarity between the feature set of the query image and those of the images stored in the database. Finally, the system ranks the relevance based on the similarity and returns the results to the user. The process is called the *initial search* for a given query. If the user is not satisfied with the initial search results, the user can conduct a relevance feedback stage. The user provides relevance feedback to the retrieval system in order to obtain better search results. The issues with regards to the design of the relevance feedback function and approaches applied for analyzing feedback data will be described in the following two sections.

3. CHALLENGES IN RELEVANCE FEEDBACK

Three specific characteristics of relevance feedback, which differentiate it from other applications of machine learning, formulate challenges in learning relevance feedback (Zhou et al., 2003).

Figure 2. The typical architecture of an image retrieval system.

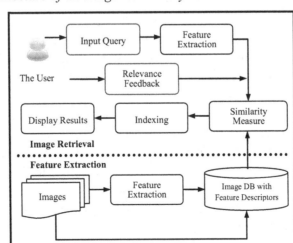

1. **A small quantity of training data:** The number of images labeled by the user is usually very small compared to the total number of images in the database. The number of training examples that can be used to investigate the user's information needs depends on the user's patience and willingness to cooperate. In general, the training examples provided by the user are less than 20 at each round of relevance feedback (Zhou & Huang, 2003). Many data analysis and machine learning theories are founded on the assumption that the amount of training data is more than the number of low-level features, and the amount of training data is unlimited. In reality, the amount of training data in a relevance feedback session is often smaller than the number of low-level features extracted to represent an image. Hence, some data analysis and machine learning approaches may not completely applicable to relevance feedback;

2. **A large asymmetry in training classes:** The number of positive examples is usually far more than that of negative examples provided in the relevance feedback process. As the set of training data lacks symmetrical proportion in the ratio of the number of the target class to the number of non-target classes, the boundary of the training classes is likely to skew more toward the target class, thereby affecting the correction of classification.

3. **Real time requirement:** Since relevance feedback is a real-time interactive process, the user has to wait for the completion of the learning approach. A search session may take several relevance feedback rounds until the user is satisfied with the result, so a short response time is required.

4. DESIGN OF RELEVANCE FEEDBACK FUNCTION

There are four fundamental requirements for implementing a relevance feedback function in an image retrieval system:

*   The feature descriptors used for representing the candidate images should contain useful features to discriminate between the relevant or irrelevant examples (Crucianu, Ferecatu, & Boujemaa, 2004).

*   When searching for a specific image, if images in the database have been displayed to the users for evaluating their relevance to the query at this relevance feedback session, those images should not be shown again. All images will be eventually displayed once if the relevance feedback session is not terminated (Laaksonen, Koskela, Laakso, & Oja, 2001).

*   When treating relevance feedback as a classification problem, images used for relevance feedback should be labeled as "relevant" or "irrelevant" to the current query example. Since training data is analyzed by finding the correlation among labeled images, it is not allowed to provide only one image or only irrelevant images as the training data (Laaksonen et al., 2001).

*   The system should have a learning mechanism to update the degree of similarity for all candidate images after obtaining the user's relevance feedback. As mentioned in Section 3, since the number of images identified as relevant/ irrelevant is smaller than the size of image population in the database, to alleviate the problem of small training set, it is desirable to involve all images identified as relevant / irrelevant since the relevance feedback session starts. Accordingly, as more images are labeled as relevant or irrelevant, the system has an increasing amount of data available to predict the user's target image or class (Laaksonen et al., 2001).

Relevance feedback in an interactive search process is obtained using an interactive interface. A user-friendly interface is a prerequisite to an interactive search. This interface not only displays the search results, but also provides an interactive mechanism to communicate with the user and convey relevance feedback. The means of obtaining relevance feedback usually fall into the following modes:

- **Binary choice:** In this type of systems, the system always return only two images and expect the user to select the more similar image as the positive example;
- **Positive examples:** This mode requires the user to select multiple relevant images as the positive examples at each round;
- **Positive, neutral, and negative examples:** In addition to selecting positive examples, the user can also label those ambiguous images as neutral, or completely irrelevant images as negative examples in order to remove other irrelevant images in the next search round;
- **Degree of relevance for each retrieved image:** The degree of relevance for each retrieved image can be used to analyze the importance of image features, thereby inferring the search target.

Once the user provides the relevance feedback to the system, the feedback examples need to be denoted as different semantic labels. Denoting feedback examples involves the choice of the learning approach and the ways of obtaining relevance feedback. For example, as a probability method is applied for inferring the user's target images from the relevance feedback under the "positive, neutral, and negative examples" mode. The feedbacks can be denoted as the different numeric values given by the following interpretation: positive = 1, neutral = 0.5 and negative = 0. The main advantage of this denotation is that the range of the numeric values corresponds to the measure space of probability. Therefore, as the probability measure function is performed, the resulting value interprets the probability of belonging to the positive class.

5. LEARNING APPROACHES TO RELEVANCE FEEDBACK

The approach used for learning relevance feedback is seen as the main factor that affects the refined retrieval results. This section will review various approaches, including the *query point movement* approach, the *re-weighting* approach, and the *classification* approach.

Query Point Movement Approach

With this approach it is assumed that there exists several images which completely convey the intentions of the user, and high-level concept of those images has been modeled in low-level feature space (Su, Zhang, Li, & Ma, 2003; Kushki, Androutsos, Plataniotis, & Venetsanopoulos, 2004). The query point movement approach is to move the point of the query toward the region of the feature space that contains the desired images. The development of query point movement approach was based on classic Rocchio algorithm, which was originally developed to improve the effectiveness of information retrieval system (Rocchio, 1971). Suppose that the user provides a set of relevance feedback documents $D(= D^+ \cup D^-)$ to a given initial query Q, where D^+ represents relevant documents and D^- represents irrelevant documents. The iterative estimation used for finding the ideal query point Q' follows the equation,

$$Q' = \alpha Q + \beta \left(\frac{1}{N_{R'}} \sum_{i \in D'_R} D_i \right) - \gamma \left(\frac{1}{N_{N'}} \sum_{i \in D'_N} D_i \right) \tag{2}$$

where α, β, γ are weight parameters, ($\alpha + \beta + \gamma = 1$), and N^+ and N^- are the number of the document set D^+ and D^-, respectively. The new query point Q' is the point that is moved toward positive example points and away from negative example points.

Since α, β, γ control the importance of the previous query point, the average of document features at the set D^+, and the average of document features at the set D^-, respectively, the setting of the weight parameters implies different assumptions as follows:

- When $\alpha = 0$, the initial query point Q will be ignored. The new query point is obtained by using the currently available image set D. The original query often conveys information, which should be retained.
- When $\gamma = 0$, the irrelevant images D^- will not be considered.

It is noted that the parameter $\beta = 0$ indicates the relevant images D^+ will not be considered for refinement and the setting is unlike to obtain effective retrieval refinement because the set of images does not reflect the common characteristics to interpret the user's information need. In addition to the requirement $\beta \neq 0$, the weight parameters should satisfy $\beta > \gamma$ in practical applications because information in D^+ is more valuable than that in D^-. The query point movement approach has been applied in many CBIR systems, such as (Zhang & Zhang, 2006; Wang, Ding, Zhou, & Hu, 2006).

Re-Weighting Approach

The idea of the re-weighting approach is to adjust the weights assigned to each feature or modify the similarity measure (Rui, Huang, & Mehrotra, 1998), i.e. giving more important features larger weights, and less important features smaller weights. A direct way to implement the idea is to exploit statistical properties of data distribution in feature space or user's relevance judgment for training examples.

When a given feature f_i is able to effectively represent a characteristic the relevant images have in common, the spread of the feature always concentrates on a specific area of the feature space. When this is not the case, i.e. when the feature has a widespread distribution, the feature is unlikely to be a discriminative descriptor for the set of relevant image set D^+. As a result, the inverse of the standard deviation σ_i for a given feature f_i can be used as the weight w_i to reflect the importance of the feature. In addition, the standard deviation σ_i can be replaced by variance to amplify the emphasis of the feature distribution.

Another re-weighting technique is to assign the weight based on the user's relevance judgment. Let $\pi = [\pi_1, \pi_2, ..., \pi_n]$ represents the degree of relevance of each of n positive feedback images. An ideal query vector q_i for each feature i is described by the weighted sum of all positive feedback images as (Rui et al., 1998)

$$q_i = \frac{\pi^T X_i}{\sum_{j=1}^{n} \pi_j} \tag{3}$$

where X_i is the $n \times K_i$ (K_i is the length of feature i) training sample matrix for feature i obtained by stacking the n positive feedback training vectors into a matrix. The system uses q_i as the optimal query to evaluate the relevance of images in the database. Similar techniques are widely used in many CBIR studies (Han & Kamber, 2001; Saha, Das, & Chanda, 2007).

Classification Approach

The classification approach regards the image retrieval task as a dichotomous classification problem, that is, one where the whole image set is classified into a positive set and a negative set. Those that belong to the positive class are considered as more similar images than those in the negative class. However, the actual goal of image retrieval is to measure the relevance degree of each single image to a query example, rather than classify images into different categories. A similarity measure needs to be included in order to rank the images in the search results.

Due to the fact that positive examples are typically clustered in certain areas in the feature space and the negative examples spread wide, Huang & Zhou (2001) defined learning from relevance feedback as a biased classification problem, where an uncertain number of classes is assumed but the user is only interested in one of them. The desired class can be separated by biased discriminant analysis and kernel-based nonlinear functions. Several methods based on support vector machines (Chen, Zhou, & Huang, 2001; Hoi, Chan, Huang, Lyu, & King, 2004) have been proposed to deal with the relevance feedback problem.

Probabilistic Estimation Approach

The approach assumes that each candidate image at each search session is associated with the estimated probabilities $P(I \in D^+)$ and $P(I \in D^-)$. Images with the highest probabilities to the query example are deemed as the most relevant images to a given query. The Bayesian probabilistic approach has been applied in many studies for learning relevance feedback (Zhang, Qian, Li, & Zhang, 2003; de Ves, Domingo, Ayala, & Zuccarello, 2007). The image retrieval problem can also be formulated as a task of probability density estimation. Suppose a CBIR system collects a set of positive example images $D^+(n)$ and applies parametric density estimation, the task is to estimate the probability density of the relevant images, which is expressed as $p(x|D^+(n); \theta)$, where θ contains the parameters of the distribution. The Gaussian mixture model and the expectation-maximization algorithm have been proposed for solving the relevance feedback problem (Meilhac & Nastar, 1999).

6. AN EXAMPLE

A content-based mammogram retrieval application is taken as an example of approaches to learning relevance feedback. The system uses a typical system architecture for image retrieval as shown in Figure 2. As mammograms usually contain a rich variety of information, including breast tissues, fat, and other noise, a total of 14 geometric and textural features were used to describe the mammogram contents. Those features are separately used in two different layers: geometric layer and textural layer.

At the relevance feedback stage the task of the system is to learn user's relevance feedback, which are formed from user's subjective judgment on returned images. The common characteristics in relevant images reveal the user's search target and are what the user is interested in. To analyze the common characteristics and make a prediction, this study proposes a learning approach shown in Figure 3.

The proposed approach firstly collects relevance feedback as the training data, which is regarded as two different data sets. The first set includes the geometric features and the second set includes the texture features. The two sets of training data are then used to develop their individual probabilistic models. Training data is firstly transformed into the high-dimension feature space and then support vector machines (SVM) is applied to find the decision boundary/hyperplane that separates the data into two classes: relevant (1) and irrelevant (-1). Next, the probabilistic model is built to enable individual images to obtain their *a-posteriori* P(class=1|image features). The parameters of the model are adapted to give the best probability outputs by minimization the cross-entropy error (Platt, 1999). As the probabilistic models are built for the training data, all of the database images are fitted into the model so that the probability of membership can be obtained for each image in the database. As two different feature layers are used to develop their individual probabilistic model, each image can obtain two different probabilities for a different feature layer. The final probability that an image belongs to the relevant class will be obtained by multiplying these two probability rates. As mentioned earlier, at the initial search stage where no relevance feedback is involved, the similarity between any two images is measured by the mathematical distance of two points in the multidimensional system using a distance metrics. At the relevance feedback stage, image similarity is completely based on the probability estimation. The detailed process is described in the following subsections.

Support Vector Machines

Suppose a set of training data belonging to two separate classes are given as $D = \{(x_i, y_i), i = 1, ..., l\} \subset X \times \Re$, where x denotes the image feature space, $y \in \{1, -1\}$ denotes the associated label, and l represents the number of training examples. The set of training data can be optimally separated by the hyperplane

Figure 3. The proposed learning approach to relevance feedback.

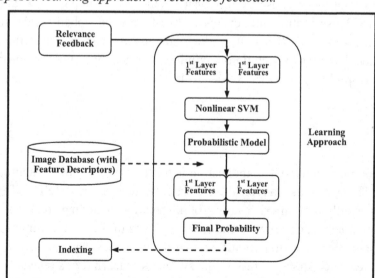

$$f(x) \; (w^T \cdot x) + b \tag{4}$$

where w is the weight vector and b is the bias. The separating hyperplane must satisfy the following constraints

$$y((w^T \cdot x_i) + b) \geq 1, i = 1, \dots, l \tag{5}$$

The hyperplane that optimally separates the data can be obtained by finding the smallest possible w without committing any error. This can be expressed as the quadratic optimization problem (Burges, 1998)

$$\min_{w,b} \; \frac{1}{2} \| w \|^2, \text{ subject to } y_i((w^T \cdot x_i) + b) \geq 1, \forall i = 1, \dots, l \tag{6}$$

The problem of obtaining the minimum of Equation can be transformed to its dual problem, which is obtaining the conditional extremum of a Lagrangian Function. For many practical applications, the data are often not linearly separable. Hence, in the transformation the slack variables ξ_i are introduced to relax the hard-margin constraints

$$\xi_i(w,b) \leq y_i((w, x_i) + b) - 1, i = 1, \dots, l, \xi_i \geq 0, \tag{7}$$

which allows for some classification errors. A term $\sum_{i=1}^{l} \xi_i$ representing the number of training errors is added to Equation to reformulate the quadratic optimization problem

$$\min_{w,b} \left(\frac{1}{2} f(w,b) + \sum_{i=1}^{l} \alpha \, \xi_i(w,b) \right) \tag{8}$$

where $\alpha = (\alpha_1, \alpha_2, \dots, \alpha_i)$ represents a Langrage multiplier. Hence, the Langrage multiplier method (Burges, 1998) can be used to obtain the conditional extremum of Equation by solving its Partial Differential Equation (PDE). The conditional extremum is the corresponding minimum of Equation .

To nonlinearly separate data, SVM maps the input data into a higher dimensional space through an underlying nonlinear mapping $\Phi(\cdot)$ and then finds an optimal hyperplane in the feature space. However, the computation of $(\Phi(x_i) \cdot \Phi(x_j))$ is intractable to work directly in the feature space. To circumvent the problem, the function $K(x_i, x_j) = (\Phi(x_i) \cdot \Phi(x_j))$ is applied to yield the inner products in feature space. Any function that satisfies Mercer's conditions can perform the implicit mapping. The kernel function is used to avoid explicitly computing features Φ. Therefore, the optimal α^* can be obtained by the following equation

$$\alpha^* = \arg \max_{\alpha} -\frac{1}{2} \sum_{i=1}^{l} \sum_{j=1}^{l} \alpha_i \alpha_j y_i y_j K(x_i, x_j) - \sum_{k=1}^{l} \alpha_k \tag{9}$$

where $K(x, x')$ is the kernel function performing the nonlinear mapping from the input space into a high dimensional feature space. Those examples $i \notin sv$ (support vector) for which $\alpha_i = 0$ are ignored. As α is determined, b^* and w^* can be obtained to find the hyperplane. Several functions such as radial basis functions (RBF), polynomial, and spline kernels, can be considered as kernel functions.

Probabilistic Scaling

Suppose y_i and f_i are the desired output and the actual output of SVM of data element i, respectively. In the binary class case, the output of the whole training data set is sigmoid, and can be interpreted as the probability of class 1. The logistic likelihood produces the cross-entropy error

$$E = -\sum \left[y_j \log f_j + (1 - y_j) \log(1 - f_j) \right], \tag{10}$$

which represents the negative log likelihood. To apply the output of SVM for logistic regression, y_i is transformed into the probabilistic value t_i with $0 \leq t_i \leq 1$, which is transformed from

$$t_i = \frac{y_i + 1}{2} \tag{11}$$

The parametric model proposed in (Platt, 1999) can fit the posterior $P(y = 1|x)$. The *a-posteriori* probability P_i of the class membership is computed using two parameters λ and η in Equation.

$$p_i = \frac{1}{1 + \exp(\lambda f_i + \eta)} \tag{12}$$

The optimal parameters λ^*, η^* are determined by minimizing the negative log likelihood of the training data

$$(\lambda^*, \eta^*) = \arg \min_{\lambda, \eta} \left(-\sum_i t_i \log(p_i) + (1 - t_i) \log(1 - p_i) \right),$$

where $p_i = \dfrac{1}{1 + \exp(\lambda f_i + \eta)}$. \tag{13}

To find the optimal parameter set $V^* = (\lambda^*, \eta^*)$ the problem is solved by Newton's method (Hagan, Demuth, & Beale, 1996). Newton's method is a numerical optimisation method that finds a minimum of a function $F: \Re^n \to \Re^2$ by approaching it with a convergent series of approximations. The search starts in an initial point and computes the step toward the next point. The termination test will be performed for minimisation until the minimum is found. The Newton's method based on the 2nd-order Taylor series of cost function can be represented as

$$F(V_0 + \Delta V) = F(V_0) + g \Delta V + \frac{1}{2} \Delta V^T H \Delta V + O(\| \Delta V \|^3)$$

$$\approx F(V_0) + g \Delta V + \frac{1}{2} \Delta V^T H \Delta V \tag{14}$$

where g is the gradient of F defined as,

$$g \equiv \nabla F = \begin{bmatrix} \dfrac{\partial F}{\partial \lambda} \\[2mm] \dfrac{\partial F}{\partial \eta} \end{bmatrix} \tag{15}$$

and H is the Hessian matrix

$$H \equiv F'' = \begin{bmatrix} \dfrac{\partial^2 F}{\partial \lambda^2} & \dfrac{\partial^2 F}{\partial \lambda \, \partial \eta} \\[3mm] \dfrac{\partial^2 F}{\partial \eta \, \partial \lambda} & \dfrac{\partial^2 F}{\partial \eta^2} \end{bmatrix} \tag{16}$$

Since V_0 represents a given value to variable V in the function $F(V_0 + \Delta V)$, Equation can be substituted by

$$G\Delta V = F(V_0 + \Delta V) \tag{17}$$

The minimum of the function $G\Delta V$ is given when its derivative $G('\Delta V) = 0$.

$$G'(\Delta V) = g + H\Delta V = 0$$
$$\Rightarrow \Delta V = -(H^{-1}g) \tag{18}$$

where ΔV determines the step size toward the next point. The optimal parameter set can be obtained as

$$V^* = V_{final-1} + \Delta V_{final} \tag{19}$$

Therefore, Equation can be used to compute the *a-posteriori* probability P_i of the class membership for each image in the database.

The advantage of the proposed approach is twofold: one is that this approach takes advantage of SVM's characteristics to effectively classify the training data into relevant and irrelevant classes; the other is that the probabilistic model can fulfill the logistic regression, which is a mathematical modeling approach that can be used to describe the relationship of real-valued independent variables to a dichotomously dependent variable. As a result, values of image feature can be converted into probability rate, indicating the likelihood of class membership.

Table 1. The four cases of relevant and irrelevant items retrieved and not retrieved

	Relevant	Irrelevant
Retrieved	A (true positive)	C (false positive)
Not-Retrieved	B (false negative)	D (true negative)

7. PERFORMANCE EVALUATION

In performance evaluation the four cases of relevant and irrelevant items that are retrieved and not retrieved are tabulated in Table 1. The most common evaluation measures used in CBIR are *precision* and *recall*, which often are presented as a precision versus recall graph. Precision P is the ratio of the number of relevant images retrieved to the total number images retrieved while recall R is the number of relevant images retrieved to the total number of relevant images stored in the database. Precision P and recall R are expressed using the following formulas:

$$P = \frac{A}{A+C} \tag{20}$$

$$R = \frac{A}{A+B} \tag{21}$$

In addition to precision and recall, a set of measures used in the TERC benchmark include the evaluation and effectiveness and efficiency (Muller, Muller, Squire, Marchand-Maillet, & Pun, 2001). These measures, as explained as follows, are proposed to compare systems based on the same image databases, and use the same queries and the same ground truth database.

- r is the ratio of the total number of images in the database to the number of relevant images for each of the query tasks. The ratio r is expressed as

$$r = \frac{A+B}{A+B+C+D} \tag{22}$$

- t is the time the system takes to perform a query.
- $Rank_1$, $\overline{Rank}$, $\widetilde{Rank}$: $Rank_1$ is the rank at which the first relevant image is retrieved, $\overline{Rank}$ is the average rank, and $\widetilde{Rank}$ is the normalized average rank of relevant images, which is defined as

$$\widetilde{Rank} = \frac{1}{NN_r}\left(\sum_{i=1}^{N_r} R_i - \frac{N_r(N_r-1)}{2}\right) \tag{23}$$

where R_i is the rank at which the ith relevant image is found, N is the collection size and N_R the number of relevant images for a given query.

- $P(20)$, $P(50)$, and $P(n)$ are precision rates after 20, 50, and n images are retrieved, where n is the number of relevant images.
- $P(R(0.5))$ and $R(100)$ are recalls at precision 0.5 and after 100 images are retrieved, respectively.

A CBIR system collects relevance feedback based on the users' relevance judgments on the initial search result. To show the system's self-adaptability to users' information needs, the initial search result and the refined search results of the first relevance feedback rounds can be compared with the same measures aforementioned. The same measures can be used for comparing the performance among different CBIR systems. It is noted that, to make those measures comparable, it is presumed that the same image databases and the same queries are used.

8. FUTURE RESEARCH ISSUES

Although incorporating relevance feedback for image retrieval has been an active research field and reasonable progress has been made in past years, many research issues remain open. This section will address some of the issues on the future research agenda.

The Optimal Dispensing Strategy

When searching a large image database for specific images, generally more than one round of user interaction is needed. It is important to select the optimal set of images at each round of asking for the user's feedback so that the total number of iterations required to reach the target image is minimized. An optimal dispensing strategy is required to provide a set of refined results at each round. However, the dispensing strategy has two conflicting goals during each feedback round (Ferecatu, Crucinu, & Boujemaa, 2004). The dispensing strategy has to provide as many relevant images as possible in the shortest time, but also has to investigate images of unknown relevance to the query example to reduce a maximal amount of uncertainty with regards to the target image. An optimal dispensing strategy can maximize the two conflicting goals.

The Use of Negative Examples

There are two schools of thought with regard to the use of negative examples. One school thinks that positive examples cluster in a certain way, but negative examples usually are not clustered together because all positive examples are alike and every negative example is different in its own way (Zhou & Huang, 2001). Assigning all negative examples to one class may mislead the learning algorithm, thereby damaging the robustness in performance, especially when the size of the training sample is small. The other school investigated the use of negative examples and indicated that the negative examples are useful in reducing false positives (i.e. irrelevant images that are retrieved) and false negatives (relevant images that are not found) (Kherfi, Ziou, & Bernardi, 2003). Another work reported that the significant improvements were made in the first four rounds using both positive and negative examples, whereas the major improvement occurred in the first round using only positive examples (Muller, Muller, March-and-Maillet, Pun, & Squire, 2000). Hence, this needs more investigation to provide more evidence for this issue.

Long-Term Learning

Long-term learning involves a user's memory and target search (i.e. looking for a specific image). The user's information need, deduced from the user's relevance feedback in an earlier query session, is used to improve the retrieval performance of later searches. Since information is not accumulated for use in different sessions, even if the user searches for a specific image they viewed before, they still have to go through the same relevance feedback process to find that image. Therefore, a long-term learning algorithm is required in order to accumulate the user's search information and utilize it to shorten the retrieval time and the relevance feedback process during future query sessions.

9. CONCLUSIONS

Content-based image retrieval systems not only require low-level visual features to effectively capture the image content, but also need to provide the maximal support to bridge the semantic gap between low-level features and human perceptions. An interactive search paradigm that has been developed for image retrieval is introducing relevance feedback into the retrieval loop for continuous learning of users' intentions. Embedding a relevance feedback function into an image retrieval system requires the integration of useful low-level feature extraction, effective learning of high-level semantics and user interface design. It is expected that reasonable progress in relevance feedback will make content-based image retrieval systems more intelligent, thus enhancing their performance.

REFERENCES

Burges, C. J. (1998). A tutorial on support vector machines for pattern recognition. *Knowledge Discovery and Data Mining, 2,* 121-167.

Chen, Y., Zhou, X. S., & Huang, T. S. (2001). One-class support vector machine for learning in image retrieval. In *Proceedings of the IEEE International Conference on Image Processing 2001* (pp. 34-37). IEEE Press.

Crucianu, M., Ferecatu, M., & Boujemaa, N. (2004). *Relevance feedback for image retrieval: a short survey.* INRIA Rocquencourt, France.

de Ves, E., Domingo, J., Ayala, G., & Zuccarello, P. (2007). A novel Bayesian framework for relevance feedback in image content-based retrieval systems. *Pattern Recognition, 39,* 1622-1632.

Feng, D., Siu, W. C., & Zhang, H. J. (2003). *Multimedia Information Retrieval and Management: Technological Fundamentals and Applications.* Berlin: Springer.

Ferecatu, M., Crucinu, M., & Boujemaa, N. (2004). *Reducing the redundancy in the selection of samples for SVM-based relevance feedback.* INRIA Rocquencourt, France.

Hagan, M. T., Demuth, H. B., & Beale, M. H. (1996). *Neural network design.* PWS Publishing.

Han, J. & Kamber, M. (2001). *Data mining: concepts and techniques.* San Diego, CA, USA: Academic Press.

Hoi, C.-H., Chan, C.-H., Huang, K., Lyu, M. R., & King, I. (2004). Biased support vector machine for relevance feedback in image retrieval. In *Proceedings of International Joint Conference on Neural Networks* (pp. 3189-3194).

Jaimes, A. (2006a). Human factors in automatic image retrieval system design and evaluation. In *Proceedings of IS&T/SPIE Internet Imaging 2006*. SPIE Press.

Jaimes, A. (2006b). Human-centered multimedia: Culture, deployment, and access. *IEEE Multimedia Magazine, 13*, 12-19.

Kherfi, M. L., Ziou, D., & Bernardi, A. (2003). Combining positive and negative examples in relevance feedback for content-based image retrieval. *Journal of Visual Communication & Image Representation, 14*, 428-457.

Kushki, A., Androutsos, P., Plataniotis, K. N., & Venetsanopoulos, A. N. (2004). Query feedback for interactive image retrieval. *IEEE Transactions on Circuits and Systems for Video Technology, 14*, 644-655.

Laaksonen, J., Koskela, M., Laakso, S., & Oja, E. (2001). Self-organising maps as a relevance feedback technique in content-based image retrieval. *Pattern Analysis & Applications, 4*, 140-152.

Liu, Y., Zhang, D., Lu, G., & Ma, W.-Y. (2007). A survey of content-based image retrieval with high-level semantics. *Pattern Recognition, 40*, 262-282.

Meilhac, C. & Nastar, C. (1999). Relevance feedback and category search in image databases. *Proceedings of IEEE International Conference on Multimedia Computing and Systems, 1*, 512-517.

Muller, H., Muller, W., Marchand-Maillet, S., Pun, T., & Squire, D. M. (2000). Strategies for positive and negative relevance feedback in image retrieval. In *Proceedings of the International Conference on Pattern Recognition* (pp. 1043-1046).

Muller, H., Muller, W., Squire, D. M., Marchand-Maillet, S., & Pun, T. (2001). Performance evaluation in content-based image retrieval: Overview and proposals. *Pattern Recognition Letters, 22*, 593-601.

Ortega-Binderberger, M. & Mehrotra, S. (2003). Relevance feedback in multimedia databases. In B.Furht & O. Marquez (Eds.), *Handbook of video databases: design and applications* (pp. 511-536). New York: CRC Press.

Platt, J. C. (1999). Probabilistic outputs for support vector machines and comparisons to regularized likelihood methods. In A.Smola, P.Bartlett, B.Scholkopf, & D.Schuurmans (Eds.), *Advance in Large Margin Classifiers* (pp. 61-74). Cambridge, MA, USA: MIT Press.

Rocchio, J. J. (1971). Relevance feedback in information retrieval. In G.Salton (Ed.), *The SMART Retrieval System-Experiments in Automatic Document Processing* (pp. 313-323). Englewood Cliffs, NJ: Prentice Hall.

Rui, Y., Huang, T. S., & Mehrotra, S. (1998). Human perception subjectivity and relevance feedback in multimedia information retrieval. In *Proceedings of IS&T/SPIE Storage and Retrieval of Image and Video Database* (pp. 25-36). SPIE Press.

Saha, S. K., Das, A. K., & Chanda, B. (2007). Image retrieval based on indexing and relevance feedback. *Pattern Recognition Letters, 28*, 357-366.

Su, Z., Zhang, H., Li, S., & Ma, S. (2003). Relevance feedback in content-based image retrieval: Bayesian framework, feature subspaces, and progressive learning. *IEEE Transaction on Image Processing, 12*, 924-937.

Vasconcelos, N. (2007). From pixels to semantic spaces: Advances in content-based image retrieval. *Computer, 40,* 20-26.

Wang, Y., Ding, M., Zhou, C., & Hu, Y. (2006). Interactive relevance feedback mechanism for image retrieval using rough set. *Knowledge-Based Systems, 19,* 696-703.

Zhang, L., Qian, F., Li, M., & Zhang, H. (2003). An efficient memorization scheme for relevance feedback in image retrieval. In *IEEE International Conference on Multimedia & Expo.* IEEE Press.

Zhang, R. & Zhang, Z. (2006). BALAS: Empirical Bayesian learning in the relevance feedback for image retrieval. *Image and Vision Computing, 24,* 211-233.

Zhou, X. S. & Huang, T. S. (2001). Comparing discriminating transformations and SVM for learning during multimedia retrieval. In *Proceedings of the ninth ACM international conference on Multimedia* (pp. 137-146). ACM Press.

Zhou, X. S. & Huang, T. S. (2003). Relevance feedback in image retrieval: A comprehensive review. *ACM Multimedia System Journal, 8,* 536-544.

ADDITIONAL READING

Chang, H. & Yeung, D.-Y. (2007). Kernel-based distance metric learning for content-based image retrieval. *Image and Vision Computing, 25*(5), 695-703.

Cheng, J. & Wang, K. (2007). Active learning for image retrieval with Co-SVM. *Pattern Recognition, 40*(1), 330-334.

Cheng, P.-C., Chien, B.-C., Ke, H.-R., & Yang, W.-P. (2007). A two-level relevance feedback mechanism for image retrieval. *Expert Systems with Applications. (*in press*).*

Cheng, S.-C., Chou, T.-C. , Yang, C.-L. & Chang, H.-Y. (2005). A semantic learning for content-based image retrieval using analytical hierarchy process. *Expert Systems with Applications, 28*(3), 495-505.

de Mauro, C., Diligenti, M., Gori, M., & Maggini, M. (2003). Similarity learning for graph-based image representations. *Pattern Recognition Letters, 24*(8), 1115-1122.

Doulamis, N. & Doulamis, A. (2006). Evaluation of relevance feedback schemes in content-based in retrieval systems. *Signal Processing: Image Communication, 21*(4), 334-357.

Duan, L., Gao, W., Zeng, W., & Zhao, D. (2005). Adaptive relevance feedback based on Bayesian inference for image retrieval. *Signal Processing, 85*(2), 395-399.

Giacinto, G. & Roli, F. (2004). Bayesian relevance feedback for content-based image retrieval. *Pattern Recognition, 37*(7), 1499-1508.

Jiang, W., Er, G., Dai, Q., & Gu, J. (2005). Hidden annotation for image retrieval with long-term relevance feedback learning. *Pattern Recognition, 38*(11), 2007-2021.

Kim, D.-H., Chung, C.-W. & Barnard, K. (2005). Relevance feedback using adaptive clustering for image similarity retrieval. *Journal of Systems and Software, 78*(1), 9-23.

King, I. & Jin, Z. (2003). Integrated probability function and its application to content-based image retrieval by relevance feedback. *Pattern Recognition, 36*(9), 2177-2186.

Kwak, J. W. & Cho, N. I. (2003). Relevance feedback in content-based image retrieval system by selective region growing in the feature space. *Signal Processing: Image Communication, 18*(9), 787-799.

Lam-Adesina, A.M. & Jones, G.J.F. (2006). Examining and improving the effectiveness of relevance feedback for retrieval of scanned text documents. *Information Processing & Management, 42*(3), 633-649.

León, T., Zuccarello, P., Ayala, G., de Ves, E., & Domingo, J. (2007). Applying logistic regression to relevance feedback in image retrieval systems. *Pattern Recognition, 40*(10), 2621-2632.

Lin, H.-C., Chiu, C.-Y. , & Yang, S.-N. (2003). Finding textures by textual descriptions, visual examples, and relevance feedbacks. *Pattern Recognition Letters, 24*(14), 2255-2267.

Lu, K. & He, X. (2005). Image retrieval based on incremental subspace learning. *Pattern Recognition, 38*(11), 2047-2054.

Nakazato, M., Manola, L., & T.S. Huang. (2003). ImageGrouper: A group-oriented user interface for content-based image retrieval and digital image arrangement. *Journal of Visual Languages & Computing, 14*(4), 363-386.

Peng, J. (2003). Multi-class relevance feedback content-based image retrieval. *Computer Vision and Image Understanding, 90*(1), 42-67.

Stejic, Z., Takama, Y., & Hirota, K. (2003). Genetic algorithms for a family of image similarity models incorporated in the relevance feedback mechanism. *Applied Soft Computing, 2*(4), 306-327.

Stejic, Z., Takama, Y., & Hirota, K. (2003). Genetic algorithm-based relevance feedback for image retrieval using local similarity patterns. *Information Processing & Management, 39*(1), 1-23.

Stejic, Z., Takama, Y., & Hirota, K. (2005). Mathematical aggregation operators in image retrieval: effect on retrieval performance and role in relevance feedback. *Signal Processing, 85*(2), 297-324.

Subramanyam Rallabandi, V.P. & Sett, S.K. (2007). Image retrieval system using R-tree self-organizing map. *Data & Knowledge Engineering, 61*(3), 524-539.

Subramanyam Rallabandi, V.P. & Sett, S.K. (2007). Knowledge-based image retrieval system. *Knowledge-Based Systems.* (in press).

Wan, C. & Liu, M. (2006). Content-based audio retrieval with relevance feedback. *Pattern Recognition Letters, 27*(2), 85-92.

Wu, S., Rahman, M.K.M. & Chow, T. W.S. (2005). Content-based image retrieval using growing hierarchical self-organizing quadtree map. *Pattern Recognition, 38*(5), 707-722.

Yager, R.R. & Petry, F.E. (2005). A framework for linguistic relevance feedback in content-based image retrieval using fuzzy logic. *Information Sciences, 173*(4), 337-352.

Yin, P.-Y., & Li, S.-H. (2006). Content-based image retrieval using association rule mining with soft relevance feedback. *Journal of Visual Communication and Image Representation, 17*(5), 1108-1125.

Yoo, H.-W., Park, H.-S. & Jang, D.-S. (2005). Expert system for color image retrieval. *Expert Systems with Applications, 28*(2), 347-357.

Zhang, Q. & Izquierdo, E. (2007). Adaptive salient block-based image retrieval in multi-feature space. *Signal Processing: Image Communication.* (in press).

Zhao, T., Tang, L.H., Ip, H.H.S., & Qi, F. (2003). On relevance feedback and similarity measure for image retrieval with synergetic neural nets. *Neurocomputing, 51,* 105-124.

Zhou, X., Zhang, Q., Liu, L., Zhang, L. & Shi, B. (2003). An image retrieval method based on analysis of feedback sequence log. *Pattern Recognition Letters, 24*(14), 2499-2508.

Chapter XI
Preference Extraction in Image Retrieval

Paweł Rotter
European Commission, Joint Research Centre, Institute for Prospective Technological Studies, Spain
& AGH-University of Science and Technology, Poland

Andrzej M.J. Skulimowski
AGH-University of Science and Technology, Poland

ABSTRACT

In this chapter, we describe two new approaches to content-based image retrieval (CBIR) based on preference information provided by the user interacting with an image search system. First, we present the existing methods of image retrieval with relevance feedback, which serve then as a reference for the new approaches. The first extension of the distance function-based CBIR approach makes it possible to apply this approach to complex objects. The new algorithm is based on an approximation of user preferences by a neural network. Further, we propose another approach to image retrieval, which uses reference sets to facilitate image comparisons. The methods proposed have been implemented, and compared with each other, and with the earlier approaches. Computational experiments have proven that the new preference extraction and image retrieval procedures here proposed are numerically efficient. Finally, we provide a real-life illustration of the methods proposed: an image-based hotel selection procedure.

1.0 INTRODUCTION

Multimedia technologies have been developing rapidly over the last few years and have yielded a large number of databases containing graphical documents. Tools for content-based search of graphical objects have been the subject of intensive research (cf. e.g. (Liu, et al. 2007)), but their performance is still unsatisfactory for many applications, opening up a field for further research and technology development. Up till now, all popular Internet search engines have been only text-based, including those that search for images. Moreover, only a few existing content-based image retrieval systems, like MARS (Rui at al. 1997), MindReader (Ishikawa, Subramanya, & Faloutsos, 1998) or VisualSeek (Smith, & Chang, 1996) allow for an interaction with the user during the search process. The idea of an interactive search consists in changing search parameters based on the user's assessment of the relevance of images presented by the search system in consecutive iterations of the search process.

In section 2, we briefly describe existing image retrieval methods and point out their limitations. The theoretical foundations of the utility function approximation for relevance feedback are given in section 3. In the following part we propose two different methodologies of content-based image retrieval, both based on elicitation of user preferences from his/her interactive feedback. They are complementary in the sense that they cover two different search problems and have different approaches to solving the problem of "semantic gap" (between low-level features extracted from the image and high-level features which the user uses to describe the image).

The first approach, presented in section 4, is designed for graphical objects which can be broken down into sub-objects with homogenous texture and colour distribution, in such a way that the main object can be classified by the low-level features of sub-objects (texture, colour distribution and shape) and spatial relations between them. The method can be used for development of multimedia atlases and thematic encyclopaedias equipped with effective visual search capabilities, so the user who does not know e.g. the name of a species, may have an option to look for it by its memorized appearance. In this approach, user preferences are approximated with an RBF neural network (Park, & Sandberg, 1991). This method has been tested with an interactive atlas of fishes, which we have developed in Matlab.

The second approach, proposed in section 5, is especially well-suited to images that cannot be recognized by directly matching sub-objects and the relations between them. The retrieval process is based on high-level features, calculated from the entire image. Depending on the set of features foreseen in a specific implementation, this method can be used either with a homogeneous database containing a specific class of images or with heterogeneous database, which most Internet search engines have to deal with. The method is based on reference sets, introduced by Skulimowski (1996; 1997). For testing purposes, we have developed a Matlab application for photo-based searching of a hotel according to user preferences.

Figure 1. Image of a butterfly is an example of an object which can be classified by low-level features of sub-objects and spatial relations between them. Segmentation into sub-objects was performed automatically with Edge Flow algorithm (Manjunath, 1997)

Another consequence of adopting the above approach is a two-stage learning scheme of image retrieval. After the assessment stage combined with learning user preferences by the retrieval algorithm, a semi-automated procedure of eliminating presumably irrelevant images and selecting candidates for the final choice follows.

2.0 A SURVEY OF EARLIER APPROACHES TO INTERACTIVE IMAGE RETRIEVAL

In this section, we review methods of interactive image retrieval, point out their advantages and limitations, and give some references to existing systems which allow interaction with a user in the search process.

We will refer to the method proposed by Rui, Huang and Mehrotra (1998) as a typical approach to image retrieval. In the next section, we will propose modifications of this method, with a view to extending its application to complex objects (with non-homogenous colour and texture). Then we will compare the performance of methods based on the approach described below with the method based on neural networks proposed in section 4.

The selection of object features to be used for calculation of similarity between images plays a crucial role in systems for image recognition and retrieval. Much work has been done on finding the features which are most useful for recognition, i.e. those that give high similarity of objects from the same class and low similarity of objects belonging to different classes. The methodology which consists of a choice of a specific similarity measure and scalarization method (e.g. by weighted sum of several similarity measures) before the recognition (retrieval) process is referred to as the *isolated approach* (Lew 2001). In the case of image retrieval, unlike image recognition, interaction with the user is possible and even desired. Some research has, therefore, been done with a view to modifying similarity measures during the retrieval process, based on information provided by the user in interactive feedback. It is assumed that users do not have any specialised knowledge on image analysis so, in interactive feedback, they only need to provide evaluation of individual images in the form of grades which express the *relevance* of images. In each iteration, the system presents several images to the user, who gives information on their relevance. This information is used as a starting point for upgrading similarity function parameters. Therefore, the images presented by the system in the next iteration better correspond to the user's preferences – in other words, to what the user is looking for. Besides the parameters of similarity function, descriptors of a query object can also be modified. Starting values are calculated based on an image provided by the user (who wants to find other images similar to the one/ones he already has) or randomly chosen in the first iteration, if a query image was not provided. The term *virtual query* means the set of descriptors corresponding to a system's guess about the image the user is looking for. In other words, virtual query is a point in descriptor space which moves when the system updates information about the desired characteristics of the searched image. The concept described above is referred to as *relevance feedback* and is depicted in Figure 2.

Rui, Huang and Mehrotra (1998) proposed an approach which was popularised in a monograph (Lew 2001). In their method, functions describing the similarity of objects are defined at three levels:

- **1° level:** Object – area with homogenous colour and texture,
- **2° level:** Feature – e.g. colour or texture,

Figure 2. A typical image retrieval system with relevance feedback

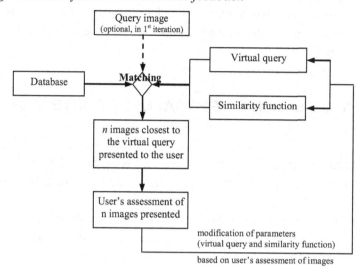

- **3° level:** Feature representation – e.g. colour histogram or average value of Gabor transform for a given area.

They assume that the user's utility function is a linear combination of preferences concerning image features (like colour, texture or shape) – for example, shape is k_1 times more relevant than texture. Moreover, they assume that preferences for a specific image feature are a linear combination of similarities of feature representations – for example for shape, the Hausdorff distance is k_2 times more relevant than similarity of Fourier descriptors. Coefficients (in our case k_1 and k_2) can be modified in every iteration of algorithm based on *relevance feedback*, provided by the user.

Based on the assumptions given above, the distance between the query object q and the model m can be expressed as a linear combination of functions Ψ_i, which define the distance for the feature representation i:

$$d(q,m) = \sum_{i=1}^{I} u_i \Psi_i(q_i, m_i, P_i) \tag{1}$$

where q and m denote the query object and model, q_i and m_i are representations (vectors, with different dimensions for different i and P_i is a set of parameters of the metric in space of representation i. For example, for scalarization by weighted Euclidean distance P_i are weights $w_{i,j}$ of components of representation i. Calculation of parameters of similarity functions was formulated as a minimisation problem:

$$\sum_{k} \sum_{i=1}^{I} \pi_k u_i \Psi_i(q_i, m_i^{(k)}, P_i) \longrightarrow \min_{u_i, q_i, P_i}, \tag{2}$$

where π_k defines the degree of k-th image relevance for the user and is positive for *relevant*, zero for *indifferent* and negative for *non-relevant* images (i.e. images with negative relevance, which are examples of what the user is not looking for).

When optimal parameters u_i^*, q_i^*, P_i^* are selected based on (2), the object sought is a solution to the optimisation problem:

$$\sum_{i=1}^{I} u_i^* \Psi_i(q_i^*, m_i^{(k)}, P_i^*) \longrightarrow \min_k. \tag{3}$$

K objects with the smallest value of (3) are presented to the user, who can again assign to them a degree of relevance in order to recalculate optimal search parameters according to (2) and perform the next iteration of the algorithm.

Many authors refer to the Rocchio formula (Rui, Huang, & Mehrotra 1998; Spink, & Losee 1996; Müller at al. 2000; Cheng P.C. at al., 2007; Doulamis & Doulamis, 2006). The idea was proposed in the 70s by J.J. Roccio (1971) and is based on moving a virtual query towards the centre of gravity of *relevant* objects (in the descriptors' space) and in the opposite direction to the centre of gravity of *non-relevant* objects:

$$q_i' = \alpha\, q_i + \beta\, \frac{1}{\# M_R} \sum_{n \in M_R} m_i^n - \gamma\, \frac{1}{\# M_{NR}} \sum_{n \in M_{NR}} m_i^n, \tag{4}$$

where α, β and γ are parameters determining what part of the modified query q' comes from the original query (if provided), *relevant* and *non-relevant* objects – provided by user feedback. In some cases, heuristics (4) can give results contrary to those expected, like in the example shown in Figure 3. According to the Rocchio formula (4), the virtual query is moved in direction opposite to the desired one. From this example, we can see that the Rocchio formula does not work properly if the distance between sets of *relevant* and *non-relevant* objects is smaller, or comparable to, the diameters of these sets (the situation is similar to gravity phenomenon: gravity of a solid can be approximated by gravity of its centre only for points that are far from the solid, in comparison with its diameter).

The Rochio formula defines how to modify descriptors of the query object but does not solve the problem of how to find parameters of similarity function. This has been done by using heuristic methods (cf. Rui, Huang, & Mehrotra 1997). Ishikawa, Subramanya and Faloutsos (1998) gave an analytical solution of (2) but only for a specific class of similarity function.

Figure 3. Example of non-relevant objects configuration in feature space when the Rocchio formula fails

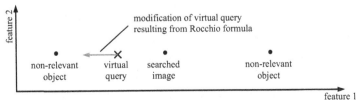

3.0 UTILITY THEORY FOUNDATIONS AND APPLICATION FOR IMAGE RETRIEVAL SYSTEMS

The methods described above are based on the assumption that the user is looking for an object with pre-specified values of descriptors and that these descriptors are combined in such a way that the aggregating function is monotone with respect to the preferences expressed verbally during the search. However, the distance function (5), and the functions (6) and (7) derived there from, can only locally approximate the preferences, as they do not possess all the properties attributed to a utility.

This section aims to provide a definition and some useful properties of a utility function, which will then serve as a theoretical base for constructing further CBIR algorithms. In both approaches, elicitation of user preferences is based on a gradual approximation of a simple deterministic user-specific utility function v, which represents the degree to which the images in the database correspond to user preferences. By definition, a deterministic utility function is a real function v, which defines the linear order $\leq_v$ in the set of alternatives assessed (here: the set D of images in the database), which conforms to the partial order $\leq$ derived from the user's preferences, i.e.

$$u_1 \leq_v u_2 \Leftrightarrow^{\mathrm{df}} v(u_1) \leq v(u_2) \tag{5}$$

and

$$u_1 \leq u_2, \Rightarrow u_1 \leq_v u_2 \tag{6}$$

where u_1 and u_2 are images in the database just surveyed.

The other properties of the relation $\leq_v$ result from the definition and the utility theory axioms:

- Completeness: $\forall u_1, u_2 \in D: u_1 \leq_v u_2 \vee u_2 \leq_v u_1$
- Reflexivity: $u_1 \leq_v u_1 \; u_1 \leq_v u_1$
- Transitivity: $u_1 \leq_v u_2 \wedge u_2 \leq_v u_3 \Rightarrow u_1 \leq_v u_3$.

Relation $\leq_v$ orders the set of images according to the user's preferences. Without the loss of generality, we presuppose that a higher value of v denotes higher user satisfaction, therefore $u_1 \leq_v u_2$ denotes that u_2 is at least as good as u_1 (weakly preferred). Level sets of a utility function will be called *indifference sets*.

It is easy to see that the notion of utility function defined above is too strong for most applications, where no total ranking of images is sought. Instead, the user wishes to select one or a few image objects $u_{c1}, u_{c2}, ..., u_{ck}$, out of the set of objects D such that:

$$\forall u \in D \setminus \{ u_{c1}, u_{c2}, ..., u_{ck} \} \; \forall x \in D: v(x) \leq v(u), \tag{7}$$

where u and x are image objects from the set D and v is the utility function. Equation (7) corresponds to the subset selection problem. The latter property means that the axiomatic properties of the utility function v need to be fulfilled only on a subset D_1 of $D \times D$. As usual in multicriteria choice, one can assume that the utility is defined for all $u \in D$, but the user's efforts to assess the preferences are concentrated on a proper subset of D. This contributes to the numerical efficiency of the utility-based retrieval algorithms.

Thus, we can assume that the user's utility function is monotonically decreasing with the distance between the vector of descriptors of a query and retrieved object. In the previous approaches, selection of a distance has been the only way to influence utility function. In virtue of the above definitions, its scope of application is very limited as indifference sets can only be spheres in the selected metric. Such an assumption about their shape usually has no justification, especially if the indifference sets are non-convex. Moreover, they even may be disconnected if the utility function is multimodal. For example, if the user wants to find one of several objects (the case of several queries combined with *OR*), for every query component there is a corresponding local maximum of the utility function.

Therefore, the typical approach to the image retrieval problem with relevance feedback presented in section 2 is based on a heuristic, yet often inconsistent, methodology, which we will try to improve now. Specifically, we will pay attention to eliminating the following deficiencies of the heretofore used methods:

- The assumption of linearity of a user's preferences is not justified; on the contrary, it seems that, in most cases, these preferences are non-linear,
- In the methods cited in section 2, search results not only depend on the ordinal structure of ranks assigned by the user to objects, but also on their values; this is incoherent with the basic assumptions of utility theory,
- The assumption that any object the user is looking for can be represented by a single point in feature space does not always correspond to real-life situations.

4.0 IMAGE RETRIEVAL SYSTEM BASED ON NEURAL NETWORKS

In this section, we propose an extension of image retrieval methods described in section 2. This modification will allow us to apply these methods to complex objects, which consist of several sub-objects with different colours and textures. Then we propose an image retrieval system based on neural networks. The methodology proposed below is designed for a specific class of objects, which can be broken down into sub-objects in such a way that the main object can be classified by shape, colour distribution and texture of the sub-objects and the spatial relations between the sub-objects in a 2-dimensional image. We also assume that translation, scaling and 2D rotation do not change the class of the object, but we do not consider 3D transformation. Therefore, photos of the same 3D object from different positions for example are considered to be objects belonging to different class. In order to exploit the approach proposed in this section, objects in a database should undergo preliminary processing: i.e. they should appear on a homogeneous background. Because of above limitations, the algorithms proposed here are not designed for search in large heterogeneous databases, neither are the suitable for applications where content-based search is motivated by lack of textual information associated with images (however, RBF networks can also be exploited for this kind of problem, (cf. Chuang S.C., et. al., 2006)). However, they can be an effective tool for retrieving knowledge from preliminary prepared databases (atlases, encyclopaedias) based on the appearance of an object memorized by the user, who is not able to provide textual information. An example of such an application is the interactive atlas of species, which we have developed in Matlab based on the method describe here.

4.1 Adaptation of Existing Image Retrieval Methods for Non-homogeneous Objects

The methods presented in section 2 are based on the assumption that values of descriptors are similar for the whole object. This means that objects must have homogeneous colour and texture – or at least classification can be done based on global distribution of these features in the image. Here we assume that we are dealing with non-homogeneous objects, which are composed of several homogeneous sub-objects. We also assume that a class of transformations (e.g. isometria, homothetia or affine transform) exists that does not change the classification of an object.

Finding similarity between a pair of objects in our adaptation of methods described in the previous section consists of:

- Finding a transformation of one of the compared objects with respect to the other which gives the best match
- Segmentation of both objects into sub-objects with homogeneous colour and texture
- Finding similarity of corresponding pairs of sub-objects
- Scalarization of sub-object similarities

Therefore, the search algorithm looks as follows:

Algorithm 1 Interactive retrieval of non-homogeneous objects based on distance from virtual query

Phase 1. Calculation/upgrade of the virtual query

Step 1: Presentation of K images to the user, who can assign to them grades (positive or negative). Value of π_k ranks the user's perception of similarity between a given image and the image $q*$, which he/she is looking for. The image with the highest value of π_k. is denoted by $m*$

Step 2: Segmentation of object $m*$. For segmentation, we used the Edge Flow algorithm, proposed by Ma and Manjunath (1997).

Step 3: For each object $m^{(k)}$ with a defined value π_k finding parameters of transformation which gives the best match to the model $m*$, e.g. by minimization of the Hausdorff distance.

Step 4: Matching of objects $m*$ and $m^{(k)}$ according to transformation found in Step 3 and calculation of local descriptors of colour (histograms) and texture (Gabor coefficients) for areas of object $m^{(k)}$ corresponding to sub-objects of $m*$.

Step 5: Calculation of new virtual query descriptors, as the sum of descriptors for K objects, weighted with π_k:

$$q_i^r = \sum_{k=1}^{K} \pi_k m_i^{(k,r)} \bigg/ \sum_{k=1}^{K} |\pi_k|,$$

where r is an index of area of object m*, i – index of representation and q_i^r, $m_i^{(k,r)}$ are i-th representations of k-th object in area corresponding to r-th sub-object of $m*$. Correspondence is determined by the best matching of $m*$ and $m^{(k)}$.

Phase 2: Calculation of ranking of images from the database

Step 6: Calculation of similarities of all images in the database to the virtual query with descriptors given by (8), as the sum of homogeneous sub-objects, weighted by their areas.

Step 7: Calculation of K images the most similar to the virtual query. If this is the same set of images as in the previous iteration, STOP. Otherwise, return to Step 1.

4.2 Image Retrieval System Based on Neural Networks

At the end of section 2, we presented the most common approach to image retrieval and pointed out its restrictions. In this section, we propose the application of neural networks with *Radial Basis Function* (RBF) (Park, & Sandberg 1991) for user preference approximation. In contrast to methods described in previous sections, we do not model the user's preferences as a distance to a query (i.e. point of set of points in feature space) but we assume that the user's preferences can be expressed by an arbitrary utility function, which we approximate with the neural network. A model of a neuron with RBF network is depicted in Figure 4. In the case of the RBF network, unlike most other neural networks, coefficients w that are changed during the learning process are not weights: the output on the neuron depends on the *distance* between vector w and the input vector. Neuron input can be interpreted as a set of descriptors of the graphical object: output is high when the object's feature represented by input is similar to the object's feature represented by the neuron (vector w). In the training process, the neuron is taught to represent any feature desired by the user. Roughly speaking, vector w corresponds to a virtual query (but

Figure 4. Model of neuron with Radial Basis function

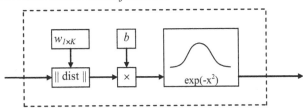

Figure 5. Structure of a neural network used for preference approximation in our image retrieval system.

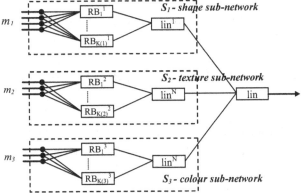

in this case, there can be many virtual queries) or in other words, it corresponds to the local maximum of utility function in a subspace of a feature space.

The network structure which we used for preference approximation is depicted in Figure 5. For every representation m_i there is a defined and separate sub-network S_i with metric adjusted to the specific kind of representation (e.g. histogram intersection for colour histogram). The number of neurons for i-*th* representation is chosen automatically in such a way that the sub-network S_i can be trained to ensure that the margin of error is below a specific threshold, therefore the network is able to approximate utility functions regardless of shape. The output neuron, which combines outputs of sub-networks (cf. Figure 5) is trained by linear regression.

Algorithm 2 Interactive retrieval of non-homogenous objects based on RBF network

Phase 1. Calculation/upgrade of the virtual query

Step 1: Presentation of K images to the user, who can assign to them grades (positive or negative). Value of π_k ranks user's perception of similarity between a given image and the image q^*, which he/she is looking for. The image with the highest value of π_k is denoted by m^*

Step 2: Segmentation of object m^* with Edge Flow algorithm.

Step 3: For each object $m^{(k)}$ with a defined value π_k finding parameters of transformation which gives the best match to the model m^*, e.g. by minimalization of the Hausdorff distance.

Step 4: Matching of objects m^* and $m^{(k)}$ according to transformation found in Step 3 and calculation of local descriptors of colour and texture for areas of object $m^{(k)}$ corresponding to sub-objects of m^*.

Step 5: Training of the network. Three sub-networks (for: shape, texture and colour) are trained separately. Training set is a set of images presented to the user. For each of these images:

    a.   Input vector of the i-th sub-network, $i=\{1$ for shape, 2 for texture, 3 for colour$\}$ is a subset of features $m_i^{(k,r)}$

    b.   Desired output of sub-network is relevance π_k. Weights of the output neuron are found using linear regression in order to minimize total error of the network.

Phase 2. Calculation of ranking of images from the database

Step 6: Simulation of the network for all images in the database and ranking them according to value of the network output.

Step 7: If the set of top K images is the same set as in the previous iteration, STOP. Otherwise, return to Step 1.

4.3 Comparison of Performance for Existing and Neural Network-based Approaches

Figure 7 shows $K=12$ images presented to the user in the first iteration of the algorithm. In Figure 7, we can see the results of the first three iterations of the algorithm based on existing methods (Algorithm 1). For each, the number of the picture within a presented set and (in brackets) within the whole database (in our case, 78 images) is given. In the experiment, the user was trying to find fishes that are most

Figure 6. The screenshot from the Matlab application which we have developed for testing of algorithms described in section 4.1. and 4.2. Image number 6 has been selected by the user as relevant in the first iteration of both compared algorithms.

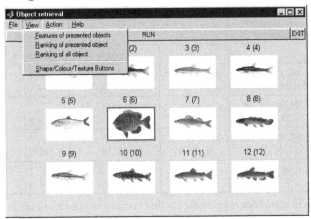

Figure 7. The results of the first three iterations of the algorithm based on existing methods (section 4.1)

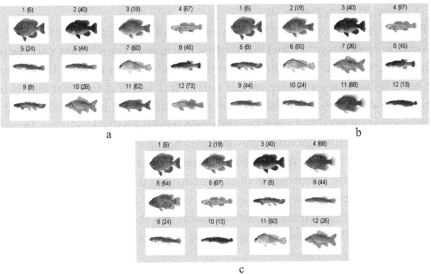

Figure 8. The result of a single iteration of the algorithm based on neural networks

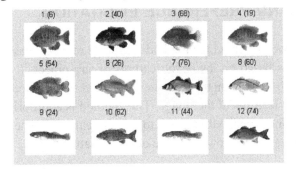

Table 1.Results of experimental comparison of Algorithm 1 based on classical methodology and Algorithm 2 based on RBF neural networks.

Number of experiment	Images, which the user considers relevant*	Relevant images retrieved after one iteration (presented to the user among top 12)		Number of images retrieved after one iteration (among top 12) divided by total number of relevant images	
		Algorithm 1	Algorithm 2	Algorithm 1	Algorithm 2
1	**06**, 19, 26, 40, 54, 62, 68, 74, 76	06, 19, 26, 40	06, 19, 26, 38, 54, 62, 68, 74, 76	4 / 9 (44 %)	9 /9 (100 %)
2	**01**, 21, 23, 28, 37, 47, 53	23, 53	1, 21, 23, 47, 53	2 / 7 (29 %)	5 / 7 (71 %)
3	**02**, **10**, **11**, 18, 29, 36, 31, 46	2, 10, 11, 29, 36, 31, 46	2, 10, 11, 29, 36, 31, 46	7 / 8 (88 %)	7 / 8 (88 %)
4	**05**, 14, 27	05, 14	05, 14, 27	2 / 3 (67 %)	3 / 3 (100 %)

* Numbers of images which were marked as relevant for the first iteration of algorithms are in bold

similar to that with the number 6. The user was looking for images similar to the 6th one in Figure 7. He ranked the following as relevant images: Image 6 from Figure 7; images 1, 2, and 3 from Figure 7a, and images 1, 2, 3, and 11 from Figure 7b.

In Figure 8, we present the results of the first iteration of the algorithm based on the RBF neural network. The result is satisfactory: we find that the first five images from Figure 8 are the most similar to the query image in the whole database (this is, of course, a subjective view, we do not present the whole database here but suppose that most users would agree). It is worth noting that the set of 12 retrieved objects contains all those representing the *Centrarchidae* family: see images 1-5 and 10 in Figure 8.

In Table 1 we present the results of experimental comparison of both algorithms. In each experiment, the users selected images from the database relevant to his/her query (identifiers of these images are listed in column 2) and then tried to retrieve them by pointing to relevant images (numbers in bold) among those presented by the system. Performance of algorithms was assessed on the basis of the percentage of relevant images which were retrieved by the system after one iteration.

Based on experiments presented above, we can claim that the image retrieval algorithm based on neural networks has proved to be much more effective than the one based on methods described in section 2 and 4.1.

5.0 IMAGE RETRIEVAL METHODS BASED ON MULTICRITERIA CLASSIFICATION AND PREFERENCE ELICITATION

In the previous section, we presented the method for image retrieval based on neural networks, where classification of objects is based on low-level features of sub-objects (colour, texture and shape) and relation between these sub-objects. In this section, we will present the approach based on reference sets, which exploits high-level features of the image. This method is appropriate for applications where the user's preferences are monotonical with respect to certain features of the image, i.e. the user is looking for images with the highest (or the lowest) value of these features.

5.1 Application of Reference Sets in Image Retrieval Systems

Let us recall first that the classification of objects based on presenting typical representatives of each class is a common approach in classification procedures. Further steps involve finding characteristic features of such representatives (see Kohavi, & John, 1997). An intrinsic part of such procedures is learning the relevance of features, the preferences, and – finally – the relevance of objects described by the features. For classification purposes, such an approach is often called 'learning from examples'. The approach here presented differs from that used for classification and recognition in the instrumental role of the 'cut-off' points used during the procedure: the reference points, that form reference sets, need not be the elements of the database to be researched, and – with the exception of status quo solutions (the class A_2 defined in the next paragraph) – they do not even need to exist. The essential is the preference relation between the elements indicated by the user, who defines the reference points. The examples point out how such a relation acts, then the retrieval algorithm learns how the preferences can be expressed by comparing individual features, and applies them to select the preferred images (semi)automatically.

Reference sets (cf. Skulimowski, 1996, 1997) constitute a tool originally designed to support decisions but, as we show below, interactive image retrieval can be seen as a kind of decision support system. Reference sets are defined as sets of characteristic points in the criteria space with similar levels of utility. There are four basic types of reference sets (cf. Skulimowski 1997):

- A_0 – bounds of optimality: upper (in the case of maximisation of criteria) borders of area where optimisation of criteria makes sense,
- A_1 – *target points*: goals of optimisation,
- A_2 – *status quo solutions*: existing solutions, which should be improved in optimisation process or lower bounds of the set of satisfactory solutions,
- A_3 – *anti-ideal point*: solutions to avoid,

which can be further split into subclasses. All, or only a few, classes of reference sets may occur in a decision problem, while the consistency of problem formulation imposes a set of conditions to be fulfilled by the reference sets (cf. Skulimowski, 1997).

The reference sets are always defined in the context of a multicriteria decision problem, i.e.

$$(F: D \rightarrow E) \rightarrow \max, \tag{9}$$

where $F=(F_1,...,F_N)$ are criteria to be optimised, E is the space of criteria values ordered by a partial order "$\leq$", which is consistent with the preference structure (1). Let us recall that the solutions to (9) are called non-dominated or "Pareto-optimal".

Below we will show below analogies between decision support systems based on reference sets and image retrieval systems with relevance feedback. It should be noted that images in a database can be seen as elements of the set of feasible solutions. Therefore, we will redefine the interpretation of reference sets in the context of image retrieval:

- A_0 is a set of graphical queries provided by the user. We assume that the goal of the user is to find an image which is most similar to one of his queries. When the user cannot provide a query, then $A_0=\varnothing$,

Figure 9. Example of a situation when, with two criteria F_1 and F_2, the solution b is dominated but becomes Pareto-optimal when a new criterion F_3 is added

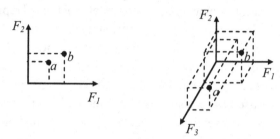

- A_1 is a set of reference images ranked by the user as *most relevant*,
- A_2 is a set of images ranked by the user as *relevant*,
- A_3 is a set of images ranked by the user as *irrelevant*,

In addition, we define the set A_4 as containing images ranked by the user as *anti-relevant*, i.e. characterised by attribute values opposite to those sought. Moreover, we assume that the vector criterion (9) need not be known a priori to the user, as the explicit user preferences constitute the primary background information. The present approach is based on an assumption that the criteria can be constructed gradually using the preference information elicited during the search process. Thus, even the number of relevance criteria cannot be assumed to be known a priori as various classes of graphical objects may be characterised by different sets of features and coefficients.

Elimination of Dominated Solutions

In an image retrieval system with a variable number of criteria, not all dominated solutions can be rejected, because some of them can become non-dominated (Pareto-optimal) in further iterations of the search process. This situation is depicted in Figure 9: when the new criterion F_3 is added, solution *b* becomes non-dominated. In order to avoid premature elimination of solutions which are temporarily dominated, in our algorithm we will eliminate only solutions dominated by images assigned by the user to sets A_3 or A_4.

Sets A_1 to A_4 change during the search process. In every iteration, K solutions are presented (e.g. $K=12$) and assigned by the user to one of sets A_i. We assume that solutions in *i*-th iteration are at least as good as in previous iterations. Therefore, the solution assigned to set A_i cannot be later assigned to A_j for $j<i$ – it follows that we can eliminate solutions dominated by images from sets A_3 or A_4 because they cannot be assigned in the future to A_1 or A_2. The opposite situation is also possible: objects originally ranked as *relevant* among K randomly chosen images can be later ranked as neutral.

Image Feature and Selection of Criteria

Criteria used for ranking images according to user preferences are modified in every iteration based on the user's evaluation of images and are calculated based on a subset of image features ς. The selection of image features depends on the class of images; we present the feature set for hotel selection in section 4.2.

Let us denote by $u_i <_A u_j$ the fact that solution u_i has been assigned by the user to a reference set with an index higher than u_j. Features f, for which the following holds:

$$u_i <_A u_j \Leftrightarrow f(u_i) < f(u_j) \tag{10}$$

will be called monotonically increasing in respect to user preferences and features for which the following holds:

$$u_i <_A u_j \Leftrightarrow f(u_i) > f(u_j) \tag{11}$$

will be called monotonically decreasing. Sets of feature monotonically increasing and decreasing will be denoted respectively: $\varsigma_\uparrow$ and $\varsigma_\downarrow$.

As criteria, we will select features from the set $\varsigma_\uparrow$ and a decreasing function of features from the set $\varsigma_\downarrow$. Utility function is calculated on the basis of two criteria: distance from the set A_1 (or A_0, if it has been defined by providing virtual queries) and distance from the set A_4. Therefore, utility function can be expressed as:

$$v(u) = 1/[d(u, A_1) + h(d(u, A_4))], \tag{12}$$

where h is a decreasing function. For implementation, we used $h(x) = 1/(x+\varepsilon)$.

Steps of the image retrieval algorithm with reference sets are presented below.

Algorithm 3 Interactive image retrieval – reference sets method

Phase 1. Calculation/upgrade of the set of criteria and utility function

Step 1. Present to the user of the set $S(i)$ of images (i is the number of the iteration), ordered according to ranking based on recently calculated information about user preferences. In the first iteration, the set $S(i)$ is chosen randomly from the database.

Step 2. The user assigns elements of the set $S(i)$ to the reference sets.

Step 3. Calculate the set of features monotonically increasing $\varsigma_\uparrow$ and monotonically decreasing $\varsigma_\downarrow$.

Step 4. Calculate criteria values based on $\varsigma_\uparrow$ and $\varsigma_\downarrow$, estimation of utility function v and calculation of utility of images from the set $S(i)$.

Step 5. Check if $\forall\, u_1, u_2 \in S(i)\; u_i <_A u_j \Rightarrow v(u_1) > v(u_2)$. If this condition is not fulfilled, the user should redefine reference sets, and we return to Step 2.

Phase 2. Upgrade of the set of dominated solutions and calculation of ranking of images from the database

Step 6. Assign images dominated by elements of $\{A_3(i) \cup A_4(i)\}$ to the set of dominated solutions.

Step 7. Calculate utility for all images in the database.

Step 8. Rank all images in the database on the basis of utility function.

Step 9. Assign $i = i+1$, return to Step 1.

Table 2. Set of image features for hotel retrieval application

no	feature description
1	area of hotel divided by area of image
2	area of forest divided by area of image
3	area of meadow divided by area of image
4	area of sea divided by area of image
5	area of swimming pool divided by area of image
6	area of beach divided by area of image
7	area of forest divided by area of hotel
8	area of meadow divided by area of hotel
9	area of sea divided by area of hotel
10	area of swimming pool divided by area of hotel
11	area of beach divided by area of hotel
12	number of segmented parts of image recognized as parts of hotel
13	width of hotel divided by width of image
14	height of hotel divided by height of image
15	height of hotel divided by its width
16	width of forest areas divided by width of image
17	height of forest areas divided by height of image
18	value of feature 17 divided by value of feature 16

5.2 An Example of Real-life Application and Performance Assessment

To evaluate the above-presented method, we have developed an interactive system *Scene Retrieval* for a Matlab environment. Tests have been done for an image-based hotel search. The set of image features depends on a specific application and class of images. The feature set for our application is presented in Table 2.

Figure 10. Images of hotels presented to the user in the first iteration of the search algorithm

Table 3. Preferences of the user, expressed by assignment of images to reference sets

no of image	no of reference set	filename
1 (a)	2	1811.jpg
2 (b)	4	1814.jpg
3 (c)	1	1818.jpg
4 (d)	1	1824.jpg
5 (e)	2	1831.jpg
6 (f)	2	1836.jpg

Table 4. Results – 6 images with the lowest value of utility function extracted from the database

no in ranking	no in database	utility
2	3	0.0053
3	4	0.0494
4	5	0.8899
5	111	0.9782
6	33	1.0472
8	36	1.2404

Figure 11. Results – 6 images with the best value of utility function. In brackets, the numbers of images within the database are given

High-level features presented in Table 2 were calculated on the basis of low-level features (colour distribution, texture and type of border) of areas segmented with the *Edge Flow* algorithm. We used supervised learning to train the software to classify objects on the basis of low-level features.

In Figure 10, we can see 6 of the 137 images of Greek hotels, available at the website: www. dilos.com.

Table 5. Image features preferred by the user, automatically calculated on the basis of examples

Image features preferred by the user	• Large area of forest (the main criterion) • Small size of buildings (additional criterion)
Preferred image features calculated by the system based on 6 examples	Low value of: • Area of hotel divided by area of image • Height of hotel divided by height of image High value of: • Area of forest divided by area of image • Area of forest divided by area of hotel • Width of forest areas divided by width of image • Height of forest areas divided by height of image
Preferred image features calculated by the system based on 12 examples	Low value of: • Width of hotel divided by width of image • Height of hotel divided by its width High value of: • Width of forest areas divided by width of image • Height of forest areas divided by height of image

Let us assume that the user – intentionally or not – selects a hotel where the image contains a lot of greenery (the main user criterion) and with small buildings (additional criterion). The images are therefore assigned:

- To the set A1, if the image contains forest and small buildings
- To the set A2, if the image contains forest and big buildings
- To the set A3, if the image contains no forest (or a small area of forest) and small buildings
- To the set A4, if the image contains no forest (or a small area of forest) and big buildings

In a single iteration, 6 images are presented to the user. Images presented in the first iteration are shown in Figure 10. Reference sets $A_1,..., A_4$ assigned by the user to these images are presented in Table 3.

Based on data presented in Table 3, our algorithm automatically found features that change monotonically with a change of utility value. Features monotonically increasing (i.e. with smaller values for higher levels of user satisfaction) are 1 and 14. Features monotonically decreasing are 2, 7, 16 and 17 – cf. Table 2. A ranking of the 6 images with the best (lowest) value of utility function is presented in Table 4 and in Figure 11.

In the next four experiments (Table 6), the users assigned each of the 12 presented images to reference sets according to their preferences. Then they assigned the images retrieved by the system, in order to assess the system's performance. In these experiments respectively, 11, 11, 9, and 11 of the retrieved images among 12 were considered by the user as belonging to reference set A_1 or A_2 - in other words, they can be considered as relevant.

Experiments, like the one described above (and others which can be found in Rotter 2004), show that the system is able to elicit user preferences on the basis of their assessment of several exemplary images. Retrieved images correspond to user expectations, therefore we can claim that the proposed method can be useful for interactive image retrieval systems. It is, however, worth noting that the preference elicitation

Table 6. Results of experiments on hotel database

Number of experiment	Description of user preferences (which were not directly revealed to the program)	Reference sets assigned by the user to the presented images		Results for 12 top images: number in ranking / number of retrieved images in database / user assessment of reference set			Number of images from reference sets 1-4 among top 12 images retrieved
1	Water (sea or swimming pool) and beach. If only one exists in the image, water is slightly more important	1 2 3 4 5 6 7 8 9 10 11 12 1	1 2 2 1 1 3 4 4 1 1 1	1 2 3 4 5 6 7 8 9 10 11 12	1 35 12 122 88 45 97 54 30 95 98 135	1 1 1 2 1 4 1 1 2 2 1 2	1: 7 2: 4 3: 0 4: 1
2	Water and greenery in the image, both elements equally preferred.	1 2 3 4 5 6 7 8 9 10 11 12 1	1 2 1 1 1 2 2 2 2 1 1	1 2 3 4 5 6 7 8 9 10 11 12 1	1 12 122 35 45 19 43 93 13 135 30 22	1 1 1 1 2 2 2 3 2 2 1	1: 6 2: 5 3: 1 4: 0
3	Big building and no water in the image.	1 2 3 4 5 6 7 8 9 10 11 12 4	3 3 4 3 3 3 1 1 3 3 3	1 2 3 4 5 6 7 8 9 10 11 12 2	7 75 86 63 78 76 20 40 134 92 62 89	1 3 1 3 2 1 1 3 1 1 1	1: 7 2: 2 3: 3 4: 0
4	Complex architecture of the building and greenery around	1 2 3 4 5 6 7 8 9 10 11 12 1	1 3 1 1 1 1 2 2 3 2 1	1 2 3 4 5 6 7 8 9 10 11 12 2	1 12 11 13 122 106 45 128 111 26 3 22	1 1 1 1 1 2 2 3 1 2 1	1: 7 2: 4 3: 1 4: 0

algorithm is only a part of the whole image retrieval system. Image analysis is another crucial part and the overall usefulness of the system depends on correct classification of image objects. The performance of an image retrieval system is therefore restricted by image recognition methods and strongly depends on the class of images. In our experiments, for example, it happened that an area of beach was erroneously interpreted as a hotel wall: umbrellas placed at regular intervals provide a texture similar to ranks of windows; if an area of beach has a similar distribution of colours and is limited with straight lines, like the walls of a building, the algorithm cannot discriminate between these two objects on the basis of low-level features. In the experiments presented in Table 6, user preferences were related to features which can, to some extent, be calculated on the basis of low-level image analysis (like distribution of colours for segmented areas). For example, the users was looking for water in the image, without distinguishing between the sea and a swimming pool. Methods of automatic understanding of 3D scenes applied here not yet advanced enough to provide a reliable set of high-level features; this creates a challenge for further research, but – for the time being – limits the performance of the search process.

Table 7. Comparison of image retrieval methods based on preference elicitation presented in this chapter

	The method based on RBF neural networks (section 4)	**The method based on reference sets (section 5)**
Examples of application areas	Atlases and thematic encyclopaedias with CBIR capabilities. E-commerce (for some classes of products). Trademark databases.	Photo albums. E-commerce (for some classes of products). Internet search engines.
Motivation for using content-based (instead of textual) search	We assume that the user remembers appearance of the searched object, but is not able to formulate a narrative description of desired features (mostly because the classification depends on low-level features, which are not directly perceived or are difficult to articulate)	Lack of sufficient description (like textual and numerical information) associated with images. The user may be not aware of some of the desired features; the method automatically finds features which coincide with user's assessment of the presented images. If the number of features is high, the selection of the best images is difficult for the user. The method includes a decision support system which helps the user to make a selection.
Type of images	Each image contains one object and homogenous background. Preferably, images are rather schematic pictures than real photos	Real scenes, containing many objects.
Type of features used for retrieval	Low-level features of sub-objects and spatial relations between them in 2D image. The searched image corresponds to a point/area of feature space.	Subset of pre-defined features of the image. Features are usually high-level (e.g. presence/size of a given type of object) but also low-level features can be defined. Features automatically selected for retrieval during search process are monotonic in respect to user's preferences (higher value – more desirable, or opposite) and do not have optimal value.
Required adaptation of the method to application	The database of images should be preliminary prepared to fulfil the constraints.	Defining of pre-selected set of features and development of algorithms for their extraction is required. Standard "universal" set of features and extraction method can be implemented (e.g. for Internet search)
Factors influencing the performance	Homogeneity of database. If images fulfil assumptions (see row "type of images"), the method is very reliable	Performance of the algorithm for extraction of high-level features (e.g. recognition of objects in the image). Aptness and number of pre-defined features.

6.0 CONCLUSION

In this chapter, we have presented two approaches to interactive visual search, designed for different applications. The first method, based on RBF neural networks, is based on breaking down graphical object into sub-objects. Low-level features of sub-objects (like colour, texture and shape) and the mutual relations between them are used for the elicitation of user queries. Target applications are mostly interactive atlases and multimedia encyclopaedias which allow the user to search for an item based on a memorized image. The second method is based on reference sets and exploits high-level features of the image. The method can be used for a specific class of images (like images of hotels in our experiments), but with a sufficiently large set of pre-defined image features, it can also be used in Internet search engines.

For testing purposes, we have implemented both methods as Matlab applications: queries in an interactive atlas of fishes and a photo-based hotel search according to user preferences. These experiments show an essential improvement in the performance of the proposed algorithms compared to classical methods.

Table 7 contains a comparison of selected properties of two image retrieval methods based on preference elicitation presented in section 4. and section 5 of this chapter.

7.0 FUTURE RESEARCH DIRECTIONS

Further development of the above presented methods constitutes a challenge from both theoretical and implementation points of view. Major improvement of IR performance has been achieved by a combined application of the image classification methods and multicriteria preference elicitation. This research direction requires further efforts, with the main targets being:

- An optimal man-machine interface when designing a query and providing feedback information, and
- Optimised navigation in the feature space, and an adaptive feature space contraction/expansion.

Further experiments are needed to find out how many pictures can be presented to the user simultaneously to achieve the most efficient preference extraction, as a function of image type (landscape, faces, artefacts), size, shape, and features (colour, black and white etc.).

Table 8. Future development prospect of the two image retrieval methods presented in this chapter

	The method based on RBF neural networks (section 4)	**The method based on reference sets (section 4)**
Future research	Research on including 3D-invariants in the IR, investigation of suitable 3D-transformations	Definition of large set of pre-defined features and methods for their extraction. Development of multimedia search method, which combines textual, numerical, sound and visual information. Research on reference 3D and 4D (moving) objects
Extensions and improvements	IR for 3D and moving objects	Development of experimental Internet search engine, extensions enabling video sequence search

As regards real-life applications, it should be remembered that the above presented methods have been implemented as prototype versions in a Matlab environment. Optimized coding of the algorithms (e.g. in C++) would allow tests on large databases and feasibility assessment of commercial applications on the basis of the proposed algorithms.

An implementation of an Internet search engine based on reference sets, with a large set of pre-defined high-level features incorporated is needed for a reliable assessment of the efficiency of the proposed method for this type of application. The performance of this method depends on the quality of high-level feature extraction, and the elaboration of a reliable feature extraction algorithm is, in itself, one of the most challenging problems of visual search. An effective search engine should incorporate both visual and text-based search. Fusion of the proposed methods with search algorithms based on textual information associated with images would be an interesting topic for future research.

A summary of future research and extensions which aim to directly improve the two image retrieval methods here presented is shown in the table below.

ACKNOWLEDGMENT

The research of P. Rotter has been partially supported by the project CHORUS (www.ist-chorus.org). The authors would like to thank to Patricia Farrer from JRC-IPTS for her help with preparation of the manuscript.

DISCLAIMER

The views expressed in this publication are purely those of the authors and may not in any circumstances be regarded as stating an official position of the European Commission.

8.0 REFERENCES

Agouris, P., Carswell, J., & Stefanidis, A. (1999). "An Environment for Content-Based Image Retrieval from Large Spatial Databases", *ISPRS Journal of Photogrammetry and Remote Sensing*, Elsevier, Vol. 54, No. 4, pp. 263-272, 1999.

Bronez, T.P., & Hughes, E.S. (1997). "Image & Video Retrieval for National Security Applications: An Approach Based on Multiple Content Codebooks", The MITRE Corporation, McLean, Virginia 1997.

Cheng, P.C. et al. (2007). "A two-level relevance feedback mechanism for image retrieval" Expert Systems with Applications, In Press, Corrected Proof, available online 4 March 2007.

Chuang, S.C., et al. (2006) "A Multiple-Instance Neural Network-based Image Content Retrieval System", in Proceedings of the First International Conference on Innovative Computing, Information and Control (ICICIC), 2006.

Doulamis, N., & Doulamis, A. (2006). "Evaluation of relevance feedback schemes in content-based in retrieval systems" Signal Processing: Image Communication, Vol. 21, Issue 4, April 2006, 334-357.

Eakins, J.P., & Graham, M.E. (1999). "Content-based Image Retrieval", A report to the JISC Technology Applications Programme, Institute for Image Data Research, University of Northumbria at Newcastle, January 1999.

Goodrum, A. (2000). "Image Information Retrieval: An Overview of Current Research" *Informing Science*, Special Issue of Information Science Research, vol. 3 no 2, 2000.

Ishikawa, Y., Subramanya, R., & Faloutsos C. (1998). "MindReader: Querying databases through multiple examples", 24th VLDB Conference, New York, 1998.

Kohavi, R., & John, G. Wrappers for feature subset selection, *Artificial Intelligence*, 97, 1997, 273-324.

Lew, M.S. (2001). *Principles of Visual Information Retrieval*. Springer-Verlag, London 2001.

Liu, Y. (2007) "A survey of content-based image retrieval with high-level semantics", Pattern Recognition, Vol. 40, Issue 1, January 2007, 262-282.

Ma, W.Y., & Manjunath, B.S. (1997). "Edge flow: a framework of boundary detection and image segmentation" Proc. IEEE International Conference on Computer Vision and Pattern Recognition, San Juan, Puerto Rico, June 1997, pp. 744-749.

Müller, H. et al. (2000). "Learning features weights from user behaviour in Content-Based Image Retrieval", In S.J. Simoff and O.R. Zaiane eds., *ACM SIGKDD International Conference on Knowledge Discovery and Data Mining* (Workshop on Multimedia Data Mining MDM/KDD2000), Boston, MA, USA, August 20-23, 2000.

Müller, H. et al. (2000a). "Strategies for positive and negative relevance feedback in image retrieval", in *Proc. of the International Conference on Pattern Recognition* (ICPR'2000), Vol. 1 of Computer Vision and Image Analysis, pp. 1043-1046, Barcelona, Spain, September 3-8 2000.

Müller, H. et al. (2001). "Performance Evaluation in Content-Based Image Retrieval: Overview and Proposals", *Pattern Recognition Letters*, Special Issue on Image and Video Indexing, 22, 5, pp. 593-601, 2001. H. Bunke and X. Jiang Eds.

Mehrotra, S. et al. (1997). "Multimedia Analysis and Retrieval System", in *Proc. of The 3rd Int. Workshop on Information Retrieval Systems*, Como, Italy, September 25-27, 1997, pp. 39-45.

Park, J., & Sandberg, I.W. (1991). "Universal approximation using radial-basis-function networks", *Neural Computation* 3, 1991, pp. 246-257.

Roccio, J.J. (1971). "Relevance Feedback in Information Retrieval", in G. Salton ed., *The SMART Retrieval System – Experiments in Automatic Document Processing*, pp. 313-323, Prentice Hall, Englewood Cliffs, N.J., 1971.

Rotter, P. (2004). *Zastosowanie metod optymalizacji wielokryterialnej w interpretacji obrazów (Application of multicriteria optimisation methods in image interpretation)*. Unpublished doctoral dissertation, AGH-University of Science and Technology, Krakow, 2004.

Rui, Y. et al. (1997). "A Relevance Feedback Architecture in Content-based Multimedia Information Retrieval Systems", in *Proc of IEEE Workshop on Content-based Access of Image and Video Libraries*, in conjunction with CVPR'97 , June 20, 1997, Puerto Rico, pp 82-89.

Rui, Y., Huang, T.S., & Chang, S.F. (1999). "Image Retrieval: Current Techniques, Promising Directions and Open Issues", Journal of Visual Communication and Image Representation, Vol. 10, 39-62, March, 1999.

Rui, Y., Huang, T.S., & Mehrotra, S. (1997). "Content-based Image Retrieval with Relevance Feedback in MARS", in *Proc. of IEEE Int. Conf. on Image Processing '97* , October 26-29, 1997 Santa Barbara, California, USA, pp. 815-818.

Rui, Y., Huang, T.S., & Mehrotra, S. (1998). "Relevance Feedback Techniques in Interactive Content-Based Image Retrieval", in Proc. of *IS&T and SPIE Storage and Retrieval of Image and Video Databases VI*, pp. 25-36, January 24-30, 1998, San Jose, CA.

Servetto, S. et al. (1998). "A Region-based Representation of Images in MARS", *Journal on VLSI Signal Processing Systems*, Special Issue on Multimedia Signal Processing (Guest Editors: Yao Wang & Amy Reibman), Volume 20, Issues 2, pp. 137-150, October 1998.

Smith, J.R., & Chang, S.F. (1996). "VisualSEEk: a fully automated content-based image query system", in *Proc. ACM Intern. Conf. Multimedia*, Boston, MA, May 1996.

Skulimowski, A.M.J. (1996). *Decision Support Systems Based on Reference Sets*, AGH-UST University Publishers, Kraków 1996, p.167.

Skulimowski, A.M.J. (1997). "Methods of Multicriteria Decision Support Based on Reference Sets", in: R. Caballero, F. Ruiz, R.E. Steuer (Eds.) *Advances in Multiple Objective and Goal Programming*, Lecture Notes in Economics and Mathematical Systems, 455, Springer-Verlag, Berlin-Heidelberg-New York, pp. 282-290, 1997.

Spink, A., & Losee, R. (1996). "Feedback in information retrieval", *Annual Review of Information Science and Technology*, vol. 31, pp. 33-78, 1996.

9.0 ADDITIONAL READING

Before presenting the additional reading recommendations, we would like to point out that the Reader should be aware of the fact that making a selection from thousands of quality papers devoted to visual information retrieval is a hard task, with an unavoidable subjectivity burden. The selection of journal papers and books listed below should thus be considered merely as a starting point for a more profound bibliographic study, using the references cited therein, and reviewing regularly key journals and conference proceedings in the field.

Al.-Ani, A. (2005). Feature Subset Selection Using Ant Colony Optimization. *International Journal of Computational Intelligence* 2(1), 2005, 53-58 (see also the references cited therein).

Alvarez, C., Oumohmed, A.I., Mignotte, M. & Nie, J.-Y. (2004). Toward Cross-language and Cross-media Image Retrieval. In Multilingual Information Access for Text, Speech and Images. Proceedings of the 5th Workshop of the Cross-Language Evaluation Forum. CLEF 2004, Bath, UK, September 2004, *LNCS* 3491, Springer, 676–687.

Angilella, S., Greco, S., Lamantia, F., & Matarazzo, B. (2004). Assessing non-additive utility for multicriteria decision aid. *European Journal of Operational Research* 158 (2004) 734–74.

Blum, A.L., & Langley, P. (1997). Selection of relevant features and examples in machine learning. Artificial Intelligence, 97, 245-271.

Brugha, C.M. (2004). Phased Multicriteria Preference finding. *European Journal of Operational Research*, 158, 2004, 308-316.

Castelli, V., & Bergman, L.D. (editors) (2001) Image Databases: Search and Retrieval of Digital Imagery. Wiley-Interscience 2001

Deb, S. (2003) Multimedia Systems and Content-Based Image Retrieval. Information Science Publishing, 2003.

Dombi, J., & Zsiros, A. (2005). Learning multicriteria classification models from examples: Decision rules in continuous space. *European Journal of Operational Research*, 160, 2005, 663-675.

Doumpos, M., & Zopounidis, C., A multicriteria classification approach based on pairwise comparisons, *European Journal of Operational Research*, 158, 2004, 378-389.

Duda, R.O., & Hart, P.E. (1973) Pattern Classification and Scene Analysis, John Wiley and Sons, New York, 1973.

Dy, J.G., Brodley, C.E., Kak, A., Broderick, L.S., & Aisen, A.M. 2003. Unsupervised Feature Selection Applied to Content-based Retrieval of Lung Images, *IEEE Transactions on Pattern Analysis and Machine Intelligence 25(3)*, 373-378.

Gagaudakis, G., & Rosin, P.L. (2002) Incorporating shape into histograms for CBIR. *Pattern Recognition*, 35 (1) (2002), 81-91.

He X., King, O., Ma, W.-Y., Li, M., & Zhang, H.-J. (2003) Learning a semantic space from user's relevance feedback for image retrieval, *IEEE Trans. Circ. Syst. Video Technol.* 13 (1), 39–48.

Huijsmans, D.P. & Sebe, N. (2005). How to Complete Performance Graphs in Content-based Image Retrieval: Add Generality and Normalize Scope. *IEEE Transactions on Pattern Analysis and Machine Intelligence 27(2)*, 245-251.

Jain, A., & Zongker, D. (1997) Feature selection: Evaluation, application, and small sample performance, *IEEE Transactions on Pattern Analysis and Machine Intelligence*, 19, 1997, 153-158.

Kailing, K., Kriegel, H.-P., & Schoenauer S. (2004) Content-based Image Retrieval Using Multiple Representations. Proc. 8th Int. Conf. on Knowledge-based Intelligent Information and Engineering Systems (KES'04), Wellington, New Zealand, Spronger, *LNAI* 3214, 2004, 982-988.

Keysers, D., Macherey, W., Ney, W.H., & Dahmen, J. (2004) Adaptation in Statistical Pattern Recognition using Tangent Vectors. *IEEE Transactions on Pattern Analysis and Machine Intelligence*, 26(2): February 2004, 269–274,

Lew, M.S., Sebe, N., Djeraba, C., & Jain, R. (2006). Content-based Multimedia Information Retrieval: State of the Art and Challenges, *ACM Transactions on Multimedia Computing, Communications, and Applications,* Feb. 2006

Lewis, P.H., Martinez, K., Abas, F.S., Fauzi, M.F.A., Chan, S.C.Y., Addis, M.J., Boniface, M.J., Grimwood, P., Stevenson, A., Lahanier, C., & Stevenson, J. (2004). An Integrated Content and Metadata-based Retrieval System for Art. *IEEE Transactions On Image Processing*, Vol. 13, No. 3, March 2004, 302-313.

Marques, O., & Furht, B. (2002) Content-based Image and Video Retrieval. Springer, 2002

Nieddu, L., & Patrizi, G. (2000). Formal methods in pattern recognition: A review. *European Journal of Operational Research*, 120, 459-495.

Smeulders, A., Worring, M., Santini, S., Gupta, A., & Jain, R. (2000). Content-based image retrieval at the end of the early years. *IEEE Transactions on Pattern Analysis and Machine Intelligence 22(12)*, 1349-1380.

Veltkamp, R.C., Burkhardt, H., & Kriegel, H.P. (editors) (2001). State-of-the-Art in Content-based Image and Video Retrieval. Springer, 2001

Wang, J.T.L., Zhang, K., Chang, G., & Shasha, D. (2002). Finding approximate patterns in undirected acyclic graphs. Pattern Recognition 35 (2002) 473–483

Wang, Z., Chi, Z., Feng, D., & Tsoi, A.C. (2003). Content-based image retrieval with relevance feedback using adaptive processing of tree-structure image representation, *Int. J. Image Graphics* 3 (1) 119–144

Xu, Y., Saber E., & Murat Tekalp, A.M. (2004) Dynamic learning from multiple examples for semantic object segmentation and search, *Computer Vision and Image Understanding* 95 (2004) 334–353

Zhang, Y. (2006) Semantic-based Visual Information Retrieval. IGI Global, 2006

Chapter XII
Personalized Content–Based Image Retrieval

Iker Gondra
St. Francis Xavier University, Canada

ABSTRACT

In content-based image retrieval (CBIR), a set of low-level features are extracted from an image to represent its visual content. Retrieval is performed by image example where a query image is given as input by the user and an appropriate similarity measure is used to find the best matches in the corresponding feature space. This approach suffers from the fact that there is a large discrepancy between the low-level visual features that one can extract from an image and the semantic interpretation of the image's content that a particular user may have in a given situation. That is, users seek semantic similarity, but we can only provide similarity based on low-level visual features extracted from the raw pixel data, a situation known as the semantic gap. The selection of an appropriate similarity measure is thus an important problem. Since visual content can be represented by different attributes, the combination and importance of each set of features varies according to the user's semantic intent. Thus, the retrieval strategy should be adaptive so that it can accommodate the preferences of different users. Relevance feedback (RF) learning has been proposed as a technique aimed at reducing the semantic gap. It works by gathering semantic information from user interaction. Based on the user's feedback on the retrieval results, the retrieval scheme is adjusted. By providing an image similarity measure under human perception, RF learning can be seen as a form of supervised learning that finds relations between high-level semantic interpretations and low-level visual properties. That is, the feedback obtained within a single query session is used to personalize the retrieval strategy and thus enhance retrieval performance. In this chapter we present an overview of CBIR and related work on RF learning. We also present our own previous work on a RF learning-based probabilistic region relevance learning algorithm for automatically estimating the importance of each region in an image based on the user's semantic intent.

INTRODUCTION

In recent years, the rapid development of information technologies and the advent of the Web have accelerated the growth of digital media and, in particular, image collections. As a result and in order to realize the full potential of these technologies, the need for effective mechanisms to search large image collections becomes evident. The management of text information has been studied thoroughly, and there have been many successful approaches for handling text databases (see Salton, 1986). However, the progress in research and development of multimedia database systems has been slow due to the difficulties and challenges of the problem.

The development of concise representations of images that can capture the essence of their visual content is an important task. However, as the saying "a picture is worth a thousand words" suggests, representing visual content is a very difficult task. The human ability to extract semantics from an image by using knowledge of the world is remarkable, though probably difficult to emulate.

At present, the most common way to represent the visual content of an image is to assign a set of descriptive keywords to it. Then, image retrieval is performed by matching the query text with the stored keywords (Rui & Huang, 1998). However, there are many problems associated with this simple keyword matching approach. First, it is usually the case that all the information contained in an image cannot be captured by a few keywords. Furthermore, a large amount of effort is needed to do keyword assignments in a large image database. Also, because different people may have different interpretations of an image's content, there will be inconsistencies (Rui & Huang, 1998). Consider the image in Figure 1. One might describe it as "mountains," "trees," and/or "lake." However, that particular description would not be able to respond to user queries for "water," "landscape," "peaceful," or "water reflection."

In order to alleviate some of the problems associated with text-based approaches, content-based image retrieval (CBIR) was proposed (see Faloutsos et al., 1993, for examples of early approaches). The idea is to search on the images directly. A set of low-level features (such as color, texture, and shape) are extracted from the image to characterize its visual content. In traditional approaches (Faloutsos et al., 1993; Gupta & Jain, 1997; Hara, Hirata, Takano, & Kawasaki, 1997; Kelly, Cannon, & Hush,

Figure 1. Sample image

Figure 2. General CBIR computational framework

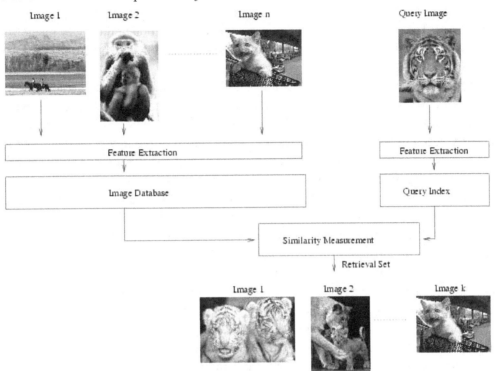

1995; Mehrotra, Rui, Ortega, & Huang, 1997; Pentland, Picard, & Sclaroff, 1994; Samadani, Han, & Katragadda, 1993; Sclaroff, Taycher, & Cascia, 1997; Smith & Chang, 1996, 1997; Stone & Li, 1996; Wang, Wiederhold, Firschein, & Sha, 1998), each image is represented by a set of global features that are calculated by means of uniform processing over the entire image and describe its visual content (e.g., color, texture). The features are then the components of a feature vector which makes the image correspond to a point in a feature space.

Users usually look for particular objects when describing the semantic interpretation of an image. Thus, due to global image properties affecting the recognition of certain objects depicted in an image, low retrieval performance is often attained when using global features. In region-based image representations (Carson, 2002; Chen & Wang, 2002; Li, Wang, & Wiederhold, 2000; Li, Chen, & Zhang, 2002; Ma & Majunath 1997; Smith & Li, 1999; Wang, Li, & Wiederhold, 2001), the use of local features that describe each of a set of segmented regions in an image provides a more meaningful characterization that is closer to a user's perception of an image's content. That is, instead of looking at the image as a whole, we look at its objects and their relationships. Many image segmentation algorithms have been proposed. However, robust and accurate segmentation remains a difficult problem.

Retrieval in CBIR is performed by image example where a query image is given as input by the user and an appropriate similarity measure is used to find the best matches in the corresponding feature space. Thus, the system views the query and database images as a collection of features. The relevance of a database image to the query image is then proportional to their feature-based similarity. The general computational framework of a CBIR system is depicted in Figure 2. In order to create the image database, images are processed by a feature extraction algorithm and their feature representations are stored in the database. The same feature extraction algorithm is used to obtain the features that represent the query image. The similarity measure compares the representation of the query image with the representation of each database image. Those feature representations deemed the most "similar" are returned to the user as the retrieval set.

This approach suffers from the fact that there is a large discrepancy between the low-level visual features that one can extract from an image and the semantic interpretation of the image's content that a particular user may have in a given situation. That is, users seek semantic similarity but we can only provide similarity based on low-level visual features extracted from the raw pixel data. The human notion of similarity is usually based on high-level abstractions such as activities, events, or emotions displayed in an image. Therefore, a database image with a high feature similarity to the query image may be completely different from the query in terms of user-defined semantics. This discrepancy between low-level features and high-level concepts is known as the *semantic gap* (Smeulders, Worring, Santini, Gupta, & Jain, 2000). This situation is exacerbated when the retrieval task is to be performed in broad image domains (e.g., the Web) where images with similar semantic interpretations may have unpredictable and large variability in their low-level visual content. In contrast, when the retrieval task is performed in narrow domains (e.g., medical images, frontal views of faces), usually there are specific assumptions particular to the application that, for a given semantic interpretation, limit the variability of its corresponding low-level visual content. As a result, it is easier to find links between low-level visual content and semantic interpretations (i.e., the semantic gap is smaller). The selection of an appropriate similarity measure is thus an important problem. Since visual content can be represented by different attributes, the combination and importance of each set of features varies according to the user's semantic intent. Thus, the retrieval strategy should be adaptive so that it can accommodate the preferences of different users.

Relevance feedback (RF) learning, originally developed for information retrieval (Rocchio & Salton, 1971), has been proposed as a learning technique aimed at reducing the semantic gap. It works by gathering semantic information from user interaction. Based on the user's feedback on the retrieval results, the retrieval scheme is adjusted. By providing an image similarity measure under human perception, RF learning can be seen as a form of supervised learning that finds relations between high-level semantic interpretations and low-level visual properties. That is, the feedback obtained within a single query session is used to personalize the retrieval strategy and thus enhance retrieval performance.

CONTENT-BASED IMAGE RETRIEVAL

As described in the previous section, early approaches to image retrieval were mainly text-based techniques consisting of the manual annotation of images with descriptive keywords. This manual annotation is very time consuming and cumbersome for large image databases. Furthermore, it is very subjective and error-prone. Recently, some approaches for automatic image labeling (Ono, Amano, Hakaridani, Satoh, & Sakauchi, 1996; Shen, Ooi, & Tan, 2000; Srihari, Zhang, & Rao, 2000) have been proposed as an attempt to improve this manual annotation process. Ono et al. (1996) use image recognition techniques to automatically assign descriptive keywords to images. Their approach uses only a limited number of keywords. Furthermore, because image recognition techniques are not completely reliable, automatically assigned keywords still must be verified by a human. Shen et al. (2000) use the textual context of images in a Web page to automatically extract descriptive keywords. The collateral text that usually accompanies an image (e.g., captions) is exploited in Srihari et al. (2000). The performance of those approaches is not as high as that obtained with manual annotation, and their applicability is limited in situations where there is no textual context (e.g., a photo album). Wenyin et al. (2001) propose a semi-automatic annotation that assigns images to keywords based on users' RF. Their approach uses both keyword- and content-based retrieval strategies. A weighted sum of the keyword-based and visual feature-based similarity measures is used to calculate the overall similarity of an image. Based on the user's RF, the annotation of each image in the retrieval set is updated. The experiments conducted in Wenyin et al. (2001) indicate that this strategy of semi-automatic annotation outperforms manual annotation in terms of efficiency and automatic annotation in terms of accuracy. However, the performance of this approach depends heavily on the performance of the particular CBIR and RF algorithms used, especially when there is no initial annotation in the database at all (Wenyin et al., 2001).

In order to overcome the above-mentioned drawbacks associated with text-based approaches, it would be more suitable to search on the images directly based on their visual content. In the early 1990s, CBIR was proposed as a way of allowing a user to search target images in terms of the content represented by visual features. Since then, many CBIR systems have been developed including Blobworld (Carson, 2002), QBIC (Faloutsos et al., 1993), IRM (Li et al., 2000), NeTra (Ma & Majunath, 1997), MARS (Mehrotra et al., 1997), Photobook (Pentland et al., 1994), WebSEEK (Smith & Change, 1997), and SIMPLIcity (Wang et al., 2001), just to name a few.

Retrieval is performed by image example, where a query image is given as input by the user and an appropriate similarity measure is used to find the best matches in the corresponding feature space. Thus, the system views the query and database images as a collection of features. The relevance of a database image to the query image is then proportional to their feature-based similarity. The general computational framework of a CBIR system is depicted in Figure 2. In order to create the image database, images are processed by a feature extraction algorithm and their feature representations are stored in the database. The same feature extraction algorithm is used to obtain the features that represent the query image. The similarity measure compares the representation of the query image with the representation of each database image. Those feature representations deemed the most "similar" are returned to the user as the retrieval set. For example, when retrieving similar images based on color, most existing techniques use a color histogram generated from the entire image (Jain & Vailaya, 1996). In Swain & Ballard (1991), image similarity was based solely on color. The distribution of color was represented by color histograms. The similarity between two images was then based on a similarity measure between their corresponding histograms called the "normalized histogram intersection."

Conversely, we can measure distance between images. In this case, small distances between feature representations correspond to large similarities, and large distances correspond to small similarities. Thus, distance is a measure of dissimilarity. One way to transform between a distance measure and a similarity measure is to take the reciprocal. Some commonly used distance measures are the Euclidean (also known as the L2-distance) and city-block distances (also known as the Manhattan distance or L1-distance) (Bimbo, 1999). For example, Netra (Ma & Majunath, 1997) uses Euclidean distance on color and shape features; MARS (Mehrotra et al., 1997) uses Euclidean distance on texture features; Blobworld (Carson, 2002) uses Euclidean distance on texture and shape features. IBM's QBIC (Faloutsos et al., 1993) was the first commercial system that implemented CBIR. It addressed the problems of non-Euclidean distance measuring and high dimensionality of feature vectors. MIT's Photobook (Pentland et al., 1994) implements a set of interactive tools for browsing and searching images. It consists of three subsystems: one that allows the user to search based on appearance, one that uses 2D shape, and one that allows search based on textural properties. While searching, these image features can be combined with each other and with keywords to improve retrieval performance.

Similarity Measure

The selection of an appropriate similarity (or distance) measure is an important problem. Since visual content can be represented by different attributes, the combination and importance of each set of features varies according to the user's semantic intent. Thus, the retrieval strategy should be adaptive so that it can accommodate the preferences of different users. Note that with (uniformly weighted) Euclidean distance, every feature is treated equally. However, some features may be more important than others. Similarly, in region-based approaches (where similarity between regions of two images must be computed), some regions may be more important than others in determining overall image-to-image similarity. Thus, the weight of each feature (or region) should be based on its discriminative power between the relevant and non-relevant images for the current query (see Figure 4). Then, the similarity measure of images can be based on a weighted distance in the feature space. The querying system developed in Smith and Li (1999) decomposes and image into regions with characterizations pre-defined in a finite pattern library. In Blobworld (Carson, 2002), images are partitioned into regions that have similar color and texture. Each pixel is then associated with a set of color, texture, and spatial features. The distribution of pixels for each region is calculated and the distance between two images is equal to the distance between their regions in terms of color and texture. In NeTra (Ma & Majunath, 1997), regions are segmented based on color. Then, texture, shape, color, and spatial properties are used to determine similarity. Both Blobworld (Carson, 2002) and NeTra (Ma & Majunath, 1997) require the user to select the region(s) of interest from the segmented query image. This information is then used for determining similarity with database images. Ravela, Manmatha, and Riseman (1996) use a system that uses a measure of correlation to indicate similarity. This system works for a variety of images, but it requires the user to select the region(s) of interest from the images.

Image Segmentation

A major problem with systems that use region-based image representations is that the segmented regions they produce usually do not correspond to actual objects in the image. For instance, an object may be partitioned into several regions, with none of them being representative of the object. Object (or strong) segmentation is defined as a grouping of the image pixels into regions such that each region contains all the pixels of a single physical object and nothing else. It is an extremely difficult image processing task mainly due to the fact that most segmentation algorithms use low-level data-driven properties to generate regions that are homogeneous according to some criterion. Unfortunately, it is very often the case that such regions do not correspond to meaningful units (i.e., physical objects). Thus, due to the great difficulty of accurately segmenting an image into regions that correspond to a human's perception of an object, several approaches have been proposed (Chen & Wang, 2002; Li et al., 2002; Smith & Li, 1999; Wang et al., 2001) that consider all regions in an image for determining similarity. As a result, the problems of inaccurate segmentation are reduced. Integrated region matching (IRM) (Li et al., 2002) is proposed as a measure that allows a many-to-many region mapping relationship between two images by matching a region of one image to several regions of another image. Thus, by having a similarity measure that is a weighted sum of distances between all regions from different images, IRM is more robust to inaccurate segmentation. Recently, a fuzzy logic approach, unified feature matching (UFM) (Chen & Wang, 2002), was proposed as an improved alternative to IRM. UFM uses the same segmentation algorithm as IRM. In UFM, an image is characterized by a fuzzy feature denoting color, texture, and shape characteristics. Because fuzzy features can characterize the gradual transition between regions in an image, segmentation-related inaccuracies are implicitly considered by viewing them as blurring boundaries between segmented regions. As a result, a feature vector can belong to multiple regions with different degrees of membership, as opposed to classical region representations in which a feature vector belongs to only one region. The similarity between two images is then defined as the overall similarity between two sets of fuzzy features.

A key factor in these types of systems that consider all the regions to perform an overall image-to-image similarity is the weighting of regions. The weight that is assigned to each region for determining similarity is usually based on prior assumptions such as that larger regions, or regions that are close to the center of the image, should have larger weights. For example, in IRM, an *area percentage scheme,* which is based on the assumption that important objects in an image tend to occupy larger areas, is used to assign weights to regions. The location of a region is also taken into consideration. For example, higher weights are assigned to regions in the center of an image than to those around boundaries. These region weighting heuristics are often inconsistent with human perception. For instance, a facial region may be the most important when the user is looking for images of people, while other larger regions such as the background may be much less relevant. Some RF approaches are motivated by the need to have a similarity measure that is flexible to user preferences. Later in this chapter, we present our previous work on a learning algorithm that can be used in region-based CBIR systems for estimating region weights in an image.

RELEVANCE FEEDBACK LEARNING

CBIR suffers from what is known as the semantic gap, or the large discrepancy between the low-level visual features that one can extract from an image and the semantic interpretation of the image's content that a particular user may have in a given situation. This situation is exacerbated when the retrieval task is to be performed in broad image domains (e.g., the Web) where images with similar semantic interpretations may have unpredictable and large variability in their low-level visual content. Thus with the exception of some constrained applications such as face and fingerprint recognition, low-level features do not capture the high-level semantics of images (Rui, Huang, & Chang, 1999). The selection of an appropriate similarity measure is thus an important problem. Since visual content can be represented by different attributes, the combination and importance of each set of features varies according to the user's semantic intent. Thus, the retrieval strategy should be adaptive so that it can accommodate the preferences of different users.

Relevance feedback learning, originally developed for information retrieval (Rocchio & Salton, 1971), has been proposed as a learning technique aimed at reducing the semantic gap. It works by gathering semantic information from user interaction. Based on the user's feedback on the retrieval results, the retrieval scheme is adjusted. By providing an image similarity measure under human perception, RF learning can be seen as a form of supervised learning that finds relations between high-level semantic interpretations and low-level visual properties. That is, the feedback obtained within a single query session is used to personalize the retrieval strategy and thus enhance retrieval performance. In order to learn a user's query concept, the user labels each image returned in the previous query round as relevant or non-relevant. Based on the feedback, the retrieval scheme is adjusted and the next set of images is presented to the user for labeling. This process iterates until the user is satisfied with the retrieved images or stops searching.

Relevance Feedback Learning Strategies

The key issue in RF is how to use the positive and negative examples to adjust the retrieval scheme so that the number of relevant images in the next retrieval set will increase. Two main RF strategies have been proposed in CBIR: query modification (Rui, Huang, & Mehrotra, 1997) and distance reweighing (Buckley & Salton, 1995; Ishikawa, Subramanys, & Faloutsos, 1998; Peng, Bhanu, & Qing, 1999; Rui & Huang, 1998; Shaw, 1995). Query modification changes the representation of the user's query in a form that is closer (hopefully) to the semantic intent of the user. In particular, query shifting involves moving the query towards the region of the feature space containing relevant images and away from the region containing non-relevant images (see Figure 3). This is based on the assumption that relevant images have similar feature vectors and cluster together in feature space. Based on RF, the next query location can be determined with the standard Rocchio formula (Salton & McGill, 1998):

$$q' \leftarrow \alpha q + \beta \left(\frac{1}{|R^+|} \sum_{x \in R^+} x \right) - \gamma \left(\frac{1}{|R^-|} \sum_{x \in R^-} x \right)$$

where q is the initial query, q' is the new query location, R^+ is the set of relevant retrievals, and R^- is the set of non-relevant retrievals. Thus, the new query location q' is a linear combination of the mean feature vectors of the relevant and non-relevant retrieved images so that q' is close to the relevant mean and far from the non-relevant mean. The values for the parameters α, β, and γ are usually chosen by experimental runs. Note that the refined query vector represents an ideal query point and not longer corresponds to any actual image.

Figure 3. Query shifting. The query is moved towards the region of the feature space containing user-labeled relevant images (squares) and away from the region containing user labeled non-relevant images (circles).

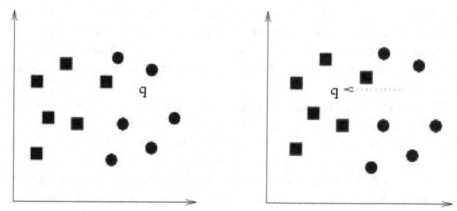

Figure 4. Features are unequal in their differential relevance for computing similarity. The neighborhoods of queries b and c should be elongated along the less relevant Y and X axis respectively. For query a, features X and Y have equal discriminating strength.

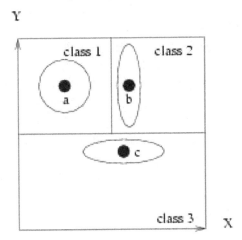

Distance reweighing changes the calculation of image to image similarity to strengthen the contribution of relevant image components in regard to the current query. Thus, the task is to determine the features that help the most in retrieving relevant images and increase their importance in determining similarity. In Rui and Huang (1998), the weight and representation of each feature is updated according to their ability to discriminate between the set of relevant and non-relevant images in the current query. Peng et al. (1999) present a probabilistic feature relevance learning (PFRL) method that automatically captures feature relevance based on RF. It computes flexible retrieval metrics for producing neighborhoods that are elongated along less relevant feature dimensions and constricted along most influential ones (see Figure 4). PFRL is an application of the approach described in Friedman (1994) for learning local feature relevance. Friedman (1994) observes that input variables of low relevance can degrade the performance of nearest-neighbor classifiers if they are allowed to be equally influential with those of high relevance in defining the distance from the point to be classified. Thus, if the relative local relevance of each input variable was known, this information would be used to construct a distance metric that provides an optimal differential weighting for the input variables (Friedman, 1994).

Some methods for incorporating both query shifting and feature relevance weighting have also been proposed (Heisterkamp, Peng, & Dai 2000; Ishikawa et al., 1998). Heisterkamp et al. (2000) propose a retrieval method that combines feature relevance learning and query shifting to achieve the best of both worlds. This method uses a linear discriminant analysis to compute the new query and exploit the local neighborhood structure centered at the new query by using PFRL.

Heisterkamp et al. (2001) further use distance in the feature space associated with a kernel to rank relevant images. An adaptive quasiconformal mapping based on RF is used to generate successive new kernels. The kernel is constructed in such a way that the spatial resolution is contracted around relevant images and dilated around non-relevant images. Then, the distance from the query to new images is measured in this new space. Instead of updating individual feature weights, we could also select from a pre-defined set of similarity measures. For example, Sclaroff et al. (1997) describe an approach that minimizes mean distance between user-labeled relevant images by selecting from a set of pre-defined distance metrics.

In PicHunter (Ingemar & Cox, 2000), a Bayesian framework is used to associate each image with a probability that it corresponds to the user's query concept. The probability is updated based on the user's feedback at each iteration. Tieu and Viola (2000) propose a "boosting" algorithm to improve RF learning. Recently, Support Vector Machine (SVM) learning has been applied to CBIR systems with RF to significantly improve retrieval performance (Chen, Zhou, & Huang, 2001; Hong, Tian, & Huang, 2000; Tong & Chang, 2001; Zhang, Goldman, Yu, & Fritts, 2002). Basically, the probability density of relevant images can be estimated by using SVMs. For instance, Chen et al. (2001) use a one-class SVM to include as many relevant images as possible into a hypersphere of minimum size. That is, relevant images are used to estimate the distribution of target images by fitting a tight hypersphere in the non-linearly transformed feature space. Zhang et al. (2002) regard the problem as a two-class classification problem, and a maximum margin hyperplane in the non-linearly transformed feature space is used to separate relevant images from non-relevant images. Many other approaches, such as Heisterkamp et al. (2002), Peng, Banerjee, and Heisterkamp (2002) and Zhou and Huang (2001), have provided improved alternatives for utilizing kernel methods in CBIR.

Other classical machine learning approaches, such as decision trees (MacArthur, Bradley, & Shyu, 2000), nearest-neighbor classifiers (Wu & Manjunath, 2001), and artificial neural networks (Laaksonen, Koskela, & Oja, 1999) have also been applied for RF learning in CBIR. MacArthur et al. (2000) use a decision tree to sequentially split the feature space until all points within a partition are of the same class. Then, images that are classified as relevant are returned as the nearest neighbors of the query image.

Although RF learning has been successfully applied to CBIR systems that use global image representations, not much research has been conducted on RF learning methods for region-based CBIR. By referring to an image as a bag and a region in the image as an instance, multiple instance learning (MIL) has been applied to image classification and retrieval (Andrews, Tsochantaridis, & Hofmann, 2003; Maron & Lakshmi Ratan, 1998; Yang & Lozano Perez, 2000; Zhang et al., 2002). The Diverse Density technique (Maron & Lozano Perez, 1997) is applied in Maron and Lakshmi Ratan (1998), Yang and Lozano Perez (2000), and Zhang et al. (2002). Basically, an objective function is used that looks for a feature vector that is close to many instances from different positive bags and far from all instances from negative bags. Such a vector is likely to represent the concept (i.e., object in the image) that matches the concept the user has in mind.

Maron and Lakshmi Ratan (1998) applied MIL to the task of learning to recognize a person from a set of images that are labeled positive if they contain the person and negative otherwise. They also used this model to learn descriptions of natural images (such as sunsets or mountains) and then used the learned concept to retrieve similar images from an image database. Their system uses the set of cumulative user-labeled relevant and non-relevant images to learn a scene concept which is used to retrieve similar images. This is done by using the Diverse Density algorithm to find out what regions are in common between the relevant images, and the differences between those and the non-relevant images. The confidence that an image is relevant to the user's query concept can be measured by the distance from the ideal point (as computed by the Diverse Density algorithm) to the closest region in the image. However, not all region features are equally important. Thus, in this approach, the distance measure is not restricted to a normal Euclidean distance, but may be defined as a weighted Euclidean distance where important features have larger weights. The Diverse Density algorithm is also capable of determining these weights. However, by introducing weights, the number of dimensions over which Diverse Density has to be maximized is doubled. This method is improved in Yang and Lozano Perez (2000) by allowing a broader range of images. Yang and Lozano Perez (2000) define the image similarity measure as the correlation coefficient of corresponding regions. This similarity measure is further refined by allowing different weights for different locations. Zhang et al. (2002) present a comparison of performance obtained with the Diverse Density and EM-DD (Zhang & Goldman, 2001) algorithms when using a wide variety of image processing techniques and a broader range of images.

Based on the assumption that important regions should appear more often in relevant images than unimportant regions, an *RF*IIF* (Region Frequency * Inverse Image Frequency) weighting scheme is proposed in Jing, Li, Zhang, Zhang, and Zhang (2003). Let $D = \{x_i\}_1^m$ be the set of all images in the da-

Figure 5. Regions are unequal in their differential relevance for computing similarity. Given that the user is looking for images of people, region R_1 may be the most important, perhaps followed by R_2 and R_3. Thus, the neighborhood of the similarity metric should be elongated along the direction of R_1 and constricted along the direction of R_3.

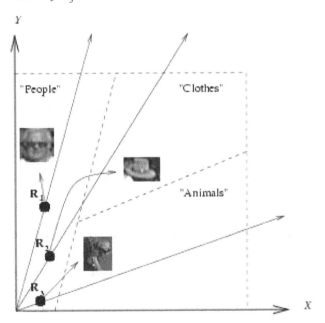

Query Image

tabase, x be the query image, $\{R_i\}_1^n$ be the set of all regions in x, and R^+ be the set of cumulative relevant retrieved images for x. The region frequency (RF) of a region R_i is defined as:

$$RF(R_i) = \sum_{x_j \in R^+} s(R_i, x_j)$$

where $s(R_i, x_j) = 1$ if at least one region of x_j is similar to R_i, and 0 otherwise. Two regions are deemed similar if their L1-distance (also known as the Manhattan distance or city-block distance) is smaller than a predefined threshold. The inverse image frequency (IIF) of R_i is defined as:

$$IIF(R_i) = \log\left(\frac{m}{\sum_{x_j \in D} s(R_i, x_j)} \right)$$

The region importance RI (i.e., weight) of R_i is then:

$$RI(R_i) = \frac{RF(R_i) * IIF(R_i)}{\sum_{j=1}^{n} (RF(R_j) * IIF(R_j))}$$

PROBABILISTIC REGION RELEVANCE LEARNING

A key factor in region-based CBIR approaches that consider all the regions to perform an overall image-to-image similarity is the weighting of regions. The weight that is assigned to each region for determining similarity is usually based on prior assumptions such as that larger regions, or regions that are close to the center of the image, should have larger weights. For example, in integrated region matching (IRM) (Li et al., 2002), an *area percentage scheme,* which is based on the assumption that important objects in an image tend to occupy larger areas, is used to assign weights to regions. The location of a region is also taken into consideration. For example, higher weights are assigned to regions in the center of an image than to those around boundaries. These region weighting heuristics are often inconsistent with human perception. For instance, a facial region may be the most important when the user is looking for images of people, while other larger regions such as the background may be much less relevant.

Based on the observation that regions in an image have unequal importance for computing image similarity (see Figure 5), we proposed a probabilistic method inspired by probabilistic feature relevance learning (PFRL) (Peng et al., 1999) and probabilistic region relevance learning (PRRL) (Gondra & Heisterkamp, 2004) for automatically capturing region relevance based on user's feedback. PRRL can be used to set region weights in region-based image retrieval frameworks that use an overall image-to-image similarity measure.

Region Relevance Measure

Given a query image $x = \{R_i\}_1^n$, where R_i represents the features extracted from a region in the image, let the class label (i.e., relevant or not relevant) $y \in \{1,0\}$ at x be treated as a random variable from a distribution with the probabilities $\{\Pr(1|x)\ \Pr(0|x)\}$. Consider the function f of n arguments:

$$f(x) \doteq \Pr(1|x) = \Pr(y=1|x) = E(y|x)$$

In the absence of any argument assignments, the least-squared estimate for $f(x)$ is simply its expected (average) value:

$$E[f] = \int f(x)p(x)dx$$

where $p(x)$ is the joint probability density. Now, suppose that we know the value of x at a particular region R_i. The least-squares estimate becomes:

$$E[f|R_i] = \int f(x)p(x|R_i)dx$$

where $p(x|R_i)$ is the conditional density of the other regions. Because $f(x) = 1$ (i.e., the query image is always relevant), $(f(x)-0)$ is the maximum error that can be made when assigning 0 to the probability that x is relevant when the probability is in fact 1. On the other hand, $(f(x)-E[f|R_i])$ is the error that is made by predicting $E[f|R_i]$ to be the probability that x is relevant. Therefore:

$$[(f(x)-0)-(f(x)-E[f|R_i])] = E[f|R_i]$$

represents a reduction in error between the two predictions. Therefore, a measure of the relevance of region R_i for x can be defined as:

$$r_i(x) = E[f|R_i] \tag{1}$$

Figure 6. The probabilistic region relevance learning (PRRL) algorithm

1. Use a segmentation method to extract regions and represent current query by $x = \{R_i\}_1^n$; initialize region weight vector w to $\left\{\dfrac{1}{n}\right\}_1^n$; $A = \phi$.
2. Compute the K most similar images to x with an overall image-to-image similarity measure using w for the weighting of regions in x.
3. User marks the K images as relevant or not relevant.
4. While more RF iterations Do
4.1. $A \leftarrow A \cup \{marked\ K\ images\}$.
4.2. Update w from Eqs. (3) and (2) using A.
4.3. Compute the K most similar images to x with an overall image-to-image similarity measure using w for the weighting of regions in x.
4.4. User marks the K images as relevant or not relevant.

Figure 7. A typical RF process

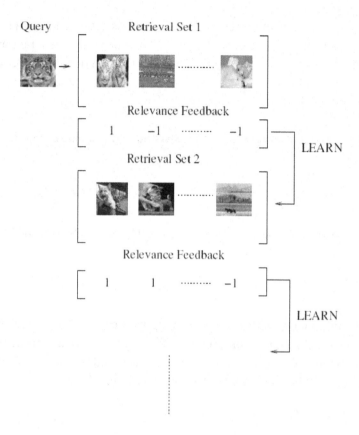

The relative relevance can then be used as the weight of region R_i in a weighted similarity measure:

$$w_i = \frac{e^{Tr_i(x)}}{\sum_{j=1}^{n} e^{Tr_j(x)}}$$

(2)

where T is a parameter that can be chosen to maximize (minimize) the influence of r_i on w_i.

Estimation of Region Relevance

Retrieved images with RF are used to estimate region relevance. Let $A = \{(x_j, y_j)\}_1^m$ be the set of cumulative retrievals for x. Let $x_j = \{R'_j\}_1^z$. Let $0 \leq s(R_i, R'_j) \leq 1$ denote the similarity between region R_i in x and region R'_j in x_j in a region-based CBIR system. Also, let $\hat{s}(R_i, x_j) = \max_{j \in \{1,2,\ldots,z\}} (s(R_i, R'_j))$. We can use A to estimate $r_i(x)$ and hence w_i. Note that $E[f | R_i] = E[y | R_i]$. However, since there may be no $x_j \in A$ for which $R'_j = R_i$ (i.e., no R'_j such that $s(R_i, R'_j) = 1$), a strategy suggested in Friedman (1994) is followed, and we look for data in the vicinity of R_i (i.e., we allow $s(R_i, R'_j)$ to be smaller than 1). Thus, w_i is estimated by:

Figure 8. Retrieval results on random query image (top leftmost) from subset of COREL image database. The images are sorted based on their similarity to the query image. The ranks descend from left to right and from top to bottom.

Initial Retrieval Set with UFM, precision = 0.3

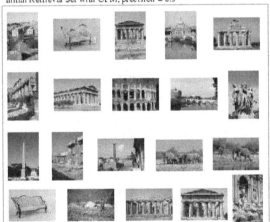

Retrieval Set with UFM+PRRL after 2 RF iterations, precision = 0.75

$$\hat{E}[y \mid R_i] = \frac{\sum_{j=1}^{m} y_j 1(\hat{s}(R_i, x_j) > \varepsilon)}{\sum_{j=1}^{m} 1(\hat{s}(R_i, x_j) > \varepsilon)} \qquad (3)$$

where $1(\cdot)$ returns 1 if its argument is true, and 0 otherwise. Thus, $0 \le \varepsilon \le 1$ is an adaptive similarity threshold that changes so that there is sufficient data for the estimation of $r_i(x)$. The value of ε is chosen so that:

$$\sum_{j=1}^{m} 1(\hat{s}(R_i, x_j) > \varepsilon) = G,$$

where $G \le m$. The probabilistic region relevance algorithm is summarized in Figure 6.

Figure 9. Image retrieval performance measures: D is the set of all database images; A is the set of all images relevant to a query; R is the retrieval set in response to the query; precision is $|R^+|/|R|$; recall is $|R^+|/|A|$.

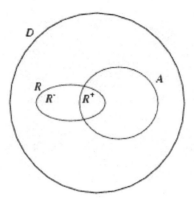

Usage Scenario

We present in this subsection a typical usage scenario in an RF-based CBIR system and show how the PRRL algorithm presented improves the retrieval performance of such system. As previously discussed, the goal of RF learning is to reduce the semantic gap by gathering semantic information from user interaction. Based on the user's feedback on the retrieval results, the retrieval scheme is adjusted. By

Figure 10. Sample images from COREL data set

providing an image similarity measure under human perception, RF learning can be seen as a form of supervised learning that finds relations between high-level semantic interpretations and low-level visual properties. That is, the feedback obtained within a single query session is used to personalize the retrieval strategy and thus enhance retrieval performance. As illustrated in Figure 7, in order to learn a user's query concept, the user labels each image returned in the previous query round as relevant (denoted by a 1 in Figure 7) or non-relevant (denoted by a -1 in Figure 7). Based on the feedback, the retrieval scheme is adjusted and the next set of images is presented to the user for labeling. After each such RF iteration, the number of relevant images (e.g., images of cats in Figure 7) in the retrieval set increases and thus retrieval performance is improved. This process iterates until the user is satisfied with the retrieved images or stops searching.

After each RF iteration, the PRRL algorithm automatically captures the relevance/importance of the different regions in an image. Suppose that a particular user of the CBIR system would like to obtain other images that are similar to a query image (e.g., the top leftmost image in Figure 8). The top box in Figure 8 shows the top 20 images that the CBIR system would return to the user if using UFM (without RF learning) as the similarity measure. The retrieval precision is only 0.3 (i.e., only 30% of the images in the retrieval set are relevant to the user's query concept). On the other hand, if the CBIR system uses the PRRL algorithm, after only two RF iterations the retrieval performance is much higher (i.e., a precision of 0.75 is obtained), as illustrated by the retrieval set in the bottom box of Figure 8.

Experimental Results

Next we present experimental results obtained with PRRL. *Precision* and *recall* are common measures that are used to evaluate the performance of an image retrieval system. Consider an image database consisting of a set of images D. Let x be a query image and $A \subset D$ be the subset of images in D that are relevant to x. Assume that a given image retrieval strategy processes x and generates $R \subset D$ as the

Figure 11. Retrieval performance at different number of RF iterations with PRRL and other methods on COREL data

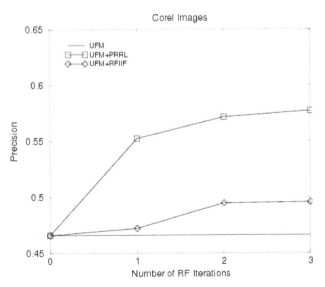

retrieval set. Then, $R^+ = R \cap A$ is the set of relevant images to x that appear in R. Similarly, $R^- = R - A$ is the set of non-relevant images to x that appear in R. Figure 9 illustrates these sets. Precision measures the ability to retrieve only relevant images and is defined as $precision = |R^+|/|R|$. Recall measures the ability to retrieval all relevant images and is defined as $recall = |R^+|/|A|$.

Both high recall and high precision are desirable, though not often obtainable. That is, in many cases, improvement of one leads to the deterioration of the other. Note that perfect recall could be achieved simply by letting $R = D$ (i.e., by retrieving all images in the database in response to x). However, obviously users would probably not be happy with this approach. Thus, recall by itself is not a good measure of the performance of an image retrieval system. Instead, users want the database images to be ranked according to their relevance to x and then be presented with only the K most relevant images so that $|R| = K < |D|$. Therefore, in order to account for the quality of image rankings, precision at a cut-off point (e.g., K) is commonly used. For example, if $K = 20$ and the top 20 ranked images are all relevant to x, then R contains only relevant images and thus precision is 1. On the other hand, if $K = 40$ and only the first top 20 images are all relevant to x, then half of the images in R are non-relevant to x and thus precision is only 0.5. A common way to depict the degradation of precision as K increases is to plot a precision-recall graph.

Ideally, in order to evaluate the practical usability of an RF-based CBIR system, large-scale experiments with real users should be conducted. However, such experiments are costly and difficult to set up. As a result, the evaluation and comparison of RF algorithms rely on the use of image ground-truth databases and on the emulation of the behaviour of real users. In an image ground-truth database, all images are labeled according to their category (i.e., all images that belong to the same category such as "cat" have the same label). Thus, it is known whether an image in a retrieval set would be labeled as relevant (in case it has the same label as that of the query image) or non-relevant (in case its label is different from that of the query image). Therefore, the user's feedback on a retrieval set can be emulated by automatically labeling all returned images as either relevant or non-relevant without any mistake.

Figure 12. Retrieval performance in initial retrieval set with PRRL and other methods on COREL data

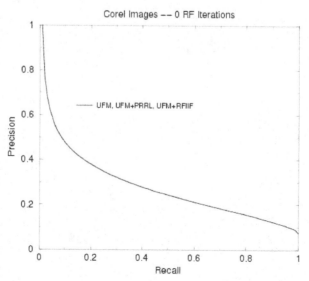

Figure 13. Retrieval performance after one RF iteration with PRRL and other methods on COREL data

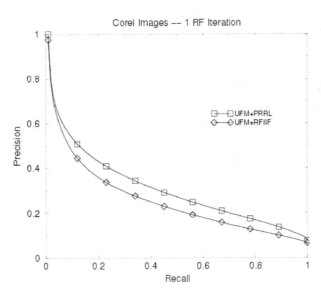

Figure 14. Retrieval performance after two RF iterations with PRRL and other methods on COREL data

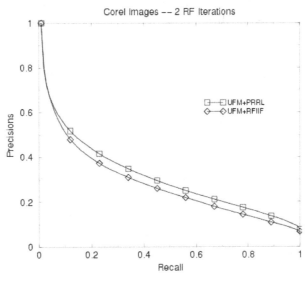

A subset of 2000 labeled images from the general purpose COREL image database was used as the ground-truth for evaluation. There are 20 image categories, each containing 100 pictures. The region-based feature vectors of those images are obtained with the IRM/UFM segmentation algorithm. Sample images are shown in Figure 10.

We tested the performance of unified feature matching (UFM) (Chen & Wang, 2002), UFM with PRRL (UFM+PRRL), and UFM with the RF*IIF method (Jing et al., 2003) (UFM+RFIIF). Every image is used as a query image. A uniform weighting scheme is used to set the region weights of each query and target images. For UFM+PRRL and UFM+RFIIF, user feedback was simulated by carrying out three RF iterations for each query. Because the images in the data set are labeled according to their category, it is known whether an image in a retrieval set would be labeled as relevant or non-relevant by a user.

The average precision of the 2000 queries with respect to different number of RF iterations is shown in Figure 11. The size of the retrieval set is 20. Figures 12 through 15 show the precision-recall curves after each RF iteration. We can observe that UFM+PRRL has the best performance. It can be seen that, even after only one RF iteration, the region weights learned by PRRL result in a very significant performance improvement.

CONCLUSION

Content-based image retrieval (CBIR) suffers from the fact that there is a large discrepancy between the low-level visual features that one can extract from an image and the semantic interpretation of the image's content that a particular user may have in a given situation. That is, users seek semantic similarity, but we can only provide similarity based on low-level visual features extracted from the raw pixel data. The selection of an appropriate similarity measure is thus an important problem. Since visual content can be represented by different attributes, the combination and importance of each set

Figure 15. Retrieval performance after three RF iterations with PRRL and other methods on COREL data

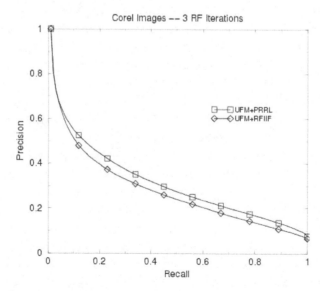

of features varies according to the user's semantic intent. Thus, the retrieval strategy should be adaptive so that it can accommodate the preferences of different users. Relevance feedback (RF) learning has been proposed as a technique aimed at reducing the semantic gap. By providing an image similarity measure under human perception, RF learning can be seen as a form of supervised learning that finds relations between high-level semantic interpretations and low-level visual properties. That is, the feedback obtained within a single query session is used to personalize the retrieval strategy and thus enhance retrieval performance. In this chapter we presented an overview of CBIR and related work on RF learning. We also presented our own previous work on an RF learning-based probabilistic region relevance learning algorithm for automatically estimating the importance of each region in an image based on the user's semantic intent.

A fundamental observation when designing a personalized CBIR system is that, ultimately, the semantic interpretation of an image is defined by humans and thus people are an indispensable part of such system. This is reinforced by the fact that, in contrast to early literature which emphasizes the search for a "single best feature," more recent research is focused on "human in the loop" approaches. Therefore, when attempting to reduce the semantic gap and thus meet the performance challenges encountered in practical CBIR applications, RF learning remains a very promising research direction.

FUTURE RESEARCH DIRECTIONS

We can distinguish two different types of information provided by RF: the short-term learning obtained within a single query session is intra-query learning; the long-term learning accumulated over the course of many query sessions is inter-query learning. By accumulating knowledge from users, long-term learning can be used to enhance future retrieval performance. The fact that two images were regarded as similar by a previous user is a cue for similarities in their semantic content. This is because, although different people may associate the same image into different concepts, there is some common semantic agreement. While short-term learning has been widely used in the literature, less research has been focused on exploiting long-term learning (several references to previous work on long-term learning are given in the Additional Reading section). Currently, PRRL only performs intra-query learning. That is, for each given query, the user's feedback is used to learn the relevance of the regions in the query, and the learning process starts from ground up for each new query. However, it is also possible to exploit inter-query learning to enhance the retrieval performance of future queries. Thus, for a new query, instead of starting the learning process from the ground up, we could exploit the previously learned region importance of similar queries. This would be very beneficial especially in the initial retrieval set since, instead of using uniform weighting or some other weighting heuristic, we could make a more informed initial estimate of the relevance of regions in the new query. We plan to investigate the possibility of incorporating inter-query learning into the PRRL framework as part of our future work

REFERENCES

Andrews, S., Tsochantaridis, I., & Hofmann, T. (2003). Support vector machines for multiple-instance learning. In S. Becker, S. Thrun, & K. Obermayer (Eds.), *Advances in neural information processing systems* (vol. 15, pp. 561–568). Cambridge, MA: MIT Press.

Bimbo, A. (1999). *Visual information retrieval.* San Francisco: Morgan Kaufmann.

Buckley, C., & Salton, G. (1995). Optimization of relevance feedback weights. In E.A. Fox, P. Ingwersen, & R. Fidel (Eds.), *Proceedings of the Annual International ACM SIGIR Conference on Research and Development in Information Retrieval* (pp. 351–357).

Carson, C. (2002). Blobworld: Image segmentation using expectation-maximization and its applications to image querying. *IEEE Transactions on Pattern Analysis and Machine Intelligence, 24*(8), 1026–1038.

Chen, Y., Zhou, X., & Huang, T. (2001). One-class SVM for learning in image retrieval. *Proceedings of the IEEE International Conference on Image Processing* (vol. 1, pp. 34–37).

Chen, Y., & Wang, J. (2002). A region-based fuzzy feature matching approach to content-based image retrieval. *IEEE Transactions on Pattern Analysis and Machine Intelligence, 24*(9), 1252–1267.

Faloutsos, C., Flicker, M., Niblack, W., Petkovic, D., Equitz, W., & Barber, R. (1993). *Efficient and effective querying by image content.* Technical Report, IBM, USA.

Friedman, J. (1994). *Flexible metric nearest neighbor classification.* Technical Report, Department of Statistics, Stanford University, USA.

Gondra, I., & Heisterkamp, D.R. (2004). Probabilistic region relevance learning for content-based image retrieval. *Proceedings of the International Conference on Imaging Science, Systems, and Technology* (pp. 434–440).

Gupta, A., & Jain, R. (1997). Visual information retrieval. *Communications of the ACM, 40*(5), 70–79.

Hara, Y., Hirata, K., Takano, H., & Kawasaki, S. (1997). Hypermedia navigation and content-based retrieval for distributed multimedia databases. *Proceedings of the NEC Research Symposium on Multimedia Computing* (pp. 133–148).

Heisterkamp, D.R. (2002). Building a latent semantic index of an image database from patterns of relevance feedback. *Proceedings of the International Conference on Pattern Recognition* (vol. 4, pp. 134–137).

Heisterkamp, D.R., Peng, J., & Dai, H.K. (2000). Feature relevance learning with query shifting for content-based image retrieval. *Proceedings of the International Conference on Pattern Recognition* (vol. 4, pp. 4250–4253).

Heisterkamp, D.R., Peng, J., & Dai, H. (2001). Adaptive quasiconformal kernel metric for image retrieval. *Proceedings of the IEEE International Conference on Computer Vision and Pattern Recognition* (vol. 2, pp. 388–393).

Hong, P., Tian, Q., & Huang, T. (2000). Incorporate support vector machines to content-based image retrieval with relevance feedback. *Proceedings of the IEEE International Conference on Image Processing* (pp. 750–753).

Ingemar, J., & Cox, J. (2000). The Bayesian image retrieval system, PicHunter: Theory, implementation, and psychological experiments. *IEEE Transactions on Image Processing, 9*(1), 20–37.

Ishikawa, Y., Subramanys, R., & Faloutsos, C. (1998). MindReader: Querying databases through multiple examples. *Proceedings of the International Conference on Very Large Databases* (pp. 218–227).

Jain, A.K., & Vailaya, A. (1996). Image retrieval using color and shape. *Pattern Recognition, 29*(8), 1233–1244.

Jing, F., Li, M., Zhang, L., Zhang, H., & Zhang, B. (2003). Learning in region-based image retrieval. *Proceedings of the International Conference on Image and Video Retrieval* (vol. 2728, pp. 206–215).

Kelly, P.M., Cannon, T.M., & Hush, D.R. (1995). Query by image example: The CANDID approach. In W. Niblack & R. Jain (Eds.), *Proceedings of the SPIE Storage and Retrieval for Image and Video Databases* (vol. 2420, pp. 238–248).

Laaksonen, J., Koskela, M., & Oja, E. (1999). Picsom: Self-organizing maps for content-based image retrieval. *Proceedings of the International Joint Conference on Neural Networks* (vol. 4, pp. 2470–2473).

Li, J., Wang, J., & Wiederhold, G. (2000). IRM: Integrated region matching for image retrieval. *Proceedings of the ACM International Conference on Multimedia* (pp. 147–156).

Li, M., Chen, Z., & Zhang, H. (2002). Statistical correlation analysis in image retrieval. *Pattern Recognition, 35*(12), 2687–2693.

Ma, W., & Majunath, B. (1997). NeTra: A toolbox for navigating large image databases. *Proceedings of the IEEE International Conference on Image Processing* (vol. 1, pp. 568–571).

MacArthur, S.D., Bradley, C.E., & Shyu, C.R. (2000). Relevance feedback decision trees in content-based image retrieval. *Proceedings of the IEEE Workshop on Content-Based Access of Image and Video Libraries* (pp. 68–72).

Maron, O., & Lakshmi Ratan, A. (1998). Multiple-instance learning for natural scene classification. In J.W. Shavlik (Ed.), *Proceedings of the International Conference on Machine Learning* (vol. 15, pp. 341–349).

Maron, O., & Lozano Perez, T. (1997). A framework for multiple-instance learning. In M.I. Jordan, M.J. Kearns, & S.A. Solla (Eds.), *Advances in neural information processing systems* (vol. 10, pp. 570–576). Cambridge, MA: MIT Press.

Mehrotra, S., Rui, Y., Ortega, M., & Huang, T. (1997). Supporting content-based queries over images in MARS. *Proceedings of the IEEE International Conference on Multimedia Computing and Systems* (pp. 632–633).

Ono, A., Amano, M., Hakaridani, M., Satoh, T., & Sakauchi, M. (1996). A flexible content-based image retrieval system with combined scene description keywords. *Proceedings of the IEEE International Conference on Multimedia Computing and Systems* (pp. 201–208).

Peng, J., Banerjee, B., & Heisterkamp, D.R. (2002). Kernel index for relevance feedback retrieval in large image databases. *Proceedings of the International Conference on Neural Information Processing* (pp. 187–191).

Peng, J., Bhanu, B., & Qing, S. (1999). Probabilistic feature relevance learning for content-based image retrieval. *Computer Vision and Image Understanding, 75*(1/2), 150–164.

Pentland, A., Picard, R., & Sclaroff, S. (1994). PhotoBOOK: Tools for content-based manipulation of image databases. In W. Niblack & R. Jain (Eds.), *Proceedings of the SPIE Storage and Retrieval for Image Databases* (vol. 2, pp. 34–47).

Ravela, S., Manmatha, R., & Riseman, E.M. (1996). Scale-space matching and image retrieval. *Proceedings of the Image Understanding Workshop* (vol. 2, pp. 1199–1207).

Rocchio, J., & Salton, G. (1971). The SMART retrieval system: Experiments in automatic document processing. In *Relevance feedback in information retrieval* (pp. 313–323). Englewood Cliffs, NJ: Prentice Hall.

Rui, Y., & Huang, T. (1998). Relevance feedback: A power tool for interactive content-based image retrieval. *IEEE Transactions on Circuits and Systems for Video Technology, 8*(5), 644–655.

Rui, Y., Huang, T., & Chang, S. (1999). Image retrieval: Past, present, and future. *Journal of Visual Communication and Image Representation, 10,* 1-23.

Rui, Y., Huang, T., & Mehrotra, S. (1997). Content-based image retrieval with relevance feedback in MARS. *Proceedings of the IEEE International Conference on Image Processing* (vol. 2, pp. 815–818).

Salton, G. (1986). Another look at automatic text-retrieval systems. *Communications of the ACM, 29*(7), 648–656.

Salton, G., & McGill, M. (1998). *Introduction to modern information retrieval.* New York: McGraw-Hill.

Samadani, R., Han, C., & Katragadda, L.K. (1993). Content-based event selection from satellite image of the aurora. In W. Niblack (Ed.), *Proceedings of the SPIE Storage and Retrieval for Image and Video Databases* (vol. 1908, pp. 50–59).

Sclaroff, S., Taycher, L., & Cascia, M.L. (1997). *ImageRover: A content-based image browser for the World Wide Web.* Technical Report No. 97-005, Computer Science Department, Boston University, USA.

Shaw, W.M. (1995). Term-relevance computations and perfect retrieval performance. *Information Processing and Management: An International Journal, 31*(4), 491–498.

Shen, H.T., Ooi, B.C., & Tan, K.L. (2000). Giving meanings to WWW images. *Proceedings of the ACM Multimedia* (pp. 39–47).

Smeulders, A.W.M., Worring, M., Santini, S., Gupta, A., & Jain, R. (2000). Content-based image retrieval at the end of the early years. *IEEE Transactions on Pattern Analysis and Machine Intelligence, 22*(12), 1349–1380.

Smith, J., & Chang, S. (1996). VisualSEEk: A fully automated content-based image query system. *Proceedings of the ACM Conference on Multimedia* (pp. 87–98).

Smith, J., & Chang, S. (1997). An image and video search engine for the World Wide Web. *Proceedings of the SPIE Storage and Retrieval for Image and Video Databases* (vol. 5, pp. 84–95).

Smith, J.R., & Li, C.S. (1999). Image classification and querying using composite region templates. *Computer Vision and Image Understanding, 75*(1/2), 165–174.

Srihari, R.K., Zhang, Z., & Rao, A. (2000). Intelligent indexing and semantic retrieval of multimedia documents. *Information Retrieval, 2,* 245–275.

Stone, H.S., & Li, C.S. (1996). Image matching by means of intensity and texture matching in the Fourier domain. In I.K. Sethi & R. Jain (Eds.), *Proceedings of the SPIE Conference on Image and Video Databases* (vol. 2670, pp. 337–349).

Swain, M., & Ballard, D. (1991). Color indexing. *International Journal of Computer Vision, 7*(1), 11–32.

Tieu, K., & Viola, P. (2000). Boosting image retrieval. *Proceedings of the IEEE Conference in Computer Vision and Pattern Recognition* (pp. 1228–1235).

Tong, S., & Chang, E. (2001). Support vector machine active learning for image retrieval. *Proceedings of the ACM International Conference on Multimedia* (pp. 107–118).

Wang, J., Li, G., & Wiederhold, G. (2001). Simplicity: Semantic-sensitive integrated matching for picture libraries. *IEEE Transactions on Pattern Analysis and Machine Intelligence, 23,* 947–963.

Wang, J., Wiederhold, G., Firschein, O., & Sha, X. (1998). Content-based image indexing and searching using Daubechies' wavelets. *International Journal of Digital Libraries, 1*(4), 311–328.

Wenyin, L., Dumais, S., Sun, Y., Zhang, H., Czerwinski, M., & Field, B. (2001). Semiautomatic image annotation. *Proceedings of the International Conference on Human-Computer Interaction* (vol. 1, pp. 326–334).

Wu, P., & Manjunath, B.S. (2001). Adaptive nearest neighbor search for relevance feedback in large image databases. *Proceedings of the ACM Conference on Multimedia* (pp. 89–97).

Yang, C., & Lozano Perez, T. (2000). Image database retrieval with multiple instance learning techniques. *Proceedings of the IEEE International Conference on Data Engineering* (pp. 233–243).

Zhang, Q., & Goldman, S.A. (2001). EM-DD: An improved multiple-instance learning technique. In T.G. Dietterich, S. Becker, & Z. Ghahramani (Eds.), *Advances in neural information processing systems* (vol. 14, pp. 1073–1080). Cambridge, MA: MIT Press.

Zhang, Q., Goldman, S.A., Yu, W., & Fritts, J. (2002). Content-based image retrieval using multiple-instance learning. In C. Sammut & A.G. Hoffmann (Eds.), *Proceedings of the International Conference on Machine Learning* (pp. 682–689).

Zhou, X., & Huang, T. (2001). Small sample learning during multimedia retrieval using BiasMap. *Proceedings of the IEEE International Conference on Computer Vision and Pattern Recognition* (vol. 1, pp. 11–17).

ADDITIONAL READING

Benitez, A.B. (1998). Using relevance feedback in content-based image metasearch. *IEEE Internet Computing, 2*(4), 59–69.

Campadelli, P., Medici, D., & Schettini, R. (1997). Color image segmentation using Hopfield networks. *Image and Vision Computing, 15*(3), 161–166.

Ciaccia, P., Patella, M., & Zezula, P. (1997). M-tree: An efficient access method for similarity search in metric spaces. *Proceedings of the International Conference on Very Large Databases* (pp. 426–435).

Cox, J., Miller, M.L., Minka, T.P., & Yianilos, P.N. (1998). An optimized interaction strategy for Bayesian relevance feedback. *Proceedings of the IEEE Conference on Computer Vision and Pattern Recognition* (pp. 553–558).

Gondra, I., & Heisterkamp, D.R. (2004). Adaptive and efficient image retrieval with one-class support vector machines for inter-query learning. *WSEAS Transactions on Circuits and Systems, 3*(2), 324–329.

Gondra, I., & Heisterkamp, D.R. (2004). Improving image retrieval performance by inter-query learning with one-class support vector machines. *Neural Computing and Applications, 13*(2), 130–139.

Gondra, I., & Heisterkamp, D.R. (2004). Learning in region-based image retrieval with generalized support vector machines. *Proceedings of the IEEE Conference on Computer Vision and Pattern Recognition Workshops.*

Gondra, I., & Heisterkamp, D.R. (2004). Semantic similarity for adaptive exploitation of inter-query learning. *Proceedings of the International Conference on Computing, Communications, and Control Technologies* (pp. 142–147).

Gondra. I., & Heisterkamp, D.R. (2004). Summarizing inter-query knowledge in content-based image retrieval via incremental semantic clustering. *Proceedings of the IEEE International Conference on Information Technology* (pp. 18–22).

Gondra, I., & Heisterkamp, D.R. (2005). A Kolmogorov complexity-based normalized information distance for image retrieval. *Proceedings of the International Conference on Imaging Science, Systems, and Technology: Computer Graphics* (pp. 3–7).

Gondra, I., Heisterkamp, D.R., & Peng, J. (2003). Improving the initial image retrieval set by inter-query learning with one-class support vector machines. *Proceedings of the International Conference on Intelligent Systems Design and Applications* (pp. 393–402).

Guttman, A. (1984). R-trees: A dynamic index structure for spatial searching. *Proceedings of the ACM SIGMOD International Conference on Management of Data* (pp. 47–57).

Guy, G., & Medioni, G. (1996). Inferring global perceptual contours from local features. *International Journal of Computer Vision, 20*(12), 113–133.

Haralick, R.M., Shanmugam, K., & Dinstein, I. (1973). Texture features for image classification. *IEEE Transactions on Systems, Man, and Cybernetics, 3*(6), 610–621.

He, X., King, O., Ma, W., Li, M., & Zhang, H. (2003). Learning a semantic space from user's relevance feedback for image retrieval. *IEEE Transactions on Circuits and Systems for Video Technology, 13*(1), 39–48.

Heisterkamp, D.R. (2002). Building a latent semantic index of an image database from patterns of relevance feedback. *Proceedings of the International Conference on Pattern Recognition* (pp. 132–135).

Koskela, M., & Laaksonen, J. (2003). Using long-term learning to improve efficiency of content-based image retrieval. *Proceedings of the International Workshop on Pattern Recognition in Information Systems* (pp. 72–79).

Lee, C., Ma, W.Y., & Zhang, H.J. (1999). Information embedding based on user's relevance feedback for image retrieval. *Proceedings of the SPIE International Conference on Multimedia Storage and Archiving Systems* (pp. 19–22).

Minka, T., & Picard, R. (1997). Interactive learning using a society of models. *Pattern Recognition, 30*(4), 565–581.

Sull, S., Oh, J., Oh, S., Song, S., & Lee, S. (2000). Relevance graph-based image retrieval. *Proceedings of the IEEE International Conference on Multimedia and Expo* (pp. 713–716).

Vasconcelos, N., & Lippman, A. (2000). Learning over multiple temporal scales in image databases. *Proceedings of the European Conference on Computer Vision* (pp. 33–47).

Yin, P., Bhanu, B., & Chang, K. (2002). Improving retrieval performance by long-term relevance information. *Proceedings of the International Conference on Pattern Recognition* (pp. 533–536).

Zhang, C., & Chen, T. (2002). An active learning framework for content-based information retrieval. *IEEE Transactions on Multimedia, 4*(2), 260–268.

Zhang, Y.J. (1996). A survey on evaluation methods for image segmentation. *Pattern Recognition, 29*(8), 1335–1346.

Zhang, Y.J. (2001). A review of recent evaluation methods for image segmentation. *Proceedings of the International Symposium on Signal Processing and its Applications* (pp. 13–16).

This work was previously published in Personalized Information Retrieval and Access: Concepts, Methods, and Practices, edited by J. Wang, pp. 194-219, copyright 2008 by Information Science Reference, formerly known as Idea Group Reference (an imprint of IGI Global).

Section IV

Chapter XIII
A Semantics Sensitive Framework of Organization and Retrieval for Multimedia Databases

Zhiping Shi
Institute of Computing Technology, Chinese Academy of Sciences, China

Qingyong Li
Beijing Jiaotong University, China

Qing He
Institute of Computing Technology, Chinese Academy of Sciences, China

Zhongzhi Shi
Institute of Computing Technology, Chinese Academy of Sciences, China

ABSTRACT

Semantics-based retrieval is a trend of the Content-Based Multimedia Retrieval (CBMR). Typically, in multimedia databases, there exist two kinds of clues for query: perceptive features and semantic classes. In this chapter, we proposed a novel framework for multimedia database organization and retrieval, integrating the perceptive features and semantic classes. Thereunto, a semantics supervised cluster-based index organization approach (briefly as SSCI) was developed: the entire data set is divided hierarchically into many clusters until the objects within a cluster are not only close in the perceptive feature space, but also within the same semantic class; then an index entry is built for each cluster. Especially, the perceptive feature vectors in a cluster are organized adjacently in disk. Furthermore, the SSCI supports a relevance feedback approach: users sign the positive and negative examples regarded a cluster as unit rather than a single object. Our experiments show that the proposed framework can improve the retrieval speed and precision of the CBMR systems significantly.

INTRODUCTION

The advances in the data capturing, storage, and communication technologies have made vast amounts of multimedia data be available to consumer and enterprise applications (Smeulders, 2002). To find needed data from multimedia databases, the initial method is the multimedia data are categorized and labeled according to human semantic understanding, then retrieved with the labeled keywords matching. It is an efficient method to organize a data collection by semantic classification according to people's custom. However, it is a difficult and expensive manual task to label a large data set with semantic concepts, and the labeling process is subjective, inaccurate and incomplete. Moreover, the amount of the data in one class is too large to looking up. So the researchers proposed a CBMR technology. In the CBMR system, multimedia objects are usually represented by high-dimensional perceptive feature vectors, for example, an image is represented by a visual perceptive feature vector with some number of dimensions, and the similarity between two objects is defined by a distance function, e.g., Euclidean distance, between the corresponding perceptive feature vectors. CBMR is the similarity query. Similarity query is usually implemented by finding k feature vectors most similar to the feature vector of the query example, namely k-nearest neighbor (k-NN) search. Now CBMR has gained a degree of succeed, and a number of techniques extracting low-level perceptive features of multimedia automatically have been brought out. However, one side, there is no efficient index methods for large-scale perceptive features data that is represented by high-dimensional vectors. On the other hand, users of multimedia search engines are generally interested in retrieving data based on semantics, such as a video clip for "shoot events in football games" and so on. But the perceptive features of some data with relevant semantics may not be located very close in the perceptive feature space, or vice versa, the objects with similar perceptive features may come from different semantic classes. The difficulty in supporting semantics lies in the gap between perceptive features and semantic concepts, the so-called **semantic gap** (Smeulders, 2002). Thus, indexing multimedia data based only on perceptive features sometimes could not provide satisfied solutions.

Typically, there exist usually two kinds of clues for query in a large-scale multimedia database: 1) semantic classes, 2) perceptive features. Intuitively, it is reasonable to develop techniques that combine the advantages of both semantics and perceptive feature index.

In this chapter, we propose a semantics supervised cluster based index approach (briefly as SSCI) to achieve the target. We model the relationship between semantic classes and perceptive feature distributions of the data set with the Gaussian mixture model (GMM). The SSCI method proceeds as follows: the entire data set is divided hierarchically by a modified clustering technique into many clusters until the objects within a cluster not only are close in the perceptive feature space but also are within the same semantic class and the cluster here is called as **index cluster**, in particular, the perceptive feature vectors in an index cluster are organized adjacently in disk; an index entry (cluster index) including semantic clue and perceptive feature clue is built for each index cluster.

Based on the SSCI, we develop our approximate nearest neighbor (NN) searching technique that consists two phases: the first phase computes the distances between the query example and each cluster index and returns the clusters with the smallest distances, the so-called candidate clusters; then the second phase retrieves the original feature vectors within the candidate clusters to gain the approximate nearest neighbors. The main character of our technique is that it distinctly improves the speed and the semantic precision of CBMR.

Furthermore, we propose a novel Bayes-based relevance feedback approach integrating the perceptive features and the semantics for CBMR. We assume that both the positive feedback space and the negative feedback space follow the Gaussian mixture distribution so we can estimate the complexity distribution of query space more accurately. The feedback examples are expanded to their index clusters. The Bayes classifiers created by the index clusters are applied to rectify similarity distance. On the other hand, the positive and negative semantic space can be estimated by feedback examples' semantic information. The probability of each database object belonging to the positive or negative semantic space can be estimated to rectify the similarity distance. The retrieval results by feedback are more consistent with the semantics.

In the next section, background including high-dimensional index, semantic classification and relevance feedback techniques are briefly reviewed. Section 3 discusses the relationship between semantic classes and perceptive features distribution of multimedia objects. In section 4, we propose the SSCI technique, and discuss multimedia semantic classification and approximate NN search approaches based on the SSCI. In section 6, the proposed relevance feedback approach is presented. In section 6, we report a performance analysis of the proposed techniques. Section 7 concludes the chapter.

BACKGROUND

The two main challenging problems of the CBMR are so called "curse of dimension"(Weber, 1998) and "semantic gap". Researchers made vast works to deal with the two problem. Thereinto, high-dimensional indexing and semantic learning are widely used methods.

High-Dimensional Index Techniques

Many high-dimensional index techniques have been proposed to speed up the k-NN search. The time cost of a retrieval session includes accessing disk time (I/O) and computing distance time. In a large-scale database, the most of the data is at disk because of the limitation of the main memory size. The accessing disk time is dominant. The method to reduce the disk I/O cost can be categorized into two general classes (Ferhatosmanoglu, 2006): 1) representative size reduction; 2) retrieved set reduction.

The dimensionality reduction (Kanth,1998) and VA-based indexing (Weber, 1998; Ferhatosmanoglu, 2000; Ye, 2003) are examples of representative size reduction. The general approach for dimensionality reduction is to transform the feature vectors from high dimension into low dimension by taking the first few leading coefficients of the transformed vectors. The low dimensional vectors instead of the original vectors are used in query process. The dimensionality reduction can overcome the curse of dimensionality to a degree. However, dimensionality reduction sacrifices some accuracy. So the dimensionality reduction is usually used with other methods together.

Weber (1998), Ferhatosmanoglu (2000) and Ye HJ (2003) proposed vector approximation based indexing approach. These approaches divided the data space into 2^b rectangle cells where b is the number of bits specified by the user for the approximation of feature vectors. A unique bit-string of length b is allocated for each cell, and the bit-string approximates the data points that fall into the cell. Through filtering by retrieving approximation vectors, the efficiency of query is improved because only a portion of original vectors need be accessed for retrieval. However, the candidate original vectors are stored randomly in the database. Visiting the candidate original vectors stored randomly need many disk head shifts, which is mechanical movement and the slowest operation in I/O. To enhance the efficiency ulteriorly, the ideal approach is that the candidate vectors is stored consecutively in the disk. If the candidate vectors fell in one or a few cells and the vectors of each cell were stored consecutively, the amount of disk head shift had been reduced. It is a pity that because the partition cells for approximation vector approach is based on each dimension, one of the most of cells is empty or has single vector. Different vectors fall into different cells. The defect is inherent in the space dividing approaches. The work of Ye HJ still shows that the Gaussian mixture model (GMM) more accurately represents the distribution of the data.

The retrieved set reduction can be achieved by limiting search in some semantics range (classes) or by cluster-based indexing approaches. The semantics range limit approach requires users know the semantics label information of the database. Cluster-based approach partitions the data set based on the distribution of data completely. The data vectors in a cluster may be organized neighborly in the disk. This can speed up retrieval assuredly. The achieved precision of query depends on the performance of the clustering algorithm. Ferhatosmanoglu et al. put forward a general framework for approximate NN search (Ferhatosmanoglu, 2006). The retrieved portion of data is reduced by using clustering, and the feature vectors within a cluster are organized to support efficient interactive approximate searching. The approach allows a user to progressively explore the approximate results with increasing accuracy. The experiments on several real data sets obtained significant speed-ups by using the cluster-based technique over other current approaches.

Semantic Learning Techniques

The ideal method of overcome semantic gap is to enable computers to understand the semantics of multimedia contents. Therefore a number of approaches have been proposed (Fischer, 1995; Chen, 2001; Mittal, 2004) to mind the relationship between perceptive features and semantic classes with machine learning technology. A.Mittal et al. (2004) presented a video classification approach using Bayesian networks. In order to extend the application of conventional Bayesian theory to the case of continuous and nonparametric descriptor space, dimension was partitioned into attributes by minimizing the discrete Bayes error. Comparison experiments with standard classification tools on video data of more than 4,000 segments showed the potential of this approach in pattern classification. However, the approach weakens the classification capability for high-dimensional vectors due to each dimension of the vector is taken into account respectively.

Relevance feedback technology plays an important role in refining the precision of CBMR (Wu, 2005). Relevance feedback technology, which deals with the relation between the perceptive features and the semantics of multimedia data through human-machine interaction, is a matter of the two-class classification of the machine learning in nature. So many machine learning theories and methods can be used in relevance feedback, for example, discriminant analysis (Ishikawa, 1998), Bayes learning based on density estimation (Cox, 2000; Su, 2002; Meilhac, 1999), support vector machine (Liang, 2006), etc..

The relevance feedback based on density estimation estimates the probability density of the positive and negative samples so as to set up decision evaluation of retrieval results. The methods proposed in (Rui, 1998, 2000; Ishikawa, 1998) can be regarded as the positive samples probability estimation based on the Gaussian distribution hypothesis. The Gaussian distribution hypothesis is too simple to represent the distribution of the samples of the multimedia database.

The method from Meilhac et al. (1999) estimates the apriori probabilities and the class-conditional probabilities of the feedback example images, and then calculates the posterior probability of each image of the image database using the Bayes decision. Each image's posterior probabilities for the positive class membership and the negative class membership are computed to decide that if it is a relevant image. The method estimates the distribution of the relevant images using the Gaussian mixture model, and each image is regarded as the center of a Gaussian distribution.

Su et al. (2002) argued that the positive examples are similar, so their distribution can be represented by a Gaussian model; but the negative examples are often isolated and independent, their distribution need to be represented by multi Gaussian models with small variances. They utilize the negative feedback information in the refined retrieval by applied a 'dibbling' process to push away the images in the database that are very close to the negative examples. They treat the negative examples and the positive ones using different probabilistic models; weaken the influence that the negative examples impacting on the positive examples, so the omission factor is reduced.

Although the relevance feedback methods mentioned previously have improved the performance of the CBMR, learning the classifier faces the following problems because of the particularity of the relevance feedback: 1) the dimensionality of features is high but the feedback examples are insufficient; 2) the positive samples and negative samples are asymmetrical; 3) there isn't any certain maps between the perceptive features distribution and the semantic concepts.

PERCEPTIVE FEATURE DISTRIBUTION AND MODELING

The objects in a multimedia database always can be categorized into some semantic classes such as news, sports, commercial and mountain etc. for videos or images. The users commonly wish query multimedia within expected semantic class. However, users hardly know the semantic classes labeled by multimedia database owners, so multimedia objects are queried by perceptive feature vectors in CBMR system.

Intuitively, the semantic gap would be reduced if the relationship between the perceptive feature vectors and the semantic classes was mined. It is often supposed that the feature vectors within a semantic class follow a single Gaussian distribution and the whole data set follows a Gaussian mixture model (Ye, 2003). In practice, data distribution in multimedia databases is complicated so the feature distribution

Figure 1. The distribution and contour lines of two semantic classes A and B. The circular points belong to A and the square points belong to B. The contour line of semantic class A is concave, so the distribution of A should be simulated by a Gaussian mixture model with multiple components

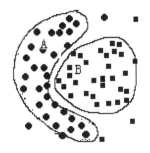

in a semantic class may be arbitrary shape. Figure 1(a) abstractly illustrates the complex distribution in the feature space where two arbitrary shaped semantic classes A and B exist. If each semantic class is simulated by a single Gaussian model, the Gaussian model for A would cover many objects of B. To alleviate this problem, the distribution of class A in Figure 1(b) is modeled by a combination of 3 small Gaussian components, which can avoid covering the objects in class B.

In this chapter, we present a reasonable hypothesis: not only the whole data set but also each semantic class follows the Gaussian mixture distribution, and a cluster of feature vectors follow a compact single Gaussian model. For an object x_i in the multimedia database, its probability density function of the Gaussian mixture distribution is:

$$f(x_i | \boldsymbol{\Theta}) = \sum_{k=1}^{K} \pi_k f_k(x_i | \theta_k).$$

(1)

Where K refers to number of Gaussian components; π_k is a factor for each mixture component referring to priori probability of each mixture component; $\boldsymbol{\Theta} = (\theta_1, \theta_2, ..., \theta_K)$, is a parameter vector for the mixture components, where $\theta_k = (\boldsymbol{\mu}_k, \boldsymbol{\Sigma}_k)$, is a parameter of a Gaussian component including mean vector and covariance matrix; $f_k(x_i | \theta_k)$ is a probability density function of the single Gaussian distribution:

$$f_k(x_i | \theta_k) = G(x_i | \boldsymbol{\mu}_k, \boldsymbol{\Sigma}_k) = \frac{1}{\sqrt{(2\pi)^d | \boldsymbol{\Sigma}_k |}} e^{-\frac{1}{2}(x_i - \boldsymbol{\mu}_k)^T \boldsymbol{\Sigma}_k^{-1}(x_i - \boldsymbol{\mu}_k)}$$

(2)

In this chapter, the expectation maximization (EM) algorithm is used to estimate the GMM parameters. For a data set X, if the probability density function format, $f(x | \theta), \theta \in \boldsymbol{\Theta}$, is known, the joint probability of the samples $x_1, x_2, ..., x_n$ is as follow

$$L(\boldsymbol{\Theta}) = L(x_1, x_2, ..., x_n | \boldsymbol{\Theta}) = \prod_{i=1}^{n} f(x_i | \boldsymbol{\Theta})$$

(3)

This is a likelihood function of the mixture model. With maximum likelihood estimation method by Fisher, let $\boldsymbol{\Theta} = \boldsymbol{\Theta}^*$ to make

$$L(x_1, x_2, ..., x_n | \boldsymbol{\Theta}^*) = \max_{\Theta} L(x_1, x_2, ..., x_n | \boldsymbol{\Theta})$$

(4)

It is usually solved through equation (5):

$$\frac{d}{d\boldsymbol{\Theta}} \ln L(\boldsymbol{\Theta}) = 0$$

(5)

Using equations (3) and (2), we obtain equation (6):

$$\ln L(\boldsymbol{\Theta}) = \ln \prod_{i=1}^{n} f(x_i | \boldsymbol{\Theta})$$

$$= \sum_{i=1}^{n} \ln f(x_i | \boldsymbol{\Theta})$$

$$= \sum_{i=1}^{n} \ln \sum_{k=1}^{K} \pi_k G(x_i | \boldsymbol{\mu}_k, \boldsymbol{\Sigma}_k)$$

(6)

Apparently the Gaussian mixture model mentioned previously is hard to solve using equations (5) and (6). Due to the data incompleteness, it is unknown which Gaussian component affected by a certain sample, that is to say, there exist some hidden data that can't be observed directly. The EM algorithm is a maximum likelihood method estimating the Gaussian mixture model parameters in the case there are hidden data.

We introduce hidden data F to define complete data Y={X, F}, so the likelihood function can be written as

$$L(\boldsymbol{\Theta}\,|\,Y) = L(\boldsymbol{\Theta}\,|\,X,F) = P(X,F\,|\,\boldsymbol{\Theta}) \tag{7}$$

where X and $\boldsymbol{\Theta}$ are regarded as constants and F is a independent variable, so the function is a random variable. Its maximum is not easy gained, but its expectation is a determinate function which optimization is easy to do. The basis framework of the EM algorithm is following.

E-Step: $\quad Q(\boldsymbol{\Theta}\,|\,\boldsymbol{\Theta}^t) = E\left[\log P(X,F\,|\,\boldsymbol{\Theta})\,|\,X,\boldsymbol{\Theta}^t\right] \tag{8}$

M-Step: $\quad \boldsymbol{\Theta}^{t+1} = \arg\max Q(\boldsymbol{\Theta},\boldsymbol{\Theta}^t) \tag{9}$

The introduced hidden data is defined as probability belongingness that stands for the probability of a sample belonging to a Gaussian component:

$$f(\theta_k\,|\,\boldsymbol{x}_i) = \frac{\pi_k G(\boldsymbol{x}_i\,|\,\boldsymbol{\mu}_k,\boldsymbol{\Sigma}_k)}{\sum\limits_{j=1}^{K}\pi_j G(\boldsymbol{x}_i\,|\,\boldsymbol{\mu}_j,\boldsymbol{\Sigma}_j)} \tag{10}$$

Thereby the recursive formula solving the Gaussian mixture model can be inferred as follow:

$$\left.\begin{aligned}
a_k^t &= \sum_{i=1}^{N} p(k\,|\,\boldsymbol{x}_i,\boldsymbol{\Theta}^t),\\[4pt]
\pi_k^t &= \frac{1}{N}a_k^t,\\[4pt]
\boldsymbol{\mu}_k^{t+1} &= \frac{1}{a_k^t}\sum_{i=1}^{N}\boldsymbol{x}_i p(k\,|\,\boldsymbol{x}_i,\boldsymbol{\Theta}^t),\\[4pt]
\boldsymbol{\Sigma}_k^{t+1} &= \frac{1}{a_k^t}\sum_{i=1}^{N} p(k\,|\,\boldsymbol{x}_i,\boldsymbol{\Theta}^t)(\boldsymbol{x}_i-\boldsymbol{\mu}_k^{t+1})(\boldsymbol{x}_i-\boldsymbol{\mu}_k^{t+1})^T
\end{aligned}\right\} \tag{11}$$

where $p(k\,|\,\boldsymbol{x}_i,\boldsymbol{\Theta}^t) = \dfrac{\pi_k^t G(\boldsymbol{x}_i\,|\,\boldsymbol{\mu}_k^t,\boldsymbol{\Sigma}_k^t)}{\sum_{j=1}^{K}\pi_j^t G(\boldsymbol{x}_i\,|\,\boldsymbol{\mu}_j^t,\boldsymbol{\Sigma}_j^t)}.$

THE SEMANTICS SENSITIVE APPROXIMATE NN SEARCH

In this section, we represent the SSCI approach and approximate NN search method based on the index approach.

The SSCI Algorithm

We expect to build an index structure based on the following principles: the entire data set is divided into many subsets; the perceptive feature vectors in a subset are organized together continuously in the disk; an index entry is built for each subset. Supposing that the mean size of the subsets is d, the population of the index file is as $1/d$ as that of the data set. The index file is small enough to fit into memory in a lump. During retrieval, the index file is accessed at first to measure the similarity between the query example and the subsets and only a few most similar subsets are accessed to gain approximate query result. Moreover, it is timesaving to access a subset which members are stored in continuous disk space.

Now, which objects should be clustered into one subset? We expect that a CBMR system returns semantic relevant results, given a perceptive feature vector as a query example. If the semantic class of the query could be estimated, we go forward to the expectation. We adopt a Bayes classifier to classify multimedia objects into certain semantic class. Let π_i denote the priori probability of a semantic class i, $1 \leq i \leq |S|$, where $|S|$ is the number of the semantic classes, and $p(x \mid s_i)$ refers to the conditional probability density of x, the feature data point for an object, given that it belongs to class i. $p(x)$, the probability distribution function of x, is given by $\sum_{i=1}^{|S|} p(x \mid s_i)\pi_i$. The Bayes error that is associated with Bayes classifier is given by:

$$E = \int \left[1 - \max_i \ p(s_i \mid x) \right] p(x) dx \tag{12}$$

Where $p(s_i \mid x)$ is the a posteriori probability of semantic class s_i, $i = 1, 2, 3,\ldots, |S|$. Because of the complexity of the relation between perceptive feature distribution and semantic classes (see section 3), $p(s_i \mid x)$ can't be accurate estimated directly. The feature data point space is partitioned into subsets $c_1,\ldots,c_{|C|}$, whose distribution is compact Gaussian component, where $|C|$ is the total number of the subsets. Then, $p(s_i \mid x)$ can be calculated by:

$$p(s_i \mid x) = \sum_{j=1}^{|C|} p(s_i \mid c_j)p(c_j \mid x) \tag{13}$$

Where $p(s_i \mid c_j)$ is the conditional probability density of semantic class s_i given cluster c_j, and the conditional probability density $p(c_j \mid x)$ is the probability of x belonging to cluster c_j and can be given by:

$$p(c_j \mid x) = \frac{p(x \mid c_j)p(c_j)}{p(x)} \tag{14}$$

So the Bayes error E can be written as:

$$E = \int [1 - \max_i \sum_j p(s_i \mid c_j) \frac{p(x \mid c_j)p(c_j)}{p(x)}]p(x)dx$$

$$= \int [p(x) - \max_i \sum_j p(s_i \mid c_j)p(x \mid c_j)p(c_j)]dx \tag{15}$$

$$= \int [\sum_j p(x \mid c_j)p(c_j) - \max_i \sum_j p(s_i \mid c_j)p(x \mid c_j)p(c_j)]dx$$

Where $p(s_i \mid c_j)$ can be estimated by:

$$p(s_i \mid c_j) = \frac{num(i \mid j)}{num(j)} \tag{16}$$

Where $num(j)$ is the total number of data points in cluster j and $num(i \mid j)$ is the total data points from semantic class i in cluster j.

The two equations imply that the Bayes error will decrease to 0 as $\max p(s_i \mid c_j)$ increases to 1, to say, when all of data points within a cluster (a single Gaussian component) are from the same semantic class, the error reaches minimum. So all data points within a subset (simulated by a compact Gaussian component) should belong to an identical semantic class. The index entry of a subset takes into account both perceptive feature and semantic classes.

According to what we discussed before, we propose SSCI algorithm to create our expected index structure. The outline of our SSCI is as follows: the entire data set is divided into k clusters (k can be determined by the number of semantic classes involved every time); those clusters which include objects of more than one semantic classes will be divided into sub-clusters moreover until all (or the most of) objects of each cluster belong to an identical semantic class; up to now, the objects of each cluster belong to an identical semantic class; if a cluster's size goes down below the lower threshold, merge the cluster into the nearest neighbor cluster within same semantic class; if a cluster's size goes above

Figure 2. The process of SSCI. A solid-line rectangle stands for a object; a dashed rectangle stands for a cluster; the dash-dot-line rectangle encircles cluster index entries

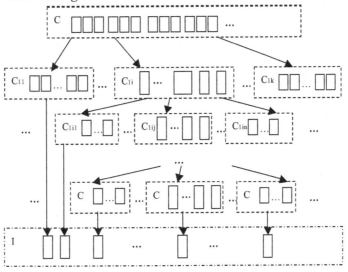

Figure 3. Hierarchical semantics and hierarchical cluster indexes

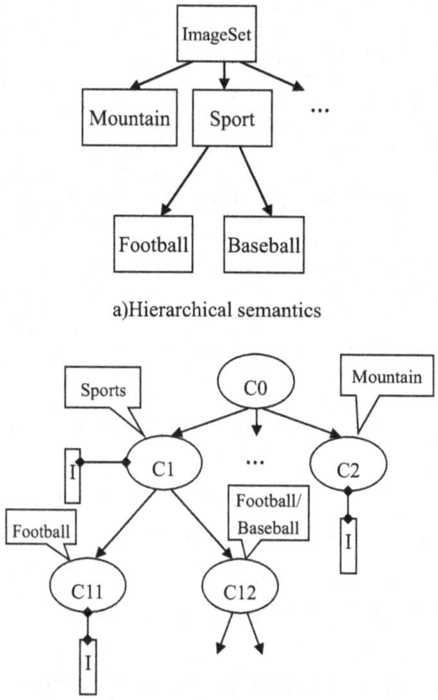

a)Hierarchical semantics

b)Hierarchical cluster index. "Ci" stand for

cluster and "I" stand for index entries.

the upper threshold, split the cluster into two; at last, the result clusters are index clusters, and an index entry including semantic class identification code and parameters of the Gaussian model (mean and variance) is created for each index cluster. The used clustering algorithm consists of two steps: in first step, K-means cluster algorithm is used to clustering the data into k clusters; in second step, the k clusters are inputted EM algorithm to fine-tune, and the parameters of the Gaussian model for the clusters are obtained. Figure 2 illustrates the process of index construction of the SSCI algorithm.

The cluster index structure is hierarchical while the semantic concepts in the multimedia database are hierarchical. For example, in an image database, there are top semantic concepts such as "mountain" and "sports", and "sports" can include lower concepts "football" and "baseball". A cluster C1, in which objects belong to sports, educes an index entry. Moreover the sports objects may be about football or baseball. So the cluster C1 is splitting into two, namely C11 and C12. The clusters C11 and C2 cannot be split because their objects belong to football and news respectively, and the football and news are the lowest level concepts.

Multimedia Semantic Classification

Using the relationship between perceptive features and semantic classes, modeled by the GMM (see subsection 4.1, a cluster is a Gaussian component), we can classify a multimedia object to a semantic class with the minimum error rate by the Bayes decision rule. Given a multimedia sample x, its class can be determined by:

$$C(\boldsymbol{x}) = \arg\max_i p(s_i \mid \boldsymbol{x}) \tag{17}$$

Where $p(s_i \mid \boldsymbol{x})$ can be computed according formulas (13),(14),(15). For simplicity, each index cluster has only identical semantic class objects in our experiments, so

$$p(s_i \mid c_j) = \begin{cases} 1 & j \in i(\text{cluster } j \text{ only inlude objects of semantic class } i); \\ 0 & j \notin i(\text{cluster } j \text{ does not inlude objects of semantic class } i) \end{cases} \tag{18}$$

Thereby formula (13) can be written as:

$$p(s_i \mid \boldsymbol{x}) = \sum_{j \in i} p(c_j \mid \boldsymbol{x}) \tag{19}$$

Each cluster is a Gaussian component, so:

$$p(\boldsymbol{x} \mid c_j) = Gauss(\boldsymbol{x} \mid \boldsymbol{\mu}_j, \boldsymbol{\Sigma}_j) \frac{1}{\sqrt{(2\pi)^d \mid \boldsymbol{\Sigma}_j \mid}} e^{-\frac{1}{2}(\boldsymbol{x}-\boldsymbol{\mu}_j)^T \boldsymbol{\Sigma}_j^{-1}(\boldsymbol{x}-\boldsymbol{\mu}_j)} \tag{20}$$

Where $\mid V \mid$ is the number of total objects.

In practical, we firstly transform the feature space with Karhunen-Loeve Transformation (KLT). After KLT, the covariance matrix becomes a diagonal matrix. Calculation is simplified and more accurate Gaussian clusters can be gained.

Approximate NN Searching Approach

For the SSCI technique, there are two different retrieval strategies as follows:

1. Classify the query example q at first using Bayes classifier, then the retrieving is limited only to the clusters within the highest likelihood semantic class. The strategy is marked as Class-q.
2. Retrieve the index file to gain the m nearest index entries (clusters) according to distance calculated with formula (14), and then retrieve the original feature vectors within the m clusters. The strategy is marked as Cluster-m, where m is the number of the accessed clusters. Obviously, the bigger the m is, the higher the precision of the retrieval result can be achieved, and the more time is spent.

Given a query, the retrieval algorithm works as follows:

1. Transforming query vector. Transform the query feature vector to KLT space domain.
2. Searching the index file. Read the index file from disk to memory, then compute the distance between the query vector and the index entries based on formula (5) (the probability of the query vector belonging to each cluster).
3. Identifying the query result candidates. For Class-q, estimate the semantic class of the query example with formula (8), and the candidates are the objects within the class. For Cluster-m, gain the m nearest index clusters and the candidates are the objects within the m clusters.
4. Searching the candidate original feature vectors. The query is answered approximately by k-NN results in the range of the candidates.

In the following of this section, we analyze the algorithm complexity of the strategy Class-q. The complexity of the strategy Cluster-m is similar.

For the large-scale high-dimensional database, the query runtime is dominated by the times of I/O because of memory limitation. On sequential retrieval method, reading the whole database needs many times I/O because of memory limitation. Supposed that the population of the multimedia database is N, and the average population of the index clusters is m, and the number of the semantic class is s. Though the populations of the index clusters (or the semantic classes) are diverse, accessing one of the index clusters (or the semantic classes) is an equiprobable event. On the Class-q algorithm, the accessed portion of data is $1/m+1/s$ of the whole data. For the most of practical application, the accessed portion of data can be fixed into memory within one I/O operation. Therefore, the retrieval speed is more than the m (or s) times of the sequential search retrieval's one.

Reasoningly, the efficiency of the SSCI-based searching is higher than that of the VA-based searching too (Weber, 1998; Ferhatosmanoglu, 2000). Because the main drawback of the VA-base approaches is that the disk I/O of accessing candidate feature vectors is random, whereas in our SSCI-based approach the disk I/O of accessing candidate feature data is sequential. Obviously, the efficiency of the sequential I/O is much higher than the random I/O, so the SSCI-based approach has better performance. Nevertheless, the SSCI-based approach is only applicable to approximate retrieval. The VA-based methods haven't the limitation.

RELEVANCE FEEDBACK

In this section, we propose the relevance feedback in perceptive features and semantics respectively.

Relevance Feedback In Perceptive Features

During the relevance feedback process, all objects in a cluster are regarded as feedback examples if one object in the cluster is marked feedback example. This can make up the insufficiency of feedback examples. The index clusters are the Gaussian components with the small variances. To say, there are many positive Gaussian components and negative Gaussian components near the query example in the perceptive feature space.

The posterior probability for the positive and/or negative Gaussian components membership of each object can be estimated and the distance of the object is amended by the margin between the posterior probability for the positive Gaussian components membership and that for the negative Gaussian components membership. Let x be a sample of the database, and c_j be an index cluster in which a feedback example has been marked. Because c_j follows a narrow Gaussian distribution, the likelihood of x is given by

$$p(x \mid c_j) = \frac{1}{\sqrt{(2\pi)^d |\Sigma_j|}} e^{-\frac{1}{2}(x-\mu_j)^T \Sigma_j^{-1}(x-\mu_j)} \tag{22}$$

Under the Bayes rules, the determining function for x belongs to c_j is given by:

$$g_j(x) = \log p(c_j \mid x)$$
$$\propto \log p(x \mid c_j) + \log p(c_j) \qquad (23)$$
$$= -\frac{1}{2}(x - \mu_j)^T \Sigma_j^{-1}(x - \mu_j) - \frac{d}{2}\log 2\pi - \frac{1}{2}\log|\Sigma_j| + \log p(c_j)$$

Let q be the query example, x be a database sample. Allowing for both the positive Gaussian distribution and the negative Gaussian distribution, the feedback function is given by:

$$sim^*(q,x) = sim(q,x) + \sum_{j\in+} g_j(x) - \sum_{j\in-} g_j(x) \qquad (24)$$

Wherein +,- stand for positive example set and negative example set respectively, $sim(q,x)$, which maybe the Euclidean distance or the intersection of the histograms commonly, stands for the similarity distance between x and q.

Allow for the feedback examples marked by users are few, and the number of the positive examples is not equal to that of the negative ones, they have only local representative. It maybe bring out uncertain errors mixing all the feedback examples to represents the distribution of the positive or negative samples. As shown in Figure 1, "+", "-" represent "is" or "is not" a query target object, and those enclosed by circles represent the feedback examples marked by the user. A query target object X is nearest from a positive example, but more negative examples around X are marked by the user. If accumulating the X' posterior probabilities for every positive Gaussian components membership and that for every negative Gaussian components membership, the effect of the negative feedback is strengthened, so X is classified a negative sample in error.

Therefore, we take into account only the nearest positive example and the nearest negative example. After the user marked feedback examples, the retrieval system calculates every object's posterior probability for the positive Gaussian models and that for the negative Gaussian models. Then the margin between the maximum posterior probability for the positive Gaussian models and the maximum one for the negative Gaussian models is used to adjust the distance of the objects.

The distance function between x and q modified by perceptive features feedback is given by

$$sim^*(q,x) = w_0 \times sim(q,x) + w_1 \times \frac{\max\limits_{j\in+} g_j(x) - \max\limits_{j\in-} g_j(x)}{\left|\max\limits_{j\in+} g_j(x) + \max\limits_{j\in-} g_j(x)\right|} \qquad (25)$$

Figure 4. The distribution of the positive and negative samples. "+", "-" represent "is" or "is not" a query target object, and those enclosed by circles represent the feedback examples marked by the user.

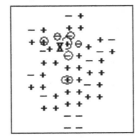

Wherein $\max_{j \in +} g_j(x)$ is the maximum $g_j(x)$ for the positive examples set, $\max_{j \in +} g_j(x)$ is the maximum $g_j(x)$ for the negative examples set, $\left| \max_{j \in +} g_j(x) + \max_{j \in -} g_j(x) \right|$ is the normalized factor, w_0, w_1 are weight factors.

Relevance Feedback in Semantics

The query results that are retrieved according to the perceptive feature similarity are with the similar perceptive features but not with the same semantics. The user's query intention points to the semantic similar objects. The user's query semantics maybe not correspond to a semantic class in the multimedia database; however the semantic classes in the database can be the important clue to optimize the query results. Although the relation of the semantic concepts is complicated, it is always that some semantic concepts are consistent and some others are repulsive. It is difficult task to figure out the relation of the semantic concepts directly. It is feasible to learn the consistent or repulsive relation between the user query semantics and the semantic classes of the database by using the positive and negative feedback examples.

Intuitively, the more positive examples are marked in a semantic class, the higher the probability that the semantic class is consistent with the query semantics is, vice versa, the more negative examples are marked in a semantic class, the higher the probability that the semantic class is repulsive with the query semantics is. So the proposed optimizing method is as follows:

1. Computing the posterior probability of the positive example semantic classes belonging to the query semantics.

$$p(S_q \mid S_i) = \frac{p(S_i \mid S_q)p(S_q)}{p(S_i \mid S_q)p(S_q) + p(S_i \mid S^-)p(S^-)} \tag{26}$$

Wherein S_i stands for the semantic class i, S_q stands for the query semantics, i.e., the positive feedback semantic space, $p(S_q)$ stands for the probability of the positive feedback examples, S^- stands for the negative feedback semantic space, $p(S^-)$ stands for the probability of the negative feedback examples.

$$p(S_i \mid S_q) = \frac{p_i}{p}. \tag{27}$$

$$p(S_q) = \frac{p}{p+n}. \tag{28}$$

$$p(S^-) = 1 - p(S_q). \tag{29}$$

Wherein p_i stands for the number of the positive examples of the semantic class i, p stands for the total number of the positive examples, n stands for the total number of the negative examples.

So the probability for the query semantics membership of the sample x is given by

$$p(S_q \mid x) = \sum_i p(S_q \mid S_i) p(S_i \mid x) \tag{30}$$

2. Computing the probability for the negative feedback semantic space membership of the sample x:

$$p(S^- \mid x) = \sum_i p(S^- \mid S_i) p(S_i \mid x) \tag{31}$$

$$p(S^- \mid S_i) = \frac{p(S_i \mid S^-) p(S^-)}{p(S_i \mid S_q) p(S_q) + p(S_i \mid S^-) p(S^-)} \tag{32}$$

$$p(S_i \mid S^-) = \frac{n_i}{n} \tag{33}$$

Wherein n_i stands for the number of the negative examples of the semantic class i

3. Updating the objects similarity distance:

$$sim'(q, x) = w_2 \times sim^*(q, x) + w_3 \times p(S_q \mid x) \tag{34}$$
$$(- w_4 \times p\ S^- \mid x)$$

Wherein w_2, w_3, w_4 are weight factors.

The probability for the semantic class i membership of x, $p(S_i \mid x)$, can be calculated by diverse methods. For example, one method is given by equation (13), and another method is that the sample x is a member of the semantic class S_i or not determinately:

$$p(S_i \mid x) = \begin{cases} 1 & x \in S_i \\ 0 & x \notin S_i \end{cases} \tag{35}$$

For the simpleness, the latter is adopted in our experiments.

EVALUATIONS

Evaluation of The SSCI-Based Searching

In this section, we evaluate the efficiency and the result quality of the SSCI-based searching approach.

We first describe the data set and the experimental system. The data set is about videos from TV, VCD-ROM, and DVD-ROM. We have already collected 150G video files for about 300 hours. We chose about 40 hours videos including 40553 key-frames. We categorized the key-frames based on their video semantics into 20 semantic classes. The 51-dimentional texture histograms (Shi, 2005) of the key-frames were clustered into 3981 clusters, a cluster index entry created for each cluster. For comparison, we employ the VA⁺-file algorithm, and create 300 bits approximate vector for each 51-dimensional texture feature vector of the data set. Our experiment system is C/S (Client/Server) structure in a local area network of 10 Mbps bandwidth. The client PC is P4 2.4G CPU with 512MB memory. The server PC is P4 1.0GHz×2CPU with 1024MB memory. The data set feature vectors are stored in SQL Server, and the query engine runs on the client PC. The index files are on the client PC.

Efficiency of the SSCI-Based searching

In this subsection, we evaluate the speedup achieved by the SSCI-based searching approach compared to the VA⁺-file based approach. Supposed $k = 90$, we queried 10 times randomly, and the mean times of the two approaches were calculated. Averagely 372 original feature vectors were accessed in the VA⁺-file based approach. For fairness, we accessed the original feature vectors of top 30 nearest neighbor clusters for the proposed method, noted Cluster-30. The mean number of the visited original feature vectors was 358 in 10 queries. The accessed data sizes of the two methods were nearly equivalent.

Table 1. The mean query times of the two index approaches (the unit is second)

Time Cost	Cluster-30	VA⁺file
IT_{index}	0.015	0.109
CT_{index}	0.015	1.286
IT_{db}	4.820	5.450
CT_{db}	0.010	
ST	4.860	6.845

Table 2. The mean precision of the video semantic classification

Semantic Class	Precision
Basketball	70
Hockey	80
Surf ride	90
Pingpong	90
Football	70
Racing car	80
Swimming	90
Running	80
Literary	100
Report	70
Commercial	80
Weather fore-cast	100
Mean	83.3

Table 1 show that the efficiency of the SSCI-based approach is higher than that of the VA⁺-file approach though both methods spend long time because C/S structure and SQL Server were used. Especially, searching the index file of the SSCI-based approach is significantly faster than searching the VA⁺-file. It is caused by two reasons: first, the population of the index file in VA⁺-file approach is equal to the population of the original feature data, N, whereas the population of the index file in the SSCI approach is N/m; second, the distances between the query object and the index entries of index file are computed directly in the SSCI-based approach, whereas in the VA⁺-file based approach, the lower and upper bounds of the distances between the query example and the approximate vectors all need to be calculated. The computing complexity t of the latter is obviously higher. At the phase of computing the distance of the original feature vectors, the distance measure of the two approaches are equivalent. The difference is that accessing the original feature vectors is performed at random disk locations in VA⁺-file but at sequential disk locations in the SSCI-based approach.

Performance of approximate *k*-NN searching

In this chapter, precision is used to measure the performance. An object of result set is correct if and only if the object belongs the same semantic class with the query example. The precision P is defined by $P = c/t$. Where c is the number of the correct result objects, and t is the number of the all result objects.

On the strategy Class-q, if the semantic class of the query object q is estimated correctly, the all result objects belong the semantic class, that is, the precision is 100%. On the contrary, if the semantic class of the query sample q is estimated wrong, the precision is 0. In a word, the retrieval precision lies on the accuracy of semantic classification of the query sample.

We chose 12 semantic classes randomly, 10 key-frames for each class, to perform semantic classification experiments. The experiment results are shown in Table 2.

The data set is full of challenge because there are some semantic classes difficult to distinguish. For example, the main backgrounds of the hockey and the football video frames are green grass court; the surf ride's and the swim's are water; the fields of running and basketball are similar too. Even then our classification experiments show a high correctness.

In the following of this sub-section, we evaluate the performance of the strategy of Cluster-m. To evaluate the quality of the approximate result set, we introduce two quality metrics: relative precision ratio and relative distance ratio. Suppose the precision of the approximate k-NN algorithm is p_a and that of the sequential k-NN algorithm is p_s. We define the precision ratio P as relative approximate precision, given by $P = p_a / p_s$. It is intuitive that the bigger P is, the higher the precision of the approximate k-NN search is. If the precision of the approximate k-NN search is higher than that of the sequential k-NN search, P is larger than 1. Or else, P is less than 1.

The precision does not capture important information about the quality of the approximation. Ferhatosmanoglu et al. (2006) introduce an error metric. Suppose the approximate k-NN algorithm returns the result set $(a_1, a_2, ..., a_k)$ and the real result set computed by the underlying distance function $d_f(q, x)$ is $(r_1, r_2, ..., r_k)$. The relative distance ratio D as error metric is given by:

$$D = \frac{\sum_{i=1}^{k} d_f(q, a_i)}{\sum_{i=1}^{k} d_f(q, r_i)} \tag{36}$$

For certainly, $D \geq 1$. Only when the result set of the approximate k-NN algorithm equal to that of the real result set computed by the distance function, the equal sign is tenable. The smaller D is, the closer the result set of the approximate k-NN algorithm is to the real result set.

We compared the Cluster-m method with the VA-LOW-k algorithm. The VA-LOW-k algorithm (Ferhatosmanoglu, 2006; Weber, 2000) is an approximate query algorithm based on VA$^+$-file. At first phase, the lower bounds of the distance between the approximate vectors and the query example were figured out. The k nearest neighbor vectors were regarded as the approximate retrieval results. At second phase, only the k original feature vectors were accessed and their accurate distances with the query example were computed for sorting the result objects. We chose 11 semantic classes randomly and do 3 queries for each class randomly, $k = 100$. For the Cluster-m method, the original feature vectors of the top 10 nearest neighbor clusters were accessed to compute the accurate distances, namely Cluster-10. The distance is measured based on the Euclidean distance.

The comparisons of performance of VA-LOW-k and Cluster-10 are presented in Table 3 for both the two metrics. On average, the Cluster-10 algorithm achieves an error of $D = 1.53$, whereas the VA-LOW-k algorithm achieves an error level of $D = 2.19$. In terms of total distance of the results, the Cluster-10 algorithm is closer to the sequential retrieval (accurate retrieval). The precision ratios of the Cluster-10 are higher than that of the VA-LOW-k. The mean precision ratio of the Cluster-10 reaches $P = 1.23$, to say, the precision ratio is 1.23 times of that of the sequential retrieval. The mean precision ratio of the VA-LOW-k reaches $P = 0.58$ that is much less than that of the sequential retrieval. Typically, the precision of the approximate retrieval is lower than that of the accurate retrieval. Because the semantic class is taken into account for the SSCI technique to create index, our *approximate* retrieval achieves higher precision than the *accurate* retrieval.

We analyze the improvement of the result quality of our technique as the number of the accessing clusters increases. The result of Cluster-m overlap to that of the accurate retrieval as the value of m increases. Meanwhile, the time cost increases as the size of the accessed original feature data grows.

Table 3. Comparison of performances of VA-LOW-k and Cluster-10

Semantic Class	P		D	
	VA-LOW-k	Cluster-10	VA-LOW-k	Cluster-10
Reports	1.0	1.55	3.29	2.62
Weather forecast	0.50	2.75	2.16	1.67
Commercial	0.86	1.05	2.94	1.53
Surf ride	0.52	0.81	2.11	1.71
Basketball	0.45	1.40	2.60	1.42
Running	0.34	1.46	1.90	1.49
Pingpong	0.50	0.73	3.17	1.75
Hockey	0.66	0.91	1.99	1.42
Gymnastics	0.57	1.71	2.80	1.83
Swimming	0.78	1.11	1.69	1.65
Football	0.77	1.33	1.68	1.22
Mean	0.58	1.23	2.19	1.53

Figure 5. Comparison of performance of Cluster-m with m=10 and m=20

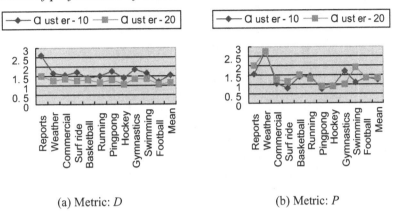

(a) Metric: *D*   (b) Metric: *P*

Figure 5 illustrates the comparison of the performances of Cluster-*m* with *m*=10 (Cluster-10) and *m*=20 (Cluster-20). The *D* of Cluster-20 is 1.16, whereas the *D* of Cluster-10 is 1.53 averagely. The *P* of Cluster-20 and Cluster-10 are average 1.33 and 1.23 respectively. The improvement of the precision is slow as *m* increases. The clusters with higher condition probability for the query example are relevant to the query semantics with higher probability. Therefore, the higher precision can be gained by accessing a few clusters of original feature vectors using our algorithm.

Compared with the idea proposed in (Ferhatosmanoglu, 2006), our approach gives attention to both perceptive clue and semantic clue of multimedia objects, improving the speed and semantic precision of CBMR systems at same time.

Performance of The Proposed Relevance Feedback Retrieval Method

In this subsection, we present experiments on an image database to show the proposed relevance feedback method performance. The image database includes 8342 images from the Internet and Corel Image Gallery, and they are classified into 23 semantic classes. The perceptive features are the 36-dimension HSV histograms of the images. The weight factors $w_0,..., w_4$ of equation (25) and (34) are assigned 0.6,0.4,0.4,0.3,0.3 ordinally. For illustrating the performance of the proposed relevance feedback method, we use sequence searching as the original retrieval, because the precisions of the SSCI-based searching are higher than.80% averagely on the database.

Figure 6 shows the progress of retrieving traditional Chinese paintings by a traditional Chinese painting example. The first retrieval results, which are retrieved by the perceptive feature, include many human photos because a man is presented on the query example image. Only after 4 cycles relevance feedback retrieval, the most of retrieval result images are traditional Chinese paintings.

We chose 4 images from the image database, which are with worse original retrieval precision, as query example images to do *k*-NN retrieval experiments. Figure 7 illustrates the performance of the proposed method, wherein *k*=90, each curve stands for a query session. The precisions of the 4 images' original retrieval (0 cycles) are not good (7%, 9%, 14%, 48% respectively), but the precisions rise to above 84%~90% quickly after 4 cycles feedback. Even when the original

Figure 6. The progress of retrieving traditional Chinese paintings

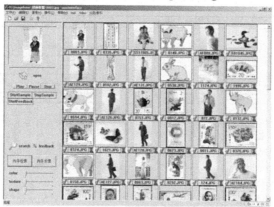

a) Original retrieval results

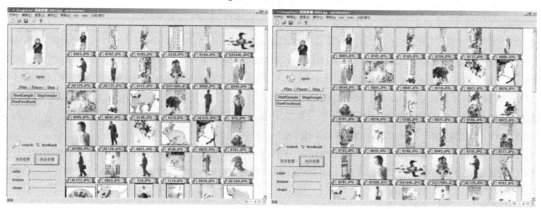

b) The results after 1ˢᵗ feedback round   c) The results after 2ⁿᵈ feedback round

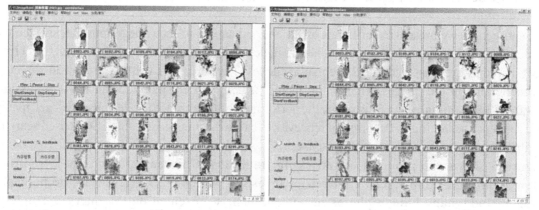

d) The results after 3ʳᵈ feedback round   e) The results after 4ᵗʰ feedback round

retrieval precision is very bad, we can get a exciting result precision after a few cycles feedback because our method integrates the visual features and semantics information.

Figure 7. The precision curves of k-NN image retrieval

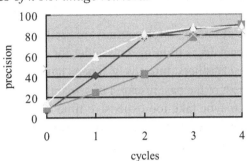

CONCLUSION AND DISCUSSION

In this chapter, we proposed a semantics supervised cluster based framework of organization and retrieval to integrate the advantages of both semantic classes and perceptive features. We analyzed the relation of semantic class and perceptive feature distribution of data set and then we modeled the relation with the GMM. We developed the SSCI-based approximate searching technique. The data set is divided into many clusters, in which the objects are similar on perceptive feature and relevant on semantics. We performed experiments to evaluate our proposed approach. Such methodology only accessing original feature vectors within the candidate clusters fastens the search procedure, and improves the retrieval precision about semantics. Meanwhile, to offset the insufficient of the feedback examples marked by users, the whole index cluster is marked as a feedback example if one object of it is marked. The query semantic space can be estimated by the semantic classes of the positive and negative index clusters because each index cluster belongs to a certain semantic class. So, the relevance feedback rises to the semantics level. Thanks to integrating the perceptive features and the semantics, the proposed method can optimize the semantic precision with a few cycles feedbacks.

Our approach can be extended to a progressive retrieval algorithm. If the index entries are created for the interim clusters, the index structure is a hierarchical tree. During query process, a user is allowed to progressively explore the results with increasing accuracy on traveling the index tree from root to leaf and from high to low probability cluster nodes.

The future work also includes finding hidden semantics corresponding to the interim clusters. For example, a cluster including objects of "football" and "grassland" possibly means "green field". This should be helpful to bridge the semantic classes and perceptive features.

FUTURE RESEARCH DIRECTIONS

Over the past decade, ambitious attempts have been made to make machines learn to understand, index and annotate images representing a wide range of concepts, with much progress. However, the CBIR is not used widely in practice because of several difficulties . To make CBIR a real-world technology, the following directions would be focused in the near future.

Large Scale Semantic Concepts Learning

It goes without saying that users of image search engines are used to express their query intention with semantic concepts. A usual framework is training a classifier for every concept on training set then labeling unsettled images with the classifiers. Intuitively, it need hundreds of concepts to labeling images in a practical application. But most of the past research of semantic learning are worked on a restricted concept set and the algorithms maybe take too expensive time or worst precision when training and labeling large scale semantic concepts. It is exigent to develop technologies of large scale semantic concepts learning. In addition to improve the efficiency and effectiveness of the existing algorithm, new framework considering concept relationship such as hierarchical, consistent and concurrent relation would be a promise solution.

Human-Computer Interactive Semantic Labeling

We must admit that machines cannot substitute human in image understanding for a long time. Image segmentation and object recognition would be longstanding difficult tasks. So manual labeling is unavoidable in practical applications. However there is not enough regard to research and develop efficient technology of human-computer interactive labeling. The more work should be done for technologies of human centered computer aided semantic labeling.

Human Cognition-Based Learning

Computers have excelled human beings in multiple sides such as computing and storing but computers are far weaker than children in sense of perception and cognition. It appears that perception and cognition are performed with different way from computing that the current computers work with. Discovering and utilizing the cognition mechanism of the human beings would be long-term promising research direction. Directly for image understanding and object recognition, the attention and feature binding etc. principles would inspire us innovative learning strategies.

ACKNOWLEDGMENT

This work is supported by the National Science Foundation of China (No. 60435010), 863 National High-Tech Program (No.2006AA01Z128), National Basic Research Priorities Programme (No. 2007CB311004).

REFERENCES

Chen, Y., & Wong, E. K. (2001). A knowledge-based approach to video content classification. *Proceedings of SPIE, 4315: Storage and Retrieval for Media Databases*, 292-300.

Cox, I. J., Miller, M. L., & Minda, T. P., et al. (2000). The Bayesian image retrieval system, PicHunter: theory, implementation, and psychophysical experiments. *IEEE Transactions on Image Proceeding, Special Issue on Image and Video Proceeding for Digital Libraries*, 9(1), 20–37.

Ferhatosmanoglu, H., Tuncel E., Agrawal D., & Abbadi A. E. (2006). High dimensional nearest neighbor searching. *Information Systems Journal, 31*(6), 512-540.

Ferhatosmanoglu, H., Tuncel, E., Agrawal, D., & Abbadi, A. E. (2000). Vector approximation based indexing for non-uniform high dimensional data sets. In *Proceedings of the 9th ACM Int. Conf. on Information and Knowledge Management*, (pp. 202–209). ACM, SIGIR, and SIGMIS.

Fischer, S., Lienhart, R., & Effelsberg, W. (1995). Automatic recognition of film genres. *Proc. ACM Multimedia 95, 295*-304. San Francisco, CA.

Ishikawa, Y., Subramanya, R., & Faloustos, C. (1998). MindReader: Query database through multiple examples. *Proceedings of the 24th international conference on very large data bases* (pp.218–227). San Fransisco.

Kanth, K. V. R., Agrawal, D., & Singh, A. (1998). Dimensionality reduction for similarity searching in dynamic databases. In Ashutosh Tiwary (Ed.), *Proceeding of ACM SIGMOD ICMD*, (pp. 166–176). ACM, New York, NY.

Liang, S., & Sun, Z. X. (2006). BSVM-based relevance feedback for sketch retrieval. *Journal of Computer-Aided Design & Computer Graphics, 18*(11), 1753-1757, (in Chinese).

Meilhac, C., & Nastar, C. (1999). Relevance feedback and category search in image databases. *Proceedings of the IEEE International Conference on Multimedia Computing and System* (pp. 512–517) Florence, Italy.

Mittal, A., & Cheong, L. F. (2004). Addressing the problems of Bayesian network classification of video using high-dimensional features. *IEEE Trans. On Knowledge and Data Engineering, 16*(2), 230–244.

Rui, Y., & Huang, T. S. (2000). Optimizing learning in image retrieval. *Proc. of IEEE Int. Conf. On Computer Vision and Pattern Recognition* (pp. 236–243) Hilton Head, SC.

Rui, Y., & Huang, T. S. (1998). Relevance feedback: A power tool for interactive content-based image retrieval. *IEEE Transactions on Circuits and System for Video Technology, Special Issue on Segmentation, Description, and Retrieval of Video Content, 8*(5), 644-655.

Shi, Z. P., Li, Q. Y., Shi, Z. Z., & Duan C. L. (2005). Texture spectrum descriptor based image retrieval. *Journal of Software, 16*(6), 1039-1045, (In Chinese).

Smeulders, A., Santini, S., Gupta, A., & Jain, R. (2002). Content-based image retrieval at the end of the early years, *IEEE Transactions on Pattern Analysis and Machine Intelligence, 22*(12), 1349-1379.

Su, Z., Zhang, H. J., & Ma, S. P. (2002). An image retrieval relevance feedback algorithm-based on the Bayesian classifier. *Journal of Software. 13*(10), 2001-2006, (in Chinese).

Weber, R., Schek, H., & Blott, S. (1998). A quantitative analysis and performance study for similarity-search methods in high-dimensional spaces. In Morgan Kaufmann (Ed.), *Proceeding of ACM VLDB'98*, (pp. 194-205). ACM. San Francisco, CA.

Weber, R., & Bohm, K. (2000). Trading quality for time with nearest-neighbor search. *Proceedings of the 7th International Conference on Extending Database Technology* (pp. 21–35) Konstanz, Germany.

Wu, H., Lu, H. Q., & Ma, S. D. (2005). A survey of relevance feedback techniques in content-based image retrieval. *Chinese Journal of Computers*, *28*(12), 1969-1979, (In Chinsese).

Ye, H. J., & Xu, G. Y. (2003). Fast search in large-scale image database using vector quantization. In *Proceedings of International Conference on Image and Video Retrieval, Lecture Notes in Computer Science, 2728*, 458–467. Berlin / Heidelberg: Springer.

ADDITIONAL READING

Weber, R., Schek, H., & Blott, S. (1998). A quantitative analysis and performance study for similarity-search methods in high-dimensional spaces. *Proceeding of ACM VLDB'98*, (pp. 194-205).

Ye, H. J., & Xu, G. Y. (2003). Fast search in large-scale image database using vector quantization. *International Conference on Image and Video Retrieval, Lecture Notes in Computer Science, 2728*, Springer, (pp. 458–467).

Ferhatosmanoglu, H., Tuncel E., Agrawal D., & Abbadi A. E. (2006). High dimensional nearest neighbor searching. *Information Systems Journal, 31(6)*, 512-540.

Lew, M. S., Sebe, N., & Djeraba, C., et al. (2006). Content-based multimedia information retrieval: State of the art and challenges. *ACM Transactions on Multimedia Computing, Communications and Applications*, *2*(1), 1-19.

Li, Q., Shi, Z., & Shi Z. (2007). Linguistic expression-based image description framework and its application to image retrieval. In Nachtegael, M., Van der Weken, D., Kerre, E. E., & Philips, W. (Eds.). Chapter 4 of *Soft Computing in Image Processing - Recent Advances Series: Studies in Fuzziness and Soft Computing*, 210, 97-120.

Carson, C., Belongie, S., & Greenspan H, et al. (2002). Blobworld: Image segmentation using expectation-maximization and its application to image querying. *IEEE Transactions on Pattern Analysis and Machine Intelligence*, *24*(8), 1026-1038.

Zhu, M., & Badii, A. (2007). Semantic-associative visual content labeling and retrieval: A multimodal approach. *Signal Processing: Image Communication*, *22*(6), 569-582.

Lu, Y., Hu, C., & Zhu, X., et al. (2000). A unified framework of semantics and feature-based relevance feedback in image retrieval systems. *Proceedings of 8th ACM International Multimedia Conference*, (pp. 31-37), Los Angeles.

Li, Q., Hu, H., & Shi, Z. (2004). Semantic feature extraction using genetic programming in image retrieval. *Proceedings of 17th International Conference on Pattern Recognition (ICPR'04)*, Beijing, (pp. 648-651).

Vailaya, A., Figueiredo, M., & Jain, A., et al. (2001). Image classification for content-based indexing. *IEEE Transactions on Image Processing*, *10*(1), 117-130.

Li, Y., & Shapiro, L. G. (2002). Consistent line clusters for building recognition in CBIR. *Proceedings of 16th IEEE International Conference on Pattern Recognition (ICPR'02)*, 952-956.

Li, J., & Wang, J. Z. (2003). Automatic linguistic indexing of pictures by a statistical modeling approach. *IEEE Transactions on Pattern Analysis and Machine Intelligence, 25*(9), 1075-1088.

Wang, J. Z., Li, J., & Wiederhold, G. (2001). SIMPLIcity: Semantics-sensitive integrated matching for picture libraries. *IEEE Transactions on Pattern Analysis and Machine Intelligence, 23*(9), 947-963.

Li, J., & Wang, J. Z. (2006). Real-time computerized annotation of pictures. *Proceedings of 14th annual ACM International Conference on Multimedia.* Santa Barbara, (pp. 911-920).

Vasconcelos, N. (2004). Minimum probability of error image retrieval. *IEEE Transactions on Signal Processing, 52*(8), 2322-2336.

Carneiro, G., Chan, A. B., & Moreno, P. J., et al. (2007). Supervised learning of semantic classes for image annotation and retrieval. *IEEE Transactions on Pattern Analysis and Machine Intelligence, 29*(3), 394-410.

Rasiwasia, N., Moreno, P. J., & Vasconcelos, N. (2007). Bridging the gap: Query by semantic example. *IEEE Transactions on Multimedia, 9*(5), 923-938.

Srihari, R. K., & Zhang, Z. (2000). Show&Tell: A semi-automated image annotation system. *IEEE Multimedia, 7*(3), 61-71.

Barnard, K., Duygulu, P., & Forsyth, D., et al. (2003). Matching words and pictures. *Journal of Machine Learning Research, 3*, 1107-1135.

Barnard, K., & Forsyth, D. (2001). Learning the semantics of words and pictures. *Proceedings of 8th IEEE International Conference on Computer Vision (ICCV'01)*, Vancouver, (pp. 408-415).

Duygulu, P., Barnard, K., & Freitas, N., et al. (2002). Object recognition as machine translation: Learning a lexicon for a fixed image vocabulary. *Proceedings of 7th European Conference on Computer Vision*, (pp. 97-112).

Jin, Y., Khan, L., & Wang, L., et al. (2005). Image annotations by combining multiple evidence and WordNet. *Proceedings of 13th annual ACM international conference on Multimedia*, Hilton, (pp. 706-715).

Blei, D. M., & Jordan, M. I. (2003). Modeling annotated data. *Proceedings of 26th annual international ACM SIGIR conference on Research and development in information retrieval*, Toronto, (pp. 127-134).

He, X., King, O., & Ma, W. Y., et al. (2003). Learning a semantic space from user's relevance feedback for image retrieval. *IEEE Transactions on Circuits and systems for video technology, 13*(1), 39-48.

Zhou, X. S., & Huang, T. S. (2002). Unifying keywords and visual contents in image retrieval. *IEEE Multimedia, 9*(2), 23-33.

Jing, F., Li, M., & Zhang, H., et al. (2005). A unified framework for image retrieval using keyword and visual features. *IEEE Transactions on Image Processing, 14*(7), 979-989.

Djordjevic, D., & Izquierdo, E. (2007). An object- and user-driven system for semantic-based image annotation and retrieval. *IEEE Transaction on Circuits and Systems for Video Technology, 17*(3), 313-323.

Sun, H., Li, S., & Li, W., et al. (2005). Semantic-based retrieval of remote sensing images in a grid environment. *IEEE Geoscience and remote sensing letters, 2*(4), 440-444.

Tang, H. L., Hanka, R., & Ip, H. H. S. (2003). Histological image retrieval based on semantic content analysis. *IEEE Transactions on Information Technology in Biomedicine, 7*(1), 26-36.

Mojsilovic, A., & Rogowitz, B. E. (2004). Semantic metric for image library exploration. *IEEE Transactions on Multimedia, 6*(6), 828-838.

Chapter XIV
Content–Based Retrieval for Mammograms

Chia-Hung Wei
Ching Yun University, Taiwan

Chang-Tsun Li
University of Warwick, UK

Yue Li
University of Warwick, UK

ABSTRACT

As distributed mammogram databases at hospitals and breast screening centers are connected together through PACS, a mammogram retrieval system is needed to help medical professionals locate the mammograms they want to aid in medical diagnosis. This chapter presents a complete content-based mammogram retrieval system, seeking images that are pathologically similar to a given example. In the mammogram retrieval system, the pathological characteristics that have been defined in Breast Imaging Reporting and Data System (BI-RADS™) are used as criteria to measure the similarity of the mammograms. A detailed description of those mammographic features is provided in this chapter. Since the user's subjective perception should be taken into account in the image retrieval task, a relevance feedback function is also developed to learn individual users' knowledge to improve the system performance.

1. INTRODUCTION

In hospitals and medical institutes, a large number of medical images are being produced in ever increasing quantities and used for diagnostics and therapy. The need for effective methods to manage and retrieve those image resources has been actively pursued in the medical community. The design of Picture Archiving and Communication Systems (PACS) is to integrate imaging modalities and interfaces with hospital and departmental information systems in order to manage the storage and distribution of images to radiologists, physicians, specialists, clinics, and imaging centers (Huang, 2003). A crucial requirement in PACS is to provide an efficient search function to access desired images. Image search in the digital imaging and communication in medicine (DICOM) protocol of PACS is currently carried out according to the alphanumerical order of the textual attributes of images (Lehmann et al., 2003). However, the information which users are interested in is the visual content of medical images rather than that residing in alphanumerical format. Traditional search requires images to be annotated with text, allowing the images to be accessed by text-based retrieval. As the size of the medical image database grows, it becomes impractical to manually annotate all contents and attributes of the images. The content of images is an informative and direct query which can be used to search for other images containing similar content. As content-based access approaches are expected to have a great impact on PACS and health database management, content-based image retrieval has been proposed for inclusion in PACS (Lehmann et al., 2003). In a PACS environment, a content-based image search system can support the usual comparisons made on images by physicians, answering similarity queries over the images stored in the distributed databases (Muller et al., 2004). The importance of searching for similar images comes from the fact that physicians usually try to recall similar cases by seeking images that are pathologically similar to a given image (Traina et al., 2005). As medical images are digitally represented in a multitude of formats based on their modality and the scanning device used, image retrieval systems have to be developed for their specific image types. Although content-based image retrieval has frequently been proposed for use in medical image management, only a few content-based retrieval systems have been developed specifically for medical images. These research-oriented systems are usually constructed in research institutes and continue to be improved, developed, and evaluated over time. Those systems include ASSERT for High-Resolution Computed Tomography (HRCT) of lungs (Shyu et al., 1999), CasImage for a variety of images from CT, MRI, and radiographs, to color photos (Muller et al., 2004), IRMA for various imaging modalities (Lehmann et al., 2004), and NHANES II for cervical and lumbar spine X-ray images (Antani et al., 2004).

Breast cancer is the most common cancer among women and affects approximately one million women worldwide. In the UK, for example, breast cancer accounts for 30 per cent of all female cancers and approximately 1 in 9 women in the UK will suffer from breast cancer sometime during their life (Beaver & Witham, 2007). Mammography has been a reliable method for the detection of breast cancer (Highnam & Brady, 1999) and women are usually asked to take mammograms regularly, and as a result many digital mammograms are produced in hospitals and breast screening centers. As distributed mammogram databases at hospitals and breast screening centers connect together through PACS, a mammogram retrieval system is needed to help medical professionals locate the mammograms they want in aid of medical diagnosis and case-based reasoning (Wei et al., 2006), thereby reducing false positives and false negatives in medical screening.

The main purpose of this chapter is to disseminate the knowledge of the content-based retrieval approach to mammogram database indexing and to attract greater interest from various research communities to rapidly advance research in medical image retrieval. The rest of the chapter is organized as follows: The second section reviews the background information and addresses the challenges of content-based mammogram retrieval. The third section presents the proposed framework for content-based mammogram retrieval. The fourth section provides more details on feature extraction methods for mass and calcification presentation. The fifth section discusses potential research issues in the future research agenda. The last section concludes this chapter.

2. BACKGROUND IN MAMMOGRAM RETRIEVAL

Mammographic feature extraction plays the most important role in developing a content-based mammogram system because its effectiveness directly determines the system performance. Due to the nature of mammograms, mammographic feature extraction is faced with low resolution and strong noise. In addition, mammograms are represented in gray level rather than color. As a result, a feature extraction method should be robust enough against low resolution and strong noise, and performed in monochrome mammograms. As the presence of masses and calcifications is often associated with a high probability of malignancy, subtle distinctions of those two signs should be included into mammographic descriptors of the retrieval system. According to Breast Imaging Reporting and Data System (BI-RADS™), masses are characterized based on shape, margin and density while calcifications are described by type and distribution. The definitions of those pathological characteristics are extracted from BI-RADS™ and listed in Table 1.

One of the most important issues in developing a mammogram retrieval system is that those extracted features have to be discriminative enough to represent different kinds of pathological characteristics. A significant amount of research work has concentrated on analysis of mammographic masses and calcifications. The rest of this section presents a brief review of the related studies for analysis of mammographic masses and calcifications.

Table 1. The classification of masses and calcification in BI-RADS (Source from BI-RADS™)

MASS	CALCIFICATION
SHAPE • **Round:** Spherical, ball-shaped, circular or globular. • **Oval:** Elliptical or egg-shaped. • **Lobular:** Contours with undulations. • **Irregular:** Cannot be characterized by any of the above.	**TYPE** (excludes typically benign) • **Punctate:** Round or oval, less than 0.5 mm with well defined margins. • **Amorphous:** Often round or "flake" shaped calcifications that are sufficiently small or hazy in appearance. • **Pleomorphic:** These are usually more conspicuous than the amorhic forms and are neither typically benign nor typically malignant irregular calcifications with varying sizes and shapes that are usually less than 0.5 mm in diameter.
MARGIN • **Circumscribed (Well-Defined or Sharply- Defined) Margins:** Sharply demarcated with an abrupt transition between the lesion and the surrounding tissue. • **Microlobulated Margins:** Undulate with short cycles producing small undulations. • **Obscured Margins:** Hidden by superimposed or adjacent normal tissue and cannot be assessed any further. • **Indistinct (Ill-Defined) Margins:** There may be infiltration by the lesion and this is not likely due to superimposed normal breast tissue. • **Spiculated Margins:** Characterized by lines radiating from the margins of a mass.	• **Round_and_Regular:** They are usually considered benign and when small (under 1 mm), they frequently are formed in the acini of lobules. • **Lucent_Center:** These are benign calcifications that range from under 1 mm to over a centimeter or more. These deposits have smooth surfaces, are round or oval, and have a lucent center. The "wall" that is created is thicker than the "rim or eggshell" type of calcifications. • **Fine_Linear_Branching:** These are thin, irregular calcifications that appear linear, but are discontinous and under 0.5mm in width.
DENSITY • **High Density:** Clearly higher than surrounding, suspicious. • **Equal (isodense) Density:** Density not appreciably different, neutral significance. • **Low Density:** Density lower, but not fat containing, neutral significance. • **Fat-Containing:** This includes all lesions containing fat such as oil cyst, lipoma, galactocele, hamartoma or fibrolipoma.	**DISTRIBUTION** • **Clustered:** Multiple calcifications occupy a small volume (less than 2 cc) of tissue. • **Linear:** Arrayed in a line that may have branch points. • **Segmental:** Deposits in a duct and its branches raising the possibility of multifocal breast cancer in a lobe or segment of the breast. • **Regional:** Calcifications scattered in a large volume of breast tissue. • **Diffuse (Scattered):** Calcifications are distributed randomly throughout the breast.

Székely et al. (2006) presented a procedure for the detection of masses in mammograms. The procedure included locating regions of interest, extracting potential lesions, and calculating features by using texture features, decision trees, and a multiresolution Markov random field model. Varela et al. (2007) studied the use of the iris filter output, gray-level pixel value, texture, contour-related, and morphological features to detect malignant masses. Yang et al. (2005) developed a method for mass detection and classification of suspicious regions using a probabilistic neural network with entropic thresholding techniques and extracting mass features of circularity, contrast, radial angle, and full width at half maximum. A local adaptive thresholding technique was also proposed for the detection of mammographic masses by Kom et al. (2007). Ozekes et al. (2005) used a mass template to determine whether masses exist in a mammogram. Varela et al. (2006) proposed a method for classifying benign and malignant masses. In this method, mammographic mass lesions were characterized by outer, border, and interior features of masses, and a neural network classifier was subsequently used to discriminate benign and malignant masses. Fauci et al. (2005) developed a method for mass detection by searching for local maxima of the pixel grey level intensity. Hejazi and Ho (2005) described a scheme for classification of mammographic tumors based on a series of classifiers of area, shape, edge distance variation, and the spread pattern. Retico et al. (2006a) reported on the use of 16 features to discriminate malignant lesions from benign massive lesions. Rangaraj et al. (2006) defined a turning angle function for capturing the characteristics of mass shape. Machine learning techniques such as genetic programming and inductive machine learning were applied for the detection and classification of malignant lesions by Panourgian et al. (2006). Alto et al. (2005) investigated the suitability of the objective measures of shape, edge sharpness, and texture for retrieving similar mass images.

Since the presence of microcalcifications has been considered as a crucial indicator for breast diagnosis, much research has been conducted for developing reliable methods for the accurate identification of microcalcifications. To detect clustered microcalcifications, Arodz et al. (2006) filter the mammogram with a filter that is sensitive to microcalcification contrast shape, and enhance the contrast by using wavelet-based sharpening algorithm. A support vector machines (SVM) method is used to detect microcalcification clusters by El-Naqa et al. (2004). The features they used include cross sectional area, compactness, eccentricity, density, scatteredness, solidity, invariant moment, moment signature, and normalized Fourier descriptor. Peng et al. (2006) incorporate a knowledge-discovery mechanism in the genetic algorithm for detecting microclacifications. Nine features are designed to characterize a bright spot in terms of its shape and texture. Linguraru et al. (2006) developed a method for microcalcification detection based on a biologically inspired adaptive model of contrast detection. An important improvement is that their algorithm can automatically estimate the parameter values from the image. As the spatial distribution and the shape of the microcalcifications have a significant impact in medical practice, Bocchi & Nori (2007) used Radon transform to develop a set of features, thereby evaluating the morphology of calcified spots. In addition, Nakayama et al. (2006) and Retico et al. (2006b) developed a computer-aided detection scheme for microcalcification cluster identification. The reader is referred to Rangayyan et al (2007), and Sampat et al (2005) for the earlier studies on the pattern recognition techniques of breast cancer

In addition to mammographic feature extraction, another crucial issue is that the development of an image retrieval system has to take human factors into account. Among human factors, subjective perception is one of the most challenging issues. An image is a symbolic presentation; people interpret an image and associate semantics with it based on their subjective perceptions, which involves the user's knowledge, cultural background, personal feelings and so on (Jaimes, 2006a). An important assumption in image retrieval is that "*each user's information need is different and time varying* (Zhou & Huang, 2003)". This assumption indicates that humans exhibiting subjective perceptions when interpreting images can be classified as different information seekers or same information seekers (Jaimes, 2006b). Different information seekers normally have different interpretations for the same image based on their individual perceptions. As a result, when different information seekers provide the same query example, they will have different satisfactory degrees for the same search results; even same information seekers have different subjective perceptions as time evolves.

To compensate for the vagueness of subjective human perceptions, image retrieval systems must be able to interactive with users and discover the current user's information needs. Due to the vagueness of subjective human perceptions, a retrieval system cannot adopt a fixed clustering structure to deal with the problem. An interactive search paradigm that has been developed for image retrieval is machine learning with a user-in-the-loop, i.e. in the search process users will be required to interact with the system in an iterative loop. The interactive search process is guided by relevance feedbacks, which refers to the notion of relevance of the individual images based on the current user's subjective judgment. Relevance feedback serves as an information carrier to convey the user's information needs to the retrieval system. For a given query, the retrieval system returns initial results based on predefined criteria. Then, the user is required to identify the positive and/or negative examples by labeling those which are relevant and/or irrelevant) to the query. A retrieval system can employ this relevance information to construct a better sketch and use it to provide better results to the user (Ortega-Binderberger & Mehrotra, 2003). Relevance feedback plays a more vital role in image-based search than in text-based search. This is because the features derived from images are more complex than the keywords used for text-based searches. As a result, in image-based search users cannot easily modify the features of the query example whereas in text-based search users can directly modify their query formulation, thereby making relevance feedback an indispensable function in image retrieval.

One of the important issues concerns approaches to learning relevance feedback, i.e. when relevance feedback is submitted to the system, how the retrieval system can realize the user's information need by analyzing the relevance feedback and connect the user's information need with low-level features in order to improve the search results. Three relevance feedback approaches are query point movement, re-weighting, and classification. The query point movement approach assumes that there exists at least one image which completely conveys the intentions of the user, and its high-level concept has been modeled in low-level feature space (Rui et al., 1998). The query point movement approach involves moving the point of the query toward the region of the feature space that contains the ideal image; since each image is represented by an n dimensional feature vector, the feature vector can be regarded as a point in an n dimensional space. The idea of the re-weighting approach is to adjust the weights assigned to each feature or modify the similarity measure used (Rui & Huang, 1999), i.e. give important features larger weights, and less important features smaller weights. Since images with similar features are located together in the feature space, images can be classified into different categories based on their features. The classification approach involves using feedback information to classify the whole set of images (Gondra et al., 2004). Those that belong to a given class can be considered as similar images.

3. OVERVIEW OF THE MAMMOGRAM RETRIEVAL FRAMEWORK

The proposed system framework as shown in Figure 1(a) can be divided into off-line feature extraction and on-line image retrieval. In off-line feature extraction, the contents of the mammograms in the database are pre-processed and described with a feature vector (Figure 1(b)). The feature vectors of the images constitute a feature dataset stored in the database. In on-line image retrieval, the user can submit a query example to the retrieval system to search for desired mammograms. Since the proposed mammogram retrieval system is designed for specific users—medical professionals, who are experts on mammography, the system predetermines the feature sets and asks its users to specify the pathology

Figure 1. a) The framework for mammogram retrieval; b) The feature extraction process; c) The predetermined feature sets; d) The learning approach to relevance feedback.

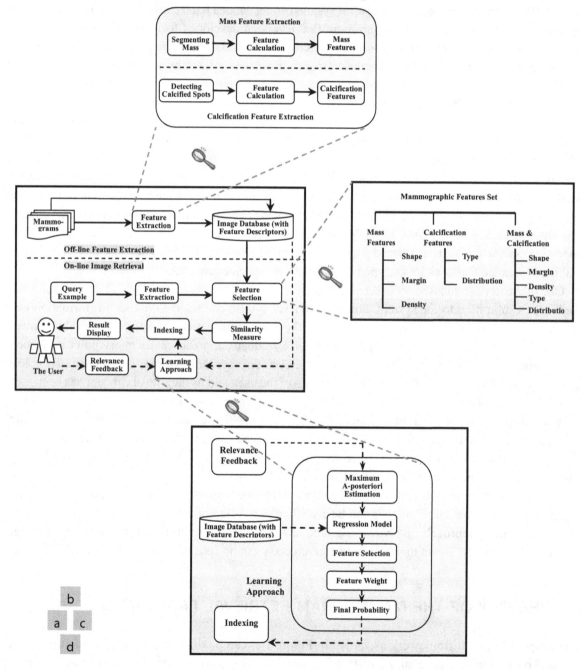

contained in the example mammogram, including "mass", "calcification", or "mass & calcification". The user's specification helps the system link and measure the most appropriate feature set shown in Figure 1(c). The similarities between the feature vector of the query example and those of the mammograms in the feature dataset are computed. Retrieval is conducted by applying an indexing scheme to provide an efficient way of searching the image database. Finally, the system ranks the similarities and returns the images that are most similar to the query example. This is called the initial search stage for a given query. If the user is not satisfied with the initial search results, the user can conduct a relevance feedback stage (Figure 1(d)). The user provides relevance feedback to the retrieval system in order to search further (following the dashed arrows in Figure 1(a)). Two of the most important issues are mammographic feature extraction and relevance feedback, which will be discussed in Section 4 and 5 in details.

4. MAMMOGRAPHIC FEATURE EXTRACTION

Mammogram representation needs to consider which pathological characteristics are most meaningful when medical professionals observe a mammogram, and which approaches can effectively encode the attributes of the images. This section will discuss how to characterize mass and calcification.

REPRESENTATION OF MASS

A mass is characterized by three characteristics: shape, margin, and density. To facilitate the development of feature extraction methods, pictorial representation of those pathological characteristics based on their definitions in BI-RADS™ is illustrated in Figure 2.

Figure 2. Characteristic spectra of mammographic masses based on the definitions of BI-RADS™

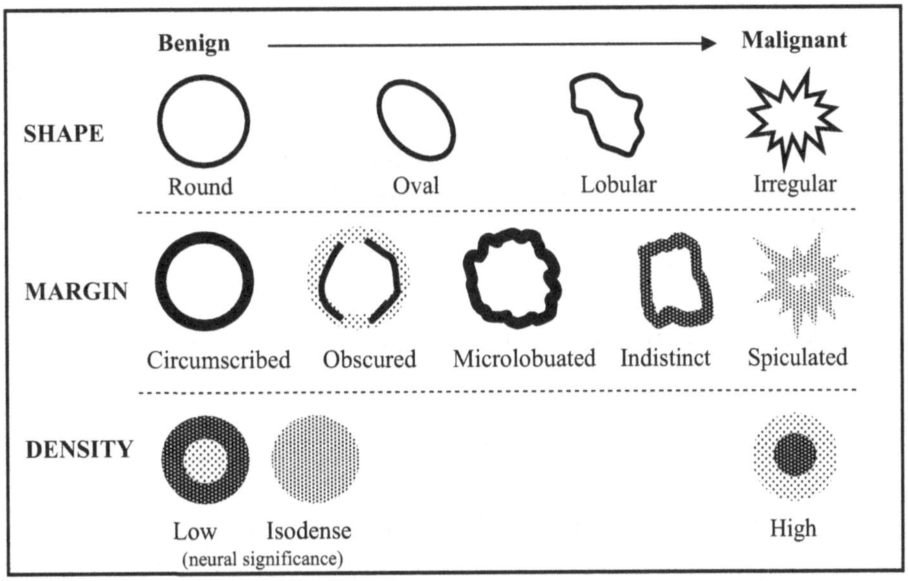

Shape Feature

In this study, the use of the Zernike moments for describing shape is motivated by the following properties: 1) The Zernike basis function satisfies the orthogonal property (Wee & Paramesran, 2007; Papakostas et al., 2007), implying that the contribution of each moment coefficient to the underlying image is unique and independent, i.e. no redundant information overlap between the moments; 2) The Zernike polynomials are usually expressed in terms of the polar coordinates in the pupil, which is defined with respect to the eye in the same way as in the conventional optometric notation for cylindrical corrections. Coefficients of the Zernike polynomials present the peculiarity of the individual eye (Charman, 2005); 3) Calculation of the Zernike moments do not require knowledge of the precise boundary of an object, making Zernike moments suitable for representing complex objects with obscure boundaries, such as mammographic masses.

The Zernike moments are derived from a set of complex polynomials orthogonal over the interior of a unit circle $U : x^2 + y^2 \leq 1$ and defined in the polar coordinates. The form of 2-dimensional Zernike polynomial V_{nm} is expressed as

$$V_{nm}(\rho, \theta) = R_{nm}(\rho)exp(jm\,\theta) \tag{1}$$

where n and m are called order and repetition, respectively. The order n is a non-negative integer, and the repetition m is an integer satisfying $n - |m| =$ an even number and $|m| \leq n$. j is an imaginary unit $\sqrt{-1}$. $R_{nm}(\rho)$ is the 1-dimensional radial polynomial, which is defined as

$$R_{nm}(\rho) = \sum_{S=0}^{\frac{(n-|m|)}{2}} (-1)^S \frac{(n-S)!}{S!\left(\frac{n+|m|}{2} - S\right)!\left(\frac{n-|m|}{2} - S\right)!} \rho^{n-2S} \tag{2}$$

As the Zernike moments are the projection of the image $I_0 = f(x, y)$ onto these orthogonal basis functions, the image I_0 can be decomposed into a weighted sum of the Zernike polynomials

$$f = \sum_{n=1}^{\infty} \sum_{m=-n}^{n} A_{nm} V_{nm} \tag{3}$$

where A_{nm} are the Zernike moments, which are the coefficients of the Zernike polynomials. The Zernike moments of a continuous image $f(x, y)$ are calculated according to the following equation

$$A_{nm} = \frac{n+1}{\pi} \iint_U f(x, y) V_{nm}(\rho, \theta) dx dy \tag{4}$$

For a digital image, the discrete form of the Zernike moments for an image is expressed as follows:

$$A_{nm} = \frac{n+1}{\lambda} \sum_{x=0}^{N-1} \sum_{y=0}^{N-1} f(x, y) V_{nm}(\rho, \theta) \tag{5}$$

where $\lambda = \delta A / \pi$ is a normalizing constant. δA is the elemental area of the square image when projected onto the unit circle of Zernike polynomials. A list of selected Zernike polynomials and their physical meanings relative to primary aberrations are shown in Table 2.

Table 2. provides a list of Zernike polynomials up to 4th order and their physical meanings relative to primary aberrations

j	n	m	Zernike Polynomial	Physical Meaning
0	0	0	1	Piston: constant term
1	1	-1	$2\rho\sin\theta$	Distortion: tilt in x direction
2	1	1	$2\rho\cos\theta$	Distortion: tilt in y direction
3	2	-2	$\sqrt{6}\rho^2\sin2\theta$	Astigmatism with axis at $\pm 45°$
4	2	0	$\sqrt{3}(2\rho^2-1)$	Spherical defocus: field curvature
5	2	2	$\sqrt{6}\rho^2\cos2\theta$	Astigmatism with axis at $0°$or $90°$
6	3	-3	$\sqrt{8}\rho^3\sin3\theta$	Triangular astigmatism, based on x-axis (Trefoil)
7	3	-1	$\sqrt{8}(3\rho^3-2\rho)\sin\theta$	Primary coma along x axis
8	3	1	$\sqrt{8}(3\rho^3-2\rho)\cos\theta$	Primary coma along y axis
9	3	3	$\sqrt{8}\rho^3\cos3\theta$	Triangular astigmatism, based on y-axis (Trefoil)
10	4	-4	$\sqrt{10}\rho^4\sin4\theta$	Quatrefoil
11	4	-2	$\sqrt{10}(4\rho^4-3\rho^2)\sin2\theta$	5th order astigmatism
12	4	0	$\sqrt{5}(6\rho^4-6\rho^2+1)$	Spherical
13	4	2	$\sqrt{10}(4\rho^4-3\rho^2)\cos2\theta$	5th order astigmatism
14	4	4	$\sqrt{10}\rho^4\cos4\theta$	Quatrefoil

As the Zernike basis functions take the unit disk as their domain, the disk must be specified before any moments are calculated. At the first step the mass is segmented and projected onto a unit circle of fixed radius. This step makes the resulting moments invariant to translation and scale, in addition to the rotation-invariance possessed by Zernike polynomials. Since the method of the Zernike moments expands an image into a series of orthogonal basis, the accuracy of shape representation depends on the number of moments used from the expansion. To human eyes, the coefficients of the orders higher than the 5th or 6th order are too small to be measurable reliably so high-order coefficients can always be ignored (Charman, 2005). For this consideration, we compute the first 4th-order Zernike moments so as to yield the most effective and reliable measurement.

Margin Feature

In a mass, margin is defined as the edge or transition between a mass and surrounding normal fatty tissue. The importance of margin analysis lies in the tendency of invasive cancer to infiltrate adjacent tissue, which results in an indistinct or frankly spiculated appearance (BI_RADS, 1998). As the development of a margin affects the shape of the mass, the similarity comparison between masses should take both shape and margin into account, rather than comparing the margin type alone. As a result, a sharpness degree for the margin is required to fully characterize a mass.

Once the margin of a segmented mass has been detected by Sobel operators, the variation of gray scale can be obtained to measure its sharpness degree, which is used as a margin feature to describe marginal characteristics. The steps of the proposed method are illustrated in Figure 3 and summarized as follows:

Step 1: Find the change of gray level with Sobel operators.

Step 2: Extract the outer ring and inner ring.

Step 3: Calculate the variation degrees *VD* of the inner and outer rings according to

$$VD = \frac{area}{the\ number\ of\ light\ pixels}.$$

Step 4: Calculate the sharpness degree *SD* according to $SD = \frac{variation\ of\ outer\ ring}{variation\ of\ inner\ ring}.$

Density Feature

The density, degree of X-ray attenuation, is defined relative to the expected attenuation of an equal volume of normal glandular tissue of the breast because most breast cancers that develop a mass appear to have attenuation equal to or greater than the surrounding fibroglandular tissue (BI_RADS, 1998). The method of calculating the density degree is similar to that of the sharpness degree mentioned in the previous section. For density feature, we divide a mass into two regions, outer and inner regions, and compare the brightness variation between these two regions, thereby finding the variation from the mass center to margins. Figure 4 shows that outer and inner regions are divided from a mass, where the

Figure 3. a) A mammographic mass; b) Change of gray level found in (a); c) A shrunken shape is obtained to produce outer ring; d) An outer ring is obtained; e) A shrunken shape is obtained to produce inner ring; f) An inner ring is obtained

a b c d e f

Figure 4. a) A high-density mass; b) The outer region of (a); c) The inner region of (a)

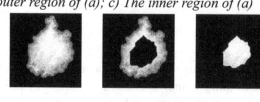

a b c

minor axis of the inner region is approximately half minor axis of the outer region. The density degree DD can be calculated according to $DD = \dfrac{\text{brightness of inner region}}{\text{brightness of outer region}}$.

REPRESENTATION OF CALCIFICATION

The contrast between the areas of calcifications and their backgrounds is usually limited and, depending on the imaging equipments and the image capturing conditions, the dynamic range of gray scale of mammograms may vary significantly. To compensate these issues, we first perform histogram equalization on all the mammograms. This pre-processing not only enhances the contrast but also normalize the gray scale of all the mammograms to the same dynamic range 0 to 255, smoothing way for feature extraction.

It is observed that calcifications usually appear as spots which are the brightest areas when compared to the other breast tissues. Three spot detectors, D_1-D_3 as shown in Figure 5, are applied to detect calcified spots of different sizes. To avoid picking up noise and misleading information in the detection process, *a priori* knowledge that calcified spots are usually brighter than the backgrounds is introduced to form the threshold T for considering the brightness variation in individual mammograms. The threshold T is defined as

$$T = \alpha \cdot \mu + (1-\alpha) \cdot M \qquad (6)$$

where μ and M are the mean and maximal gray scales of the mammogram and α determines where between the mean and maximum the threshold T should lie. If α is set to 0.5, this will take the average of the mean and maximum as the threshold. The spot detectors will skip those pixels with their gray scale lower than the threshold T by setting their corresponding responses to 0. Denoting the (i,j)th pixel of a mammogram g as $g(i,j)$, the response $r(i,j)$ of $g(i,j)$ to the kth spot detector D_k can be defined as

$$r(i,j) = \begin{cases} 0 & , \text{if } g(i,j) < T \\ \sum_{x=1}^{X_k} \sum_{y=1}^{Y_k} D_k(x,y) \cdot g(i+x, j+y) & , \text{if } g(i,j) \geq T \end{cases} \qquad (7)$$

where X_k and Y_k are the numbers of rows and columns of spot detector D_k. The strength of the response at each pixel is taken as the degree of calcification at that pixel. The effect of the thresholding is clearly shown in Figure 6. Figure 6(a) is a mammogram before pre-processing (i.e., histogram equalization). Figure 6(b) shows the response map of the pre-processed mammogram to the spot detector D_1 without thresholding while Figure 6(c) illustrates the response map of the mammogram with thresholding. By comparing Figure 6(b) and (c), it can be seen that most of the non-useful information has been filtered out by the thresholding operation.

Once calcified spots have been detected, the resulting output can be used to calculate its calcification features using Equation (8) – (19). Utilization of these features is based on BI-RADS□ definitions mentioned in Table 1.

Figure 5. a) Detector D1; b) Detector D2; c) Detector D3;

-1	-1	-1
-1	8	-1
-1	-1	-1

-1	-1	-1	-1
-1	3	3	-1
-1	3	3	-1
-1	-1	-1	-1

-1	-1	-1	-1	-1
-1	1	2	1	-1
-1	2	4	2	-1
-1	1	2	1	-1
-1	-1	-1	-1	-1

Figure 6. a): The original image; b): Response map resulted from convolving D1 with the histogram equalized mammogram without thresholding; c): Response map resulted from convolving D1 with the histogram equalized mammogram with thresholding.

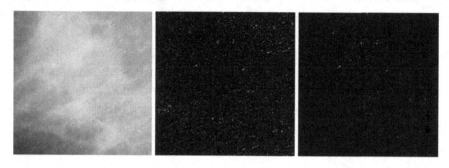

Number of spots = the number of calcification spots detected   (8)

Size = size of each calcification spot   (9)

$$\text{Margin} = \frac{\text{average gray value in contour}}{\text{gray value inside contour}}$$ (10)

$$\text{Contrast} = \frac{\text{average gray value of calcification spots}}{\text{average gray value of an overall mammogram}}$$ (11)

Calcification area = minimum area of covering all calcification spots   (12)

$$\text{Eccentricity} = \frac{\text{major axis of a minimum oval}}{\text{minor axis of a minimum oval}}$$ (13)

$$\text{Compactness} = \frac{\pi \cdot (\text{perimeter of calcification area})^2}{4 \cdot \text{calcification area}}$$ (14)

$$\text{Calcification density} = \frac{\text{number of calcification spots}}{\text{area}}$$ (15)

Mean of scatterness = the mean distance between neighboring calcification spots   (16)

Standard deviation of scatterness =
standard deviation of the distance between neighboring calcification spots   (17)

$$\text{Solidity} = \frac{\text{calcification area}}{\text{area of convex hull formed by calcification spots}} \qquad (18)$$

$$\text{Shape} = \text{Zernike moments of the calcification area} \qquad (19)$$

5. RELEVANCE FEEDBACK

The use of logistic regression (see Figure 7) is motivated by the following factors: 1) The range of the logistic function $f(z)$ can be directly mapped to a probability space within the range [0, 1]. As the logistic function $f(z)$ provides estimates that must lie in the range between zero and one, the estimates present the relevance to the query example in the application of image retrieval; 2) the shape of the logistic function $f(z)$: As the variable z is viewed as representing an index that combines the contributions of several features extracted from images, $f(z)$ represents the relevance for a given value of z. The s-shape of $f(z)$ indicates that the relevance of z on a candidate image is minimal for low z's until some critical point is reached. The relevance then rises rapidly over a certain range of intermediate z values, and then remains high around 1 once z becomes large enough. Hence, the s-shape model can be applied for considering multiple features of an image retrieval question.

The main steps of the proposed approach are described as follows:

Step 1: Collects relevance feedback as the training data for developing a logistic regression model.
Step 2: Apply the iteratively re-weighted least squares (IRLS) algorithm to estimate the parameters of the regression curve.
Step 3: Fit all database images into the regression model.
Step 4: Use goodness-of-fit statistics to select discriminating features.
Step 5: Determine the weights of the discriminating features based on the individual contributions of the features to the maximum likelihood.
Step 6: Estimate the probability of the relevant-class membership of each image from the logistic regression model

Details of logistic regression, the maximum *a-posteriori* parameter estimate, feature selection, and feature weighting are presented in the following subsections.

Figure 7. A logistic curve.

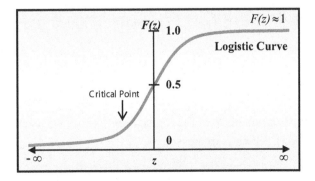

5.1. Logistic Regression

Logistic regression is a mathematical modeling approach that can be used to describe the relationship of real-valued independent variables to a dichotomously dependent variable (Kleinbaum, 2002). Suppose the label y of an image can take one of two possible values 0 and 1. $y = 1$ if the image is relevant to the query example; otherwise $y = 0$. As $y = f(z) = \dfrac{1}{1+e^{-z}}$ is introduced as a logistic regression function, the *a posteriori* probability of the class membership can be estimated. As exemplified in Figure 7, the logistic regression forms an s-shaped curve in which $f(z)$ approaches 1 as $z \rightarrow \infty$, or 0 as $z \rightarrow -\infty$. Let $x = (x_1, x_2,...,x_k)^T$ be the feature descriptor of an image. The input variable z of the logistic regression function is calculated using the linear function of x, $z = \beta_0 + \beta_1 x_1 + \beta_2 x_2 + ... + \beta_k x_k$, where $\beta = (\beta_0, \beta_1,..., \beta_k)$ represents the weight vector. Since the output variable y only takes on values $\in \{0, 1\}$ for the retrieval result, the expectation value of the logistic function can be used to represent $E(y \mid x)$. The conditional probability of the label y given the feature vector x is expressed as

$$P(y=1 \mid x, \beta) = \mu(x \mid \beta) = \frac{e^{\beta x}}{1+e^{\beta x}} = \frac{1}{1+e^{-\beta x}} = \frac{1}{1+e^{-z}}. \tag{20}$$

The set of adjustable parameters β of the regression curve is the key to the development of the regression model. The maximum *a posteriori* parameter estimate can be obtained by several algorithms, such as iteratively re-weighted least squares (IRLS), Newton's method, and Fixed-Hessian Newton method (Minka, 2003).

In our system, relevant images from each round have to be identified as relevance feedback which will be accumulated throughout the whole session. Therefore, the more relevance feedback rounds the user performs, the more feedback information the system will obtain, and the better the results that are expected.

5.2. Maximum A-Posteriori Estimation

The iteratively re-weighted least squares (IRLS) algorithm is applied to solve a least squares problem in order to estimate the maximum *a-posteriori* parameters. Suppose a logistic regression model is fit to a set of n samples $X = (x^1, x^2,..., x^n)^T$ and $Y = (y^1, y^2,..., y^n)^T$ where x^i and y^i represents a set of features and the label of the ith image, respectively. As these n samples are randomly drawn from a binomial distribution, the conditional likelihood of a single observation can be expressed as

$$P(y^i \mid x^i, \beta) = \mu(x^i \mid \beta)^{y^i} (1 - \mu(x^i \mid \beta))^{1-y^i} \tag{21}$$

The conditional log-likelihood is

$$l(\beta \mid X, Y) = \sum_{i=1}^{n} (y^i \log \mu(x^i \mid \beta) + (1 - y^i) \log(1 - \mu(x^i \mid \beta)) \tag{22}$$

To obtain the optimal parameter β of the logistic regression, we use the Newton-Raphson algorithm (Komarek & Moor, 2005), which is expressed as.

$$\beta_{t+1} = \beta_t - H^{-1} \nabla_\beta l(\beta_t \mid X, Y) \tag{23}$$

where $\nabla_\beta l(\beta_t \mid X, Y)$ represents the vector of partial derivatives of the log-likelihood equation, and $H_{ij} = \dfrac{\partial^2 l(\beta_t \mid X, Y)}{\partial \beta_i \beta_j}$ represents the Hessian matrix of second order derivatives. Then, Fisher's scoring method is applied to find the solution to the conditional log-likelihood equation. Taking the second derivative of the likelihood score equations gives us

$$\frac{\partial^2 l(\beta \mid X, Y)}{\partial \beta \beta^T} = -\sum_{i=1}^{n} x^i (x^i)^T \mu(x^i \mid \beta)(1 - \mu(x_i \mid \beta)). \tag{24}$$

Since the Newton-Raphson algorithm can be expressed as an equation group of x^i in the form of Equation (24), the coefficient group of Equation (24) is an $n \times n$ diagonal matrix, which is expressed as

$$W = \begin{bmatrix} \mu(x_1 \mid \beta)(1 - \mu(x_1 \mid \beta)) & 0 & \cdots & 0 \\ 0 & \mu(x_2 \mid \beta)(1 - \mu(x_2 \mid \beta)) & & 0 \\ \vdots & & \ddots & \vdots \\ 0 & 0 & \cdots & \mu(x_n \mid \beta)(1 - \mu(x_n \mid \beta)) \end{bmatrix} \tag{25}$$

Let $P = (\mu(x^1 \mid \beta) \, \mu(x^2 \mid \beta), ..., \mu(x^n \mid \beta)$ be the corresponding vector of the fitted probability of X. The gradient of the log likelihood can be expressed in a matrix form as

$$\frac{\partial l(\beta \mid X, Y)}{\partial \beta} = \sum_{i=1}^{n} x^i (y^i - \mu(x^i \mid \beta)) = X^T (Y - P). \tag{26}$$

The Hessian matrix can be expressed as

$$\frac{\partial l(\beta \mid X, Y)}{\partial \beta_i \beta_i} = -X^T W X \tag{27}$$

The Newton-Raphson algorithm then becomes

$$\beta^{new} = \beta^{old} + (X^T W X)^{-1} X^T (Y - P) = (X^T W X)^{-1} X^T W (X \beta^{old} + W^{-1}(Y - P)) \tag{28}$$

5.3. Feature Selection and Feature Weights

Since a typical CBIR system only requires the user to submit images as query examples, no assumptions are made with regard to the characteristics of the content. To look for images with various characteristics, the system has to extract as many low-level features as possible from the images in the databases. Although discriminating features may be extracted, more redundant features may simultaneously undermine the retrieval performance if they are included into feature descriptor set for further similarity measurement. This study proposes a feature selection process that automatically selects a subset of discriminating features at the relevance feedback stage. As the whole set of database images is fitted to the regression model and the value of the maximum likelihood is estimated, this system can perform null hypothesis testing using a measure of the goodness-of-fit. The measure of the goodness-of-fit, also called a likelihood ratio test (Montgomery et al., 2004), compares a relatively more complex model, called complete model *c*, to a simpler model, called reduced model *r*, in order to assess whether the simpler model fits the dataset significantly better. The likelihood ratio test begins with a measure of deviance between the complete model that contains all the features, and the reduced model that is the same as the complete one except that the observed features are not included. The statistical deviance is defined as −2 times the log-likelihood. The difference *D* in the deviance between the two nested models can be compared to a chi-square distribution (Montgomery et al., 2004). Hence, as the *i*th feature D_i is observed, it can be express as

$$D_i = -2(logL_c - logL_r)$$
(29)

where L_c and L_r represent the maximum log-likelihood for the complete model and the reduced model, respectively. To assess the importance of a specific feature x_i, the remaining features are used to account for it and the observed feature x_i is removed from the complete model to obtain the reduced model. The system automatically assesses the contribution from each discriminating feature and then determines the individual weighting based on the contribution. If feature x_i is assessed to have significant contributions on the maximum likelihood score, the weight w_i is computed via an exponential function

$$w_i = e^{-D_i}.$$
(30)

Therefore, the original value of feature x_i is substituted for the new value computed by $w_i \times x_i$. At the interactive search process, the logistic regression can provide each image of the database with the probability of membership of the relevant-image class.

6. EXPERIMENTS

6.1. Ground Truth of Data Set

The data set consists of 2,563 mammograms from the DDSM, including 1,919 mass mammograms and 644 calcification mammograms. The ground truth of the data set following the BI-RADS specification has been tabulated in Table 3 and Table 4 in terms of lesion types, mass characteristics, and calcification characteristics. To make the relevance judgment consistent, this study evaluates the similarity according to the ground truth of the DDSM mammogram databases, identified by experienced radiologists. The ground truth of the DDSM mammogram dataset indicates mass shape and margin characteristics for each mass mammogram, and calcification type and distribution characteristics for each calcification mammogram.

6.2. Relevance Judgment and Measure

Since masses and calcifications are both characterized by two pathological characteristics, respectively, this study uses three similarity levels to describe the degree of similarity of these cases. The proposed

Table 3. Ground truth of the mass mammograms used for performance evaluation

Shape	Margin	Number	Percentage	Abbreviation
Irregular	Ill Defined	265	13.81%	irr-ill
Lobulated	Circumscribed	178	9.28%	lob-cir
Oval	Obscured	152	7.92%	ova-obs
Oval	Circumscribed	134	6.98%	
Lobulated	Obscured	105	5.47%	
Oval	Ill Defined	102	5.32%	
Lobulated	Ill Defined	91	4.74%	
Round	Circumscribed	59	3.07%	rou-cir
Lobulated	Microlobulated	56	2.92%	
Round	Obscured	42	2.19%	
Oval	Microlobulated	33	1.72%	
Round	Ill Defined	33	1.72%	
Irregular	Obscured	25	1.30%	
Oval	Spiculated	25	1.30%	
Miscellaneous		619	32.26%	
Total		1919	100.00%	

Table 4. Ground truth of the calcification mammograms used for performance evaluation

Type	Distribution	Number	Percentage	Abbreviation
Pleomorphic	Clustered	255	39.60%	ple-clu
Pleomorphic	Segmental	92	14.29%	ple-seg
Pleomorphic	Linear	55	8.54%	ple-lin
Amorphous	Clustered	39	6.06%	amo-clu
Punctate	Clustered	28	4.35%	pun-clu
Fine Linear Branching	Linear	27	4.19%	fin-lin
Fine Linear Branching	Clustered	25	3.88%	
Pleomorphic	Regional	19	2.95%	
Fine Linear Branching	Segmental	16	2.48%	
Amorphous	Segmental	10	1.55%	
Miscellaneous		78	12.11%	
Total		644	100.00%	

criteria for performance evaluation are listed in Table 5. For example, suppose the retrieved image matches one of two pathological characteristics, the image is given a score of 0.5. If the retrieved image fully matches all characteristics, it is given a score of 1.

The precision-recall (P-R) graph is commonly used for evaluating the performance of CBIR systems. In P-R graphs, the x-axis and y-axis represent recall and precision rates respectively. Precision is the ratio of the number of relevant images retrieved to the total number images retrieved, while recall is the ratio of the number of relevant images retrieved to the total number relevant images stored in the database. The formulae for precision P and recall R are expressed, respectively, as follow:

$$P = \frac{\sum_{i=1}^{n} s_i}{A+C} \tag{31}$$

where, s_i is the score assigned to the i-th retrieved image, and $A + C$ is the number of top n images retrieved.

$$R = \frac{\sum_{i=1}^{n} s_i}{A+B} \tag{32}$$

where $A + B$ is the total number of relevant images stored in the data set. The two measurements can objectively evaluate the system performance.

6.3. Evaluation Procedure

The evaluation of the proposed mammogram retrieval system is conducted in the query-by-example (QBE) only mode and the QBE plus relevance feedback learning (QBE + RF) mode, respectively. In the QBE mode, a query image is submitted to seek images similar to the query example, while in a relevance feedback (RF) learning mode, relevance feedback is provided to refine the search results by applying the logistic regression function. The detailed evaluation procedure is described as follows: When the user provides a query image to perform QBE retrieval, the system returns the initial retrieval results for the query. Subsequently, the user provides relevance feedback to the retrieval system so it can apply the relevance feedback learning function, which, in this system, is the logistic regression function, as proposed in Section 5. Finally, the system returns the refined search results after performing relevance feedback learning.

For each query image presented to the system, the system returns ten pages of hits with descending similarity rankings, each page containing nine mammograms (i.e. $A + C$ in Equation (31) equals 90). This allows the performance of the system to be evaluated in a page-wise manner. However in order to obtain a more objective picture of the system's performance, instead of plotting the precision-recall graph for each individual query image, the average performance of the system is plotted after 15 query

Table 5. Criteria of relevance judgement of performance evaluation of CBIR

Score	Criteria
1.0	The retrieved image matches all of the pathological characteristics of query example.
0.5	The retrieved image matches only one pathological characteristic, appeared in query example.
0	The retrieved image does not match any pathological characteristic of the query example.

images of the same class have been presented to the system. In a precision-recall graph, the first point, the leftmost point in a curve, represents the average precision rate and the average recall rate for the first result page (i.e. the first 9 returned images). The second point explains the precision and recall for the first page plus the second one (i.e. the first 18 returned images). Therefore, the tenth point takes into account the precision and recall of the first 10 pages, where a total of 90 images have been examined. A precision-recall graph with a higher initial value that tails off more quickly indicates that the corresponding algorithm performs relatively better.

6.4. Performance Evaluation

The proposed system was tested and evaluated for image retrieval and relevance feedback learning under various pathological characteristics. The evaluation results for mass lesions and calcification lesions are presented in Sections 6.4.1 and 6.4.2, respectively.

6.4.1 Evaluation of Mass Similarities

Shape and margin characteristics are both taken into consideration in this evaluation, where the similarity is given a score of 1 only when the two features are both matched and the similarity for those images with a partial match is give a score of 0.5. The number of image in each class used in this evaluation can be seen in Table 3. In the evaluation, four mass lesion classes are, namely the "irregular shape and ill-defined mass (irr-ill)", "lobulated shape and circumscribed margin (lob-cir)", "oval shape and obscured margin (ova-obs)", and "round shape and circumscribed margin (rou-cir)" classes, which have been described in Table 3. Figure 8 shows the precision rates of the rou-cir (Figure 8(a)), ova-obs (Figure 8(b)), and irr-ill (Figure 8(d)) classes can be greatly increased with relevance feedback learning, especially in the first few pages. Though the RF curve of the lob-cir class (Figure 8(c)) is significantly improved in the first three pages, it can only have better performance than QBE curve for the first 5 pages where the feedback images have highly homogeneous characteristics in common, making the system narrow down its target images. Because it contains only 59 images, the rou-cir class significantly increases its recall rates when compared with the other three classes with larger numbers of image. From the evaluation results, we find that the mass mammograms with irregular shape and ill-defined margin achieve the best. It can also be seen that feedback learning can rapidly increase the precision rates, especially for the first few points of the P-R curves.

6.4.2 Evaluation of Calcification Similarities

The calcification lesion classes selected to evaluate their performance include pleo-morphic type and clustered distribution (ple-clu), pleomorphic type and segmental distri-bution (ple-seg), pleomorphic type and linear distribution (ple-lin), amorphous type and clustered distribution (amo-clu), punctate and clustered distribution (pun-clu), and fine linear branching linear (fin-lin). The detailed information about the four classes has been indicated in Table 4.

Two pathological characteristics, calcification type and distribution, are both taken into consideration in this evaluation. The evaluation results in our pilot experiments indicate that the pleomorphic class and clustered class perform best in type and distribution evaluations, respectively. These classes related to pleomorphic type or clustered distribution may display better performance. This explains the

Figure 8. Evaluation of two mass characteristics based on the following classes. (a) rou-cir for round shape and circumscribed margin; (b) ova-obs for oval round and obscured margin; (c) lob-cir for lobulated shape and circumscribed margin; (d) irr-ill for irregular shape and ill-defined margin

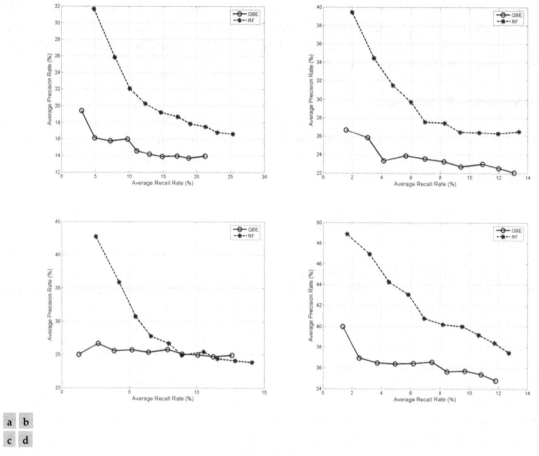

results in Figure 9, where the fin-lin class obtains poorer precision in QBE than other classes that are related to either pleomorphic type or clustered. The evaluation results indicate that, when the system is used to locate a single calcification characteristic, or both characteristics in calcification mammograms, querying the calcification mammograms with the pleomorphic type or clustered distribution can obtain better precision, when compared with other characteristics in QBE and RF.

7. FUTURE RESEARCH ISSUES

Although content-based image retrieval has made reasonable progress in recent years, many research issues regarding mammograms retrieval remain open and require further efforts to be made. This section addresses some of the issues on the future research agenda.

Figure 9. Evaluation of two calcification characteristic based on the following classes. (a) amo-clu for amorphous type and cluster distribution; (b) fin-lin for fine linear branch type and linear distribution; (c) ple-clu for pleomorphic type and cluster distribution; (d) ple-lin for pleomorphic type and linear distribution; (e) ple-seg for pleomorphic type and segmental distribution; (f) pun-clu for punctate type and cluster distribution

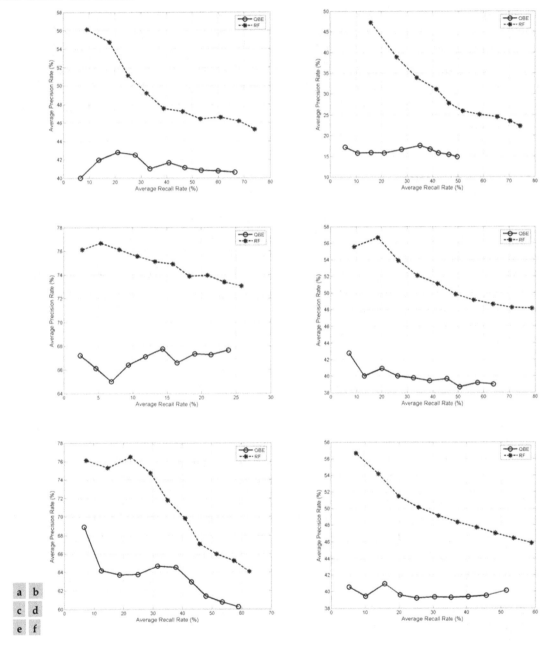

RECOGNITION OF ALL MAMMOGRAPHIC PATHOLOGY

It is desirable that a mammogram retrieval system is able to effectively recognize any pathological characteristics in support of medical professionals' information needs. In addition to two of the most important signs—masses and malignant calcifications, architectural distortion, typically benign calcifications, and special cases should also be included in the descriptor of mammograms. To represent those pathological characteristics, mammographic image processing techniques need to be developed for them, such as detection, segmentation, and feature extraction methods. However, another issue may be raised as if a retrieval system collects too many features, this may distort its similarity measure and diminish the retrieval precision. Therefore, a mechanism for measuring individual features may be needed in order to maximize the effectiveness of those features extracted for representation of pathological characteristics.

LONG-TERM LEARNING

Long-term learning involves a user's memory and target search (i.e. looking for a specific image). The user's information need, deduced from the user's relevance feedback in an earlier query session, is used to improve the retrieval performance of later searches. Since information is not accumulated for use in different sessions, even if the user searches for a specific image they reviewed before, they still have to go through the same relevance feedback process to find that image. Therefore, a long-term learning algorithm is required in order to accumulate the user's search information and utilize it to shorten the retrieval time and the relevance feedback process during future query sessions.

HUMAN-CENTERED COMPUTING

Since the ultimate aim of image retrieval systems is to satisfy the user's information need, computing and computational artifacts relating to the user's condition should be taken into account. For instance, most users have limited patience and are reluctant to provide too mcuh feedback in the interactive search process. Human factors and interface design should be investigated to improve the effectiveness of human-computer interaction. How to encourage the user to provide more feedback, or what multimodel can be added to the interactive search process are potential factors to the success of interactive search. In addition to the retrieval effectiveness, the usability of the human-computer interaction should be evaluated for the retrieval system. Usability attributes evaluated for the user interface include efficiency, memorability, errors and satisfaction.

8. CONCLUSION

The contribution of this chapter is two-fold: Firstly, a complete content-based mammogram retrieval system has been realized, which makes maximal utilization of PACS's medical image resource possible and achieves the aim of developing PACS. With the development of this mammogram retrieval system, we expect to attract more attention from various research communities to devote more efforts to other kinds of medical images. Secondly, this chapter not only applies image processing techniques for mammogram representation, but also presents a machine learning method for solving the problem of subjective perception from different users.

REFERENCES

Alto, H., Rangayyan, R. M., & Desautels, J. E. L. (2005). Content-based retrieval and analysis of mammographic masses. *Journal of Electronic Imaging, 14*(2), 1-17.

Antani, S., Lee, D. J., Long, L. R., & Thoma, G. R. (2004). Evaluation of shape similarity measurement methods for spine X-ray images. *Journal of Visual Communication and Image Representation, 15*(3), 285-302.

Arodz, T., Kurdziel, M., Popiela, T. J., Sevre, R. O. D., & Yuen, D. A. (2006). Detection of clustered microcalcifications in small field digital mammography, *Computer Methods and Programs in Biomedicine, 81*(1), 56-65.

Beaver, K., & Witham, G. (2007). Information needs of the informal carers of women treated for breast cancer. *European Journal of Oncology Nursing, 11*(1), 16-25.

BI-RADS, Breast Imaging Reporting and Data System. (1998). 3rd edition. American College of Radology, Reston, VA, USA.

Bocchi, L., & Nori, J. (2007). Shape analysis of microcalcifications using Radon transform. *Medical Engineering & Physics, 29*(6), 691-698.

Charman, W. N. (2005). Wavefront technology: Past, present, and future. *Contact Lens and Anterior Eye, 28*(2), 75-92.

El-Naqa, I., Yang, Y., Galatsanos, N. P., Nishikawa, R. M., & Wernick, M. N. (2004). A similarity learning approach to content-based image retrieval: Application to digital mammography. *IEEE Transactions on Medical Imaging, 23*(10), 1233-1244.

Fauci, F., Raso, G., Magro, R., Forni, G., Lauria, A., Bagnasco, S., Cerello, P., Cheran, S. C., Lopez Torres, E., Bellotti, R., De Carlo, F., Gargano, G., Tangaro, S., De Mitri, I., De Nunzio, G., & Cataldo, R. (2005). A massive lesion detection algorithm in mammography. *Physica Medica, 21*(1), 23-30.

Gondra, I., Heisterkamp, D. R., & Peng, J. (2004). Improving image retrieval performance by inter-query learning with one-class support vector machines. *Neural Computing & Applications, 13*(2), 130-139.

Hejazi, M. R., & Ho, Y. S. (2005). Automated detection of tumors in mammograms using two segments for classification. In *Proceedings of the 6th Pacific-Rim Conference on Multimedia, 1(3767),* 910-921. New York: Springer.

Highnam, R., & Brady, M. (1999). *Mammographic Image Analysis*, London: Kluwer Academic Publishers.

Huang, H. K. (2003). PACS, image management, and imaging informatics. In D. Feng, W. C. Siu, & H. J. Zhang (Eds.), *Multimedia information retrieval and management: Technological fundamentals and applications* (pp.347-365). New York: Springer.

Jaimes, A. (2006a). Human-centered multimedia: Culture, deployment, and access. *IEEE Multimedia Magazine, 13*(1), 12-19.

Jaimes, A. (2006b). Human factors in automatic image retrieval system design and evaluation. In *Proceedings of IS&T/SPIE Internet Imaging 2006*, San Jose, CA, 2006.

Kleinbaum, D. G. (2002). *Logistic regression.* New York: Springer-Verlag.

Kom, G., Tiedeu, A., & Kom, M. (2007). Automated detection of masses in mammograms by local adaptive thresholding. *Computers in Biology and Medicine, 37*(1), 37-48.

Komarek, P., & Moor, A. W. (2005). Making logistic regression a core data mining tool with TR-IRLS. In *Proceedings of the Fifth IEEE International Conference on Data Mining* (pp. 685-688). IEEE Press.

Lehmann, T. M., Guld, M. O., Keysers, D, Deselaers, T., Schubert, H., Wein B. B., & Spitzer, K. (2004). Similarity of medical images computed from global feature vectors for content-based retrieval. *Lecture Notes in Artificial Intelligence*, 989-995.

Lehmann, T.M., Wein, B.B., & Greenspan, H. (2003). Integration of content-based image retrieval to picture archiving and communication systems. In *Proceedings of Medical Informatics Europe.* IOS Press.

Linguraru, M. G., Marias, K., English, R., & Brady, M. (2006). A biologically inspired algorithm for microcalcification cluster detection. *Medical Image Analysis, 10*(6), 850-862.

Minka, T. (2003). *A comparison of numerical optimizers for logistic regression* (Tech. Rep. No. 758). USA: Carnegie Mellon University, Department of Statistics.

Montgomery, D. C., Runger, G.C., Hubele, N.F. (2004). *Engineering statistics.* New York: John Wiley & Sons.

Muller, H., Michous, N., Bandon, D., & Geissbuhler, A. (2004). A review of content-based image retrieval systems in medical applications—Clinical benefits and future directions. *International Journal of Medical Informatics, 73*(1), 1-23.

Muller, H., Rosset, A., Vallee, J.-P., & Geissbuhler, A. (2004). Comparing features sets for content-based image retrieval in a medical-case database. In *Proceedings of IS&T/SPIE Medical Imaging 2004: PACS and Imaging Informatics* (pp. 99-109).

Nakayama, R., Uchiyama, Y., Yamamoto, K., & Watanabe, R., & Namba, K. (2006). Computer-aided diagnosis scheme using a filter bank for detection of microcalcification clusters in mammograms. *IEEE Transactions on Biomedical Engineering, 53*(2), 273-283.

Ortega-Binderberger, M., & Mehrotra, S. (2003). Relevance feedback in multimedia databases, In B. Furht & O. Marquez (Eds.), *Handbook of video databases: design and applications*, (pp. 511-536), New York: CRC Press.

Ozekes, S., Osman, O., & Camurcu, A. Y. (2005). Mammographic mass detection using a mass template. *Korean Journal of Radiology, 6*(4), 221-228.

Panourgias, E., Tsakonas, A., Dounias, G., & Panagi, G. (2006). Computational intelligence for the detection and classification of malignant lesions in screening mammography. *Oncology Reports, 15*, 1037-1041.

Peng, Y., Yao, B., & Jiang, J. (2006). Knowledge-discovery incorporated evolutionary search for micro-calcification detection in breast cancer diagnosis. *Artificial Intelligence in Medicine, 37*(1), 43-53.

Rangayyan, R. M., Ayres, F. J. & Leo Desautels, J. E. (2007). A review of computer-aided diagnosis of breast cancer: Toward the detection of subtle signs. *Journal of the Franklin Institute, 344*(3-4), 312-348.

Retico, A., Delogu, P., Fantacci, M. E., & Kasae, P. (2006a). An automatic system to discriminate malignant from benign massive lesions on mammograms. *Nuclear Instruments and Methods in Physics Research Section A: Accelerators, Spectrometers, Detectors and Associated Equipment, 569*(2), 596-600.

Retico, A., Delogu, P., Fantacci, M. E., Martinez, A. P., Stefanini, A., & Tata, A. (2006b). A scalable computer-aided detection system for microcalcification cluster identification in a pan-European distributed database of mammograms. *Nuclear Instruments and Methods in Physics Research A: Accelerators, Spectrometers, Detectors and Associated Equipment, 569*(2), 601-605.

Rui, Y. & Huang, T. (1999). A novel relevance feedback technique in image retrieval. In *Proceedings of the Seventh ACM International Conference on Multimedia, 2*, 67-70. New York: ACM Press.

Rui, Y., Huang, T. S., & Mehrotra, S. (1998). Human perception subjectivity and relevance feedback in multimedia information retrieval. In *Proceedings of IS&T/SPIE Storage and Retrieval of Image and Video Databas*e, 6, 25-36.

Sampat, M. P., Markey, M. K., and Bovik, A. C. (2005). Computer-aided detection and diagnosis in mammography. In Bovik, A.C. (Ed): *Handbook of Image and Video Processing*, Elsevier Academic Press: London, UK, pp. 1195–1217.

Shyu, C., Brodley, C., Kak, A., Kosaka, A., Aisen, A., & Broderick, L. (1999). ASSERT: A physician-in-the-loop content-based image retrieval system for HRCT image databases. *Computer Vision and Image Understanding, 75*(1/2), 111-132.

Székely, N., Tóth, N., & Pataki, B. (2006). A hybrid system for detecting masses in mammographic images. *IEEE Transactions on Instrumentation and Measurement, 55*(3), 944-952.

Traina Jr., C., Traina, A. J. M., Araujo, M. R. B., Bueno, J. M., Chino, F. J. T., Razente, H., & Azevedo-Marques, P. M. (2005). Using an image-extended relational database to support content-based image retrieval in a PACS. *Computer Methods and Programs in Biomedicine, 80*(1), S71-S83.

Varela, C., Timp, S., & Karssemeijer, N. (2006). Use of border information in the classification of mammographic masses. *Physics in Medicine and Biology, 51*(2), 425-441.

Wee, C.-Y., & Paramesran, R. (2007). On the computational aspects of Zernike moments. *Image and Vision Computing, 25*(6), 967-980.

Wei, C.-H., Li, C.-T., & Wilson, R. (2006). A content-based approach to medical image database retrieval. In: Z. M. Ma (Ed): *Database Modeling for Industrial Data Management*, (pp. 258–291), Hershey, PA: Idea Group Publishing.

Yang, S.-C., Wang, C.-M., Chung, Y.-N., Hsu, G.-C., Lee, S.-K., Chung, P.-C., & Chang, C.-I, (2005). A computer-aided system for mass detection and classification in digitized mammograms. *Biomedical Engineering-Applications, Basis & Communications, 17*(5), 215-228.

Zhou, X. S., & Huang, T. S. (2003). Relevance feedback in image retrieval: A comprehensive review. *ACM Multimedia System Journal, 8*(6), 536-544.

ADDITIONAL READING

Astley, S. M., &Gilbert, F. J. (2004). Computer-aided detection in mammography. *Clinical Radiology, 59*(5), 390-399.

Ayres, F. J., & Rangayyan, R. M. (2005). Characterization of architectural distortion in mammograms. *IEEE Engineering in Medicine and Biology Magazine, 24*(1), 59–67.

Baker, J. A., Rosen, E. L., Lo, J.Y., Gimenez, E.I., Walsh, R., & Soo, M. S. (2003). Computer-aided detection (CAD) in screening mammography: Sensitivity of commercial CAD systems for detecting architectural distortion. *American Journal of Roentgenology, 181*(4), 1083–1088.

Cady, B., & Chung, M. (2005). Mammographic screening: No longer controversial. *American Journal of Clinical Oncology: Cancer Clinical Trials, 28*(1), 1-4.

Cheng, H. D., Cai, X., Chen, X., Hu, L., & Lou, X. (2003). Computer-aided detection and classification of microcalcifications in mammograms: A survey. *Pattern Recognition, 36*(12), 2967–2991.

Ciatto, S., Turco, M. R. D., Burke, P., Visioli, C., Paci, E., & Zappa, M. (2003). Comparison of standard and double reading and computer-aided detection (CAD) of interval cancers at prior negative screening mammograms: blind review. *British Journal of Cancer, 89*(9), 1645–1649.

Freer, T. W., & Ulissey, M. J. (2001). Screening mammography with computer-aided detection: Prospective study of 12,860 patients in a community breast center. *Radiology, 220*(3), 781–786.

James, .J. (2004). The current status of digital mammography. *Clinical Radiology, 59*(1), 1–10.

Li, L., Clark, R. A., & Thomas, J. A. (2002). Computer-aided diagnosis of masses with full-field digital mammography. *Academic Radiology, 9*(1), 4–12.

Mavroforakis, M. E., Georgiou, H. V., Dimitropoulos, N., Cavouras, D., & Theodoridis, S. (2006). Mammographic masses characterization based on localized texture and dataset fractal analysis using linear, neural and support vector machine classifiers. *Artificial Intelligence in Medicine, 37*(2), 145-162.

Pisano, E. D. (2000). Current status of full-field digital mammography. *Radiology, 214*(1), 26–28.

Rangayyan, R. M. (2005). *Biomedical Image Analysis*. Boca Raton, FL: CRC Press.

Rangayyan, R. M., & Ayres, F. J. (2006). Detection of architectural distortion in mammograms using Gabor filters and phase portraits. *Medical and Biological Engineering and Computing, 44*(10), 883–894.

Saha, P. K., Udupa, J. K., Conant, E. F., Chakraborty, D. P., & Sullivan, D. (2001). Breast tissue density quantification via digitized mammograms. *IEEE Transactions on Medical Imaging, 20*(8), 792–803.

Sivaramakrishna, R., Obuchowski, N. A., Chilcote, W.A., Cardenosa, G., & Powell, K.A. (2000). Comparing the performance of mammographic enhancement algorithms—A preference study. *American Journal of Roentgenology, 175*(1), 45–51.

Soltanian-Zadeh, H., Rafiee-Rad, F., & Pourabdollah-Nejad, S. (2004). Comparison of multiwavelet, wavelet, Haralick, and shape features for microcalcification classification in mammograms. *Pattern Recognition, 37*(**10**), 1973–1986.

Sun, Y., Suri, J., Desautels, J., & Rangayyan, R. (2006). A new approach for breast skin-line estimation in mammograms. *Pattern Analysis and Applications 9*(1), 34–47.

Tourassi, G. D., Delong, D. M., & Floyd Jr., C. E. (2006). A study on the computerized fractal analysis of architectural distortion in screening mammograms. *Physics in Medicine and Biology, 51*(5), 1299–1312.

Ursin, G., Hovanessian-Larsen, L., Parisky, Y., Pike, M. C., & Wu, A. H. (2005). Greatly increased occurrence of breast cancers in areas of mammographically dense tissue. *Breast Cancer Research, 7*(**5**), R605–R608.

Verma, B. & Zhang, P. (2007). A novel neural-genetic algorithm to find the most significant combination of features in digital mammograms. *Applied Soft Computing, 7*(2), *612-625.*

Wei, L., Yang, Y., Nishikawa, R. M., Vernick, M. N., & Edwards, A. (2005). Relevance vector machine for automatic detection of clustered microcalcifications. *IEEE Transactions on Medical Imaging, 24*(**10**), 1278–1285.

Yu, S., & Guan, L. (2000). A CAD system for the automatic detection of clustered microcalcifications in digitized mammogram films. *IEEE Transactions on Medical Imaging, 19*(**2**), 115–126.

Yu, S.-N., Li, K.-Y., & Huang, Y.-K. (2006). Detection of microcalcifications in digital mammograms using wavelet filter and Markov random field model. *Computerized Medical Imaging and Graphics, 30*(3), 163–173.

Zheng L., & Chan, A. K. (2001). An artificial intelligent algorithm for tumor detection in screening mammogram. *IEEE Transactions on Medical Imaging, 20*(7), 559–567.

Zwiggelaar, R., Astley, S. M., Boggis, C. R. M., & Taylor, C. J. (2004). Linear structures in mammographic images: detection and classification. *IEEE Transactions on Medical Imaging, 23*(9), 1077–1086.

Chapter XV
Event Detection, Query, and Retrieval for Video Surveillance

Ying-li Tian
IBM T. J. Watson Research Center, USA

Max Lu
IBM T. J. Watson Research Center, USA

Arun Hampapur
IBM T. J. Watson Research Center, USA

Andrew Senior
IBM T. J. Watson Research Center, USA

Lisa Brown
IBM T. J. Watson Research Center, USA

Chiao-fe Shu
IBM T. J. Watson Research Center, USA

Rogerio Feris
IBM T. J. Watson Research Center, USA

Yun Zhai
IBM T. J. Watson Research Center, USA

ABSTRACT

Video surveillance automation is used in two key modes: watching for known threats in real-time and searching for events of interest after the fact. Typically, real-time alerting is a localized function, for example, an airport security center receives and reacts to a "perimeter breach alert," while investigations often tend to encompass a large number of geographically distributed cameras like the London bombing, or Washington sniper incidents. Enabling effective event detection, query and retrieval of surveillance video for preemption, and investigation, involves indexing the video along multiple dimensions. This chapter presents a framework for event detection and surveillance search that includes: video parsing, indexing, query and retrieval mechanisms. It explores video parsing techniques that automatically extract index data from video indexing, which stores data in relational tables; retrieval which uses SQL queries to retrieve events of interest and the software architecture that integrates these technologies.

1. INTRODUCTION

Video analysis and video surveillance are active areas of research. The key challenges are video-based event detection and large-scale data management and retrieval. While detecting and tracking objects is a critical capability for smart surveillance, the most critical challenge in video-based surveillance (from the perspective of a human intelligence analyst) is retrieval of the analysis output to detect events of interest and identify trends. In this chapter, we describe a specific system, the IBM Smart Surveillance Solution, in order to detail an open and extensible framework for extracting events in video which can be used for real-time alerting, searching during investigations with unpredictable characteristics, or exploring normative (or anomalous) behaviors.

Current systems have begun to look into automatic event detection. These are often point solutions for detecting license plate numbers, abandoned objects, or motion in restricted locations. However, the area of context-based interpretation of the events in a monitored space is still in its infancy. Challenges here include: using knowledge of time and deployment conditions to improve video analysis, using geometric models of the environment and other object and activity models to interpret events, and using learning techniques to improve system performance and detect unusual events. The first hurdle that must be overcome is to provide extensible search capabilities based on the broadest possible set of meaningful event metadata which can be provided by state-of-the-art point solutions.

This chapter explores these issues using as an example the IBM Smart Surveillance Solution. Its architecture is outlined as an example of a system which addresses the problems of indexing event metadata and providing extensible search. Its components provide examples of video parsing, indexing and retrieval methods which are deployed by the system. Lastly, its interface shows many examples of how an end-user may search for specific information regarding a real-world investigation.

2. BACKGROUND

Video surveillance systems which run 24/7 (24 hours a day and seven days a week) create a large amount of data including videos, extracted features, alerts, statistics etc. Designing systems to manage this extensive data and make it easily accessible for query and search is a very challenging and potentially rewarding problem. However, the vast majority of research in video indexing has taken place in the field of multimedia, in particular for authored or produced video such as news or movies, and spontaneous but broadcast video such as sporting events. Efforts to apply video indexing to completely spontaneous video such as surveillance data are still emerging.

The work in video indexing of broadcast video has focused on such tasks as shot boundary detection, story segmentation and high level semantic concept extraction. The latter is based on the classification of video, audio, and text into a small (10-20) but increasing number of semantically interesting categories such as outdoor, people, building, road, vegetation, and vehicle. For broadcast video, the goal is to find a high level indexing scheme to facilitate retrieval. The task objectives are very different for surveillance video. For surveillance video, the primary interest is to learn higher level behavior patterns. In both broadcast and surveillance video, there exists a semantic gap between the feasible low level feature set and the high level semantics or ontology desired by the system users.

Because of its practical nature, surveillance video analysis has been extensively explored. However, compared to the vast amount of research in broadcast video search, such as (Hauptmann, 2006; Naphade,

2004), very few systems address the issue of search in surveillance video. Lee (2005) describes a user interface to retrieve simple surveillance events like presence of person and objects. Stringa (1998) proposed a content-based retrieval system for abandoned objects detected by a subway station surveillance system. In their system, similar abandoned objects can be retrieved using feature vectors of position, shape, compactness, etc. Berriss (2003) utilized the MPEG-7 dominant color descriptor to establish an efficient retrieval mechanism to search for the same person from surveillance systems deployed in retail stores. Meesen (2006) analyzed the instantaneous object properties in surveillance video key-frames, and performed content-based retrieval using a generic dissimilarity measure which incorporates both global and local dissimilarities between the query and target video key-frames. There is significant effort in industrial surveillance systems (ObjectVideo; PyramidVision) targeted toward real-time event detection. Very few of these systems have focused on video search. 3VR (3VR) does provide capabilities to search for a person based on face recognition. In summary, there is a very limited number of both research and commercial systems focused on searching surveillance video. As surveillance systems grow in scale and utility, there is an increasingly critical need to provide the corollary search capabilities.

While applying video analytics to provide real-time alerting based on predetermined event definitions, such as "tripwire," has been explored both in the research literature and in commercial systems, the challenges of searching through surveillance video remain largely unaddressed. While video analysis and pattern recognition technologies are at the core of "intelligent" or "smart" surveillance, effective search of surveillance video requires research into searchable meta-data representations for video based features, data models for indexing and correlating diverse types of meta-data, and architectures for integrating technologies into large scale systems.

Searching surveillance video essentially revolves around the following key search criteria: (1) Specific search for people and vehicles and (2) Generic search for objects and events of interest. Search applications require a combination of these criteria to create composite queries and the ability for the search to be applied across multiple cameras distributed over a spatial region.

In this chapter, we use the IBM Smart Surveillance System (SSS) as an example system for discussing various aspects of the technology involved in event detection, query and retrieval. The IBM Smart Surveillance Solution (SSS) is a IBM middleware offering for use in surveillance systems and provides video based behavioral analysis capabilities. It offers not only the capability to automatically monitor a scene but also the ability to manage the surveillance data, perform event based retrieval, receive real time event alerts through a standard web infrastructure and extract long term statistical patterns of activity. The IBM SSS is an open and extensible framework designed so that it can easily integrate multiple independently developed event analysis. Section 2 describes the architecture of the IBM SSS including a description of the two main components: the SSE (Smart Surveillance Engine) which takes the camera inputs and produces event metadata, and MILS (Middleware for Large Scale Surveillance) which provides data management and retrieval capabilities. Section 3 presents the underlying processes which comprise the video parsing (or analytics) performed by the SSE to create event metadata. Section 4 describes MILS in more detail including the services it provides and the data structure used. Section 5 presents the user interface of the system. Sections 6 and 7 explore the various aspects of searching for people, events and objects. Sections 8 and 9 present examples of compound queries and the concept of spatio-temporal searching. Section 10 shows some performance results for searching in the Smart Surveillance System. We conclude the chapter with a discussion of the significant research challenges that remain in enabling large scale searching of surveillance video.

3. THE IBM SSS

The IBM SSS includes two components: (1) ***Smart Surveillance Engine (SSE)*** which provides video analysis capabilities; (2) ***Middleware for Large Scale Surveillance (MILS)*** which provides data management and retrieval capabilities. These two components support the following features:

- **Local Real-time Surveillance Event Notification:** This set of functions provides real-time alerts to the local application, which is running the SSE.
- **Web-based Real-time Surveillance Event Notification:** This set of functions provides a web-based real-time event notification within 3 seconds of the occurrence of a specified event in the monitored area; for example "Speeding Vehicle."
- **Web-based Surveillance Event Retrieval:** This set of functions provides the ability to retrieve surveillance events based on various attributes like object type, speed, or color.
- **Web-based Surveillance Event Statistics:** This set of functions provides the ability to compute a variety of statistics on the event data. For example distribution of people arriving and leaving a building over a day.

Figure 1 shows the software architecture of IBM SSS. For details, refer to Shu (2005). which supports the aforementioned four features with the following software components:

Figure 1. An open and extensible architecture for IBM SSS. The smart surveillance engine (SSE) provides a plug and play framework for video analytics. The event meta-data generated by the engines are sent to the database as XML files. Web services API's allow for easy integration and extensibility of the meta-data. Various applications like event browsing and real time alerts can use an SQL-like query language through web services interfaces to access the event meta-data from the data base

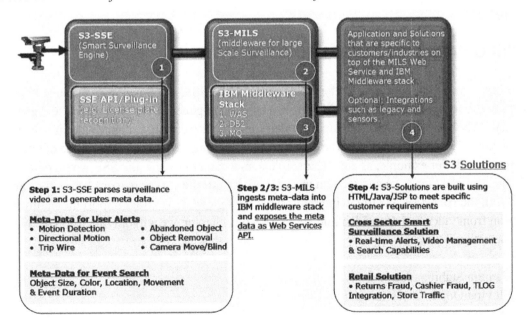

Smart Surveillance Engine (SSE) The SSE is designed to process one stream of video in real-time, extracting object meta-data and evaluating user defined alerts. The SSE uploads messages in XML to the central data repository. The SSE provides the software framework for hosting a wide range of video analytics like behavior analysis, face recognition, license plate recognition etc. One computer can run multiple SSEs.

Middleware for Large Scale Surveillance (MILS) MILS provides the algorithms needed to take the event meta-data and map it into tables in a relational database. Additionally, MILS provides event search services, meta-data management, system management, user management and application development services. MILS uses off the shelf data management (IBM DB2), a web server (IBM Websphere Application Server) and messaging software (IBM MQ) to provide these services.

Solutions These are mainly web applications (written in HTML, Java, JSP, applets, Javascript, and AJAX) which use the web services provided by MILS to provide the functionality needed by the user to query the database and view the results.

The data flow in the IBM SSS architecture is summarized as following:

1. Sensor data from a variety of sensors is processed in the Smart Surveillance Engines (SSEs). Each SSE can generate real-time alerts and generic event meta-data.
2. The meta-data generated by the SSE is represented using XML. The XML documents have some set of fields which are required and common to all engines and others which are specific to the particular type of analysis being performed by the engine.
3. The meta-data generated by the SSEs is transferred to the backend MILS system. This is accomplished via the use of web services data ingest APIs provided by MILS.
4. The XML meta-data is received by MILS and indexed into predefined tables in the IBM DB2 database. This is accomplished using the DB2 XML extender. This allows for fast searching using the primary keys.
5. MILS provides a number of query and retrieval services based on the types of meta-data available in the database.

4. VIDEO PARSING PERFORMED BY THE SSE

In the first item in the data flow of the architecture of the SSS, the Smart Surveillance Engine (SSE) processes the sensor data (typically video from a camera) to generate real-time alerts and generic event meta-data. The basic approach used to extract alerts and events from surveillance video involves detection and tracking. The specific nature of the detection and tracking vary based on the type of video analysis technique used. For example, as a car (person) enters a camera's view, the SSE would detect the entry of the license plate (or face) and recognize and track it until the car (or person) leaves the camera field of view. In the IBM SSE, the following main steps are followed to extract important features for event detection from video and non-video information. In this chapter, we will only focus on the video-based event detection:

*   Camera Stabilization
*   Moving Object Detection and Tracking
*   Object Classification

- Color Classification
- Alert Detection
- Compound Spatio-Temporal Event Detection
- Face Capture and Tracking
- People Counting
- Behavior Analysis

4.1 Camera Stabilization

In order to achieve robust event detection results for complex environments such as outdoor video surveillance on windy days, camera calibration techniques (Jin, 2001) have been applied to the input video streams to correct the subtle camera motion. We use a point tracking method (tracking salient feature points from frame to frame) similar to the method used by Lucas (1981) to estimate the camera movement and output stabilized video for further processing.

4.2 Moving Object Detection and Tracking

The most widely applicable form of surveillance video parsing uses moving object detection and tracking. In common with most video surveillance systems, we use background subtraction (Tian, 2005) to detect changes in a video stream. Background subtraction works by maintaining a statistical model of the observed values of a pixel and modeling the variations to distinguish a change caused by a moving object from changes due to lighting changes or camera vibrations. The detected objects are tracked over their life within a single camera using a tracking system (Senior, 2006). The tracker associates multiple detections of the same object over time and constructs tracks which each represent the movement of a single object (or sometimes the coherent motion of a group of objects). Since it corresponds to a physical object, the track (which designates a time interval) is the fundamental representation in the database. For a given object, we can derive characteristics, such as the object's type, appearance and identity, which are assumed to be constant over time, although our estimates of these characteristics may be derived from accumulations of multiple observations of the object over time. The following sections discuss how the various attributes of objects can be extracted to enable searching.

4.3 Object Classification

After moving object detection and tracking have been performed, object classification is used to determine if object tracks belong to people or vehicles. We deploy a two-phase system in order to achieve classification for an arbitrary scene. In the first phase, human/vehicle recognition is attained using classical feature-based classification based on shape and motion of the detect object. Classical features include the aspect ratio, compactness (ratio of perimeter squared over area), speed and variation in speed. This phase is used to initialize view-normalization parameters for each view. The parameters allow the second phase to perform improved classification based on normalized features, i.e, features which are scaled according to the view. The normalization also enables absolute identification of size and speed which can be used in various ways including identifying vehicles of a certain size and searching for objects traveling at specific speeds across different locations in the image and across different viewpoints/cameras.

4.4 Color Classification

Object tracks are also classified as one of six colors: red, yellow, green, blue, black or white. Color is computed incrementally over the life of the object. When the object first appears, a color histogram is initialized. This histogram is updated periodically if the object remains in the scene. The histogram is computed based on (1) converting RGB to HSI color space and (2) quantizing HSI space to the six colors based on user-defined parameters. These parameters include the thresholds used to determine if saturation is high enough for different bands of intensity. The ultimate dominant color of the object is determined based on ad hoc rules which take into account object type (vehicle, person) and lighting conditions. These rules are based on thresholds for each color and the balance between black and white. If the object contains large amounts of black (because of shadows or object type) then the balance between black and white can be modified. Similarly, if only a small amount of hue is necessary for it to be the dominant color of an object (as in the case of vehicles) these thresholds can be lowered accordingly.

4.5 Alert Detection

Based on the object detection and tracking outputs, eight types of basic alerts can be currently detected in our system. The parameters of these alerts can be specified on the user interface.

Motion detection: Defines an event where a specified number of moving objects, satisfying the specified parameter values, is detected in a region of interest (ROI). The parameters for this event are the ROI, the minimum and maximum sizes for the detected objects, minimum number of frames the motion should last, and the minimum number of moving objects to detect.

Directional motion: Defines an event where a moving object is detected in the specified region and in the specified direction. The parameters are the ROI, the direction of motion in that region, and the tolerance in direction in terms of angle.

Abandoned object: Defines an event where an object satisfying the desired parameters is left in the specified region. The parameters are the region of interest, the minimum and maximum detected object sizes, and the waiting time before considering the object abandoned.

Object removal: Defines an event where an object, selected by drawing a region around it, is removed. The parameters are the region drawn around the object, and the sensitivity level. The sensitivity level is the threshold used to determine if the object is removed. This threshold is based on the amount of change measured in the region.

Trip wire: Defines an event where the line drawn is crossed in the specified direction. The parameters are the line of interest, the direction of crossing, and the minimum and maximum object sizes.

Camera blind/camera moved: This primitive event detects if/when the camera is moved or blinded.

Region alert: This alert detects which part of the moving object enters or leaves the specified region.

Camera motion stopped: This primitive event detects if/when the moved camera is stopped.

4.6 Compound Spatio-Temporal Event Detection

We define multiple events or activities which may occur across different times or multiple cameras based on heterogeneous meta-data as compound events. Examples include: a person leaving a building (seen from one camera) and entering a region (seen in another camera) or tailgating (one person entering using a badge entry system, followed by another not using the badge entry system). In order to provide the flexibility to specify customized events with varying complexity, and enter them to the database in a generic way, we introduce a spatio-temporal event detection system which lets the users specify multiple composite events of high-complexity, and then detects their occurrence automatically. Events can be defined on a single camera view or across multiple camera views. Semantically higher level event scenarios can be built by using the building blocks which we call the primitive events (such as the basic alerts). Primitive events are connected to each other by an operator using a user-friendly interface. Operators include: AND, OR, SEQUENCE (one event follows another), and XOR. More importantly, the newly defined composite events can be combined with each other. For example, an event may be defined as either a car OR a person in a certain region. Another example could be an event defined as a car in region 1 AND a person crossing into region 2. This layered structure makes the definition of events with ever higher complexity possible. The event definitions are written to an XML file, which is then parsed and communicated to the tracking engines running on the videos of the corresponding cameras. For example, when multiple events are combined by a SEQUENCE operator, a time interval can be defined among them. With the proposed system, we can not only detect "a person exiting the building," we can also detect "a person coming from the south corridor of the building and then exiting the building." Later in Section 10 of this chapter, the interface and results for an example of a compound spatio-temporal event are shown.

4.7 Face Capture and Tracking

Faces are the key to identifying people. Automatically recognizing people from surveillance cameras still remains a challenging problem for face recognition technologies (FRVT, 2006; Senior, 2007). The first step in achieving automatic face recognition is the indexing of video with a "presence of people" index. While face-based people detection is valuable, in most realistic scenes, it isn't sufficient to enable people searching because people:

- Could be entering the scene with a pose which limits the visibility of the face from the camera,
- People could be facing away from the camera, in which case face capture / reco will fail

Our approach to creating a "presence of people" index uses a combination of face and people detection to ensure a very low rate of false negatives.

Our face detection method relies on extracting adapted features to encode the local geometric structures of training samples prior to learning. Local feature adaptation is carried out by a non-linear optimization method that determines feature parameters such as position, orientation and scale in order to match the geometric structure of each training sample. This non-linear optimization is similar to the Levenberg-Marquadt method which is a well-known numerical method which minimizes an objective function over a space of parameters of the function. In a second stage, Adaboost learning is applied to the pool of adaptive features in order to obtain general features, which encode common characteristics of all training face images and thus are suitable for detection. Compared to other techniques e.g., Viola (2001), our method (Feris, 2007) offers faster learning time and improved detection rate for quantitative evaluation on standard datasets).

As described in Feris (2007), after detecting a face in the field of view of a surveillance camera, we apply a correlation-based tracking algorithm to track the face in the subsequent video frames. More specifically, when a face is detected, the correlation-based tracker is triggered. For the subsequent frame, if the face detection fails, tracking is updated with the window given by the correlation tracker, i.e. the window with highest correlation to the previous window. Otherwise, if the face detector reports a window result with a close position and size to the current tracking window, then this face detection window result is used to update tracking. This mechanism is important to avoid drifting. Continuous face detection is used to re-initialize the tracker, using multiple view-based classifiers (frontal and profile) interleaved along the temporal domain in the video sequence. Each view-based classifier is based on the two stage Adaboost learning method described before – one for frontal views and another for profile views. By using two classifiers, the face detector will more robustly detect all faces regardless of pose.

4.8 People Counting

Automatic counting of people, entering or exiting a region of interest, is a very important feature for video surveillance systems. We developed an automatic and robust people counting system which can count multiple people who interact in the region of interest, by using only one camera mounted overhead. Two-level hierarchical tracking is employed. An example of hierarchical tracking can be found in Funahashi (2005). For cases not involving merges or splits, a fast blob tracking method is used. See Francois (2004) as a related example. In order to deal with interactions among people in a more thorough and reliable way, the system uses the mean-shift tracking algorithm (Comaniciu, 2000). Using the first-level blob tracker in general, and employing the mean shift tracking only in the case of merges and splits saves power and makes the system computationally efficient. The system setup parameter can be automatically learned in a new environment from a 3 to 5 minute video with people going in or out of the target region one at a time. We tested the proposed method with video sequences which contain many interactions (such as merges/splits, shaking hands, and hugging) between people in the ROI. Most of these interactions occur right in the vicinity of the entry/exit line, thus successfully resolving them is essential to determine direction and perform counting accurately. The system runs at about 33fps on 320x240 images without code optimization on 2GHz Pentium machines. Average accuracy rates of 98.5% and 95% are achieved on videos with normal traffic flow and videos with many cases of merges and splits, respectively. More details of the algorithm can be found in paper by Velipasalar (2006a).

4.9 Behavior Analysis

In IBM SSS, we have a preliminary structure for detecting trajectory anomalies. This system shown in Figure 2 analyses the paths of tracked objects, learns a set of repeated patterns that occur frequently, and detects when an object moves in a way inconsistent with these normal patterns.

The system begins by detecting object entrance and exit locations. Here the start and end points of tracks are clustered to find regions where tracks often end or begin. These points will tend to be where paths or roads reach the edge of the camera's field of view. Having clustered these locations, we have a simple classification for trajectories by labeling a track with its start and end location (or as an anomaly when it starts or ends in an unusual location such as a person walking through the bushes). For example, when we cluster trajectories for our camera which views the entrance to our building, trajectories are classified into one of 5 classes – entering/exiting into the left side (from the road on the left or from

Figure 2. (a) Summary view showing the retrieval of trajectories all events that occurred in the parking lot over a 24 hour period. Trajectory color coding, start white and end is red. (b): Activity distribution over extended time period, X-axis is time, Y-sxis is the number of people in the area. Each day of the week is shown with a different line. (c): Unsupervised behavior analysis. Object entrance/departure zones (green ellipses) and prototypical tracks (brown curves) with typical variation (crossbars)

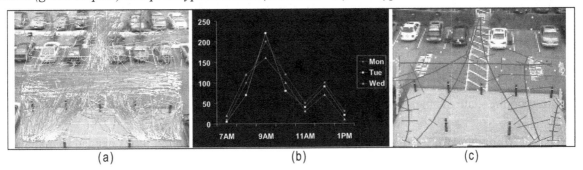

(a)   (b)   (c)

the center), enter/exiting to the right side (from the road on the right or from the center), or moving horizontally across the road. We then apply a secondary clustering scheme to further detect anomalous behavior. This scheme operates as follows: the trajectories of all tracks with a given start/end location labeling are resampled and clustered together. This gives an average or "prototypical track" together with standard deviations, as shown in Figure 3. Thus most tracks from a given entry location to a given exit will lie close to the prototypical track, with typical normal variation indicated by the length of the crossbars. Tracks that wander outside this normal area can be labeled as anomalous and may warrant further investigation. Principal components of the cluster can also indicate typical modes of variation or "eigentracks" giving a more accurate model of normal vs. abnormal.

5. THE IBM MIDDLEWARE FOR LARGE SCALE SURVEILLANCE

In the previous section, we described the components of the IBM Smart Surveillance Engine (SSE) which extracts event metadata from the camera input. In this section, we describe the other major component of the IBM Smart Surveillance Solution (SSS), the IBM Middleware for Large Scale Surveillance or MILS. We first describe in 5.1 the services provided by MILS which comprise the MILS Application Programming Interface. In subsection 5.2 we describe the data structures used within MILS to store the information used to index the data and perform relevant searches.

5.1 Services Provided by the MILS

MILS provides the data management services needed to build a large scale smart surveillance application and to enable extensive search capabilities. While MILS builds on the extensive capabilities of the IBM DB2 database system, it is essentially independent of this product and can be implemented on top of 3rd party relational databases. It supports the indexing and retrieval of spatio-temporal event data. MILS also provides analysis engines with the following support functionalities via standard web services interfaces using XML documents.

A: **Meta-data Ingestion Services:** These are web services calls which allow an engine to ingest events into the MILS system. There are two categories of ingestion services
    A.1: Index Ingestion Services
    A.2: Event Ingestion Services

B: **Schema Management Services:** These are web services which allow a developer to manage their own meta-data schema. A developer can create a new schema or extend the base MILS schema to accommodate the metadata produced by their analytical engine.

C: System Management Services: These services provide a number of facilities needed to manage a surveillance system including
    C.1: Camera Management Services
    C.2: Engine Management Services
    C.3: User Management Services
    C.4: Content Based Search Services

5.2 Data Structures in MILS

The MILS system has three types of data structures, namely, (1) the system data structure which captures the specification of a given monitoring system, including details like geographic location of the system, number of cameras, physical layout of the monitored space, etc. (2) the user data structure which contains user names, privileges and user functionality, (3) the event data structure which contains the events that occur in a specific sensor or zone in the monitored space. Each of these data structures is briefly described in the following subsections.

A. System Data Structure

The system data structure has a number of components.
    A.1: Sensor/Camera Data Structure
    A.2: Engine Data Structures

B. User Data Structure

The user data structure captures the privileges of a given user. These include

- Selective access to camera views
- Selective access to camera / engine configuration and system management functionality
- Selective access to search and query functions.

C. Event Data Structure

This data structure represents the events that occur within a space that may be monitored by one or more cameras or other sensors. IBM SSS uses the timeline data structure which uses time as a primary synchronization mechanism for events that occur in the real world between sensors. The basic MILS schema allows multiple layers of annotations for a given time span. The following is a description of the schema:

- **Event:** An event is defined as an interval of time.
- **StartTime:** Time at which the event starts.
- **Duration:** This is the duration of the event. Events with zero duration are permitted, for example snapping a picture or swiping a badge through a reader.
- **Event ID:** This is a unique number which identifies a specific event.
- **Event Type:** This is a event type identifier.
- **Other descriptors:** Every analysis engine can generate its own set of tags such as basic types or more complex types. If the tags are basic types CHAR, INT, FLOAT, they can be searched using the native search capabilities of the database. However, if the tag is a special type (for example color histogram) the developer needs to supply a mechanism for searching the field.

The most fundamental index into surveillance video is the time of occurrence of an event. The challenge is to automatically derive the time of occurrence of "events of interest" by analyzing the video. Once an event is detected in video, the time interval of the event can be annotated with additional metadata which captures a more detailed description of the event. Hence, the most basic data structure for surveillance events is a time interval. Table 1 shows the basic data model for two types of surveillance events (1) a car driving through a parking lot captured on camera 23 and (2) the license plate of a car recognized on camera 35

Each unique event that occurs within a scene is assigned an event identifier which is guaranteed to be unique across all cameras that are being indexed into a single database instance. The event ID is

Table 1. Event time is used as the basis for annotation surveillance events

Example Data Models	
Behavior Meta -data	**License Plate Meta -data**
Camera ID: 23	Camera ID: 35
Unique EventID: 2379406	Unique EventID: 4926402
Start: 9/10/06:02:22:15:100	Start: 9/10/06:02:12:15:100
End: 9/10/06:02:22:55:300	End: 9/10/06:02:12:25:453
Keyframe: 23567.jpg	Keyframe: 563783.jpg
Video : //mils/xx/file1.wmv	Video : //mils/xx/file3.wmv
Object Type: Car	License Plate #: 525sds
Additional Fields: (trajectory, color, shape, size, etc)	Additional Fields: (e.g State of Origin)

used as the primary key to select from and join across multiple tables in the database. The time of occurrence of the event is used to correlate events across multiple cameras that exist in the system. This data structure can easily be extended to accommodate new types of meta-data as new types of video analytics are added to the system. If the meta-data is one of the basic types (INT, CHAR, FLOAT etc.) supported by the database it can be searched using SQL. For special types of meta-data, like color histograms additional user defined search functions have to be developed.

Figure 3. An Interface showing the various camera views currently available in the system

Figure 4. An interface showing the results from a "Find Person" query

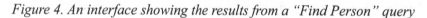
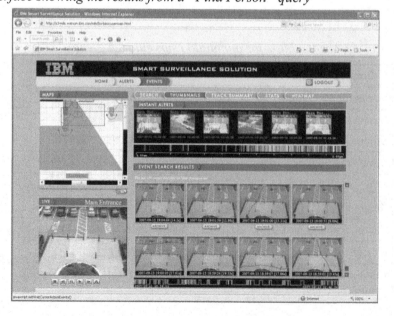

6. INTERFACE OF IBM SSS

Figure 3 – 8 show some interfaces of IBM SSS for the list of camera views, query results of car, query results of person, face capture, license platecolor recognition, and specific alert definition for the pilot in Hawthorne NY. In all the figures, the upper left region contains a map of the facility showing the locations of the cameras. The upper right region contains instant alerts. Alerts are updated in real-time as they occur. The lower left region contains a video player. Initially it contains a live video of the cur-

Figure 5. An Interface showing the results of "Find Faces"

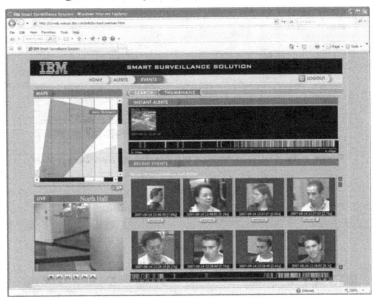

Figure 6. An interface showing the results of "License Plate Recognition"

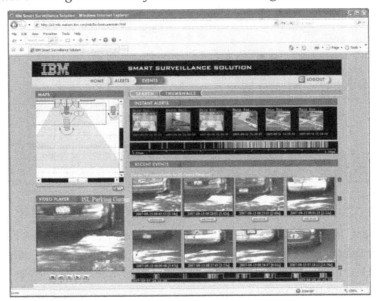

Figure 7. An Interface showing the Results of "Red Car" search

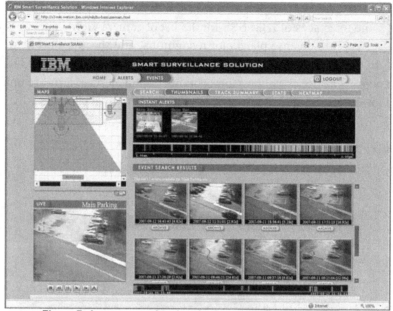

Figure 7: An   howing the Results of "Red Car" search

Figure 8. An Interface showing the track summary of one day data

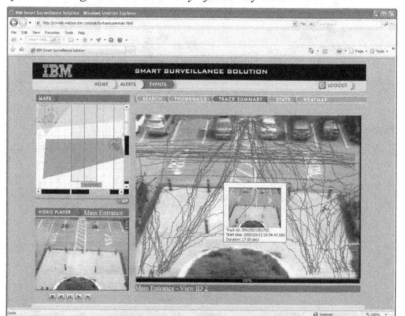

rently selected camera. But this player can also show a selected alert or event. The lower right region changes as the user selects what he/she would like to search. This region can contain either the page to specify the search criteria or the results of a search. In the figures, the lower right region differs depending on the search criteria.

7. SPECIFIC PEOPLE AND VEHICLE SEARCH

As shown in the user interface, the SSS can be used to search for events based on a large set of attributes provided by the engines (SSEs) and stored in the database and retrieval system (MILS). In this section and the next three sections, we detail the search functionality and search performance of the system. In this section, we describe the search capabilities for finding people and vehicles and determining the number of people crossing through a region. In Section 8, we describe the generic search capabilities including object color, object class, object size, object shape, object location, object movement, time of event of occurrence and event duration. In Section 9 we give an example of compound search while in Section 10 we give examples of more complex searches which we call compound spatio-temporal search. Finally in Section 11 we give some results evaluating the performance of the system in both precision and recall and for time to recall for detecting and tracking objects and executing specific search queries.

7.1 Searching for People

After detecting and tracking human faces, we also store a keyframe for each captured face image in the database, associated with a timestamp. This allows the user to query the system like ``Show me all people who entered the facility yesterday from 1pm to 5pm.'' An example of this search is shown at the right of Table 2.

Ideally, for every person passing through the scene, a face keyframe would be generated and stored in the database. However, due to false negatives in face detection and face pose and person orientation issues, important events might be missed. We address this problem by using a keyframe selection technique that combines a face classifier with a person classifier. If a face is detected and tracked in the video sequence, a face keyframe is stored in the database. Otherwise, a person keyframe is generated if a person is detected and tracked in the video.

We analyzed ten hours of data (from 10 days), with each hour corresponding to the peak hour (i.e., the hour with most people entering the facility) in each day. Table 2 shows our results. Out of 445 people

Table 2: Results obtained from ten hours of surveillance video. Example faces (frontal and profile) captured by our system (blurred to preserve privacy)

Total # of people approaching camera		445
Total # of people receding from camera		40
Face Detection	Faces Captured	351
	Faces Missed	94
	False Poitives	7
Person Detection	Persons captured	134
	Approaching	94
	Receding	40
	False Positives	19
Overall People False Negatives		0
Overall People False Positives 26/445		5.6%

entering the facility (not walking back to the camera), we captured 351 faces, with only 7 false positives. The reason that some faces were missed is that sometimes people enter the door looking down, occluding the face from the camera, which is placed on the ceiling. By running our keyframe selection technique (using face and person detectors), we can capture all remaining 94 persons, as well as 40 persons walking back to the camera, with an additional 19 false positives.

7.2. Searching for Vehicles

Searching for vehicles based on license plates is achieved using license plate recognition technology, which is very advanced when compared to the state of face recognition. An example system used in the IBM SSS was developed by Hi Tech Solution (HiTech, website). Unlike human faces, license plates vary widely based on geography. Variations include language, font, background and numbering scheme. Typically, there is no single algorithm or company which can recognize license plates across wide geographies. One approach to handling this variation is to standardize the interfaces to the license plate algorithms (such as Hi Tech's SeeCar algorithm) and standardize the meta-data representation for the license plate. The software architecture of IBM SSS supports this approach.

Figure 9. Results of people counting for a week in the IBM Hawthorne cafeteria

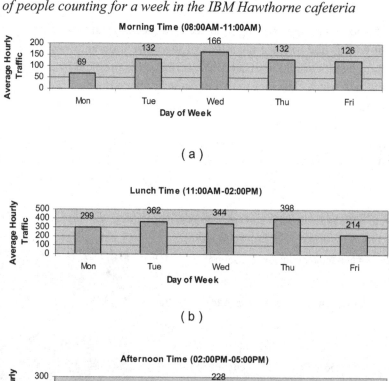

(a)

(b)

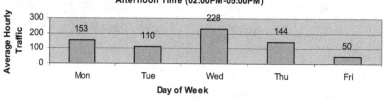

(c)

7.3 People Count

Figure 9 shows the result of one-week long testing in IBM Hawthorne cafeteria, we found: 1) the morning time (8:00am-11:00am) has the lowest traffic load in a day; 2) the lunch time (11:00am-2:00pm, especially 12:00pm-2:00pm) has the highest traffic load, (as expected for a cafeteria); 3) Friday has relatively lower traffic than the other four days in the week.

8. GENERIC SEARCH CRITERIA

Generic search includes search for objects and behaviors of objects over time. This search can be qualified by one or more of the following: object color, object class, object size, object shape, object location, object movement, time of event of occurrence and event duration.

8.1 Search by Object Color

Object color is determined by (1) converting RGB object colors to a 6 color Hue/Saturation/Intensity (HSI) space, (2) periodically updating and normalizing the 6 color HSI cumulative histogram over the life of the object and (3) determining the three dominant colors and their percentages. For vehicle color estimation, the final primary color is determined based on hue if sufficient (regardless of the amount of achromatic pixels), and the relative amount of black and white. Table 3 shows the results of color classification for vehicles entering and exiting our facilities for a total of 8 hours (4 hours for two days). The overall correct color classification is 80%. Over half the misclassified vehicles are black or white vehicles misclassified as white or black respectively. Although this may be improved with parameter tuning taking into consideration the variations in lighting conditions, the most significant issue here is due to the variable amount of shadows included in the object segmentation and the percent of the true black components for each vehicle (i.e. windshield size, tires, accessories etc.) Figure 10 and 11 show illustrative examples of vehicles classified correctly and incorrectly.

Figure 11. Keyframes 1,2,3 show errors from searching for black objects. Keyframes 4,5,6 are results of searching for white objects. For 1,2,3 notice the dark shadows and color of windows etc which lead to misclassification. The garbage truck appears to be black in the keyframe (5) but in playing , it appears that the truck, including the lower body, is white.

Table 3. Color Results: BL-Black, WH-White, RE-Red, YE- Yellow, BU-Blue, GR-Green

		COLOR SEARCH→GROUND TRUTH						
		BL	WH	RE	YE	BU	GR	
COLOR SEARCH→RESULTS	BL	119	36	20	0	1	0	165
	WH	3	102	1	0	1	0	107
	RE	0	0	18	0	0	0	18
	YE	0	0	0	1	0	0	1
	BU	0	0	0	0	7	0	7
	GR	0	0	0	0	0	2	2
		122	138	39	1	9	2	

Figure 10. Retrieved keyframes (cross indexed to video by time) (1) yellow, (2) green, (3) blue, (4) red, (5) black and (6) white vehicles. (Trajectory color indicates direction of movement, blue is track start, red is track end)

Figure 11. Keyframes 1,2,3 show errors from searching for black objects. Keyframes 4,5,6 are results of searching for white objects. For 1,2,3 notice the dark shadows and color of windows etc which lead to misclassification. The garbage truck appears to be black in the keyframe (5) but in playing, it appears that the truck, including the lower body, is white

8.2 Search by Object Class

Object classification is performed using a view invariant classifier (Brown 2004). An object can be classified as either a person or a vehicle based on shape features such as compactness and principal axis ratio, and motion features such as speed and degree of recurrent motion. Table 4 (left) shows results for vehicles and people entering the front of our laboratory for 4 hours one morning. (May 16 2007, Camera #2, between 8am and 12pm). Overall 307/334 or 92% of the vehicle/person object tracks were correctly classified.

Table 4. **Left:***Object Classification Result: V: Vehicles, P: Person, O: Other* **Right:** *Search using object size. P: Person, C: Car, MS-T: Medium Sized Truck, L-T: Large Truck, O: Other*

OBJECT CLASS RESULTS	Object Class Ground Truth			
		V	P	O
	V	77	0	1
	P	9	230	19
	O	1	18	53
		86	248	73

SIZE SEARCH → RESULTS	SIZE SEARCH → GROUND TRUTH				
		P	C	MS-T	L-T	O
	P	17	2			
	C	3	39			20
	MS-T		3	1		
	L-T				1	
	O					11
	Total	20	43	1	1	31

8.3 Search by Object Size

Object size is often useful to determine object class for objects moving orthogonal to the camera viewpoint. Object size was used to distinguish pedestrians from vehicles and to distinguish standard vehicles (cars, SUVs, minivans) from mid-size vehicles (delivery trucks, large pickups) and large trucks (such as garbage trucks and tractor trailers) for our camera looking orthogonal to the entry road. Table 4 (right) shows the results of a size search used for object classification.

8.4 Search by Object Shape

Currently our system does not support explicit search by shape. However as described in the object classification section, shape of objects is used to determine the class.

8.5 Search by Object Movement

Object movement can be qualified by several parameters such as speed, acceleration, direction, and extended properties of the objects trajectory (like finding all people walking in a zigzag manner through the parking lot). The SSE computes several of these parameters for use in evaluating user specified events like directional motion of the object. At this time, our search interface only provides the ability to search based on the speed of the object.

8.6 Search by Object Location

This is achieved by storing the entire trajectory of the object into the database. The tracker (described in 4.2) generates a trajectory for each moving object in the scene in image coordinates. When the user selects a region of interest (ROI) within an image (yellow box), this is used to generate an SQL query which retrieves all the objects whose trajectories intersect with the ROI. Figure 12 (left) shows the results of events recovered when the user selects the yellow region outlined in the image.

Figure 12. (Left) Results of spatial search, showing the trajectories of all objects that passed through the user-selected yellow region. The user can click on the trajectory to index into the video clip. (Right) Loitering events (note the long person trajectories) retrieved by using the event duration query

8.7 Search by Time of Occurrence of Events

Every event indexed into the database is required to have an event start timestamp and event end time-stamp (see section on data structure). These time stamps are used to retrieve events within the user specified time of interest. Currently we only support retrieval of events that occurred: a) before a user specified time b) after a user specified time c) during a user specified interval.

8.8 Search by Duration of Event

Every event recorded by the system has an associated time duration. The duration of an event can be used for multiple purposes. The following are sample events from a query for events of duration longer than 50 seconds. These sample events demonstrate how loitering can be detected by using the event duration query (figure 12 right).

9. COMPOUND SEARCH

All the criteria discussed previously can be combined into a single query to search for events of much higher degree of complexity. Consider the following scenario: Employees at a facility have registered a complaint that one of the drivers from an express mail company is driving very fast in the parking lot. Since it is known that the delivery truck is yellow, we can use the composite query as follows:

FIND ALL, Object Type = "VEHICLE", Object Size > X1 and Object Size <X2, Object Color = Yellow, Object Speed > S1

Figure 13. Detecting a "tailgate" event

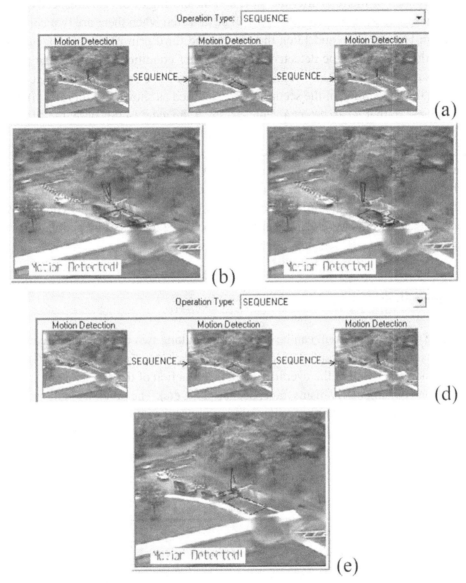

Applying such a query to events over a month would help establish a pattern of speeding violations committed by the delivery truck, thus narrowing down the specific driver.

10. COMPOUND SPATIO-TEMPORAL SEARCH

In a number of applications, the events of interest are a combination of basic events over space (cameras) and time. Figure 13 shows a detected tailgate event at the entrance by using the spatio-temporal event detection method. First, the tailgate event is described by using the building blocks and operators shown in Fig. 13(a). The three primitives here correspond to the opening of the gate, detection of two cars in the ROI (Region of Interest) after the gate, and the closing of the gate respectively. The middle primitive event in Fig. 13(a) is defined so that it will be detected when there are two objects in the ROI. As can be seen in Figures 13(b) and 13(c), the second and third primitives are detected successfully. The opening of the gate cannot be detected due to weather conditions affecting the performance of the background subtraction algorithm. (This refers to subsection 4.2 on Moving Object Detection and Tracking.)Then, the description of the scenario was modified as shown in Figure 13(d) where the first primitive is changed so that it can detect a vehicle right at the gate. In this case, the first primitive can be detected successfully as well.

Many complex events, such as a person entering the building and then removing an object or a person jumping over a fence and entering a specified region, can be expressed in terms of primitive events and be detected by using the proposed system. We also tested our system successfully with several scenarios like people tailgating to enter the building and a truck following an unusual path defined on the views of four cameras. These events were defined and introduced to the system by people with no technical expertise by using the proposed scheme and the interface.

11. SEARCH PERFORMANCE

The performance of a search system can be characterized along two dimensions: precision and recall. These dimensions provide a measure of how well the system is meeting the requirements of the user's query. The precision and recall of the overall system is a function of the precision and recall of each of the individual video parsing mechanisms (face, license plate, etc). The previous sections have presented the results for people detection. The precision and recall of all of the other retrieval techniques such as color, size, location, event time, and event duration are dependent on the precision and recall of the

Table 5. Test set description

Test Data Set Description with ground truth	
Data volume	4 cameras, 10 sequences, 36 minutes (2267 frames)
Total # of hand marked objects	2964 objects in 2267 frames
Total # of objects tracks FOV	90 objects

Table 6. Object detection performance summary

Object Detection or Background Subtraction Results	
False Positives	0.03 objects per frame
False Negatives (missed object)	628 of 2964 = 21.2%
Avg size of missed object	226 sq-pixels

Table 7. Object tracking performance summary

Object Tracking Results	
False Positives (spurious tracks)	25 with average length of 77 frames
False Negatives (missed tracks)	24/90 = 26.6%
Avg size of missed tracks	169 sq-pixels

Table 8. Retrieval time summary

Database Server, Dual Xeon, 3.8Ghz with 4GB Ram running IBM DB2	
Total number of events on Main Parking Lot Camera	From Apr 30, 07 to May 14, 07 10997 events over 15 days
Red car search	219 events retrieved in under 5 secs

underlying event parsing system (object detection and tracking). A detailed evaluation of event parsing (detection and tracking) can be found in (Brown 2005a, 2005b)

As shown in Table 5, we used a test set of videos which was hand marked by a person for objects in each frame and tracks over the sequence. The results of running our base object detection and tracking algorithms are shown in Tables 6 and 7. At the selected operating point (set of thresholds of object size, sensitivity of detection thresholds, track match thresholds, etc.) the base performance of the detection and tracking algorithms is good on objects that are of significant size (above 169 sq. pixels). The false positives when measured at a track level tend to be very short lived trajectories (77 frames, less than 3s). Typically, events that occur in the real world are of significantly longer duration. While improvement in the base event parsing is always desirable, the current level of performance is more that adequate for a search and real-time alert in retail and city surveillance.

Table 8 shows a summary of retrieval time for the system. This is the time between the user launching a query and the system responding with results. This time varies widely based on the type of query, with location searches being the most expensive and searches based on native SQL types falling into a different bucket. The following is a sample performance result for color retrieval, which is a native SQL query.

12. CONCLUSION

Enabling effective search of surveillance video is a challenging problem, as it involves not only the challenges of extracting events and activities in video, but also the challenges of generating searchable meta-data, efficient indexing into a database and intuitive search and visualization mechanisms. The current activities in research and industry have only begun to scratch the surface of the challenges involved in surveillance video.

This chapter presented a framework for addressing detection, query and retrieval issues in surveillance video using the IBM Smart Surveillance System. This system has a broad range of detection capabilities which can be used to automatically monitor a scene in real-time including person/vehicle recognition, color identification, complex alert detection, face capture, and people counting. This framework can also manage the unwieldy amount of surveillance data, perform event-based retrieval and receive real time event alerts through a standard web infrastructure. This latter capability enables large distributive systems which can scale to a large number of cameras and facilities. The system can also extract long term statistical patterns of activity to facilitate traffic monitoring and improved understanding of operational conditions. Lastly, the system is an open and extensible framework which can easily integrate multiple independently developed event analysis technologies in a common infrastructure.

Many challenges and research opportunities remain open in the space of surveillance video analysis and search. Examples include dealing with the challenges of searching for color across varying scene conditions such as time of day, camera settings, tinted lighting etc., searching for people who have been seen earlier (in different cameras, on different days, under different lighting conditions) or dealing efficiently with indexing large amounts of video and providing intuitive interfaces for enabling search and interaction. The Holy Grail might be to reduce the time to investigate situations like the London bombings or the Washington sniper incident and find the perpetrators in a timely fashion.

13. FUTURE RESEARCH DIRECTIONS

We are planning to investigate on-line learning techniques to improve the performance of our algorithms in specific scenarios. Conventional offline methods are designed for generic scenarios, often involving large training sets with samples drawn independently from some probabilistic distribution. Offline training can be very computationally expensive, like the adaboost learning process for face detection, which can take order of weeks to be completed in conventional machines. In contrast, on-line learning methods use one example at a time to update the learning parameters and thus are more suitable to process large amounts of data. A key advantage of these techniques is adaptation to new environments. Consider as an example a face detector which is deployed in a particular camera. With online learning, the detector would continuously tune its parameters to adapt to the particular camera conditions (like lighting, background, etc.) as new data arrives.

Currently, our visual object tracker is restricted to a single camera. We plan to extend our approach to track objects across multiple cameras. This is a very challenging problem, as objects can change their appearance dramatically from one camera view to another, due to different camera viewpoints and camera intrinsic properties like different color responses. Obtaining reliable solutions for this problem will allow us to better monitor sites such as retail stores, where we may desire to analyze the complete trajectories of people across multiple cameras.

We also plan to incorporate other computer vision modules in our system, such as face analysis for gender and age classification, activity recognition (e.g., detection of a person falling down), more sophisticated trajectory analysis and clustering, tracking and object classification in crowded environments, and many others. All these new modules can be easily integrated in our system framework as DLL plug-ins.

Thus far our system relies on static cameras, which allows us to use background modeling techniques to segment moving objects. In many cases, however, this segmentation may be very poor due to crowded scenarios or extreme lighting changes. A more interesting issue happens when we consider moving cameras, rather than static cameras. In this case, background modeling is meaningless. We are currently investigating analytics modules that work well in these circumstances.

14. REFERENCES

3VR, http://www.3vr.com/Products/#smartsearch.

Berriss, W.P., Price, W.G., & Bober, M.Z. (2003). Real-Time Visual Analysis and Search Algorithms for Intelligent Video Surveillance, International Conference on Visual Information Engineering (pp. 226-229).

Brown, L.M. (2004). View independent vehicle/person classification, ACM 2nd International Workshop on Video Surveillance and Sensor Networks (pp. 114-123) New York, NY.

Brown, L.M., Lu, M., Shu, C., Tian, Y., & Hampapur, A. (2005a) Improving performance via post track analysis. IEEE International Workshop on Visual Surveillance and Performance Evaluation of Tracking and Surveillance (pp. 341 – 347) Beijing, China.

Brown, L., Senior, A., Tian, Y., Connell, J., Hampapur, A., Shu, C., Merkl, H., & Lu, M. (2005b). Performance evaluation of surveillance systems under varying conditions, IEEE International Workshop on Performance Evaluation of Tracking and Surveillance (pp. 79-87) Breckenridge, CO.

Comaniciu, D., Ramesh, V. & Meer, P. (2000). Real-time tracking of non-rigid objects using mean shift, In Proc. IEEE Conference on Computer Vision and Pattern Recognition, 2, 142-149.

Feris, R., Tian, Y., & Hampapur, A. (2007). Capturing people in surveillance video, The Seventh International Workshop on Visual Surveillance (pp. 1-8.)

FRVT, (2006). Face recognition vendor test (FRVT), http://www.frvt.org/FRVT2006/.

Francois, A. (2004). Real-time multi-resolution blob tracking, Institute for Robotics and Intelligent Systems, University of Southern California, Los Angeles, California, from http://handle.dtic.mil/100.2/ADA447622.

Funahashi, T., Fujiwara, T., & Koshimizu, H. (2005). **Coarse to fine hierarchical tracking system for face recognition**. IEEE International Conference on Systems, Man and Cybernetics, 4, 3454-3459.

Hauptmann, A. (2006). Lessons for the future from a decade of infomedia video analysis research, International Conference on Image and Video Retrieval (pp. 1-10.)

HiTech, http://www.htsol.com/Products/SeeCar.html.

Jin, J., Zhu, Z., Xu, G. (2001). Digital video sequence stabilization-based on 2.5-D motion estimation and inertial motion filtering, Real-Time Imaging, 7(4), 357-365, Academic Press.

Lee, H., Smeaton, A., O'Connor, N., & Murphy, N., (2005). User interface for CCTV search system, The IEE International Symposium on Imaging for Crime Detection and Prevention (pp. 39-43.)

Lucas, B. D., & Kanade, T. (1981). An iterative image registration technique with an application to stereo vision. Proceedings of Imaging understanding workshop, (pp 121—130.)

Marcenaro, L., Oberti, F., Foresti, G.L., & Regazzoni, C.S. (2001). Distributed architectures and logical-task decomposition in multimedia surveillance systems, Proceedings of IEEE, 89(10), 1419-1440.

Meessen, J., Coulanges, M., Desurmont, X., & Delaigle, J.F., (2006). Content-based retrieval of video surveillance scenes, Multimedia Content Representation, Classification and Security. (pp. 785-792.)

Naphade, M., & Smith, J.R. (2004). On the detection of semantic concepts at TRECVID, ACM International Conference on Multimedia. (pp. 660-667.)

ObjectVideo, http://www.objectvideo.com/products/vew/.

PyramidVision, http://www.pyramidvision.com/.

Senior, A., Hampapur, A., Tian, Y., Brown, L., Pankanti, S., & Bolle, R. (2006). Appearance models for occlusion handling, In Journal of Image and Vision Computing, 24(11), 1233-1243.

Senior, A., Brown, L., Shu, C., Tian, Y., Lu, M., Zhai, Y., & Hampapur, A. (2007). Visual person searches for retail loss detection: Application and evaluation, International Conference on Vision Systems.

Shu, C., Hampapur, A., Lu, M., Brown, L., Connell, J. Senior, A., & Tian, Y. (2005). IBM smart surveillance system (S3): A open and extensible framework for event based surveillance, IEEE Conference on **Advanced Video and Signal Based Surveillance** (pp. 318 – 323.)

Stringa, E., & Regazzoni, C.S. (1998). Content-based retrieval and real time detection from video sequences acquired by surveillance systems, IEEE International Conference on Image Processing, 3, 138-142.

Tian, Y., Lu, M., & Hampapur, A. (2005). Robust and efficient foreground analysis for real-time video surveillance, IEEE International Conference on Computer Vision and Pattern Recognition. 1, 1182-1187.

Velipasalar, S., Brown, L. & Hampapur, A. (2006a). Specifying, interpreting and detecting high-level, spatio-temporal composite events in single and multi-camera systems, Conference on Computer Vision and Pattern Recognition Workshop, (pp. 110-116.)

Velipasalar, S., Tian, Y., & Hampapur, A. (2006b). Automatic counting of interacting people by using a single uncalibrated camera, IEEE International Conference on Multimedia and Expo, (pp. 1265-1268.)

Viola, P., & Jones, M. (2001). Rapid object detection using a boosted cascade of simple features, IEEE Conference on Computer Vision and pattern Recognition (pp. 511-518.)

15. ADDITIONAL READING

Ali, S., & Shah, M. (2007). A lagrangian particle dynamics approach for crowd flow segmentation and stability analysis, IEEE Conference on Computer Vision and Pattern Recognition, Minneapolis.

Auvinet, E., Grossman, E., Rougier, C., Dahmane, M., & Meunier, J. (2006). Left-luggage detection using homographies and simple heuristics. PETS2006 Proceedings.

Bose, B., &. Grimson, E. (2004). Improving object classification in far-field video. IEEE Computer Society Conference on Computer Vision and Pattern Recognition (CVPR'04), 2, 181-188, Washington, D.C..

Buxton, H. (2003). Learning and understanding dynamic scene activity: A review. Image and Vision Computing, 21, 125-136.

Davis, J. W. (2004). Sequential reliable-inference for rapid detection of human actions. IEEE Computer Society Conference on Computer Vision and Pattern Recognition Workshops (CVPRW'04), Washington, D.C.

Ferryman, J., & Thirde, D. (2006). An overview of the PETS2006 dataset. PETS2006 Proceedings.

Gray, D., Brennan, S., & Tao, H. (2007). Evaluating Appearance Models for Recognition, Reacquisition, and Tracking. PETS2007 Proceedings.

Hongeng, S., & Nevatia, R. (2003). Large-scale event detection using semi-hidden markov models, IEEE International Conference on Computer Vision, Nice, France.

Joo, S., & and R. Chellappa (2006). Attribute grammar-based event recognition and anomaly detection. International Workshop on Semantic Learning Applications in Multimedia, New York , NY.

Katz, B., Lin, J., Stauffer, C., & Grimson E. (2005). Answering questions about moving objects in surveillance videos. AAAI Spring Symposium on New Directions in Question Answering.

Khan, S., & Shah, M. (2005). Detecting group activities using rigidity of formation. Proceedings of ACM Multimedia.

Krahnstoever, N., Tu, T., Sebastian, T., Perera, A., & Collins, R. (2006). Multi-view detection and tracking of travelers and luggage in mass transit environments. PETS2006 Proceedings.

Martinez-del-Rincon, J., Herrero-Jaraba, J., Gomez, J. & Orrite-Urunuela, C. (2006). Automatic left luggage detection and tracking using multi-camera UKF. PETS2006 Proceedings.

Pound, M., Naeem, A., French, A. & Pridmore, T. (2007). Quantitative and qualitative evaluation of visual tracking algorithms using statistical tests. PETS 2007 Proceedings.

Remagnino, P. & Jones, G.A. (2001). Classifying surveillance events from attributes and behaviour, British Machine Vision Conference, Manchester, pp. 685-694. ISBN/ISSN 1901725162.

Ramanathan, N. & Chellappa, R. (2006). Face verification across age progression", In IEEE Transactions on Image Processing, 15, 3349-3361.

Rodriguez, M., & Shah, M. (2007) Detecting and segmenting humans in crowded scenes. Proceedings of ACM Multimedia.

Shao J., Zhou, S., & Chellappa, R. (2004). Appearance-based tracking and recognition using the 3-D trilinear tensor. IEEE Intl. Conf. on Acoust., Speech and Signal Processing, Montreal, Canada.

Sheikh, Y., Li X., & Shah, M. (2007). Trajectory association across non-overlapping moving cameras in planar scenes, IEEE Conference on Computer Vision and Pattern Recognition, Minneapolis, USA.

Stauffer, C. (2003). Estimating tracking sources and sinks. IEEE Workshop on Event Mining.

White, B., & Shah, M. (2007). Automatically tuning background subtraction parameters using particle swarm optimization, IEEE International Conference on Multimedia & Expo, Beijing, China.

Yin, F., Makris, D., & Velastin, S. (2007). Performance evaluation of object tracking algorithms. PETS2007 Proceedings.

Zhao, T., & Nevatia, R. (2004). Tracking multiple humans in crowded environment. IEEE Computer Society Conference on Computer Vision and Pattern Recognition, (pp. 406-413.)

Zhou, S. & Chellappa, R. (2005). Image-based face recognition under illumination and pose variations ", Jl. Optical Society of America, A, Vol. 22, pp. 217-229.

Zhu, X. et al. Video data mining: Semantic indexing and event detection from the association perspective. IEEE Trans. on Knowledge and Data Engineering, 17(5), 665-677.

Chapter XVI
MMIR:
An Advanced Content–Based Image Retrieval System Using a Hierarchical Learning Framework

Min Chen
Florida International University, USA

Shu-Ching Chen
Florida International University, USA

ABSTRACT

This chapter introduces an advanced content-based image retrieval (CBIR) system, MMIR, where Markov model mediator (MMM) and multiple instance learning (MIL) techniques are integrated seamlessly and act coherently as a hierarchical learning engine to boost both the retrieval accuracy and efficiency. It is well-understood that the major bottleneck of CBIR systems is the large semantic gap between the low-level image features and the high-level semantic concepts. In addition, the perception subjectivity problem also challenges a CBIR system. To address these issues and challenges, the proposed MMIR system utilizes the MMM mechanism to direct the focus on the image level analysis together with the MIL technique (with the neural network technique as its core) to real-time capture and learn the object-level semantic concepts with some help of the user feedbacks. In addition, from a long-term learning perspective, the user feedback logs are explored by MMM to speed up the learning process and to increase the retrieval accuracy for a query. The comparative studies on a large set of real-world images demonstrate the promising performance of our proposed MMIR system.

INTRODUCTION

Content-based image retrieval (CBIR), which was proposed in the early 1990s, has attracted a broad range of research interests from many computer communities in the past decade. Generally speaking, in a CBIR system, each image is first mapped to a point in a certain feature space, where the features can be categorized into color (Stehling, Nascimento, & Falcao, 2000), texture (Kaplan et al., 1998), shape (Zhang & Lu, 2002), and so forth. Next, given a query in terms of image examples, the system retrieves images with regard to their features (He, Li, Zhang, Tong, & Zhang, 2004). Though extensive research efforts have been directed into this area, it still remains a big challenge and an open issue in terms of retrieving the desired images from the large image repositories effectively and efficiently. In short, some of the major obstacles can be summarized as follows.

- First, it is widely accepted that the major bottleneck of CBIR systems is the large semantic gap between the low-level image features and high-level semantic concepts, which prevents the systems from being applied to real applications (Hoi & Lyu, 2004).
- Second, the perception subjectivity problem poses additional challenges for CBIR systems. In other words, in viewing the same image (e.g., Figure 1a), different users might possess various interests in either a certain object (e.g., the house, the tree, etc.) or the entire image (e.g., a landscape during the autumn season). In this case, Figure 1b, Figure 1c, or Figure 1d, respectively, might be considered as the relevant image with regard to Figure 1a. In addition, even a same user can have different perceptions toward the same image at various situations and with different purposes.

To address the earlier-mentioned challenges and issues, a certain form of adaptive (i.e., data-driven) description is required to capture the salient meaning of each image. In addition, the system should be able to expedite the navigation process through a large image database with the facilitation of users' relevance feedbacks. In other words, the search engine should be equipped with an inference engine to observe and learn from user interactions. To this extent, we believe that there are both a need and an opportunity to systematically incorporate machine learning techniques into an integrated approach for content-based image retrieval. In this chapter, we introduce an advanced content-based image retrieval system called MMIR, where Markov model mediator (MMM) and multiple instance learning (MIL)

Figure 1. Example images

(a) (b)

(c) (d)

techniques are integrated seamlessly and act coherently as a hierarchical learning engine to boost both the retrieval accuracy and efficiency.

Markov model mediator (MMM) is a statistical reasoning mechanism, which adopts the mathematically sound Markov model and the concept of mediators. As presented in our earlier studies (Shyu, Chen, Chen, Zhang, & Shu, 2003; Shyu, Chen, & Rubin, 2004a), MMM possesses the extraordinary capability in exploring the semantic concepts in the image level from the long-term learning perspective. In contrast, multiple instance learning (MIL) incorporated with the neural network (NN) technique aims at learning the region of interests based on the users' relevance feedbacks on the whole image in real time. Integrating the essential functionalities from both MMM and MIL has the potential in constructing a robust CBIR system, which is the attempt of this study.

The remainder of this chapter is organized as follows. The next section, *Background and Related Work*, gives a broad background introduction as well as the literature review. The system is detailed in the *Hierarchical Learning Scheme* section and the *Experimental Results* section, followed by the discussions of the possible future trends in terms of the CBIR research in the *Future Trends* section. Finally, the chapter ends with the *Conclusions* section.

BACKGROUND AND RELATED WORK

The existing work in CBIR can be roughly classified into the following four categories:

- **Feature Analysis and Similarity Measures:** Many early-year studies on CBIR focused primarily on feature analysis and similarity measures (Pass, 1997; Zhou, Rui, & Huang, 1999). However, due to the semantic gap and the perception subjectivity issues, it is extremely difficult to discriminate the images by solely relying on the similarity measure upon the low-level features in the real-world image databases (Hoi et al., 2004).
- **Relevance Feedback (RF):** A variety of RF mechanisms from heuristic techniques to sophisticated learning techniques have been proposed and actively studied in recent years to mitigate the semantic gap issue (Rui, Huang, & Mehrotra, 1997; Tong & Chang, 2001). The principle of RF is to adjust the subsequent queries by altering the position of the query point (or called the query center) and/or the feature weights based on the information gathered from the user's feedback, which can be regarded as a form of supervised learning. From the past research studies, RF has been shown as an effective scheme to improve the retrieval performance of CBIR and has already been incorporated as a key part in designing a CBIR system. However, it typically takes quite a number of iterations to converge the learning process to obtain the high-level concepts. Moreover, in case when the relevant samples are scarce in the initial query or the relevant images are widely scatted in the feature space, the RF technique is often inadequate in learning the concepts (Jin & French, 2003). Furthermore, most of the existing RF based applications regard each image as a whole, which often fails to produce satisfactory results when the user's query interest is just the salient region(s) in the image.
- **Region-Based Approaches:** With the assumption that human discernment of certain visual contents could be potentially associated with the semantically meaningful object(s) in the image, region-based retrieval (Chen & Wang, 2004; Jing, Li, Zhang, & Zhang, 2000) and MIL (Chen, Rubin, Shyu, & Zhang, in press; Huang, Chen, Shyu, & Zhang, 2002) techniques offer an alternative solution by

decomposing the images into a set of homogeneous regions for analysis. It is worth noting that, as will be discussed in a later section, to some extent, the MIL technique might be considered as a hybrid of the RF technique and the region-based approach. In fact, semantically accurate image segmentation is an ambitious long-term goal for computer vision researchers, which highly limits the performance of these approaches. Here, semantically accurate image segmentation means the capability of building a one-to-one mapping between the segmented regions and the objects in the image (Chen et al., 2004). In addition, the assumption of the existence of salient object(s) in the images does not always hold.

- **Log-Based Retrieval (or called Long-Term Learning):** Due to the complexity of image understanding, the regular learning techniques, such as RF and MIL, need quite a number of rounds of feedbacks to reach satisfactory results. Consequently, log-based retrieval was proposed recently (Hoi et al., 2004; Shyu, Chen, Chen, & Zhang, 2004b; Zhou et al., 1999), which seeks to speed up the convergence of the learning process in terms of the high-level semantic concepts in a query with the assistance of the historical feedback logs accumulated in the system from the long-term learning perspective. However, most of the existing log-based retrieval frameworks solely capture the general user concepts but fail to adjust or customize the high-level semantic concepts in a query with regard to a specific user. Also, similar to most of the RF techniques, they have difficulties in propagating the feedback information across the query sessions toward the region or object level.

From these discussions, we observe that by acting alone, the earlier-mentioned approaches have certain limitations in terms of retrieval accuracy and/or processing costs. However, via the intelligent integration, we aim at offering a potentially promising solution for the CBIR system with the assistance of MIL (the region-based learning approach with NN as the core) and MMM (a statistical reasoning and log-based retrieval mechanism). We will detail these two techniques in the next section. To this extent, we seek to develop a unified framework that (1) explores the high-level semantic concepts in a query from both the object-level and the image-level and (2) addresses the needs of serving the specific user's query interest as well as reducing the convergence cycles.

To our best knowledge, very few efforts have been directed to serve this purpose. In He, King, Ma, Li, and Zhang (2003), the authors suggested to incorporate the RF technique with the singular value decomposition (SVD) based long-term learning. In addition, Hoi et al. (2004) studied the log-based relevance feedback for the purpose of improving the retrieval performance and reducing the semantic gap in CBIR. In our earlier study (Shyu, Chen, Chen, Zhang, & Shu, 2006), we also proposed a unified framework which integrates the MMM mechanism with the RF technique. However, these approaches solely direct the focus on the image level. In our recent work (Chen, Zhang, Chen, & Chen, 2005), we extended our research efforts to the object level by incorporating the latent semantic indexing (LSI) based long-term learning and one-class support vector machine (SVM) based MIL technique. However, to record the query logs, the users are asked to pick the interested region in the segmented image, which imposes a heavy burden to the users.

HIERARCHICAL LEARNING SCHEME

As discussed earlier, integrating the essential functionalities from both MMM and MIL has the potential in constructing a robust CBIR. In the following two sub-sections, we will introduce MIL and MMM, respectively, followed by the detailed discussions of the proposed hierarchical learning framework in our proposed MMIR system.

Multiple Instance Learning

Motivated by the *drug activity prediction problem*, Dietterich, Lathrop, and Lozano-Perez (1997) introduced the multiple instance learning model. Since its introduction, it has become increasingly important in machine learning.

In a traditional supervised learning problem, the task is to learn a function

$$y = f(x_1, x_2, ..., x_n) \qquad , \tag{1}$$

given a group of examples $(y_i, x_{i1}, x_{i2},...,x_{in})$, $i = 1,2,...Z$.

Here, Z represents the number of input examples and n denotes the number of features for each example object. In other words, each set of input values $(x_{i1}, x_{i2},...x_{in})$ is tagged with the label y_i, and the task is to learn a hypothesis (function f) that can accurately predict the labels for the unseen objects.

In MIL, however, the input vector $(x_{i1}, x_{i2},...x_{in})$ (called an *instance*) is not individually labeled with its corresponding y_i value. Instead, one or more instances are grouped together to form a *bag* $B_b \in \beta$ and are collectively labeled with a $Y_b \in L$. Here, β denotes the bag space and L represents the label space with $L = \{0(\text{Negative}), 1(\text{Positive})\}$ for binary classification. Let α be the instance space and assume there are m instances in B_b, the relation between the bag label Y_b and the labels $\{y_{bj} \mid y_{bj} \in L\}$ ($j = 1,...,m$) of all its instances $\{I_{bj} \mid I_{bj} \in \alpha\}$ is defined as follows.

$$Y_b = \begin{cases} 1 & \text{if } \exists_{j=1}^{m} y_{bj} = 1 \\ 0 & \text{if } \forall_{j=1}^{m} y_{bj} = 0 \end{cases} \tag{2}$$

In other words, the label of a bag (i.e., Y_b) is a disjunction of the labels of the instances in the bag (i.e., Y_b where $j = 1,...,m$). That is, the bag is labeled as positive if and only if at least one of its instances is positive; whereas it is negative when all the instances in that bag are negative. The goal of the learner is to generate a hypothesis $h : \beta \rightarrow L$ to accurately predict the label of a previously unseen bag.

In terms of image representations in the region-based retrieval, images are first segmented into regions, where each of them is roughly homogeneous in color and texture and is characterized by a feature vector. Consequently, each image is represented by a collection of feature vectors. From the perspective of learning, the labels (positive or negative) are directly associated with images instead of individual regions. It is reasonable to assume that if an image is labeled as positive, at least one of its regions is of user's interest. Intuitively, the basic idea is essentially identical to the MIL settings, where a *bag* refers to an *image*; whereas an *instance* corresponds to a *region*. With the facilitation of MIL, we can expect a reasonably good query performance by discovering and applying the query-related objects in the process and filtering out the irrelevant objects.

In this study, for the sake of accuracy, the real-valued MIL approach developed in our earlier work (Huang, Chen, & Shyu, 2003) is adopted. The idea is to transfer the discrete label space $L = \{0(\text{Negative}), 1(\text{Positive})\}$ to a continuous label space $L_R = [0, 1]$, where the value indicates the degree of positive for a bag, with label "1" being 100% positive. Therefore, the goal of the learner is to generate a hypothesis h_R

$: \beta \rightarrow L_R$. Consequently, the label of the bag (i.e., the degree of the bag being positive) can be represented by the maximum of the labels of all its instances and Eq. (2) is then transformed as follows.

$$Y_b = \max_j \{y_{bj}\}. \tag{3}$$

Let $h_I : \alpha \rightarrow L_R$ be the hypothesis to predict the label of an instance, we have the relationship between hypotheses h_R and h_I as depicted in Equation (4).

$$Y_b = h_R(B_b) = \max_j \{y_{bj}\} = \max_j \{h_I(I_{bj})\}. \tag{4}$$

Then the minimum square error (MSE) criterion is used. That is, we try to learn the hypotheses $\hat{h}_R$ and $\hat{h}_I$ to minimize the following function.

$$S = \sum_b \left(Y_b - \hat{h}_R(B_b) \right)^2 = \sum_b \left(Y_b - \max_j \{\hat{h}_I(I_{bj})\} \right)^2. \tag{5}$$

In this study, the multilayer feed-forward neural network is adopted to represent the hypothesis $\hat{h}_I$ and the back-propagation learning method is used to train the neural network to minimize S. More detailed discussion can be found in Huang et al. (2003). In the *Experimental Results* section, we will discuss the structure and parameter settings of the neural network.

It is worth noting that to some extent, the MIL approach can be considered as a hybrid of the RF technique and the region-based retrieval. In other words, MIL intends to achieve better query results in the next round by analyzing the training bag labels (i.e., user's feedback), which resembles the RF concepts. Nevertheless, the main focus of MIL is to explore the region of users' interest, which is the reason that we classify MIL as a region-based approach.

Markov Model Mediator

Markov model mediator (MMM) is a statistical reasoning mechanism, which adopts the mathematically sound Markov model and the concept of the mediators. The Markov model is one of the most powerful tools used to analyze the complicated systems, whereas a mediator is defined as a program to collect and combine information from one or more sources to yield the resulting information (Wiederhold, 1992).

Generally speaking, an MMM is a stochastic finite state machine with a stochastic output process attached to each state to describe the probability of the occurrences of the output symbols (states) (Shyu et al., 2004b). Its structure and settings are determined by three model parameters, that is, state transition probability distribution, observation symbol probability distribution, and initial state probability distribution denoted by A, B and Π, respectively. The parameter B is determined by the states' characteristics (or attributes), whereas parameters A and Π are defined by two kinds of information extracted from the historical database query logs, namely access patterns P and access frequencies F.

Let q_k be a query in the logs that accessed a certain number of states, $f_k \in F$ represents the number of such query q_k issued and recorded, and $P_{m,k} \in P$ denotes the access pattern of state m with respective to q_k, where

$$p_{m,k} = \begin{cases} 1 & \text{if state } m \text{ is accessed by } q_k \\ 0 & \text{otherwise} \end{cases} \tag{6}$$

Let $a_{m,n} \in A$ be the transition probability between two states m and n, we have

$$a_{m,n} = \frac{\sum\limits_{k} p_{m,k} \times p_{n,k} \times f_k}{\sum\limits_{n}\sum\limits_{k} p_{m,k} \times p_{n,k} \times f_k} \tag{7}$$

The initial state probability $\pi_m \in \Pi$ for state m is defined as follows.

$$\pi_m = \frac{\sum\limits_{k} p_{m,k}}{\sum\limits_{n}\sum\limits_{k} p_{n,k}} \tag{8}$$

Then a dynamic programming based stochastic output process is carried out to produce the probability of the occurrences of the output states. A more detailed discussion can be found in Shyu et al. (2003). Owing to its strong reasoning capability, it has been widely applied to a variety of domains including database clustering (Shyu et al., 2004a), multimedia database management (Shyu et al., 2004b), and so forth.

Intuitively, in terms of the applications in image retrieval, an MMM can be readily converted to model the semantic network by regarding the images as the states and accumulating the users' feedbacks in the query logs. It is worth noting that because of the perception subjectivity issue, each user's feedback will be recorded distinctly in the logs. In other words, the access frequency $f_k \in F$ is set to 1, and Equation (6) is redefined as

$$p_{m,k} = \begin{cases} 1 & \text{if image } m \text{ is positive in the } k^{th} \text{ feedback} \\ 0 & \text{otherwise} \end{cases} \tag{9}$$

Then given a query image (the starting state), the stochastic output process is applied to traverse the network to yield the probability of the occurrences (or the similarity values) of the output states (the other images), where the greater the probability is, the higher the image is ranked in the retrieved image set. It is worth noting that as a statistical reasoning mechanism, MMM effectively learns the concepts adopted by the majority of users (or called general concepts), which has been fully demonstrated in Shyu et al. (2003, 2004b). However, it fails to serve the specific user's query need if it is far from the general concepts. In addition, if the query image has no access record in the query logs, the retrieval process will end up using solely the low-level image features to calculate the similarity values.

Hierarchical Learning Framework in the MMIR System

In this sub-section, we will present the basic idea and procedure of constructing the hierarchical learning framework (for short, MMM_MIL framework) by integrating these two techniques for the MMIR sys-

Figure 2. The hierarchical learning framework

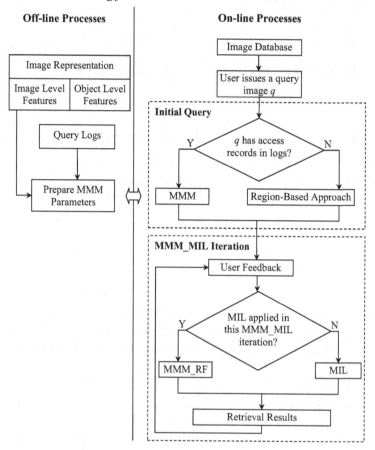

tem, which is illustrated in Figure 2. As can be seen in this figure, the MMM_MIL framework consists of an off-line process which aims at extracting the image and object-level features to obtain the MMM parameters, and an online retrieval process. These two processes work closely with each other in the sense that the off-line process prepares the essential data for the online process to reduce the online processing time. In addition, the feedbacks provided in the online process can be accumulated in the logs for the off-line process to update the MMM parameters periodically. In this section, we will focus on the online retrieval process.

Initial Query

In most of the existing CBIR systems, given a query image, the initial query results are simply computed using a certain similarity function (e.g., Euclidean distance, Manhattan distance, etc.) upon the low-level features either in the image or the object level. For instance, in the general MIL framework, since there is no training data available for the outset of the retrieval process, a simple distance-based metric is applied to measure the similarity of two images (Huang et al., 2003). Formally, given a query image q with R_q regions (denoted as $q = \{q_i\}$, $i = 1, ..., R_q$), its difference with respect to an image m consisting of R_m regions (denoted as $m = \{m_j\}$, $j = 1, ..., R_m$) is defined as:

$$Dist(q,m) = \sum_i \min_j \left\{ \left| q_i - m_j \right| \right\} \qquad (10)$$

Here, $\left| q_i - m_j \right|$ represents the distance between two feature vectors of regions q_i and m_j.

However, due to the semantic gap issue, it is highly possible that the number of "positive" images retrieved in the initial run is relatively small (e.g., less than five positives out of the top 30 images). This lack of positive samples greatly hinders the learning performance for most of the learning algorithms, including the NN-based MIL approach we discussed earlier. In contrast, MMM possesses the capability of representing the general concepts in the query and outperforms the region-based approach defined in Equation (10) on the average. One exception, though, is that any query image that has not been accessed before will force the MMM mechanism to perform the Euclidean distance function upon the low-level image features (discussed earlier). In this case, the region-based approach will be applied as it captures more completed information. Therefore, in our proposed hierarchical learning framework, the initial query is carried out as illustrated in Figure 2. It is worth noting that the test of whether an image q has been accessed before (its access record) in the log can be formally transformed to test whether $\sum_j a(q, j)$ equals 0, where $a(q, j) \in A$.

MMM_MIL Iteration

With the initial query results, the users are asked to provide the feedbacks for the MMM_MIL iteration, which is defined as an MIL process followed by MMM. The basic idea is that based on the region of interest (e.g., instance I_p in image or bag B_p) MIL learned for a specific user, the semantic network represented by MMM is intelligently traversed to explore the images which are semantically related to B_p. Obviously, it can be easily carried out by treating B_p as the query image and using the algorithms described earlier. However, in case that a group of positive bags (images) are identified, which is actually the general case, the situation becomes relatively complicated in the sense that a number of paths need to be traversed and the results are then aggregated to reach the final outputs.

Therefore, an extended MMM mechanism called MMM_RF (Shyu et al., 2006) is used to solve this problem. In brief, the difference between MMM and MMM_RF is that MMM considers only the direct relationship between the query image q and the other images in the database; whereas MMM_RF adopts an additional relationship called indirectly related (RI) relationship which denotes the situation when two images are connected to a common image. With the introduction of RI, the multiple paths mentioned earlier can be effectively merged into a new path, where the same dynamic programming based stochastic output process can be applied to produce the final results (please refer to Shyu et al., 2006).

EXPERIMENTAL RESULTS

Experimental Datasets

To perform rigorous evaluation of our proposed framework, we chose 9,800 real-world images from the COREL image CDs, where every 100 images represent one distinct topic of interest. Therefore, our data set contains 98 thematically diverse image categories, including antique, balloon, car, cat, firework, flower, horse, and so forth, where all the images are in JPEG format with size 384*256 or 256*384.

Experimental Setup

In order to evaluate the performance of the proposed MMIR system, the off-line process needs to be carried out first, which includes feature extraction and query log collection. In addition, the neural network structure for MIL should be defined before the online process can be conducted.

Image Representation

Each image is represented by the color and texture features extracted from both the image and object levels.

- **Color:** Color feature is widely adopted in a CBIR system for its simplification and effectiveness. In addition, HSV color space and its variants are proven to be particularly amenable to color image analysis. Also as discussed in Goldstein (1999), though the wavelength of visible light ranges from 400 to 700 nanometers, the colors that can be named by all the cultures are generally limited to be around 11. Therefore, we quantify the color space using color categorization based on H, S, V value ranges and identify 13 representative colors. Besides *black* and *white*, 10 discernible colors (*red, red-yellow, yellow, yellow-green, green, green-blue, blue, blue-purple, purple* and *purple-red*) are extracted by dividing the Hue into five main color slices and five transition color slices. Here, each transition color slice like *red-yellow, yellow-green*, and so forth, is considered between two adjacent main color slices. In addition, we add a new category *gray* for the remaining value ranges.
- **Texture:** Texture is an important cue for image analysis. It has been shown in a variety of studies (Smith & Chang, 1995; Tong et al., 2001) that characterizing texture features in terms of structure, orientation, and scale fits perfectly with the models of human perception. A number of texture analysis approaches have been proposed. In this study, a one-level wavelet transformation using Daubechies wavelets is used to generate the horizontal detail sub-image, the vertical detail sub-image, and the diagonal detail sub-image. The reason for selecting Daubechies wavelet transform lies in the fact that it is proven to be suitable for image analysis. For the wavelet co-efficients in each of the earlier-mentioned three sub-bands, the mean and variance values are collected respectively. Therefore, six texture features are extracted.

In terms of image-level features, the extraction process is relatively straightforward when an image is considered as a whole and a vector of 19 features (13 color features and 6 texture features) is generated as discussed earlier. As far as the region level features are considered, an image segmentation process needs to be carried out beforehand.

- **Image Segmentation:** In this study, the *WavSeg* algorithm proposed in our earlier work (Zhang, Chen, & Shyu, 2004) is applied to partition the images. In brief, *WavSeg* adopts a wavelet analysis in concert with the SPCPE algorithm (Chen, Sista, Shyu, & Kashyap, 2000) to segment an image into a set of regions. By using Daubechies wavelets, the high-frequency components will disappear in larger scale sub-bands and the possible regions will be clearly evident. Then by grouping the salient points from each channel, an initial coarse partition is obtained and passed as the input to the SPCPE segmentation algorithm, which has been proven to outperform the random initial partition based SPCPE algorithm. In addition, this wavelet transform process can actually produce the region-level texture features together with the extraction of the region-of-interest within one entry scanning through the image data.

Once the region information becomes available, the region-level color features can be easily extracted.

Query Logs

The collection of query logs is a critical process for learning the essential parameters in this framework. Therefore, in MMIR, a group of seven users were asked to create the log information. In other words, the users are requested to perform the query-by-example (QBE) execution on the system and provide their feedbacks on the retrieved results.

In order to ensure that the logs cover a wide range of images, each time a query image is randomly seeded from the image database and the system returns the top 30 ranked images by employing the region-based approach defined earlier. The user then provides the feedbacks (positive or negative) on the images by judging whether they are relevant to the query image. Such information is named as a query log and is accumulated in the database. Currently, we have collected 896 query logs. It is worth noting that though the users may give noisy information to the logs, it will not significantly affect the learning performance as long as it only accounts for a small portion of the query logs.

Neural Network

As discussed earlier, a three-layer feed-forward neural network is used in our study to map an image region with a low-level feature vector into the user's high-level concept.

As can be seen from Figure 3, the network consists of an input layer, a hidden layer, and an output layer. Here, the input layer contains 19 input units, where each of them represents a low-level feature of an image region. Therefore, the notations $f_1, f_2, \ldots, f_{19}$ correspond to the 19 low-level features described previously. The hidden layer is composed of 19 hidden nodes with w_{ij} being the weight of the connection between the ith input unit I_i and the jth hidden node H_j (where $i, j = 1, \ldots, 19$). Note that the output layer contains only one node, which outputs the real value $y \in L_R = [0, 1]$ indicating the satisfactory level of an image region with regard to a user's concept. The weight between the output node and the jth hidden node H_j is in turn denoted as w_j. The Sigmoid function with slope parameter 1 is used as the activation function and the back-propagation (BP) learning method is applied with a learning rate of 0.1 with no momentum. The initial weights for all the connections (i.e., w_{ij} and w_j) are randomly set with relatively small values (e.g., in the range of [-0.1, 0.1]) and the termination condition of the BP algorithm is defined as follows.

$$\left| S^{(k)} - S^{(k-1)} \right| < \alpha \times S^{(k-1)}. \tag{11}$$

Here, $S^{(k)}$ denotes the value of S at the kth iteration and α is a small constant, which is set to 0.005 in our experiment.

Figure 3. The three-layer feed-forward neural network

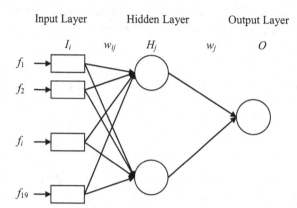

Performance Comparison

The performance measurement metric employed in our experiments is *accuracy*, which is defined as the average ratio of the number of relevant images retrieved over the number of total returned images (or called scope). In order to evaluate the performance of the hierarchical learning framework (denoted as MMM_MIL), we compare it with the neural network-based MIL technique with relevance feedback (for short, MIL_RF) which does not support the log-based retrieval. In addition, we also compare the performance of our system with another general feature re-weighting algorithm (Rui et al., 1997) with relevance feedback using both Euclidean and Manhattan distances, denoted as RF_Euc and RF_Mah, respectively.

Fifty query images are randomly issued. For each query image, the initial query results are first retrieved and then followed by two rounds of user feedbacks with regard to MIL_RF, RF_Euc and RF_Mah algorithms. Correspondingly, besides the initial query, one MMM_MIL iteration is performed as each iteration consists of two rounds of feedbacks. In our database log, totally 896 distinct queries have been recorded which are used by MMM_MIL. In addition, the region-level features used by MIL_RF are the same as the ones used by MMM_MIL. Similarly, the image-level features used by RF_Euc, RF_Mah and MMM_MIL are also identical.

The accuracy within different scopes, i.e., the percentages of positive images within the top 6, 12, 18, 24, and 30 retrieved images are calculated. The results are illustrated in Figure 4, where Figures 4a and 4b show the initial query results and the second query (or the first round of MMM_MIL) results, respectively.

As can be seen from this figure, the accuracy of MMM_MIL greatly outperforms all the other three algorithms in all the cases. More specifically, with regard to the initial query results (Figure 4a), MMM_MIL (represented by the red line) performs far better than the remaining three algorithms with more than 10% difference in accuracy on average, which demonstrates MMM's strong capability in capturing the general concepts. Furthermore, by comparing Figure 4a and Figure 4b, we observe that the MMM_MIL results improve tremendously where the increment of the accuracy rate reaches 30% on

Figure 4. Experimental results

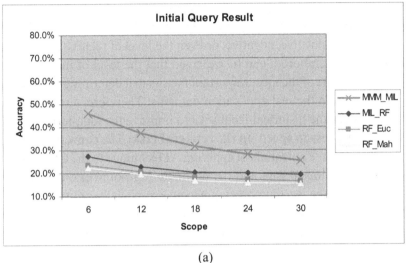

(a)

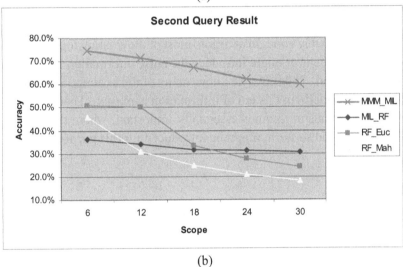

(b)

average. In contrast, the improvements of the other approaches are relatively small (with the improvement of the accuracy rate ranging from 10% to 20%), which indicates that MMM_MIL can achieve an extremely fast convergence of the concept.

FUTURE TRENDS

Machine learning and other artificial intelligence (AI) approaches have attracted increasing interests in the content-based image retrieval (CBIR) area. Many research works have been conducted, which led to quite a few encouraging achievements. However, there remain a number of emerging challenges and open issues to be addressed. Correspondingly, we list some of the future trends as follows.

- **Better interaction scheme to alleviate the manual efforts:** Generally, for an interactive CBIR system, the query performance is achieved at the cost of huge human efforts. Take the relevance feedback system as an example. Normally, the users are asked to go through 3 to 4 iterations to provide their feedbacks (positive, negative, or even the level of relativity in some approaches) for tens of images in each iteration. It can be expected that the level of manual efforts required for image retrieval will be one of the most important factors that determine the potential and popularity of the CBIR system in the real application domains. Therefore, a trend has been emerged to accumulate and analyze the historical feedbacks to improve the long-term system performance.

- **Faster converging process to speed up the retrieval task:** The converging speed is another important issue that affects the potentials of applying AI technique to the CBIR system. Considering the explosive growth of image data and the normally high-dimensional image representations, the converging speed of the learning process becomes especially critical for the real-time image retrieval process. The singular value decomposition (SVD) has been used for dimension reduction and noisy data removal to facilitate the converging process. More studies for this issue are certainly expected.

- **Noise-tolerate mechanism:** In the current CBIR research, various assumptions are made in terms of the amount of noise data contained in the image database. For instance, we presume that the image quality is of reasonably good. In addition, most of the existing log-based CBIR frameworks assume that while a certain user might introduce the noise information into the query log, the rate is negligibly low (Hoi et al., 2004). As we know, many of the assumptions do not hold in the real-world applications, especially in this era of information explosion. Therefore, the construction of the noise-tolerate mechanism becomes essentially important, where the techniques like outlier detection, fuzzy logic, and so forth, might be introduced for this purpose.

CONCLUSION

As an emerging topic, the application of the learning techniques in the CBIR system has attracted increasing attentions nowadays. With the aim of addressing the semantic gap and the perception subjectivity issues, in this chapter, we introduced an advanced content-based image retrieval system called MMIR that is facilitated with a hierarchical learning framework called MMM_MIL. The unique characteristic of the proposed MMM_MIL learning framework is that it not only possesses the strong capabilities in real-time capturing and learning the object and image semantic concepts, but also offers an effective solution to speed up the learning process by intelligently exploring the feedback logs. The comparative experiments with the well-known learning techniques fully demonstrate the effectiveness of the proposed MMIR system.

REFERENCES

Chen, S.-C., Rubin, S. H., Shyu, M.-L., & Zhang, C. (in press). A dynamic user concept pattern learning framework for content-based image retrieval. Accepted for publication, *IEEE Transactions on Systems, Man, and Cybernetics: Part C.*

Chen, S.-C., Sista, S., Shyu, M.-L., & Kashyap, R. L. (2000). An indexing and searching structure for multimedia database systems. In the *Proceedings of the IS&T/SPIE International Conference on Storage and Retrieval for Media Databases,* San Jose, CA, January 23-28 (pp. 262-270). Bellingham, WA: SPIE Press.

Chen, Y., & Wang, J. Z. (2004). Image categorization by learning and reasoning with regions. *Journal of Machine Learning Research*, 5, 913-939.

Chen, X., Zhang, C., Chen, S.-C., & Chen, M. (2005). A latent semantic indexing based method for solving multiple instance learning problem in region-based image retrieval. In the *Proceedings of IEEE International Symposium on Multimedia,* Irvine, CA, December 12-14 (pp. 37-44). Los Alamitos, CA: IEEE Computer Society.

Dietterich, T. G., Lathrop, R. H., & Lozano-Perez, T. (1997). Solving the multiple-instance problem with axis-parallel rectangles. *Artificial Intelligence*, *89*, 31-71.

Goldstein, E. B. (1999). *Sensation and perception* (5th ed.). Pacific Grove, CA: Brooks/Cole.

He, X., King, O., Ma, W.-Y., Li, M., & Zhang, H. J. (2003). Learning a semantic space from user's relevance feedback for image retrieval. *IEEE Transactions on Circuits and Systems for Video Technology*, *13*(1), 39-49.

He, J., Li, M., Zhang, H.-J., Tong, H., & Zhang, C. (2004). Mean version space: A new active learning method for content-based image retrieval. In the *Proceedings of ACM International Conference on Multimedia,* New York, NY, October 10-16 (pp. 15-22). New York: ACM Press.

Hoi, C.-H., & Lyu, M. R. (2004). A novel log-based relevance feedback technique in content-based image retrieval. In the *Proceedings of ACM International Conference on Multimedia,* New York, NY, October 10-16 (pp. 24-31). New York: ACM Press.

Huang, X., Chen, S.-C., & Shyu, M.-L. (2003). Incorporating real-valued multiple instance learning into relevance feedback for image retrieval. In the *Proceedings of the IEEE International Conference on Multimedia & Expo,* Baltimore, MD, July 6-9 (pp. 321-324). Los Alamitos, CA: IEEE Computer Society Press.

Huang, X., Chen, S.-C., Shyu, M.-L., & Zhang, C. (2002). User concept pattern discovery using relevance feedback and multiple instance learning for content-based image retrieval. In the *Proceedings of the Third International Workshop on Multimedia Data Mining,* Edmonton, Alberta, Canada, July 23 (pp. 100-108). Edmonton, Alberta, Canada: University of Alberta.

Jin, X., & French, J. C. (2003). Improving image retrieval effectiveness via multiple queries. In the *Proceedings of ACM International Workshop on Multimedia Database,* New Orleans, LA, November 7 (pp. 86-93). New York: ACM Press.

Jing, F., Li, M., Zhang, H.-J., & Zhang, B. (2000). An effective region-based image retrieval framework. In the *Proceedings of ACM International Conference on Multimedia,* Los Angeles, CA, October 30-November 3 (pp. 456-465). New York: ACM Press.

Kaplan, L. M. et al. (1998). Fast texture database retrieval using extended fractal features. In the *Proceedings of IS&T/SPIE Conference on Storage and Retrieval for Media Databases,* San Jose, CA, January 28-30 (pp. 162-173). Bellingham, WA: SPIE Press.

Pass, G. (1997). Comparing images using color coherence vectors. In the *Proceedings of ACM International Conference on Multimedia,* Seattle, WA, November 9-13 (pp. 65-73). New York: ACM Press.

Rui, Y., Huang, T. S., & Mehrotra, S. (1997). Content-based image retrieval with relevance feedback in MARS. In the *Proceedings of the International Conference on Image Processing,* Washington D.C., October 26-29 (pp. 815-818). Piscataway, NJ: IEEE Press.

Shyu, M.-L., Chen, S.-C., Chen, M., & Zhang, C. (2004b). Affinity relation discovery in image database clustering and content-based retrieval. In the *Proceedings of ACM International Conference on Multimedia,* New York, NY, October 10-16 (pp. 372-375). New York: ACM Press.

Shyu, M.-L., Chen, S.-C., Chen, M., Zhang, C., & Shu, C.-M. (2003). MMM: A stochastic mechanism for image database queries. In the *Proceedings of the IEEE Fifth International Symposium on Multimedia Software Engineering,* Taichung, Taiwan, ROC, December 10-12 (pp. 188-195). Los Alamitos, CA: IEEE Computer Society Press.

Shyu, M.-L., Chen, S.-C., Chen, M., Zhang, C., & Shu, C.-M. (2006). Probabilistic semantic network-based image retrieval using MMM and relevance feedback. *Multimedia Tools and Applications, 30*(2), 131-147.

Shyu, M.-L., Chen, S.-C., & Rubin, S. H. (2004a). Stochastic clustering for organizing distributed information source. *IEEE Transactions on Systems, Man and Cybernetics, Part B, 34*(5), 2035-2047.

Smith, J., & Chang, S.-F. (1995, July). Automated image retrieval using color and texture. Technical report CU/CTR 408-95-14, Columbia University.

Stehling, R. O., Nascimento, M. A., & Falcao, A. X. (2000). On shapes of colors for content-based image retrieval. In the *Proceedings of ACM International Workshop on Multimedia Information Retrieval,* Los Angeles, CA, November 4 (pp. 171-174). New York: ACM Press.

Tong, S., & Chang, E. (2001). Support vector machine active learning for image retrieval. In the *Proceedings of ACM International Conference on Multimedia,* Ottawa, Ontario, Canada, September 30-October 5 (pp. 107-118). New York: ACM Press.

Wiederhold, G. (1992). Mediators in the architecture of future information systems. *IEEE Computers, 25*(3), 38-49.

Zhang, C., Chen, S.-C., & Shyu, M.-L. (2004). Multiple object retrieval for image databases using multiple instance learning and relevance feedback. In the *Proceedings of IEEE International Conference on Multimedia and Expo,* Taipei, Taiwan, ROC, June 27-30 (pp. 775-778). Los Alamitos, CA: IEEE Computer Society Press.

Zhang, D. S., & Lu, G. (2002). Generic fourier descriptors for shape-based image retrieval. In the *Proceedings of IEEE International Conference on Multimedia and Expo,* Lausanne, Switzerland, August 26-29 (pp. 425-428). Los Alamitos, CA: IEEE Computer Society Press.

Zhou, X. S., Rui, Y., & Huang, T. (1999). Water-filling: A novel way for image structural feature extraction. In the *Proceedings of IEEE International Conference on Image Processing: Vol. 2,* Kobe, Japan, October 25-28 (pp. 570-574). Piscataway, NJ: IEEE Press.

388

Compilation of References

3VR, http://www.3vr.com/Products/#smartsearch.

Aach, J., & Church, G. M. (2001). Aligning gene expression time series with time warping aalgorithms. *Bioinformatics, 17*(6), 495-508.

Agouris, P., Carswell, J., & Stefanidis, A. (1999). "An Environment for Content-Based Image Retrieval from Large Spatial Databases", *ISPRS Journal of Photogrammetry and Remote Sensing*, Elsevier, Vol. 54, No. 4, pp. 263-272, 1999.

Agrawal, R., Lin, K.-I., Sawhney, H. S., & Shim, K. (1995). Fast similarity search in the presence of noise, scaling, and translation in time-series databases. *Proceedings of 21th International Conference on Very Large Data Bases* (pp. 490-501). San Francisco, CA, USA: Morgan Kaufmann Publishers Inc.

Ahuja, N., & Rosefeld, A. (1978). A note on the use of second-order gray-level statistics for threshold selection. *IEEE Transactions on Systems, Man, and Cybernetics, 8*, 895-898.

Alto, H., Rangayyan, R. M., & Desautels, J. E. L. (2005). Content-based retrieval and analysis of mammographic masses. *Journal of Electronic Imaging, 14*(2), 1-17.

Anderson, E. (1935). The irises of the Gaspé Peninsula. *Bulletin of the American Iris Society, 59*, 2–5.

Andrews, S., Tsochantaridis, I., & Hofmann, T. (2003). Support vector machines for multiple-instance learning. In S. Becker, S. Thrun, & K. Obermayer (Eds.), *Advances in neural information processing systems* (vol. 15, pp. 561–568). Cambridge, MA: MIT Press.

Androutsos, D., Plataniotis, K. N., & Venetsanopoulos, A. N. (1999). A novel vector-based approach to color image retrieval using vector angular-based distance measure. *Computer Vision and Image Understanding,* 1/2, 46-58.

Andrysiak T., & Choras M. (2005). Image retrieval based on hierarchical Gabor filters. *International Journal of Applied Mathematics and Computer Science. 15*(4), 471-480.

Ankerst, M., Breunig, M.M., Kriegel, H.-P., & Sander, J. (1999). Optics: Ordering points to identify the clustering structure. In Proceedings ACM SIGMOD International Conference on Management of Data, pp. 49–60.

Ansia, F., Penedo, M. Mariño, C., López, J., & Mosquera, A. (2000). Automatic 3D shape reconstruction of bones using active net-based segmentation. In *15th International Conference on Pattern Recognition,* Barcelona, Spain.

Ansia, F., Penedo, M., Mariño, C., López, J., & Mosquera, A. (1999). Morphological analysis with active nets. In *4th International Conference on Advances in Pattern Recognition and Digital Techniques.*

Antani, S., Lee, D. J., Long, L. R., & Thoma, G. R. (2004). Evaluation of shape similarity measurement methods for spine X-ray images. *Journal of Visual Communication and Image Representation, 15*(3), 285-302.

Arbter, K., et al. (1990). Application of affine-invariant Fourier descriptors to recognition of 3D objects. IEEE PAMI, 12, 640-647.

Arivazhagan S., Ganesan L., & Priyal S. P. (2006). Texture classification using Gabor wavelets-based rotation invariant features. *Pattern Recognition Letters, 27*(16), 1976-1982.

Arodz, T., Kurdziel, M., Popiela, T. J., Sevre, R. O. D., & Yuen, D. A. (2006). Detection of clustered microcalcifications in small field digital mammography, *Computer Methods and Programs in Biomedicine, 81*(1), 56-65.

Arunkumar, S. (2004). *Neural network and its application in pattern recognition* (Dissemination Report). Department of Computer Science and Engineering, Indian Institute of Technology, Bombay.

Assent, I., Wenning, A., and Seidl, T., (2006). Approximation techniques for indexing the earth mover's distance in multimedia databases. In Proc. of IEEE ICDE.

Attar, R., & Fraenkel, A. S. (1977). Local feedback in full-text retrieval systems. *Journal of the ACM, 24*(3), 397-417.

Bach, J., Fuller, C., Gupta, A., Hampapur, A., Gorowitz, B, Humphrey, R., Jain, R., & Shu, C. (1996). Virage image search engine: An open framework for image management. In Poceedings of the SPIE Conference on Storage and Retrieval for Image and Video Databases IV, pp. 76–87.

Bar-Joseph, Z., Gerber, G., Gifford, D. K., Jaakkola, T. S., & Simon, I. (2002). A new approach to Aanalyzing gene expression time series data. *Proceedings of 6th Annual International Conference on Computational Biology* (pp. 39 - 48). Washington, DC, USA: ACM.

Barnard, K., & Forsyth, D. A. (2001). Learning the semantics of words and pictures. In *Proceedings of the International Conference on Computer Vision (ICCV)* (pp. 408–415).

Barnard, K., Duygulu, P., & Forsyth, D. A. (2001). Clustering art. *Computer Vision and Pattern Recognition (CVPR), 2,* 434–441.

Barreira, N., & Penedo, M. G. (2004). Topological active volumes for segmentation and shape reconstruction of medical images. In *Lecture Notes in Computer Science: Image Analysis and Recognition* (pp. 132-140).

Barreira, N., Penedo, M. G., Ibázes, O., & Santos, J. (2007). Automatic topological active net division in genetic-greedy hybrid approach. In *Lecture Notes in Computer Science: Pattern Recognition and Image Analysis* (pp. 226-233).

Baumberg, A. (2000). Reliable feature matching across widely separated views. CVPR, pp.774-781.

Bazan, J., Skowron, A., & Synak, P. (1994). Dynamic reducts as a tool for extracting laws from decision tables. In *Proceedings of the Symposium on Methodologies for Intelligent Systems*, 346-355.

Beaver, K., & Witham, G. (2007). Information needs of the informal carers of women treated for breast cancer. *European Journal of Oncology Nursing, 11*(1), 16-25.

Beckmann, N., et al. (1990). The R*-tree : An efficient and robust access method for points and rectangles. Proc. of ACM SIGMOD.

Bei, C.-D., & Gray, R. M. (1985). An improvement of the minimum distortion encoding algorithm for vector quantization. *IEEE Transactions on Communications, 33,* 1132–1133.

Belkhatir, M. (2005). A symbolic query-by-example framework for the image retrieval signal/semantic integration. In *Proceedings of the 17th IEEE International Conference on Tools with Artificial Intelligence, ICTAI* (pp. 348-355). Washington, DC, IEEE Computer Society Press.

Belkhatir, M., Chiaramella, Y., & Mulhem, P. (2005). A signal/semantic framework for image retrieval. In *Proceedings of the 5th ACM/IEEE-CS Joint Conference on Digital Libraries, JCDL '05* (pp. 368-368). Denver, CO, USA, ACM Press.

Belongie, S., Malik, J., & Puchiza, J. (2001). Matching Shapes. In *Proceeeding International Conference on Computer Vision.*

Belongie, S., Malik, J., & Puzicha, J. (2002). Shape matching and object recognition using shape contexts. *IEEE PAMI 24*(24), 509-522.

Bentley, J. L. (1975). Multidimensional binary search trees used for associative searching. *Communication of the ACM, 18*(9), 509–517.

Berchtold, S., Böhm, C., Keim, D.A., & Kriegel, H.-P. (1997). A cost model for nearest neighbor search in high-dimensional data space. In *Proceedings of the 16th ACM SIGACT-SIGMOD-SIGART Symposium on Principles of Database Systems* (pp. 78–86).

Berchtold, S., Keim, D., & Kriegel, H.P. (1996). The X-tree: An index structure for high-dimensional data. Proc. of VLDB.

Berndt, D. J., & Clifford, J. (1994). Using dynamic time warping to find patterns in time series. *AAAI Workshop on Knowledge Discovery in Databases* (pp. 229-248).

Berretti, S., Del Bimbo, A., & Vicario, E. (2001). Efficient matching and indexing of graph models in content-based retrieval. *IEEE Transactions on Pattern Analysis and Machine Intelligence, 23*(10), 1089-1105.

Berriss, W.P., Price, W.G., & Bober, M.Z. (2003). Real-Time Visual Analysis and Search Algorithms for Intelligent Video Surveillance, International Conference on Visual Information Engineering (pp. 226-229).

Besag, J. (1986). On the statistical analysis of dirty pictures. *Journal Royal Statistical Society, Series B, 33*(3), 259-302.

Bigün, J., & du Buf, J. M. H. (1994). N-folded symmetries by complex moments in Gabor space and their application to unsupervised texture segmentation. *IEEE Transactions on Pattern Analysis and Machine Intelligence, 16*(1), 80-87.

Bimbo, A. (1999). *Visual information retrieval.* San Francisco: Morgan Kaufmann.

BI-RDS, Breast Imaging Reporting and Data System. (1998). 3rd edition. American College of Radology, Reston, VA, USA.

Blom, G. (1989). *Probability and Statistics: Theory and Applications.* London, U. K.: Springer Verlag.

Bocchi, L., & Nori, J. (2007). Shape analysis of microcalcifications using Radon transform. *Medical Engineering & Physics, 29*(6), 691-698.

Boerrs, E. J., & Kuiper, H., (1992). *Biological metaphors and the design of modular artificial neural networks.* Master's thesis, Department of Computer Science and Experimental Psychology, Leiden University.

Boggess, A., & Narcowich, F.J. (2001). A first course in wavelets with Fourier analysis, chapter Haar wavelet analysis, pp. 155-178. Prentice Hall.

Bovik, A. C., Gopal, N., Emmoth, T., & Restrepo, A. (1992). Localized measurement of emergent image frequencies by Gabor wavelets. *IEEE Transactions on Information Theory, 38*(2), 691-712.

Bozkaya, T., & Ozsoyoglu, M. (1997). Distance-based indexing for high-dimensional metric spaces. *ACM SIGMOD*, 357-368.

Breiman, L., Friedman, J. H., Olshen, R. A., & Stone, C. J. (1984). *Classification and regression trees.* Belmont, CA: Wadsworth International Group.

Brin, S. (1995). Near neighbor search in large metric spaces. *VLDB*, 574-584.

Bronez, T.P., & Hughes, E.S. (1997). "Image & Video Retrieval for National Security Applications: An Approach Based on Multiple Content Codebooks", The MITRE Corporation, McLean, Virginia 1997.

Bro-Nielsen, M. (1994) *Active nets and active cubes.* (Tech. Rep. No. 94-13). IMM.

Brown, L., Senior, A., Tian, Y., Connell, J., Hampapur, A., Shu, C., Merkl, H., & Lu, M. (2005b). Performance evaluation of surveillance systems under varying conditions, IEEE International Workshop on Performance Evaluation of Tracking and Surveillance (pp. 79-87) Breckenridge, CO.

Brown, L.M. (2004). View independent vehicle/person classification, ACM 2nd International Workshop on Video Surveillance and Sensor Networks (pp. 114-123) New York, NY.

Brown, L.M., Lu, M., Shu, C., Tian, Y., & Hampapur, A. (2005a) Improving performance via post track analysis. IEEE International Workshop on Visual Surveillance and Performance Evaluation of Tracking and Surveillance (pp. 341 – 347) Beijing, China.

Brown, M., Szeliski, R., & Winder, S. (2005). Multi-image matching using multi-scale oriented patches. *CVPR*, 510-517.

Brumby, S. P., Theiler, J., Perkins, S., Harvey, N. R., & Szymanski, J. J. (2002). *Genetic programming approach to extracting features from remotely sensed imagery*. Paper presented at the internal meeting of Space and Remote Sensing Sciences, Los Alamos National Laboratory, Los Alamos, New Mexico.

Brumby, S. P., Theiler, J., Perkins, S. J., Harvey, N., Szymanskia, J. J., Bloch, J. J., & Mitchellb, M. (1999). *Investigation of image feature extraction by a genetic algorithm*. Paper presented at the internal meeting of the Los Alamos National Laboratory, Space and Remote Sensing Sciences, Santa Fe Institute.

Buckley, C., & Salton, G. (1995). Optimization of relevance feedback weights. In E.A. Fox, P. Ingwersen, & R. Fidel (Eds.), *Proceedings of the Annual International ACM SIGIR Conference on Research and Development in Information Retrieval* (pp. 351–357).

Burges, C. J. (1998). A tutorial on support vector machines for pattern recognition. *Knowledge Discovery and Data Mining, 2,* 121-167.

Burr, D. C., Morrone, M. C., & Spinelli, D. (1989). Evidence for edge and bar detectors in human vision. Vision Research, *29*(4), 419-431.

Caiani, E. G., Porta, A., Baselli, G., Turiel, M., Muzzupappa, S., Pieruzzi, F., et al. (1998). *Warped-average template technique to track on a cycle-by-cycle basis the cardiac filling phases on left ventricular volume, computers in cardiology* (pp. 73-76). Cleveland, OH, USA.

Carson, C. (2002). Blobworld: Image segmentation using expectation-maximization and its applications to image querying. *IEEE Transactions on Pattern Analysis and Machine Intelligence, 24*(8), 1026–1038.

Carson, C., Belongie, S., Greenspan, H., & Malik, J. (2002). Blobworld: Image segmentation using expectation-maximization and its application to image querying. *IEEE Transactions on Pattern Analysis and Machine Intelligence, 24*(8), 1026-1038.

Carson, C., et al. (1999). Blobworld : A system for region-based image indexing and retrieval. Proc. of International Conference on Visual Information Systems.

Carson, C., Thomas, M., Belongie, S., Hellerstein, J. M., & Malik, J. (1999). Blobworld: *A system for region-based image indexing and retrieval*. Third International Conference on Visual Information Systems, 509-516.

Chan, F. K.-P., Fu, A. W.-C., & Yu, C. (2003). Haar wavelets for efficient similarity search of time-series: With and without time warping. *IEEE Transactions on Knowledge and Data Engineering, 15*(3), 686-705.

Chang, C.C., & Lin, C.J. (2001). Libsvm: a library for support vector machines. Software available at http://www.csie.ntu.edu.tw/~cjlin/libsvm.

Chang, S.K., & Hsu, A. (1992). Image information systems: Where do we go from here? *IEEE Trans. on Knowledge and Data Engineering, 5*(5), 431-442.

Chang, T., & Jay, C.C., & Kuo. (1993). Texture analysis and classification with tree-structured wavelet transform. *IEEE Transactions on Image Processing, 2*(3), 429–441.

Charman, W. N. (2005). Wavefront technology: Past, present, and future. *Contact Lens and Anterior Eye, 28*(2), 75-92.

Chen, S.-C., Sista, S., Shyu, M.-L., & Kashyap, R. L. (2000). An indexing and searching structure for multimedia database systems. In the *Proceedings of the IS&T/SPIE International Conference on Storage and Retrieval for Media Databases,* San Jose, CA, January 23-28 (pp. 262-270). Bellingham, WA: SPIE Press.

Chen, S.-C., Rubin, S. H., Shyu, M.-L., & Zhang, C. (in press). A dynamic user concept pattern learning framework for content-based image retrieval. Accepted for publication, *IEEE Transactions on Systems, Man, and Cybernetics: Part C.*

Chen, X., Zhang, C., Chen, S.-C., & Chen, M. (2005). A latent semantic indexing based method for solving multiple instance learning problem in region-based image retrieval. In the *Proceedings of IEEE International Symposium on Multimedia,* Irvine, CA, December 12-14 (pp. 37-44). Los Alamitos, CA: IEEE Computer Society.

Chen, Y. D., & Dougherty, E. R. (1994). Gray-scale morphological granulometric texture classification. *Optical Engineering, 33*(8), 2713-2722.

Chen, Y., & Wang, J. (2002). A region-based fuzzy feature matching approach to content-based image retrieval. *IEEE Transactions on Pattern Analysis and Machine Intelligence, 24*(9), 1252–1267.

Chen, Y., & Wang, J. Z. (2004). Image categorization by learning and reasoning with regions. *Journal of Machine Learning Research*, 5, 913-939.

Chen, Y., & Wong, E. K. (2001). A knowledge-based approach to video content classification. *Proceedings of SPIE, 4315: Storage and Retrieval for Media Databases*, 292-300.

Chen, Y., and Zhou, X., & Huang, T. (2001). One-class SVM for learning in image retrieval. In *Proceedings of the IEEE International Conference on Image Processing.*

Chen, Y., Zhou, X. S., & Huang, T. S. (2001). One-class support vector machine for learning in image retrieval. In *Proceedings of the IEEE International Conference on Image Processing 2001* (pp. 34-37). IEEE Press.

Chen, Y., Zhou, X., & Huang, T. (2001). One-class SVM for learning in image retrieval. *Proceedings of the IEEE International Conference on Image Processing* (vol. 1, pp. 34–37).

Cheng, M. Y. K., Micacchil, C., & Cohen, R. (2005). Adjusting the autonomy of collections of agents in multiagent Ssystems. In *Advances in Artificial Intelligence, 3501, 2005* (pp. 33-37). Springer Berlin / Heidelberg Publisher.

Cheng, P.C. et al. (2007). "A two-level relevance feedback mechanism for image retrieval" Expert Systems with Applications, In Press, Corrected Proof, available online 4 March 2007.

Chien, Y. P., & Fu, K. S. (1974). Recognition of X-ray picture patterns. *IEEE Transactions on Systems Man and Cybernetics. 4*(2), 145-156.

Chiu., S.-T. (1996). A comparative review of bandwidth selection for kernel density estimation. *Statistica Sinica,* 16:129–145.

Chiueh, T.-C. (1994). Content-based image indexing. In *Very large databases* (pp. 582–593).

Chu, S., Keogh, E., Hart, D., & Pazzani, M. (2002). Iterative deepening dynamic time warping. *Proceedings of 2nd SIAM International Conference on Data Mining.* Maebashi City, Japan.

Chuang, S.C., et al. (2006) "A Multiple-Instance Neural Network-based Image Content Retrieval System", in Proceedings of the First International Conference on Innovative Computing, Information and Control (ICICIC), 2006.

Ciaccia, P., Patella, M. & Zezula, P. (1997). M-Tree: An efficient access method for similarity search in metric spaces. *VLDB Journal*, 426-435.

Cios, K., Pedrycz, W., & Swiniarski, R. (1998). *Data mining methods for knowledge discovery.* Norwell, MA: Kluwer Academic Publishers.

Clark, M., Bovik, A. C., & Geisler, W. S. (1987). Texture segmentation using Gabor modulation/demodulation. *Pattern Recognition Letters, 6*(4), 261-267.

Columbia University. WebSeek. Available at http://persia.ee.columbia.edu:8008/

Comaniciu, D., Ramesh, V. & Meer, P. (2000). Real-time tracking of non-rigid objects using mean shift, In Proc. IEEE Conference on Computer Vision and Pattern Recognition, 2, 142-149.

Conners R. W., & Harlow C. A. (1980). Towards a structural textural analyzer based on statistical methods. *Computer Graphics and Image Processing, 12*(3), 224-256.

Convera. Purchasing RetrievalWare. Available at http://www.convera.com/.

COREL. Corel images. Accessed on 12/3/2005. Available at http://wang.ist.psu.edu/docs/related.

Cost, R. S., & Salzberg, S. (1993). A weighted nearest neighbor algorithm for learning with symbolic features. *Machine Learning, 10*, 57–78.

Cover, T. M., & Hart, P. E. (1967). Nearest neighbor pattern classification. *IEEE Transaction in Information Theory, 13*, 57–67.

Cox, I. J., Miller, M. L., & Minda, T. P., et al. (2000). The Bayesian image retrieval system, PicHunter: theory, implementation, and psychophysical experiments. *IEEE Transactions on Image Proceeding, Special Issue on Image and Video Proceeding for Digital Libraries, 9*(1), 20–37.

Cox, I.J., Miller, M.L., Minka, T.P., Papathomas, T.V., & Yianilos, P.N. (2000). The Bayesian image retrieval system, PicHunter: Theory, implementation and psychophysical experiments. *IEEE Trans. on Image Processing, 9*(1):20–37.

Crucianu, M., Ferecatu, M., & Boujemaa, N. (2004). *Relevance feedback for image retrieval: a short survey.* INRIA Rocquencourt, France.

Cui, B., Ooi, B.C., Su, J., & Tan, T. (2005). Indexing high-dimensional data for efficient in-memory similarity search. *IEEE Trans. on Knowledge and Data Engineering, 17*(3), 339-353.

Dagli, C., & Huang, T. S. (2004). A framework for grid-based image retrieval. *17th International Conference on Pattern Recognition, 2, ICPR'04* (pp. 1021-1024). IEEE Computer Society Press.

Das, G., Lin, K.-I., Mannila, H., Renganathan, G., & Smyth, P. (1998). Rule discovery from time series. *Proceedings of 4th International Conference on Knowledge Discovery and Data Mining* (pp. 16-22). New York, NY, USA: AAAI Press.

Dasgupta, D., & Forrest, S. (1996). Novelty detection in time series data using ideas from immunology. *Proceedings of 5th International Conference on Intelligent Systems* (pp. 82-87). Reno, Nevada, USA.

Datar, M., et al. (2004). Locality-sensitive hashing scheme-based on P-Stable distributions. *ACM SoCG.*

Datta, R., Joshi, D., Li, J., & Wang, J.Z. (in press). Image retrieval: Ideas, influences, and trends of the new age. *ACM Computing Surveys.*

de Ves, E., Domingo, J., Ayala, G., & Zuccarello, P. (2007). A novel Bayesian framework for relevance feedback in image content-based retrieval systems. *Pattern Recognition, 39*, 1622-1632.

Deerwester, S. C., Dumais, S. T., Landauer, T. K., Furnas, G. W., & Harshman, R. A. (1990). Indexing by latent semantic analysis. *Journal of the American Society for Information Science (JASIS), 41*(6), 391–407.

Del Bimbo, A. (1999). *Visual Information Retrieval.* San Francisco, CA: Morgan kaufmann Pub.

Del Buono, A. (2007). *An overview about sophisticatedf-Face recognition systems.* (Tech. Rep No. 1). National Research Centre, Computer Science and Knowledge Laboratory (CSK Lab).

Deng, Y., Manjunath, B.S. (2001). Unsupervised segmentation of color-texture regions in images and video. *IEEE Trans. PAMI, 23*(8), 800-810.

Deselaers, T., Keysers, D., & Ney, H. (2003). Clustering visually similar images to improve image search engines. *Proceedings of Informatiktage 2003 der Gesellschaft für Informatik.* Bad Schussenried, Germany.

Dietterich, T. G., Lathrop, R. H., & Lozano-Perez, T. (1997). Solving the multiple-instance problem with axis-parallel rectangles. *Artificial Intelligence, 89*, 31-71.

Diez, J. J. R., & González, C. A. (2000). Applying boosting to similarity literals for time series classification. *Proceedings of 1st International Workshop on Multiple Classifier Systems* (pp. 210-219). Cagliari, Italy.

Dillon, W.R., & Goldstein, M. (1984). *Multivariate Analysis, Mehtods and Applications.* New York: John Wiley and Sons.

Doi, A., Fujiware, S., Matsuda, K., & Kameda, M. (2002). 3D Volume extraction and mesh generation using energy minimization techniques. In *Proceedings of the first International on 3D Data Processing Visualization and Transmission* (pp. 83-86).

Dol, Z., Salam, R. A., & Zainol, Z. (2006). Face feature extraction using Bayesian network. *Proceedings of the 4th International Conference on Computer Graphics and Interactive Techniques* (pp. 261-264). ACM Press.

Doulamis, N., & Doulamis, A. (2006). "Evaluation of relevance feedback schemes in content-based in retrieval systems" Signal Processing: Image Communication, Vol. 21, Issue 4, April 2006, 334-357.

Dowe, J. (1993). Content-based retrieval in multimedia imaging. In *Poceedings of the SPIE Conference on Storage and Retrieval for Image and Video Databases*.

Duc, B., Fischer, S., & Bigun, J. (1999). Face authentication with Gabor information on deformable graphs. *IEEE Transactions on Image Processing, 8*(4), 504-516.

Duce, D. (Ed.). W3C Portable Network Graphics Specification Version 2.0. Available at http://www.w3.org/TR/PNG-Glossary.html.

Duda, R.O., & Hart, P.E. (1973). *Pattern Classification and Scene Analysis*. New York: John Wiley and Sons.

Duygulu, P., Barnard, K., De Freitas, J. F. G., & Forsyth, D. A. (2002). Object recognition as machine translation: Learning a lexicon for a fixed image vocabulary. In *Proceedings of the European Conference on Computer Vision, (ECCV)* (pp. 97–112).

Eakins, J.P., & Graham, M.E. (1999). "Content-based Image Retrieval", A report to the JISC Technology Applications Programme, Institute for Image Data Research, University of Northumbria at Newcastle, January 1999.

Eleuteri, A., Tagliaferri, R., & Milano, L. (2005). A novel information geometric approach to variable selection in MLP Networks. *International Journal on Neural Network, 18*(10), 1309-1318, Elsevier Science Publishing.

El-Naqa, I., Yang, Y., Galatsanos, N. P., Nishikawa, R. M., & Wernick, M. N. (2004). A similarity learning approach to content-based image retrieval: Application to digital mammography. *IEEE Transactions on Medical Imaging, 23*(10), 1233-1244.

Faloutsos, C., et al. (1994). Efficient and effective querying by image content. *Journal of Intelligent Information Systems, 3*(3/4), 231–262.

Faloutsos, C., Flicker, M., Niblack, W., Petkovic, D., Equitz, W., & Barber, R. (1993). *Efficient and effective querying by image content*. Technical Report, IBM, USA.

Faloutsos, C., Ranganathan, M., & Manolopoulos, Y. (1994). Fast subsequence matching in time-series databases. *Proceedings of the 1994 ACM SIGMOD International Conference on Management of Data* (pp. 419-429). Minneapolis, Minnesota, United States: ACM.

Fauci, F., Raso, G., Magro, R., Forni, G., Lauria, A., Bagnasco, S., Cerello, P., Cheran, S. C., Lopez Torres, E., Bellotti, R., De Carlo, F., Gargano, G., Tangaro, S., De Mitri, I., De Nunzio, G., & Cataldo, R. (2005). A massive lesion detection algorithm in mammography. *Physica Medica, 21*(1), 23-30.

Fayyad, U. M., Piatetsky-Shapiro, G., & Smyth, P. (1996). From data mining to knowledge discovery: An overview. In *Advances in Knowledge Discovery and Data Mining* (pp. 1–34). Menlo Park: AAAI Press.

Feng, D., Siu, W. C., & Zhang, H. J. (2003). *Multimedia Information Retrieval and Management: Technological Fundamentals and Applications*. Berlin: Springer.

Ferecatu, M., Crucinu, M., & Boujemaa, N. (2004). *Reducing the redundancy in the selection of samples for SVM-based relevance feedback*. INRIA Rocquencourt, France.

Ferhatosmanoglu, H., Tuncel E., Agrawal D., & Abbadi A. E. (2006). High dimensional nearest neighbor searching. *Information Systems Journal, 31*(6), 512-540.

Ferhatosmanoglu, H., Tuncel, E., Agrawal, D., & Abbadi, A. E. (2000). Vector approximation based indexing for non-uniform high dimensional data sets. In *Proceedings of the 9th ACM Int. Conf. on Information and Knowledge Management*, (pp. 202–209). ACM, SIGIR, and SIGMIS.

Feris, R., Tian, Y., & Hampapur, A. (2007). Capturing people in surveillance video, The Seventh International Workshop on Visual Surveillance (pp. 1-8.)

Filho, R.F.S., Traina, A.J.M., Traina, C., & Faloutsos, C. (2001). Similarity search without tears: The OMNI family of all-purpose access ,ethods. *ICDE*, 623-630, 2001.

Finlayson, G. D., Hordley, S. D., & Hubel, P. M. (2001). Color by correlation: A simple, unifying framework for color constancy. *IEEE Transactions on Pattern Analysis and Machine Intelligence, 23*(11), 1209-1221.

Fischer, S., Lienhart, R., & Effelsberg, W. (1995). Automatic recognition of film genres. *Proc. ACM Multimedia 95*, 295-304. San Francisco, CA.

Fisher, R. (1936). The use of multiple measurements in taxonomic problems. *Annals of Eugenics, 7*, 179–188.

Fix, E., & Hudges, J. L. (1951). *Discriminatory analysis: Nonparametric discrimination: Consistency properties* (Tech. Rep. No. 21-49-004). Randolph Field, TX: USAF School of Aviation Medicine.

Flickner, M., et al. (1995). Query by image and video content : The QBIC system. *IEEE Computer, 28*(9), 23-32.

Flickner, M., et al. (1995). Query by image and video content: The QBIC system. *IEEE Computer, 28*(9), 23–32.

Flickner, M., Niblack, W., Sawhney, H., Ashley, J., Huang, Q., Dom, B., Gorkani, M., Hafner, J., Lee, D., Petkovic, D., Steele, D., & Yanker, P. (1995). Query by image and video content: The QBIC system. *IEEE Computer, 28*(9), 23-32.

Flickner, M., Sawhney, H., Niblack, W., Ashley, J., Huang, Q., Dom, B., Gorkani, M., Hafner, J., Lee, D., Petkovic, D., Steele, D., & Yanker, P. (1995). Query by image and video content: The QBIC system. *IEEE Computer Magazine, 28*(9), 23-32.

Florack, L.M.J., et al. (1993). Cartesian differential invariants in scale-space. J. mathematical imaging and vision, 3, 327-348.

Florack, L.M.J., et al. (1994). General intensity transformation and differential invariants. *J. Mathematical Imaging and Vision, 4*(2), 171-187.

Fogel, I., & Sagi, D. (1989). Gabor filters as texture discriminator. *Biological Cybernetics, 61*(2), 103-113.

Forstner, W. (1994). A framework for low level feature extraction. *ECCV*, 383-394.

Francois, A. (2004). Real-time multi-resolution blob tracking, Institute for Robotics and Intelligent Systems, University of Southern California, Los Angeles, California, from http://handle.dtic.mil/100.2/ADA447622.

Freitas, A. A. (2002). A survey of evolutionary algorithms for data mining and knowledge discovery. *Advances in evolutionary computation: Theory and application, natural computing series* (pp. 819-845). Springer Publisher.

Friedman, J. (1994). *Flexible metric nearest neighbor classification*. Technical Report, Department of Statistics, Stanford University, USA.

Friedman, J. H., Baskett, F., & Shustek, L. J. (1975). An algorithm for finding nearest neighbors. *IEEE Transactions on Computers, 24*(10), 1000–1006.

FRVT, (2006). Face recognition vendor test (FRVT), http://www.frvt.org/FRVT2006/.

Fu, A.W.-C., et al. (2000). Dynamic VP-tree indexing for N-Nearest search given pair-wise distances. *VLDB Journal*.

Funahashi, T., Fujiwara, T., & Koshimizu, H. (2005). Coarse to fine hierarchical tracking system for face recognition. IEEE International Conference on Systems, Man and Cybernetics, 4, 3454-3459.

Gabriel, K. R., & Sokal, R. R. (1969). A new statistical approach to geographic variation analysis. *Systematic Zoology, 18*, 259–278.

Gandi, A. (2002). *Content-based image retrieval: Plant species identification.* Oregon State University.

García-Pérez, D. Mosquera, A., Berretti, S., & Del Bimbo, A. (2006b). Topological active-nets for object-based image retrieval. In *International Conference on Image Analysis and Recognition* (pp. 636-647). Pòvoa de Varzim, Portugal.

García-Pérez, D., Mosquera, A., Berretti, S., & Del Bimbo, A. (2006a). Object-based image retrieval using active nets. In *Proceedings International Conference on Pattern Recognition* (ICPR'06), (pp. 750-753). Honk-Kong, China.

Gavrila, D. M., & Davis, L. S. (1995). Towards 3-D model-based tracking and recognition of human movement: A multi-view approach. *Proceeding of International Workshop on Face and Gesture Recognition* (pp. 272-277).

Gebara, D., & Alhajj, R. (2007). WaveQ: Combining wavelet analysis and clustering for effective image retrieval. Proceedings of IEEE International Symposium on Data Mining and Information Retrieval.

Geman, D., & Moquet, R. (2000). A stochastic model for image retrieval. In *Proceedings of RFIA 2000*, Paris, France.

Geman, S., & Geman, D. (1984). Stochastic relaxation, Gibbs distributions, and the Bayesian restoration of images. *IEEE Transactions on Pattern Analysis and Machine Intelligence, 6*(6).

Gersho, A., & Gray, R. M. (1991). *Vector quantization and signal compression.* Boston: Kluwer Academic.

Geusebrock, J., Burghouts, G., & Smeulders, A. (2006). The Amsterdam library of object images. *International Journal of Computer Vision, 66*(1), 103-112.

Gevers, T., & Smeulders, A. W. M. (1999). Color-based object recognition. *Pattern Recognition*, 32, 453-464.

Gevers, T., & Smeulders, A. W. M. (2000). Pictoseek: Combining color and shape invariant features for image retrieval. *IEEE Transactions on Image Processing, 9*(1), 102-110.

Gionis, A., Indyk, P., Motwani, R. (1999). Similarity search in high dimensions via hashing. Proc. of VLDB.

Glatard, T., Montagnat, J., & Magnin, I.E. (2004). Texture-based medical image indexing and retrieval: application to cardiac imaging. In *Proceedings of ACM SIGMM international workshop on Multimedia information retrieval* (pp. 135-142). New York, NY: Association for Computing Machinery.

Goldstein, E. B. (1999). *Sensation and perception* (5th ed.). Pacific Grove, CA: Brooks/Cole.

Gollmer, K., & Posten, C. (1996). Supervision of bioprocesses using a dynamic time warping algorithm. *Control Engineering Practice, 4*(9), 1287-1295.

Gondra, I., & Heisterkamp, D.R. (2004). Probabilistic region relevance learning for content-based image retrieval. *Proceedings of the International Conference on Imaging Science, Systems, and Technology* (pp. 434–440).

Gondra, I., Heisterkamp, D. R., & Peng, J. (2004). Improving image retrieval performance by inter-query learning with one-class support vector machines. *Neural Computing & Applications, 13*(2), 130-139.

Goodrum, A. (2000). "Image Information Retrieval: An Overview of Current Research" *Informing Science*, Special Issue of Information Science Research, vol. 3 no 2, 2000.

Google Image Search. http://www.google.com/imghp.

Graham, M. E. (2004). Enhancing visual resources for searching and retrieval: Is content based image retrieval solution? *Literary and Linguistic Computing, 19*(3), 321-333.

Grzymala-Busse, J., Pawlak, Z., Slowinski, R., & Ziarko, W. (1999). Rough sets. Communications of the ACM, 38(11), 88-95.

Guan, L., & Kamel, M. (1992). Equal-average hyperplane partitioning method for vector quantization of image data. *Pattern Recognition Letters, 13*(10), 693–699.

Gupta, A., & Jain, R. (1997). Visual information retrieval. *Communications of the ACM, 40*(5), 70-79.

Gupta, L., Molfese, D. L., Tammana, R., & Simos, P. G. (1996). Nonlinear alignment and averaging for estimating the evoked potential. *IEEE Transactions on Biomedical Engineering, 43*(4), 348-356.

Guttman, A. (1984). R-trees: A dynamic index structure for spatial searching. In *Proceedings of the SIGMOD Conference* (pp. 47–57).

Hacid, H., & Zighed, A.D. (2005). An effective method for locally neighborhood graphs updating. *Database and Expert Systems Applications* (LNCS 3588, 930-939).

Hagan, M. T., Demuth, H. B., & Beale, M. H. (1996). *Neural network design.* PWS Publishing.

Haley, G. M., & Manjunath, B. S. (1999). Rotation invariant texture classification using a complete space-frequency model. *IEEE Transactions on Image Processing, 8*(2), 255-269.

Han, J. & Kamber, M. (2001). *Data mining: concepts and techniques.* San Diego, CA, USA: Academic Press.

Hara, Y., Hirata, K., Takano, H., & Kawasaki, S. (1997). Hypermedia navigation and content-based retrieval for distributed multimedia databases. *Proceedings of the NEC Research Symposium on Multimedia Computing* (pp. 133–148).

Haralick, R. M. (1979). Statistical and structural approaches to texture. In *Proceedings of the IEEE, 67*(5), 786-804.

Haralick, R. M., & Shanmugam, K. (1973). Textural features for image classification. *IEEE Transaction on Systems Man Cysbern, 3*(6), 610-621. IEEE Press.

Haralick, R. M., Shanmugam, K., & Dinstein, I. (1973). Texture features for image classification. *IEEE Transactions on Systems Man and Cybernetics. 3*(6), 610-621.

Harris, C., & Stephens, M. (1988) A combined corner and edge detector. In Alvey Vision Conference.

Hassanien, A., & Ali, J. (2004). Enhanced rough sets rule reduction algorithm for classification digital mammography. *Intelligent System Journal, 13*(2), 117-151.

Hauptmann, A. (2006). Lessons for the future from a decade of infomedia video analysis research, International Conference on Image and Video Retrieval (pp. 1-10.)

He, J., Li, M., Zhang, H.-J., Tong, H., & Zhang, C. (2004). Mean version space: A new active learning method for content-based image retrieval. In the *Proceedings of ACM International Conference on Multimedia,* New York, NY, October 10-16 (pp. 15-22). New York: ACM Press.

He, X., King, O., Ma, W.-Y., Li, M., & Zhang, H. J. (2003). Learning a semantic space from user's relevance feedback for image retrieval. *IEEE Transactions on Circuits and Systems for Video Technology, 13*(1), 39-49.

Healey, C.G., & Enns, J.T. (1999). Large datasets at a glance: Combining textures and colors in scientific visualization. *IEEE Transactions on Visualization and Computer Graphics, 5*(2), 145–167.

Heeger, D. J., & Bergen, J. R. (1995). Pyramid-based texture analysis/synthesis. *In Proceedings of the 22nd Annual Conference on Computer Graphics and Interactive Techniques* (pp. 229-238). ACM Press.

Heidemann, G. (2004). Combining spatial and colour information for content-based image retrieval. *Computer Vision and Image Understanding, 94*(1-3) 234-270.

Heisterkamp, D.R. (2002). Building a latent semantic index of an image database from patterns of relevance feedback. *Proceedings of the International Conference on Pattern Recognition* (vol. 4, pp. 134–137).

Heisterkamp, D.R., Peng, J., & Dai, H. (2001). Adaptive quasiconformal kernel metric for image retrieval. *Proceedings of the IEEE International Conference on Computer Vision and Pattern Recognition* (vol. 2, pp. 388–393).

Heisterkamp, D.R., Peng, J., & Dai, H.K. (2000). Feature relevance learning with query shifting for content-based image retrieval. *Proceedings of the International Conference on Pattern Recognition* (vol. 4, pp. 4250–4253).

Hejazi, M. R., & Ho, Y. S. (2005). Automated detection of tumors in mammograms using two segments for classification. In *Proceedings of the 6th Pacific-Rim*

Conference on Multimedia, 1(3767), 910-921. New York: Springer.

Hettich, S., Blake, C., & Merz, C. (1998). UCI repository of machine learning databases.

Highnam, R., & Brady, M. (1999). *Mammographic Image Analysis,* London: Kluwer Academic Publishers.

Hillier, F.S., & Liberman, G.J. (1990). Introduction to mathematical programming. McGraw-Hill.

Hitchcock, F.L. (1941). The distribution of a product from several sources to numerous locations. *J. Math. Phys.,* 20, 224-230.

HiTech, http://www.htsol.com/Products/SeeCar.html.

Hoi, C.-H., & Lyu, M. R. (2004). A novel log-based relevance feedback technique in content-based image retrieval. In the *Proceedings of ACM International Conference on Multimedia,* New York, NY, October 10-16 (pp. 24-31). New York: ACM Press.

Hoi, C.-H., Chan, C.-H., Huang, K., Lyu, M. R., & King, I. (2004). Biased support vector machine for relevance feedback in image retrieval. In *Proceedings of International Joint Conference on Neural Networks* (pp. 3189-3194).

Hoiem, D., Sukthankar, R., Schneiderman, H., & Huston, L. (2004). Object-based image retrieval Using the statistical structure of images. In *IEEE Conference on Computer Vision and Pattern Recognition.*

Hong, D., Wang, J., & Gardner, R. (2004). Real analysis with an introduction to wavelets and applications, chapter Orthonormal wavelet basis, pp. 209-270. Academic Press.

Hong, P., Tian, Q., & Huang, T. (2000). Incorporate support vector machines to content-based image retrieval with relevance feedback. *Proceedings of the IEEE International Conference on Image Processing* (pp. 750–753).

Hopgood, A. A. (2005). The state of artificial intelligence. In M. V. Zelkowitz (Ed.), *Advances in Computers* (pp. 1-75). Elsevier Publishing.

Horaud, R., Skordas, T., & Veillon, F.. (1990). Finding geometric and relational structures in an image. *ECCV,* 374-384.

Howarth, P., & Rüger, S. (2004). Evaluation of texture features for content-based image retrieval. In International Conference on Image and Video Retrieval, pp. 326–334.

Hu, N., Dannenberg, R. B., & Tzanetakis, G. (2003). Polyphonic audio matching and alignment for music retrieval *Proceedings of the 2003 IEEE Workshop on Applications of Signal Processing to Audio and Acoustics* (pp. 185-188).

Huang, H.K. (2003). PACS, image management, and imaging informatics. In D. Feng, W. C. Siu, & H. J. Zhang (Eds.), *Multimedia information retrieval and management: Technological fundamentals and applications* (pp. 347-365). New York: Springer.

Huang, J., et al. (1997). Image indexing using color correlogram. *CVPR,* 762-768.

Huang, J., Kumar, S.R., Mitra, M., Zhu, W.-J., & Zabih, R. (1997). Image indexing using color correlograms. In *IEEE Int'l Conf. Computer Vision and Pattern Recognition Proceedings,* Puerto Rico.

Huang, T.S., Mehrotra, S., & Ramchandran, K. (1996). Multimedia analysis and retrieval system (MARS) project. In Proceedings of 33rd Annual clinic on Library Application of Data Processing - Digital Image Access and Retrieval.

Huang, W., Tan, C. L., & Loew, W. K. (2003). Model-based chart image recognition. In *Proceedings of the International Workshop on Graphics Recognition (GREC),* 87-99.

Huang, X., Chen, S.-C., & Shyu, M.-L. (2003). Incorporating real-valued multiple instance learning into relevance feedback for image retrieval. In the *Proceedings of the IEEE International Conference on Multimedia & Expo,* Baltimore, MD, July 6-9 (pp. 321-324). Los Alamitos, CA: IEEE Computer Society Press.

Huang, X., Chen, S.-C., Shyu, M.-L., & Zhang, C. (2002). User concept pattern discovery using relevance feedback and multiple instance learning for content-based image retrieval. In the *Proceedings of the Third International Workshop on Multimedia Data Mining,* Edmonton, Alberta, Canada, July 23 (pp. 100-108). Edmonton, Alberta, Canada: University of Alberta.

Hubbard, B. (1998). The World According to Wavelets. A K Peters, Ltd Natick.

Hubel, D. H., & Wiesel, T.N. (1974). Sequence Regularity and Geometry of Direction Columns in the Monkey Striate Cortex. *Journal of Comparative Neurology, 158*(3), 267-293.

Ibáñez, O., Barreira, N., Santos, J., & Penedo, M. G. (2006). Topological active nets optimization using genetic algorithms. In *Lecture Notes in Computer Science: Image Analysis and Recognition* (pp. 272-282).

IBM. QBIC IBM's Query by Image Content. Available at http://wwwqbic.almaden.ibm.com.

Indyk, P., & Motwani, R. (1998). Approximate nearest neighbors: Towards removing the curse of dimensionality. *Proc. of ACM STOC.*

Ingemar, J., & Cox, J. (2000). The Bayesian image retrieval system, PicHunter: Theory, implementation, and psychological experiments. *IEEE Transactions on Image Processing, 9*(1), 20–37.

Ishikawa, Y., Subramanya, R., & Faloustos, C. (1998). MindReader: Query database through multiple examples. *Proceedings of the 24th international conference on very large data bases* (pp.218–227). San Fransisco.

Ishikawa, Y., Subramanya, R., & Faloutsos, C. (1998). Mindreader: Query databases through multiple examples. In *the 24ᵗʰ VLDB Conference Proceedings*, New York.

Ishikawa, Y., Subramanys, R., & Faloutsos, C. (1998). MindReader: Querying databases through multiple examples. *Proceedings of the International Conference on Very Large Databases* (pp. 218–227).

Itakura, F. (1975). Minimum prediction residual principle applied to speech recognition. *IEEE Transactions on Acoustics, Speech, and Signal Processing, 23*(1), 67-72.

Jagadish, H.V., el al. (2005). iDistance: An adaptive B+-tree based indexing method for nearest neighbor search. *ACM Trans. Database Syst., 30*(2), 364-397.

Jaimes, A. (2006a). Human-centered multimedia: Culture, deployment, and access. *IEEE Multimedia Magazine, 13*(1), 12-19.

Jaimes, A. (2006b). Human factors in automatic image retrieval system design and evaluation. In *Proceedings of IS&T/SPIE Internet Imaging 2006*, San Jose, CA, 2006.

Jaimes, A. (2006b). Human-centered multimedia: Culture, deployment, and access. *IEEE Multimedia Magazine, 13,* 12-19.

Jain, A. K., & Namboodiri, A. M. (2003). Indexing and retrieval of on-line handwritten documents. *Proceedings 7th International Conference on Document Analysis and Recognition* (pp. 655-659).

Jain, A.K., & Vailaya, A. (1996). Image retrieval using color and shape. *Pattern Recognition, 29*(8), 1233–1244.

Jennings, N. R., Sycara, K., & Wooldridge M. (1998). A roadmap of agent research and development. *International Journal on Autonomous Agents and Multi-Agent Systems, 1*(1), 7-38. Boston, Kluwer Academic Publishers.

Jeon, J., Lavrenko, V., & Manmatha, R. (2003). Automatic image annotation and retrieval using cross-media relevance models. In *Proceedings of the SIGIR* (pp. 119–126).

Jhanwar, N., Chaudhuri, S., Seetharaman, G., & Zavidovique, B. (2004). Content based image retrieval using motif cooccurrence matrix. *Image and Vision Computing, 22*(14), 1211-1220.

Jin, J., Zhu, Z., Xu, G. (2001). Digital video sequence stabilization-based on 2.5-D motion estimation and inertial motion filtering, Real-Time Imaging, 7(4), 357-365, Academic Press.

Jin, X., & French, J. C. (2003). Improving image retrieval effectiveness via multiple queries. In the *Proceedings of ACM International Workshop on Multimedia Database*, New Orleans, LA, November 7 (pp. 86-93). New York: ACM Press.

Jing, F., *et al.* (2004). An efficient and effective region-based image retrieval framework. *IEEE Transactions on Image Processing, 13*(5), 699-709.

Jing, F., Li, M., Zhang, H.-J., & Zhang, B. (2000). An effective region-based image retrieval framework. In the *Proceedings of ACM International Conference on Multimedia,* Los Angeles, CA, October 30-November 3 (pp. 456-465). New York: ACM Press.

Jing, F., Li, M., Zhang, H.-J., & Zhang, B. (2003). Support vector machines for region-based image retrieval. In *Proceedings of the IEEE International Conference on Multimedia & Expo*, Baltimore, MD.

Jing, F., Li, M., Zhang, L., Zhang, H., & Zhang, B. (2003). Learning in region-based image retrieval. *Proceedings of the International Conference on Image and Video Retrieval* (vol. 2728, pp. 206–215).

Julesz, B. (1975). Experiments in the Visual Perception of Texture. *Scientific American, 232*(4): 34-43.

Kadir, T., & Brady, M. (2001), Saliency, scale, and image description. *IJCV 45*(2), 83-105.

Kadir, T., Zisserman, A., & Brady, M. (2004). An affine invariant salient region detector. *ECCV, 1,* 228-241.

Kadous, M. W. (1999). Learning Comprehensible Descriptions of Multivariate Time Series. *Proceedings of 16th International Conference on Machine Learning* (pp. 454-463). Bled, Slovenia: Morgan Kaufmann Publishers Inc.

Kanth, K. V. R., Agrawal, D., & Singh, A. (1998). Dimensionality reduction for similarity searching in dynamic databases. In Ashutosh Tiwary (Ed.), *Proceeding of ACM SIGMOD ICMD*, (pp. 166–176). ACM, New York, NY.

Kaplan, L. M. et al. (1998). Fast texture database retrieval using extended fractal features. In the *Proceedings of*

IS&T/SPIE Conference on Storage and Retrieval for Media Databases, San Jose, CA, January 28-30 (pp. 162-173). Bellingham, WA: SPIE Press.

Kass, M., Witkin, A., & Terzopoulos, D. (1988) Snakes: Active contour models. *International Journal of Computer Vision, 1,* 312-331.

Käster, T., Wendt, V., & Sagerer, G. (2003). Comparing Clustering Methods for Database Categorization in Image Retrieval. *Proceedings of 25th Deutsche Arbeitsgemeinschaft für Mustererkennung Symposium* (pp. 228-235). Magdeburg, Germany.

Katajainen, J. (1988). The region approach for computing relative neighborhood graphs in the LP metric. *Computing, 40,* 147–161.

Katamaya, N., & Satoh, S. (1997). The SR-tree: An index structure for high-dimensional nearest neighbor queries. *Proc. of ACM SIGMOD.*

Kavallieratou, E., Dromazou, N., Fakotakis, N., & Kokkinakis, G. (2003). An Integrated System for Handwritten Document Image Processing. *International Journal of Pattern Recognition and Artificial Intelligence, 17*(4), 617 - 636

Kelly, P.M., Cannon, T.M., & Hush, D.R. (1995). Query by image example: The CANDID approach. In W. Niblack & R. Jain (Eds.), *Proceedings of the SPIE Storage and Retrieval for Image and Video Databases* (vol. 2420, pp. 238–248).

Kent, R. E. (1994). Rough concept analysis, rough sets, fuzzy sets knowledge discovery. In *Proceedings of the International Workshop on Rough Sets, Knowledge, Discovery,* 248-255.

Keogh, E. (2002). Exact indexing of dynamic time warping. *Proceedings of 28th International Conference on Very Large Data Bases* (pp. 406 - 417). Hong Kong, China.

Keogh, E., & Kasetty, S. (2003). On the need for time series data mining benchmarks: A survey and empirical demonstration. *Data Mining and Knowledge Discovery, 7*(4), 349-371.

Keogh, E., & Pazzani, M. (1999). Relevance feedback retrieval of time series data. *Proceedings of 22nd Annual International ACM SIGIR Conference on Research and Development in Information Retrieval* (pp. 183-190). Berkeley, CA, USA: ACM.

Keogh, E., & Pazzani, M. (2000). Scaling up dynamic time warping for data mining applications. *Proceedings of 6th ACM SIGKDD International Conference on Knowledge Discovery and Data Mining* (pp. 285-289). Boston, MA, USA: ACM.

Keogh, E., & Ratanamahatana, C. A. (2005). *Exact Indexing of Dynamic Time Warping. Knowledge and Information Systems, 7*(3), 358-386.

Keogh, E., Chakrabarti, K., Pazzani, M., & Mehrotra, S. (2001a). Dimensionality reduction for fast similarity search in large time series databases. *Knowledge and Information Systems, 3*(3), 263-286.

Keogh, E., Chakrabarti, K., Pazzani, M., & Mehrotra, S. (2001b). Locally adaptive dimensionality reduction for indexing large time series databases. *Proceedings of the 2001 ACM SIGMOD International Conference on Management of Data* (pp. 151-162). Santa Barbara, California, United States: ACM Press.

Keogh, E., Wei, L., Xi, X., Lee, S.-H., & Vlachos, M. (2006). LB_Keogh Supports Exact Indexing of shapes under rotation invariance with arbitrary representations and distance measures. *Proceedings of 32nd International Conference on Very Large Data Bases* (pp. 882-893). Seoul, Korea.

Kherfi, M. L., Ziou, D., & Bernardi, A. (2003). Combining positive and negative examples in relevance feedback for content-based image retrieval. *Journal of Visual Communication & Image Representation, 14*, 428-457.

Kim, S.-W., Park, S., & Chu, W. W. (2001). An index-based approach for similarity search supporting time warping in large sequence databases. *Proceedings 17th International Conference on Data Engineering* (pp. 607-614). Heidelberg, Germany.

Kleinbaum, D. G. (2002). *Logistic regression.* New York: Springer-Verlag.

Ko, B., & Byun, H. (2002). Integrated region-based image retrieval using region's spatial relationships. *EEE ICPR.*

Koenderink, J.J. (1984). The Structure of images. *Biological Cybernetics, 50*, 363-370.

Koenderink, J.J., & van Doorn, A.J. (1987) Representation of local geometry in the visual system. *Biological Cybernetics, 55*, 367-375.

Kohavi, R., & John, G. Wrappers for feature subset selection, *Artificial Intelligence*, 97, 1997, 273-324.

Kohonen, T. (2001). *Self-organizing maps* (Vol. 30). New York: Springer.

Kom, G., Tiedeu, A., & Kom, M. (2007). Automated detection of masses in mammograms by local adaptive thresholding. *Computers in Biology and Medicine, 37*(1), 37-48.

Komarek, P., & Moor, A. W. (2005). Making logistic regression a core data mining tool with TR-IRLS. In *Proceedings of the Fifth IEEE International Conference on Data Mining* (pp. 685-688). IEEE Press.

Konar, A. (Ed.). (2000). Artificial intelligence and soft computing - Behavioral and cognitive modeling of the human brain. CRC Press.

Konstantinos, N. P., & Rastislav, L. (Eds.). (2006). *Color image processing: Methods and applications.* CRC Press

Korn, F. *et al.* (1996). Fast nearest neighbor search in medical image databases. *VLDB*, 215-226.

Korolev, L. N. (2007). On evolutionary algorithms, neural-network computations, and genetic programming. Mathematical problems. *International Journal on Automation and Remote Control, 68*(5), 811-821. Plenum Press.

Koskela, M., Laaksonen, J., & Oja, E. (2004). Entropy-based measures for clustering and SOM topology preservation applied to content-based image indexing and retrieval. In *Proceedings of 17th International Conference on Pattern Recognition* (ICPR 2004), 1005-1009.

Kriegel, H.P., *et al*. (2007). Optimal multi-step K-Nearest neighbor search. In Proc. of the International Symposium on Spatial and Temporal Databases.

Krishnamachari, S., & Abdel-Mottaleb, M. (1999). Image Browsing Using Hierarchical Clustering. *Proceedings of the 1999 IEEE International Symposium on Computers and Communications* (pp. 301-307).

Kruizinga, P., & Petkov, N. (1995). A computational model of periodic-pattern-selective cells. In: J. Mira & F. Sandoval, (Eds.), *International Workshop on Artificial Neural Networks* (pp. 90-99). Berlin: Springer-Verlag.

Kruizinga, P., & Petkov, N. (1998). Grating cell operator features for oriented texture segmentation. In A. Jain, S. Venkatesh, & B. Lovell, (Eds.), *International Conference on Pattern Recognition* (pp. 1010-1014). Brisbane: IEEE Press.

Kruizinga, P., & Petkov, N. (1999). Non-linear operator for oriented texture. *IEEE Transactions on Image Processing, 8*(10), 1395-1407.

Kruskall, J. B., & Liberman, M. (1983). The Symmetric Time Warping Algorithm: From Continuous to Discrete. Time Warps, String Edits, and Macromolecules.

Kryszkiewicz, M., & Rybinski, H. (1994). Finding reducts in composed information systems, rough sets, fuzzy sets knowledge discovery. In *Proceedings of the International Workshop on Rough Sets, Knowledge, Discovery*, 261-273.

Kubo, M., Aghbari, Z., & Makinouchi, A. (2003). Content-based image retrieval technique using wavelet-based shift and brightness invariant edge feature. *International Journal of Wavelets, Multiresolution and Information Processing, 1*(2) 163–178.

Kundu, A., & Chen, J. L. (1992). Texture classification using QMF Bank-based subband decomposition. *CVGIP: Graphical Models and Image Processing, 54*, 369-384.

Kushki, A., Androutsos, P., Plataniotis, K. N., & Venetsanopoulos, A. N. (2004). Query feedback for interactive image retrieval. *IEEE Transactions on Circuits and Systems for Video Technology, 14*, 644-655.

Kwong, S., He, Q. H., & Man, K. F. (1996). Genetic Time warping for isolated word recognition. *International Journal of Pattern Recognition and Artificial Intelligence, 10*(7), 849-865.

Laakdonen, J., Koskela, M., & Oja, E. (1999). Picsom: Self-organizing maps for content-based image retrieval. In *IJCNN'99 Proceedings*, Washington DC.

Laaksonen, J., Koskela, M., & Oja, E. (1999). Picsom: Self-organizing maps for content-based image retrieval. *Proceedings of the International Joint Conference on Neural Networks* (vol. 4, pp. 2470–2473).

Laaksonen, J., Koskela, M., Laakso, S., & Oja, E. (2001). Self-organising maps as a relevance feedback technique in content-based image retrieval. *Pattern Analysis & Applications, 4*, 140-152.

Laine, A., & Fan, J. (1993). Texture classification by wavelet packet signatures. *IEEE Trans. PAMI, 15*(11), 1186-1191.

Lau, P.Y., & Ozawa, S. (2004). An image-based analysis for classifying multimodal brain images in the image-guided medical diagnosis model. In: D. Hudson (Ed.), *Annual International Conference of the IEEE Engineering in Medicine and Biology Society: Vol. 26*. (pp. 3400-3403). New, Jersey: Institute of Electrical and Electronics Engineers Inc.

Laudon, K. C., & Laudon, J. P. (2006). *Management information systems: Managing the digital FIRM* (9th ed.). NJ: Prentice Hall.

Lazebnik, S., Schmid, C., & Ponce, Jean. (2005). A sparse texture representation using local affine regions. *IEEE PAMI, 27*(8).

Lee, C.-H., & Chen, L.H. (1994). Fast closest codeword search algorithm for vector quantisation. In *IEEE Proceedings: Vision, Image, and Signal Processing* (Vol. 141, pp. 143–148).

Lee, H., Smeaton, A., O'Connor, N., & Murphy, N., (2005). User interface for CCTV search system, The IEE International Symposium on Imaging for Crime Detection and Prevention (pp. 39-43.)

Lehmann, T. M., Guld, M. O., Keysers, D, Deselaers, T., Schubert, H., Wein B. B., & Spitzer, K. (2004). Similarity of medical images computed from global feature vectors for content-based retrieval. *Lecture Notes in Artificial Intelligence*, 989-995.

Lehmann, T. M., Wein, B. B., & Greenspan, H. (2003). Integration of content-based image retrieval to picture archiving and communication systems. In *Proceedings of Medical Informatics Europe*. IOS Press.

Lei, Y. S., Wang, M. S., & Qin R. (2007). Edge information extraction algorithm of CT cerebrovascular medical image based on imaginary part of gabor filter. *Journal of Tianjin University Science and Technology*, *40*(7), 833-838.

Leibe, B., & Schiele, B. (2003). Analyzing appearance and contour-based methods of object categorization. In *Proceedings of the IEEE Computer Society Conference on Computer Vision and Pattern Recognition (CVPR'03)*.

Leveson, N. G., & Weiss, K. A. (2004). Making embedded software reuse practical and safe. *Proceedings of the Twelfth International Symposium on ACM SIGSOFT* (pp. 171-178). ACM Press.

Levine, M. (Ed.). (1985). Vision in Man and Machine. New, York: McGraw-Hill.

Lew, M. S., Sebe, N., Djeraba, C., & Jain, R. (2006). Content-based multimedia information Retrieval: State-of-the-art and Challenges. *ACM Transactions on Multimedia Computing, Communications and Applications*, *2*(1), 1-19.

Lew, M.S. (2001). *Principles of Visual Information Retrieval*. Springer-Verlag, London 2001.

Li, C.S., Smith, J.R., Castelli, V., & Bergman, L. (1999). Comparing texture feature sets for retrieving core images in petroleum applications. In *Proceedings of Storage and Retrieval for Image and Video Databases VII: Vol. 3656. The International Society for Optical Engineering* (pp. 2-10). Bellingham, WA: Society of Photo-Optical Instrumentation Engineers.

Li, J., & Wang, J. Z. (2003). Automatic linguistic indexing of pictures by a statistical modeling approach. *IEEE Transactions on Pattern Analysis and Machine Intelligence, 25*(9), 1075–1088.

Li, J., Gray, R. M., & Olshen R. A. (2000). Multiresolution image classification by hierarchical modeling with two-dimensional hidden Markov models. *IEEE Transactions on Information Theory, 46*(5), 1826-1841.

Li, J., Wang, J., & Wiederhold, G. (2000). Classification of textured and non-textured images using region segmentation. In Proc. of the 7th International Conference on Image Processing, pp. 754–757.

Li, J., Wang, J., & Wiederhold, G. (2000). IRM: Integrated region matching for image retrieval. *Proceedings of the ACM International Conference on Multimedia* (pp. 147–156).

Li, J., Wang, J.Z., & Wiederhold, G. (2000). Irm: Integrated region matching for image retrieval. *ACM Multimedia*.

Li, M., Chen, Z., & Zhang, H. (2002). Statistical correlation analysis in image retrieval. *Pattern Recognition, 35*(12), 2687–2693.

Li, Q., Hu, H., & Shi, Z. (2004). Semantic feature extraction using genetic programming in image retrieval. *Proceedings of the 17th International Conference on Pattern Recognition, ICPR 2004, 1(23-26)*, pp. 648-651. IEEE Computer Society Press.

Liang, S., & Sun, Z. X. (2006). BSVM-based relevance feedback for sketch retrieval. *Journal of Computer-Aided Design & Computer Graphics, 18*(11), 1753-1757, (in Chinese).

Lienhart, R., & Hartmann, A. (2002). Classifying images on the Web automatically. *Journal of Electronic Imaging, 11*, 31-40.

Limin, W. (2006). Learning Bayesian-neural network from mixed-mode data. In *Neural information processing* (pp. 680-687). Springer Publisher.

Lin H. C., Chiu C. Y., & Yang S. N. (2003). Finding textures by textual descriptions, visual examples, and relevance feedbacks. *Pattern Recognition Letters, 24*(14), 2255-2267.

Lin, K., Jagadish, H.V., & Faloutsos, C. (1994). The TV-tree: An idex structure for high-dimensional data. *VLDV Journal, 3*, 517-542.

Lin, K.-I., Jagadish, H. V., & Faloutsos, C. (1994). The TV-tree: An index structure for high-dimensional data. *Very Large Databases Journal, 3*(4), 517–542.

Lindeberg, T. (1998). Feature detection with automatic scale selection. *IJCV, 26*(3), 79-116.

Lindeberg, T. (1994). Scale-space theory: A basis tool for analyzing structures at different scales. *Journal of Applied Statistics, 21*(2), 225-270.

Lindeberg, T., & Garding, J. (1997). Shape-adapted smoothing in estimation of 3-d shape cues from affine distortions of local 2-D brightness structure. *Image and Vision Computing, 15*(6), 415-434.

Lindgren, D., & Spangeus, P. (2004). A novel feature extraction algorithm for asymmetric classification. *IEEE Sensors Journal*, 4(5):643–650.

Ling, H., & Jacobs, D.W. (2005). Deformation invariant image matching. *ICCV*.

Linguraru, M. G., Marias, K., English, R., & Brady, M. (2006). A biologically inspired algorithm for microcalcification cluster detection. *Medical Image Analysis, 10*(6), 850-862.

Liu, F., & Picard, R. (1996). Periodicity, directionality, and randomness: World features for image modeling and retrieval. *IEEE Transactions on Pattern Analysis and Machine Intelligence, 18*(7), 722-733.

Liu, J., & Yin, J. (2000). Multi-agent integer programing. *Proceedings of the Second International Conference on Intelligent Data Engineering and Automated Learning* (pp. 301-307), Springer Press.

Liu, J., & Zhao, Y. (2002). On adaptive agentlets for distributed divide-and-conquer: A dynamical systems approach. *IEEE Transactions on Systems, Man and Cybernetics, 32(*2), 214-227. IEEE Press.

Liu, Y. (2007) "A survey of content-based image retrieval with high-level semantics", Pattern Recognition, Vol. 40, Issue 1, January 2007, 262-282.

Liu, Y., Rothfus, W., & Kanade, T. (1998). Content-based 3D neuroradiologic image retrieval: Preliminary results. In *IEEE International Workshop on Content-based Access of Image and Video Databases*, pages 91 – 100, January 1998. in conjunction with International Conference on Computer Vision (ICCV98).

Liu, Y., Zhang, D. S., Lu, G. J., & Ma, W. Y. (2007). A survey of content-based image retrieval with high-level semantics. *Pattern Recognition, 40*(1), 262-282.

Lowe, D. G. (2004). Distinctive image features from scale-invariant keypoints. *International Journal of Computer Vision, 60*(2), 91-110.

Lowe, D.G. (2004). Distinctive image features from scale invariant features. *IJCV, 60*(2), 91-110.

Lucas, B. D., & Kanade, T. (1981). An iterative image registration technique with an application to stereo vision. Proceedings of Imaging understanding workshop, (pp 121—130.)

Lv, Q., et al. (2007). Multi-probe LSH: Efficient indexing for high-dimensional similarity Search. *Proc. of VLDB*.

Ma, W. Y., & Manjunath, B. S. (1996). Texture-based pattern retrieval from image databases. *Journal Multimedia Tools and Applications, 2*(1), 35-51.

Ma, W. Y., & Manjunath, B. S. (1999). NeTra: A toolbox for navigating large image databases. *Multimedia Systems, 7*(3), 184-198.

Ma, W., & Majunath, B. (1997). NeTra: A toolbox for navigating large image databases. *Proceedings of the IEEE International Conference on Image Processing* (vol. 1, pp. 568–571).

Ma, W.Y., & Manjunath, B.S. (1997). "Edge flow: a framework of boundary detection and image segmentation" Proc. IEEE International Conference on Computer Vision and Pattern Recognition, San Juan, Puerto Rico, June 1997, pp. 744-749.

Ma, W.Y., & Manjunath, B.S. (1999). Netra: A toolbox for navigating large image databases. *Multimedia Systems, 7*(3), 184–198.

MacArthur, S.D., Bradley, C.E., & Shyu, C.R. (2000). Relevance feedback decision trees in content-based image retrieval. *Proceedings of the IEEE Workshop on Content-Based Access of Image and Video Libraries* (pp. 68–72).

MacArthur, S.D., Brodley, C.E., & Shyu, C. (2000). Relevance feedback decision trees in content-based image retrieval. In *IEEE Workshop CBAIVL Proceedings*, South Carolina.

Manjunath B.S., Wu P., Newsam S., and Shin H.D. (2000). A texture descriptor for browsing and similarity retrieval. *Signal Processing: Image Communication, 16*(1-2), 33-43.

Manjunath, B. S., & Chellappa, R. (1993). A unified method to boundary perception: Edges, textures and illusory contours. *IEEE Transactions on Neural Networks, 4*(1), 96-108.

Manjunath, B. S., & Ma, W. Y. (1996). Texture features for browsing and retrieval of image data. *IEEE Transactions on Pattern Analysis and Machine Intelligence, 18*(8), 837-842.

Manjunath, B. S., Ohm, J. R., vasudevan, V. V., & Yamada, A. (2001). Color and texture descriptors. *IEEE Transactions on Circuits and Systems for Video Technology, 11*(6), 703-715.

Manmatha, R., & Rath, T. M. (2003). *Indexing handwritten historical documents - recent progress, the 2003 symposium on document image understanding* (pp. 77-86).

Mao, J., & Jain, A.K. (1992). Texture classification and segmentation using multiresolution simultaneous autoregression models. *Pattern Recognition, 25*(2), 173-188.

Marcenaro, L., Oberti, F., Foresti, G.L., & Regazzoni, C.S. (2001). Distributed architectures and logical-task decomposition in multimedia surveillance systems, Proceedings of IEEE, 89(10), 1419-1440.

Mari, P., Bogdan, C., Moncef, G., & Ari, V. (2002, October). *Rock texture retrieval using gray level co-occurrence matrix.* Paper presented at the NORSIG-2002, Fifth NORDIC Signal Processing Symposium, Hurtigruten from Tromsø to Trondheim, Norway.

Maron, O., & Lakshmi Ratan, A. (1998). Multiple-instance learning for natural scene classification. In J.W. Shavlik (Ed.), *Proceedings of the International Conference on Machine Learning* (vol. 15, pp. 341–349).

Maron, O., & Lozano Perez, T. (1997). A framework for multiple-instance learning. In M.I. Jordan, M.J. Kearns, & S.A. Solla (Eds.), *Advances in neural information processing systems* (vol. 10, pp. 570–576). Cambridge, MA: MIT Press.

Maron, O., & Ratan, A. L. (1998). Multiple-instance learning for natural scene classification. In *Proceedings of the International Conference on Machine Learning* (pp. 341–349).

Marsicoi, M.D., Cinque, L., & Levialdi, S. (1997). Indexing pictorial documents by their content: a survey of current techniques. *Imagee and Vision Computing,* 15:119–141.

Matas, J., Chum, O., Urban, M., & Pajdla, T. (2004). Robust wide-baseline stereo from maximally stable external regions. *Image and Vision Computing, 22,* 761-767.

Materka, A., & Strzelecki, M. (1998). *Texture Analysis Methods-A Review* (Tech. Rep. No. COST B 11). Brussels: Technical University of Lodz, Institute of Electronics.

Meessen, J., Coulanges, M., Desurmont, X., & Delaigle, J.F., (2006). Content-based retrieval of video surveillance scenes, Multimedia Content Representation, Classification and Security. (pp. 785-792.)

Mehrotra, S. et al. (1997). "Multimedia Analysis and Retrieval System", in *Proc. of The 3rd Int. Workshop on Information Retrieval Systems*, Como, Italy, September 25-27, 1997, pp. 39-45.

Mehrotra, S., Rui, Y., Ortega, M., & Huang, T. (1997). Supporting content-based queries over images in MARS. *Proceedings of the IEEE International Conference on Multimedia Computing and Systems* (pp. 632–633).

Mehta, M., Agrawal, R., & Rissanen, J. (1996). SLIQ: A fast scalable classifier for data mining. In *Proceed-*

ings of the Fifth International Conference on Extending Database Technology, Avignon, France.

Meilhac, C. & Nastar, C. (1999). Relevance feedback and category search in image databases. *Proceedings of IEEE International Conference on Multimedia Computing and Systems, 1,* 512-517.

Meilhac, C., & Nastar, C. (1999). Relevance feedback and category search in image databases. *Proceedings of the IEEE International Conference on Multimedia Computing and System* (pp. 512–517) Florence, Italy.

Mikolajczyk, K., & Schmid, C. (2001). Indexing based on scale invariant interest points. *ICCV.*

Mikolajczyk, K., & Schmid, C. (2004). Scale & affine invariant point detectors. *IJCV 60*(1), 63-86.

Mikolajczyk, K., & Schmid, C. (2005). A performance evaluation of local descriptors. *IEEE PAMI, 27*(10), 1615-1630.

Mikolajczyk, K., et al. (2006). A comparison of affine region detectors. *IJCV.*

Minka, T. (2003). *A comparison of numerical optimizers for logistic regression* (Tech. Rep. No. 758). USA: Carnegie Mellon University, Department of Statistics.

Mitchell, T. M. (2003). Machine learning meets natural language. In *Proceedings of the Progress in Artificial Intelligence 8th Portuguese Conference on Artificial Intelligence, EPIA '97* (p. 391).

Mitra, S., Pal, S. K., & Mitra, P. (2002). Data mining in soft computing framework: A survey. *IEEE Transactions on Neural Networks, 13*(1), 3-14.

Mittal, A., & Cheong, L. F. (2004). Addressing the problems of Bayesian network classification of video using high-dimensional features. *IEEE Trans. On Knowledge and Data Engineering, 16*(2), 230–244.

Molinier, M., Laaksonen, J., Ahola, J., & Häme, T. (2005, October). Self-organizing map application for retrieval of man-made structures in remote sensing data. In *Proceedings of ESA-EUSC 2005, Image Information Mining: Theory and Application to Earth Observation,* Frascati, Italy.

Monay, F., & Gatica-Perez, D. (2003). On image auto-annotation with latent space models. In *Proceedings of the ACM International Conference on Multimedia (ACM MM),* Berkeley, CA (pp. 275–278).

Montgomery, D. C., Runger, G.C., Hubele, N.F. (2004). *Engineering statistics.* New York: John Wiley & Sons.

Moreau, V., Cohen, L. D., & Pellerin, D. (2002). Estimation and analysis of the deformation of the cardiac wall using Doppler tissue imaging. In *Proceedings International Conference on Pattern Recognition.*

Mori, Y., Takahashi, H., & Oka, R. (1999). Image-to-word transformation based on dividing and vector quantizing images with words. *Proceedings of the International Workshop on Multimedia Intelligent Storage and Retrieval Management* (pp. 341–349).

Moyo T., Bangay S., & Foster G. (2006). The identification of mammalian species through the classification of hair patterns using image pattern recognition. In *Proceedings of the 4th international conference on Computer graphics, virtual reality, visualisation and interaction in Africa.* (pp. 177-181). Cape Town: ACM Press.

Müller, H. et al. (2000). Learning features weights from user behaviour in Content-Based Image Retrieval, In S.J. Simoff and O.R. Zaiane eds., *ACM SIGKDD International Conference on Knowledge Discovery and Data Mining* (Workshop on Multimedia Data Mining MDM/KDD2000), Boston, MA, USA, August 20-23, 2000.

Müller, H. et al. (2000a). Strategies for positive and negative relevance feedback in image retrieval, in *Proc. of the International Conference on Pattern Recognition* (ICPR'2000), Vol. 1 of Computer Vision and Image Analysis, pp. 1043-1046, Barcelona, Spain, September 3-8 2000.

Müller, H. et al. (2001). "Performance Evaluation in Content-Based Image Retrieval: Overview and Proposals", *Pattern Recognition Letters,* Special Issue on Image and Video Indexing, 22, 5, pp. 593-601, 2001. H. Bunke and X. Jiang Eds.

Muller, H., Michous, N., Bandon, D., & Geissbuhler, A. (2004). A review of content-based image retrieval systems in medical applications—Clinical benefits and future directions. *International Journal of Medical Informatics, 73*(1), 1-23.

Muller, H., Muller, W., Marchand-Maillet, S., Pun, T., & Squire, D. M. (2000). Strategies for positive and negative relevance feedback in image retrieval. In *Proceedings of the International Conference on Pattern Recognition* (pp. 1043-1046).

Muller, H., Muller, W., Squire, D. M., Marchand-Maillet, S., & Pun, T. (2001). Performance evaluation in content-based image retrieval: Overview and proposals. *Pattern Recognition Letters, 22,* 593-601.

Muller, H., Rosset, A., Vallee, J.-P., & Geissbuhler, A. (2004). Comparing features sets for content-based image retrieval in a medical-case database. In *Proceedings of IS&T/SPIE Medical Imaging 2004: PACS and Imaging Informatics* (pp. 99-109).

Munich, M. E., & Perona, P. (1999). Continuous dynamic time warping for translation-invariant curve alignment with applications to signature verification. *Proceedings of 7th IEEE International Conference on Computer Vision* (Vol. 1, pp. 108-115). Kerkyra, Greece.

Murase, H., & Naya, S. K. (1995). Visual learning and recognition of 3D objects for appearance. *International Journal of Computer Vision,* 14, 5-14.

Myers, C., Rabiner, L., & Rosenberg, A. (1980). Performance tradeoffs in dynamic time warping algorithms for isolated word recognition. *IEEE Transactions on Acoustics, Speech, and Signal Processing, 28*(6), 623-635.

Nakayama, R., Uchiyama, Y., Yamamoto, K., & Watanabe, R., & Namba, K. (2006). Computer-aided diagnosis scheme using a filter bank for detection of microcalcification clusters in mammograms. *IEEE Transactions on Biomedical Engineering, 53*(2), 273-283.

Naphade, M., & Smith, J.R. (2004). On the detection of semantic concepts at TRECVID, ACM International Conference on Multimedia. (pp. 660-667.)

Nastar, C., Mitschke, M., & Meilhac, C. (1998). Efficient query refinement for image retrieval. In *IEEE Conf.*

Computer Vision and Pattern Recognition Proceedings, CA.

Natsev, A., Rastogi, R., & Shim, K. (2004). WALRUS: A similarity retrieval algorithm for image databases. *IEEE Transactions on Knowledge and Data Engineering, 16*(3), 301-316.

Nayar, S. K., & Bolle, R. M. (1996). Reflectance-based object recognition. *International Journal of Computer Vision,* 17(3), 219-240.

Nene, S. A., Nayar, S. K., & Murase, H. (1996). (Tech. Rep. No. CUCS-006-96). Columbia Object Image Library (coil-100).

Niblack, W., Barber, R., Equitz, W., Flickner, M., Glasman, E., Petkovic, D., Yanker, P.,Faloutsos, C., & Taubin, G. (1993). The QBIC project: Quering images by content using color, texture, and shape. In *Poceedings of the SPIE Conference on Storage and Retrieval for Image and Video Databases,* pp. 173–187.

Niblack, W., *et al.* (1993). Querying images by content, using color, texture, and shape. SPIE Conference on Storage and Retrieval for Image and Video Databases.

Nievergelt, J., Hinterberger, H., Sevcik, K.C.. (1984). The grid file: An adaptable, symmetric multikey file structure. ACM Trans. *Database Syst.* 9(1).

ObjectVideo, http://www.objectvideo.com/products/vew/.

Ogawa, K., Fukushima, M., Kubota, K., & Hisa, N. (1998). Computer-aided diagnostic system for diffused liver diseases with ultrasonography by neural networks. *IEEE Transactions on Nuclear Science, 45*(6), 3069-3074.

Ojala, T., Pietikainen, M., & Maenpaa, T. (2002). Multiresolution gray-scale and rotation invariant texture classification with local binary patterns. *IEEE Transactions on Pattern Analysis and Machine Intelligence, 24*(7), 971–987.

Ono, A., Amano, M., Hakaridani, M., Satoh, T., & Sakauchi, M. (1996). A flexible content-based image retrieval system with combined scene description keywords. *Proceedings of the IEEE International Conference on Multimedia Computing and Systems* (pp. 201–208).

Ortega-Binderberger, M. & Mehrotra, S. (2003). Relevance feedback in multimedia databases. In B.Furht & O. Marquez (Eds.), *Handbook of video databases: design and applications* (pp. 511-536). New York: CRC Press.

Ozekes, S., Osman, O., & Camurcu, A. Y. (2005). Mammographic mass detection using a mass template. *Korean Journal of Radiology, 6*(4), 221-228.

Pagel, B.-U., Korn, F., & Faloutsos, C. (2000). Deflating the dimensionality curse using multiple fractal dimensions. *Proc. of IEEE ICDE*, 589-598.

Panourgias, E., Tsakonas, A., Dounias, G., & Panagi, G. (2006). Computational intelligence for the detection and classification of malignant lesions in screening mammography. *Oncology Reports, 15*, 1037-1041.

Parekh, R., Yang, J., & Honavar, V. (2000). Constructive neural network learning algorithms for pattern classification. *IEEE Transactions on Neural Networks, 11*(2), 436-451.

Park, J., & Sandberg, I.W. (1991). "Universal approximation using radial-basis-function networks", *Neural Computation* 3, 1991, pp. 246-257.

Pass, G. (1997). Comparing images using color coherence vectors. In the *Proceedings of ACM International Conference on Multimedia,* Seattle, WA, November 9-13 (pp. 65-73). New York: ACM Press.

Pawlak, Z. (1982). Rough sets. *International Journal of Computer and Information Science, 11*, 341-356.

Pawlak, Z. (1991). *Rough sets: Theoretical aspect of reasoning about data.* Norwell, MA: Kluwer Academic Publishers.

Pawlak, Z., Grzymala-Busse, J., Slowinski, R., & Ziarko, W. (1995). Rough sets. *Communications of the ACM, 38*(11), 89-95.

Peng, J., Banerjee, B., & Heisterkamp, D.R. (2002). Kernel index for relevance feedback retrieval in large image databases. *Proceedings of the International Conference on Neural Information Processing* (pp. 187–191).

Peng, J., Bhanu, B., & Qing, S. (1999). Probabilistic feature relevance learning for content-based image retrieval. *Computer Vision and Image Understanding, 75*(1/2), 150–164.

Peng, Y., Yao, B., & Jiang, J. (2006). Knowledge-discovery incorporated evolutionary search for microcalcification detection in breast cancer diagnosis. *Artificial Intelligence in Medicine, 37*(1), 43-53.

Pentland, A., Picard, A., & Sclaroff, S. (1994). Photobook: Tools for content-based manipulation of image databases. In *Proc. of SPIE.*

Pentland, A., Picard, R., & Sclaroff, S. (1994). Photobook: Tools for content-based manipulation of image databases. In Proceedings of the SPIE Conference on Storage and Retrieval for Image and Video Databases II.

Pentland, A., Picard, R., & Sclaroff, S. (1994). PhotoBOOK: Tools for content-based manipulation of image databases. In W. Niblack & R. Jain (Eds.), *Proceedings of the SPIE Storage and Retrieval for Image Databases* (vol. 2, pp. 34–47).

Perkins, S., Theiler, J., Brumby, S. P., Harvey, N. R., Porter, R., Szymanski, J. J., & Bloch, J. J. (2000). *GENIE - A hybrid genetic algorithm for feature classification in multi-spectral images.* Los Alamos National Laboratory Internal Proceeding, SPIE 4120 (pp. 52-62).

Petkov, N., & Kruizinga, P. (1997). Computational Models of Visual Neurons Specialized in the Detection of Periodic and Aperiodic Oriented Visual Stimuli: Bar and Grating Cells. *Biological Cybernetics, 76*(2), 83-96.

Picard, R. W., & Minka, T. P. (1995). Vision texture for annotation. *Multimedia Systems, 3*(1), 3–14.

Picard, R.W., Minka, T.P., & Szummer, M. (1996). Modeling user subjectivity in image libraries. In *IEEE International Conference on Image Processing Proceedings,* Lausanne, Switzerland.

Platt, J. C. (1999). Probabilistic outputs for support vector machines and comparisons to regularized likelihood methods. In A.Smola, P.Bartlett, B.Scholkopf, &

D.Schuurmans (Eds.), *Advance in Large Margin Classifiers* (pp. 61-74). Cambridge, MA, USA: MIT Press.

Porkaew, K., Mehrotra, S., & Ortega, M. (1999). Query reformulation for content based multimedia retrieval in MARS. In *IEEE Int'l Conf. Multimedia Computing and Systems.*

Porter, R., Eads, D., Hush, D., & Theiler, J. (2003). Weighted order statistic classifiers with large rank-order margin. *Proceedings of the Twentieth International Conference on Machine Learning, ICML 20*, 600-607. Los Alamos National Laboratory, Washington DC.

Preparata, F., & Shamos, M. I. (1985). *Computational Geometry: Introduction.* New York: Springer-Verlag.

Pressman, N. J. (1976). Markovian analysis of cervical cell images. *Journal of Histochemistry and Cytochemistry. 24*(1), 138-144.

PyramidVision, http://www.pyramidvision.com/.

Quin, L. (Ed.). (1999). *XML Specification Guide.* John Wiley Press.

Rabiner, L., & Juang, B.-H. (1993). *Fundamentals of speech recognition.* Prentice-Hall, Inc.

Rangayyan, R. M., Ayres, F. J. & Leo Desautels, J. E. (2007). A review of computer-aided diagnosis of breast cancer: Toward the detection of subtle signs. *Journal of the Franklin Institute, 344*(3-4), 312-348.

Ratan, A.L., & Grimson, W.E.L. (1997). Training templates for scene classification using a few examples. In *IEEE Workshop on Content-Based Access of Image and Video Libraries Proceedings*, pages 90–97.

Ratanamahatana, C. A., & Keogh, E. (2004). Making Time-Series Classification More Accurate Using Learned Constraints. *Proceedings of 4th SIAM International Conference on Data Mining* (pp. 11-22). Lake Buena Vista, FL, USA.

Ratanamahatana, C. A., & Keogh, E. (2005). Three Myths about Dynamic Time Warping. *Proceedings of 5th SIAM International Conference on Data Mining* (pp. 506-510). Newport Beach, CA, USA.

Rath, T. M., & Manmatha, R. (2003). Word image matching using dynamic time warping. *Proceedings of the 2003 IEEE Computer Society Conference on Computer Vision and Pattern Recognition* (Vol. 2, pp. 512-527). Madison, WI, USA.

Ravela, S., Manmatha, R., & Riseman, E.M. (1996). Scale-space matching and image retrieval. *Proceedings of the Image Understanding Workshop* (vol. 2, pp. 1199–1207).

Retico, A., Delogu, P., Fantacci, M. E., & Kasae, P. (2006a). An automatic system to discriminate malignant from benign massive lesions on mammograms. *Nuclear Instruments and Methods in Physics Research Section A: Accelerators, Spectrometers, Detectors and Associated Equipment, 569*(2), 596-600.

Retico, A., Delogu, P., Fantacci, M. E., Martinez, A. P., Stefanini, A., & Tata, A. (2006b). A scalable computer-aided detection system for microcalcification cluster identification in a pan-European distributed database of mammograms. *Nuclear Instruments and Methods in Physics Research A: Accelerators, Spectrometers, Detectors and Associated Equipment, 569*(2), 601-605.

Rickman, J. T. (1972). Design considerations for a boolean search system with automatic relevance feedback processing. *Proceedings of the ACM Annual Conference* (pp. 478 - 481). Boston, MA, USA: ACM.

Ripley, B.D., & Venables, W.N. (2002). *Modern Applied Statistics with S.* New York: Springer Verlag.

Ro, Y. M. Matching pursuit: Contents featuring for image indexing. (1998). In *Proceedings of Multimedia Storage and Archiving Systems III: Vol. 3527. The International Society for Optical Engineering* (pp. 89–100). Boston, MA: The International Society for Optical Engineering.

Ro, Y. M., Kim M., Kang H. K., Manjunath B. S., & Kim J. (2001). MPEG-7 Homogeneous Texture Descriptor. *ETRI Journal, 23*(2), 41-51.

Robinson, J.T. (1981). The K-D-B tree: A search structure for large multi-dimensional dynamic indexes. *Proc. of ACM SIGMOD*, 10-18.

Rocchio, J. (1971). Relevance feedback in information retrieval. In G. Salton (Ed.), *The SMART Retrieval System - Experiments in Automatic Document Processing* (pp. 313-323): Prentice-Hall, Inc.

Rocchio, J. J. (1971). Relevance feedback in information retrieval. In G.Salton (Ed.), *The SMART Retrieval System-Experiments in Automatic Document Processing* (pp. 313-323). Englewood Cliffs, NJ: Prentice Hall.

Rocchio, J., & Salton, G. (1971). The SMART retrieval system: Experiments in automatic document processing. In *Relevance feedback in information retrieval* (pp. 313–323). Englewood Cliffs, NJ: Prentice Hall.

Rocchio, J.J.J. (1971). Relevance feedback in information retrieval. In *The SMART Retrieval System—Experiments in Automatic Document Processing*, pages 313–323. Englewood Cliffs, NJ: Prentice Hall, Inc.

Rosenfeld, A., and Kak, A. (Ed.). (1982). *Digital Picture Processing*. New, York: Academic Press.

Rotter, P. (2004). *Zastosowanie metod optymalizacji wielokryterialnej w interpretacji obrazów (Application of multicriteria optimisation methods in image interpretation)*. Unpublished doctoral dissertation, AGH-University of Science and Technology, Krakow, 2004.

Roussopoulos, N., Kelly, S., & Vincent, F. (1995). Nearest neighbor queries. In *ACM SIGMOD*, (pp. 71–79).

Rubner, Y., Tomasi, C. & Guibas, L. (2000). The earth mover's distance as a metric for image retrieval. *IJCV, 40*(2), 99-121.

Rui, Y. & Huang, T. (1999). A novel relevance feedback technique in image retrieval. In *Proceedings of the Seventh ACM International Conference on Multimedia, 2*, 67-70. New York: ACM Press.

Rui, Y. et al. (1997). "A Relevance Feedback Architecture in Content-based Multimedia Information Retrieval Systems", in *Proc of IEEE Workshop on Content-based Access of Image and Video Libraries*, in conjunction with CVPR'97 , June 20, 1997, Puerto Rico, pp 82-89.

Rui, Y., & Huang, T. (1998). Relevance feedback: A power tool for interactive content-based image retrieval.

IEEE Transactions on Circuits and Systems for Video Technology, 8(5), 644–655.

Rui, Y., & Huang, T.S. (2000). Optimizing learning in image retrieval. In *IEEE Conf. Computer Vision and Pattern Recognition*, South Carolina.

Rui, Y., Huang, T. S., & Chang, S. F. (1999). Image retrieval: Current techniques, promising directions, and open issues. *Journal of Visual Communication and Image Representation, 10*(1), 39-62.

Rui, Y., Huang, T. S., & Chang, S.-F. (1999). Image retrieval: Current techniques, promising directions, and open issues. *Journal of Visual Communications and Visual Representations, 10*, 39-62.

Rui, Y., Huang, T. S., & Mehrotra, S. (1997). Content-based image retrieval with relevance feedback in MARS. In the *Proceedings of the International Conference on Image Processing,* Washington D.C., October 26-29 (pp. 815-818). Piscataway, NJ: IEEE Press.

Rui, Y., Huang, T. S., & Mehrotra, S. (1998). Human perception subjectivity and relevance feedback in multimedia information retrieval. In *Proceedings of IS&T/SPIE Storage and Retrieval of Image and Video Database* (pp. 25-36). SPIE Press.

Rui, Y., Huang, T. S., & Mehrotra, S. (1998). Human perception subjectivity and relevance feedback in multimedia information retrieval. In *Proceedings of IS&T/SPIE Storage and Retrieval of Image and Video Database, 6,* 25-36.

Rui, Y., Huang, T., & Chang, S. (1999). Image retrieval: Past, present, and future. *Journal of Visual Communication and Image Representation, 10,* 1-23.

Rui, Y., Huang, T., & Mehrotra, S. (1997). Content-based image retrieval with relevance feedback in MARS. *Proceedings of the IEEE International Conference on Image Processing* (vol. 2, pp. 815–818).

Rui, Y., Huang, T.S., & Chang, S.F. (1999). "Image Retrieval: Current Techniques, Promising Directions and Open Issues", Journal of Visual Communication and Image Representation, Vol. 10, 39-62, March, 1999.

Rui, Y., Huang, T.S., & Mehrotra, S. (1997). "Content-based Image Retrieval with Relevance Feedback in MARS", in *Proc. of IEEE Int. Conf. on Image Processing '97*, October 26-29, 1997 Santa Barbara, California, USA, pp. 815-818.

Rui, Y., Huang, T.S., & Mehrotra, S. (1998). "Relevance Feedback Techniques in Interactive Content-Based Image Retrieval", in Proc. of *IS&T and SPIE Storage and Retrieval of Image and Video Databases VI*, pp. 25-36, January 24-30, 1998, San Jose, CA.

Rui, Y., Huang, T.S., Ortega, M., & Mehrotra, S. (1998). Relevance feedback: A power tool in interactive content-based image retrieval. *IEEE Trans. on Circuits and Systems for Video Tech*, 8(5):644–655.

Saad, A., Avineri, E., Dahal, K., Sarfraz, M., & Roy, R. (Eds.). (2007). *Soft computing in industrial applications: Recent and emerging methods and techniques*. Springer Verlag Press.

Saber, E., & Tekalp, A. M. (1998). Integration of color, edge, shape and texture features for automatic region-based image annotation and retrieval. *Electronic Imaging, 7*, 684-700.

Safabakhsh, R., & Zamani, F. (2006). A robust multi-direction Gabor based system for discriminating touching white and red cells in microscopic blood image. In *Proceedings of the International Conference on Information & Communication Technologies: Vol. 1. from Theory to Applications* (1135- 1139). Damascus: IEEE Press.

Saha, S. K., Das, A. K., & Chanda, B. (2007). Image retrieval based on indexing and relevance feedback. *Pattern Recognition Letters, 28*, 357-366.

Sakoe, H., & Chiba, S. (1978). Dynamic programming algorithm optimization for spoken word recognition. *IEEE Transactions on Acoustics, Speech, and Signal Processing, 26*(1), 43-49.

Sakurai, Y., Yoshikawa, M., & Faloutsos, C. (2005). FTW: Fast Similarity Search under the Time Warping Distance. *Proceedings of 24th ACM SIGMOD-SIGACT-SIGART Symposium on Principles of Database Systems* (pp. 326 - 337). Baltimore, MD, USA: ACM.

Salden, A.H., et al. (1992). A complete and irreducible set of local orthogonally invariant features of 2-dimensional images. *ICPR*, 180-184.

Salton, G. (1986). Another look at automatic text-retrieval systems. *Communications of the ACM, 29*(7), 648–656.

Salton, G., & Buckley, C. (1997). Improving Retrieval Performance by Relevance Feedback. *Journal of the American Society for Information Science, 41*(4), 288-297.

Salton, G., & McGill, M. (1998). *Introduction to modern information retrieval.* New York: McGraw-Hill.

Samadani, R., Han, C., & Katragadda, L.K. (1993). Content-based event selection from satellite image of the aurora. In W. Niblack (Ed.), *Proceedings of the SPIE Storage and Retrieval for Image and Video Databases* (vol. 1908, pp. 50–59).

Sampat, M. P., Markey, M. K., and Bovik, A. C. (2005). Computer-aided detection and diagnosis in mammography. In Bovik, A.C. (Ed): *Handbook of Image and Video Processing*, Elsevier Academic Press: London, UK, pp. 1195–1217.

Santini, S., & Jain, R. (2000). Integrated browsing and querying for image databases. *IEEE Multimedia*, 7:26–39.

Sarfraz, M. (Ed.). (2005). *Computer-aided intelligent recognition techniques and applications.* John Wiley Press.

Schiele, B., & Crowley, J. L. (2000). Recognition without correspondence using multidimensional receptive field histograms. *International Journal of Computer Vision, 36*(1), 31-52.

Schmid, C., & Mohr, R. (1997) Local gray value invariants for image retrieval. *IEEE PAMI, 19*(5), 530-535.

Schmid, C., Mohr, R., & Bauskhage, C. (1998). Comparing and evaluating interest points. *ICCV*, 230-235.

Schmill, M., Oates, T., & Cohen, P. (1999). Learned Models for Continuous Planning. *Proceedings of 7th*

International Workshop on Artificial Intelligence and Statistics (pp. 278-282).

Schroeter, P., & Bigün, J. (1995). Hierarchical image segmentation by multidimensional clustering and direction adaptive boundary refinement. *Pattern Recognition, 28*(5), 695-709.

Sclaroff, S., & Pentland, A. (1995). Modal matching for correspondence and recognition. *IEEE PAMI, 17*(6), 545-561.

Sclaroff, S., Taycher, L., & Cascia, M.L. (1997). *ImageRover: A content-based image browser for the World Wide Web*. Technical Report No. 97-005, Computer Science Department, Boston University, USA.

Scuturici, M., Clech, J., Scuturici, V. M., & Zighed, A. D. (2005, January-June). Topological representation model for image databases query. *Journal of Experimental and Theoretical Artificial Intelligence (JETAI), 17*(1-2), 145–160.

Seidl, T., & Kriegel, H.P. (1998). Optimal multistep K-Nearest neighbor search. *SIGMOD*.

Senior, A., Brown, L., Shu, C., Tian, Y., Lu, M., Zhai, Y., & Hampapur, A. (2007). Visual person searches for retail loss detection: Application and evaluation, International Conference on Vision Systems.

Senior, A., Hampapur, A., Tian, Y., Brown, L., Pankanti, S., & Bolle, R. (2006). Appearance models for occlusion handling, In Journal of Image and Vision Computing, 24(11), 1233-1243.

Servetto, S. et al. (1998). "A Region-based Representation of Images in MARS", *Journal on VLSI Signal Processing Systems*, Special Issue on Multimedia Signal Processing (Guest Editors: Yao Wang & Amy Reibman), Volume 20, Issues 2, pp. 137-150, October 1998.

Shaft, U., & Ramakrishnan, R. (2005). When is nearest neighbors indexable? *ICDT*, 158-172.

Shaw, W.M. (1995). Term-relevance computations and perfect retrieval performance. *Information Processing and Management: An International Journal, 31*(4), 491–498.

Shen, H.T., Ooi, B.C., & Tan, K.L. (2000). Giving meanings to WWW images. *Proceedings of the ACM Multimedia* (pp. 39–47).

Shi, J., & Malik, J. (2000). Normalized cuts and image segmentation. *IEEE Transactions on Pattern Analysis and Machine Intelligence, 22*(8), 888–905.

Shi, Z. P., Li, Q. Y., Shi, Z. Z., & Duan C. L. (2005). Texture spectrum descriptor based image retrieval. *Journal of Software, 16*(6), 1039-1045, (In Chinese).

Shu, C., Hampapur, A., Lu, M., Brown, L., Connell, J. Senior, A., & Tian, Y. (2005). IBM smart surveillance system (S3): A open and extensible framework for event based surveillance, IEEE Conference on **Advanced Video and Signal Based Surveillance** (pp. 318 – 323.)

Shyu, C., Brodley, C., Kak, A., Kosaka, A., Aisen, A., & Broderick, L. (1999). ASSERT: A physician-in-the-loop content-based image retrieval system for HRCT image databases. *Computer Vision and Image Understanding, 75*(1/2), 111-132.

Shyu, M.-L., Chen, S.-C., & Rubin, S. H. (2004a). Stochastic clustering for organizing distributed information source. *IEEE Transactions on Systems, Man and Cybernetics, Part B, 34*(5), 2035-2047.

Shyu, M.-L., Chen, S.-C., Chen, M., & Zhang, C. (2004b). Affinity relation discovery in image database clustering and content-based retrieval. In the *Proceedings of ACM International Conference on Multimedia*, New York, NY, October 10-16 (pp. 372-375). New York: ACM Press.

Shyu, M.-L., Chen, S.-C., Chen, M., Zhang, C., & Shu, C.-M. (2003). MMM: A stochastic mechanism for image database queries. In the *Proceedings of the IEEE Fifth International Symposium on Multimedia Software Engineering*, Taichung, Taiwan, ROC, December 10-12 (pp. 188-195). Los Alamitos, CA: IEEE Computer Society Press.

Shyu, M.-L., Chen, S.-C., Chen, M., Zhang, C., & Shu, C.-M. (2006). Probabilistic semantic network-based image retrieval using MMM and relevance feedback. *Multimedia Tools and Applications, 30*(2), 131-147.

Silverman, B.W. (1986). *Density Estimation for Statistics and Data Analysis.* New York: Chapman and Hall.

Sivic, J., & Zisserman, A. (2003). Video google: A text retrieval approach to object matching in videos. In *Proceedings of the International Conference on Computer Vision.*

Skulimowski, A.M.J. (1996). *Decision Support Systems Based on Reference Sets*, AGH-UST University Publishers, Kraków 1996, p.167.

Skulimowski, A.M.J. (1997). "Methods of Multicriteria Decision Support Based on Reference Sets", in: R. Caballero, F. Ruiz, R.E. Steuer (Eds.) *Advances in Multiple Objective and Goal Programming*, Lecture Notes in Economics and Mathematical Systems, 455, Springer-Verlag, Berlin-Heidelberg-New York, pp. 282-290, 1997.

Slowinski, R. (1995). Rough set approach to decision analysis. *AI Expert Magazine, 10*(3), 18-25.

Smeulders, A. W. M., Worring, M., Santini, S., Gupta, A., & Jain, R. (2000). Content-based image retrieval at the end of the early years. *IEEE Transactions on Pattern Analysis and Machine Intelligence, 22*(12), 1349-1380.

Smeulders, A., Worring, M., Santini, S., Gupta, A., & Jain, R. (2000). Content-based image retrieval at the end of the early years. *IEEE Transactions on Pattern Analysis and Machine Intelligence, 22*, 1349-1380.

Smeulders, A., Worring, M., Santini, S., Gupta, A., & Jain, R. (2000). Content-based image retrieval at the end of the early years. *IEEE Transactions on Pattern Analysis and Machine Intelligence, 22*(12), 1349-1380.

Smeulders, A.W.M., Worring, M., Santini, S., Gupta, A., & Jain, R. (2000). Content-based image retrieval at the end of the early years. *IEEE Transactions on Pattern Analysis and Machine Intelligence, 22*(12), 1349–1380.

Smith, J. R. (1998). Image retrieval evaluation. In *Proceedings of IEEE Workshop on Content-based Access of Images and Video Libraries*, 112-113.

Smith, J. R., & Chang, S. F. (1996). VisualSEEk: a Fully Automated content-based image query system. In *ACM Multimedia '96.* Boston, MA.

Smith, J., & Chang, S. (1997). An image and video search engine for the World Wide Web. *Proceedings of the SPIE Storage and Retrieval for Image and Video Databases* (vol. 5, pp. 84–95).

Smith, J., & Chang, S.-F. (1995, July). Automated image retrieval using color and texture. Technical report CU/CTR 408-95-14, Columbia University.

Smith, J.R., & Chang, S.F. (1996). "VisualSEEk: a fully automated content-based image query system", in *Proc. ACM Intern. Conf. Multimedia*, Boston, MA, May 1996.

Smith, J.R., & Chang, S.F. (1997). Visually searching the Web for content. *IEEE Multimedia Magazine, 4*(3), 12-20.

Smith, J.R., & Li, C.S. (1999). Image classification and querying using composite region templates. *Computer Vision and Image Understanding, 75*(1/2), 165–174.

Smith, W. D. (1989). *Studies in computational geometry motivated by mesh generation* [doctoral thesis]. Princeton University.

Spink, A., & Losee, R. (1996). "Feedback in information retrieval", *Annual Review of Information Science and Technology*, vol. 31, pp. 33-78, 1996.

Srihari, R.K., Zhang, Z., & Rao, A. (2000). Intelligent indexing and semantic retrieval of multimedia documents. *Information Retrieval, 2*, 245–275.

Starzyk, J. A., Dale, N., & Sturtz, K. (2000). A mathematical foundation for improved reduct generation in information systems. *Knowledge and Information Systems Journal, 2*, 131-147.

Stefanowski, J. (1993). Classification support based on the rough sets. Foundations of Computing and Decision Sciences, 18, 371-380.

Stehling, R. O., Nascimento, M. A., & Falcao, A. X. (2000). On shapes of colors for content-based image retrieval. In the *Proceedings of ACM International Workshop on Multimedia Information Retrieval,* Los Angeles, CA, November 4 (pp. 171-174). New York: ACM Press.

Stone, H.S., & Li, C.S. (1996). Image matching by means of intensity and texture matching in the Fourier domain. In I.K. Sethi & R. Jain (Eds.), *Proceedings of the SPIE Conference on Image and Video Databases* (vol. 2670, pp. 337–349).

Stricker, M.A., & Oregno, M. (1996). Similarity of color images. In *SPIE Storage and Retrieval of Still Image Video Databases IV*, volume 2420, pages 381–392.

Stringa, E., & Regazzoni, C.S. (1998). Content-based retrieval and real time detection from video sequences acquired by surveillance systems, IEEE International Conference on Image Processing, 3, 138-142.

Su, Z., Zhang, H. J., & Ma, S. P. (2002). An image retrieval relevance feedback algorithm-based on the Bayesian classifier. *Journal of Software. 13*(10), 2001-2006, (in Chinese).

Su, Z., Zhang, H., Li, S., & Ma, S. (2003). Relevance feedback in content-based image retrieval: Bayesian framework, feature subspaces, and progressive learning. *IEEE Transaction on Image Processing, 12,* 924-937.

Swain, M. J., & Ballard, D. H. (1991). Color indexing. *International Journal of Computer Vision, 7*(1), 11-32.

Swets, D., & Weng, J. (1999). Hierarchical discriminant analysis for image retrieval. *IEEE Transactions on Pattern Analysis and Machine Intelligence, 21*(5), 386-401.

Székely, N., Tóth, N., & Pataki, B. (2006). A hybrid system for detecting masses in mammographic images. *IEEE Transactions on Instrumentation and Measurement, 55*(3), 944-952.

Szummer, M. & Jaakkola, T. (2002). Information regularization with partially labeled data. In *Proceedings of the Neural Information Processing Systems (NIPS).*

Szummer, M., & Jaakkola, T. (2000). Kernel expansions with unlabeled examples. In *Proceedings of the Neural Information Processing Systems (NIPS).*

Takanashi, T., Muraki, S., & Kaufman, A. (1998) Three-dimensional active Net for volume extraction. In *Proceedings of SPIE 3289* (pp. 184-193).

Tamura, H., et al. (1978). Texture features corresponding to visual perception. IEEE Trans. on Systems, Man, and Cybernetics.

Tamura, H., Mori, S., & Yamawaki, T. (1978). Texture features corresponding to visual perception. *IEEE Transactions on Systems Man and Cybernetics, 8*(6), 460-473.

Tan, T. N. (1995). Texture edge detection by modeling visual cortical channels. *Pattern Recognition, 28*(9), 1283-1298.

Tao, D., & Tang, X. (2004). Random sampling based SVM for relevance feedback image retrieval. In *Proceedings of the IEEE Conf. Computer Vision and Pattern Recognition.*

Tappert, C., & Das, S. (1978). Memory and Time Improvements in a Dynamic Programming Algorithm for Matching Speech Patterns. *IEEE Transactions on Acoustics, Speech, and Signal Processing, 26*(6), 583-586.

Tax, D.M.J., & Duin, R.P.W. (2001). Combining one-class classifiers. In *Proceedings of the Second International-Workshop Multiple Classifier systems*, pages 299–308.

Terrell, G.R., & Scott, D.W. (1992). Variable kernel density estimation. *The Annals of Statistics,* 20:1236–1265.

Tian, Y., Lu, M., & Hampapur, A. (2005). Robust and efficient foreground analysis for real-time video surveillance, IEEE International Conference on Computer Vision and Pattern Recognition. 1, 1182-1187.

Tieu, K., & Viola, P. (2000). Boosting image retrieval. In *IEEE Conf. Computer Vision and Pattern Recognitin Proceedings*, South Carolina.

Tieu, K., & Viola, P. (2000). Boosting image retrieval. *Proceedings of the IEEE Conference in Computer Vision and Pattern Recognition* (pp. 1228–1235).

Tomai, C. I., Zhang, B., & Govindaraju, V. (2002). Transcript Mapping for Historic Handwritten Document Images. *Proceedings of 8th International Workshop on Frontiers in Handwriting Recognition* (pp. 413-418).

Tong, S., & Chan, E. (2001). Support vectormachine active learning for image retrieval. In *ACM Multimedia 2001 Proceedings*, Ottawa, Canada.

Tong, S., & Chang, E. (2001). Support vector machine active learning for image retrieval. In the *Proceedings of ACM International Conference on Multimedia,* Ottawa, Ontario, Canada, September 30-October 5 (pp. 107-118). New York: ACM Press.

Tourassi, G. D., & Floyd, C. E. (2004). Computer-assisted diagnosis of mammographic masses using an information-theoretic image retrieval scheme with BIRADs-based relevance feedback. In *Proceedings of Progress in Biomedical Optics and Imaging - Medical Imaging 2004*: *Vol. 5370(2). Imaging Processing* (pp. 810-817). Bellingham, WA: International Society for Optical Engineering.

Toussaint, G. T. (1980). The relative neighborhood graphs in a finite planar set. *Pattern Recognition, 12,* 261–268.

Toussaint, G. T. (1991). Some unsolved problems on proximity graphs. In *Proceedings of the First Workshop on Proximity Graphs,* Las Cruces, NM.

Traina Jr., C., Traina, A. J. M., Araujo, M. R. B., Bueno, J. M., Chino, F. J. T., Razente, H., & Azevedo-Marques, P. M. (2005). Using an image-extended relational database to support content-based image retrieval in a PACS. *Computer Methods and Programs in Biomedicine, 80*(1), S71-S83.

Traina, C., et al. (2000). Slim-Trees: High performance metric trees minimizing overlap between nodes. *EDBT,* 51-65.

Tsumiyama, Y., Sakane, K., & Yamamoto, K. (1989). Active net: Active Net model for region extraction. *IPSJ SIG Notes,* 89(96), 1-8.

Turk, M., & Pentland, A. (1991). Eigenfaces for recognition. *Journal of Cognitive Neuroscience,* 3, 71-86.

Turner, M. R. (1986). Texture discrimination by Gabor functions. *Biological Cybernetics*, 55(2-3), 71-82.

Tuytelaars, T., & van Gool, L. (2004). Matching widely separated views based on affine invariant regions. *IJCV, 59*(1), 61-85.

Uchiyama, T., & Arbib, M. (1994). Color image segmentation using competitive learning. *IEEE Transactions on Pattern Analysis and Machine Intelligence, 10*(12), 1197-1206.

Uhlmann, J.K. (1991). Satisfying general proximity/similarity queries with metric trees. *Information Processing Letters, 40,* 175-179.

Unser, M., & Blu, T. (2000). Wavelets and radial basis functions: A unifying perspective. In Proceedings of the SPIE Conference on Mathematical Imaging: Wavelet Applications in Signal and Image Processing VIII, pp. 487-493.

Vadivel, A., Sural, S., & Majumdar, A. K. (2007). An integrated color and intensity co-occurrence matrix. *Pattern Recognition Letter, 28,* 974-983. Elsevier Science Inc. Publisher.

Vapnik, V. (1995). *The Nature of Statistical Learning Theory.* New York: Springer.

Varela, C., Timp, S., & Karssemeijer, N. (2006). Use of border information in the classification of mammographic masses. *Physics in Medicine and Biology, 51*(2), 425-441.

Vasconcelos, N. (2007). From pixels to semantic spaces: Advances in content-based image retrieval. *Computer, 40,* 20-26.

Vasconcelos, N., & Lippman, A. (2000). Learning from user feedback in image retrieval. In S. A. Solla, T. K. Leen, and K. R. Muller, editors, *Adv. in Neural Information Processing Systems 12.* MIT Press.

Velipasalar, S., Brown, L. & Hampapur, A. (2006a). Specifying, interpreting and detecting high-level, spatiotemporal composite events in single and multi-camera systems, Conference on Computer Vision and Pattern Recognition Workshop, (pp. 110-116.)

Velipasalar, S., Tian, Y., & Hampapur, A. (2006b). Automatic counting of interacting people by using a single uncalibrated camera, IEEE International Conference on Multimedia and Expo, (pp. 1265-1268.)

Veltkamp, R. C., & Tanase, M. (2000). *Content-based image retrieval systems: A survey* (Tech. Rep. No. UU-CS-2000-34). Utrecht University.

Veltkamp, R.C., & Tanase, M. Content-based image retrieval systems: Available at http://give-lab.cs.uu.nl/cbirsurvey/.

Venkateswaran, J. et al. (2006). Reference-based indexing of sequences databases. *VLDB.*

Vieira, M.R., et al. (2004). DBM-Tree : A dynamic metric access method sensitive to local density data. In *SBBD*, 163-177.

Viitaniemi, V., & Laaksonen, J. (2006). Techniques for still image scene classification and object detection. In *Proceedings of 16th International Conference on Artificial Neural Networks* (ICANN 2006).

Vincent, L., & Soille, P. (1991). Watershed in digital spaces : an efficient algorithm based on immersion simulations. *IEEE PAMI, 13*(6), 583-598.

Viola, P., & Jones, M. (2001). Rapid object detection using a boosted cascade of simple features, IEEE Conference on Computer Vision and pattern Recognition (pp. 511-518.)

Viskin, S. (2000). Cardiac pacing in the long QT syndrome: Review of available data and practical recommendations. *Journal of Cardiovascular Electrophysiology, 11*(5), 593-600.

Vlachos, M., Kollios, G., & Gunopulos, D. (2002). Discovering similar multidimensional trajectories. *Proceedings of 18th International Conference on Data Engineering* (pp. 673-684). San Jose, CA, USA.

Vu, K., Hua, K. A., & Jiang, N. (2003). Improving image retrieval effectiveness in query-by example environment. *Proceedings of the 2003 ACM Symposium on Applied Computing,* (pp. 774-781). Melbourne, Florida, USA, ACM Press.

Wang, J. Z. , Li, J., & Wiederhold, G. (2001). SIMPLIcity: Semantics-sensitive integrated matching for picture libraries. *IEEE Transactions on Pattern Analysis and Machine Intelligence*, 23, 947–963.

Wang, J. Z., Li, J., & Wiederhold, G. (2001). Simplicity: Semantics-sensitive integrated matching for picture libraries. *IEEE Transactions on Pattern Analysis and Machine Intelligence, 23*(9), 947-963.

Wang, J., Wiederhold, G., Firschein, O., & Sha, X. (1998). Content-based image indexing and searching using Daubechies' wavelets. *International Journal of Digital Libraries, 1*(4), 311–328.

Wang, J., Yang, W.-J., & Acharya, R. (1997). Color Clustering Techniques for Color-Content-Based Image Retrieval from Image Databases. *Proceedings of the 1997 IEEE International Conference on Multimedia Computing and Systems* (pp. 442-449). Ottawa, Canada.

Wang, J.Z., Wiederhold, G., Firschein, O., & Wei, S.X. (1997). Content-based image indexing and searching using Daubechies' wavelets. *International Journal on Digital Libraries, 1*, 311–328.

Wang, L., Chan, K.L., & Zhang, Z. (2003). Bootstrapping SVM active learning by incorporating unlabelled images for image retrieval. In *Proceedings of IEEE International Conference on Computer Vision and Pattern Recognition (CVPR)*, Madison, WI.

Wang, Y., Ding, M., Zhou, C., & Hu, Y. (2006). Interactive relevance feedback mechanism for image retrieval using rough set. *Knowledge-Based Systems, 19,* 696-703.

Weber, R., & Bohm, K. (2000). Trading quality for time with nearest-neighbor search. *Proceedings of the 7th International Conference on Extending Database Technology* (pp. 21–35) Konstanz, Germany.

Weber, R., Schek, H., & Blott, S. (1998). A quantitative analysis and performance study for similarity-search methods in high-dimensional spaces. In Morgan Kaufmann (Ed.), *Proceeding of ACM VLDB'98,* (pp. 194-205). ACM. San Francisco, CA.

Wee, C.-Y., & Paramesran, R. (2007). On the computational aspects of Zernike moments. *Image and Vision Computing, 25*(6), 967-980.

Wei, C. H., Li, C. T., & Wilson, R. (2005). A content-based method to medical image database retrieval. In Z. M. Ma (Ed.), *Database Modeling for Industrial Data Management* (pp. 258-292). Hershey, PA: Idea Group publishing.

Wei, C.-H., Li, C.-T., & Wilson, R. (2006). A content-based approach to medical image database retrieval. In: Z. M. Ma (Ed): *Database Modeling for Industrial Data Management*, (pp. 258–291), Hershey, PA: Idea Group Publishing.

Weliwitage, C., Harvey, A., & Jennings, A. (2003). Whole of Word Recognition Methods for Cursive Script. *Proceedings of the 2003 APRS Workshop on Digital Image Computing* (pp. 111-116). Brisbane, Australia.

Wenyin, L., Dumais, S., Sun, Y., Zhang, H., Czerwinski, M., & Field, B. (2001). Semiautomatic image annotation. *Proceedings of the International Conference on Human-Computer Interaction* (vol. 1, pp. 326–334).

White, D. A., & Jain, R. (1996). Similarity indexing: Algorithms and performance. *Storage and Retrieval for Image and Video Databases (SPIE)*, 62–73.

White, D.A., & Jain, R. (1996). Similarity indexing with the ss-tree. Proc. of IEEE ICDE.

Wied, G., Bahr, G., & Bartels, P. (1970). Automatic analysis of cell images. In G. Wied, & G. Bahr (Ed.), Automated Cell Identification and Cell Sorting (pp. 195-360). New, York: Academic Press.

Wiederhold, G. (1992). Mediators in the architecture of future information systems. *IEEE Computers, 25*(3), 38-49.

Williams, D., & Shah, M. (1992). A fast algorithm for active contours and curvature estimation. *CVIGP: Image Understanding, 55*(1), 1-26.

Wong, T. S. F., & Wong, M. H. (2003). Efficient subsequence matching for sequences databases under time warping. *Proceedings of 7th International Database Engineering and Applications Symposium* (pp. 139-148).

Wood, M.E.J., Campbell, N.W., & Thomas, B.T. (1998). Iterative refinement by relevance feedback in content-based digital image retrieval. In *ACM Multimedia 98 Proceedings*, Bristol, UK.

Woods, J. W. (Ed.). (2006). *Multidimensional signal, image, and video processing and coding*. Elsevier Press.

Wu, H., Lu, H. Q., & Ma, S. D. (2005). A survey of relevance feedback techniques in content-based image retrieval. *Chinese Journal of Computers, 28*(12), 1969-1979, (In Chinsese).

Wu, P., & Manjunath, B. S. (2001). Adaptive nearest neighbor search for relevance feedback in large image databases. *Proceedings of 9th ACM International Conference on Multimedia* (pp. 89-97). Ottawa, Canada: ACM.

Wu, P., Ma, W., Manjunath, B.S., Shin, H., & Choi, Y. (1999). MPEG-7 Document, ISO/IEC JTC1/SC29/WG11/P77.

Wu, P., Manjunath, B. S., Newsam, S., & Shin, H. D. (2000). A texture descriptor for browsing and image retrieval. *Signal Processing: Image Communication, 16*(1-2), 33-43.

Wu, Q. T., & Huang, T. (2000). Discriminant algorithm with application to image retrieval. In *Proceedings to the IEEE Conference on Computer Vision and Pattern Recognition, 1*, 222-227.

Yahoo! Search. http://images.search.yahoo.com/.

Yan, R., Hauptmann, A., & Jin, R. (2003). Negative pseudo-relevance feedback in content based video retrieval. In *Proceedings of the ACM Multimedia 2003*, Berkeley, CA.

Yang, C., & Lozano Perez, T. (2000). Image database retrieval with multiple instance learning techniques. *Proceedings of the IEEE International Conference on Data Engineering* (pp. 233–243).

Yang, L., & Algregtsen, F. (1994). Fast computation of invariant geometric moments: A new method giving correct results. Proc. IEEE Int. Conf. on Image Processing.

Yang, S.-C., Wang, C.-M., Chung, Y.-N., Hsu, G.-C., Lee, S.-K., Chung, P.-C., & Chang, C.-I, (2005). A computer-aided system for mass detection and classification in digitized mammograms. *Biomedical Engineering-Applications, Basis & Communications, 17*(5), 215-228.

Yang, Z., & Kuo, C.-C. J. (2000). Learning image similarities and categories from content analysis and relevance feedback. *Proceedings the 2000 ACM Workshops on Multimedia* (pp. 175-178). Los Angeles, CA, USA: ACM.

Yang, Z., & Laaksonen, J. (2005). Partial relevance in interactive facial image retrieval. In *Proceedings of 3rd International Conference on Advances in Pattern Recognition* (ICAPR 2005), 216-225.

Ye, H. J., & Xu, G. Y. (2003). Fast search in large-scale image database using vector quantization. In *Proceedings of International Conference on Image and Video Retrieval, Lecture Notes in Computer Science, 2728,* 458–467. Berlin / Heidelberg: Springer.

Yeung, M. M., & Liu, B. (1995). Efficient Matching and Clustering of Video Shots. *Proceedings of the 1995 International Conference on Image Processing* (Vol. 1, pp. 338-341). Washington D.C., WA, USA.

Yi, B.-K., & Faloutsos, C. (2000). Fast time sequence indexing for arbitrary Lp norms. *Proceedings of 26th International Conference on Very Large Data Bases* (pp. 385-394). San Francisco, CA, USA: Morgan Kaufmann Publishers Inc.

Yi, B.-K., Jagadish, H. V., & Faloutsos, C. (1998). Efficient Retrieval of Similar Time Sequences under Time Warping. *Proceedings of 14th International Conference on Data Engineering* (pp. 201-208). Washington D.C., WA, USA.

Yianilos, P. (1993) Data structures and algorithms for nearest neighbor search in general metric spaces. *Proceedings of the third annual ACM-SIAM symposium on Discrete Algorithms,* 311-321.

Yining, D., & Manjuncth, B. S. (1999). An efficient low-dimensional color indexing scheme for region-based image retrieval. In *Proceedings of the IEEE International*

Conference on Acoustics, Speech, and Signal Processing (ICASSP), 3017-3020.

Zachary, J.M., & Iyengar, S.S. (1999). Content-based image retrieval systems. In Proceedings of the IEEE Symposium on Application-Specific Systems and Software Engineering and Technology, pp. 136–143.

Zayan, M. A. (2006). Satellite orbits guidance using state space neural network. *Aerospace Conference, 4, AERO 2006.* 16-22. IEEE Press.

Zhang G., Ma Z.M., & Cai Z.P. (2007). Directed filter for dominant direction fuzzy set in content-based image retrieval. In *Proceedings of the 22th ACM Symposium on Applied Computing.* (pp. 76–77). Seoul: ACM Press.

Zhang, C., Chen, S.-C., & Shyu, M.-L. (2004). Multiple object retrieval for image databases using multiple instance learning and relevance feedback. In the *Proceedings of IEEE International Conference on Multimedia and Expo,* Taipei, Taiwan, ROC, June 27-30 (pp. 775-778). Los Alamitos, CA: IEEE Computer Society Press.

Zhang, D. S., & Lu, G. (2002). Generic fourier descriptors for shape-based image retrieval. In the *Proceedings of IEEE International Conference on Multimedia and Expo,* Lausanne, Switzerland, August 26-29 (pp. 425-428). Los Alamitos, CA: IEEE Computer Society Press.

Zhang, G. Ma, Z.M., Cai, Z. P., & Wang, H. L. (2007). Texture analysis using modified computational model of grating cells in content-based medical image retrieval. In *Proceedings of International Conference on Medical Imaging and Informatics* (pp. 184-191). Beijing: Middlesex University Press.

Zhang, G., & Ma, Z.M. (2007). Texture feature extraction and description using Gabor wavelet in content-based medical image retrieval. In *Proceedings of International conference on wavelet analysis and pattern recognition* (pp. 169-173). Beijing: IEEE Press.

Zhang, G., Ma, Z. M., Deng, L. G., & Cai, Z. P. (2007). Oriented Filter Based on Dominant Directions in Content-based Image Retrieval. *Journal of Northeastern University, 28*(7), 978-981.

Zhang, H., Gong, Y., Low, C. Y., & Smoliar, S. W. (1995). Image retrieval based on color feature: An evaluation study. In *Proceedings of SPIE, 2606*, 212-220.

Zhang, L., Qian, F., Li, M., & Zhang, H. (2003). An efficient memorization scheme for relevance feedback in image retrieval. In *IEEE International Conference on Multimedia & Expo*. IEEE Press.

Zhang, Q., & Goldman, S.A. (2001). EM-DD: An improved multiple-instance learning technique. In T.G. Dietterich, S. Becker, & Z. Ghahramani (Eds.), *Advances in neural information processing systems* (vol. 14, pp. 1073–1080). Cambridge, MA: MIT Press.

Zhang, Q., Goldman, S.A., Yu, W., & Fritts, J. (2002). Content-based image retrieval using multiple-instance learning. In C. Sammut & A.G. Hoffmann (Eds.), *Proceedings of the International Conference on Machine Learning* (pp. 682–689).

Zhang, R. (2005). *Semantics-Oriented Modeling and Retrieval in Image Databases*, SUNY Binghamton PhD Dissertation.

Zhang, R., & Zhang, Z. (2003). Addressing CBIR efficiency, effectiveness, and retrieval subjectivity simultaneously. In *the 5th ACM Int'l Workshop on Multimedia Information Retrieval*, Berkeley, CA, November 2003. in conjunction with ACM Multimedia (ACM MM).

Zhang, R. & Zhang, Z. (2006). BALAS: Empirical Bayesian learning in the relevance feedback for image retrieval. *Image and Vision Computing, 24*, 211-233.

Zhang, R., & Zhang, Z. (2004). Hidden semantic concept discovery in region based image retrieval. In *IEEE International Conference on Computer Vision and Pattern Recognition (CVPR)*.

Zhang, Y. J. (Ed.). (2006). *Advances in image and video segmentation*. Idea Group Inc (IGI) Press.

Zhao, C.G., Cheng, H.Y., Huo, Y.L., & Zhuang, T.G. (2004). Liver CT-image retrieval based on Gabor texture. In *Proceedings of the 26th Annual International Conference of the IEEE Engineering in Medicine and Biology Society: Vol. 26 II.* (pp. 1491-1494). San Francisco, CA: Institute of Electrical and Electronics Engineers Inc.

Zheng, B., & Li, Y. (2007). New model for multi-objective evolutionary algorithms. *Computational Science–ICCS 2007, 4490, 2007*, 037-1044. Springer Berlin/Heidelberg Publisher.

Zhong, N., & Skowron, A. (2000). Rough sets in KDD: Tutorial notes. *Bulletin of International Rough Set Society, 4*(1/2), 9-30.

Zhou, X. S. & Huang, T. S. (2001). Comparing discriminating transformations and SVM for learning during multimedia retrieval. In *Proceedings of the ninth ACM international conference on Multimedia* (pp. 137-146). ACM Press.

Zhou, X. S. & Huang, T. S. (2003). Relevance feedback in image retrieval: A comprehensive review. *ACM Multimedia System Journal, 8*, 536-544.

Zhou, X. S., & Huang, T. S. (2003). Relevance feedback in image retrieval: A comprehensive review. *ACM Multimedia System Journal, 8*(6), 536-544.

Zhou, X. S., Rui, Y., & Huang, T. (1999). Water-filling: A novel way for image structural feature extraction. In the *Proceedings of IEEE International Conference on Image Processing: Vol. 2*, Kobe, Japan, October 25-28 (pp. 570-574). Piscataway, NJ: IEEE Press.

Zhou, X., & Huang, T. (2001). Small sample learning during multimedia retrieval using BiasMap. *Proceedings of the IEEE International Conference on Computer Vision and Pattern Recognition* (vol. 1, pp. 11–17).

Zhou, Z. H., Jiang, Y., & Chen, S. F. (2000). A general neural framework for classification rule mining. *International Journal of Computers, Systems, and Signals, 1*(2), 154-168.

Zhu, Y., & Shasha, D. (2003). Warping Indexes with Envelope Transforms for Query by Humming. *Proceedings of the 2003 ACM SIGMOD International Conference on Management of Data* (pp. 181-192). San Diego, CA, USA: ACM.

Zhu, Y., Shasha, D., & Zhao, X. (2003). Query by humming: In action with its technology revealed. *Proceedings of the 2003 ACM SIGMOD International Conference on Management of Data* (pp. 675-675). San Diego, CA, USA: ACM.

About the Contributors

Zongmin Ma (Z. M. Ma) received the PhD degree from the City University of Hong Kong in 2001 and is currently a full professor in College of Information Science and Engineering at Northeastern University, China. His current research interests include intelligent database systems, knowledge representation and reasoning, the Semantic Web and XML, knowledge-bases systems, and engineering database modeling. He has published over 80 papers in international journals, conferences and books in these areas since 1999. He also authored and edited several scholarly books published by Springer-Verlag and IGI Global, respectively. He has served as member of the international program committees for several international conferences and also spent some time as a reviewer of several journals. Dr. Ma is a senior member of the IEEE.

* * *

Reda Alhajj is professor of computer science at the University of Calgary. He published over 250 papers in refereed international journals and conferences. He served on the program committee of several international conferences including IEEE ICDE, IEEE ICDM, IEEE IAT, SIAM DM. He is associate editor of IEEE SMC- Part C. His primary work and research interests are in the areas of biocomputing and biodata analysis, data mining, multiagent systems, schema integration and re-engineering, social networks and XML. Dr. Alhajj recently received with Dr. Jon Rokne donation of equipment valued at $5 million from RBC and Teradata for their research on computational intelligence and bioinformatics research.

Danilo Avola received his degree in computer science at the University of Rome "La Sapienza". His research activity is sponsored by a fellowship (assegno di ricerca) at the Multi Media & Modal Laboratory (M3L) of the IRPPS-CNR of Italy. He is mainly interested in human-computer interaction, multimodal interaction, visual languages, visual interfaces, sketch-based interfaces, image and video processing, pattern recognition.

Stefano Berretti received the "Laurea" degree in electronic engineering and the Ph.D. in information and telecommunications engineering from the University of Firenze, Italy, in 1997 and 2001, respectively. Since 2002 he is an assistant professor at the "Dipartimento di Sistemi e Informatica," of the University of Firenze. His current research activities mainly focus on pattern recognition, image and 3D objects databases, and multimedia information retrieval. He serves as a frequent reviewer of many conferences and journals in the area of pattern recognition, artificial intelligence and multimedia. He is a member of the International Association for Pattern Recognition (IAPR) and of the IEEE.

Alberto Del Bimbo is Professor of computer engineering and the director of the master's degree in multimedia of the University of Florence, Italy. He was the director of the Department of Systems and Information, from 1997 to 2000 and the deputy rector for research and innovation transfer of the University of Florence from 2000 to 2006. From 2007 he has been the president of the Foundation for Research and Innovation, promoted by the University of Florence. His scientific interests are pattern recognition, image databases, human–computer interaction and multimedia applications. He has published over 230 pages in some of the most distinguished scientific journals and presented at international conferences, and is the author of the monograph *Visual Information Retrieval*, on content-based retrieval from image and video databases, published by Morgan Kaufmann in 1999. From 1996 to 2000, he was the president of the IAPR Italian Chapter, and, from 1998 to 2000, member at large of the IEEE Publication Board. He was the general chair of IAPR ICIAP'97, the International Conference on Image Analysis and Processing, IEEE ICMCS'99, the International Conference on Multimedia Computing and Systems, AVIVDiLib'05, the International Workshop on Audio-Visual Content and Information Visualization, and VMDL07, the International Workshop on Visual and Multimedia Digital Libraries, and was on the board of many other primary scientific conferences. He is associate editor of *Pattern Recognition, Journal of Visual Languages and Computing, Multimedia Tools and Applications, Pattern Analysis and Applications* and *International Journal of Image and Video Processing*, and was Associate Editor of *IEEE Transactions on Multimedia* and *IEEE Transactions on Pattern Analysis and Machine Intelligence*. Email: delbimbo@dsi.unifi.it.

Lisa Brown received her PhD in computer science from Columbia University in 1995. She wrote her thesis on medical image registration while working in the Computer Assisted Surgery Group at the IBM T.J Watson Research Center. For the past decade she has been a research staff member at IBM. She worked for three years in the Education Group creating software which enables students to take measurements on images and videos.She is currently in the Exploratory Computer Vision Group. She is well known for her ACM survey paper in image registration, which was extensively cited and translated into several languages. She has also published extensively, been an invited speaker and panelist to various workshops and has filed several patents. Her primary interests are in head tracking, head pose estimation and more recently in object classification and performance evaluation of tracking in surveillance.

Rogerio Feris is currently a research staff member at IBM TJ Watson Research Center. He received a PhD in computer science from the University of California, Santa Barbara, an MS in computer science from University of Sao Paulo, Brazil, and a BS in computer engineering from the Federal University of Rio Grande, Brazil. His research interests include computer vision and graphics, with particular emphasis on visual surveillance, intelligent user interfaces, and computational photography.

Fernando Ferri received degrees in electronics engineering in 1990 and the PhD in medical informatics in 1993 from the University of Rome "La Sapienza". He is actually senior researcher at the National Research Council of Italy (2001-2007). From 1993 to 2000 he was professor of "Sistemi di Elaborazione" at the University of Macerata. From 1996 to 2001 he was researcher at the National Research Council of Italy. He is the author of more than 100 papers in international journals, books and conferences. His main methodological areas of interest are: human-computer interaction visual languages, visual interfaces, sketch-based interfaces, and multimodal interfaces, data and knowledge bases, geographic information systems. He was responsible of several projects funded by Italian Ministry of University and Research and European Commission.

David García-Pérez received the "Laurea" degree in Physics from the University of Santiago de Compostela in 2001. He is right now a PhD student in the area of "languages and computer systems" of the University of Santiago de Compostela. His current research activities focus in two areas. Mainly, he is working on the design of new solutions of image retrieval system, also, he started to work on automatic analysis of fundus eye digital image.

Dany Gebara received her BSc in from the American University of Beirut, Lebanon. She completed her MSc in computer science at the University of Calgary. Her main areas of research include image mining and content-based image retrieval.

Patrizia Grifoni received the degrees in electronics engineering in 1990 and from the University of Rome "La Sapienza". She is researcher at the National Research Council of Italy. From 1994 to 2000 she was professor of "Elaborazione digitale delle immagini" at the University of Macerata. She is the author of more than 70 papers in international journals, books and conferences. Her scientific interests have evolved from query languages for statistical and geographic databases to the focal topics related to human-computer interaction, multimodal interaction, visual languages, visual interfaces, sketch-based interfaces and accessing web information. She was responsible of several projects funded by Italian and International Institutions.

Arun Hampapur is the chief technology officer for physical security in IBM's Global Technology Services Division. In this role, he has responsibility for technology offerings in the physical security space, including digital video surveillance, biometrics, access control and related technologies. Dr Hampapur also oversees the development of advanced video analysis technologies for the IBM Smart Surveillance Solution. Prior to joining Global Services, Dr. Hampapur lead the research team which invented IBM Smart Surveillance System (S3) at IBM T.J Watson Research Center. He has led the S3 effort from its inception as an exploratory research effort, thru the building of the first lab prototype, first customer pilot engagement, to the commercialization as a services offering. He has developed several algorithms for video analytics and video indexing. He has published more than 40 papers on various topics related to media indexing, video analysis, and video surveillance and holds 8 US patents. He is also active in the research community and serves on the program committees of several IEEE International conferences. Dr. Hampapur is an IEEE Senior Member. He is one of the early researchers in the field of applied computer vision and multimedia database management. Dr Hampapur obtained his PhD from the University of Michigan in 1995. Before moving to IBM he was leading the video effort at Virage Inc (1995 – 1997).

Qing He received his BSc degree from Department of Mathematics, Hebei Normal University in China, and MSc degree from the Department of Mathematics, Zhengzhou University, and the PhD degree from Beijing Normal University in 2000. He has been an Associate Professor of the Key Laboratory of Intelligent Information Processing, Institute of Computing Technology, Chinese Academic of Sciences (KLIIP, ICT, CAS) since 2000. His research interests are in the areas on machine learning, data mining artificial intelligence, neural computing, and cognitive science.

Eamonn Keogh is an associate professor at Department of Computer Science and Engineering, University of California, Riverside, USA. He received his Ph.D. from the University of California, Irvine. His research interests include artificial intelligence, data mining, and information retrieval.

Chang-Tsun Li received the BS degree in electrical engineering from Chung-Cheng Institute of Technology (CCIT), National Defense University, Taiwan, in 1987, the MS degree in computer science from US Naval Postgraduate School, USA, in 1992, and the PhD degree in computer science from the University of Warwick, UK, in 1998. He was an associate professor of the Department of Electrical Engineering at CCIT during 1999-2002 and a visiting professor of the Department of Computer Science at U.S. Naval Postgraduate School in the second half of 2001. He is currently an associate professor of the Department of Computer Science at the University of Warwick, UK, editor-in-chief of the *International Journal of Digital Crime and Forensics (IJDCF)* and associate editor of the *International Journal of Applied Systemic Studies (IJASS)*. He has involved in the organization of a number of international conferences and workshops and also served as member of the international program committees for several international conferences. His research interests include multimedia security, bioinformatics, image processing, pattern recognition, computer vision and content-based image retrieval.

Qingyong Li is a lecturer in School of Computer and Information Technology at Beijing Jiaotong University. He holds a PhD from the institute of computing technology, Chinese Academy of Sciences. His research interests include cognitive informatics, machine learning and image processing.

Yue Li has been a PhD candidate with the department of computer science at the University of Warwick, UK. He obtained his master's degree from the University of Nottingham, UK, in 2005 and bachelor's degree from the Nankai University, China, in 2003. He has published more than 8 refereed research papers. His research interests include digital watermarking, steganography, pattern recognition, and content-based image retrieval.

Max Lu is a senior software engineer of IBM GTS (Global Technology Service). He received his MS in computer pattern recognition from National Lab of Pattern Recognition, Chinese Academy of Sciences, and BA in EE from HuaZhong University of Science and Technology, China. He designed and implemented the framework of IBM Smart Surveillance Solution. He has also worked on computer numeric control (CNC), 3D model construction, and wafer defect detecting etc. He has published some papers and filed a number of patents.

Antonio Mosquera received the "Laurea" degree in physics and the PhD in physics from the University of Santiago de Compostela, Spain, in 1989 and 1995, respectively. Between 1991 and 2001 he worked on different teacher and research positions in the University of Santiago de Compostela. Since 2001, he is an assistant professor at the "Departamento de Electrónica y Computación" of the University of Santiago de Compostela. His research activities mainly focus on image processing: feature extraction, development of automatic image diagnostic systems, image information retrieval, etc.

Vit Niennattrakul is a PhD candidate in computer engineering at Chulalongkorn Unversity, Thailand, where he received his BEng degrees in computer engineering. His research interests include data mining, especially on time series data, information retrieval, and machine learning.

Chotirat Ann Ratanamahatana is a lecturer at Computer Engineering Department, Chulalongkorn University, Bangkok, Thailand. She received her undergraduate and graduate studies from Carnegie Mellon University and Harvard University, respectively, and received her Ph.D. from the University of California, Riverside. Her research interests include time series data mining, information retrieval, machine learning, and human-computer interaction.

Paweł Rotter completed his MSc degree in electronic and telecommunication (1999) at AGH-University of Science and Technology in Kraków. He followed this with post-graduate studies in automatic control and robotics (AGH-UST 2003) and a PhD degree in computer science (AGH-UST 2004). From 2001 to 2004 he worked at the Artificial Intelligence and Information Analysis Laboratory of Aristotle University of Thessaloniki and the Institute of Transport Management and Control at the Cracow University of Technology (CUT). In 2004, he became an Assistant Professor at the Chair of Automatic Control at AGH-University of Science and Technology in Krakow. Since September 2005, he has been on leave from AGH-UST, while doing research at the Institute for Prospective Technological Studies (IPTS), Joint Research Centre of the European Commission in Seville. He has been involved in research projects related to audiovisual search, biometrics and radio frequency identification. other areas of his research interests are: computer vision, multicriteria optimisation and automatic control.

Andrew Senior received his PhD on "offline handwriting recognition" from the University of Cambridge. Having worked at LIMSI at the University of Paris XI on continuous speech recognition, he joined IBM Research in 1994 where he has worked in the areas of handwriting, audio-visual speech, face and fingerprint recognition. He has co-authored a book: *Guide to Biometrics*, holds twelve patents and has published over sixty scientific papers. Most recently he has worked on video privacy and visual tracking, which have been commercialized as part of the IBM Smart Surveillance System. He is an adjunct professor at Columbia University. His research interests range across pattern recognition, computer vision and new-media art.

Zhiping Shi received the BS degree in engineering at Inner Mongolia University of Technology in Huhhot, China in 1995, the MS degree in application of computer science from Inner Mongolia University, China in 2002, and the PhD degree in computer software and theory from Institute of Computing Technology Chinese Academy of Science in 2005. From 1995 to 1999 year, He had been a faculty member at Inner Mongolia University of Technology. He is an assistant professor at the Key Lab of Intelligent Information Processing of Institute of Computing Technology, Chinese Academy of Science. His research interests include content-based visual information retrieval, image understanding, machine learning and cognitive informatics.

Zhongzhi Shi is a professor at the Key Laboratory of Intelligent Information Processing, Institute of Computing Technology, Chinese Academy of Sciences, Beijing, China. His research interests include intelligence science, multiagent systems, and semantic web. He has published 10 books, edited 11 books, and more than 300 technical papers. Professor Shi is a member of the AAAI. He is the chair of WG 12.3 of IFIP. He also serves as vice president of the Chinese Association for Artificial Intelligence. He received the 2nd Grade National Award of Science and Technology Progress in 2002. In 1998 and 2001 he received the 2nd Grade Award of Science and Technology Progress from the Chinese Academy of Sciences.

Chiao-Fe Shu has received his PhD from computer science and engineering department of University of Michigan in 1993. He is an expert programmer and researcher with over 10 years of industrial experience. He has co-founded Virage Inc. in 1994. His research covers the areas of oriented texture pattern analysis, classification, and segmentation, in-situ wafer inspection system based on fourier imaging, and multimedia indexing and retrieval. Since joined Virage, he focused on developing viable commercial applications based on content-based retrieval technology. They include stock photo image system, trademark search system, image informatics system, audio/video indexing/retrieval system. The image informtics application developed by him has led to another well-funded private company called Scimagix. Dr. Chiao-Fe Shu has published extensively in his researh areas and owns 9 US patents. Dr. Chiao-Fe Shu also has solid software product development and management experience through all phases of development cycle. He is currently the chief architect and commercialization lead for IBM Smart Surveillance System.

Andrzej M.J. Skulimowski is a professor at the Chair of Automatic Control, AGH University of Science and Technology, Kraków, Poland. He graduated Electronics, specialisation Automatic Control, at the AGH University and Pure Mathematics at the Jagiellonian University, Kraków, Poland, getting MSc degrees in electrical engineering in 1981 and in mathematics in 1982, respectively. He got his PhD in automatic control with honours in 1985 and a DSc degree in operations research in 1997, both from the AGH University. He was also granted *de venia legendi* from the University of St. Gallen, Switzerland, in 1991. His main field of expertise is multicriteria decision analysis, decision support systems, AI methods in forecasting, risk management, and foresight. From 1987 to 1996, he lived in Switzerland, where he was first a fellow of the Swiss Confederation at the Swiss Federal Institute of Technology (ETH) in Zurich (1987-88), a SNF Research Associate at the Institute of Communication Technology at the ETH (1988-90) and a Visiting Professor at the Institute of Information Management at the University of St. Gallen (since 1990). Since May 2002, Mr. Skulimowski has been a senior expert of ESTO, providing consulting support to the European Commission. He is the author of over 120 scholarly papers and three monographs.

Ying-Li Tian received her PhD from the Chinese University of Hong Kong in 1996. She is experienced in computer vision topics ranging from object recognition, photometric modeling and shape from shading, to human identification, 3D reconstruction, motion/video analysis, digital video surveillance, and facial expression analysis. After she worked in National Laboratory of Pattern Recognition, Chinese Academy of Sciences, Beijing, China, Dr. Tian joined the Robotics Institute in Carnegie Mellon University as a postdoctoral fellow. She focused on automatic facial expression analysis. She proposed and developed robust and powerful methods for facial feature detection, tracking, and automated facial expression analysis. Since 2001, Dr. Tian is working at IBM T. J. Watson Research Center and focusing on moving object detection, tracking, and event and activity analysis. She is one of the inventors of the IBM Smart Surveillance System (S3). Dr. Tian published more than 60 papers in journals and conferences. She is a senior member of IEEE.

Chia-Hung Wei has been a PhD candidate with the Department of Computer Science at the University of Warwick, UK, and expects to obtain his PhD degree in 2008. He obtained his master's degree from the University of Sheffield, UK, in 2000 and bachelor's degree from the Tunghai University, Taiwan, in 1996. He has published more than 10 refereed research papers. He is a reviewer of a number of journals and conferences. His research interests include content-based image retrieval, image processing, pattern recognition, and information retrieval.

Li Yan received the PhD degree from Northeastern University, China in 2008 and is now an associate professor at Northeastern University, China. Her research interests include XML databases, intelligent information processing and fuzzy database modeling. Dr. Yan has published over 30 papers in these areas.

Yun Zhai received his BS degree in computer science from the Bethune-Cookman College in 2001, and his PhD in computer science from the University of Central Florida in 2006. He has been working at IBM since September 2006. His research interests are in the fields of computer vision and multimedia. Some of his research focuses are surveillance video analysis, temporal video segmentation, spatiotemporal visual attention analysis, content-based image/video retrieval and semantic video linking.

Gang Zhang received the BS degree from Northeastern University, China in 2000 and the MS degree from Northeastern University, China in 2004. Now he is a PhD candidate at Northeastern University, china and a faculty member at Shenyang University of Technology, China. His research interests include content-based image retrieval, image analysis and understanding, artificial intelligence, etc.

Ming Zhang received the bachelor's degree in computer science and engineering in 1995 from Zhejiang University, China, and the master's degree in computer science in 2005 from University of Regina, Canada. He is currently a PhD candidate in the department of computer science, the University of Calgary, Canada. His research interests include image processing, database and data mining.

Ruofei Zhang is a Computer Scientist at Yahoo! Inc. His research fields are in machine learning, data mining, optimization, and multimedia information retrieval in large scale data set. He has filed six patents on search relevance, search result page click modeling, multimedia content analysis, and NLP based query rewriting, and published two dozen papers on multimedia information retrieval, machine learning, and data mining on leading academic journals and top international conferences. He received a Ph. D. in computer science with Distinguished Dissertation Award from State University of New York at Binghamton, USA, a M.S. in electronics from Tsinghua University, China, and a B.S. in computer science and engineering from Xi'an Jiaotong University, China.

Zhongfei (Mark) Zhang is an associate professor at the Computer Science Department at State University of New York (SUNY) at Binghamton. He was on the faculty of Computer Science and Engineering Department at SUNY Buffalo. He has been PIs/Co-PIs for many projects in the area of multimedia data mining supported by the US federal government, the New York State government, as well as private industries. He has many publications and inventions and served as reviewers/PC members for many conferences and journals, organizers for several well-known international workshops, and Associate Editor for Pattern Recognition and Guest Editors for several other journals.

Ji-feng Zhu received the BS degree from Shenyang Industrial Institute, China in 1997 and the MS degree from Northeastern University, China in 2008. Now she is a faculty member at Shenyang University, China. Her research interests include Semantic Web, artificial intelligence, etc.

Index